Data Structures, Algorithms, and Program Style Using C

The PWS-KENT Series in Computer Science

Advanced Structured BASIC: File Processing with the IBM PC, Payne

Assembly Language for the PDP-11: RT-RSX-UNIX, Second Edition, Kapps and Stafford

Data Structures, Algorithms, and Program Style, Korsh

Data Structures, Algorithms, and Program Style Using C, Korsh and Garrett

FORTRAN 77 for Engineers, Borse

FORTRAN 77 and Numerical Methods for Engineers, Borse

Logic and Structured Design for Computer Programmers, Rood

Microprocessor Systems Design: 68000 Hardware, Software, and Interfacing, Clements

Modula-2, Beidler and Jackowitz

Problem Solving with Pascal, Brand

Problem Solving Using Pascal: Algorithm Development and Programming Concepts, Skvarcius

Programming Using Turbo Pascal, Riley

Structured BASIC for the IBM PC with Business Applications, Payne

Structured Programming in Assembly Language for the IBM PC, Runnion

Turbo Pascal for the IBM PC, Radford and Haigh

Using BASIC: An Introduction to Computer Programming, Third Edition, Hennefeld

Using Microsoft and IBM BASIC: An Introduction to Computer Programming, Hennefeld

VAX Assembly Language and Architecture, Kapps and Stafford

Data Structures, Algorithms, and Program Style Using C

James F. Korsh
Temple University
Leonard J. Garrett
Temple University

PWS-KENT Publishing Company
Boston

PWS-KENT
Publishing Company

20 Park Plaza
Boston, Massachusetts 02116

PWS-KENT Publishing Company is a division of Wadsworth, Inc.

Library of Congress Cataloging-in-Publication Data

Korsh, James F.
Data structures, algorithms, and program style using C / James F. Korsh, Leonard J. Garrett.
p. cm.
Bibliography: p.
Includes index.
ISBN 0-87150-099-X
1. C (Computer program language) 2. Data structures (Computer science) 3. Algorithms. I. Garrett, Leonard J. II. Title.
QA76.73.C15K67 1988
005.13′3--dc19 87-27019
CIP

Printed in the United States of America.
88 89 90 91 92 — 10 9 8 7 6 5 4 3 2

Sponsoring Editor *Bob Prior*
Production Coordinator *Elise Kaiser*
Production *Hoyt Publishing Services*
Composition *Bi-Comp, Incorporated*
Cover Design *Julie Gecha*
Cover Printer *New England Book Components*
Text Printer/Binder *Halliday Lithograph*

Preface

One must learn by doing the thing,
for though you can think you know it
you have no certainty until you try it.

Sophocles

Data Structures, Algorithms, and Program Style Using C is intended for use in a second programming course, such as CS2 of the ACM curriculum, as well as in a Data Structures course. It will also be invaluable for computer professionals who wish to develop applications using the C programming language. All programs appear in C, although the concepts and methods presented are independent of the language used. The book emphasizes current techniques for the creation and testing of programs and stresses the importance of writing programs that are general enough to be readily adapted for use in the solution of complex problems. Data abstraction and modularity are stressed throughout. Complex concepts are presented in a concise, informal way; theory is coupled with concrete examples.

The book is written to provide a significant amount of flexibility in the order in which the material is covered, as illustrated in the accompanying chart. For a second programming/introductory data structures class, the **fundamental concepts** of structured programming and data structures are presented in Chapters 1 through 7. These chapters, combined with selected topics from Chapters 8 and 9, provide a challenging course. Chapters 8 through 13 deal with the **application of the concepts** to more complex problems and also introduce some advanced data structures. Where data structures are taught after the second programming course, selected material from Chapters 1 through 8 can serve as a quick review of the basics, followed by an in-depth study of Chapters 9 through 13. Care has been taken throughout to include sets of exercises that are graduated by degree of difficulty and complexity. Also included are suggested assignments that incorporate the essential concepts of each chapter.

Just as knowing the grammar of a natural language does not ensure quality writing, knowing the grammar of a programming language does not ensure quality programs. Learning to program well entails utilizing principles of good style and requires skill in the use of a wide variety of tools. It is an advanced task, beyond simply learning the grammar of a language. A master mechanic, upon opening the hood of an automobile, does not see a jumble of wires and metal, but rather essential components linked together and aligned in a systematic fashion. A knowledgeable programmer must learn not only to write programs but to read them in the same fashion as a master mechanic looks at an automobile engine. He or she has to be able to see the major components and linkages of the program. Program structure can enhance or obscure a program's intelligibility.

This book explains and demonstrates the tools needed to craft good programs and to solve substantial problems. These tools, although few in number, must be used with care and forethought. The tools include the basic paradigms for

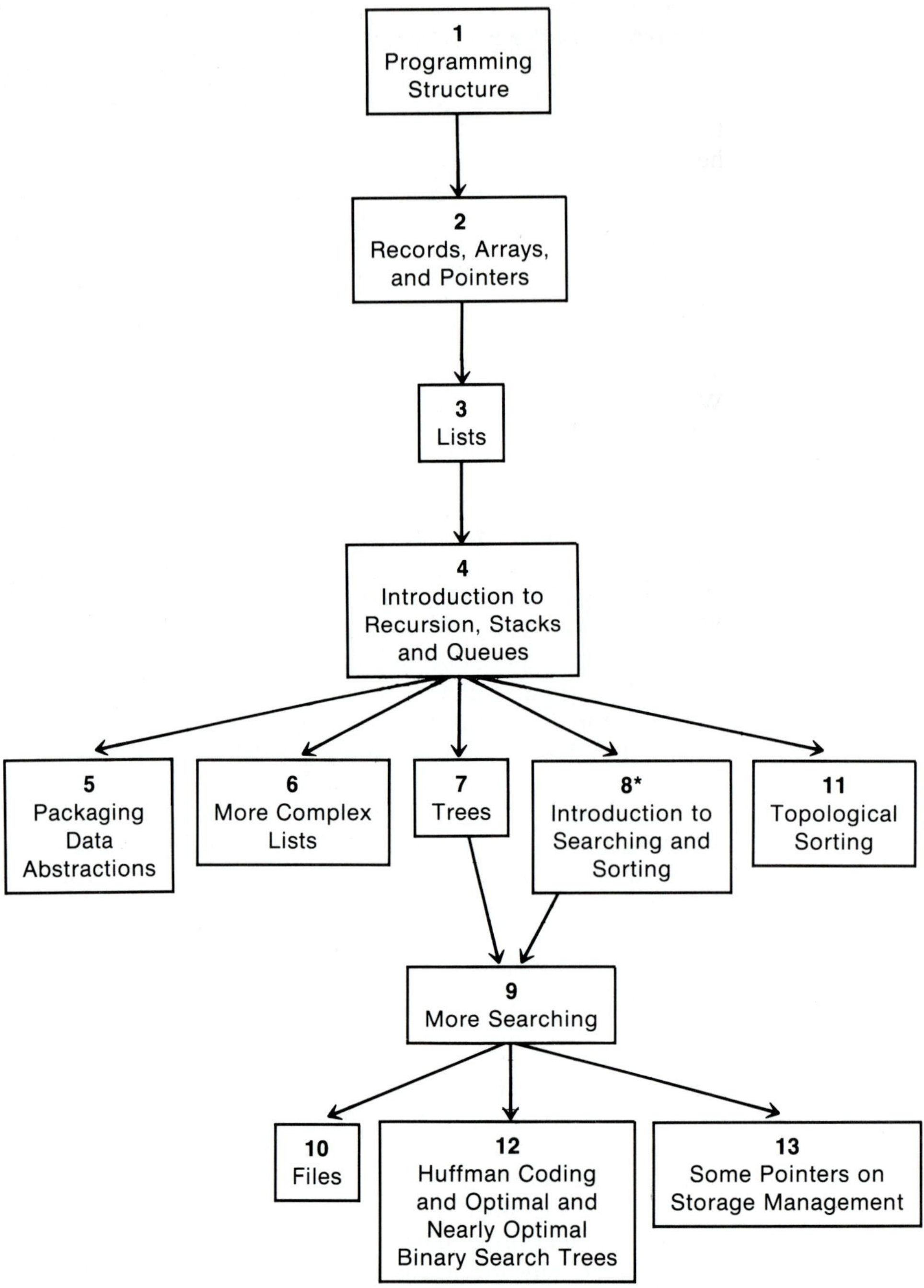

* Heapsort requires Chapter 7.

problem solving, for structuring programs, and for structuring data. Their proper use involves data abstraction, modularization, and the appropriate choice of data structures. Because the book emphasizes the entire program development process, readers will learn how to write well-designed programs and how to recognize them. They will, at the same time, develop insight into program analysis and learn how to analyze programs in order to determine their correctness and efficiency.

Many individuals contributed to this book. Special thanks are due to Sharon Doherty, Mary Helen Fein, Giorgio Ingargiola, and Paul LaFollette for their help, as well as to the students who labored through the early versions of the manuscript. The staff of PWS-KENT Publishing Company, including Bob Prior and Elise Kaiser, all provided valuable support and guidance. We would also like to thank David Hoyt for help during the production process. It is also a delight to acknowledge the painstaking and helpful work of the reviewers: James Calhoun, Western Illinois University; Michael Driscoll, DePaul University; Terry Hamberger, York College of Pennsylvania; Marek Holynski, Boston University; Sam C. Hsu, Florida Atlantic University; Paul W. Ross, Millersville University of Pennsylvania; Shai Simonson, University of Illinois at Chiçago; John B. Tappen, University of Southern Colorado; and Therril Valentine, McNeese State University. Finally, and certainly most important, we deeply appreciate and thank our wives Nina and Judy and our children, who suffered from us and with us, avoided us and supported us, during the time this book was being written.

James F. Korsh
Leonard J. Garrett

Contents

□□□□□ Fundamentals

□□□□□ Applications

8 Introduction to Searching and Sorting 358

9 More Searching: Insertion and Deletion 406

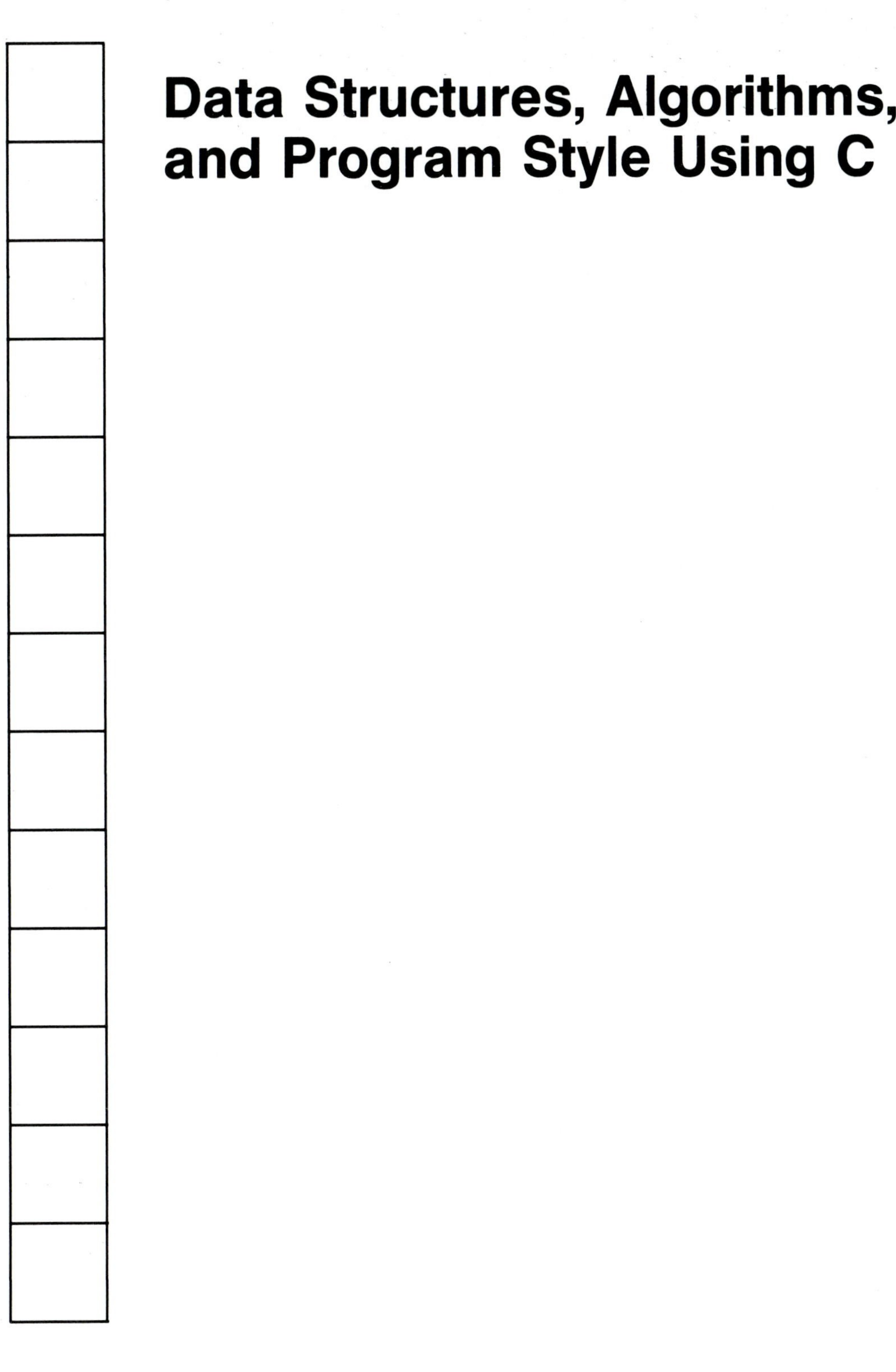

Data Structures, Algorithms, and Program Style Using C

2 3 4 5 6 7 8 9 10 11 12 13

1 Programming Structure

Emphasizes the importance of
- *structuring programs*
- *using an explicit problem solving methodology and top-down design to create programs*
- *good program style*

Introduces and illustrates the components of good programming style
- *data abstraction*
- *functional modularization*
- *verification and debugging*
- *documentation*

Begins the discussion of program time and storage requirements and how to determine them

Case study—scoring bowling games
- *illustrates the concepts introduced in the chapter*

1.1 Structure: Data and Program

Two programs doing exactly the same task may look entirely different. One may be highly readable, concise, and easily adjusted to carry out related tasks. The other may be impenetrable, lengthy, and difficult to modify. The same two may differ so much in execution time and storage needs that one program executes while the other aborts, having exceeded time or space restrictions. Experience has shown such differences to be traceable to choice of program structure and data structure.

Programs are written to solve real problems. ***Program structure*** breaks the problem and its solution down into simpler, more easily understood parts. The information to be processed is stored in ***data structures*** (arrays, records, lists, stacks, trees, and files) provided by the programming language. A data structure groups data. The right data structure for an operation can make it simple and efficient; the wrong one can make the operation cumbersome and inefficient.

Data structures contain information and are operated on during the execution of a program. Programs are said to process information when, in fact, they process data structures. Thus it is not surprising that data and program structure are important and need to be properly related to achieve the goal of successful programming. How this is done is the subject of this book. The story is fascinating and sometimes involved, but it has a happy ending: you master practical programming techniques. These techniques provide the programmer with the means to keep a tight rein on programs so that they remain understandable, maintainable, and efficient, even as they grow in size.

There is structure, then, in both the data and the program itself, and both program and data structure must be appropriate to their tasks. This book presents data structures, not as an isolated theoretical subject, but as an essential object of the problem-solving process leading to the creation of a good program. Three main themes are stressed.

1. Data structures and their impact on programs
2. Programming methodology and its impact on programs
3. Consolidation and extension of knowledge of a high-level language

Data structures are important because the way the programmer chooses to represent data significantly affects the clarity, conciseness, speed of execution, and storage requirements of the program. The text shows how to use particular data structures to create correct and efficient programs. You will see that the operations to be performed on the data determine the best data structures to use.

Developing programs is difficult, especially when done without good guidelines. Creating programs entails solving problems. ***Top-down programming,*** another name for ***structured programming,*** makes program development easier and leads to well-structured programs. It is the controlled breaking down of a complex task into simpler ones whose individual solutions easily combine to carry out the original task. This process gives structure to the development of programs (hence its name). The top-down, or structured, approach, combined with good programming style, is emphasized in this text. Elements of good programming style include the use of data abstractions and functional modularization, which significantly enhance the readability and changeability of programs.

Data abstraction treats a collection of data by abstracting its important aspects while ignoring as much detail as possible. A data abstraction reduces data to a collection, and to those processing operations directly allowed on that collection. The effect is as though the collection were in an impenetrable black box, the only access to the contents of the box being through the invocation of one or more of the allowed operations. How the collection is actually stored within the box, and how the operations are actually performed, become irrelevant details. Such details determine the efficiency of a program but do not affect its logic.

Functional modularization is the use of a special program unit to carry out a task. In FORTRAN such a unit would be a function or subroutine, in Pascal a function or procedure, in COBOL a paragraph, and in C a function. These program units are used to carry out meaningful processing tasks. C programmers use the word *modularization* in two ways. One means functional modularization, and the other has to do with packaging a data abstraction using one or more related files. When the first meaning is intended, this book uses *functional modularization.* The second interpretation appears only in Chapter 5 and will be addressed there.

Practice may not make perfect but seems to be the best way to make problem solvers and programmers out of computer science students. As a student you must repeatedly practice creating programs, because repetition is what facilitates learning. As in learning to dance, draw, or drive, no matter how closely you watch others perform, you can develop skills only by practice.

Finally, whatever high-level programming language you use, studying and understanding the material in this text will enhance your knowledge of that language and your ability to use it effectively. It is assumed that you are familiar with some high-level programming language. Such languages share many features, but each is unique. Although this text occasionally indulges in comparative investigations, all programs herein are written in VAX C, version 2.2, and run on a VAX 11/780 under VMS.

Horowitz [1983] is a collection of reprints of the landmark papers in programming languages. For background in C, see the introductory texts by Kelley and Pohl [1986], Miller and Quilici [1986], and the classic book by Kernighan and Ritchie [1978]. A good reference is Harbison and Steele [1987]. Advanced topics can be found in Berry [1986] and Lapin [1987]. For interesting reading in structured programming, the reader should study the texts by Dahl, Dijkstra, and Hoare [1972] and Wirth [1973].

1.2 A Look Ahead

A nucleus of commonly used data structures will be introduced. These include arrays and records, which are ***static*** structures that change only their values, and stack, lists, trees, and files, which are ***dynamic*** structures whose size and shape change as well as their values. Specific ways to implement each structure will be explained and typical and important operations on them investigated. These operations include selection, traversal, insertion, deletion, searching, and sorting. Although particular methodologies and data structures are important, it is more important to acquire skill in applying a methodology and in determining which data structures are appropriate for a given problem.

Programs are built from data structures. Yet the methodology an expert programmer uses makes the data structures invisible and makes the program structure clear and understandable. Neither good program structure nor good data structure selection alone produces good programs. Both must be done well, but they cannot be done independently. Obtaining a good program requires a well-designed solution, expressed first as an algorithm. The final step is writing the program in a programming language.

Determining what information is required to implement the algorithm and how to store it for efficient use and processing are perhaps the most crucial aspects of that facet of problem solving that is commonly called *computer programming*. The aim of this text is to illustrate good algorithm design, data structure selection, and programs.

If you do not know how to solve a given problem, then you cannot magically write a program to do so. In other words, *if you don't know where you are going, then it doesn't matter how you get there*. Moreover, as H. L. Mencken said, "Every complex problem has a simple easy-to-understand wrong answer." So before you begin writing a program, you will need to understand the problem and write a step-by-step solution, or ***algorithm.***

Unfortunately, there is no algorithm for finding algorithms. There isn't even an algorithm for checking a candidate to see if it really is an algorithm. But there are some helpful techniques for developing algorithms. For example, it is useful to recognize when a known algorithm or program can be modified to give a solution to a new problem. One way to enhance this recognition is to solve problems in general or abstract terms. Sometimes a problem requires finding an object stored in computer memory that has certain properties. One technique is to search through the set of all objects until one with the desired properties is found. Alternatively, objects without the desired properties may be eliminated. The latter approach is used to develop a prime number algorithm in Section 1.3. At other times it may be possible to avoid searching altogether by constructing the desired object directly. Thinking up an algorithm is usually more difficult than programming it.

1.3 The Need for Structure

Imagine that you are a census taker charged with visiting all the homes in Spokesville and Squaresville (Figure 1.1). In each town, you must start and finish at home 1, after visiting each home once. All roads are the same length, and there are the same number of homes in each town. Nonetheless, in Spokesville you will travel a total distance exactly twice the distance required in Squaresville! The difference is due to structure.

It is easy to find the telephone number of a company whose name you know, even in the telephone directory of a large city. But finding the name of a company when you know only its telephone number is a tedious and time-consuming chore. The information in the telephone directory is structured in such a way that one task is easy while the other causes tension headache and eyestrain!

Two maps of the continental United States appear in Figure 1.2; part (a) gives a clear overview, while (b) gives a more detailed view. Structure clarifies, and detail obscures. Still, both are needed for a complete picture. Notice that drawing a border around and naming each state in the overview, in the absence of other distracting details, makes the composition of the country discernible. It is the plethora of detail and subordination of structure that is overwhelming in the other map. The less detailed map is analogous to a functionally modularized program, the other to an unmodularized program.

An algorithm for a given problem specifies a series of operations to be performed that eventually leads to a correct result. Algorithms express solutions step by step. In stating an algorithm, care must be taken to avoid ambiguity and to be sure that it is clear how each step is to be done. When the solution is translated

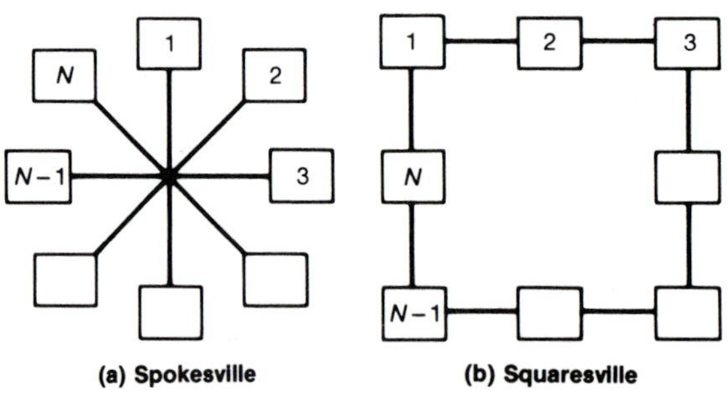

Figure 1.1 A Tale of Two Cities

into a programming language for execution by a computer, even more care and attention to detail are needed. But first, the solution is usually expressed in English or flowchart form, before the details required by the programming language are introduced. The next example illustrates the effect of structure in this context.

An integer larger than 1 is a ***prime number*** if it cannot be written as the product of two integers, each larger than 1. Suppose we must find a way to print all prime numbers between 2 and some integer n. Thus if n is 12, the primes are 2, 3, 5, 7, and 11. Compare the following two algorithms for accomplishing this task.

primes(n)

1. Create a collection called `candidates`, consisting of all integers from 2 to n.
2. Remove all nonprime integers from `candidates`.
3. Print all integers that remain in `candidates`.

anotherprimes(n)

1. Set $X_1, X_2, \ldots, X_n$ to zero.
2. Set k to 2.
3. If X_k is 1, go to step 7.
4. Print k.
5. Set m to the integer part of n/k.
6. Set $X_k, X_{2k}, \ldots, X_{mk}$ to 1.
7. Set k to $k + 1$.
8. If $k \le \sqrt{n}$, go to step 3.
9. If X_k is zero, print k.
10. Set k to $k - 1$.
11. If $k \le n$, go to step 9.

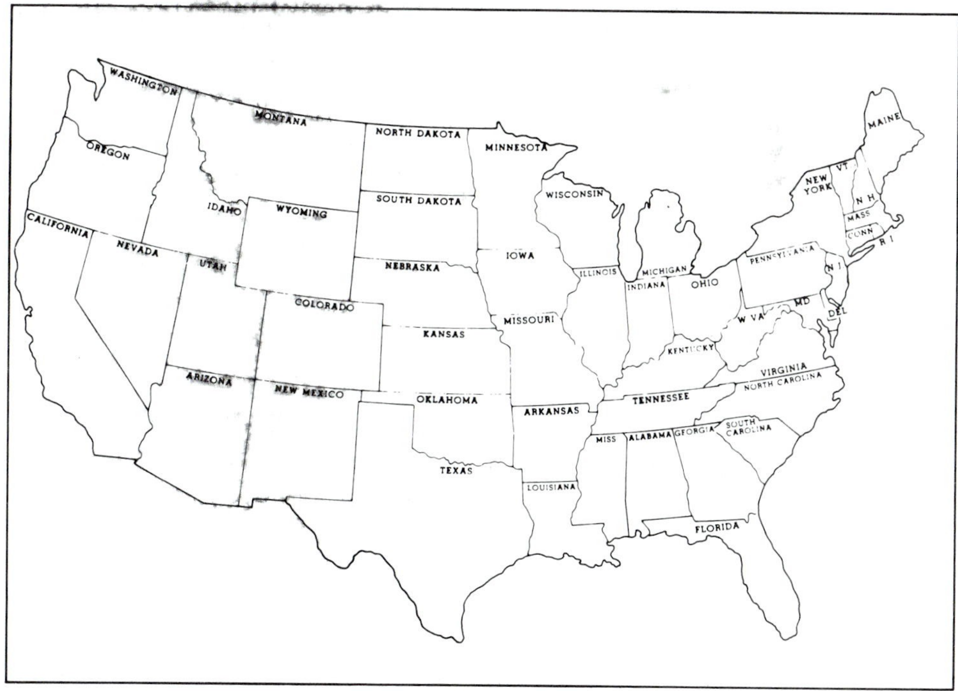

(a) Overview

Figure 1.2(a) Courtesy: Hammond Incorporated, Maplewood, NJ 07040.

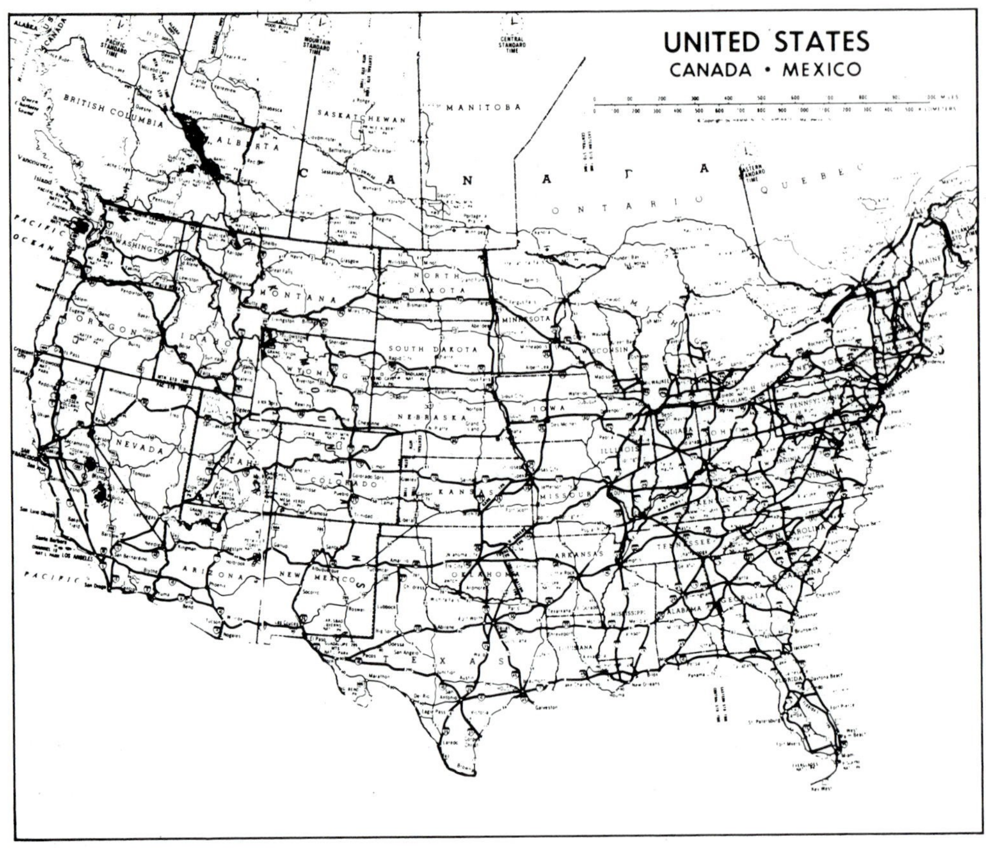

(b) Detailed View

Figure 1.2(b) Courtesy: Hammond Incorporated, Maplewood, NJ 07040.

It is not difficult to see that if each step of the first algorithm can be carried out, the correct result will be printed. It is considerably more difficult to see that the same is also true of the second algorithm. The first is structured to provide clarity, while the second is poorly structured and provides too much detail. These examples indicate why structure is needed in each stage of program design. Structured solutions are easier to understand, expand, and alter, and structured data make the operations of the algorithm easier and faster to perform.

1.3.1 Using Structure

Well-designed, clear programs are based on the explicit underlying methodology called ***structured*** programming. As problems and their solutions become more sophisticated, the brute-force or ad hoc method of programming becomes much less effective. Compilers, operating systems, business management systems, and word processing systems consist of many thousands of program statements. Just as writing a lengthy book is several magnitudes more difficult than writing a paragraph, so is the process of developing a large programming system much more involved than writing a short program. There must be an overall structure.

An example of a large and complex program is an operating system. Many years ago it was thought that operating systems could not be implemented without errors. The immensity of the task was believed to cause inherent problems that could not be isolated and debugged in advance of system implementation. Hence system failure seemed inevitable and getting the system up and running meant a long trial-and-error period of testing and debugging. A new methodology of system design based on the concept of structured programming has demonstrated, however, that error-free operating systems are possible.

Since the programs you see as a student may be relatively trivial, the need for a well-founded methodology of programming may not be evident. However, imagine a large program (twenty pages long, and over a thousand lines of program statements) that you did not write. If you were assigned the task of modifying the program to add a new feature, how or where would you start? Certainly you must have a full understanding of what the program does, how it does it, and how it relates to other programs that use it or are used by it. Anyone who intends to read, write, modify, or correct any programming systems with more than a few dozen statements should use structured programming.

1.3.2 A Prime Example

The example of prime numbers is presented here in more detail to illustrate the process and benefits of structuring and the concept of data abstraction. To do this a group of functions is developed from the first prime number algorithm:

primes(*n*)

1. Create a collection called `candidates,` consisting of all integers from 2 to *n*.
2. Remove all nonprime integers from `candidates.`
3. Print all integers that remain in `candidates.`

Consider first a simple function called `primes`.

```
primes(n)
int n;
{
    collection candidates;
    create(n,candidates);
    remove(n,candidates);
    print(n,candidates);
}
```

`Primes` may be obtained directly from the prime number algorithm when `create`, `remove`, and `print` are interpreted as functions carrying out steps 1, 2, and 3 of the algorithm, respectively. Note that no assumptions about `candidates` have been made. At this point it is of type `collection`, which has not yet been defined. Later in the process of developing the algorithm and program, `collection`, and thereby `candidates`, will be defined, after the basic operations on `candidates` become clear. Note that `collection` is a type, whereas

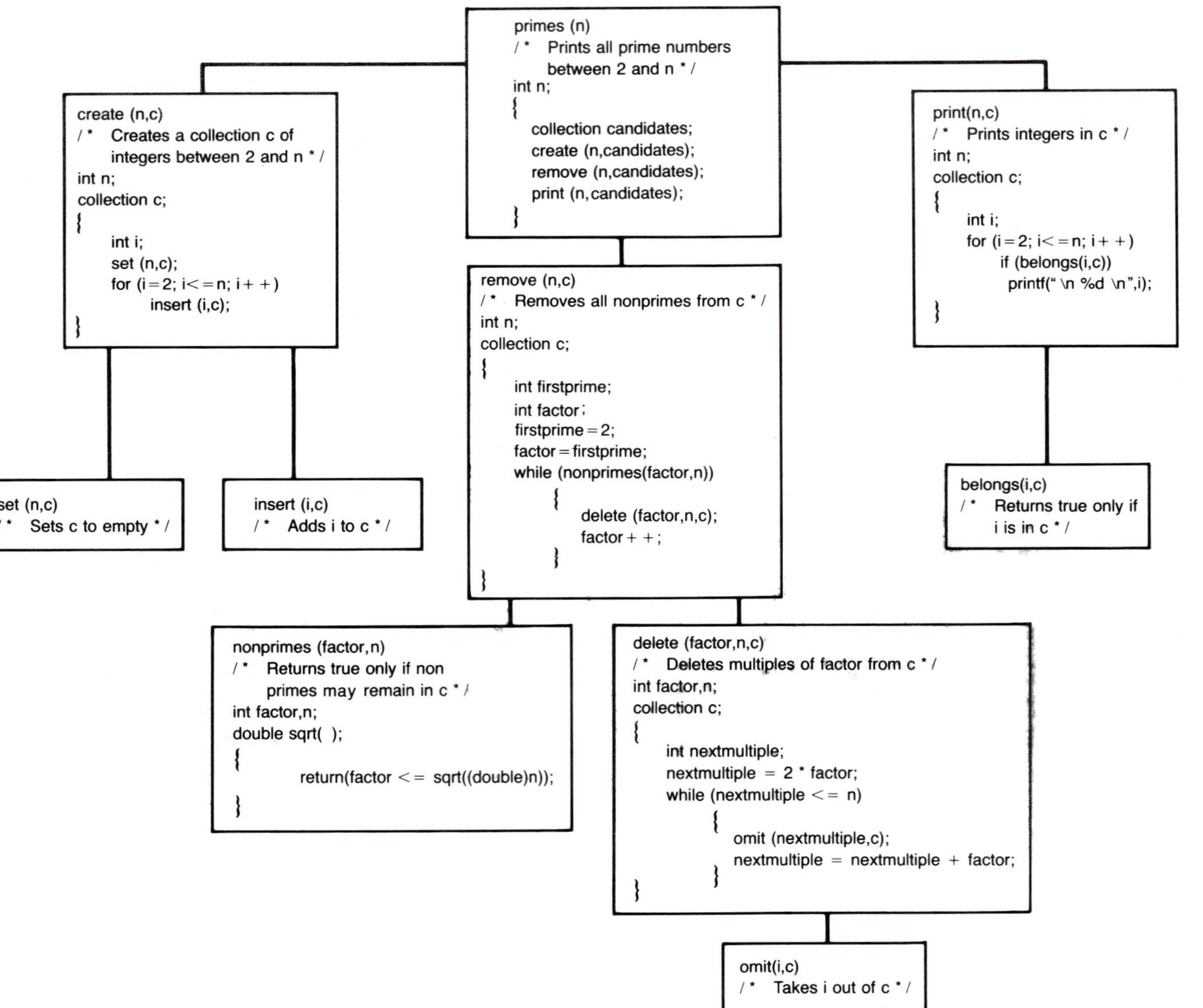

Figure 1.3 PRIMES Modularized

`candidates` is a variable whose type must be declared. The next step is to refine and verify each function of `primes`. ***Refine*** means to express or define in more detail; ***verify*** means to confirm that a refinement does indeed do its job. To refine and verify `create` and `print` is straightforward enough, but to refine and verify `remove` is more difficult. If you want to know more about a state than you see in the first map of Figure 1.2, you may consult another map containing more information on the state's geography. Similarly, if you want to know how to carry out `remove`, a more detailed description may be available. If not, as is the case here, `remove` may be treated as a new problem whose solution must be found. One solution is this:

remove(*n*, candidates)

Set `factor` to the first prime.
While (nonprimes remain in `candidates`),
    Delete from `candidates` all integers that are multiples of `factor`, and
    Increase `factor` by 1.

It is again easy to see that, as long as each step is done correctly, the desired effect is obtained.

Still, more examination is needed to determine whether "nonprimes remain in `candidates`." It can be shown that nonprimes may remain in `candidates` only when `factor` is less than or equal to the square root of `n`. Consequently the condition (nonprimes remain in `candidates`) may be replaced by the condition (`factor` $\leq \sqrt{n}$). But doing this will make `remove` more difficult to understand. It is better to consider the evaluation of the condition as a new task that must be refined. We are now ready to write the function for `remove` and to verify it. The three functions appear in Figure 1.3, where `set` initializes the collection `candidates` to empty, `insert` adds the integer `i` to the collection, `nonprimes` is a function assumed to return the value *true* when `factor` $\leq \sqrt{n}$ and *false* otherwise, `delete` removes all integers from `candidates` that are multiples of `factor`, and `belongs` returns the value *true* if `i` is in `candidates` and *false* otherwise.

`Delete` is refined next (Figure 1.3). You should verify that this function correctly performs its task as long as `omit` takes `nextmultiple` out of `candidates`. It may help to simulate the execution of `delete` when `n` is 40 and `factor` is 2, and then 3.

Each task of function `primes` has now been defined and is, in fact, a complete C function. All other tasks, except for `set`, `insert`, `belongs`, and `omit`, have also been defined. `Primes` and all other tasks have been written ***modularly (functionally)***, meaning that for each task there is a function. For example, new functions have been introduced for each of the three tasks of `primes`: `create`, `remove`, and `print`. Had `primes` along with `remove` and `delete` not been functionally modularized, it would appear as follows:

```
primes(n)
int n;
{
   collection candidates;
   int factor,i,nextmultiple;
   int firstprime;
   firstprime = 2;
   double sqrt();
   set(n,candidates);                          ] initialize candidates to empty
   for (i=2;i<=n;i++)                          ] inserts integers 2 to n into candidates
      insert(i,candidates);
   factor = firstprime;
   while (factor <= sqrt((double)n))
         {                                     ] removes nonprimes
            nextmultiple = 2 * factor;           from candidates
            while (nextmultiple <= n)
               {
                  omit(nextmultiple,candidates);
                  nextmultiple = nextmultiple + factor;
               }
            factor++
         }
   for (i=2;i<=n;i++)                          ] prints the primes
      if(belongs(i,candidates))
         printf("\n %d\n",i);
}
```

This version is also a refinement of `primes`, but instead of defining new functions for its three tasks, the tasks have been replaced by ***program segments.*** Thus there are two basic ways to refine any task: (1) define a new function for the task, or (2) replace the task directly by its refinement expressed as a program segment in code. Compare this version with the functionally modularized form, the simple function `primes` given earlier. Notice that functional modularization suppresses detail.

Deciding how to modularize a program functionally is often a matter of individual taste, but as this text unfolds, the process will become clearer, and you will be able to develop your own style. Functional modularization is intended to highlight and isolate important tasks. The advantage of using functions may not be apparent with this simple prime number problem but will be striking in more complex problems.

Finally, the low-level tasks `set`, `insert`, `omit`, and `belongs` must be coded. To do this requires deciding how to implement `candidates`—that is, deciding which data structures shall be used to store `candidates` and how to write the basic functions that operate on `candidates`. Recall that data structures such as `candidates` contain information and are operated on during the execution of a program. No matter how `candidates` is implemented, none of the functions already defined needs to be changed. They are independent of `candidates` implementation (except for the data declaration). As long as `set`, `insert`, `omit`, and `belongs` do their tasks correctly, no function invoking them needs to be changed. This is because we have written them treating `candidates` as a ***data abstraction.*** That is, we have assumed that `candidates` and the basic operations on it are available via functions (`set`, `insert`, `omit`, and `belongs`) and further, that any other operations on `candidates` have been expressed in terms of these functions. For instance, `delete` uses `omit`, and `create` uses `insert`. If, instead of calls to `set`, `insert`, `omit`, and `belongs`, the code defining them had been used, all functions containing these codes *would* be dependent on the implementation. Later, if we changed to a better implementation, it would be necessary to hunt through each function, find any code that would be affected by the change, and modify that code appropriately. A data abstraction consists of a data structure, to store data, and allowed operations on the data structure, to manipulate it. As a result, wherever one of these operations is invoked in a program, the data structure is being affected. Just as important, the data structure is *not* being affected unless one of these operations is invoked.

The use of data abstraction and functional modularization not only enhances understanding, but also simplifies *maintaining* a program. Maintenance is a crucial aspect of programming. It involves changing a program to do something new, to stop doing something, or to do better what it now does.

Using data abstractions as outlined above hides implementation details and makes the program independent of those details. On the other hand, the program's speed of execution and storage requirements will be greatly influenced by the implementation of the data abstraction. Consequently, the selection of an implementation should be based on the data abstraction's operations. Sometimes the choice that minimizes execution time and storage will be evident. More typically, conflicts arise, and the choice will involve trade-offs between time and storage. How to make this choice properly is a major focus of this text.

Consider two ways to implement `candidates`. It might be implemented as an integer array with the *i*th element of the array containing the value *true* if *i* is a prime and *false* if it is not. Alternatively, `candidates` could be implemented as an integer that is made up of contributions from each number in `candidates`. If the number *i* is in `candidates`, it contributes 2^i. Thus if `candidates` consisted of 2, 3, 5, 7, and 9, its value would be 684(4 + 8 + 32 + 128 + 512). The integer is stored in an integer array of size one. `Candidates` could also be implemented as a dynamic list or tree and, indeed, one of these might be preferred. You might want to return to this problem after studying lists and trees, to verify that it can be converted to these structures. However, at this stage, arrays that are more familiar to you will be used. The code below defines the operations on `candidates` for the two array implementations. Each implementation should have its type declaration for `collection` global to `primes` and all its functions, as follows:

Candidates Implemented as an Array

```
typedef int collection[MAXN];

set(n,c)
/* Sets c to empty */
int n;
collection c;
```

Candidates Implemented as an Integer

```
typedef int collection[1];

set(n,c)
/* Sets c to empty */
int n;
collection c;
```

```
{
   int i;
   for (i=1;i<=n;i++)
      c[i] = FALSE;
}

insert(i,c)
/* Inserts i into c */
int i;
collection c;
{
   c[i] = TRUE;
}

omit(i,c)
/* Removes i from c */
int i;
collection c;
{
   c[i] = FALSE;
}

belongs(i,c)
/* Returns true only
   if i is in c
*/
int i;
collection c;
{
   return(c[i]);
}
```

```
{
   c[0] = 0;
}

insert(i,c)
/* Inserts i into c */
int i;
collection c;
{
   int p,q;
   p = power(2,i);
   q = (c[0]/p)%2;
   c[0] = c[0] + (1-q)*p;
}
```

if `i` *is not in* `c`*, adds* 2^i *to* `c[0]`

```
omit(i,c)
/* Removes i from c */
int i;
collection c;
{
   int p,q;
   p = power(2,i);
   q = (c[0]/p)%2;
   c[0] = c[0] - q*p;
}
```

if `i` *is in* `c`*, subtracts* 2^i *from* `c[0]`

```
belongs(i,c)
/* Returns true only
   if i is in c
*/
int i;
collection c;
{
   return((c[0]/power(2,i))%2);
}

power(x,y)
/* Returns x to the power y */
int x,y;
{
   int i,p;
      p = 1;
   for (i=1;i<=y;++i)
      p = p*x;
   return(p);
}
```

Note that the terms **TRUE** and **FALSE** are used in the boolean version. Since C does not have a type boolean, **TRUE** and **FALSE** must be defined before they are used in the program. In C, a *true* statement returns a non-zero value, and a *false* statement returns a zero. For consistency, write

```
# define TRUE  1
# define FALSE 0
```

TRUE and **FALSE** will be used for programming style in many places in the text. Programs that use them merely require the above statements. In the second version the function `power(2,i)` returns 2^i.

Each implementation specifies a data structure for **candidates** and defines the same four basic operations allowed on it. Each entails some explicit restriction on the size of **candidates**. Such restrictions can be avoided by using the dynamic data structures introduced in later chapters.

The first implementation of **candidates** allows **insert**, **omit**, and **belongs** to be written so that they take constant time to execute. However, the amount of storage required will depend directly on n. The second implementation for **candidates** increases the execution times of the basic operations on **candidates** but reduces its storage requirement. In general, the choice of implementation for a data abstraction may be critical, determining whether a program will run to completion or abort because of insufficient time or storage. Section 1.8 discusses the selection of program and data structure in more detail. In any case, once the decision is made, the data declaration for **candidates** must appear in **primes**. The final result is a well-structured program. A complete program to run primes using the array implementation follows.

```
#include <stdio.h>

main()
{
   int n;
   printf("\n n = ? \n");
   scanf("%d",&n);
   primes(n);
}
```

reads in an integer n *and calls* **primes** *to print all prime numbers* ≤ n

```
#define TRUE 1
#define FALSE 0
#define MAXN 500
typedef int collection[MAXN];

set(n,c)
/* Sets c to empty */
int n;
collection c;
{
   int i;
   for (i=1;i<=n;i++)
      c[i] = FALSE;
}
```

These definitions and functions give a specific implementation of a data abstraction: `collection` *with operations* `set`, `insert`, `omit`, *and* `belongs` *allowed. This is the* ***only*** *portion of the program that needs to be changed when the implementation of the data abstraction is changed.* **MAXN** *sets a limit on the size of arrays of type* `collection`, *so it sets a limit for* n.

```
insert(i,c)
/* Inserts i in c */
int i;
collection c;
{
   c[i] = TRUE;
}

omit(i,c)
/* Removes i from c */
int i;
collection c;
{
   c[i] = FALSE;
}

belongs(i,c)
/* Returns true only
   if i is in c
*/
int i;
collection c;
{
   return(c[i]);
}

primes(n)
/* Prints all prime numbers between 2 and n */
int n;
{
   collection candidates;
   create(n,candidates);
   remove(n,candidates);
   print(n,candidates);
}

create(n,c)
/* Creates a collection of integers between 2 and n */
int n;
collection c;
{
   int i;
   set(n,c);
   for (i=2;i<=n;i++)
      insert(i,c);
}

remove(n,c)
/* Removes all nonprimes from c */
int n;
collection c;
{
```

This portion of the program is independent of the specific implementation of the data abstraction. It does not have to be changed if the implementation of the data abstraction changes. `Candidates` *is an instance of the data structure of type* `collection`.

sets `c` *to empty*

inserts integers 2 to `n` *in* `c`

```
    int firstprime;
    int factor;
    firstprime = 2;
    factor = firstprime;
    while (nonprimes(factor,n))
        {
            delete(factor,n,c);
            factor++;
        }
}

nonprimes(factor,n)
/* Returns true only if non
   primes may remain in c
*/
int factor,n;
double sqrt();
{
    return(factor <= sqrt((double)n));
}

delete(factor,n,c)
/* Deletes multiples of factor from c */
int factor,n;
collection c;
{
    int nextmultiple;
    nextmultiple = 2 * factor;
    while (nextmultiple <= n)
        {
            omit(nextmultiple,c);
            nextmultiple = nextmultiple + factor;
        }
}

print(n,c)
/* Prints integers in c */
int n;
collection c;
{
    int i;
    for (i=2;i<=n;i++)
        if (belongs(i,c))
            printf("\n %d\n",i);
}
```

For all values of `factor` *from 2 to* `n`*, invokes* `delete` *to remove multiples*

returns true *as long as* `factor` *is not larger than the square root of* `n`

invokes `omit` *to remove each nonprime from* `c` *that is a multiple of* `factor`

invokes `belongs` *for each integer from 2 to* `n` *to determine if it is a prime, and if so prints it*

As noted, the first implementation for `collection` is used in the program. Notice that the declarations and definitions needed for the collection appear together in the program. Simply replacing that portion of the program with another implementation is all that is required to change to the new implementation. In Chapter 5 another way to package the collection and its operations for this program will be presented.

Abstraction allows us to focus on concepts rather than concrete details. The architects planning a building assume an elevator as part of the plan. They know the elevator will hold passengers and freight. They know the elevator will convey its contents between floors, respond to call buttons, and be warm in winter and cool in summer. The initial building plans can proceed using only these essential concepts regarding the elevator. Later, the detailed choices necessary to build the elevator will be made. They will determine its size, shape, and structure, as well as its speed, responsiveness, and reliability. Notice that, as long as the elevator is treated as an abstraction, any specific implementation can be substituted for another without requiring changes to the plan.

Similarly, data abstraction allows us to focus on what is needed rather than how it will be assembled and packaged. Planning a program, we assume that we have specific means to store and operate on data. Only later must an implementation be selected. The implementation determines how well the job is done, but does not affect its logical design. The longer this choice can be delayed in program development, the more independent of this specific choice our program will be. This is highly desirable, making program changes much easier to effect.

1.4 Basic Constructs

The richness and power of a language are related to the variety and ease of expression that the language allows. Thus high-level computer languages provide more expressive power than more limited languages, such as assembly languages. However, it is theoretically possible to state any algorithm using only three basic constructs and the rules for their combination. In this discussion three basic constructs have been chosen for the sake of conciseness, but others are used freely when appropriate.

The three constructs indicate different types of *flow of control*. Each construct determines the order in which its tasks are processed, and each was chosen for its logic and clarity.

The first is the ***sequence*** construct, in which each task follows the previous one without altering the order of the tasks. Each task is executed once. Notice that `primes` (Figure 1.3) is based on this construct. The second is the ***decision*** construct, which allows only one of two tasks to be carried out, depending on a controlling logical condition. The appropriate task is executed once. It is the true task when the condition is true and the false task when the condition is false. The final construct is the ***loop,*** which enables a task to be repeated until a controlling condition no longer holds. Obviously, the loop must at some point end so that the next task can be executed. Failure to change the value of the controlling condition in order to end the loop task results in the infamous "infinite loop." Examples of algorithms formulated according to the three basic constructs appear in Figure 1.4 as structured flowcharts, along with their structured English equivalents. The corresponding versions are obvious.

Each construct has exactly one entry and one exit point. The constructs may

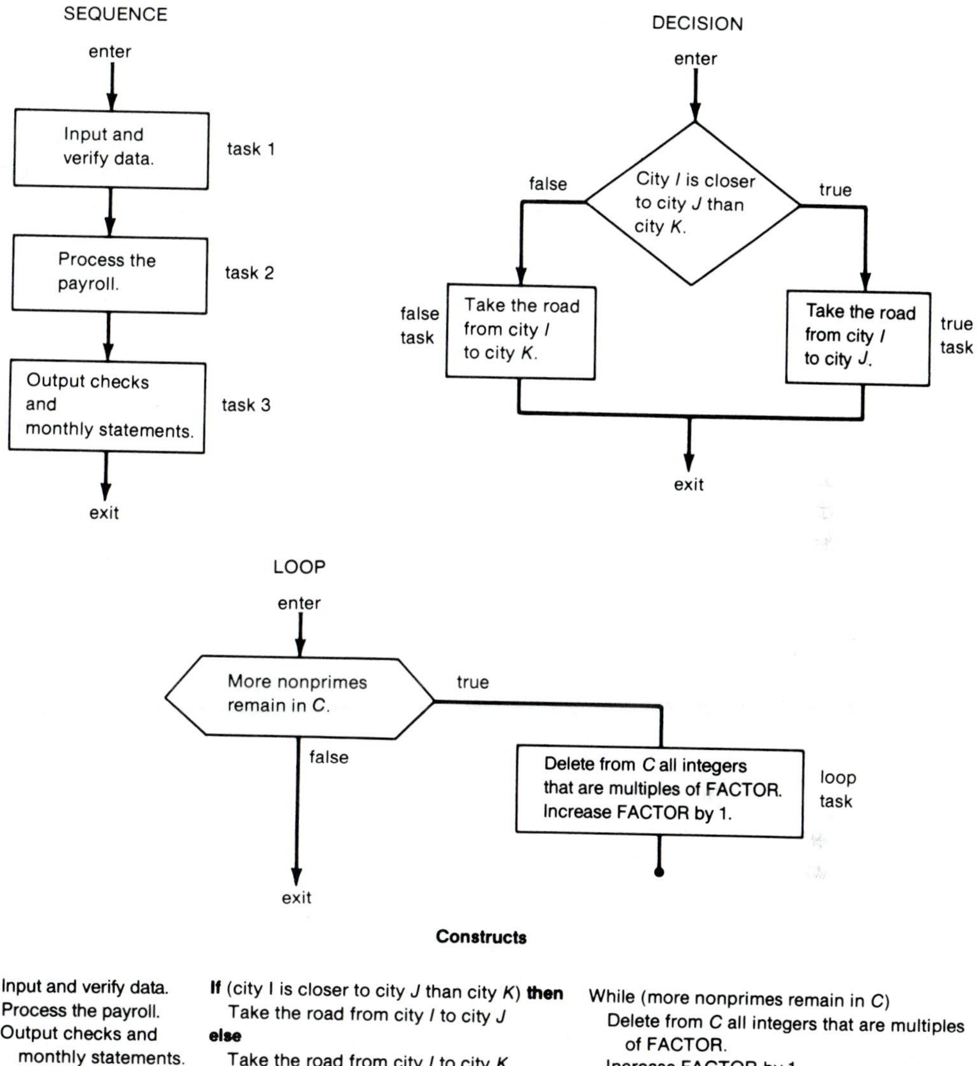

Input and verify data.
Process the payroll.
Output checks and
monthly statements.
	If (city I is closer to city *J* than city *K*) **then**
	Take the road from city *I* to city *J*
	else
	Take the road from city *I* to city *K*.
		While (more nonprimes remain in *C*)
		Delete from *C* all integers that are multiples of FACTOR.
		Increase FACTOR by 1.

English Equivalents

Figure 1.4 The Basic Control Constructs and Their English Equivalents

be combined only by making the exit arrow of one the entrance arrow of another. This results in complex constructs that are sequences of constructs. The only allowed modification of a construct is the replacement of any of its tasks by one of the three basic constructs. This amounts to incorporating the task's refinements into the construct, producing a more complex construct.

There are two different ways to express a solution using these constructs and rules for their combination. One is to start with a basic construct and repeatedly apply modifications to it. Each modification corresponds to the use of a program segment for its implementation. This results in a final unmodularized flowchart, English equivalent, or program. See the unmodularized version of `primes` for an example. The second is to start with a basic construct, and, instead of modifying it, express the solution for each of its tasks as a separate function. This amounts to functionally modularizing each task's refinement, with the complete solution consisting of the collection of individual solutions. This results in a final collection of functionally modularized flowcharts, their English equivalents, or program components. Usually a combination of the two is better than using one method only. It is wise to keep each part of a solution to a reasonable size, say one page. This can serve as a guide to whether or not ***functional modularization*** (the use of a function) or ***modification*** (the use of a program segment) is appropriate. But remember: the primary goal is clarity.

1.5 Top-Down Design

The purpose of structured programming is to create programs that are

- *Understandable,* meaning the logic is readily followed
- *Reliable,* so the program performs as intended
- *Adaptable,* so modifications can be made with reasonable effort

Structured programming is a method of approaching a problem rather than adhering to a rigid set of rules.

As Dijkstra [1972] observed, the "art of programming is the art of organizing complexity, of mastering multitude and avoiding its bastard chaos as effectively as possible." The essential concept of structured programming is that dealing with complexity requires simplicity.

Regarding terminology, note that the tasks performed by a program solve problems. In this book the words *task* and *problem* are used interchangeably. Each programming task entails defining the input information to be processed, defining the output information to be produced, and stating clearly the precise instructions as to *what,* but not *how,* it is to be done.

Simplicity and clarity are achieved in a complex program by focusing attention on just one task at a time. To show *how* the task is done, it is broken down into smaller meaningful subtasks. The combination of smaller tasks to perform the given task is called a ***refinement*** of that task. The next step is verifying that the refinement is correct—that is, that the refinement indeed accomplishes the task, as long as each of its components does its job. This verification may be done even without knowing *how* each component works. This is important. How the components of a refinement work is irrelevant to verification. The goal is to ensure that, if they work correctly, then the refinement itself works correctly.

Top-down design begins with the original problem and involves a loop: repeated refining and verifying of the problem and its refinements until only implementable problems remain. ***Implementable*** means simple enough to be directly coded in a programming language. Review the development in Section 1.3.2 for `primes` to see that this loop was, in fact, being used. With this approach the programmer can be sure the final program is correct even though he or she has considered only one manageable piece at a time.

If the total number of tasks needed to complete a detailed solution is proportional to the complexity of the initial problem (as we hope), then the effort to create, understand, and verify a solution to a complex problem will also be proportional to its complexity. This is a very desirable situation. If the cost of a solution increased more drastically with complexity, then the complexity of problems we could solve would be much more severely limited.

Think about building a jigsaw puzzle. You probably use the top-down approach. You break up the picture conceptually into components—say, the border and recognizable objects with distinct shapes and colors. Then you build each component and combine them all. Surely the most difficult puzzles are those with no distinguishable objects. They prevent refinement, forcing one to deal with all the complexity at one time. Perhaps this is why all the problems humans solve have structure; they are the only ones we can handle.

Two caveats must be added:

1. At each level of refinement, keep the number of component tasks small and keep them independent. This is critical because human beings can deal well with only a few things at a time, and can do so more readily when the things are not intertwined. Psychological studies suggest a "magic number": a maximum of seven tasks, plus or minus two. *Independence* means that how one task is accomplished need not be a consideration in how another task is done. Sometimes independence must be given up for other considerations, such as efficiency. These trade-offs should be considered carefully.

2. Control carefully how tasks of a refinement are combined. Simplicity requires structure that makes the logic of a program easily discernible. Certain combinations or constructs foster such clarity. Some programs present a bewildering panorama of program statements, but what is needed are programs that appear as a logical sequence of tasks to be executed. Some ways of expressing the order in which tasks are to be executed are more understandable than others. Constructs that are well designed allow anyone working with a program to grasp quickly what is intended. This is the hallmark of the basic constructs—sequence, decision, and loop—introduced in Section 1.4.

1.6 High-Level Languages

High-level languages provide basic data structures and operations and the capability of using these to build more complex data structures and operations. With some languages it can be hard to realize this capability, while with others it is relatively effortless. In addition, languages have different idiosyncrasies and subtle shortcomings. In this text, the focus is not on the language but on the more general topics of program structure and data structure selection. Still, whatever background you have in high-level languages may be helpful.

A program written in a high-level language specifies a series of operations to be performed on data structures. Think of a high-level language as having an associated *high-level computer* that carries out those operations and stores those data structures in its memory. Such high-level computers are just a concept—normally they are not built. The conventional computer is not specifically a C, Cobol, Pascal, or FORTRAN machine; we rely on compilers to translate programs from high-level languages into the languages of existing computers. The translated version is then executed by the conventional computer. The compiler, in effect, makes the conventional computer appear to be a high-level computer for the high-level language.

To do this translation, the compiler must find a way to represent the program's data structures, using those in the conventional computer's language. It must also apply operations of the conventional computer's language to these representations to simulate the program's operations on its data structures. How this is done, or what the actual computer is, does not affect the correctness of programs written in the high-level language. This is data abstraction par excellence! However, the way this is done will influence the storage requirements and execution time of the program. It can also cause problems for the unwary user.

1.6.1 Data Types

Programs use ***variables*** to refer to storage elements in the memory of the high-level computer. Each variable has a ***name,*** which refers to its storage elements, and a ***value,*** which is the content of those elements. For example, the C assignment statement

```
sum = sum + increment;
```

uses two variables with names `sum` and `increment`. Individual variables, which correspond to a single storage element, are the simplest type of data structure. More complex structures are built from variables. In turn, operations on the more complex structures are built from operations on the simpler structures. High-level languages differ in the kinds of basic data structures they provide. For example, FORTRAN includes individual variables and dimensioned arrays. C adds records and pointers and, significantly, allows the definition of new data types and data structures. The Ada language allows new basic operations to be introduced as well.

Each variable must be defined by a declaration that gives its name and data type. The ***data type*** indicates the actual values that may by assumed by the variable. For example, the C declaration

```
int sum, increment;
char check;
```

specifies that `sum` and `increment` are the names of variables whose values will be integers, and that `check` is the name of a variable whose values will be a character.

1.6.2 Data Representation

Data types must be specified. An example will show why. Suppose a compiler represents integer and real variables (floats) using seven decimal digits. Then in storage that is designated type integer, the value 1230045 represents the integer number 1,230,045. In storage that is designated type float the value 1230045 represents the real number 0.30045×10^{12}. In general, the compiler interprets

$d_1\, d_2 \ldots d_7$ of type integer as the integer number $d_1\, d_2 \ldots d_7$.

and

$d_1\ d_2\ .\ .\ .\ d_7$ of type float as the real number $0.d_3\ d_4\ .\ .\ .\ d_7 \times 10^{d_1 d_2}$

Given this situation, suppose the compiler must cause the contents of `sum` = `1230045` to be added to the contents of `increment` = `1250047`, where they are both of type integer. The compiler might apply the usual column-by-column addition algorithm:

```
sum          1230045
+
increment    1250047
             -------
             2480092
```

Here, 2480092, when stored in `sum`, represents the correct result. If `sum` and `increment` are of type real, then the content of `sum` represents the real number 0.30045×10^{12} and the content of `increment` represents the real number 0.50047×10^{12}. Their sum is 0.80092×10^{12}. However, if the above column-by-column addition algorithm is applied and the result stored in `sum`, then its contents will still be 2480092, but this now represents the real number 0.80092×10^{24}. This is incorrect by a factor of 10^{12}. To represent the correct result, `sum` should contain 1280092. The difficulty is, of course, that the same algorithm should not be applied for the addition of numbers of both type integer and type float. Two distinct algorithms are needed, because two distinct representations are used. In general, the algorithms used must depend on the data types of the variables involved. The compiler can choose the correct algorithm only when it knows the data types.

Thus it is essential to declare the data type of each variable so that the compiler can choose the proper algorithm to achieve the intended result. Type declarations also allow high-level language compilers to build in checks for validity. Such checks may generate error messages during compilation or during execution of the program. Languages with more restrictive rules for the manipulation of different data types, called ***strongly typed languages,*** allow more checking. For example, Pascal's strong typing prevents the contents of a variable of one type from being copied into a variable of a different type. C, FORTRAN, and COBOL allow this to be done in some cases but not in others.

The C data types ***integer, float,*** and ***char*** or their equivalents are now standard in most high-level languages. The values they may assume, and the operations that may be performed on variables of these types, are specified in each language.

1.7 Elements of Style

Individual writers, even whole magazines or journals, have their own writing style. Often a glimpse at a few paragraphs can give clues to the author or the type of publication. Still, there are general rules to follow for acceptable style; entire books have been devoted to this subject. Style will always be in style.

Dress, carriage, and response are parts of personal style, as are straightness of teeth, polished or scuffed shoes, and a fast or slow gait. Program style is determined by overall appearance as well as by details of implementation. We want to see the logical structure of a program clearly; too many details cloud the picture. Data abstraction and functional modularization are tools for sharpening the picture. Hiding information, so that only parts of a program that need it can see it, also provides better focus. People react differently to unexpected situations: some become erratic while others remain calm, going cheerfully about their business. Programs should react to unexpected data with aplomb, letting us know about errors, but getting on with the job when possible. Details of a program should not affect its logical structure, only its efficiency. Details can make an otherwise stylish program sloppy, slow, and in need of repair, or they can finish the design so it is elegant, sleek, and well-tuned. What we see isn't always what we get, but stylish programs suggest a better thought-out design and product.

Since good programs must be written with style, guidelines are offered here for this purpose. A good program is correct, easy to read, and changeable through a reasonable amount of effort. Whether or not it should be efficient depends on the application. In some cases an efficient program may be written with the same effort as an inefficient one. In other cases it will be necessary to put in more effort to achieve efficiency, so the additional programming may be done only if it will bring substantial (or required) savings in computation time.

1.7.1 Expressing Purpose

What's in a name? "A rose is a rose is a . . . ." "There's more form than substance." Perhaps these sentiments are true, but in a well-presented program there is a great deal in a name. One function is not another function, and understanding of substance is enhanced by form.

Indentation and proper spacing serve to delineate significant components of a program. Choosing names to convey and delineate purpose is also extremely important. Even without the descriptions given for the functions of Figure 1.3, the names of each function, variable, and constant almost provide, by themselves, enough information to see what each does. On the other hand, inappropriate names can be very misleading and distracting.

Reading identifiers to understand what a program does requires reading the entire program. This is too demanding. After all, when selecting a book, no one wants to be forced to read from cover to cover just to see what it is about. The same holds for a program; program documentation must be provided for this purpose. Good name selection is not enough. The main program and each of its functions must start with comments that allow users (including its author) to understand readily what it does and what its inputs, outputs, and parameters are. The main program's documentation then tells immediately *what* it does. No further reading is necessary unless someone wants to know *how* it is done. Similar comments can precede program segments that implement tasks of some complexity. To a great extent, the structure of a function, coupled with the documentation of each of its tasks, explains *how* the function does what it does. In this sense, structured programs (with proper comments) are self-documenting. Functional modularization and data abstraction help to elucidate structure by obscuring detail. Some programmers are free to develop their own style for delineation and documentation; for others it may be specified rigidly. The case study presented later gives a complete program with documentation as a guide for annotating your own programs. As a rule, complete documentation is not included in programs appearing in this book, since in effect the text itself serves as documentation, discussing completely each program presented. Still, programs will be annotated for clarity. Proper documentation is a prominent aspect of every good program and should become a habit of the programmer. Since the top-down approach requires a description for each task, the documentation for a task may be done as it is introduced, even before it is written.

1.7.2 Communication between Functions

High-level languages allow the definition of three kinds of variables: local, nonlocal, and global. A C program consists of functions. A function of a program may reference

1. ***Local*** variables, to which it alone has access
2. ***Nonlocal*** variables, to which it and some other functions of the program have access
3. ***Global*** variables, to which all functions of the program have access

A variable is referenced by a function in order to copy, modify, or simply look at its value.

High-level languages treat variables in differing ways. FORTRAN, for example, considers variables to be local to a function unless they appear as formal parameters of that function (in which case they are nonlocal). Variables stored in special common areas of memory are global. C determines whether a variable is local, nonlocal, or global by using block rules. In Figure 1.3 `candidates` is local to `primes`, `factor` is local to `remove`, and `nextmultiple` is local to `delete`, while `n` is nonlocal or global to each.

Each high-level language has its own rules to give one function access to variables of another. Merely using the same variable name in two functions will not normally allow one to reference a variable in another. For example, `i` in `create` and `i` in `print` (Figure 1.3) do not represent the same variable; each is local to its function. If this were not so, functions could not be written independently. Once a complex problem has been refined, different individuals or groups should be able to develop components independently. Otherwise, each time a group used a new variable name, it would have to check that no other group used the same name.

The issue here is really communication between functions of a program. ***Communication between functions***—allowing one to reference variables also used by another—occurs in two basic ways: using nonlocal or global variables, or using formal parameters in defining functions.

When a function changes the value of a variable used by another, and the variable is not communicated (or passed) between them as a parameter, a ***side effect*** has occurred. Side effects make it extremely difficult to understand what functions do. It is easier to see what a function does when we can be sure that only the parameters and the local variables will be affected by the execution of the function. The communication structure of a program is clearer when information is communicated explicitly by the use of parameters. This shows "who is doing what to whom." For example, in `delete` (Figure 1.3), no side effects can occur, since the only nonlocal variables `factor`, `n`, and `candidates` all appear as parameters. Thus the only variables not local to `delete` that it can reference are `factor`, `n`, and `candidates`.

At one extreme, it is possible to make all variables global—every function may then reference any variable. Making all variables global requires extremely careful adherence to the use of variable names and increases the probability of side effects. COBOL programs are typically written this way. However, such programs use well-defined file structures, deal with high-volume input and output, and use relatively simple algorithms, so this method may not cause difficulty.

The other extreme is to use only parameters between functions. This may not always be possible. For example, storage considerations may intrude, as with arrays in Pascal.

Communication between functions by using parameters may be a one-way or a two-way street. In some high-level languages, like FORTRAN, any change in the value of a parameter in a called function is passed or reflected back to the calling function. Other languages, such as C, allow one component to communicate information to another yet never reflect changes made to the parameter's value. Upon return, the parameter's value is the same as prior to the call. Also, upon return from a call, different languages treat local variables of functions differently. Some preserve their values between calls, while others do not. In FORTRAN it is possible to have local variables retain their values between invocations of a function; in Pascal it is not. In C either case may apply. Values may be preserved or erased as desired.

1.7.3 Ensuring against Data Errors: Defensive Programming

Functions receive and output data. In `primes`, what happens if `n` is negative or so large that it exceeds the storage capacity allocated to the data structure implementing `candidates`? Think how upset a company's personnel would be if no one received paychecks because the input data for one employee was not valid. Or suppose each employee received an output check equal to the entire payroll. Defensive programming is ensuring that your programs guard against such outcomes by checking for invalid data, incoming or outgoing, and doing something reasonable when such data are discovered. What is reasonable can vary from signaling an error and stopping further processing to simply outputting an error message, ignoring the invalid data, and continuing processing. Sometimes the correct data may be inferred from the invalid data, but this approach must be taken with great caution. The important point is to ensure that errors are discovered. It is safer to have no output than output that is in error but thought to be correct. Invalid data is a very serious problem, regardless of whether it is due to design or to happenstance. Validation functions for input and output should be used, even though it is not always easy to see how to guard against all possible errors. This text does not have space to dwell on the issue of data validation, but it should always be in your mind.

1.7.4 Changing Programs

Consider a new problem: count and print the number of primes that are no greater than n. Instead of immediately attempting a solution, can you think of a program that already solves a related problem? You've already seen one: `primes`. Perhaps it can be changed to help with the solution. Looking at the refinement of `primes` (Figure 1.3), you can see that replacing function `print` by a `count` function that prints the proper count does the trick. The solution `countprimes`, using the changed `primes` and `count`, is as follows.

```
countprimes(n)
/* This function counts the prime
   numbers between 2 and n
   and prints the count.
*/
int n;
{
   collection candidates;
   create(n,candidates);
   remove(n,candidates);
   count(n,candidates);
}

count(n,c)
/* Prints the number of integers
   in c between 2 and n.
*/
int n;
collection c;
{
   int i,counter;
   counter = 0;
   for (i = 2; i<=n;i++)
      if (belongs(i,c))
         counter++;
   printf("\n The number of primes between 2 and %d is %d\n",
          n, counter);
}
```

Solutions are rarely obtained so easily. Yet this example teaches us something. Programs that have been designed wisely, with an eye to generality, may often be used as tools in the solution of related problems. When beginning the development of a solution to a problem, see first if a program for a related problem is already known, and if so whether it can be adapted. This can save significant time, effort, and money compared to writing a new program or function.

It was easy to see what to change and how to change it in our example, because `primes` is functionally modular, with narrowly defined tasks and independent functions. Changes are rarely as straightforward as this; for contrast, consider changing the algorithm `anotherprimes` to a program for `countprimes`. In general, though, isolating functions that carry out a single narrowly defined task tends to generate lower-level functions that are clear, simple, and of moderate size. At higher levels, such single-task functions need not be simple. For example, a function to "Select the best next chess move" is such a function, but it is not simple. The lower the level of a function that needs changing, the less the effort required. However, the higher the level of the task for which one can adapt a known program, the greater the savings, since much refinement is avoided. In an ideal situation, changes require little effort and benefits are great.

Often a programmer's assignment or goal is to increase the efficiency of a program, and this will involve changing the way data are stored. If the program has been written using data abstractions, it is much easier to see exactly which functions need changing. For example, in `primes`, to change the implementation of `candidates` involves changing only its declaration and `set`, `insert`, `omit`, and `belongs`.

1.7.5 Verification and Debugging

Verifying a solution means checking that program segments and functions do their tasks correctly. It is difficult to verify programs, although some formal methods are known. This text will illustrate how a program can be verified informally, but rigorously, for appropriate examples. For most of the small examples, verification is left to the reader.

Although only proper verification can ensure the correctness of a program, debugging can help in locating mistakes. Your goal should be not to run or even code programs until you are sure the algorithm is correct. Even if you are sure of the algorithm, debugging tools should be employed. Then, when your program fails to work correctly (as you know by now it will), you can track down the cause without the help of a Holmes or Watson.

In addition to debugging aids provided by your computer system and compiler, good programming techniques facilitate debugging. For example, it is important to learn to display appropriate error messages and information. The top-down approach includes debugging individual functions or program segments as they are refined, so that debugging proceeds as the program is developed. Verifying, debugging, and documenting all require basic understanding of the program and much the same information. To a large extent, then, they should be done concurrently with program development. During development you have the concepts and information fresh in your mind.

The main program and the other functions may each be debugged independently, just as they may be verified and documented independently. This requires stubs and drivers.

A ***stub*** takes the place of a function. It should have the same name and parameters as the function and, when called, should output a message indicating it was called. For example,

```
remove(n,c)
/* This is a stub for remove */
int n;
collection c;
{
   printf("\n remove was called \n");
}
```

A ***driver*** plays the role of a function that calls another function, and is used to debug the called function. The driver should set up test values for the parameters used by the function it calls, output those values, call the function, and output the returned values. For example,

```
removedriver()
/* This is a driver for remove */
{
   collection candidates;
   int n;
   int sentinel = -1;
   printf("\n enter a value for n between 2 and 27 \n");
   scanf("%2d",&n);
   while (n != sentinel)
      {
         printf("\n remove has been called with n = %d\n",n);
         create(n,candidates);
         print(n,candidates);
         remove(n,candidates);
         printf("\n remove returns n = %d ", n);
         printf(" and candidates: \n");
         print(n,candidates);
         printf("\n enter a new value for n or -1 to stop \n");
         scanf("%2d",&n);
      }
}
```

Using drivers and stubs allows any individual function to be tested and debugged even though the functions that call it and are called by it have not yet been written. Within the function, program segments that correspond to algorithmic tasks can be isolated. A statement can be inserted before and after each of these segments to output a message indicating that the segment was reached during execution, giving the values of variables it worked on, specifying that it was exited during execution, and giving the modified values of the variables.

In this way, you can see the progress of a program during its execution by studying the output of the drivers, stubs, and function being tested. With this approach, you never find yourself with a program that has not run correctly and for which you have no output, or output that gives no clue as to what went wrong or where. Suppose function *M* has just been refined and is to be tested and debugged. Its refinement may include calls to other functions not yet written or debugged. To test and debug *M* you must

1. Write a driver to call *M* and feed it test data on which to work
2. Replace each function of *M*'s refinement by its own stub

For example, to test and debug **remove** (Figure 1.3) requires

1. A driver to call **remove** and feed it test values for **n** and **candidates**
2. Replacing **nonprimes** and **delete** by their individual stubs

This assumes that **primes** (which calls **remove**) and **nonprimes** and **delete** (which **remove** calls) have not yet been verified or even written.

Instead, suppose **primes** has already been debugged. **Primes**, in conjunction with the driver used to debug it, could then be taken as the basis for **remove**'s driver. Next, this driver plus **remove** could be used as the basis for **delete**'s driver. This way of proceeding parallels the top-down development of the program. It amounts to inserting one new function at a time into an already debugged program.

To illustrate the proper way to use debugging statements, a complete listing and output is given for an execution of the case study program later in the chapter.

1.7.6 In a Nutshell

The discussion of good programming style may be summarized with the following guidelines.

1. Take care to present programs well.
   Don't choose a name without a purpose.
   Don't leave a component's purpose unspecified.
   Descriptions should be simple even if tasks are not.
2. Communicate well.
   Store data only where it is needed (use local variables).
   Pass information explicitly when needed elsewhere (use parameters).
   Avoid side effects.
3. Use data abstraction.
   This is the basic way to make programs independent of data implementation, and it makes implementation changes easier and more reliable.
4. Functionally modularize programs.
   Functions should execute a simple, narrowly defined task.
   It should be possible to determine what a function does by looking only at it.
   Changes to a function should not necessitate changes in other functions.
   Prevent unreasonable input and output data by defensive programming.
5. Use debugging aids.
   Also verify your programs.

Of course, strict adherence to rules may not always be possible or even yield the best results. Knowing how or to what extent to apply programming rules comes only from experience in using them and in studying their effects.

1.8 Time and Storage Requirements

Sometimes the time of execution or the storage required by a program, or both, are limited. Analysis helps pinpoint parts of a program whose efficiency may be worth trying to improve, because they are executed frequently or require large amounts of storage. Such analysis can be very difficult, and simulation of the program may be needed for estimates. ***Simulation*** means that the program is executed repeatedly for appropriately chosen data, and the results are averaged or otherwise statistically analyzed. Sometimes it is possible to analyze how these requirements increase as the amount or size of the data increases, even though we cannot say what happens exactly for smaller amounts or sizes. This is called ***asymptotic analysis.*** When exact analysis cannot be done, we settle for bounds on the time and storage required.

1.8.1 Analyzing the Prime Example

The nonmathematically inclined reader may want to skip the following analysis of `primes` (Figure 1.3), which demonstrates how to go about informally analyzing a program and shows how trade-offs arise. Even such simple programs do not necessarily have simple analyses.

When a statement is said to take *constant time,* it means that the statement is always executed in the same amount of time, whatever the current values of the variables it processes. Clearly, the execution time of `primes` is given by the sum of the execution times of its three components. In what follows it is assumed that `insert`, `belongs`, and `omit` all take constant time (notice that for the array implementation for `candidates` (Section 1.3.2) this will be true, but `set` takes time proportional to n).

`Create` executes `set` once and `insert` exactly $n - 1$ times. Similarly, `print` executes its if statement $n - 1$ times. The amount of time the **if** statement takes depends on whether `belongs` is *true* or *false* but requires, at most, the time for `belongs` plus the time for `printf`.

`Remove` is more complex. Its initial assignment statement takes constant time, to which must be added the loop time. The loop is executed $\sqrt{n} - 1$ times, so the loop condition is evaluated $\sqrt{n}$ times. Assuming, for simplicity, that `sqrt(n)` takes constant time C, then $C \times \sqrt{n}$ is the total time for the evaluation of the condition. If the loop task took constant time, then the total loop time would be the product of this constant and $(\sqrt{n} - 1)$. Unfortunately `delete`'s time varies, depending on the value of `factor`. Nonetheless, the total time for `delete` can still be derived.

`Delete`'s own loop is executed for each multiple of `factor` between 2 × `factor` and m × `factor`, where m is the largest number of times that `factor` divides into n. m is the integer part of n/`factor` denoted by ⌊n/`factor`⌋. Hence `delete`'s loop is executed ⌊n/`factor`⌋ times for this value of `factor`. Since `factor` takes on values 2, 3, 4, . . . , $\sqrt{n}$, the total number of `delete`'s loop executions is

$$n/2 + n/3 + n/4 + \cdots + n/\lfloor\sqrt{n}\rfloor$$

or

$$n \times [1/2 + 1/3 + \cdots + 1/\lfloor\sqrt{n}\rfloor]$$

But $1/2 + 1/3 + \cdots + 1/n$ is roughly the natural logarithm of n, denoted by $\ln n$. Thus the entire time for the loop of `delete` is a constant (for `omit` and the assignment statement) times $n\ln\lfloor\sqrt{n}\rfloor$. The condition of this loop contributes roughly its own constant times $n\ln\lfloor\sqrt{n}\rfloor$. The initialization of `nextmultiple` in `delete` contributes its constant times $\sqrt{n}$.

Adding everything, we get a good execution time estimate of

$$C_1 + C_2\sqrt{n} + C_3 n + C_4 n\ln n$$

where C_1, C_2, C_3, and C_4 come from the times for condition evaluation, assignment statement execution, and `set`, `insert`, `omit`, and `belongs`.

For large n, this expression is dominated by the term $C_4 n\ln n$. In fact, for large enough values of n, the expression will be no greater than $C\, n\ln n$ for an appropriate value of C. We describe this concisely by saying the expression is $O(n\ln n)$, read "order $n\ln n$"; this notation will be used throughout the text.

By the storage requirements of `primes` is meant the total storage required for its data structures. Except for a few variables, the storage is required primarily for `candidates` and will be determined by its implementation. The analysis reveals that the bulk of the execution time for `primes` is spent executing the loop in `delete`. Consequently, to improve its time we speed up the time of the loop itself, or reduce the number of times it needs to be executed. For the array implementation, the storage required will be proportional to n, and this is where the bulk of the storage required is needed.

`Primes` can be improved in a number of obvious ways. Except for 2, no primes are even. Hence all other even numbers can be eliminated from consideration. This means that `factor` need never take on even values, so it can be increased by 2 instead of 1 in `remove` and can also be initialized to 3. `Delete` can be changed so that `nextmultiple` takes on only odd multiples of `factor`. With a little more work, `candidates` can be cut to roughly half its size by eliminating even integers. This will necessitate changes to `set` as well as changes to the **for** loops in `create` and `print`, but it reduces the storage needed by about one-half and the time by more than one-half.

Perhaps a less obvious improvement is to modify the increase of `factor` in `remove` so that, instead of increasing by 1 (or 2), `factor` increases to the value of the next prime in `candidates` (see Exercise 8). To realize this saving fully, it is necessary to use a new data structure, the list or the balanced binary tree, for the collection. Lists are discussed in Chapter 3, balanced binary trees in Chapters 7 and 9. These would save not only time but storage as well. Borrowing a result from mathematics about the distribution of prime numbers, we can state that any version of `primes` that stores all the primes from 2 to n in a collection will need $n/\ln n$ storage locations, since there are about that many such primes. Thus we will run out of storage before we run out of time!

`Primes` may be written so that its execution time increases but its storage needs decrease, or vice versa. Thus time is traded for storage, as is often done. `Primes` represents one extreme where all the primes are saved. A version of `primes` in which no primes are saved is at the other extreme (see Exercise 10). This version would require significantly more time.

1.8.2 Limits on Time and Storage

Programs carry out certain basic operations. For example, `primes` executes assignment statements, evaluates conditions, and executes `set`, `insert`, `omit`, and `belongs`. In fact, its total execution time equals the number of times each of the operations is executed multiplied by the time taken by that operation. Determining the number of basic operations performed by a program to solve a problem allows evaluation of its practicality. For illustration, suppose that 1,000,000 basic operations can be carried out in 1 second by a computer. Then the number of basic operations that it can carry out in 1 year is

1,000,000 basic operations/second × 60 seconds/minute × 60 minutes/hour × 24 hours/day × 365 days/year

This is fewer than 10^{13} basic operations/year, and this is assuming that the computer is available for the exclusive use of the program and that it will never fail during the year. Thus 10^{13} can be taken as a benchmark figure—any program that requires a number of operations on this order to solve a problem is not feasible!

How much storage is available is determined by your computer system. The amount needed is surely not feasible when your program aborts during execution with a message indicating insufficient storage, or when the compiler tells you there is insufficient storage. If you run out of time or storage, you must then abandon the problem (and perhaps your job), find a more efficient program, or trade time for storage.

1.9 Case Study: Bowling Scores

This section illustrates the way a flowchart and a program are developed for a problem connected with the game of bowling. The way in which the spirit of the structured programming philosophy is followed is more important than the particular development.

Bowling, as you may know, consists of ten *frames*. In each frame, there is a chance to knock down ten pins by throwing one or two balls down the bowling alley. To start, you roll the first ball of a given frame. If all ten pins are knocked down, a *strike* is achieved for that frame, and you earn a frame score of 10 plus the total number of pins knocked down on the next two rolls. If any pins remain standing, you roll a second ball for the frame. After this roll, if all pins are down, you have a *spare,* and a frame score of 10 plus the number of pins knocked down on the next roll. If any pins remain standing after the second roll, then the result is an *open frame,* and the frame score obtained is given by the total number of pins knocked down on the two rolls of the frame. A strike or spare occurring on the last (the tenth), results in two or one additional rolls, respectively. The total score for a game is the sum of all the individual frame scores.

Getting twelve strikes in a row results in the maximum attainable score of 300. In this case, twelve rolls are made. The least number of rolls possible is eleven and the greatest is twenty-one. In fact there is a correlation between the number of rolls in a game and the game score. Many rolls correspond to low scores and few rolls to high scores. The better a bowler you are, the fewer rolls you get!

Example 1.1 The problem is to print the total score for each of a series of games, as well as the minimum, average, and maximum scores. Assume the input is given as a series of roll scores for each game and includes at least one game. ■

1.9.1 Algorithm

An initial flowchart might be as shown in Figure 1.5(a). If the three tasks can be carried out correctly, in the sequence indicated, then the problem is solved. The flowchart breaks down the original problem into three smaller problems. Obtaining their solutions and sequencing them correctly provides the solution to the original problem. This is the top-down approach to problem solving. Next, it is applied to each of the three problems.

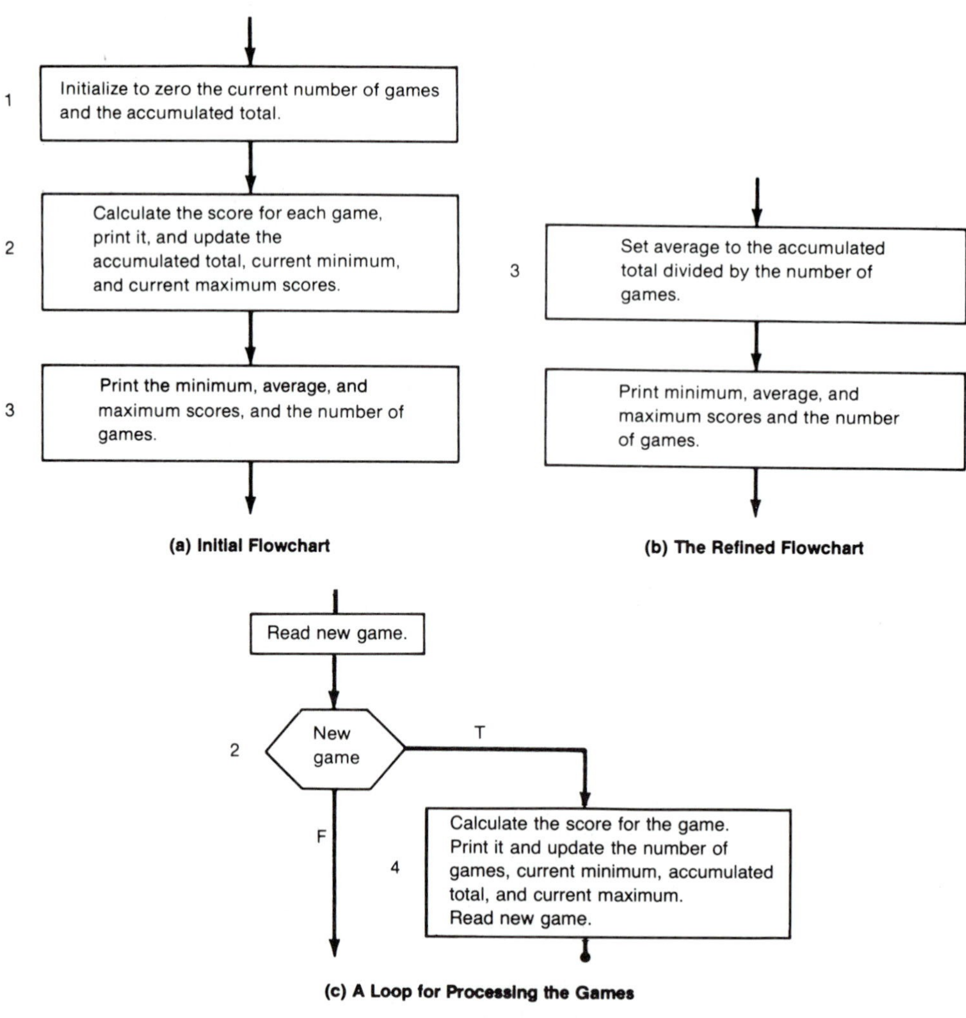

Figure 1.5 Flowcharts of the Bowling Scores Algorithm

Problem 1 is transparent enough. Problem 3 is clearly solved by the expanded or refined flowchart shown in Figure 1.5(b).

Problem 2 needs to be refined. It seems clear that the basic structure for its solution is a loop, within which each game is processed. When all games have been processed, the loop should be exited. (See Figure 1.5(c).)

The new problem introduced as task 4 must be solved next. The input for this new problem will be the roll scores that must be processed for the new game. A basic looping structure can accomplish the task. The loop task will be executed ten times, once for each frame. Each execution calculates the score for the current frame and updates the game score and a frame counter, **`frame`**. Prior to entering the loop, **`frame`** must be initialized to 1, and **`gamescore`** to 0. Other initialization may be required. After the loop is exited, the game score must be printed, and proper updating must occur. This refinement is shown in Figure 1.6.

Suppose that each time the programmer expands a task, the expanded version of the task does in fact solve the problem introduced by that task. Then the programmer knows that, whatever the current structured flowchart, it must repre-

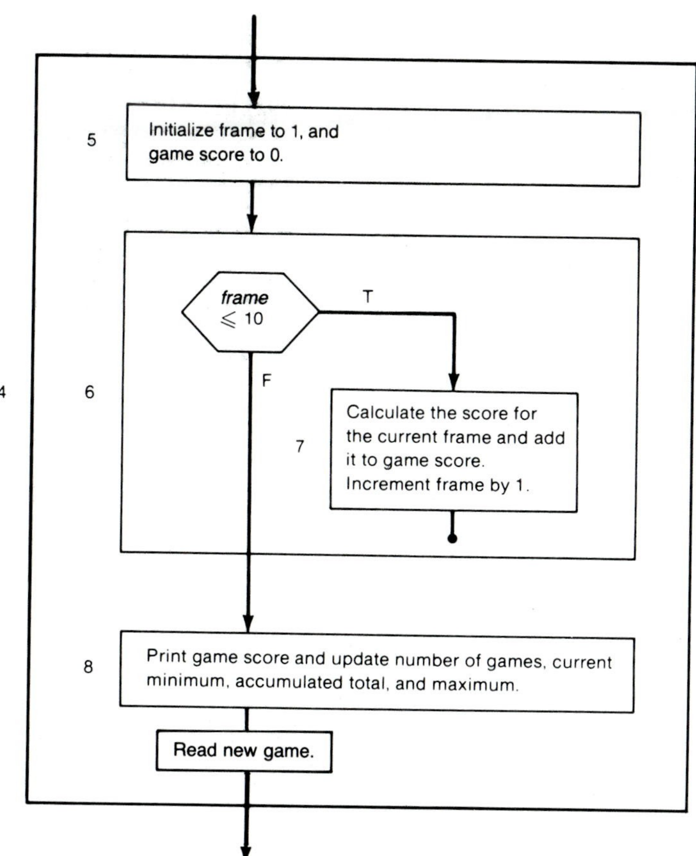

Figure 1.6 Refinement of Task 4

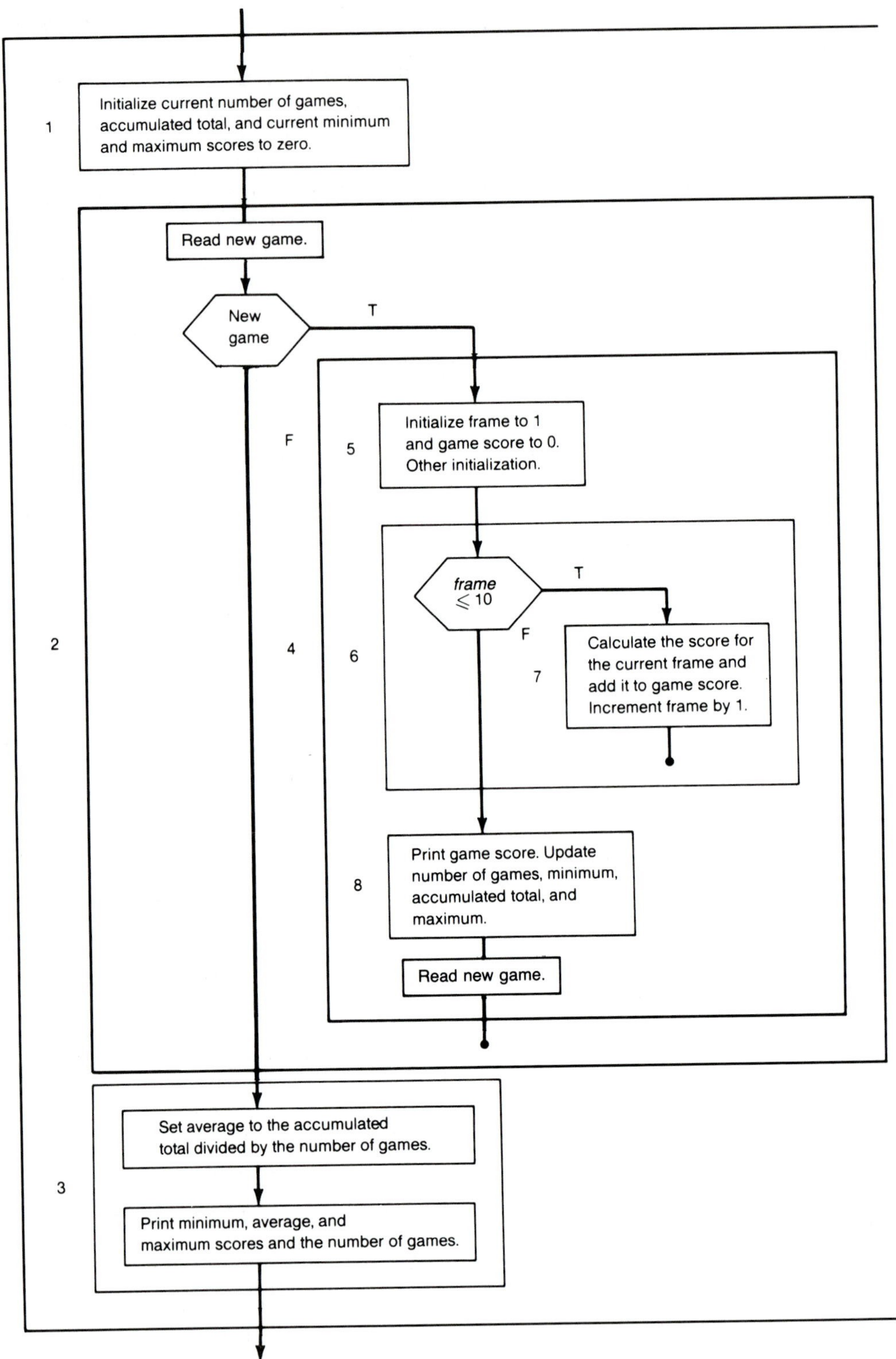

Figure 1.7 Refinement of Initial Flowchart

sent a solution to the original problem as long as each of its tasks can be carried out correctly. The detailed structured flowchart of Figure 1.7 is thus a solution to the problem, as long as each of its tasks can be carried out correctly. It is detailed enough so that we know how to carry out (or program) each of its tasks except for 5, 6, 7, and 8. However, if the high-level language chosen for the program allows direct implementation of those tasks, then no more detail is needed to complete the solution.

Instead of increasing the complexity of the flowchart of Figure 1.7, tasks 5–8 can be functionally modularized.

Functions for tasks 7 and 8 appear in Figures 1.8 and 1.9. The solution to the original problem will then consist of Figure 1.7 plus the functions for tasks 5–8. This illustrates the application of structured programming to a relatively simple problem. Note again the importance of choosing variable names that convey

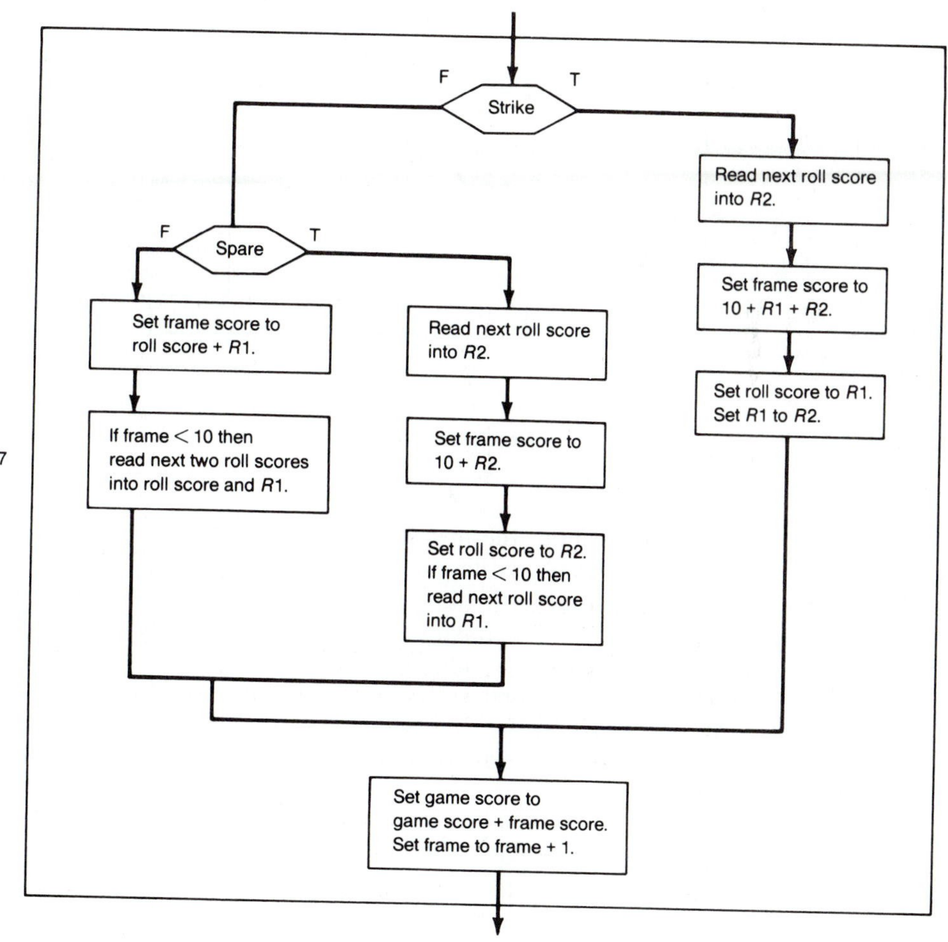

Figure 1.8 Refinement of Task 7

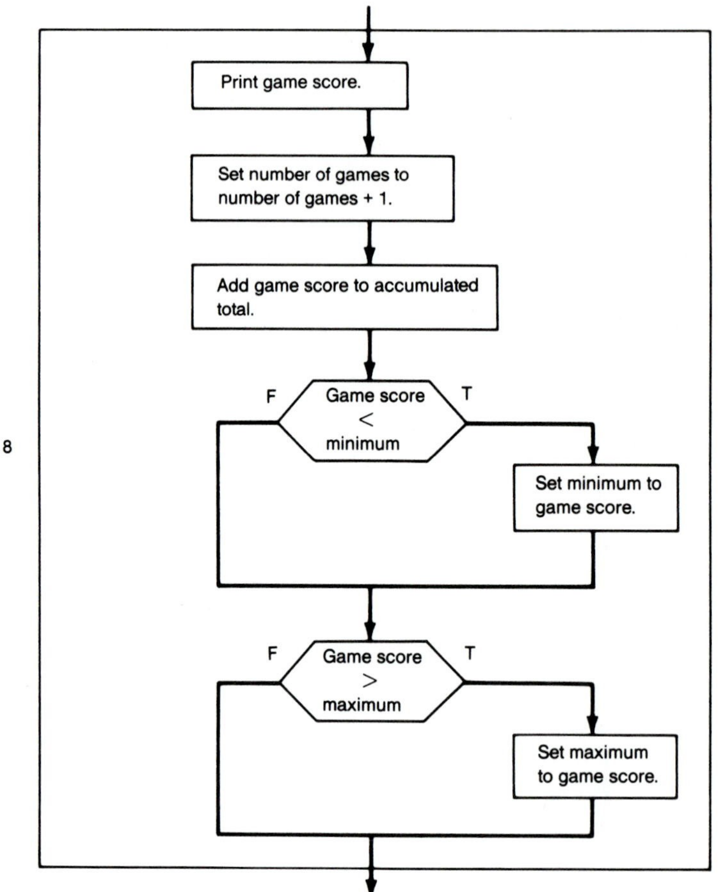

Figure 1.9 Refinement of Task 8

information about the meaning and use of the variables. Good names make the algorithm clearer. Note that C compilers normally treat names as distinct only when they differ in the first eight characters, so some care must be taken. In this text, however, this constraint is ignored for clarity.

When task 7 is entered, the variables `rollscore` and `r1` must contain, respectively, the first roll score of the current frame and the next roll score. Consequently, before entering task 6, the first two roll scores of the game must be read into `rollscore` and `r1`. This is the "other initialization" required of task 5.

The conditions "strike" and "spare" (Figure 1.8) are actually implemented as "`rollscore` equals 10" and "(`rollscore` + `r1`) equals 10," respectively. To emphasize the fact that complexity in a flowchart should be limited, Figure 1.10 is the complete detailed flowchart for the solution as it could appear without functional modularization. Descriptions do not appear; the chart simply indicates the structure of the solution. The flowchart can be derived by adding the detailed expansions of tasks 5–8 to Figure 1.7.

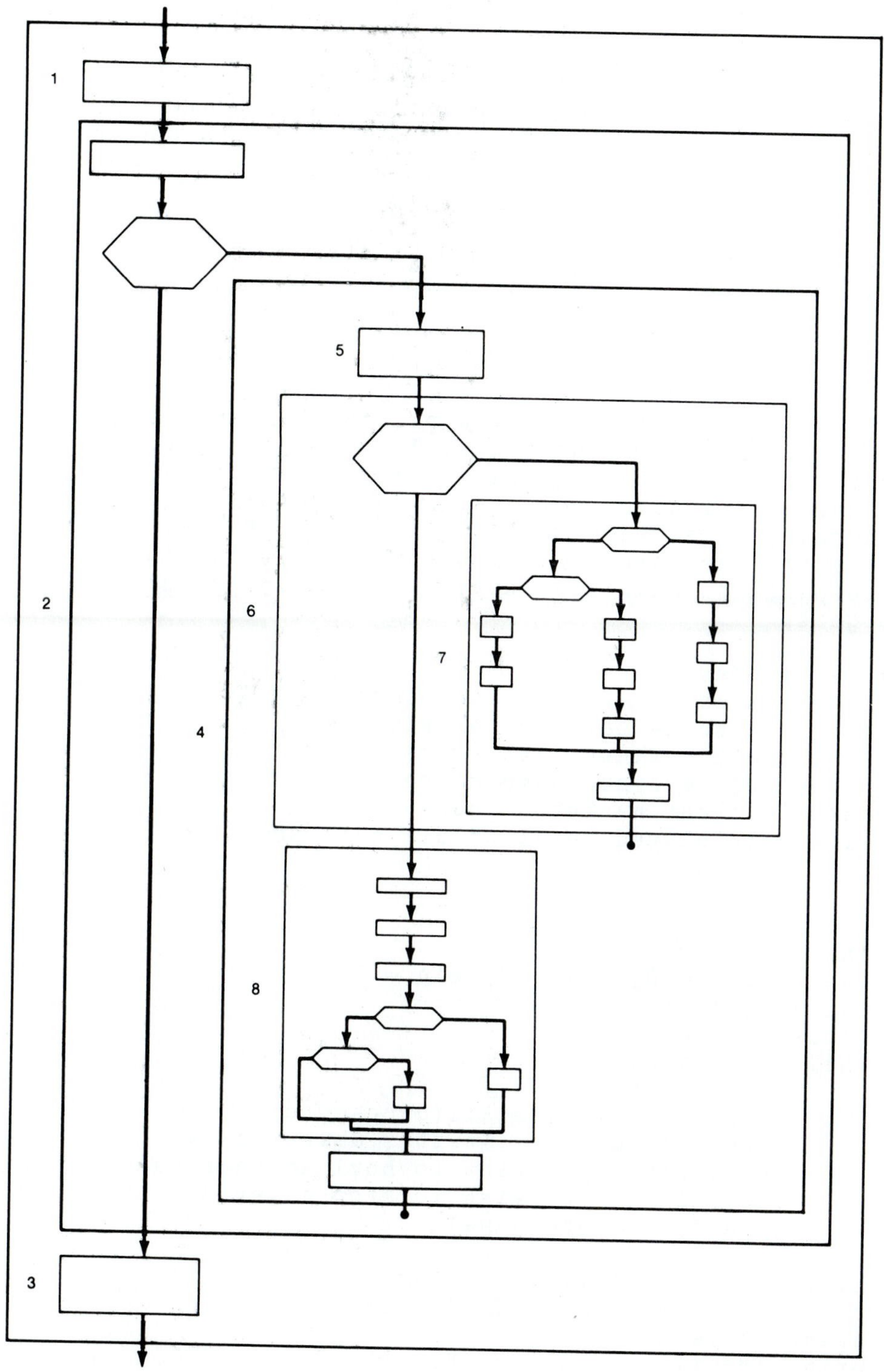

Figure 1.10 Too Detailed a Refinement

1.9.2 Program

The program now follows directly from the flowcharts. Notice that its structure parallels the flowcharts', that we have attempted to minimize side effects by passing information between components explicitly as parameters, and that information needed only by a component is kept local to that component.

```
#include <stdio.h>
#define TRUE 1
#define FALSE 0

main()
/*
Bowling Scores calculates and prints the game scores
for a series of bowling games. It also prints the
number of games bowled, the minimum, average, and
maximum of all game scores. The input consists, for
each game, of a sequence of roll scores. Each roll
represents the number of pins knocked down on the
corresponding roll. Its input must consist of at least
one game.

Main Variables
average - average of all game scores
gamescore - score for the current game
max - current maximum game score
min - current minimum game score
number - current number of games played
total - accumulated total of all game scores
*/

{
   int gamescore;
   int number = 0, max = 0, min = 300;
   int newgame = TRUE;
   float average;
   while (newgame)
      {
         gamescore = gamecalc(gamescore);
         update(gamescore,&number,&min,&max,&total);
         printf("If you want to bowl another game enter a 1\n");
         printf("If you wish to stop enter a 0\n");
         scanf("%d",&newgame);
      }
   average = ((float)total)/number;
   printf("Minimum game %d\n",min);
   printf("Average game %f\n",average);
   printf("Maximum game %d\n",max);
   printf("Number of games %d\n",number);
}
```

```
gamecalc(gamescore)
/* calculates gamescore for the current game.

Main variables
frame - the current frame
gamescore - score for the current game
rollscore - first roll score of the current frame
r1 - succeeding roll score after rollscore
*/

int gamescore;
{
   int frame, rollscore, r1;
   gamescore = 0;
   frame = 1;
   printf("Please enter the number of pins down on this roll\n");
   scanf("%d",&rollscore);
   printf("Please enter the number of pins down on this roll\n");
   scanf("%d",&r1);
   while (frame <= 10)
      framecalc(&gamescore,&frame,&rollscore,&r1);
   return(gamescore);
}

framecalc(pgamescore,pframe,prollscore,pr1)
/* Calculates the framescore for the current game,
   adds it to gamescore, increases frame by 1 and
   updates rollscore and r1.

Main variables
pframe - pointer to the current frame
pgamescore - pointer to the score for the current game
prollscore - pointer to first rollscore of current frame
pr1 - pointer to next rollscore of current frame
framescore - score for current frame
r2 - rollscore after r1
*/

int *pgamescore,*pframe,*prollscore,*pr1;
{
   int framescore, r2;
   if (*prollscore == 10) /* it is a strike */
      {
         printf("Please enter the number of pins down on this");
         printf(" roll\n");
         scanf("%d",&r2);
         framescore = 10 + *pr1 + r2;
         *prollscore = *pr1;
         *pr1 = r2;
      }
   else if ((*prollscore + *pr1) == 10) /* it is a spare */
      {
         printf("Please enter the number of pins down on this");
```

```
         printf(" roll\n");
         scanf("%d",&r2);
         framescore = 10 + r2;
         *prollscore = r2;
         if (*pframe < 10)
            {
               printf("Please enter the number of pins down");
               printf("on this roll\n");
               scanf("%d",pr1);
            }
      }
   else /* it is an open frame */
      {
         framescore = *prollscore + *pr1;
         if (*pframe < 10)
            {
               printf("Please enter the number of pins");
               printf("down on this roll\n");
               scanf("%d",prollscore);
               printf("Please enter the number of pins");
               printf("down on this roll\n");
               scanf("%d",pr1);
            }
      }
   *pgamescore = *pgamescore + framescore;
   *pframe = *pframe + 1;
}

update(gamescore,pnumber,pmin,pmax,ptotal)
/* This prints gamescore, and updates number, min, max,
   and total to reflect gamescore.

Main variables
gamescore - current game score
pnumber - pointer to current number of games
pmin - pointer to current minimum game score
pmax - pointer to current maximum game score
ptotal - pointer to total of all game scores
*/

int gamescore, *pnumber, *pmin, *pmax;
int *ptotal;
{
   printf("gamescore \n");
   printf("%d\n",gamescore);
   *pnumber = *pnumber + 1;
   *ptotal = *ptotal + gamescore;
   if (gamescore < *pmin)
      *pmin = gamescore;
   if (gamescore > *pmax)
      *pmax = gamescore;
}
```

1.9.3 Debugging

The following is a complete listing and output of a version of the Bowling Scores program that contains statements used as debugging aids (the boxed lines). This listing demonstrates how to use such statements and what they can tell us as we peruse the output. The roll scores of the two games that served as input are

game 1—5, 4, 6, 4, 2, 4, 1, 4, 3, 4, 8, 1, 9, 0, 10, 10, 9, 0

game 2—9, 1, 10, 7, 3, 9, 0, 10, 10, 5, 4, 6, 4, 10, 10, 10, 8

The prompts for input are in the program. They have been omitted from the output.

```
#include <stdio.h>
#define TRUE 1
#define FALSE 0

main()
/* Bowling Scores calculates and prints the game scores
for a series of bowling games. It also prints the
number of games bowled, the minimum, average, and
maximum of all game scores. The input consists, for
each game, of a sequence of roll scores. Each roll
represents the number of pins knocked down on the
corresponding roll. Its input must consist of at least
one game.

Main Variables
average - average of all game scores
gamescore - score for the current game
max - current maximum game score
min - current minimum game score
number - current number of games played
total - accumulated total of all game scores
*/

{
   int gamescore;
   int number = 0, max = 0, total = 0, min = 300;
   int newgame = TRUE;
   float average;
   while (newgame)
      {

      printf("\n CALLING GAMECALC FOR GAME #%2d",number+1);
      printf("\n-----------------------------\n");

      gamescore = gamecalc(gamescore);
```

```
printf("-===>RETURNING FROM GAMECALC WITH GAMESCORE");
printf(" =%3d FOR GAME #%2d\n",gamescore, number+1);
printf("CALLING UPDATE WITH;  MIN TOTAL MAX NUMBER\n");
printf("%26d%5d%5d%5d\n",min,total,max,number);

    update(gamescore,&number,&min,&max,&total);
    printf("If you want to bowl another game enter a 1 \n");
    printf("If you wish to stop enter a 0 \n");
    scanf("%d",&newgame);

printf("-===>RETURNING FROM UPDATE:  MIN TOTAL MAX ");
printf("NUMBER\n");
printf("%33d%6d%6d%5d\n",min,total,max,number);

    }
  average = ((float)total)\number;

printf("FINAL RESULTS FOR ALL GAMES FOLLOW:\n");
printf("************************************\n");
printf("  ACCUMULATED TOTAL = %5d\n\n",total);
printf("     MINIMUM GAME = %5d\n",min);
printf("     AVERAGE GAME = %10.4f\n",average);
printf("     MAXIMUM GAME = %5d\n\n",max);
printf("NUMBER OF GAMES PLAYED = %3d\n",number);

}

gamecalc(gamescore)
/* calculates gamescore for the current game.

Main variables
frame - the current frame
gamescore - score for the current game
rollscore - first roll score of the current frame
r1 - succeeding roll score after rollscore
*/

int gamescore;
{
    int frame, rollscore, r1;
    gamescore = 0;
    frame = 1;
    printf("Please enter the number of pins down on this roll\n");
    scanf("%d",&rollscore);
    printf("Please enter the number of pins down on this roll\n");
    scanf("%d",&r1);
    while (frame <= 10)
       {
```

```
        printf("  IN GAMECALC, GOING TO FRAMECALC WITH:  GAMESCORE");
        printf("  FRAME ROLLSCORE R1\n");
        printf("%49d%9d%9d%7d\n",gamescore,frame,rollscore,r1);

          framecalc(&gamescore,&frame,&rollscore,&r1);

          printf("  IN GAMECALC, RETURNING FROM FRAMECALC WITH:");
          printf("GAMESCORE FRAME ROLLSCORE R1\n");
          printf("%53d%9d%9d%7d\n\n",gamescore,frame,rollscore,r1);

      }
   return(gamescore);
}

framecalc(pgamescore,pframe,prollscore,pr1)
/* Calculates the framescore for the current game,
   adds it to gamescore, increases frame by 1 and
   updates rollscore and r1.

Main variables
pframe - pointer to the current frame
pgamescore - pointer to the score for the current game
prollscore - pointer to first rollscore of current frame
pr1 - pointer to next rollscore of current frame
framescore - score for current frame
r2 - rollscore after r1
*/

int *pgamescore,*pframe,*prollscore,*pr1;
{
   int framescore, r2;

    printf("  STARTING FRAMECALC WITH: GAMESCORE FRAME");
    printf(" ROLLSCORE R1\n");
    printf("%36d%9d%9d%7d\n",*pgamescore,*pframe,*prollscore,*pr1);

 if(*prollscore == 10) /* it is a strike */
    {
       printf("Please enter the number of pins down on this");
       printf(" roll\n");
       scanf("%d",&r2);
       framescore = 10 + *pr1 + r2;
       *prollscore = *pr1;
       *pr1 = r2;

       printf("AFTER STRIKE, FRAMESCORE = %2d\n",framescore);
```

```
        }
    else if ((*prollscore + *pr1) == 10) /* it is a spare */
        {
            printf("Please enter the number of pins down on this");
            printf(" roll\n");
            scanf("%d",&r2);
            framescore = 10 + r2;

            printf("AFTER SPARE, FRAMESCORE= %2d\n",framescore);

            *prollscore = r2;
            if (*pframe < 10)
                {
                    printf("Please enter the number of pins down");
                    printf(" on this roll\n");
                    scanf("%d",pr1);
                }
        }
    else /* it is an open frame */
        {
            framescore = *prollscore + *pr1;

            printf("OPEN FRAME, FRAMESCORE  %2d\n",framescore);

            if (*pframe < 10)
                {
                    printf("Please enter the number of pins");
                    printf(" down on this roll\n");
                    scanf("%d",prollscore);
                    printf("Please enter the number of pins");
                    printf(" down on this roll\n");
                    scanf("%d",pr1);
                }
        }
    *pgamescore = *pgamescore + framescore;
    *pframe = *pframe + 1;

    printf("  LEAVING FRAMECALC WITH: GAMESCORE FRAME");
    printf(" ROLLSCORE R1\n");
    printf("%35d%9d%9d%7d\n\n",*pgamescore,*pframe,*prollscore,*pr1);

}

update(gamescore,pnumber,pmin,pmax,ptotal)
/* This prints gamescore, and updates number, min, max
   and total to reflect gamescore.
```

```
Main variables
gamescore - current game score
pnumber - pointer to current number of games
pmin - pointer to current minimum game score
pmax - pointer to current maximum game score
ptotal - pointer to total of all game scores
*/

int gamescore, *pnumber, *pmin, *pmax;
int *ptotal;
{

   printf("\n BEGINNING TO UPDATE WITH:  GAMESCORE");
   printf(" NUMBER MIN MAX TOTAL\n");
   printf("%37d%8d%8d%4d%6d\n",
           gamescore, *pnumber, *pmin, *pmax, *ptotal);

   *pnumber = *pnumber + 1;
   *ptotal = *ptotal + gamescore;
   if (gamescore < *pmin)
      *pmin = gamescore;
   if (gamescore > *pmax)
      *pmax = gamescore;

   printf("   LEAVING UPDATE WITH: GAMESCORE NUMBER");
   printf(" MIN MAX TOTAL\n");
   printf("%35d%8d%8d%5d%6d\n\n",
           gamescore,*pnumber,*pmin,*pmax,*ptotal);

}
```

The output of the program is as follows.

```
CALLING GAMECALC FOR GAME # 1
-----------------------------
    IN GAMECALC, GOING TO FRAMECALC WITH:     GAMESCORE   FRAME   ROLLSCORE   R1
                                                      0       1           5    4
    STARTING FRAMECALC WITH:    GAMESCORE   FRAME   ROLLSCORE   R1
                                        0       1           5    4
OPEN FRAME, FRAMESCORE = 9
    LEAVING FRAMECALC WITH:    GAMESCORE   FRAME   ROLLSCORE   R1
                                       9       2           6    4
    IN GAMECALC, RETURNING FROM FRAMECALC WITH:    GAMESCORE   FRAME   ROLLSCORE   R1
                                                           9       2           6    4
    IN GAMECALC, GOING TO FRAMECALC WITH:     GAMESCORE   FRAME   ROLLSCORE   R1
                                                      9       2           6    4
    STARTING FRAMECALC WITH:    GAMESCORE   FRAME   ROLLSCORE   R1
                                        9       2           6    4
```

```
AFTER SPARE, FRAMESCORE = 12
   LEAVING FRAMECALC WITH:      GAMESCORE  FRAME  ROLLSCORE  R1
                                    21         3       2        4
   IN GAMECALC, RETURNING FROM FRAMECALC WITH:    GAMESCORE  FRAME  ROLLSCORE  R1
                                                     21         3       2        4
   IN GAMECALC, GOING TO FRAMECALC WITH:    GAMESCORE  FRAME  ROLLSCORE  R1
                                               21         3       2        4
   STARTING FRAMECALC WITH:     GAMESCORE  FRAME  ROLLSCORE  R1
                                    21         3       2        4
OPEN FRAME, FRAMESCORE = 6
   LEAVING FRAMECALC WITH:      GAMESCORE  FRAME  ROLLSCORE  R1
                                    27         4       1        4
   IN GAMECALC, RETURNING FROM FRAMECALC WITH:    GAMESCORE  FRAME  ROLLSCORE  R1
                                                     27         4       1        4
   IN GAMECALC, GOING TO FRAMECALC WITH:    GAMESCORE  FRAME  ROLLSCORE  R1
                                               27         4       1        4

   STARTING FRAMECALC WITH:     GAMESCORE  FRAME  ROLLSCORE  R1
                                    27         4       1        4
OPEN FRAME, FRAMESCORE = 5
   LEAVING FRAMECALC WITH:      GAMESCORE  FRAME  ROLLSCORE  R1
                                    32         5       3        4
   IN GAMECALC, RETURNING FROM FRAMECALC WITH:    GAMESCORE  FRAME  ROLLSCORE  R1
                                                     32         5       3        4
   IN GAMECALC, GOING TO FRAMECALC WITH:    GAMESCORE  FRAME  ROLLSCORE  R1
                                               32         5       3        4
   STARTING FRAMECALC WITH:     GAMESCORE  FRAME  ROLLSCORE  R1
                                    32         5       3        4
OPEN FRAME, FRAMESCORE = 7
   LEAVING FRAMECALC WITH:      GAMESCORE  FRAME  ROLLSCORE  R1
                                    39         6       8        1
   IN GAMECALC, RETURNING FROM FRAMECALC WITH:    GAMESCORE  FRAME  ROLLSCORE  R1
                                                     39         6       8        1
   IN GAMECALC, GOING TO FRAMECALC WITH:    GAMESCORE  FRAME  ROLLSCORE  R1
                                               39         6       8        1
   STARTING FRAMECALC WITH:     GAMESCORE  FRAME  ROLLSCORE  R1
                                    39         6       8        1
OPEN FRAME, FRAMESCORE = 9
   LEAVING FRAMECALC WITH:      GAMESCORE  FRAME  ROLLSCORE  R1
                                    48         7       9        0
   IN GAMECALC, RETURNING FROM FRAMECALC WITH:    GAMESCORE  FRAME  ROLLSCORE  R1
                                                     48         7       9        0
   IN GAMECALC, GOING TO FRAMECALC WITH:    GAMESCORE  FRAME  ROLLSCORE  R1
                                               48         7       9        0
   STARTING FRAMECALC WITH:     GAMESCORE  FRAME  ROLLSCORE  R1
                                    48         7       9        0
OPEN FRAME, FRAMESCORE = 9
   LEAVING FRAMECALC WITH:      GAMESCORE  FRAME  ROLLSCORE  R1
                                    57         8      10       10
   IN GAMECALC, RETURNING FROM FRAMECALC WITH:    GAMESCORE  FRAME  ROLLSCORE  R1
                                                     57         8      10       10
```

```
    IN GAMECALC, GOING TO FRAMECALC WITH:    GAMESCORE  FRAME  ROLLSCORE  R1
                                                    57      8         10     10
    STARTING FRAMECALC WITH:    GAMESCORE  FRAME  ROLLSCORE  R1
                                        57      8         10     10
AFTER STRIKE, FRAMESCORE = 29
    LEAVING FRAMECALC WITH:    GAMESCORE  FRAME  ROLLSCORE  R1
                                       86      9         10      9
    IN GAMECALC, RETURNING FROM FRAMECALC WITH:    GAMESCORE  FRAME  ROLLSCORE  R1
                                                          86      9         10      9
    IN GAMECALC, GOING TO FRAMECALC WITH:    GAMESCORE  FRAME  ROLLSCORE  R1
                                                    86      9         10      9
    STARTING FRAMECALC WITH:    GAMESCORE  FRAME  ROLLSCORE  R1
                                        86      9         10      9
AFTER STRIKE, FRAMESCORE = 19
    LEAVING FRAMECALC WITH:    GAMESCORE  FRAME  ROLLSCORE  R1
                                      105     10          9      0
    IN GAMECALC, RETURNING FROM FRAMECALC WITH:    GAMESCORE  FRAME  ROLLSCORE  R1
                                                         105     10          9      0

    IN GAMECALC, GOING TO FRAMECALC WITH:    GAMESCORE  FRAME  ROLLSCORE  R1
                                                   105     10          9      0
    STARTING FRAMECALC WITH:    GAMESCORE  FRAME  ROLLSCORE  R1
                                       105     10          9      0
OPEN FRAME, FRAMESCORE = 9
    LEAVING FRAMECALC WITH:    GAMESCORE  FRAME  ROLLSCORE  R1
                                      114     11          9      0
    IN GAMECALC, RETURNING FROM FRAMECALC WITH:    GAMESCORE  FRAME  ROLLSCORE  R1
                                                         114     11          9      0
-===>RETURNING FROM GAMECALC WITH GAMESCORE=114 FOR GAME # 1
CALLING UPDATE WITH;    MIN  TOTAL  MAX  NUMBER
                        300     0     0       0
    BEGINNING TO UPDATE WITH:    GAMESCORE  NUMBER  MIN  MAX  TOTAL
                                       114       0  300    0      0
        LEAVING UPDATE WITH:    GAMESCORE  NUMBER  MIN  MAX  TOTAL
                                      114       1  114  114    114
-===>RETURNING FROM UPDATE:    MIN  TOTAL  MAX  NUMBER
                               114    114  114       1

CALLING GAMECALC FOR GAME # 2
-------------------------------
    IN GAMECALC, GOING TO FRAMECALC WITH:    GAMESCORE  FRAME  ROLLSCORE  R1
                                                     0      1          9      1
    STARTING FRAMECALC WITH:    GAMESCORE  FRAME  ROLLSCORE  R1
                                         0      1          9      1
AFTER SPARE, FRAMESCORE = 20
    LEAVING FRAMECALC WITH:    GAMESCORE  FRAME  ROLLSCORE  R1
                                       20      2         10      7
    IN GAMECALC, RETURNING FROM FRAMECALC WITH:    GAMESCORE  FRAME  ROLLSCORE  R1
                                                          20      2         10      7
    IN GAMECALC, GOING TO FRAMECALC WITH:    GAMESCORE  FRAME  ROLLSCORE  R1
                                                    20      2         10      7
    STARTING FRAMECALC WITH:    GAMESCORE  FRAME  ROLLSCORE  R1
                                        20      2         10      7
```

```
AFTER STRIKE, FRAMESCORE = 20
   LEAVING FRAMECALC WITH:     GAMESCORE  FRAME  ROLLSCORE  R1
                                  40        3        7       3
   IN GAMECALC, RETURNING FROM FRAMECALC WITH:    GAMESCORE  FRAME  ROLLSCORE  R1
                                                     40        3        7       3
   IN GAMECALC, GOING TO FRAMECALC WITH:    GAMESCORE  FRAME  ROLLSCORE  R1
                                               40        3        7       3
   STARTING FRAMECALC WITH:    GAMESCORE  FRAME  ROLLSCORE  R1
                                  40        3        7       3
AFTER SPARE, FRAMESCORE = 19
   LEAVING FRAMECALC WITH:     GAMESCORE  FRAME  ROLLSCORE  R1
                                  59        4        9       0
   IN GAMECALC, RETURNING FROM FRAMECALC WITH:    GAMESCORE  FRAME  ROLLSCORE  R1
                                                     59        4        9       0
   IN GAMECALC, GOING TO FRAMECALC WITH:    GAMESCORE  FRAME  ROLLSCORE  R1
                                               59        4        9       0

   STARTING FRAMECALC WITH:    GAMESCORE  FRAME  ROLLSCORE  R1
                                  59        4        9       0
OPEN FRAME, FRAMESCORE = 9
   LEAVING FRAMECALC WITH:     GAMESCORE  FRAME  ROLLSCORE  R1
                                  68        5       10      10
   IN GAMECALC, RETURNING FROM FRAMECALC WITH:    GAMESCORE  FRAME  ROLLSCORE  R1
                                                     68        5       10      10
   IN GAMECALC, GOING TO FRAMECALC WITH:    GAMESCORE  FRAME  ROLLSCORE  R1
                                               68        5       10      10
   STARTING FRAMECALC WITH:    GAMESCORE  FRAME  ROLLSCORE  R1
                                  68        5       10      10
AFTER STRIKE, FRAMESCORE = 25
   LEAVING FRAMECALC WITH:     GAMESCORE  FRAME  ROLLSCORE  R1
                                  93        6       10       5
   IN GAMECALC, RETURNING FROM FRAMECALC WITH:    GAMESCORE  FRAME  ROLLSCORE  R1
                                                     93        6       10       5
   IN GAMECALC, GOING TO FRAMECALC WITH:    GAMESCORE  FRAME  ROLLSCORE  R1
                                               93        6       10       5
   STARTING FRAMECALC WITH:    GAMESCORE  FRAME  ROLLSCORE  R1
                                  93        6       10       5
AFTER STRIKE, FRAMESCORE = 19
   LEAVING FRAMECALC WITH:     GAMESCORE  FRAME  ROLLSCORE  R1
                                 112        7        5       4
   IN GAMECALC, RETURNING FROM FRAMECALC WITH:    GAMESCORE  FRAME  ROLLSCORE  R1
                                                    112        7        5       4
   IN GAMECALC, GOING TO FRAMECALC WITH:    GAMESCORE  FRAME  ROLLSCORE  R1
                                              112        7        5       4
   STARTING FRAMECALC WITH:    GAMESCORE  FRAME  ROLLSCORE  R1
                                 112        7        5       4
OPEN FRAME, FRAMESCORE = 9
   LEAVING FRAMECALC WITH:     GAMESCORE  FRAME  ROLLSCORE  R1
                                 121        8        6       4
   IN GAMECALC, RETURNING FROM FRAMECALC WITH:    GAMESCORE  FRAME  ROLLSCORE  R1
                                                    121        8        6       4
```

```
        IN GAMECALC, GOING TO FRAMECALC WITH:   GAMESCORE  FRAME  ROLLSCORE  R1
                                                   121       8        6       4
        STARTING FRAMECALC WITH:   GAMESCORE  FRAME  ROLLSCORE  R1
                                      121       8        6       4
     AFTER SPARE, FRAMESCORE = 20
        LEAVING FRAMECALC WITH:   GAMESCORE  FRAME  ROLLSCORE  R1
                                     141       9       10      10
        IN GAMECALC, RETURNING FROM FRAMECALC WITH:   GAMESCORE  FRAME  ROLLSCORE  R1
                                                         141       9       10      10
        IN GAMECALC, GOING TO FRAMECALC WITH:   GAMESCORE  FRAME  ROLLSCORE  R1
                                                   141       9       10      10
        STARTING FRAMECALC WITH:   GAMESCORE  FRAME  ROLLSCORE  R1
                                      141       9       10      10
     AFTER STRIKE, FRAMESCORE = 30
        LEAVING FRAMECALC WITH:   GAMESCORE  FRAME  ROLLSCORE  R1
                                     171      10       10      10
        IN GAMECALC, RETURNING FROM FRAMECALC WITH:   GAMESCORE  FRAME  ROLLSCORE  R1
                                                         171      10       10      10
        IN GAMECALC, GOING TO FRAMECALC WITH:   GAMESCORE  FRAME  ROLLSCORE  R1
                                                   171      10       10      10
        STARTING FRAMECALC WITH:   GAMESCORE  FRAME  ROLLSCORE  R1
                                      171      10       10      10
     AFTER STRIKE, FRAMESCORE = 28
        LEAVING FRAMECALC WITH:   GAMESCORE  FRAME  ROLLSCORE  R1
                                     199      11       10       8
        IN GAMECALC, RETURNING FROM FRAMECALC WITH:   GAMESCORE  FRAME  ROLLSCORE  R1
                                                         199      11       10       8
     -===>RETURNING FROM GAMECALC WITH GAMESCORE = 199 FOR GAME # 2
     CALLING UPDATE WITH:   MIN  TOTAL  MAX  NUMBER
                            114   114   114    1
        BEGINNING TO UPDATE WITH:   GAMESCORE  NUMBER  MIN  MAX  TOTAL
                                       199        1    114  114   114
           LEAVING UPDATE WITH:   GAMESCORE  NUMBER  MIN  MAX  TOTAL
                                     199        2    114  199   313
     -===>RETURNING FROM UPDATE:   MIN  TOTAL  MAX  NUMBER
                                   114   313   199    2

     FINAL RESULTS FOR ALL GAMES FOLLOW:
     ************************************

        ACCUMULATED TOTAL =   313
             MINIMUM GAME =   114
             AVERAGE GAME =   156.5000
             MAXIMUM GAME =   199
     NUMBER OF GAMES PLAYED = 2
```

1.10 Summary

Structure is important for algorithms, programs, and data. Structured programming is a philosophy as well as a defined methodology to guide the construction of algorithms and programs. It involves a top-down approach: starting with a given problem, then using stepwise refinement, and breaking problems into smaller component problems that then may be solved independently and subsequently combined. The overall goal is to write programs that are easily understood, debugged, and changed. Data abstraction and functional modularity are important elements of programming style to be incorporated into this approach. Algorithm and program structure have been stressed in this chapter and will continue to be emphasized throughout the book, as will the equally important choice of data structures. The next chapter discusses record and array information and pointers.

■ Exercises

1. In Figure 1.1 suppose there are $n = 100$ houses and you must visit houses 3, 10, 50, 7, and 82 (in this order). How much distance must you travel in each town?

2. Why do no more nonprimes remain in `candidates` when `factor` $> \sqrt{\mathtt{n}}$?

3. Explain the difference between a function and program segment implementation of a refinement.

4. a. What determines the largest value of n for which each of the two array implementations for `candidates` will work?

b. Discuss any significant differences between `set`, `insert`, `omit`, and `belongs` for the two implementations of `candidates`.

c. Modify the second implementation so that it works for larger n—say 20 times its current limit.

d. Write a function `copy` with parameters `c1` and `c2`. It must treat them as data abstractions with the operations `set`, `insert`, `omit`, and `belongs` and is to return with `c2`'s contents identical to `c1`'s and `c1`'s contents unaltered.

5. Change `primes` so that even numbers are not considered as values for `factor` or `nextmultiple`.

6. Change your solution to Exercise 5 so that even numbers, except 2, do not appear in `candidates`. Use only enough storage for 2 and the odd numbers between 2 and n.

7. This is the same as Exercise 6 except that `candidates` must use only enough storage for 2 and the odd primes between 2 and n.

8. Change `remove` so that instead of increasing `factor` by 1, `factor` is increased to the value of the next prime in `candidates`. You may choose to do this by starting with `remove` from your solution to Exercise 7.

9. Analyze the time and storage required for your solutions to Exercises 5 to 8.

10. For the prime problem, find a solution that stores no primes.

11. Explain why we must know the data type of the information stored in variables A and B in order to multiply their contents correctly.

12. Suppose that integers are represented as in the example of Section 1.3.2. Write an algorithm, in English, that will allow someone who knows addition tables up to 9 to compute the correct sum of the contents of A and B. The algorithm must yield the correct result no matter what integers are stored in A and B.

13. This is the same as Exercise 12 except that reals are represented, and the algorithm should yield the correct sum represented as a real number.

14. Express the Bowling Scores program just as the prime number solution is expressed in Figure 1.3. What are its local, nonlocal, and global variables?

15. Modify the flowcharts and program for the bowling problem to obtain flowcharts and a program solving the same problem but also printing out the number of rolls for each game.

16. What functions might be inserted in Bowling Scores to check the validity of its input and output? Where would they go in the program?

17. What elements of style have been incorporated in the programs of Sections 1.9.2 and 1.9.3?

■ Suggested Assignments

1. Write and run a program to print all perfect numbers no greater than n. A number is perfect if it is equal to the sum of its factors; thus 6 is a perfect number ($6 = 1 + 2 + 3$). The program is to create a collection **`candidates`** of all candidates for perfect numbers, remove those that are not perfect from **`candidates`**, and print the numbers remaining in it. The program must treat the collection with operations **`set`**, **`insert`**, **`omit`**, and **`belongs`** as a data abstraction.

2. Write a program to read in integers, store them in a collection, then read in more integers, remove each of these from it, and finally print all the integers remaining in it. The program is to treat the collection of integers as a data abstraction with the operations of **`set`**, **`insert`**, **`omit`**, and **`belongs`**.

3. a. Why does the Bowling Scores program require that the input consist of at least one game?

b. Change the program so that it handles the case of no games as input in a reasonable way.

2 Records, Arrays, and Pointers

3 4 5 6 7 8 9 10 11 12 13 1

Presents the first serious consideration of data structuring
Focuses on
- *two data structures for grouping related information*
  - *records and arrays*
- *two important operations on arrays*
  - *randomly accessing an array element*
  - *traversing an array*
- *pointers and their use*
  - *as indices to arrays*
  - *to access information stored in dynamic memory*
- *pointer arrays*
  - *their application and benefits*
- *representations of two-dimensional arrays*
  - *to show different implementations*
  - *to evaluate the benefits of these implementations*

Case study—stable marriages
- *highlights the benefits of carefully selecting both the information to be stored and the data structure in which to store it*

2.1 Bricks

Now that the context in which problems will be solved and programs written has been presented, it is time to start studying seriously the effect of choice of data structure on the problem solution. Before we explore some simple examples, the two basic data structures—records and arrays—must be understood, along with the two basic operations on them—selection and traversal.

A ***record*** is a data structure made up of a fixed number of information items, not necessarily of the same type. In C records are of the type structure. In the text the two words *record* and *structure* will be used interchangeably. An ***array*** is a data structure made up of a fixed number of information items *in sequence;* all items are required to be of the same type. Records and arrays have boundless applications. Records are useful when the items are to be referred to by name, while arrays are useful when the items are to be referred to by their positions in the sequence. The fundamental importance of the array was recognized quite early in the development of programming languages; the structure, or record, has only recently been incorporated in many languages. ***Pointers*** are variables that

1. Refer or point to memory locations for variables
2. Point to data structures, or
3. Link the components of a data structure together

Records and arrays are the bricks out of which more complex data structures are built, and pointers are the mortar holding them together.

Just as a builder asks for bricks and mortar, programmers in a high-level language ask for data structures to help build their solutions. A data structure is specified by declaring a variable name to be of a specific ***type.*** Some languages restrict the choice of type to individual variables or to arrays of type *int, float,* or *char.* C includes these, plus other types such as records, pointers, and unions. However, it does not have type *boolean,* which is found in other languages. C does allow the user to give new names to types.

Records and arrays allow related items of information to be treated as a group. The individual pieces of information in a record (structure) are called ***members*** in C. In most languages they are termed *fields,* but this word has a special meaning in C. Since that meaning is never utilized in this text, both *member* and *field* will be used for the elements of a record. In the case of arrays the individual pieces of information are called ***entries.*** The merit of records and arrays lies in the fact that they allow random access to any one of their fields or entries. ***Random access*** is accomplished by direct location of the desired piece of information, without regard to sequence. This means that access to an item may be accomplished in a fixed amount of time, no matter what item was previously accessed. This contrasts with ***sequential access,*** where the time required to access an item depends on the number of items stored between that item and the last item accessed, since each of the intermediate items must be accessed. With random access, any member of a record or any entry of an array may be accessed in a fixed amount of time, typically a few millionths or billionths of a second.

Both records and arrays provide the means to treat related items as a unit, and both generalize the idea of variables containing one item to variables containing many items. Records will be discussed next, then arrays.

2.1.1 Structures or Records in C

In C, memory can be thought of as consisting of storage elements of different length and complexity. Their complexity is determined by their type. The simplest storage elements have one of the three basic types, ***int, float,*** and ***char.*** Up one level in complexity are storage elements that have type ***structure.*** Among these, the simplest have exactly one member, which in turn has one of the basic types. A storage element of type structure for a book would be more complex; it might include members for its title, author, cost, and number of pages. Members are not restricted to one of the basic types but may themselves have type structure.

Consider the following C declarations:

```
float amount;        struct book                   struct book text;
                     {
                        char title[35];
                        struct name author;
                        float cost;
                        int pages;
                     };
```

```
struct balance          struct name
{                       {
   float amount;           char last[15];     ] note that, for example, char last[15] denotes a
}bankbalance;              char middleinit;     character string 15 characters long
                           char first[15];
                        }
```

Storage for the three variables **amount**, **bankbalance**, and **text** may be pictured as in Figure 2.1. From the figure it is clear that storage must differ in complexity for different variables. The simplest is obviously the one that stores only one piece of information, as does the storage element for the variable **amount**. The structure **bankbalance** is obviously more complex; it could also be made longer by adding more fields such as **lastdeposit** and **lastwithdrawal**. Of course, more memory is needed to store the variable **text** than to store **bankbalance**. The type structure generalizes the idea of an individual variable containing only one piece of information to variables containing related pieces of information. The amount of storage required determines the ***length*** of a record, while the record's structure determines its ***complexity.***

It is now possible to write C statements that refer to the entire record **text**, its **author** field, or its **last** field, using the names **text**, **text.author**, and **text.author.last**, respectively. In earlier versions of C it was not possible to write statements that referred to entire structures.

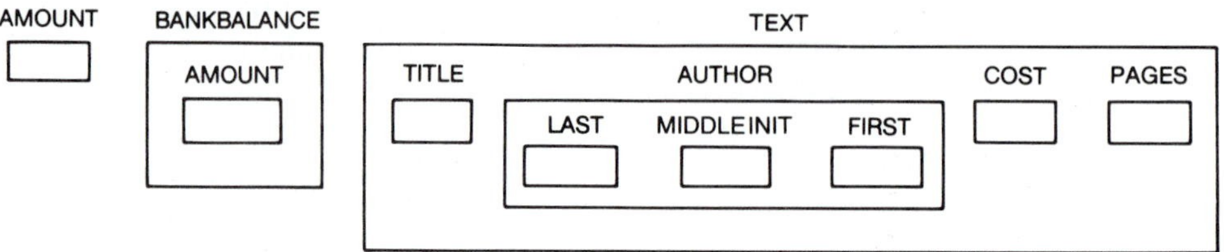

Figure 2.1 Three Variables

2.1.2 Arrays in C

Arrays provide another way to group either individual items or records. An array stores a sequence of entries; an entry in an array is referred to and located by its position in the sequence. An array has a fixed size and is homogeneous (that is, its entries must all be of the same type—say, of type integer or book). This contrasts with a record, whose fields may be of different types. An array entry is identified by qualifying the array name by the entry's position. To identify a member in a structure, the structure name is qualified by the member name. (Note that arrays can have entries of type structure, and structures can have members of type array.)

Consider the following declarations:

```
int book_number[80];
struct name author[40];
float prices[80];
char library[30];
```

The declaration specifies the name of each variable (e.g., `book_number`) and its type for each of four variables. It also specifies the range of values for an array index for each of the four arrays. An ***array index*** refers to a position of the array. `Book_number`, `author`, `prices`, and `library` have array indexes that may take on values in the range 0 to 79, 0 to 39, 0 to 79, and 0 to 29, respectively. In C the first position in an array is always the zero position. `Book_number[3]`, `author[9]`, and `prices[5]` refer to the fourth, tenth, and sixth entries, respectively, and `library[12]` refers to the thirteenth character in the character string `library`.

It has already been mentioned that arrays are very useful when entries must be accessed randomly. This occurs when the order in which requests for access to entries cannot be predicted. Suppose an array stores the initial mileage for each car of a fleet of rental cars. As a car is returned, its initial mileage is needed to prepare a bill based on mileage used. The next car to be returned can be *any* rented car. To access its initial mileage directly requires the random access capability of arrays. Processing time is saved, since the information entry is located directly—no time is lost searching through other entries to find it. When information is accessed directly, in a constant time, it is said to be ***selected.*** Thus any array entry whose position is known can be selected.

Instead of accessing a single array entry, a programmer may wish to process an entire array by accessing and processing each entry in turn. Moving sequentially through the entries is a *traverse*. In this case, the program is said to ***traverse*** the array. Such a traversal would be required in order to print out, in order, the initial mileage of each car in the fleet. A complete traversal is accomplished when each entry has been processed exactly once. A simple loop, starting at the first entry and finishing at the last, will accomplish this. Another use of traversal is to find an array entry whose position is unknown. In this case, the loop is terminated when the entry is found. If the traversal is completed, it means the desired entry was not present.

Selection and traversal are two ways to access an array entry. If the entry's position is known, selection is the efficient way to access it. When successive array positions must be examined to find the entry, selection is not possible, but traversal may be used.

If the traversal terminates at the ith entry (because it is the desired one), then a time proportional to i is required, since the $i - 1$ preceding entries must be accessed before the ith entry is obtained. Selection, on the other hand, takes constant time. This is an important distinction between these two basic operations on arrays. Selection means you can go directly to what is wanted; traversal means you must rummage around to find it. Use selection when one or more accesses must be made in arbitrary order and traversal when each entry is to be accessed in sequence.

Example 2.1 Suppose that data, such as integers in the range 1 to 100, are stored in an array `a`, as shown in Figure 2.2. Given any valid index value in the variable `i`, print the number stored in the `i`th position of the array `a`. ■

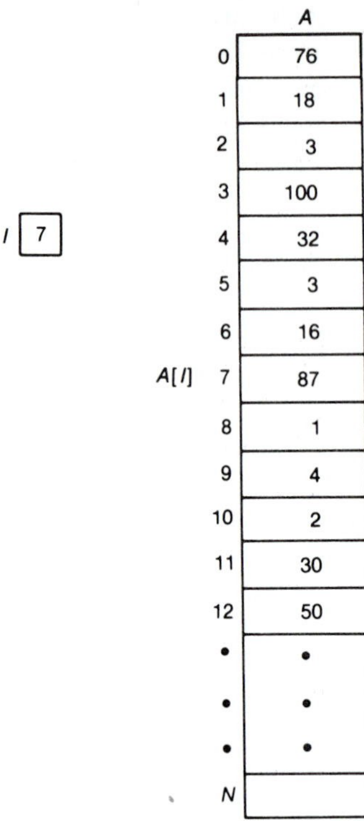

Figure 2.2 The Array for Example 2.1

This may be done by executing the C statement

```
printf("%d\n",a[i]);
```

This is a concise, easy-to-understand solution to Example 2.1. It takes a constant amount of time to execute, since it selects the desired entry of **a**. Note that when the value of the index **i** is 7, then the array entry with the value 87 is printed; when the value of **i** is 5, then the entry with the value 3 is printed. The index **i** is a variable that *points to* a particular entry of **a**. The current value of the index **i** determines the entry currently selected. Changing the value of **i** changes the entry to which it points. Thus the solution can be interpreted as the command "Print the entry of **a** to which the index **i** currently points."

Example 2.2 Let **a** be an array of length **n**, and let **k** be a variable containing an integer in the range 1 to 100. If there is some value of **i** for which **a[i]** contains **k**, then print that value of **i**; if there is more than one such value, print any one of them. If the value of **k** is nowhere in **a**, then print "−1." ■

Array **a** might represent the information kept by a car rental agency. For each **i**, array entry **a[i]** contains the account number, **k**, of the individual or firm currently renting car **i**. Example 2.1 thus requires finding the account now leasing car **i**. Example 2.2 requires finding the car being used by account **k**.

Example 2.2 could certainly be solved by traversing the array **a**, searching for an entry whose value equals the value of **k**. If one is found, its position in **a** would be printed. If the traversal is completed without success, "−1" would be printed. This solution is easy to code and could be written as follows:

```
found = FALSE;
loc = 0;
while (found != TRUE && loc <= n)
   if (a[loc] != k)
      loc++ ;
   else
      found = TRUE;
if (found)
   printf("\n %d\n",loc);
else
   printf("\n - 1 \n");
```

traverses the array until an entry containing account k *is found or until the last array entry has been considered*

Although this program segment for array traversal is simple, it is more complex than that for Example 2.1. Its execution time is proportional to the number of entries searched before the number in **k** is found, and if it is not found, the execution time is proportional to **n**.

Is it possible to find another way to solve this problem, one that will be as concise and clear as that for Example 2.1 and also execute in constant time? The answer is yes, if the information stored in **a** is represented in such a way that the program can *select* the correct value to print.

Such a program would start with creation of an array **pointer** of length 101, as follows. For each integer **k** (account number) between 1 and 100, if **k** does not appear in **a**, place "−1" in **pointer[k]**. If **k** does appear in **a** (it is an active account), place in **pointer[k]** the position of an entry of **a** that contains **k**. That is, place in **pointer[k]** the index value of an entry in **a** containing **k**. Thus, in Figure 2.3, **pointer[3]** contains 5, since **a[5]** contains 3.

With the array **pointer** available, the solution to Example 2.2 may be written as

```
printf("%d\n",pointer[k]);
```

This is the concise, easy-to-understand solution desired, and it executes in constant time. Again, the way in which the relevant information was represented in the program—that is, the way in which the data was structured—allows this solution to be achieved. Even in such a simple example, the way data is represented has a substantial impact on the resulting program.

Note that the use of the **pointer** array instead of **a** may cause some information available in **a** to be lost. This is because **pointer** captures only one of **a**'s positions that contains a specific number, even though that number may appear in **a** more than once. Finally, a price in execution time must be paid to create **pointer** from **a** in the first place. However, if the solution to Example 2.2 needed to be executed repeatedly, for many values of **k**, then it probably would be worth the price. It is frequently the case that prior processing to extract or restructure data saves later processing time.

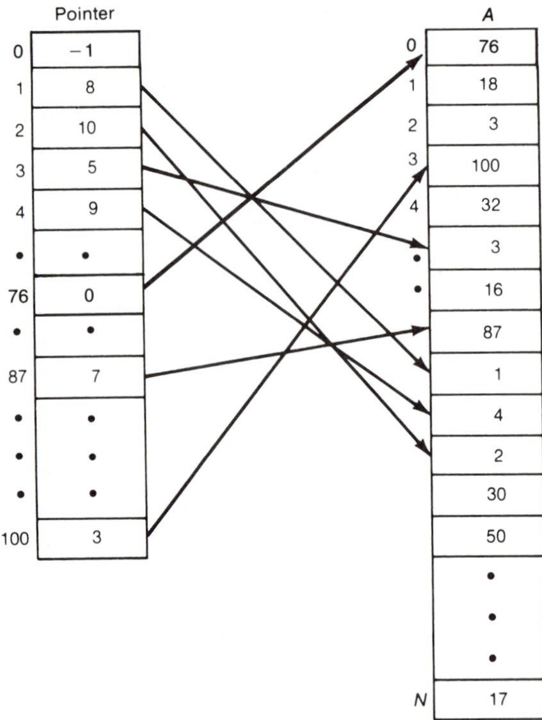

Figure 2.3 A Pointer Array for Example 2.2

In terms of storage required, `a` takes up `n` storage entries, and `pointer` takes up 101 storage entries. If `n` is much larger than 101, then `pointer` even saves storage; if `n` is much smaller, it requires more storage. Thus it is possible to trade time for storage. It will become apparent that this is generally true: saving execution time requires more storage, and vice versa.

When the choice of data structure was the array `a`, Example 2.1 was solved using selection, but traversal was required to find a solution to Example 2.2. When the `pointer` array was chosen to represent information, selection could be used to solve Example 2.2 more efficiently. However, if we had wanted to know *all* the cars leased by account `k`, `pointer` would not have been sufficient. It would have been necessary to traverse `a` to find all the occurrences of account number `k`. Can you find a way to avoid this traversal?

2.1.3 Two-Dimensional Arrays

Until now we have discussed one-dimensional arrays. High-level languages also provide arrays of more than one dimension. Thus the C declaration

```
int a[5][3];
```

defines a two-dimensional array of 5×3 or 15 entries, each of type integer. This array `a` can also be viewed as a collection of 5 one-dimensional arrays, each of length 3, or 3 one-dimensional arrays, each of length 5. Again, we can think of two variables `i` and `j` of the correct index type as pointing to an entry of the array.

Thus a[i][j] refers to the entry of the ith row and jth column, or to the entry of a currently pointed to by i and j. We assume that the (i,j)th entry can be accessed in constant time, no matter what the value of i or j. That is, the (i,j)th entry may be selected. Traversal of two-dimensional arrays is also easy.

A two-dimensional array is ***symmetric*** if a[i][j] and a[j][i] contain the same value for all i and j between 0 and n − 1. Suppose a collection of n^2 numbers, representing the distances between n(≤50) cities, is stored in a two-dimensional array a. Thus a[i][j] contains the distance between city i and city j. For this example, which involves distances, the array must be symmetric. However, the array a shown in Figure 2.4 is not symmetric, because a[2][3] does not equal a[3][2]. The n entries a[0][0], a[1][1], . . . , a[n - 1][n - 1] are called its ***diagonal*** entries. In the city-distance array, the diagonal entries must, of course, be zero.

A

	0	1	2	3
0	1	5	-7	10
1	5	2	6	11
2	-7	6	0	8
3	10	11	9	3

Figure 2.4 An Asymmetric Two-Dimensional Array

Example 2.3 Suppose a programmer wished, perhaps as part of an input validation function for the data of an array, to check the array for symmetry. The programmer might choose to write a function check to return the value *true* if the array is symmetric and *false* otherwise. A simple traversal, as follows, will do the checking. ■

```
typedef int collection[50][50];
check(a,n)
/* Returns true only if the first n
   rows and columns of a represent
   a symmetric array
*/
collection a;
int n;
{
   int i,j,ck;
   ck = TRUE;
   for (i = 0; i<n; i++)
      for (j = 0; j<n; j++)
         if (a[i][j] != a[j][i])
            ck = FALSE;
   return(ck);
}
```

collection *is the* ***type*** *name for an integer array of size 50 × 50*

a *is an* ***instance*** *of* collection, *an integer array of size 50 × 50*

i *is the row and* j *the column index*

traverses the first n *rows and columns of* a *and sets* ck *to false if any* a[i][j] *is not equal to* a[j][i]

This program does a complete traversal of the appropriate n entries of the array a. However, it is inefficient as a solution for a number of reasons. First, it does not exit immediately from the loops, even though it may have just found that a was not symmetric. Second, it checks the diagonal elements, which will always satisfy a[i][j] = a[j][i]. Finally, it double-checks each off-diagonal entry. For instance, when i = 2 and j = 3, it checks a[2][3] against a[3][2], and when i = 3 and j = 2, it checks a[3][2] against a[2][3] again. A better version would be a modified traversal, such as

```
typedef int collection[50][50];
check(a,n)
/* Returns true only if the first n
   rows and columns of a represent
   a symmetric array
*/
collection a;
int n;
{
   int i,j,ck;
   ck = TRUE;
   for(i=1; i<n && ck; i++)
      for(j=0; j <i && ck; j++)
         if(a[i][j] != a[j][i])
            ck = FALSE;
   return(ck);
}
```

the traversal is aborted when a *is known not to be symmetric; it makes only necessary comparisons*

Be sure you understand why the modified lines of code eliminate the inefficiencies.

2.1.4 Representation of Records in Arrays

In C the record, or structure, is a basic data structure. In some languages the record is not a built-in feature but must be constructed from the data structures (such as arrays) that are available. To see how this construction might be done, assume C designers had provided the integer, float and char data types, and only one-dimensional arrays. Not only would records have to be constructed, but so would arrays of more dimensions if they were needed. There are two reasons for looking at ways to build data structures.

1. It affords insight into how compilers implement records and higher-dimensional arrays.
2. It demonstrates how programmers build new structures from those that are given in order to tailor data structures to specific needs.

Moreover, even though records and higher-dimensional arrays *are* available in C, there are times when programmers may find it preferable to use these construction techniques.

Let us consider how to represent n records, each composed of m fields of the same fixed type. Suppose m is 3. A natural solution is to take an array of length $3 \times n$, of the same type as the fields, and store the records in the array. The first record takes up the first three entries, the second record the next three entries, and so on, as in Figure 2.5. Each field of a record will be stored in the corresponding one of its three entries.

The ith record begins in position $3*(i - 1)$ of the array. Thus we may *select* the ith record. To access a specific field of the ith record (say, the third) requires that position $3*(i - 1) + 2$ of the array be accessed. Although this is the $(3*(i - 1) + 2)^{\text{th}}$ array element, it contains the third field value of the ith record. Thus we may select any field of any record too.

It is also easy to *traverse* the records, using a loop. For example, the following function traverses the `n` records stored in the array `a` and prints the value in their `k`th field, where `k` may be 1, 2, or 3.

```
typedef int fieldtype;
typedef fieldtype array[30];
printfield(a,n,k)
/* Prints the contents of the
   kth field of each of the first
   n records stored in array a.
*/
array a;
int n,k;
{
   int length = 3, i;
   for(i=0; i<n; i++)
      printf("\n %d\n",a[length * i + (k-1)]);
}
```

`fieldtype` *is now another name for the type: integer—it is used to clarify its intended use;* `array` *is the name for the type: array of* `fieldtype` *of size 30*

`a` *is an instance of type* `array`

`length` *is initialized to the number of fields in each record*

In C, since arrays must be homogeneous (consisting of entries of the same type), this method is applicable only to *homogeneous* records—those whose fields are all of the same type. How then to handle the more general case of records whose fields are not homogeneous? The following example demonstrates the general concept and then how it is achieved in C.

Example 2.4 Consider Figure 2.6, which represents an array `cars` containing a record for each car of an automobile rental agency. The record for each car has an entry for the `make` (characters), monthly `rate` (a real number), current `mileage` (an integer), and the `rentee` (characters). As noted, this array, with entries of different types, could not be constructed in C. For the sake of simplicity, the following discussion does not deal with the actual storage taken by a character, float, or integer variable, but assumes that each takes one element of memory. All the records in the array are 42 elements long, using 15 elements for the `make`, 1 element each for the monthly `rate` and current `mileage`, and 25 elements for the `rentee` field. ■

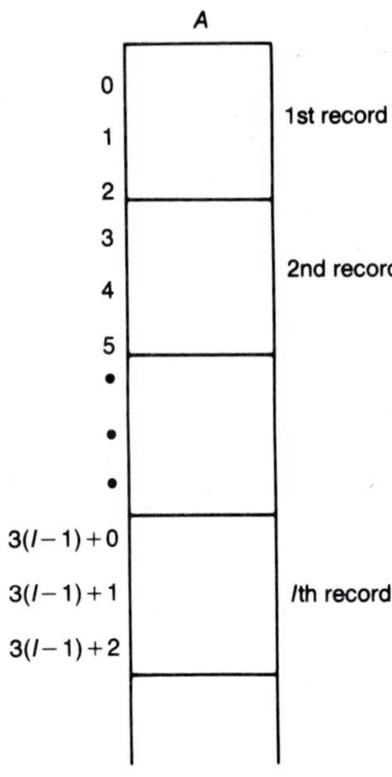

Figure 2.5 An Array of Records (of Length 3)

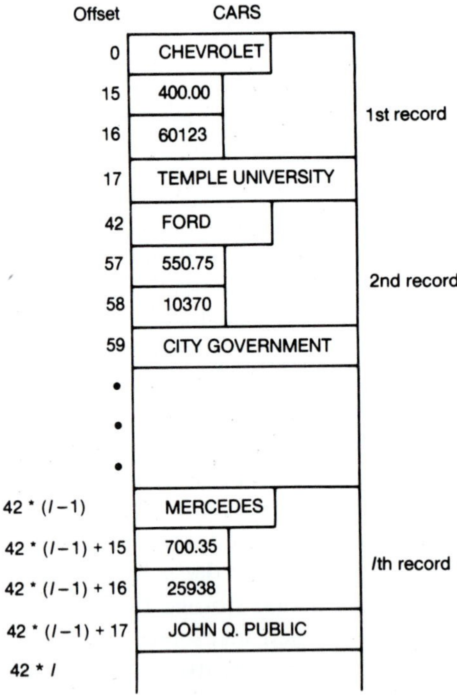

Figure 2.6 Records of a Car Rental Agency Stored in an Array CARS

An offset gives the position of a data item with respect to a given reference point. When you say, "the third house from the corner," you are using an offset reference point. Each field has a ***field offset*** from the beginning of the record. In this case, the field offsets are 0, 15, 16, and 17, respectively, for `make`, monthly `rate`, current `mileage`, and `rentee`. The ith record has a ***record offset*** of $42\times(i - 1)$ from the beginning of the array. The offset for its `rentee` field from the beginning of the array is $42\times(i - 1) + 17$, the sum of the record offset for the ith record and the field offset for the `rentee`.

In order to reference, for example, the current mileage field of the ith record, the programmer may refer to `cars[42*(i-1)+16]`, assuming the first record starts in element zero of the array. Only the fields may be referred to by the programmer; the record itself cannot be dealt with directly as a unit. In C the task is simplified for the programmer by the use of structures and arrays of structures. `Carrecord` is defined as a structure and `cars[100]` as an array of 100 `carrecords`.

```
struct carrecord
{
   char make[15];
   float rate;
   int mileage;
   char rentee[25];
}cars[100];
```

Then the C programmer may refer to the (`i` + 1)th record as a unit as `cars[i]`, and to its mileage field by `cars[i].mileage`. Treating a record as a unit allows intentions to be stated more clearly in a program. It also allows for the contents of one record to be assigned to the storage for another record more efficiently. This is analogous to being able to refer to an automobile and say "Move that automobile from here to there," rather than specifying the automobile or the move by referring to each of its parts individually. Languages that do not provide the record data structure prevent the programmer from referring to a record as a unit in this way.

Note that the record referred to during the execution of a program may be changed merely by changing the value of `i`, but the field referred to cannot be changed, since field names may not be changed during execution. The variable names `cars[i].mileage` shows this. The value of array index `i` can be changed, but the name `cars` cannot be. This means that code referring to the `i`th position of an array, such as `cars[i]`, may refer to different array entries as a program executes, by computing a new value for `i`. Code using a field name will always refer to that particular field.

This example gives a technique for sorting records in languages without strong typing constraints. Even in languages with such constraints, the *compiler* might implement `cars` in the actual computer memory as illustrated in Figure 2.6. In this case, if the initial array address in memory is 100 rather than 0, then the offset (or relative position) for the (`i` + 1)th record is added to 100 instead of to 0.

The compiler can produce commands that calculate the actual position in memory of any field of the `i`th record by adding the record offset and field offset to 100. Then a programmer's reference to `cars[1]` is interpreted as a reference to the 42 consecutive locations 142 to 183. Similarly, `cars[1].rate` refers to the entry in location 157. This assumes the array starts at memory location 100. The offsets are independent of the starting location. When applied to homogeneous records, this method requires that `cars` be defined to be the same type as the record's fields.

Observe that the `cars` array preserves the homogeneity of type that is required of all arrays in C. Its entries are now all of the same specific record type. The array entries just happen to be of type `carrecord`, even though a record itself is not homogeneous. C allows operations to be performed directly on structures, treating them as a unit. Of course, the compiler hides the details of the records' implementation from readers of the program and provides facility in handling records.

The method just discussed is a single-array implementation. The second method of representing the `n` records is a multiarray implementation, shown in Figure 2.7. The method simply uses a different array for each field. Each array then contains information of the appropriate type only. There is no *direct* way to refer to the collective notion `cars[2]`. Instead, its data are given by `make[2]`, `rate[2]`, `mileage[2]`, and `rentee[2]`. Selection of the `i`th record and traversal through the records is also possible for this method.

The single-array technique may cause problems when all entries are not of the same type. As noted, however, Example 2.4 shows offset calculations of the type that may be used by a compiler but are invisible to the programmer. The multiarray technique is useful in any language that provides arrays. Both techniques fail to give the programmer means to refer directly to, or to manipulate as a unit, an entire record composed of more than one field. The C approach provides the record data structure and makes the underlying details transparent to the C programmer, thus providing an elegant solution to the problem of treating information of different types as a unit.

MAKE	RATE	MILEAGE	RENTEE
CHEVROLET	400.00	60123	TEMPLE UNIVERSITY
FORD	550.75	10370	CITY GOVERNMENT
•			
•			
•			
MERCEDES	700.35	25938	JOHN Q. PUBLIC

Figure 2.7 A Multiarray Storage of Records of a Car Rental Agency

2.1.5 Variable-Length Records

When the records of a collection are not necessarily of the same length, they are called ***variable-length records.*** Looking back at the single-array and the multiarray representations for a collection of records, it is clear that selection of the `ith` record was possible only under the tacit assumption that the records were all the same length.

Suppose a field is added to `carrecord` for each previous rentee. Surely some newer cars will have few previous rentees, while older cars will have a long history of rentees. The programmer could decide to represent each car's record by using a single-length record large enough to accommodate the largest possible number of past rentees. This would aid in processing, as uniformity always does, but would waste a great deal of storage if many records actually have short histories.

With variable-length records, shorter records use fewer locations than longer records, as shown in Figure 2.8. Details of the implementation of such a collection of records must somehow specify where one record ends and the next starts. Separators between records would do, or a field associated with each record could give its total length. Using separators, the last element of the storage for a record would contain a special value denoting the end of the record's storage. If associated fields are used, the first storage element of each record would

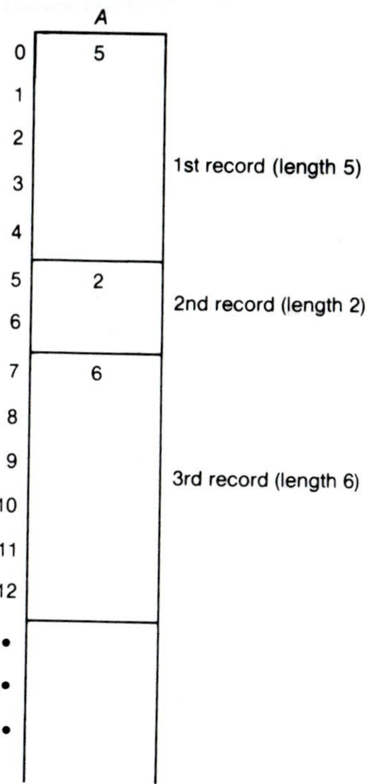

Figure 2.8 Variable-Length Records Stored in Array *A*

contain the record's length and would allow a determination of the last element of its storage. In either case, the `i`th record may no longer be selected, because its location cannot be calculated. However, given the position of the `i`th record, one can calculate the position of the (`i` + 1)th record.

Assuming the first element of each record contains its length, as in Figure 2.8, the following function accomplishes the traversal. A record of zero length is used as a sentinel to indicate that there are no more records in the array.

```
#define SENTINEL 0
traverse(a)
/* Traverses an array a */
int a[];
{
   int i;
   i = 0;
   while(a[i] != SENTINEL)
      {
         process(a,i);
         i = i+a[i];
      }
}
```

a *is the array of records to be traversed*

traverses the records until the last has been processed; does the necessary processing of the (`i` + 1)*th record*

The record array here is simply an array of individual elements. The *programmer* imposes the record structure. Each field of the record must thus have the same type in C. `Process` is a function that does whatever processing is called for. Thus, traversal through the records can be used to access the `i`th record, but this takes time proportional to `i`.

2.1.6 The Use of Unions in C

No facility is provided in C to handle variable length records directly, though *unions* do afford a means of handling some variability. A ***union*** in C may contain data that can have different types and sizes at different times. Thus unions provide a means of using a single storage area for distinct purposes. Unions are declared in the same manner as structures. The compiler allocates enough memory to hold the largest member that can be stored in the union. Unions are consequently of fixed size but allow variation in the type of data stored. The programmer has to keep track of which type is currently stored in the union. Unions would not be of significant help in Example 2.4 with the list of rentees. In this case there can be more than a few distinct rentees for each car, and unions do not fit this type of variability. Lists, the topic of the next chapter, would be used for this example.

```
union book_lookup
{
   float location;
   char title[50];
};
```

Variables of type `book_lookup` could contain either the title of a book or its location in a library (based on the Dewey Decimal System). Unions thus give some measure of variability in records. However, the records do not have variable lengths; they are of fixed length.

Unions may occur in structures, and structures may occur in unions.

```
struct
{
    int library_id;
    union book_lookup information;
}catalog[100];
```

Each individual structure of the `catalog` array can contain an "i.d." number and either a real number or character strings of length 50 in any of its entries. Then, for example, `catalog[40].information.title` refers to the member `title` in entry 40 of `catalog`.

2.1.7 Address Calculation without Access

Calculating the address of an item of data is not the same thing as accessing the item of data. The ***address*** of an item is its storage position, not its value. To ***access*** the item means to read its current value from memory or to store a value in its memory location.

Many authors associate the process of selection with the idea of access to an item, rather than with the calculation of the storage address of the item. They say that the `i`th item of a structure can be selected if, given the value of `i`, the program can access the item in a time that is independent of `i`. Such a structure is called a *random access* structure. This definition served well for early computers, in which arrays could reside in a single homogeneous memory. However, current practice includes radically different memory architectures.

Modern computers have memory hierarchies—that is, different kinds of memory—whose access times vary by one or two orders of magnitude from one level of the hierarchy to the next. It may well be the case that some portion of an array is stored in fast memory, such as high-speed cache memory, and some portion in slower central memory. Then the access time for an array element would depend on the index of the element (that is, its position in the sequence of the array), but the time required to *compute the storage address* would still be independent of the value of the index. Consequently, the process of address calculation should be thought of as separate from the process of access to the data. ***Selection*** thus denotes address calculation without access. Although it is important to grasp this distinction between address calculation and actual access, it is generally ignored in the explanations here, as in other texts, for convenience of exposition.

Our interest in the effect of data structures on program efficiency concerns the *timing* of various algorithms. Because access times may vary, depending on features of the physical computer that are completely hidden from the language, time will be measured here as if each program were executed on a computer that has a single homogeneous central memory.

The special techniques necessary to write efficient programs for computers with hierarchical memories are not within the scope of this text. Some computers even allow the exploitation of any parallelism inherent in an algorithm, which means that more than one operation may be carried out at a time. This text also largely ignores this possibility of parallel processing, although it is currently a topic of computer research.

If this array of material leaves you in disarray, keep going. Pointers will point the way!

2.2 Mortar

2.2.1 Pointers

In C, records can be stored in arrays. They can also be stored in an area of memory called the ***dynamic memory.*** Dynamic memory is managed automatically for the programmer, who can request and release storage as needed. ***Pointers*** are variables that point to data items. Those that point to array entries, as noted earlier, are called *array indexes*. Those that point to individual data items, or structures, are called ***pointer variables.*** By following a pointer, you can access a record. Sometimes it is necessary to access a record by following a sequence of pointers.

Pointers and pointer variables afford flexibility in structuring data but must be used with great care, since they can introduce subtle errors that cause difficulty in the debugging of a program. The errors are problems that arise when collections of records can expand or contract in unpredictable ways. Storage for such records must be managed carefully.

To understand pointers and pointer variables, it is practical to examine them in a more static context. They are useful even then, in solving problems involving variable-length records and the representation of arrays. A good way to become familiar with the workings of pointers and pointer variables is to solve the following problem: *Is there a way to store* `n` *variable-length records in a one-dimensional array so that traversal through the records is possible, and, more important, so that the* (`i` + 1)*th one can be selected?*

The solution is not difficult conceptually. Suppose a pointer array `pa` is created, as in Figure 2.9. The information in `pa[i]` should state where the base, or origin, of the (`i` + 1)th record is in `a`. Thus `pa[3]` is 13, because the fourth record begins in `a[13]`. One describes this by saying that `pa[i]` contains a pointer to the (`i` + 1)th record in `a`. The variable `i` can be thought of as pointing indirectly to a record in `a`; to get to it requires an access to `pa` along the way.

Recall that records are represented by a sequence of consecutive entries, so `pa[i]` points to the first entry of the (`i` + 1)th record, its base. Once the base of a record and its field offsets are known, any field of the record can be selected. This technique of using pointer arrays is an old and very important technique in computer science. This kind of pointer is just an array index; it is also known as a *relative pointer,* because it indicates the position of the record in relation to the other records within the same array. This is different from the other type of pointer, the *pointer variable,* which refers to actual memory locations.

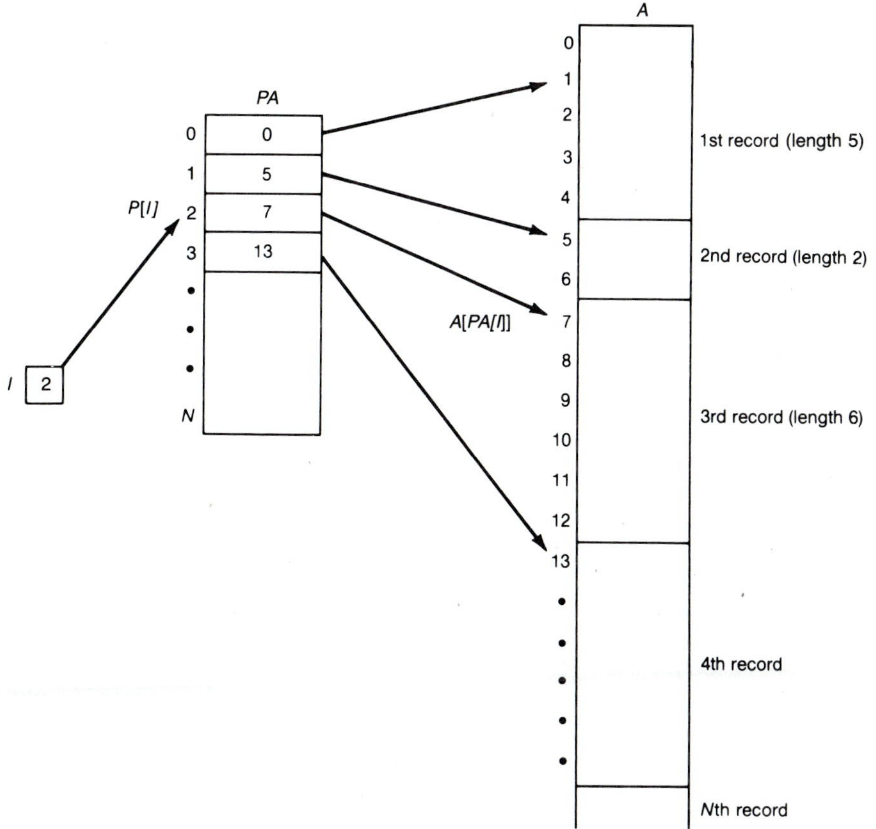

Figure 2.9 Pointer Array *PA*, with Pointers Stored in *A*

Selecting the (**i** + 1)th record is now possible by accessing **pa[i]** and following the pointer found there to the entry of **a** in which the (**i** + 1)th record begins. The base of this record has the name **a[pa[i]]**. Note that selection is being applied first to array **pa**, and then to array **a**. Each takes constant time, which is why we say the (**i** + 1)th record may be selected. It is also easy to traverse through the records using **pa**, as shown by the following program.

```
traverse(a,pa,n)
/* Traverses through the n
   records stored in a which
   are pointed to by indices
   stored in the pointer array pa
*/
int a[],pa[],n;
{
   int i;
   for (i=0; i<n; i++)
      process(a,pa,i);
}
```

Using the pointer array costs additional storage but solves the problem posed for variable-length records. Relative pointers to records stored in an array are easy to use when language typing constraints are not violated.

2.2.2 Pointer Variables and Dynamic Memory

As a programmer you may need to store a collection of records that are not all of the same type. In C they cannot be kept in a single array, since that would violate the array typing constraint, but there is a way out: simply declare each different type to correspond to one of the members of a union occurring in the record. With this trick, C treats records of different types as records of the same type. Another difficulty in C is how to store a collection of records of the same type when the maximum number of such records is not known in advance. Storing them in an array requires specifying the length of the array, but the programmer may not know what this should be. A practical solution to this problem is provided by the dynamic memory.

So far, by grouping records in arrays, it has been possible to refer to a record by its position in the array. This eliminates the need to attach a separate name to each record of the group. ***Dynamic memory*** may be viewed as a collection of storage elements that are on call for the storage of information. However, records stored in dynamic memory do not have individual names *or* array positions to be used for their reference. Instead, *pointer variables* are used to point to an individual record. A record in dynamic memory can be accessed only through its pointer variable. A pointer is like a string attached to a record: follow it and you get to the record. The pointers previously examined point to a record's position in an array, whereas pointer variables point to a record's location in dynamic memory. Both play the same role: they lead to a record.

Declaring a record type for records to be stored in dynamic memory is the same as for individual records or records stored in arrays. However, an associated variable of type pointer must be declared and used to refer to the record. For example, to store a record of type `carrecord` to be referenced by the pointer variable `pcar 1` requires the following declaration:

```
struct carrecord *pcar1,car2;
```

An important distinction exists between the variable `pcar1`, which is a pointer, and `car2` of type carrecord. The variable `car2` is not stored in dynamic memory. Storage is allocated to `car2` as soon as the component of the program in which it is declared is executed. The programmer need do nothing other than declare it to ensure this allocation of storage; statements assigning values to it may immediately be written.

This is *not* the case for the record pointed to by `pcar1`, which is to be stored in dynamic memory; `pcar1` itself is not stored in dynamic memory, but the record it will point to is. This is because `pcar1` was declared to be a pointer. The prefix, *, denotes this. No storage is allocated for the record that `pcar1` will point to until a specific request made by the programmer is executed. This is done by an invocation of the C function `malloc`. Thus,

```
pcar1 = malloc(sizeof(struct carrecord));
```

when executed, places a pointer value into **pcar1** and also allocates storage in dynamic memory for a record of type **carrecord** to which that pointer points. Until this is done, **pcar1**'s value is undefined. After the function is executed, the situation may be pictured as in Figure 2.10.

The record may be referenced by **pcar1** and its members referenced by **pcar1->make**, **pcar1->rate**, **pcar1->mileage**, and **pcar1->rentee**. At this point, though, the contents of the fields are undefined. Storage has simply been allocated for them in dynamic memory. They may be assigned values by using the assignment statement. Each field of the record pointed to by **pcar1** can be given a value. Thus

```
pcar1->rate = 20.25;
```

assigns a value of 20.25 to the rate field of the record pointed to by **pcar1**. You must be sure before assigning values to a record stored in dynamic memory that you have assigned a value to the pointer variable pointing to that record.

One advantage of pointer variables in C is that the value of a pointer can be printed. It means that a programmer can see the value of a pointer for debugging purposes. Other advantages of using pointer variables (that is, of storing records in dynamic memory) will soon become apparent.

Selection and traversal of a collection of records stored in dynamic memory may be accomplished using an array of pointers. The array entries are pointers that point to records in dynamic memory.

Example 2.5 The definition

```
struct carrecord *pcar[100];
```

establishes an array of 100 pointers that can address 100 records stored in dynamic memory. A reference to a member of a record is done by first specifying the pointer to the record, **pcar[i]**, and then the desired member of the record, say **make**. The resultant reference would then be written as **pcar[i]->make**. This references the **make** member of the (**i** + 1)th record. ■

Arrays of pointers to records in dynamic memory are not as easy to use as relative pointers to records in an array, but they provide significant flexibility. You shall see, though, that considerable care is needed to use them properly.

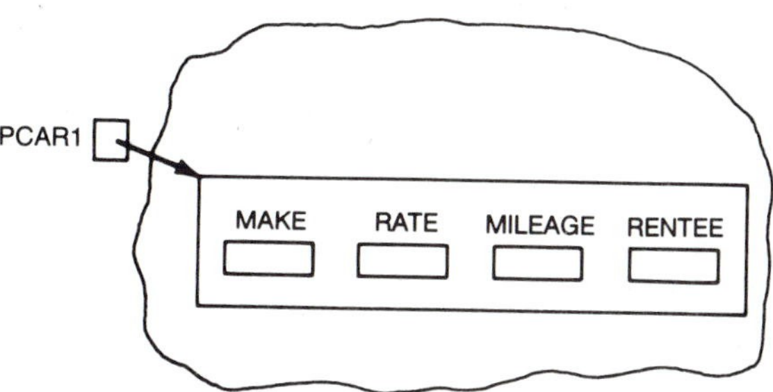

Figure 2.10 Dynamic Memory

2.3 Representations of Two-Dimensional Arrays

It is time to return to the problem of how to represent higher-dimensional arrays in terms of one-dimensional arrays. For simplicity, only two-dimensional arrays are discussed, but the techniques can be readily extended for higher dimensions. Two techniques will be studied: 1) rowwise and columnwise representation and 2) pointer array representation.

What exactly is meant by representing a two-dimensional array `a` in terms of a one-dimensional array (say, `data`), and why is it done? The idea is that the problem to be solved may involve the use of `a`, but the language being used may not provide two-dimensional arrays, or the programmer may choose not to use them for some other reason. Instead, the entries of `a` are stored in `data`. This must be done so that whenever reference is to be made to the entry in position `(i,j)` of `a` in the program, the corresponding position of `data` in which it is stored is referenced instead. For example, the `check` functions of Example 2.3 referred to a two-dimensional array `a`. If its information were stored in `data`, then the functions would have to be rewritten, replacing each reference to `a[i][j]` with a reference to the correct entry in `data` that corresponds to it. Of course, the declarations involving `a` would also have to be replaced by declarations involving `data`.

2.3.1 Rowwise and Columnwise Representation

Suppose `a` has `r` rows and `c` columns, with row index range 0 . . . (`r` − 1) and column index range 0 . . . (`c` − 1). A ***rowwise representation*** for `a` uses a `data` array of length `r` × `c` and stores the first row of `a` in the first `c` consecutive entries of `data`, the second row in the next `c` entries, and so on.

Rowwise representation in arrays is similar to the first method discussed for storing records. In fact, it is logically the same as viewing each row as a record of length `c`. Thus the offset of the entry in position (`i,j`) of `a` is `i * c + j` in `data`. This is because rows 0, 1, . . . , `i` − 1 precede the `i`th row in `data`, and take up `i` × `c` entries. The `j`th position of the `i`th row is offset an additional `j` entries.

For the array `a` shown in Figure 2.11, with `c` = 5, the offset of `a[2][3]` is 2 ∗ 5 + 3, or 13, and the third row of `a` starts at `data[10]`. `a[2][3]` is represented by `data[13]`. In C the offset and index are the same, since index values start at zero.

With this representation, function `check` of Example 2.3 would be written as

```
#define TRUE 1
#define FALSE 0
check(data,n)
/* Returns true only if an nxn
   two-dimensional array stored in
   rowwise representation in array
   data is symmetric
*/
int data[];
int n;
```

] `data` *is a one-dimensional array*

```
{
    int i,j,ck;                                    ] i is the row and j the column index
    ck = TRUE;
    for(i=1; i<n && ck ; i++)
       for(j=0; j<i && ck ; j++)
          if(data[(i*n+j)] != data[(j*n+i)])       ] compares the entries in positions
             ck = FALSE;                             [i][j] and [j][i] of the n × n
    return(ck);                                      two-dimensional array being checked
}                                                    by comparing their values, which are
                                                     stored in data[i*n+j] and in
                                                     data[j*n+i]
```

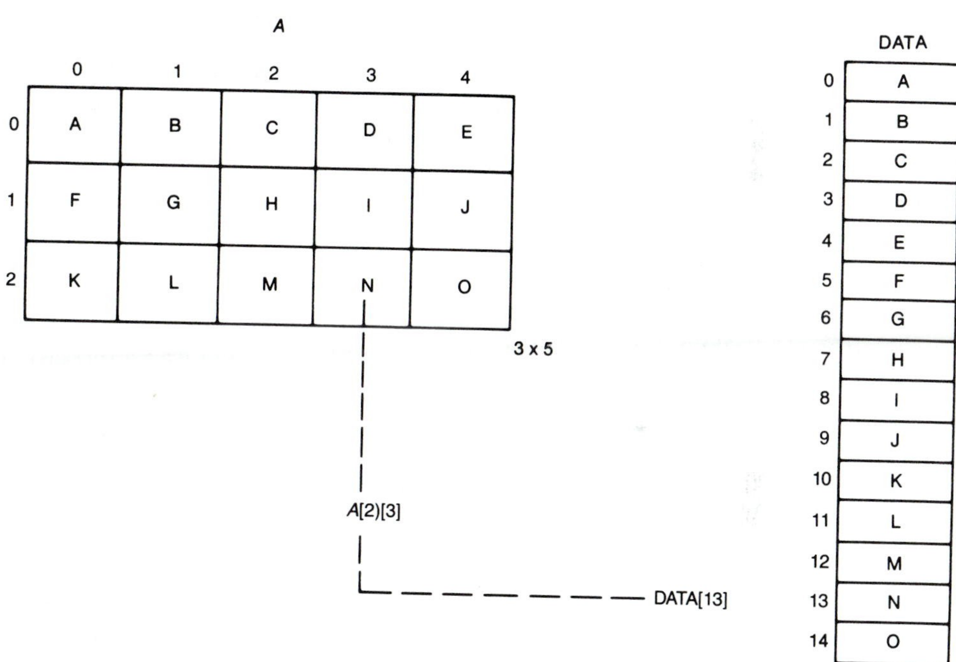

Figure 2.11 Representing a Two-Dimensional Array as a One-Dimensional Array

Obviously, this representation in `data` allows `a` to be traversed, as well as allowing its (`i`,`j`)th entry to be selected.

The *columnwise representation* of a two-dimensional array is similar, except that the columns rather than the rows of `a` are stored sequentially in `data`. The offset for the entry in position (`i`,`j`) with the columnwise representation is `j * r + i`.

2.3.2 Symmetric Array Representation

Example 2.6 Suppose a program involves an $n \times n$ array `a` that is always symmetric. In other words, it is initially symmetric, and any processing performed on `a` does not disturb its symmetry. When n is small, both the rowwise and columnwise representations are feasible, even though roughly one-half of the information being stored is superfluous. For large values of n (say, 400), the computer system may not provide the required 160,000 storage elements, so the program could not execute. One remedy may be to store only the diagonal entries of `a` and the entries below the diagonal (those whose row index `i` exceeds the column index `j`). This requires $((n \times n) + n)/2$ entries, or 80,200 instead of 160,000.

Although high-level languages could have provided a data-type, symmetric array to be used in this way, no language does. Instead, the programmer can construct a `data` array of length $((n \times n) + n)/2$ to store the entries. The idea is the same as for a rowwise representation, except that only those entries of a row in the lower half or on the diagonal of `a` are stored. Thus for the row in position `i`, entries `a[i-1][0]`, `a[i-1][1]`, . . . , `a[i][i]` are stored in consecutive entries of `data`, each row's entries following those of the preceding row. ■

To use this representation of `a`, the programmer needs to be able to refer, for given `i` and `j`, to the proper position of `data` that corresponds to `a[i][j]`, just as was done in the `check` function. Finding the offset formula is a little more complex than for the rowwise representation but is done in the same way.

Preceding the entries for the row in position `i` are the entries for rows in positions 0, 1, . . . , `i` − 1. The entry in position `j` of this row is then an additional `j` entries down in `data`. Thus the offset for `a[i][j]` is 1 + 2 + 3 + · · · + `i` + `j`. Any reference we want to make to `a[i][j]` is made, instead, by a reference to `data[1 + 2 + ... + i + j]`. This, of course, is true only for `i` ≥ `j`, since `a[i][j]`, when `i` < `j`, is not stored in `data` directly. Its symmetric entry in `a`, `a[j][i]`, is stored in `data[1 + 2 + ... + j + i]`. So if `i` < `j`, a reference to `a[i][j]` must be achieved by referring to `a[j][i]`.

The polynomial (1 + 2 + · · · + `i` + `j`) (or ((1 + 2 + · · · + `i`) + `j`) appears at first glance to require a loop for its calculation, requiring time proportional to `i`. However,

$$(1 + 2 \cdots + \mathtt{i}) \quad \text{is actually the same as} \quad \frac{\mathtt{i} \times (\mathtt{i} + 1)}{2} \quad \text{for } \mathtt{i} >= 0$$

The division is integer division, so the polynomial may be evaluated in constant time. This means that the entry in position (`i`,`j`) of `a` can be selected using the index,

$$\frac{(\mathtt{i} \times (\mathtt{i} + 1))}{2} + \mathtt{j} \quad \text{when } \mathtt{i} \geq \mathtt{j} \quad \text{and} \quad \frac{(\mathtt{j} \times (\mathtt{j} + 1))}{2} + \mathtt{i} \quad \text{when } \mathtt{i} < \mathtt{j}$$

Traversal may also be accomplished easily. Consider that the entries are stored in `data` for each row as records of variable length, yet they can be selected and traversed conveniently with no pointer array. The reason is that their lengths, and the order in which they are stored, are regular enough that the requisite calculations for positions can be made. In the *general* case of variable-length records, there is no way to do this.

2.3.3 Pointer Array Representation

The second technique for representing a two-dimensional array in terms of one-dimensional arrays uses a pointer array `p`. ***Pointer arrays*** have pointers as their entries. The entries of the pointer array point to the rows of `a`, which may be stored in one of two ways: in `data` (a one-dimensional array) or in the dynamic memory. The number of rows, `r`, of `a` must be known. Then `p`, `data`, and `r` represent `a` when the array is used, and `p` and `r` represent `a` when dynamic memory is used. In the array case, `p` is of integer type, as in Section 2.2.1. In fact, this is just an application of that method.

Clearly, there is no need to store the rows one after another in `data`; they can be anywhere in the array as long as they do not overlap. This feature provides considerable flexibility in the use of storage.

A variation of the array technique would treat the rows stored in `data` as row records. In the dynamic memory case, `p` is of type pointer, and the row records are stored in dynamic memory. Selection and traversal are thus both easily achieved. The corresponding versions (storing rows in `data`, storing row records in `data`, storing row records in dynamic memory) of the function `check` would appear as follows.

Version 1—Storing Rows in *Data*

```
#define TRUE 1
#define FALSE 0
typedef int pointerarray[50];
typedef int dataarray[2500];

check(p,data,r) /* storing rows in data */
/* Returns true only if the rxr
   two-dimensional array, whose rows
   are stored in data and are pointed to
   by pointers stored in p, is symmetric.
*/
pointerarray p;
dataarray data;
int r;
{
   int i,j,ck;
   ck = TRUE;
   for(i=1;i<r && ck;i++)
      for(j=0;j<i && ck;j++)
         if(data[p[i]+j] != data[p[j]+i])
            ck = FALSE;
   return(ck);
}
```

type names for array of pointers to rows and array containing the rows

`p` *is an instance of type* `pointerarray` *and* `data` *is an instance of type* `data-array`

`i` *is the row and* `j` *the column index*

the entries of the `r` × `r` *two-dimensional array checked are stored in positions* `p[i]+j` *and* `p[j]+i` *of* `data`

Version 2—Storing Row Records in *Data*

```
#define TRUE 1
#define FALSE 0
typedef struct
{
   int row[50];
}rowrecord;
typedef int pointerarray[50];
typedef rowrecord dataarray[50];
```

type names for row records, for array of pointers to row records, and array containing the row records

```
check(p,data,r) /* storing row records in data */
/* Returns true only if the rxr
   two-dimensional array, whose rows
   are stored in row records in data and
   are pointed to by pointers stored
   in p, is symmetric.
*/
pointerarray p;
dataarray data;
int r;
{
   int i,j,ck;
   ck = TRUE;
   for(i=1;i<r && ck;i++)
      for(j=0;j<i && ck;j++)
         if(data[p[i]].row[j] !=
            data[p[j]].row[i])

            ck=FALSE;
   return(ck);
}
```

`p` *is an instance of type* `pointerarray`, *and* `data` *is an instance of type* `data-array`

`i` *is the row and* `j` *the column index*

the entries of the `r` × `r` *two-dimensional array checked are stored in field* `row` *in records in positions* `p[i]` *and* `p[j]` *of* `data`

The third version (storing row records in dynamic memory) is a complete program with a driver for `check(p,r)`. It illustrates reading and printing of `r` and the array represented by `r` and `p`. The input and output from its execution might appear as follows.

Typical Input and Output

```
Enter an integer between 1 and 50 for r
4
Enter the next rowrecord
  3   4  -67   8
Enter the next rowrecord
  4   5   23  57
Enter the next rowrecord
-67  23   -6   4
Enter the next rowrecord
  8  57    4   0
r is 4
The row records are:
  3   4  -67   8
  4   5   23  57
-67  23   -6   4
  8  57    4   0
The array is symmetric
```

The program reads the two-dimensional input array, represents it, checks it for symmetry, and outputs the result.

Version 3—Storing Row Records in Dynamic Memory

```
#include <stdio.h>
#define TRUE 1
#define FALSE 0
typedef struct                              ] type names for row records, for pointers
{                                             to row records, and an array of pointers
   int row[50];                               to row records
}rowrecord, *rowpointer;
typedef rowpointer pointerarray[50];         ]

main()
/* Driver for check(p,r) */
{
   pointerarray p;                          ] p is an instance of type pointerarray
   int r;
   int i,j;                                 ] i is the row and j the column index
   rowpointer malloc();                     ] malloc must return a pointer to storage
                                              of type rowpointer
   printf("Enter an integer between 1 and 50 for r\n");
   scanf("%d",&r);
   for(i=0;i<r;i++)
      {
         p[i]=malloc(sizeof(rowrecord));    ] sets p[i] to storage for next row record
         printf("Enter the next rowrecord\n");
         for(j=0;j<r;j++)                   ] reads in the next row record
            scanf("%d",&(p[i]->row[j]));    ]
      }
   printf("\n r is %d \n",r);
   printf("The row records are: \n");
   for (i=0;i<r;i++)
      {
         printf("\n");
         for (j=0;j<r;j++)                  ] prints the next row record
            printf("%3d",p[i]->row[j]);     ]
      }
   if(check(p,r))
      printf("\n The array is symmetric \n");
   else
      printf("\n The array is not symmetric \n");
}

check(p,r) /* Storing row records in dynamic memory */
/* Returns true only if the rxr
   two-dimensional array, whose rows
   are stored in row records in dynamic
   memory and are pointed to by pointers
   stored in p, is symmetric.
*/

pointerarray p;
int r;
```

```
{
   int i,j,ck;
   ck=TRUE;
   for(i=1;i<r && ck;i++)
      for(j=0;j<i && ck;j++)
         if(p[i]->row[j] != p[j]->row[i])
            ck=FALSE;
   return(ck);
}
```

`i` is the row and `j` the column index

the entries of the `r` × `r` *two-dimensional array checked are stored in the field* `row` *of the records in dynamic memory pointed to by the pointers in* `p[i]` *and* `p[j]`

The pointer array technique may be used storing columns instead of rows. Then `p`'s entries point to the column records.

Example 2.7 It is often desirable to store information in an array in a specific order. Algorithms to rearrange the information to achieve the order may require repeated interchange of rows. Suppose the programmer wants to interchange the `i`th and `j`th rows of the array `a` when it is represented using the pointer array `p`. This can be accomplished quickly, taking advantage of the pointers, by executing

```
temp = p[i];
p[i] = p[j];
p[j] = temp;
```

Note that the data in each row are not moved; only the pointers change. The time it takes the computer to switch rows is independent of their length. Contrast this with the processing involved for the rowwise method of representing `a` (Section 2.3.1). Even if `a` actually is available directly as a two-dimensional array, the pointer array representation is more efficient. Swapping columns, of course, is a much more involved task, unless the programmer has chosen to store columns rather than rows. ■

The pointer array method offers the advantage of convenience in storing rows of different lengths. Thus it can be used to construct arrays with rows of different lengths easily. Also, if many rows of `a` are the same, they need not be duplicated in `data` or in dynamic memory. Their pointer entries in pointer array `p` need merely point to the same record, resulting in significant storage savings. The means should fit the ends as much as possible! In programming, the ends (the desired operations) determine the means (the data structures to be used).

2.4 Advantages and Disadvantages of the Techniques

If you think of the rows (or columns) of a two-dimensional array as records, then what has been demonstrated amounts to five basic ways to store records so that selection and traversal are possible. The methods for storing a collection of records are as follows:

1. Fixed-length records of the same type are stored sequentially in a single array and accessed by calculating record and member offsets.

2. In the C structure, each array entry is a record, perhaps including unions.
3. Fixed-length records of the same type are stored in multiarrays, each of appropriate type to match a member type.
4. Use relative pointer arrays to records stored in an array.
5. Use pointer variable arrays to records stored in the dynamic memory.

The first approach is enlightening because it makes explicit the offset calculations that are usually provided invisibly by the compiler. A severe disadvantage of this approach is that the representation of different type records causes difficulties—awkward in some languages, and impossible in others.

The second approach is the elegant form of this representation. It is possible in a language that provides the record data structure in which calculations are provided by the compiler. The disadvantage of the first approach then disappears.

The method of multiple arrays is applicable to all languages that provide arrays, whether or not they have strong typing or the record data structure. This method, and the first, sacrifice the ability to refer to an entire record by a single term, as provided by the newer C compilers.

The two pointer-oriented methods work for collections of variable-length records but are convenient only when the number of distinct lengths is small. (The more general case is treated in the next chapter.) Relative pointers are easy to use but have the drawback that embedding records in an array raises the problems of data types clashing.

Pointers to dynamic memory are more difficult and dangerous to use, for reasons mentioned later, but they provide extra flexibility. In any event, storing records in an array or in dynamic memory eliminates the need to declare a variable name for them at the outset of a program; records can thus be created dynamically during program execution.

The array is limited in the number of records it can store by its fixed length, which must be declared prior to program execution. The capacity of dynamic memory can be much larger and need not be declared a priori, but it is determined by the computer system. As will become more apparent, dynamic memory allows more efficient use of available storage.

In solving a problem, the programmer is free to use any data abstraction that is helpful. In deciding which data structure to use for its implementation, one must consider such factors as the possibility of carrying out the required operations, storage efficiency, execution time, and proneness to error. There is often a trade-off between storage efficiency and execution time. For example, pointers use extra storage and require some time to maintain, but they typically give fast access. Developing your appreciation of such trade-offs in programming is one of the goals of this text.

2.5 Case Study: Stable Marriages

To bring together the concepts presented in this chapter, a case study on stable marriages will now be analyzed. The aims of this study are to

1. Show how a program is designed using the top-down approach
2. Show that storing the "right" information in the "right" way has an

important effect on the design of a program, on the execution time, and on the memory requirements
3. Demonstrate the concept of data abstraction by treating data and basic operations on it as a unit
4. Illustrate the treatment of arrays and array indices

Consider Table 2.1. It represents the preferences that each of five men and five women has expressed for the five members of the opposite sex. For example, the first man has ranked the women in the order 2, 4, 3, 1, 5.

Table 2.1 Preferences

Men's						Women's					
*M*1	2	4	3	1	5	*W*1	1	5	3	4	2
*M*2	3	5	2	1	4	*W*2	4	5	3	2	1
*M*3	1	5	4	2	3	*W*3	3	1	4	2	5
*M*4	3	1	2	5	4	*W*4	4	2	5	1	3
*M*5	2	5	1	4	3	*W*5	1	3	2	4	5

Now suppose the group has paired off and married, as in Table 2.2. M_i is said to be stable with respect to W_j if there is no other woman preferred by M_i to W_j who, in turn, prefers M_i to her mate. Similarly, W_j is stable with respect to M_i if there is no other man W_j prefers to M_i who prefers W_j to his mate. *Any pair* (say, M_i–W_j) *is stable* if each is stable with respect to the other. An *entire pairing is stable* if all its pairs are stable; an entire pairing is *not* stable if there exist a man and a woman who are not mates but who prefer each other to their mates.

Table 2.2 Pairings

Men	Women
1	4
2	3
3	1
4	2
5	5

Consider the pair M_3–W_1 of Table 2.2. Since M_3 prefers W_1 to all others, he is stable with respect to W_1. W_1 prefers M_1 and M_5 to M_3. M_1 is married to W_4 and does not prefer W_1 to W_4. M_5 is married to W_5 and does not prefer W_1 to W_5. Thus W_1 is also stable with respect to M_3. Hence the pair is stable. The entire pairing is *not* stable. For instance, M_2 and W_3 are paired, but W_3 prefers M_4 to her mate, and M_4 prefers W_3 to his mate, so M_2–W_3 is not a stable pair. Determining whether or not an entire pairing such as that of Table 2.2 is stable may appear frivolous as stated, but there are other applications. Instead of using the terms men, women, and marriage preferences, we might consider tasks, employees, the employees' preferences for performing the tasks, and the ranking of employees by how well they perform the tasks. Or students might provide their preferences for majors while each department gives its preferences for each student.

2.5.1 The Problem—Stability of an Entire Pairing

Suppose the problem is to write a program to check whether or not a given entire pairing is stable for a given set of preferences. After this is done the problem of generating a stable entire pairing from a set of preferences will be considered. Assume that there are n men and n women.

2.5.2 The Algorithm

To determine whether an entire pairing is stable, the solution must traverse through all the pairs, testing each for stability. The following high-level algorithm does this.

Set `stable` to *true*.
For each man, as long as `stable` is *true*
    set `stable` to *false* if the man is not stable with respect to his wife or the wife is not stable with respect to her husband.

The next question is how to determine whether a person is stable. A person is stable if every individual preferred by the person to the person's mate prefers his or her mate to the person. Let `stable` hold the result of this determination and refine the task:

1. Set individual to whoever is most preferred by person.
2. While (`stable` and individual ≠ person's mate)
    If the individual prefers person to individual's mate, then
        set `stable` to *false*
    else
        set individual to whoever is next most preferred by person.

This assumes `stable` is initially *true*. Note that the refinement requires

Determining the mate of any person

Choosing the individual most preferred by a person

Determining whether an individual prefers a person to the individual's mate

Finding the individual next most preferred by a person

To follow the dictates of good programming style, the pairings and preference tables should be treated as data abstractions, with their implementation put off until the basic operations on them have become clear. These operations correspond to the four tasks required by the refinement. They will be developed, respectively, as the functions `mate`, `mostpreferred`, `prefers`, and `nextpreferred`. Before these functions can be written, the implementation of the pairings and the preference data must be decided upon.

Task 1 is to determine a person's mate. This requires the data for the entire pairing, which is given as input to the program and must be read in. However, how should this data be stored? If the mens' pairings are kept in an array `mpairs`, relating a man to his mate, then the mate of a man can be *selected* from the array. For the data of Table 2.2, `mpairs` would be

mpairs
4
3
1
2
5

Thus the mate of man 3 is woman 1. More generally, the mate of man *i* is found in `mpairs[i]`, the position of `mpairs` indexed by `i`. To find the mate of a woman, however, requires a traversal of `mpairs`. For example, the mate of woman 1 is found by traversing `mpairs` until an entry with value 1 is located. The array index of this entry, 3, gives the woman's mate. Rather than spending time traversing whenever a woman's mate is needed, storage can be traded for time. To do this, create another array, `wpairs`, so selection may be used in this case too. Of course, one traversal will still be necessary to generate `wpairs`, but this is done just once. The `wpairs` generated from `mpairs` would be

wpairs
3
4
2
1
5

Task 2 is to find out who is most preferred by a person. Suppose the preferences are implemented as two-dimensional arrays `mpref` and `wpref`. If the given preferences are those of Table 2.1, then `mpref` and `wpref` would be

mpref					wpref				
2	4	3	1	5	1	5	3	4	2
3	5	2	1	4	4	5	3	2	1
1	5	4	2	3	3	1	4	2	5
3	1	2	5	4	4	2	5	1	3
2	5	1	4	3	1	3	2	4	5

Task 2 is then straightforward and can also be done by *selection*. In each row of these arrays the first entry is the most preferred mate and the last entry is the least preferred. Thus for man 3, `mpref[3][1]` contains his most preferred mate.

To perform task 3, determining if an individual prefers a person to the individual's mate, the row for that individual in the proper preference array (`mpref` for a man and `wpref` for a woman) may be traversed until either the person or the individual's mate is encountered. If the person is encountered first, `prefers` must return *true*, and *false* otherwise.

Finally, task 4, finding the next preferred individual, can be done by using an index to point to the current individual and, after increasing the index by 1, selecting the (person, index) entry from the appropriate preference array.

The task, determining whether a person is stable, can now be further refined.

1. Set individual to `mostpreferred` (person, `pref`).
2. Set index to 1.
3. While (`stable` and individual ≠ person's mate)
   a. set individual's mate to `mate` (individual, `pairs`),
   b. if `prefers` (individual, person, individual's mate, `pref`), then
      set `stable` to *false*
      else
      i. Increase index by 1,
      ii. Set individual to `nextpreferred` (person, index, `pref1`).

This assumes that the person's mate is initially set correctly. The implementation for the functions used follows.

```
mate(person,pairs)
/* Returns person's mate
   as specified by pairs.
*/
int person;
pairings pairs;
{
   return(pairs[person]);
}
```

Task 1

selects the mate from `mpairs` *or* `wpairs`

```
mostpreferred(person,pref)
/* Returns the mate most
   preferred by person as
   specified by pref.
*/
int person;
preferences pref;
{
   return(pref[person][1]);
}
```

Task 2

selects the mate most preferred from `mpref` *or* `wpref`

```
prefers(individual,person,individualsmate,pref)
/* Returns true only if individual prefers person
   to the individual's mate as specified by pref.
*/
int individual,person,individualsmate;
preferences pref;
{
   int index,next;
   index = 1;
   next = pref[individual][1];
   while(next != person && next != individualsmate)
     {
        index++;
        next = pref[individual][index];
     }
   if(next == person)
     return(TRUE);
```

Task 3

`index` *is a column index for* `mpref` *or* `wpref`

traverses the row for individual in `mpref` *or* `wpref` *until person or individual's mate is found and returns* true *only if person is found first*

```
    else
        return(FALSE);
}

nextpreferred(person,index,pref)
/* Returns the mate next most
   preferred by person as specified
   by pref.
*/
int person,index;
preferences pref;
{
   return(pref[person][index]);
}
```

Task 4

selects next most preferred from **mpref** *or* **wpref**

To get an idea of the time required for this solution, note that the **while** loop used in determining `stable` can require a traversal through a row of `pref`. This loop may thus be executed (n − 1) times, since rows of `pref` are of length n (recall that there are n men and n women). During each of these executions, `prefers` is invoked and can traverse through a row of `pref`, which is also of length n. The determination of `stable` can thus take $O(n^2)$ time. Since `stable` may need to be calculated 2n times (twice for each pair), the total time of this solution could be $O(n^3)$. We can do better!

The traversal through `pref` in `prefers` can be eliminated. It is done simply to determine if the current individual prefers person to individual's mate, and this information can be ferreted out beforehand from `pref` and summarized in a priority array. This needs to be done only *once*. Thus the priority array can be produced before the algorithm is invoked, or can be created initially in the main function. One priority array must be created from `mpref` and another from `wpref`. The `mpriority` array can be created from `mpref` by traversing `mpref` and processing its (i,j)th entry by setting `mpriority[i][mpref[i][j]]` to j. Similarly, `wpriority` can be obtained from `wpref`. Then an individual prefers person to individual's mate if

`priority`[individual][person] < `priority`[individual][individual's mate]

For our example, these arrays are as follows:

mpriority					wpriority				
4	1	3	2	5	1	5	3	4	2
4	3	1	5	2	5	4	3	1	2
1	4	5	3	2	2	4	1	3	5
2	3	1	5	4	4	2	5	1	3
3	1	5	4	2	1	3	2	4	5

This version of `prefers` may be expressed as follows:

```
prefers(individual,person,individualsmate,priority);
/* Returns true only if individual prefers person
   to the individual's mate as specified by priority.
*/
```

Task 3—more efficient implementation

```
int individual,person,individualsmate;
preferences priority;
{
   return(priority[individual][person]<
      priority[individual][individualsmate]);
}
```

selects from `mpriority` *or* `wpriority`*; traversal not needed here*

When person is male, the parameter **priority** must be **wpriority**, and when person is female, priority must be **mpriority**. The priority arrays result in $O(\mathtt{n})$ time for determining **stable**, since one traversal is avoided. This reduces the total time of the solution to $O(\mathtt{n}^2)$. Again, storage has been traded for time. Extracting precisely the relevant information and implementing it properly, just as was done in Example 2.2, is what produced this time saving. Also, this version is clearer and more concise.

2.5.3 The Program

The algorithm, expressed as a function **stabilitycheck**, is implemented in the following program. The program first inputs **n**. Next it reads in **mpairs**, creates **wpairs** from it, reads in **mpref** and **wpref**, then creates **mpriority** and **wpriority**, calls **stabilitycheck** to check the pairings, and finally prints the result along with the pairings.

```
#include <stdio.h>

#define MAXN 50
typedef int pairings[MAXN];

mate(person,pairs)
/* Returns person's mate
   as specified by pairs.
*/
int person;
pairings pairs;
{
   return(pairs[person]);
}

read_mens_mates(n,pairs)
/* Reads the n mates of the
   men into pairs.
*/
int n;
pairings pairs;
{
   int i;
   printf("\n mpairs = ? \n");
   for(i=1;i<=n;i++)
      scanf("%d",&pairs[i]);
```

data abstraction `pairings` *and the allowed operations on it—*`mate`*,* `read_mens_mates`*, and* `create_womens_mates`

used to input data and to build `mpairs`

```
}

create_womens_mates(n,pairs1,pairs2)
/* Creates in pairs2 the women's mates
   based on the men's mates as specified
   by pairs1.
*/
int n;
pairings pairs1,pairs2;
{
   int i,j;
   for(i=1;i<=n;i++)
      {
         for(j=1;pairs1[j] != i;j++)
            {
            }
         pairs2[i] = j;
      }
}
```

used to create `wpairs` *from* `mpairs`

```
typedef int preferences[MAXN][MAXN];

mostpreferred(person,pref)
/* Returns the mate most
   preferred by person as
   specified by pref.
*/
int person;
preferences pref;
{
   return(pref[person][1]);
}

nextpreferred(person,index,pref)
/* Returns the mate next most
   preferred by person as specified
   by pref.
*/
int person,index;
preferences pref;
{
   return(pref[person][index]);
}

prefers(individual,person,individualsmate,priority)
/* Returns true only if individual prefers person
   to the individual's mate as specified by priority.
*/
int individual,person,individualsmate;
preferences priority;
```

data abstraction `preferences` *and the allowed operations on it—* `mostpreferred`, `nextpreferred`, `prefers`, `read_preferences`, *and* `create_priorities`

```
{
   return(priority[individual][person]
         < priority[individual][individualsmate]);
}

read_preferences(n,pref)
/* Reads n rows of
   preferences into pref.
*/
int n;
preferences pref;
{
   int i,j;
   for(i=1;i<=n;i++)
      for(j=1;j<=n;j++)
         scanf("%d",&pref[i][j]);
}


create_priorities(n,pref,priority)
/* Creates n individual priorities in
   priority based on the individual
   preferences specified by pref.
*/
int n;
preferences pref,priority;
{
   int i,j;
   for(i=1;i<=n;i++)
      for(j=1;j<=n;j++)
         priority[i][pref[i][j]] = j;
}

#define TRUE 1
#define FALSE 0
main()
{
   pairings mpairs,wpairs;
   preferences mpref,wpref,mpriority,wpriority;
   int i,j,n;
   printf("\n n=?\n");
   scanf("%d",&n);
   read_mens_mates(n,mpairs);
   create_womens_mates(n,mpairs,wpairs);
   printf("\n Enter mens preferences \n");
   read_preferences(n,mpref);
   printf("\n Enter womens
         preferences \n");
   read_preferences(n,wpref);
   create_priorities(n,mpref,mpriority);
   create_priorities(n,wpref,wpriority);
```

used to create `mpriority` *and* `wpriority`

`mpairs` *and* `wpairs` *are instances of type* `pairings`; `mpref`, `wpref`, `mpriority`, *and* `wpriority` *instances of type* `preferences`

inputs the number of men (and women)

reads into `mpairs`

creates `wpairs`

reads into `mpreferences`

reads into `wpreferences`

creates `mpriority`

creates `wpriority`

```
    if(stabilitycheck(n,mpairs,wpairs,mpref,wpref,
                       mpriority,wpriority))
       printf("The pairings are stable \n");
    else
       printf("The pairings are not stable \n");
    printf("The pairings are: \n");
    printf("man wife \n");
    for(i=1;i<=n;i++)
       printf("%d  %d \n",i,mate(i,mpairs));
}
```

checks stability of the entire pairing and outputs the result; outputs the entire pairing checked

```
stabilitycheck(n,mpairs,wpairs,mpref,wpref,mpriority,wpriority)
/* Checks the entire pairing specified by
   the parameters and returns true only
   if it is stable.
*/
int n;
pairings mpairs,wpairs;
preferences mpref,wpref,mpriority,wpriority;
{
   int man,wife,individual,individualsmate,index,stable;
   stable = TRUE;
   for(man=1;(stable && man<=n);man++)
      {
         wife = mate(man,mpairs);
         individual = mostpreferred(man,mpref);
         index = 1;
         while(stable &&(individual != wife))
            {
               individualsmate = mate(individual,
                  wpairs);
               if(prefers(individual,man,
                  individualsmate,wpriority))
                  stable = FALSE;
               else
                  {
                     index++;
                     individual = nextpreferred(man,
                        index,mpref);
                  }
            }
         individual = mostpreferred(wife,wpref);
         index = 1;
         while(stable &&(individual != man))
            {
               individualsmate = mate(individual,
                  mpairs);
               if(prefers(individual,wife,
                  individualsmate,mpriority))
                  stable = FALSE;
               else
                  {
```

determines whether the entire pairing is stable

determines if the man in the pair man–wife is stable

determines if the wife in the pair man–wife is stable

```
                index++;
                individual = nextpreferred(wife,
                    index,wpref);
            }
        }
    }
    return(stable);
}
```

2.5.4 Review of the Program's Development

At this point let's review the process followed in creating the program. First an algorithm was conceived and refined, moving from the original problem to the subtasks into which it was broken down: the four tasks for operating on the data abstractions, plus the task of determining **stable**. The refinement for this last task was specified, treating the pairings and preferences as data abstractions. Next the functions embodying the operations on the data abstractions were specified. In doing so, the trade-off between storage (adding the priority arrays) and execution time (requiring a traversal of rows of **mpref** or **wpref** if there were no priority arrays) came into play. This led to the "right" information to be stored and the "right" choice of data structure in which to store it—the priority arrays.

Finally, the solution was packaged into a main program that (1) created and input data to the data structures chosen; (2) called **stabilitycheck** to check the entire pairing. The functions **main** and **stabilitycheck** were written, treating the pairs and preferences as data abstractions. As a result, should their implementations need to be changed, the changes are localized to the data structure definitions and the functions operating on them.

2.5.5 Generating Stable Pairings

As explained earlier, the program only *checks* a particular entire pairing for stability. It does not generate, for given preferences, an entire pairing that *is* stable. The task of generating such a stable entire pairing is known as the **stable marriage problem.**

Some simple cases allow a stable entire pairing to be written by inspection:

1. *People have a unique way of looking at the world.* This case comes up when the first column of **mpref** has **n** distinct entries: every man most prefers a different woman. Simply pair each man with his heart's desire. The case where **wpref** has this property is similar.

2. *People are all the same.* This case occurs when the rows of **mpref** are all exactly alike: every man has exactly the same preferences. Pair the most preferred woman with the man she most prefers. Pair the next most preferred woman with the man she most prefers among those not yet paired, and so on. For example:

mpref				wpref			
2	4	3	1	3	1	2	4
2	4	3	1	3	1	4	2
2	4	3	1	4	2	1	3
2	4	3	1	4	3	2	1

Pair W_2 with M_3, W_4 with M_4, W_3 with M_2, and W_1 with M_1. The case where `wpref` has this property has a similar solution.

Not only is an algorithm for generating a stable entire pairing not apparent; it is not even evident that one always exists. The following algorithm does construct one; you might try your hand at convincing yourself that it *always* does so.

1. Set man to 1.
2. While (man is not paired)
   a. find the woman most preferred by man who is not yet paired, or, if paired, prefers man to her current mate
   b. if the woman is not yet paired, then
      i. pair man to woman,
      ii. set man to an unpaired man if there is one

      else

      i. break the pair between the woman and her current mate,
      ii. pair woman to man,
      iii. set man to her ex-mate

To illustrate this algorithm, apply it to the preferences of Table 2.1. The sequence of pairs generated by the algorithm is as shown in Table 2.3. Asterisks indicate conflicts that cause breaks when they occur. The final pairings are then 3–1, 4–3, 2–5, 5–2, 1–4.

This is a good example of a correct algorithm that surely requires both a proof of correctness (produces the proper result) and a proof that it will eventually stop. These are the essential ingredients of an algorithm. (The proofs are left as exercises.)

Table 2.3 Sequence of Pairs

	Man	Active Pairs	
	1	1	2
1	2	2	3*
	3	3	1
	4	4	3*
		1	2*
2		3	1
		4	3
	2	2	5
	5	5	2*
		3	1
		4	3
3		2	5
		5	2
	1	1	4

Exercises

1. **a.** Do users of the subway system of a large city reach their destinations by a process analogous to selection or a process analogous to traversal? Why?
   b. Do users of the telephone system of a large city reach their parties by a process analogous to selection or one like traversal? Why?

2. Suppose you are interested in processing English text in the following way:
  a. Input is in the form of an English sentence.
  b. The program is to check the sentence looking for violations of the spelling rule, " 'i' before 'e' except after 'c'." (Do not worry about exceptions such as *neighbor, weigh,* etc.) Would an array be a convenient data structure to use in your program, and would traversal be a relevant process?

3. Write a program to print out how many elements of an integer array (of length *n*) contain even integers. Did you use the process of traversal?

4. In Example 2.2 suppose the `pointer` array were stored in memory and there were no `a` itself. If you are told that `a[5]` and `a[9]` have been interchanged, then what changes would you have to make to `pointer` to reflect this interchange? What if `a[2]` and `a[5]` were interchanged?

5. Write a function to update the `pointer` array of Example 2.2 to reflect the fact that the `i`th and `j`th columns of `a` have been interchanged.

6. **a.** Suppose the `cars` array (Example 2.4) represents the fleet information for the cars of one rental agency. For a group of several such agencies, would the record data structure be convenient to represent all the information?
  b. Assume the information is represented in an array that stores records, with each record containing all the information for a particular agency. In general, are these records fixed or variable length?

7. For Example 2.4 assume the alternate multiarray implementation. Write a function to interchange the `i`th and `j`th records.

8. Create a function that prints out the rentees of all cars that have been driven more than 50,000 miles for the multiarray implementation of Example 2.4.

9. Write a function to read in a sequence of at most twenty characters into an array. They are all digits (0, or 1, or 2, . . . , or 9) except for one character that will be a decimal point. After execution of the function the variable `dp` should point to the array element that contains the decimal point, and variable `l` should point to the last digit of the input sequence. The decimal point will always have at least one digit on each side.

10. Produce a function similar to that of Exercise 2.3 except that the array of integers is two-dimensional.

11. Suppose a checkerboard is represented as a two-dimensional array. Write a function that is given the current configuration of the board and the move to be made by the player whose turn it is. The function is to return the value *true* if the move is legal and *false* otherwise. (Do not forget that a move can consist of many jumps.)

12. **a.** Is there an analogy between tabs in your home telephone directory and pointers?
  b. If a song on a tape cassette is like a record data structure type, can a particular song be indexed, or must a traverse be used to find it? How about a song on a phonograph record?

13. Explain the differences between a record stored in an array and in dynamic memory.

14. Define a function to copy the array of Example 2.5 into an array indexed by a pointer array of integers.

15. Write a function to interchange two records of the array of Example 2.5.

16. Assume the row representation for two-dimensional arrays has been extended to three-dimensional arrays. Determine the formula for the offset of `a[i][j][k]`.

17. The array `a` with `r` rows and `c` columns is stored using the rowwise representation, with `a[0][0]` corresponding to the actual base location of `a`, `abase`. Given an integer number `k` (`abase` $\leq$ `k` $\leq$ `abase` + `r` $\times$ (`c` $-$ 1)), write formulas that will yield the row and column of `a` to which actual location `k` corresponds. That is, if `a[i][j]` is stored in `k`, then your formula for the row will yield `i` and for the column will yield `j`.

18. An ***antisymmetric*** array `a` is a square array that satisfies the condition that `a[i][j]` = `-a[j][i]` for all $0 \leq$ `i`, `j` $< n$. Hence the diagonal elements must be zero. Storing the antisymmetric array can be done just as storing the symmetric array was done, except that now the diagonal entries can be omitted, since they are known. Determine the formula for the offset of a[i][j].

19. An array a is said to be *tridiagonal* if the nonzero entries of a fall along the three diagonals a[i][i], a[i][i+1], and a[i][i-1], where i goes, respectively, from 0 to $n - 1$, 0 to $n - 2$, and 1 to $n - 1$.

a. Construct a rowwise representation of the nonzero entries of a, and find a formula for the offset of a[i][j] in this array.

b. Construct a *diagonal* representation of the nonzero entries of a tridiagonal array, and find a formula for the offset of a[i][j] in the array.

20. Write a function that takes a two-dimensional array represented in terms of p and data, as in Section 2.3.3, and changes p so that any duplicate rows of a are stored only once in data. Thus, if rows 2 and 7 are identical, the contents of p[1] and p[6] are made equal.

21. Define a function to output the n diagonal elements of the array a of Section 2.3.3 when the array is represented in terms of p and data.

22. Produce a function to print out the jth column of array a when it is represented in terms of p and data as in Section 2.3.3.

23. Write a function to interchange a[i][j] and a[j][i], for all i, j, when a is represented in terms of p and data as in Section 2.3.3.

24. Create a function that takes any array a of integers with at most twenty entries and creates a pointer array p that has in p[i] a pointer to the (i + 1)th largest entry of a. Thus p[0] points to the largest entry of a.

25. Do the same as in Exercise 24, except the array a will be two-dimensional and the ith record in p must contain two pointers, one for the row and one for the column of a's ith largest entry.

26. Do Exercises 20 to 25, except use pointers and dynamic memory. Print the pointers.

27. What pairs are not stable in the example pairings?

28. Give a function to create wpairs from mpairs.

29. Write a function to create a priority array, given a pref array.

30. What function will create a pref array given a priority array?

31. **a.** Give a function to produce stable marriages.

b. How much time does your answer to Exercise 31a require?

32. **a.** Why must the algorithm to produce stable marriages terminate eventually?

b. Why does it produce stable marriages?

■ Suggested Assignments

1. **a.** Implement the collection data abstraction of Chapter 1 using an array to store the actual integers in the collection. That is, implement the operations set, insert, omit, and belongs.

b. Implement a collection c of carrecords as a data abstraction with the operations set(c), insert(p,c), omit(i,c), and printrecord(i,c). Use the carrecords defined in Section 2.1.3 but add an additional field for an identification number for each car. Then, insert(p,c) adds the carrecord pointed to by p to the collection c, omit(i,c) deletes the carrecord with the identifier i from c, and then printrecord(i,c) prints the contents of the carrecord with identifier i.

c. This is the same as (b), except the records are to be stored in dynamic memory with a pointer array used to contain pointers to them.

2. Suppose the amount of precipitation has been recorded over a region at n locations. In general each record consists of one to five numbers. You are to write and run six programs. Each is to produce the average precipitation. For example, if the input is

```
3.6
2.1
2.7
record sentinel
.67
1.2
record sentinel
1.9
record sentinel
final sentinel
```

the output should be the sum [(3.6 + 2.1 + 2.7) + (.67 + 1.2) + 1.9] divided by 6. Always ***echo print*** the input (that is, output the input as it is read in), and annotate all output so that you, or anyone, will know what the output means. Assume $n \leq 100$.

a. Two of the programs should assume all records are of the same length (say, 3). Program 1 will represent the records as fixed-length homogeneous records stored in a single array (method 1 of Section 2.4). Program 3 will represent them as fixed-length records stored in multiarrays (method 3 of Section 2.4). For method 3, assume an additional record field giving the specific location where it was recorded.

b. Three of the programs should assume the general case of C structures that contain a union and store them in an array (method 2 of Section 2.4). Program 4 will use a relative pointer array whose entries point to records stored in an array (method 4 of Section 2.4). The fifth program uses pointer variable arrays whose entries point to records stored in dynamic memory. For methods 4 and 5, output the contents of the pointer arrays and the records to which each pointer points. Your programs 4 and 5 should work correctly no matter where the records are stored in the one-dimensional array.

c. Finally, one program should assume all records are of length 1 and represent entries in an $n \times n$ symmetric array. This program uses the symmetric array representation of Example 2.6. No two-dimensional array should be used in your solution.

The input and output for each program might appear as follows:

		Input	Output
Programs A	1.	3.6 2.1 2.7 RS .67 1.2 1.9 RS FS	Echo print of the precipitation records: 3.6, 2.1, 2.7 .67, 1.2, 1.9 The average precipitation of the 6 values is 2.028 inches. The number of records is 2.
	3.	White House 3.6 2.1 2.7 RS Lincoln Memorial .67 1.2 1.9 RS FS	Echo print of the precipitation records: White House 3.6, 2.1, 2.7 Lincoln Memorial .67, 1.2, 1.9 The average precipitation of the 6 values is 2.028 inches. The number of records is 2.

		Input	Output
Programs B	2.	3.6 2.1 2.7 RS 1.2 RS 1.9 RS FS	Echo print of the precipitation records: 3.6, 2.1, 2.7 .67, 1.2 1.9 The average precipitation of the 6 values is 2.028 inches. The number of records is 3.
	4.	3.6 2.1 2.7 RS .67 1.2 RS 1.9 RS FS	Echo print of the precipitation records: 3.6, 2.1, 2.7 .67, 1.2 1.9
	5.	This is the same as for 4, except it will print the pointer array (that is, the actual pointers).	Records in dynamic storage 3.6 2.1 2.7 .67 1.2 1.9
Programs C		3.6 2.1 2.7 .67 1.2 1.9 0.0 1.1 .15	Echo print of the precipitation records as a 3 × 3 array: 3.6 2.1 2.7 .67 1.2 1.9 0.0 1.1 .15 The average precipitation of the 9 values is 2.028 inches.

Output for 4 (continued):

Pointer array		Data array	
1	10	10	3.6
2	1	11	2.1
3	16	12	2.7
		1	.67
		2	1.2
		16	1.9

The average precipitation of the 6 values is 2.028 inches. The number of records is 3.

3. Modify the program of Section 2.5.2 so that its input consists of the men's and women's preferences and then a *series* of entire pairings. For each of the pairings, it is to call **`stabilitycheck`** and print the result for the pairing.

3 Lists

Presents the list data structure for
efficient traversals
arbitrary insertions and deletions
imposing an ordering on the collection of information it holds
Discusses the limitations of lists for random access
Compares the advantages and disadvantages of lists and arrays for storing data
Discusses the implementation of lists using
records
arrays
pointers
dynamic memory
Stresses the importance of writing functional modules to solve general programming problems and
uses list traversal to convey these techniques
shows how such functional modules can be used as tools and adapted to solve related problems
Explains dynamic storage and its management
Case study—the perfect shuffle
illustrates the use of lists and arrays

3.1 Why Are Lists Needed?

Imagine you are a financial wizard and want to store information about your stock portfolio as records. Table 3.1 lists the information. How should these records be stored? The book so far has shown how to store them in

Individual storage elements with individual names

An array, so they can be referenced by position or from a pointer array

Dynamic memory, where they can be referenced by individual pointer variables or from an array of pointer variables

Having more than a few records rules out using individual names, a method that would also be inadequate because it does not allow the records to be treated as a group. The same is true for individual pointer variables.

The other three methods, two kinds of arrays and dynamic memory, allow not only grouping but also selection of records, as well as traversal through all the records. Figure 3.1 represents storage of the stock portfolio in each of these three ways. The three methods are called (a) sequential arrays, (b) sequential pointer arrays, and (c) sequential pointer variable arrays. Collectively they are known as ***sequential array methods*** for record storage.

The sequential array methods are convenient for recording the daily transactions common in the buying and selling of stocks, but only when

Table 3.1 A Stock Portfolio

Name	# Shares	Value	Date Bought
Apple	300	$ 7,512.46	3/15/84
CBS	100	8,000.55	6/16/83
Digital	200	18,400.00	9/20/83
IBM	100	11,213.25	1/20/83
IBM	200	21,400.00	4/17/84
Sears	100	3,100.00	2/10/82
Sears	100	3,200.00	4/6/84

records are kept in arbitrary order. A new record can then be inserted directly as the new last record. This means that in the method of sequential arrays (Figure 3.1(a)), a new record is inserted after Sears. In the method of sequential pointer arrays (Figure 3.1(b)), it can be placed in any unused slot, but the corresponding pointer goes in the seventh position of `p`. For the method of sequential pointer variable arrays (Figure 3.1(c)), the function `malloc` provides dynamic storage that is available to store the record, but again, its associated pointer variable value also goes in position 7 of `p`.

Usually order *does* matter. In reality the stocks are kept in alphabetical order. In this case the sequential array methods provide neither easy nor rapid insertion or deletion capability for the records. Suppose Chrysler stock is bought, and its new record must be inserted into the portfolio; Chrysler must be inserted in its proper place as the new third record. In sequential arrays this means that all five records below its new position must be moved down. In the two pointer array methods, this means that the five pointers below its new location (position 2) must be moved down. The pointer array methods afford flexibility of record storage position, but they still require shifting, although it is pointers that are moved rather than records. Shifting takes time proportional to the number of records

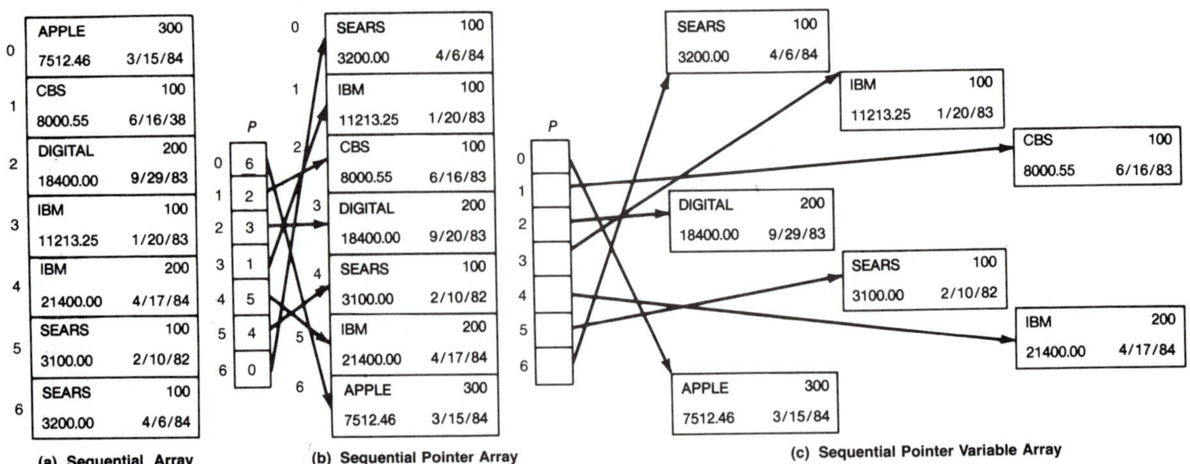

Figure 3.1 Sequential Methods of Storing Records in Arrays

moved. If n records are to be inserted, then the total time can be proportional, not to n, but to n^2. For example, suppose the n records each require insertion at the top. Even if there are no records stored initially, insertion of n records requires $0 + 1 + 2 + \cdots + (n - 1)$ moves. The time adds up to $n(n - 1)/2$, and so the time is $O(n^2)$. Even if each insertion requires only half the information to be shifted, the time is reduced merely by a factor of 2; it is still $O(n^2)$. When n is large, this can take significant time. Of course, for one trader, n will be small, but for larger brokerage houses n might be hundreds of thousands. If they were not designed to be efficient, these insertions might take hours or even days ($(300{,}000)^2$ operations $\times 10^{-6}$ seconds per operation = 25 hours).

Selling a stock, say Digital, requires that its record be deleted in the sequential array (a) or that its pointer entries be set to -1 or `null` in the pointer arrays (b) and (c). Either course would leave gaps of unused storage, which is undesirable. Leaving gaps soon uses up all the slots in an array, and unless wasting storage is tolerable and affordable, this is impractical. Instead, the gap would be filled by moving up all the records below a deleted record. But again, this could take $O(n^2)$ time for the deletion of n records.

What is needed is a way to store records so that their number can grow or shrink in response to an arbitrary number of insertions and deletions, in such a way that storage is not wasted and the time for insertion and deletion is reduced. The *list* data structure introduced in this chapter provides one solution to this problem. A ***list*** is a collection of records linked by pointers. Even with lists, it is still necessary, as with the sequential array methods, for the program to spend time deciding where to make an insertion or deletion in the first place. To make these operations efficient when large numbers of records are involved requires more advanced data structures (introduced later). For a moderate number of records, the time taken to locate the point of insertion or deletion is tolerable. Lists called *stacks* and *queues,* where insertion and deletion occur only at the beginning and end of the lists, are especially useful even when there are many records. These will be considered in the next chapter.

Chapter 2 showed that the key advantage of the sequential array methods is selection in constant time. As just shown in this chapter, the disadvantage is that inserting or deleting entries from the interior of an array is costly. Another drawback is that arrays have fixed lengths that must be declared to the compiler. Thus, the maximum number of items to be stored in the array must be known in advance of execution. No such a priori limit need be declared for the number of items on a list. Lists provide a way to insert new items or to delete existing ones at a known point of the list, in constant time. However, selection of an arbitrary ith list item will take time proportional to i.

3.2 Keeping Track of List Pointers

The pointers in lists are what is manipulated by programs, because lists are collections of records linked by pointers. A special element, called the ***head*** or ***name*** of the list, points to the beginning of the list, and each record in the list has a pointer to the next one. The final record, which has no successor, has an empty link, denoted by a special pointer value called the ***null pointer.***

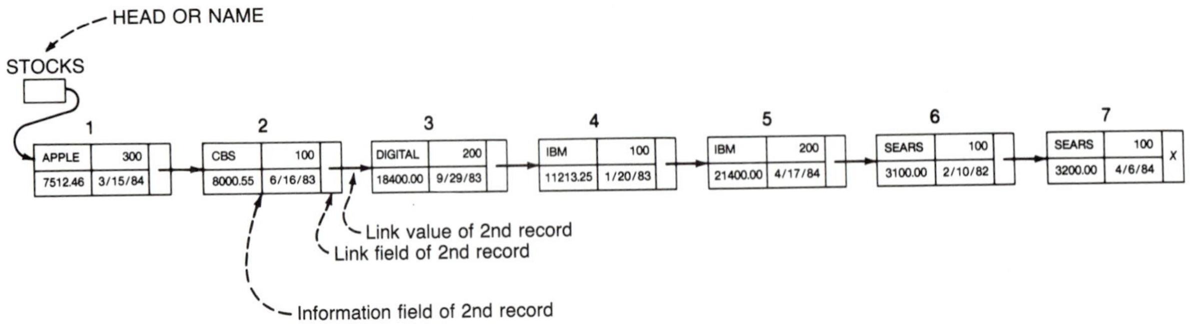

Figure 3.2 Graphic Representation of the List STOCKS

The stock portfolio example is represented in a list in Figure 3.2. The variable labeled `head` contains a pointer to the first record in the list. Each record is composed of two fields: 1) an ***information field,*** which may itself be made up of subfields such as `name`, `shares`, `value`, `datebought` (or `accountnumber`, `balance`, `address`); and 2) a ***link field,*** which contains the pointer to the next record. The *x* in the link field of the last record denotes the null pointer and indicates that this is the last record on the list. The list with no records is called the ***null list,*** and is denoted by a head containing the null pointer.

It does no good to know that a phone number (say, 642-3715) contains the digits 1, 2, 3, 4, 5, 6, and 7, unless the order 6, 4, 2, 3, 7, 1, 5 is retained as well. Notice that the list data structure, besides being a new way to store information, allows the information to be remembered in a specific order—the order in which the records appear on the list. Arrays provide this ability as well. The order in which records (or the pointers to them) are stored does this, but the operations that make lists interesting and powerful are insertion and deletion.

In effect, a list works as if the pointers from a pointer array were incorporated into the records to which they point. This is the crucial advantage of lists compared to arrays. The price of the added convenience is the loss of the capability to select an arbitrary record. Instead of access to the list records being through the pointer array, the list records must now be accessed via the pointer to the first list record (in head or name). Knowing only the head of a list means that only the first record is immediately visible. To access another list record, the chain of pointers linking list records must be followed until the desired record is encountered.

Consider the simple list `l` in Figure 3.3(a). Two situations are depicted in Figure 3.3(b,c): (b) is the case when the list head `l` is known, and (c) the case when a pointer, `ptr`, to a list record is known. In each case only the record to which the known pointer points is visible.

When only one pointer points to a record, if that pointer value is changed, then the record cannot be accessed. It is as if the programmer had stored something somewhere but had no hope of remembering where. If that pointer happens to be in the head of a list, then access to the list is lost. Suppose the programmer must start with the situation depicted in Figure 3.3(a) and must create two lists. One, `l`, is to consist of all records of the original list, from the record pointed to by

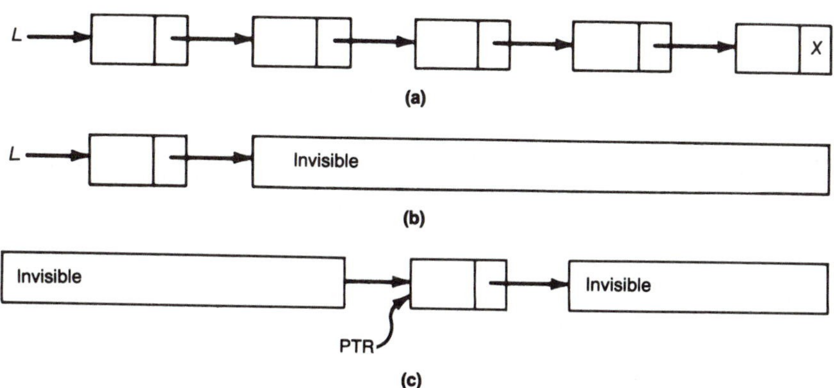

Figure 3.3 Simple Lists

`ptr` to the last record. Another, `newl`, is to consist of the original list records, from the first to the record prior to that pointed to by `ptr`. Simply copying the value of `ptr` into `l` creates the correct modified version of `l`. However, `newl` cannot be created since the pointer to the original first record that had been stored in `l` has been lost. Such a predicament must be avoided.

Keeping track of pointers in processing lists is extremely important. One reason is that more than one pointer can point to a record. The only way to see if two pointers point to the same record is to see if their pointer values are equal.

3.2.1 Insertion and Deletion of Records in Lists

Consider the effects of inserting and deleting on a conceptual list. The effect of inserting a new record is shown in Figure 3.4. The new record is inserted between the records labeled `predecessor` and `successor`. This requires changing `predecessor`'s link to point to the new record, and setting the new record's link to point to `successor`.

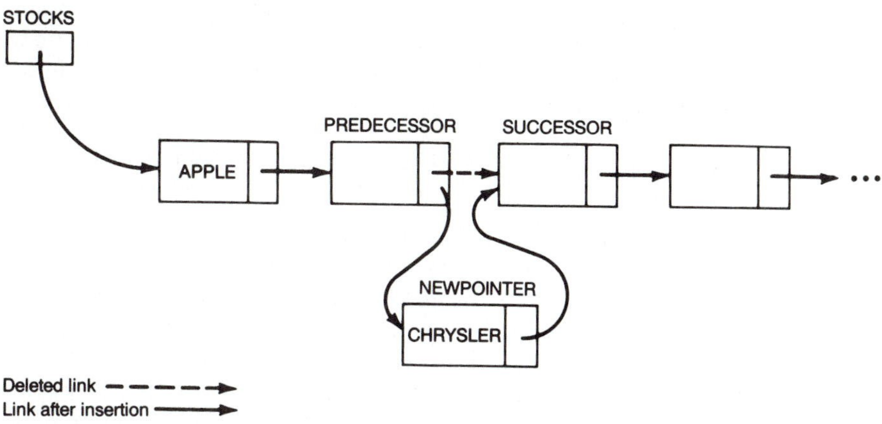

Figure 3.4 Insertion of a New Record in a Conceptual List

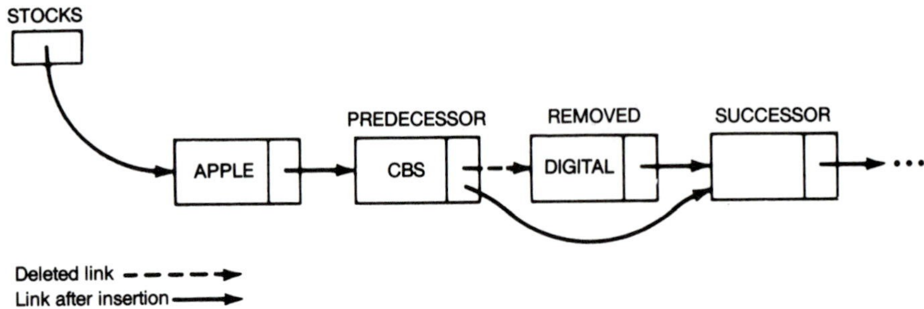

Figure 3.5 Deletion of a Record from a Conceptual List

The deletion of a record from a list is shown in Figure 3.5. The record labeled `removed` is deleted from the list by arranging `predecessor`'s link to point to `successor`. The rearrangement of links for insertion or deletion is independent of where in the list the operation occurs. Each operation can be performed in constant time. Lists, unlike arrays, readily accommodate change; they exhibit no growing pains (or contraction pains).

3.3 Expanding and Contracting Lists

3.3.1 Insertion

Suppose you wish to insert a new record for CHRYSLER. It is always a good idea to sketch an image like Figure 3.6(a) to show both the situation at the outset and the situation desired after the task is carried out. Since only the head of the list, `stocks`, is assumed known, normally each record of the list must be accessed in turn, starting from the first, in order to determine where to make the insertion. For now, assume there is a given pointer `predecessor` that points to the record after which the new record is to be inserted. In the example, this is the second record. The value of its link field must be copied into the link field of the new record, so the new record's link field points to the successor of the predecessor record. The link field of the `predecessor` record must end up pointing to the new record, so the value of `newpointer` must be copied into the `predecessor`'s link field. The code to accomplish this may be written as

```
setlink(newpointer,next(predecessor));
setlink(predecessor,newpointer);
```

where `setlink` is a function that copies the value of its second parameter into the link field of the record pointed to by its first parameter, and `next` is a function whose value is a copy of the link field value of the record pointed to by its parameter. Why is it incorrect to interchange these two statements?

Notice that no assumptions have been made about the implementation of the list. The code is thus independent of how the list is implemented. Of course, `setlink` can be written only when the implementation is known, and it will depend on the details. However, this code *will not*. The list is thus a data abstraction with insertion as one of its operations; deletion is another.

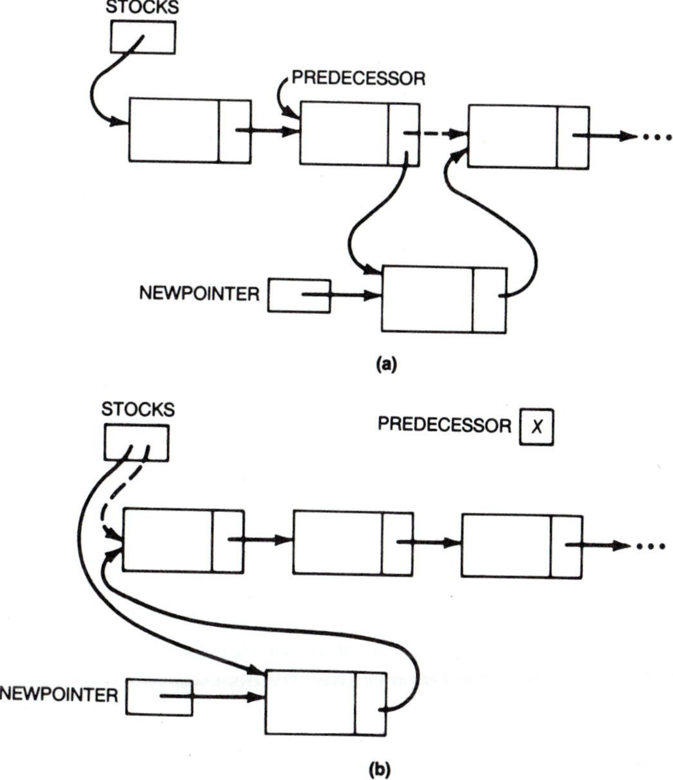

Figure 3.6 Insertion of a New Record (a) in the Interior of a List and (b) at the Front of a List

3.3.2 Special Cases

It is evident that this code is correct for insertion into the interior of the list or at its end. Special cases must always be sniffed out and dealt with. By definition, a special case means a situation requiring code different from the current solution. The existing solution must be modified to handle special cases. The special case here, shown in Figure 3.6(b), represents insertion at the front of the list. Obviously there is no predecessor record, so the solution cannot properly handle this case. It is reasonable to assume that this special condition is represented by a null value for `predecessor`. Then it is the value of head that must be copied into the link field of the new record. Also, it is the head itself that must receive the copy of `newpointer` and end up pointing to the new record. The correct function to handle all situations is as follows:

```
insert(phead,predecessor,newpointer)
/* Inserts, in list head, the record pointed to
   by newpointer as the successor of the
   record pointed to by predecessor.
*/
```

inserts a new record into a list

```
listpointer *phead,predecessor,newpointer;
{
   listpointer setnull(),next();
   if(predecessor == setnull())
      {
         setlink(newpointer,*phead);            ] inserts as a new first record
         *phead = newpointer;
      }
   else
      {
         setlink(newpointer,next(predecessor)); ] inserts in the body of the list
         setlink(predecessor,newpointer);
      }
}
```

Note: listpointer is a type which is explained in Sections 3.6.1 and 3.6.2.

where **setnull** returns the null value. What is used for the null value is determined by the list implementation (Section 3.6). When **insert** is invoked, its actual first parameter, corresponding to **phead**, must be a pointer to the head of the list. Thus to have **insert** work on a list **l**, the call would be **insert(&l,predecessor,newpointer)**. Whenever a parameter of a function must return a value (be modified by the function) the convention in this text is to *prefix* the name of the parameter in the function definition with a **p**. Thus, since the value of the pointer to head in **insert** must be changed, it is referred to as **phead**. Notice that the code for **insert** refers to ***phead**. Think of ***phead** as another name for **head**. We say that **head** has been passed to **insert** by pointer.

This version of **insert** is independent of how the list is actually implemented. In practice, **insert** might be made to execute more efficiently by writing it so that its code *does* depend on the list implementation. **Insert** might then be the level at which the list implementation is hidden instead of in **setnull**, **setlink**, and **next**. However, the version above is clearer and can be readily modified if desired.

3.3.3 Header Records

An alternative that avoids the special case of inserting a new first record assigns a special record, called a ***header record,*** to every list as its first record. This record is a ***dummy*** record. The dummy is so called because it is not part of the conceptual list of records being created. Used to make processing easier, the dummy record is never deleted, and no record is ever inserted in front of it. Then the special case never occurs, and the original code, requiring no check for the special case, can be used. Actually the header record can be a smart dummy, used to contain important information about the list, such as the number of records. When this alternative is used, the null list can no longer be recognized by a null value in the list head. It is recognized by a null pointer in the link field of the dummy record.

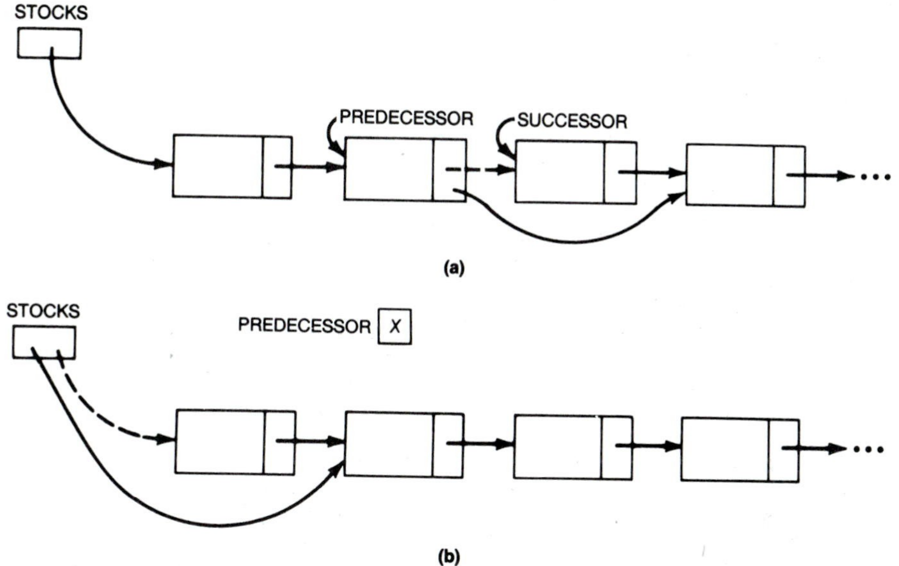

Figure 3.7 Deletion of a Record (a) from the Interior of a List and (b) from the Front of a List

3.3.4 Deletion

To delete the record following `predecessor` (Figure 3.7(a)), only the link field value of its successor must be copied into the predecessor's link field:

```
setlink(predecessor,next(next(predecessor)));
```

Thus `next(next(predecessor))` is the value that must be copied into the predecessor's link field. It is clearer to write the code as

```
successor = next(predecessor);
setlink(predecessor,next(successor));
```

even if it is slower, requiring an additional memory access. Again, either code is independent of any implementation for the list. After checking for special cases (Figure 3.7(b)), the correct function is found to be

```
delete(phead,predecessor)                                    ❘ deletes a record from a list
/* Deletes, in list head, the successor of
   the record pointed to by predecessor.
*/
listpointer *phead,predecessor;
{
   listpointer successor,null,setnull(),next();
   null = setnull();
   if(*phead != null)                                        ❘ if the list is not null
      if(predecessor == null)
         *phead = next(*phead);                              ❘ deletes the first record
```

```
    else
        {
            successor = next(predecessor);         ] deletes from the body of
            if(successor != null)                  ] the list
            setlink(predecessor,next(successor));  ]
        }
}
```

Sometimes, instead of having a pointer to the predecessor of a record to be deleted, only a pointer to the record itself is available. Deletion can still be accomplished; all that is required is to copy the entire successor record (the successor to the record to be deleted, that is) into the record to be deleted. It is necessary to assume, however, that the last list record is never deleted. Why? Whether or not this is better than keeping track of the predecessor depends on how much time is required to effect this copying operation. The larger the record, the greater the time. However, if the information field of a record is kept elsewhere, and a pointer to it stored in the record itself, then the operation reduces to copying just this pointer and the value of the link field.

Are you listing from all this list information?

3.4 Traversal of Lists

Traversing a list's records is another operation performed on the data abstraction called the list. Traversal is useful when the records are to be processed one after another in the same order in which they appear in the list. A traversal may be accomplished by following the pointer in the list's head to the first record and processing it, then following the first record's link field pointer to the next record and processing it, and so on, until the last record has been processed.

3.4.1 List Reversal Using a Loop

Example 3.1 Consider the list **l** in Figure 3.8(a). The task is to write a function **reverse**, to reverse such a list. This means that when **reverse** is applied to **l**, the result should be as shown in Figure 3.8(b). ■

At first glance, this may seem to be a complicated task involving a great deal of record and pointer manipulation. However, there is a simple solution: the information fields of each record need not be considered at all. Instead, as in Figure 3.8(c), the link field of *F* can be set to null, the link field of *O* can be set to point to *F*, the link field of *R* can be set to point to *O*, and so on. Finally, **l** itself can be set to point to *D*. The result would be as sketched in Figure 3.8(c), the correct reversed list. This procedure can be stated more generally:

1. Set the link field of the first record to null.
2. Set the link field of each record to point to its original predecessor.
3. Finally, set the list head to point to the original last record.

Even without the details of implementing the list and carrying out the procedure, it is easy to be certain that this procedure, when successfully carried out, does

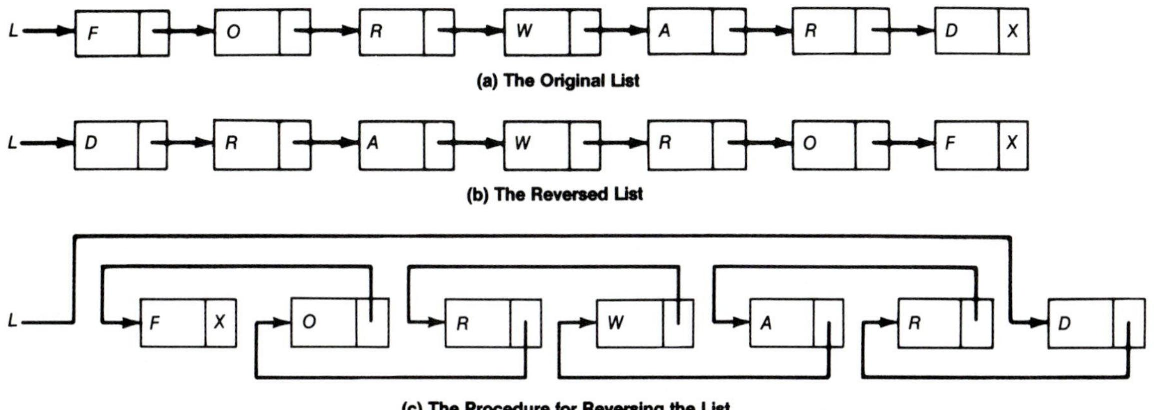

(c) The Procedure for Reversing the List

Figure 3.8 A List before, after, and during Reversal

solve the problem. This is so except for the case of a null list; the procedure does not specify what is to be done, since there is no first or last record in a null list. Since the first record of any list has no predecessor, the procedure can be specified somewhat differently.

1. Set the link field of each record to point to its original predecessor.
2. Then set the list head to point to the original last record, or to predecessor if the list is null.

Now we have a procedure that is correct for all cases, the first record's predecessor being assumed null.

The next step is to detail how this procedure is actually to be done. The basic structure involved is a loop, since the same process is to be carried out repeatedly, but on a different record each time. In general, loops need a beginning ***(initialization)*** and an end ***(finalization)***. The finalization here is specified explicitly in the procedure: namely, set the list head to point to the original last record, or to predecessor if the list is null. The initialization, as usual, cannot be specified until the loop is specified in more detail. Refining task 1 makes the algorithm read as follows:

1. Initialization
   While (there is a current record)
   a. set the link field of the current record to point to its original predecessor, and
   b. update the current record.
2. Set the head of the list to point to the original last record, or to predecessor if the list is null.

To implement the loop requires a pointer (call it `recordpointer`) to keep track of the current record to be processed within the loop by its loop task. Imagine that the first three records have already been processed correctly and the fourth is about to be processed. It is pointed to by `recordpointer`, as depicted in Figure 3.9(a).

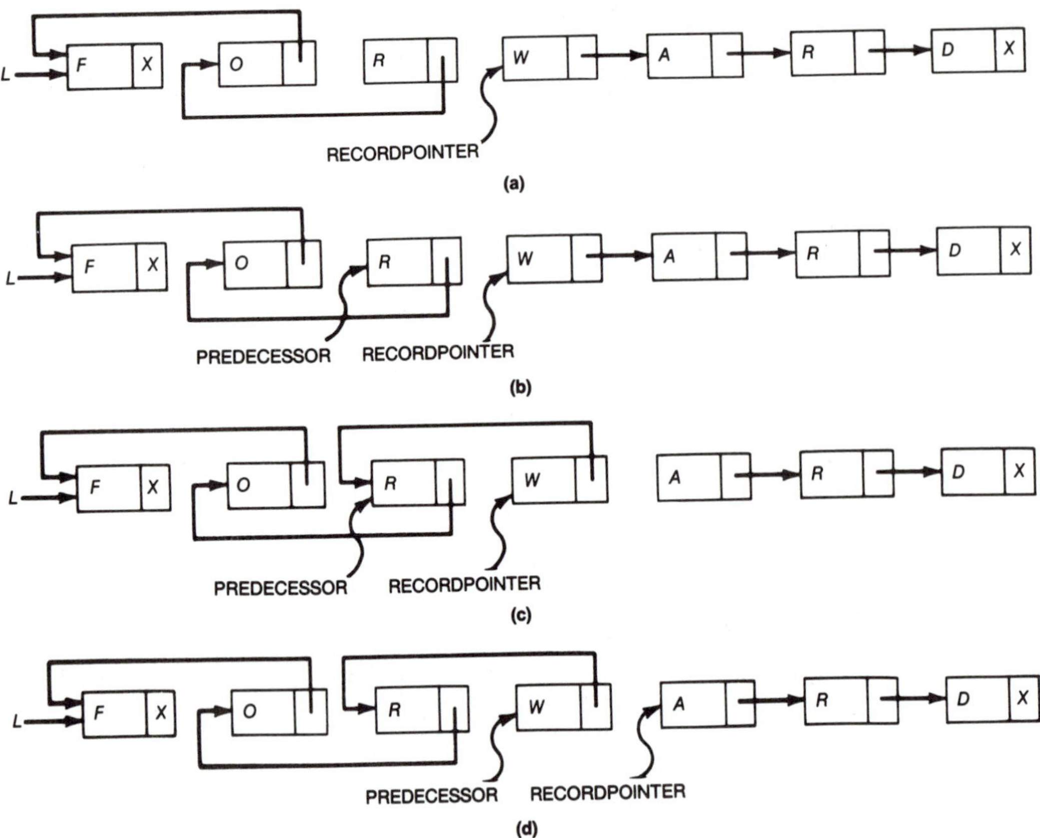

Figure 3.9 Achieving Proper Loop Implementation

Processing W requires setting its link field to point to *W*'s predecessor *R*. To do this requires knowing where its predecessor *R* is located. Thus another pointer, `predecessor`, is needed. It is so named because it will contain a pointer to the predecessor of the current record to be processed. (See Figure 3.9(b).)

Suppose someone attempts to process *W* now, copying `predecessor` into *W*'s `nextpointer` field to set it properly. The result is shown in Figure 3.9(c).

`Predecessor` and `recordpointer` must now be updated so that they point to *W* and *A*, respectively. Then *A* can be processed next when the loop is repeated. However, the link field of *W* no longer points to *A*, but instead to *R*. Thus the location of *A* has been lost. Care is required when changing pointer values so that such important information is not lost. To remedy this, introduce another pointer `hold` in which the pointer to *A* can be saved before changing *W*'s link field value. The processing of the record pointed to by `recordpointer` may now be done by sequentially

1. copying its link field value into `hold`,
2. copying `predecessor` into `recordpointer`'s link field
3. copying `hold` into `recordpointer`.

This produces the result depicted in Figure 3.9(d).

The test or condition for another repetition of the loop becomes `(recordpointer != null)`. The initialization involves setting `recordpointer` to `l`, to make it point to the first record, and setting `predecessor` to `null`. Why is it unnecessary to initialize `hold`?

When the loop is exited, `predecessor` will point to the original last record, and the finalization can be completed by copying `predecessor` into `l`. Refining again:

1. Set `predecessor` to `null`.
   Set `recordpointer` to `l`.
   While (`recordpointer` is not `null`),
   a. set `hold` to the link field value of the record pointed to by `recordpointer`, and
      set `recordpointer`'s link field to `predecessor`,
   b. set `predecessor` to `recordpointer`, and
      set `recordpointer` to `hold`.
2. Set `l` to `predecessor`.

This algorithm actually involves a complete traversal through the records of the list `l`. As it is carried out, `recordpointer` accesses each record of `l` in turn and processes it within the **while** loop. The processing is done by the loop task. In order for the loop to work correctly, some initialization had to be done, and some finalization was required after each record of the list had been processed.

3.4.2 A General List Traversal Using a Loop

Our intention now is to write a general function `traverse`, to carry out a traversal of a list, given its head, `listname`. The code for `traverse` should be independent of the list implementation, as was the code for insertion and deletion. To make `traverse` independent of the particular application as well, the processing to be done on each record will be functionally modularized in a function `process`. Its details are thus irrelevant; simply invoke `process` within `traverse`. However, to do its job, this function may need access to the list head, `listname`. It will surely need to know what record it is currently to process; `recordprinter` will be used to point to this record.

Often, the traversal must proceed through *all* the list records. To allow for the possibility of a partial traversal, however, a variable `done` can be introduced. `Done` may be set by `process` so that the traversal does not continue beyond the current record. Finally, `process` cannot retain any information between calls unless that information is kept nonlocal to it, is passed as one of its parameters, or is a static variable. So `process` is given the parameters `listname`, `recordpointer`, `done`, and `other`. `Other` denotes those parameters whose values must be preserved between calls to `process`.

The heart of a traversal is repeated access of the record pointed to by `recordpointer`, processing of the record, and updating of `recordpointer` to point to the next record. Clearly, a loop is its main construct. The function for a general traversal of a list is as follows:

```
traverse(listname)                          ] a general list traversal function
listpointer listname;
{
   listpointer recordpointer,next();
   moreparameters other;
   int done;
   initialize(listname,&other);             ] does the needed initialization for process
   recordpointer = listname;
   done = FALSE;
   while(!done&&anotherrecord(listname,
         recordpointer))
      {
         process(listname,recordpointer,    ] processes a record
                &other,&done);
         recordpointer =                    ] updates recordpointer to point to the
            next(recordpointer);            ] next record
      }
   finalize(listname,other);                ] does the finalization needed after all rec-
}                                           ] ords have been processed
```

`Initialize` may be used to set the initial value of any parameters that require initialization. **`Anotherrecord`** is a function returning *true* if **`recordpointer`** points to the next record to be processed, and returning *false* if the last record has already been processed. **`Finalize`** is used to carry out any tasks required after all list records have been processed—for instance, to print an appropriate message.

It is a good idea to check a program for correctness, in lieu of a formal proof, by seeing if it handles all special cases (and the typical case) correctly. You should check `traverse` in this way for the case of a null list, a one-record list, and a list with more than one record. For example, if the list is null, the **while** loop is never executed as long as `anotherrecord` is correct (which is assumed), and the program terminates properly as long as `finalize` is correct (which is assumed). So `traverse` does work correctly for the special case of a null list.

3.4.3 The Merits of Functional Modularization

`Traverse` has been written in this general way so that it can be used as a tool readily adaptable to the solution of a large class of problems. How to adapt this function to the solution of seemingly disparate problems is the purpose of the next section. It is important to recognize the basic technique used to render the program independent of the list implementation: embedding those details in lower level functions. This is the reason for `anotherrecord` and **`next`**, **`initialize`**, **`process`**, and **`finalize`**; these functions allow `traverse` to be adapted to specific applications.

All the functions that must reflect implementation and application details in their definitions are lower-level functions. Changes to them do not affect the correctness of `traverse`, but they do affect what `traverse` does. The functions call attention to *what* is being done instead of how it is being done. Furthermore, if the programmer consistently uses a function such as **`next`** or `process` to carry out specific tasks, then no matter how many places the task is required in a program, the definition of that task is localized in one place, and it is clear where to look for the code that implements it. The functions may then all be written independently to suit the immediate purpose. As long as they are correct, `traverse` must be correct too.

3.5 Using the `Traverse` Function for Lists

Sometimes a solution to a new problem can be obtained by modifying a known program that solves a related problem. Also, maintenance or adaptation of programs frequently involves small changes to current programs. Changes are easier, quicker, and more likely to be error-free if exactly that function or task that requires change has been localized as a program function.

`Traverse` adheres to two important elements of programming style.

1. High-level descriptions and programs should be as independent of the details of data abstraction implementation and of the application as possible.
2. High-level descriptions and programs should be functionally modular so that special lower-level functions or tasks carried out within the high-level description or program may be easily isolated.

To illustrate the use of `traverse`, and the effect of these principles, this section presents four examples. Although each could be solved in isolation, from scratch, a different approach is taken here. In each case it should be easy to see that `traverse` may be *adapted* to provide an almost immediate solution. This will be done by writing specific versions of `traverse`'s functions for each application, so that these functions turn `traverse` into a solution. This means that it will then do the required task when executed. Of course, the functions, when invoked by `traverse`, will do exactly what the programmer specifies in their definition.

Example 3.2 A sentence is stored in a list, with each record storing one character. Thus the sentence, THIS SENTENCE HAS EXACTLY 60 CHARACTERS COUNTING BLANKS AND ., is stored in a list with 60 records. For simplicity, assume the period character "." does not occur within a sentence (as it does in this one). The task is to write a function to print the length of the sentence. ■

The solution can be achieved by traversing the list and counting the number of records. `Initialize` can set a counter, `length`, to zero, and `process` can increment it by 1 each time it is invoked. `Finalize` can do the printing. The functions are readily defined.

```
initialize(listname,plength)        ] initializes length to zero
listpointer listname;
moreparameters *plength;
{
   *plength = 0;
}
```

```
process(listname,recordpointer,plength)     ] adds one to length to count the next record
listpointer listname,recordpointer;
moreparameters *plength;
{

   (*plength)++;
}

finalize(listname,length)                   ] prints the result
listpointer listname;
moreparameters length;
{
   if(length != 0)
      printf("\n The sentence has length %d \n",length);
   else
      printf("\n There is no sentence \n");
}
```

Either `anotherrecord` and `next` must be supplied to the programmer, or the details of the list implementation must be specified such that the programmer can write them. The task of the example is then carried out by the invocation `traverse(sentence)`. In this example `traverse` must be modified to the following function.

```
#define TRUE 1
#define FALSE 0
typedef int moreparameters;

traverse(listname)
/* Prints the length of the sentence
   stored in the list, listname.
*/
listpointer listname;
{
   listpointer recordpointer,next();
   moreparameters other;
   int done;
   initialize(listname,&other)                  ] other corresponds to
   recordpointer = listname;                      length
   done = FALSE;
   while(!done&&anotherrecord(listname,recordpointer))
      {
         process(listname,recordpointer,&other);  ] the only modification—
         recordpointer = next(recordpointer);       done is not needed
      }
   finalize(listname,other);
}
```

There are two ways to view `traverse`. One is as a program that can be used but not modified in any way. This would require that the functions be written as they appear and the type `moreparameters` be declared prior to `traverse`.

The second is as a program that may be used or changed in any desirable way. In this case, for clarity, the function names can be changed: **traverse** to **count-characters**, **initialize** to **zerocounter**, **process** to **increment-counter**, **finalize** to **printcounter**, and **anotherrecord** to **anothercharacter**, for example. It may be desirable to remove parameters that are not needed. Since **listname** is not needed by **initialize**, **process**, or **finalize**, and **recordpointer** is not needed by **process**, they may be omitted from the definitions and invocations of these functions. **Other** may be changed to **length**. Finally, **done** may be eliminated, since it is not needed. Having made this distinction, the programmer is free to take either view, or a view that falls between the two. The one chosen should be clear from the context.

Suppose the sentence were stored in the list with three characters per record instead of just one per record. The solution would require a new version of **process** to reflect this change, but **initialize** and **finalize** remain as is. **Next** might have to reflect the new record format. The new process is

```
process(listname,recordpointer,plength)     ] updates length to reflect the number of
listpointer listname,recordpointer;           characters in the record pointed to by
moreparameters *plength;                      recordpointer
{
   listpointer next();
   int lastrecord;
   char char1(),char2();
   lastrecord = !anotherrecord(listname,next(recordpointer));
   if(!lastrecord)                          ] not the last record, so it contains three char-
      *plength = *plength + 3;                acters
   else if(char1(recordpointer) == '.')     ] the last record has only a period
      (*plength)++;
   else if(char2(recordpointer) == '.')
      *plength = *plength + 2;              ] has two characters
   else
      *plength = *plength + 3;              ] has three characters
}
```

where **char1** returns a copy of the first character in the record pointed to by its parameters, and **char2** returns a copy of the second character in the record pointed to by its parameters. Like **next** and **anotherrecord**, they must be supplied, or the programmer must write them given list implementation details.

Finally, suppose the list is implemented as a circular list (Figure 3.10). In ***circular lists,*** the null pointer of the last record is replaced by a pointer that points to the first record. To illustrate the difference in the implementations between a

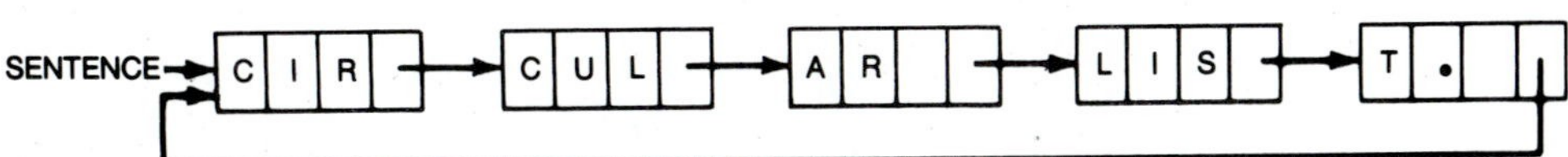

Figure 3.10 A Circular List

standard list and a circular list, the two distinct versions required for **anotherrecord** are presented.

Standard List

```
anotherrecord(listname,recordpointer)
listpointer listname,recordpointer;
{
   listpointer setnull();
   return(recordpointer != setnull());   ] when recordpointer is not null, there is
}                                           another record
```

Circular List

```
anotherrecord(listname,recordpointer)
listpointer listname,recordpointer;
{
   return(listname != recordpointer);   ] when recordpointer does not point to the
}                                          first record, or is not null, there is another
                                           record
```

Actually, the solution is not as general as possible. Suppose the list were implemented using a dummy header record. Then **process** must recognize when it is processing this record (the first) and not change **length**, since no characters are stored in the header record. You should modify **process** to account for this possibility. It is necessary to assume that the header may be distinguished from the other records in some way.

Example 3.3 Earlier in the chapter a way to reverse a list was developed from scratch. We now build a program to reverse a list utilizing **traverse**. **Traverse** may be turned into a solution for the list reversal by defining **initialize**, **process**, and **finalize**, as follows:

```
initialize(listname,psave,ppredecessor)         ] initializes save and predecessor
listpointer listname,*psave,*ppredecessor;
{
   listpointer setnull();
   *psave = setnull();
   *ppredecessor = setnull();
}

process(plistname,recordpointer,psave,          ] sets the link field of the record
        ppredecessor)                             pointed to by predecessor to
listpointer *plistname,recordpointer,*psave,      save, which points to that record's
            *ppredecessor;                        predecessor and updates save
{                                                 and predecessor
   listpointer setnull();
   if(*ppredecessor != setnull())
      setlink(*ppredecessor,*psave);
   *psave = *ppredecessor;
   *ppredecessor = recordpointer:
}
```

```
finalize(plistname,save,predecessor)
listpointer *plistname,save,predecessor;
{
   listpointer setnull();
   if(predecessor != setnull())
      {
         setlink(predecessor,save);
         *plistname = predecessor;
      }
}
```

when the list has more than one record, reverses the link of the last record and sets the list name to point to the original last record

```
traverse(plistname)
/*Reverses the list listname.*/
listpointer *plistname;
{
```

the parameter of **traverse** *has been modified to a pointer to* **listname**, *since it may need to be changed;* **save** *and* **predecessor** *are now parameters of* **initialize**, **process**, *and* **finalize**

```
   listpointer recordpointer,*psave,*ppredecessor,next();
   initialize(listname,&psave,&ppredecessor);

   recordpointer = *plistname;
   while(anotherrecord(*plistname,recordpointer))
      {
         process(*plistname,recordpointer,&psave,&ppredecessor);
         recordpointer = next(recordpointer);
      }
         finalize(&plistname,*psave,*ppredecessor);
}
```

Notice that the parameter of **traverse** is now a pointer to the **listname**. This is necessary since **listname** may need to be changed by **traverse**. Here **process** works on the record preceding the record pointed to by **recordpointer**, while the original solution worked on the record pointed to by **recordpointer**. This was necessary because that solution changed **recordpointer's** link field before updating **recordpointer**. ■

Example 3.4 Insert a new record into a list **stocks**, which is kept in alphabetical order by name. Assume the data for the new record may be accessed by a function **getnextrecord**, which returns a pointer to the new record. ■

To turn **traverse** into a solution requires simply that **process** compare the new record's name field value with that of the current record. If it precedes the current record's name field value, it must be inserted before the current record and **done** set to *true*. To make the insertion conveniently, a pointer, **predecessor**, to the predecessor of the current record will be kept by **process** and updated each time **process** is invoked. **Initialize** must allocate storage for the new record, set its data field values, and set **predecessor** to null. Assume that a function **avail** is given, returning a pointer to a storage element that may be used to store the new record. **Finalize** must insert the new record in the event that the list is null. The solution for these functions follows:

```
initialize(pnewpointer,ppredecessor)
listpointer *pnewpointer,*ppredecessor;
{
   listpointer avail(),setnull(),getnextrecord();
   *pnewpointer = avail();
   setinfo(*pnewpointer,getnextrecord());
   *ppredecessor = setnull();
}
```

sets `newpointer` *to point to storage for the new record, reads in its data and places it into the new record, initializes* `predecessor`

where `setinfo` copies the contents of the record pointed to by its second parameter into the information field of the record pointed to by its first parameter, so it depends on the list implementation details.

```
finalize(plistname,predecessor,newpointer)
listpointer *plistname,predecessor,newpointer;
{
   listpointer setnull();
   if(*plistname == setnull())
      insert(plistname,predecessor,newpointer);
}
```

inserts the new record if the list is null

```
process(plistname,recordpointer,newpointer,ppredecessor,
        pdone)
listpointer *plistname,recordpointer,newpointer,
            *ppredecessor;
int *pdone;
{
   listpointer setnull(),next();
   if(precedes(newpointer,recordpointer))
      {
         insert(plistname,*ppredecessor,newpointer);
         *pdone = TRUE;
      }
   else if(next(recordpointer) == setnull())
      {
         insert(plistname,recordpointer,newpointer);
         *pdone = TRUE;
      }
   else
         *ppredecessor = recordpointer;
}
```

inserts the record if the proper place is after `predecessor` *and sets* `done` *to true, else just updates* `predecessor`

insert in list body

insert as new last record

not the place to insert

where `precedes` returns *true* if its first parameter points to a record whose name precedes, in alphabetical order, the name in the record pointed to by its second parameter. To insert a new record, invoke `traverse(&stocks)`. However, `traverse` must be modified in a way similar to Example 3.2 as follows. A better name for this modified `traverse` would be `orderedinsert`, so we use it.

```
orderedinsert(plistname)
/*Inputs and inserts a new record
  in the list listname in alphabetical
  order.
*/
listpointer *plistname;
{
   listpointer recordpointer,newpointer,predecessor,next();
   int done;
   initialize(&newpointer,&predecessor);
   recordpointer = *plistname;
   done = FALSE;
   while(!done&&anotherrecord(*plistname,recordpointer))
      {
         process(plistname,recordpointer,newpointer,
                 &predecessor,&done);
         recordpointer = next(recordpointer);
      }
   finalize(plistname,predecessor,newpointer);
}
```

inserts a new record in the proper place in a list

Suppose you wanted to insert the new record into a list of stocks kept in order by date bought, instead of by name. Rather than keep another list distinct from **stocks**, you could add another link field to its records. Call it the **datelink** field, and assume each record's **datelink** field points to the correct successor as in Figure 3.11. **Stockdate** is a new head, pointing to the first record of that list when date bought is used as the criterion for ordering.

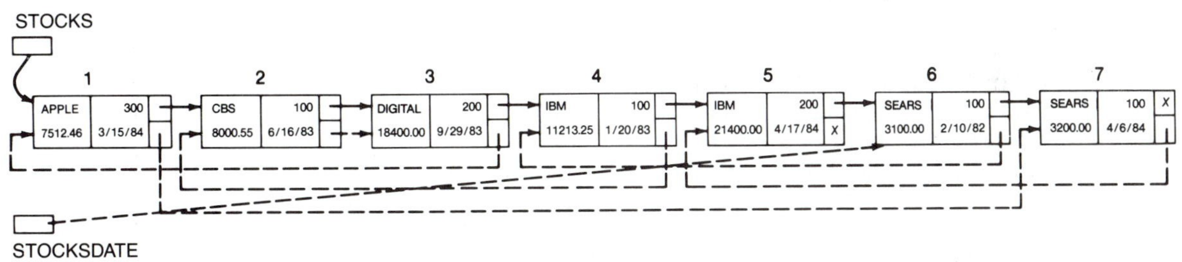

Figure 3.11 Two Orders for a List Using Two Heads and Two Link Fields

To solve this problem: 1) define **precedes** so that it compares dates instead of names; 2) replace each reference in **insert** to the **setlink** function by a reference to the **setdatebought** function and define it to work on the **datelink** field instead of the link field; and 3) redefine **next** to return a copy of the **datelink** field of the record pointed to by its parameter. A call to **orderedinsert(&stocksdate)** then carries out the task.

Example 3.5 Create a list **stocks**, to store a portfolio of stock records. ■

To solve this problem, assume the data are already stored on some input medium and **getnextrecord** gives access to each record in turn, as it is invoked. The desired list may be created by traversing the records stored on the input medium. The job of **process** is to fill in the information field of the storage allocated for the new record, and fill in the link field of the new record with a pointer to storage allocated for the next new record. However, it is assumed that the last input data is a sentinel value that indicates there are no more records. When the sentinel is input, **getnextrecord** returns a null pointer value. Consequently, **process** must first check for this case and, when it occurs, simply return after setting **done** to *true* and the link field of the predecessor of the new record to **null**, unless the list is null. If it is null, **process** must set **done** to *true* and **listname** to **null**. **Initialize** must allocate storage for the first record and set **listname** to it. **Finalize** is not needed. We have

```
initialize(plistname)
listpointer *plistname;
{
   listpointer avail();
   *plistname = avail();
}
```

allocates storage for the list and sets **listname** *to point to it*

```
process(plistname,recordpointer,pdone)
listpointer *plistname,recordpointer;
int *pdone;
{
   static listpointer predecessor;
   listpointer setnull(),avail(),getnextrecord(),
               pointer;
   pointer = getnextrecord();
   if(pointer != SENTINEL)
      {
         setinfo(recordpointer,pointer);
         setlink(recordpointer,avail());
         predecessor = recordpointer;
      }

   else if(*plistname != recordpointer)
      {
         setlink(predecessor,setnull());
         *pdone = TRUE;
      }
   else
      {
         *plistname = setnull();
         *pdone = TRUE;
      }
}
```

reads the information for the new record, fills in its information and link fields, and updates **predecessor**, *so that on the next call it can access the new record's predecessor when necessary; special handling is needed when the input is the sentinel*

the sentinel was input and the list is not null, so the link field of the new record's predecessor (the last list record) must be set to null and **done** *to true*

the sentinel was input and the list is null, so the list name must be set to null and **done** *to true*

Invoking a correctly modified **traverse(&stocks)** creates the list. Notice that this **traverse** will copy a list whenever **getnextrecord** obtains its information from the next record of the list to be copied. A better name for this function would be **readlist** or **copylist**. At this point you may want to see a complete program that creates the **stocks** list and also prints it. The program is in Section 3.6.1.

Suppose the records are given in arbitrary order, but the **stocks** list must be created with the records appearing in alphabetical order. To turn **traverse** into a solution to this problem, **initialize**, **finalize**, and **anotherrecord** are not needed; neither are the variables **recordpointer** and **other**. This problem is solved by the following version of **traverse**, which we call **expand**. The name **expand** was chosen because, when called to work on an existing ordered list, it simply expands the list by adding the new inputs to the list in the proper places. When the call **expand(&listname)** is made with **listname** set to null, it creates the ordered list.

```
expand(plistname)
/*Inputs a series of records and
  inserts them in alphabetical
  order in the ordered list listname.
*/
listpointer *plistname;
{
   int done;
   done = FALSE;
   while(!done)
      processrecord(plistname,&done);
}
```

this modified **traverse** *inserts all records of an arbitrarily ordered input list of records into an ordered list,* **listname**, *maintaining ordering*

processes the next record of the input list

```
processrecord(plistname,pdone)
listpointer *plistname;
int *pdone;
{
   listpointer pointer,getnextrecord();
   pointer = getnextrecord();
   if(pointer != SENTINEL)
      insertinorder(plistname,pointer);
   else
      *pdone = TRUE;
}
```

gets the next record of the input and inserts it into **listname**

inserts the record pointed to by **pointer** *into the list,* **listname**

Notice that **expand** has no need for the functions **initialize**, **finalize**, and **anotherrecord**, nor for the variables **recordpointer** and **other**.

Processrecord must obtain the next input record and insert it in the list at the correct place. It invokes **insertinorder**, which has the task of creating and inserting the new record into its proper place in **listname**; **pointer** points to the record whose content is to be placed in the new record's information field. **Insertinorder** itself requires a traversal of **listname**. The version below is a modification of **orderedinsert**, obtained by adding a second parameter, **pointer**. **Orderedinsert** uses **getnextrecord** to obtain the next input record and then inserts it, while **insertinorder** is given a pointer to the new record and needs only insert it. The additional task of obtaining the new input record is handled outside of `insertinorder`. Consequently its `process` and `finalize` functions can be used directly in `insertinorder`. Only its `initialize` function needs changing, but all are given below for easy reference.

```
insertinorder(plistname,pointer)
/*Inserts the record pointed to by pointer
  in the ordered list listname.
*/
listpointer *plistname,pointer;
{
   listpointer recordpointer,predecessor,newpointer,
               next();
   int done;
   initialize(&newpointer,&predecessor,pointer);
   recordpointer = *plistname;
   done = FALSE;
   while(!done&&anotherrecord(*plistname,
         recordpointer))
      {
         process(plistname,recordpointer,newpointer,
                &predecessor,&done);
         recordpointer = next(recordpointer);
      }
   finalize(plistname,predecessor,pointer);
}
```

this modification of `traverse` *inserts the input record at the correct place*

creates the new record

processes the new record

deals with insertion in a null list

```
initialize(pnewpointer,ppredecessor,pointer)
listpointer *pnewpointer,*ppredecessor,pointer;
{
   listpointer setnull(),avail();
   *pnewpointer = avail();
   setinfo(*pnewpointer,pointer);
   *ppredecessor = setnull();
}
```

creates the new record and initializes `predecessor`

```
process(plistname,recordpointer,newpointer,
        ppredecessor,pdone)
listpointer *plistname,recordpointer,
            newpointer,*ppredecessor;
int *pdone;
{
   listpointer setnull(),next();
   if(precedes(newpointer,recordpointer))
      {
         insert(plistname,*ppredecessor,newpointer);
         *pdone = TRUE;
      }
   else if(next(recordpointer) == setnull())
      {
         insert(plistname,recordpointer,newpointer);
         *pdone = TRUE;
      }
```

inserts the record if the proper place is after `predecessor` *and sets* `done` *to true; else just updates* `predecessor`

insert in list body

insert as new last record

```
    else
        *ppredecessor = recordpointer;              ] not the place to insert
}

finalize(plistname,predecessor,newpointer)        ] inserts the new record
listpointer *plistname,predecessor,newpointer;      if the list is null
{
    listpointer setnull();
    if(*plistname == setnull())
        insert(plistname,predecessor,newpointer);
}
```

3.5.1 Why Traverse Was Useful

It is very important to recognize that **traverse** of Section 3.4.2 is a *tool* that could be used in solving the example problems. The tool was applicable because

It was written using data abstractions that allowed writing or using required implementation functions without changing **traverse**.

It was written using functional modularization, which allowed isolation of functions for relevant tasks so that they could be written to satisfy specific needs.

Recognizing and applying tools is a major aspect of programming methodology. For a tool to be convenient to use, it must be written according to the two elements of programming style just stated. Of course, in the simple examples using the tool may not save much time, effort, or cost, but for complex tasks the savings can be great.

Note that the use of **getnextrecord** makes the solutions to Examples 3.4 and 3.5 independent of the input medium or the format of the input. Thus any changes in the input are not reflected in **traverse**; only **getnextrecord** and **SENTINEL** can require modification. In fact, the same should be done for any output. It is better to use a function rather than specify input and output in the basic functions, in case the input or output medium is changed.

3.6 Implementing Lists

So far this chapter has covered lists in the abstract. Lists are implemented in two basic ways, differentiated by where the records of the lists are stored: 1) in an array of records or 2) in dynamic memory. These are similar, but dynamic memory allows for more efficient use of storage and is easier to use.

3.6.1 Lists Stored in Dynamic Memory

The simplest implementation is to store all list records in the dynamic memory. The declarations required are illustrated below for the example of the stock portfolio. For storage in dynamic memory, the records of a list are defined as usual, and an additional field is added to contain the link field pointer. Since it will point to a successor record stored in dynamic memory, it must be defined as a pointer. In this case, the null value for a pointer is always given by the value **NULL**, with **NULL** having the value 0. Variables of type **listpointer** will contain pointers to records of type **stockrecord**.

```
#define MAXSIZE 5
#define NULL 0
#define SENTINEL -1
typedef struct
{
   int month;
   int day;
   int year;
}date;
typedef struct
{
   char name[MAXSIZE];
   int shares;
   float value;
   date datebought;
}infofield;
typedef struct listrecord
{
   infofield info;
   struct listrecord *link;
}stockrecord,*listpointer;
```

The following complete program reads in and creates a list of stockrecords as in Example 3.5 and, in addition, prints out the information fields of the list records. Both the creation and printing portion of the code are appropriately modified versions of **traverse**. The **initialize** and **process** functions of Example 3.5 are used in the creation portion, but **process** has been given the name **addrecord**. The program treats the list as a data abstraction. The data abstraction list, with its allowed operations—**next**, **setlink**, **setinfo**,

Table 3.2 Sample Input

	Explanation	Actual Input
Record 1	Number of shares	100
	Stock name	abc
	Price of a share	56.25
	Month day year of purchase	1 23 1978
Record 2	Number of shares	50
	Stock name	wxyz
	Price of a share	5.50
	Month day year of purchase	11 4 1986
	.	
	.	
	.	
Terminal record	Sentinel (where next number of shares would otherwise appear)	−1

`avail`, `anotherrecord`, `getnextrecord`, and `printrecord`, appear together in the program.

Typical input to the program is shown in Table 3.2.

The program that follows reads in the records of a list, creates the list, and prints the records in the list.

This portion of the program specifies the implementation of the list and its allowed operations. It is the only part of the program that needs to be changed should the list implementation change.

```
#define MAXSIZE 5
#define NULL 0
#define SENTINEL -1
typedef struct
{
   int month;
   int day;
   int year;
}date;
typedef struct
{
   char name[MAXSIZE];
   int shares;
   float value;
   date datebought;
}infofield;
typedef struct listrecord
{
   infofield info;
   struct listrecord *link;
}stockrecord,*listpointer;

listpointer next(pointer)
/* Returns a copy of the
   link field in the record
   pointed to by pointer
*/
listpointer pointer;
{
   return(pointer->link);
}

listpointer setnull()
/* Returns a null pointer */
{
   return(NULL);
}

setlink(pointer1,pointer2)
/* Sets the link field of the
   record pointed to by pointer1
   to the contents of pointer2
*/
listpointer pointer1,pointer2;
```

```
{
   pointer1->link = pointer2;
}

setinfo(pointer1,pointer2)
/* Sets the infofield of the record
   pointed to by pointer1 to the
   infofield of the record
   pointed to by pointer2
*/
listpointer pointer1,pointer2;
{
   int i;
   for(i=0;i<MAXSIZE;i++)
       pointer1->info.name[i] = pointer2->
          info.name[i];
   pointer1->info.shares = pointer2->
      info.shares;
   pointer1->info.value = pointer2->info.value;
   pointer1->info.datebought.month = pointer2->
      info.datebought.month;
   pointer1->info.datebought.day = pointer2->
      info.datebought.day;
   pointer1->info.datebought.year = pointer2->
      info.datebought.year;
}

listpointer avail()
/* Returns a pointer to storage
   allocated for a record of type
   stockrecord
*/
{
   listpointer malloc();
   return(malloc(sizeof(stockrecord)));
}

anotherrecord(recordpointer)
/* Returns true if there is
   another record
*/
listpointer recordpointer;
{
   listpointer setnull();
   return(recordpointer != setnull());
}

listpointer getnextrecord()
/* Inputs the data for the new
   record and returns a pointer
   to a record containing the data
   in its infofield or if there
```

```
    are no new records,returns
    a null pointer
*/
{
    listpointer setnull();
    static stockrecord nextrecord;
    printf(" Enter number of shares\n");
    scanf("%d",&(nextrecord.info.shares));
    if(nextrecord.info.shares != SENTINEL)
       {
          printf(" Enter the stock name - less than
                   %d characters\n",MAXSIZE);
          scanf("%s",nextrecord.info.name);
          printf(" Enter the price of one share of
                   the stock\n");
          scanf("%f",&(nextrecord.info.value));
          printf(" Enter the month day year of the
                   stock purchase\n");
          scanf("%d %d %d",&(nextrecord.info.
                datebought.month),
                &(nextrecord.info.datebought.day),
                &(nextrecord.info.datebought.year));
          return(&nextrecord);
       }
    else
       return(setnull());
}

printrecord(recordpointer)
/* Prints the contents of the infofield
   of the record pointed to by recordpointer
*/
listpointer recordpointer;
{
   printf(" The stock is %s\n",
          recordpointer->info.name);
   printf(" The number of shares is %d\n",
          recordpointer->info.shares);
   printf(" The value of a share is %f\n",
          recordpointer->info.value);
   printf(" The date of purchase is %d %d %d\n\n",
          recordpointer->info.datebought.month,
          recordpointer->info.datebought.day,
          recordpointer->info.datebought.year);
}

#include <stdio.h>
#define TRUE 1
#define FALSE 0

main()
```

this portion of the program is independent of the list implementation

```
/* Inputs a series of stockrecords,
   creates a list of the records, and
   prints the contents of each list
   record's infofield
*/
{
   listpointer stocks,recordpointer,next();
   int done;
   initialize(&stocks);
   recordpointer = stocks;
   done = FALSE;
   while(!done&&anotherrecord(recordpointer))
      {
         addrecord(&stocks,recordpointer,&done);
         recordpointer = next(recordpointer);
      }
```

this is the traversal to input data and create the list

fills in the current record, allocates storage for the next and adds it to the list, and if there is no data for the current record, terminates the list and sets `done` *to true*

```
   recordpointer=stocks;
   while(anotherrecord(recordpointer))
      {
         printrecord(recordpointer);
         recordpointer = next(recordpointer);
      }
}
```

this is the traversal to print the list

prints the record

```
initialize(plistname)
/* Allocates storage for the first record
   and sets listname to point to it
*/
listpointer *plistname;
{
   listpointer avail();
   *plistname = avail();
}

addrecord(plistname,recordpointer,pdone)
/* Fills in the current record's data, and allocates
   storage for the next record and adds it to the
   list. If there is no data for the current record
   it sets the link field of the last list record
   to null, or the list head to null, and done to
   true.
*/
listpointer *plistname,recordpointer;
int *pdone;
```

```
{
   static listpointer predecessor;
   listpointer setnull(),avail(),getnextrecord(),
               pointer;
   pointer =getnextrecord();
   if(pointer != setnull())
      {
         setinfo(recordpointer,pointer);          ] there is data for the
         setlink(recordpointer,avail());            current record
         predecessor = recordpointer;
      }
   else if(*plistname != recordpointer)
      {
         setlink(predecessor,setnull());          ] there is no data for the
         *pdone = TRUE;                             current record, and the
      }                                             list is not null
   else
      {
         *plistname = setnull();                  ] there is no data for the
         *pdone = TRUE;                             current record, and the
      }                                             list is null
}
```

3.6.2 Lists Stored in an Array of Records

Instead of being stored in dynamic memory, list records may be stored in an array of records. The declarations required are illustrated for the example of stocks.

```
#define MAXSIZE 5
#define MAX 100
#define NULL -1
typedef struct
{
   int month;
   int day;
   int year;
}date;
typedef struct
{
   char name[MAXSIZE];
   int shares;
   float value;
   date datebought;
}infofield;
typedef struct listrecord
{
   infofield info;
   int link;                     ] link is now an array index
}stockrecord;
stockrecord records[MAX];
typedef int listpointer;         ] listpointer is now an array index
```

For this implementation the null pointer value is −1. Here, variables of type `listpointer` contain integer array indices. The implementation for some of the functions operating on the list are

```
next(pointer)
/* Returns a copy of the
   link field in the record
   pointed to by pointer
*/
listpointer pointer;
{
   return(records[pointer].link);
}

setnull()
/* Returns a null pointer */
{
   return(-1);
}

setlink(pointer1,pointer2)
/* Sets the link field of the
   record pointed to by pointer1
   to the contents of pointer2
*/
listpointer pointer1,pointer2;
{
   records[pointer1].link = pointer2;
}
```

This implementation assumes that `records` is declared nonlocally to these functions, so that they may reference it. With this implementation, the `records` array plays the role of the dynamic memory. It is necessary to write an `avail` function that must keep track of those slots in `records` that are not in use, and hence can be allocated when storage for a list record is requested.

3.6.3 Lists Stored in Languages without Records

In some languages, such as FORTRAN, there is no dynamic memory, nor are there pointer variables or records. In such a language, the records themselves must be implemented by the programmer. They may be stored in single or multiple arrays, as discussed in Chapter 2. Since the list records now have an additional link field indicating their successor, they need not be stored sequentially and may be located anywhere in the array or multiarrays, as long as they do not overlap. An additional variable is needed for the head of the list. Once these arrays are set up, the programmer may write functions to access each field of a record and functions to copy one record's value into another record, or to copy a record's field value into another record's field. These might include

> `next(pointer)`
> Returns a copy of the link field value of the record pointed to by `pointer`.
> `setlink(pointer1,pointer2)`
> Sets the value of the link field of the record pointed to by `pointer1` to `pointer2`.
> `setlinfo(pointer1,pointer2)`
> Sets the value of the information field of the record pointed to by `pointer1` to the value of the information field of the record pointed to by `pointer2`.

In FORTRAN, the array or multiarray in which the records are kept could be declared to be stored in the FORTRAN common area or else must be passed as parameters to these functions. Once they are written, for all intents and purposes the language has records. These records can be accessed, copied, or modified by using these functions. Although the programmer must do all this work initially, from this point on the situation is conceptually the same as in Section 3.6.2. That is, the actual implementation of the records may be forgotten; they are treated as if stored in an array of records, just as in C. The problem of writing an `avail` function still remains, and it is addressed in the next section.

In FORTRAN, although storage for records kept in lists must be managed, the programmer does not need to manage storage for individual elements or for arrays of elements. To refer in a program to an element `n`, or an array `data`, simply declare `n` to be an element, and `data` to be an array. Then use the operations available in FORTRAN to enter specific values into `n` or `data`. This works because individual elements and arrays are data structures directly available in FORTRAN. Lists, on the other hand, are not directly available and must be built up explicitly by storing their records in arrays. Consequently, the programmer must determine where storage is available to create a record when the need arises.

In C it is not necessary to implement records of lists explicitly in arrays. Instead, dynamic data structures may be used. A data structure is dynamic if it is built during execution of a program and storage is allocated for its components at that time. Dynamic data structures are built simply by asking for storage to be allocated for a record in dynamic memory. A pointer will then be assigned to point to that storage. Using the pointer, appropriate values may be assigned to the fields of the new record. These fields may be referred to directly, using naming conventions in the language. Special functions to store or access information from the fields of the record need not be written.

Records still need to be inserted properly in a dynamic data structure. Commands directly available in the language may be used to create or reclaim records, or reclamation may be left to the implicit storage reclamation provided by the language. Thus the definition, creation, reclamation, and manipulation of dynamic data structures become easier.

3.7 Keeping Track of Available Records

Keeping track of and allocating storage that is needed during the execution of a program is called ***dynamic storage management.*** In some languages, notably FORTRAN, storage for arrays is allocated before the program's execution, and no dynamic storage management is present. In languages like C, storage is allocated to the local variables of a function at the start of its execution and remains assigned until the function (or block) completes its execution. The space can then be reassigned to the next executing function (or block). In effect, it disappears. This is why values of local variables are not preserved between invocations of a function, unless they are declared as static, in which case they are preserved between calls. Management of this storage during the execution of a program is not what is meant by dynamic storage management. Contrast this situation to dynamic memory, which is assigned or taken away from records in dynamic memory during the execution of a function itself. This captures the true flavor of dynamic storage allocation.

If the array in which records are to be kept (as in Sections 3.6.2 and 3.6.3) is to function as dynamic memory, then allocating storage in the array for a record requires dynamic storage management. In fact, this amounts to an implementation of a C-like dynamic memory. Although storage can thus be managed explicitly for a specific program, dynamic memory can manage storage for many programs and is hence more efficient use of storage. The difference is that one large array may function as storage to be used by all the programs, instead of dedicating separate smaller arrays to each program.

3.7.1 Why Dynamic Memory?

Why is storage efficiency important? Why not find storage for a new record in the array simply by placing it sequentially below the last new record's storage? After all, this would be very easy to do and would certainly use the storage as efficiently as possible. The answer is that this simple solution is a great idea—provided that all the storage needed for the array to be of sufficient length is available. The catch is that this proviso is rarely the case. Often, the amount required isn't known in advance; even when it is known, not enough storage may be available.

Reconsider the prime number example of Chapter 1. It is probably evident by now that the list is a good data structure to use for `collection`. The program to generate all the primes between 2 and n uses very little storage besides that needed for the list, but how large should you make the array in which to store the list? It is possible to modify the program so that it need not actually store all integers between 2 and n in the list, but only those that are prime. Still, how many primes are there no greater than n? It is even possible to write such a program so that it efficiently generates and prints all primes $\leq n$ yet stores only those $\leq\sqrt{n}$ in the list, but again, how many of these are there?

Suppose you are a programmer asked to store the contents of ten manuscripts in ten lists. If each can have a maximum length of 50,000 words, then storage for 500,000 words is needed. How long is the longest word? You see the problem. Even if the amount of storage could be estimated, sufficient storage may not be available. You might conclude that the task cannot be done, or you might use secondary storage (magnetic tape, disks). However, in secondary storage access is relatively slow, and it requires techniques different from those described so far. One possibility remains. Maybe the manuscripts to be stored, perhaps even more than 10, are compatible (in the sense that they are not all of great length simultaneously). Perhaps the lengths will vary as the manuscripts are processed by a program, so that at any one time the manuscripts being stored can fit. This means that they may be growing and shrinking in length at different points in the program. If the storage no longer needed for one manuscript is relinquished and reused for another, then the total array length may not ever be exceeded. In other words, if storage can be allocated, then reused for new allocations when no longer needed for its original purpose, problems may be solved that are otherwise out of range. This is the reason to manage storage.

This also explains why dynamic memory makes better use of storage than individual program management using arrays of records. Each program may, to ensure its execution, ask for a large amount of storage to be used for its array. The total amount needed by all the programs may not be at hand. It is better to take all available storage and dole it out to each program as needed, the hope being that whenever some programs need a great deal of storage, the others need little. Instead of dedicating amounts to each user for each one's worst case, the programmer manages the storage and gives out only what is needed at any moment.

3.7.2 Using Dynamic Memory

Having taken this relevant digression, let's return to the job of managing dynamic memory. This will show how dynamic memory itself might function, and give us the means to create our own when desirable. In fact, you will see when this might be advantageous.

Pointers are used in C to eliminate the problem of dynamic storage management for the programmer. Pointers allow the declaration of a variable of a complex data type and allocate storage for it by merely assigning to its pointer a value that points to that storage. The C function `malloc` is used for this purpose. This section develops a function `avail` that will have the same effect as `malloc` but will manage storage in the `records` array for Section 3.6.2.

In the general case of list processing, records need to be inserted in and deleted from lists. It is deletion, you may recall, that makes the solution of larger problems feasible. When records are deleted, their storage in the `records` array may be reused. Reclaiming storage in this way allows larger problems to be solved than would otherwise be possible, by allowing the program to execute to completion.

Records of one or more lists may be stored in the `records` array at any moment during the execution of a program. Assume that all these records have the same length, and that no sharing of storage occurs. No sharing means that no list record has more than one pointer to it at any time. The more typical case of variable-length records and sharing of storage is more complex and will be dealt with in a later chapter. The issue is now how to implement `avail`.

Suppose that, by looking at a record, you can tell whether or not it is in use. This would be the case if, whenever a record were deleted from a list, it were marked *unused*. An available record could be found by traversing the `records` array until a record marked unused were found. **Avail** could then return a pointer to that record, after marking it as now in use. In Figure 3.12, this would require the first three records to be accessed before **avail** could return to point to position 2. The time to carry out this procedure is proportional to the length of the **records** array in the worst case.

A very significant improvement would be to keep track of the available records so that the search may be avoided and the time for **avail** to do its task reduced to a constant. This is achieved by using the link fields of each unused record to create a list of available records. Initially all entries of **records** are unused, so the list should contain every record of the array. Figure 3.13 shows how this list might appear for the configuration of Figure 3.12, with **availist** taken as its head. **Avail** now carries out its task by simply deleting the first record from **availist** and returning a pointer to the deleted record. This yields the desired constant time for **avail**.

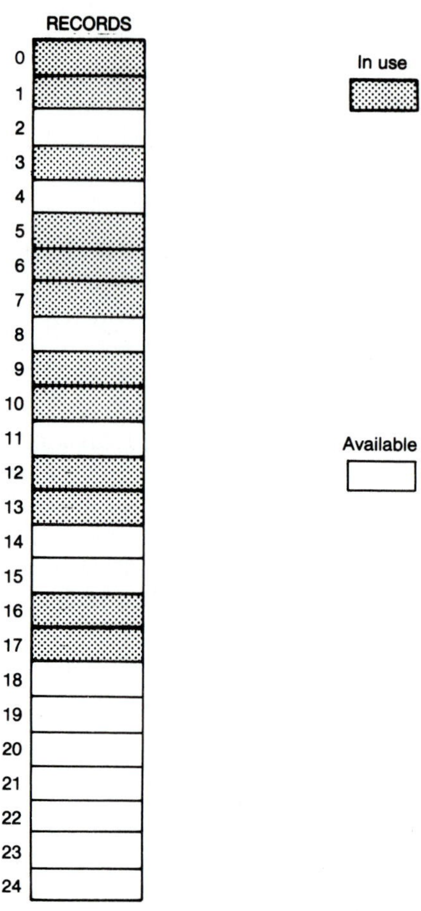

Figure 3.12 Typical Configuration of Used and Unused List Records in the RECORDS Array

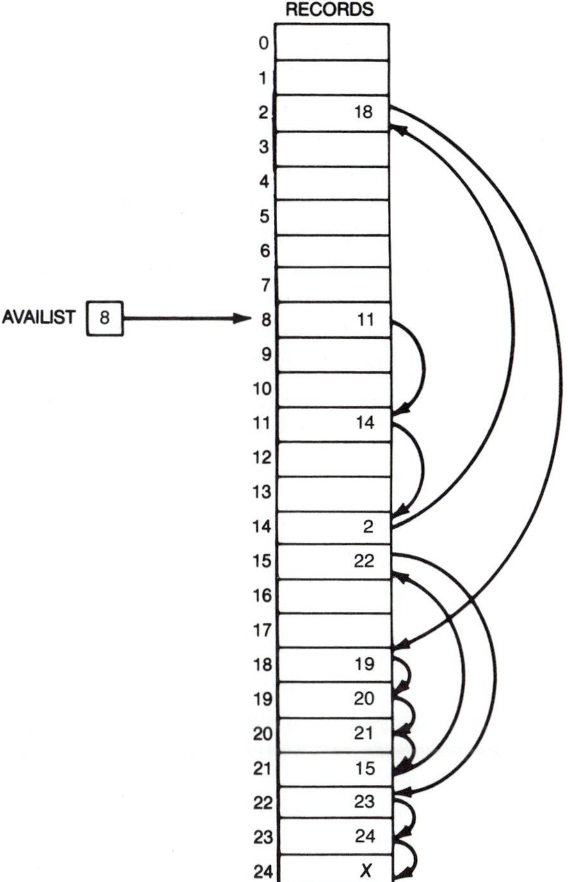

Figure 3.13 The List of Available Records Corresponding to Figure 3.12

When records are deleted from a list in programs, it is convenient to keep track of their storage for future use. This requires inserting the deleted records' storage on `availist`. Again, this operation can be done in constant time if the newly available record is inserted at the front of `availist`—as its new first record. The function that carries out this task will be called `reclaim`. What time is required for insertion if the record is inserted in the list other than at the front?

The programmer invokes `p = avail()` to request storage for a record to be stored in `records`, and `p` points to that storage when `avail` returns. The programmer invokes `reclaim(p)` to request that the storage in `records` pointed to by `p` be inserted on `availist`. By employing `avail` and `reclaim` appropriately, the programmer can dynamically allocate and reclaim storage for lists. This means that `records` can be viewed as the repository of all list records, thus acting as a miniature dynamic memory. Such routines are the heart of storage management algorithms. When the records of a list are not all of the same length, more complex management techniques must be used. When records can be shared, still more complexity is added to the storage management problem, as will be illustrated subsequently.

`Malloc` is the general C allocation function provided for the programmer's use, so that dynamic memory appears as an abstract facility for storing records. When no memory is available to be allocated, `malloc` returns a `NULL` value. Consequently, on each call to `malloc` the value returned should be checked to be certain it is not the `NULL` value. `Avail` may be written to abort or take whatever action is necessary for your application in the event memory is not available.

The C function `free` is provided to carry out the general task of `reclaim`. `Free` deallocates memory that was previously allocated by `malloc`. The argument to `free` has to be a pointer previously returned by `malloc` that has not already been freed. Once memory is freed, it can be used to satisfy new requests through `malloc`.

In languages such as FORTRAN, which do not provide dynamic memory, you can implement it through `avail` and `reclaim`. Once `avail` and `reclaim` are written, for all intents and purposes the language has dynamic memory for record storage. You have tailored it to your needs.

3.8 Sequential Arrays versus Lists for Record Storage

Arrays allow records to be stored contiguously and to be accessed randomly. With pointer arrays, random access is possible even for variable-length records. Lists are also data structures containing records. Lists provide the flexibility, when needed, to separate records—enhancing the ability to insert or delete, but reducing the capability of accessing records at random. Stored records can be traversed using either the sequential array or list implementation. The time to carry out the traversal need not be significantly different for the two methods.

Suppose that instead of processing the records in sequential order, as in a traversal, your program must access the records in arbitrary order. (In an airplane reservation system, for example, seat reservations must be processed immediately, in random order.) Having to access the records in arbitrary order means that the program must access and process the records even though the programmer cannot predict the order in which this must be done. The sequential representation, because it allows selection for fixed-length records, allows this random accessing to be accomplished in constant time. The list representation requires that random accessing be done by traversing to the needed record, starting from the first and accessing each succeeding record until the desired one is reached. If the required record is the ith, traversal will take time proportional to i. Thus randomly accessing records takes constant time for each record accessed with the sequential implementation, but time proportional to the desired record number for the list representation. This can result in significantly greater processing time for the list implementation when you are randomly processing records.

To insert one record in the collection (say, after the ith record) when using the sequential implementation, all succeeding records (the $(i + 1)$th, $(i + 2)$th, . . . , nth) must be moved down in the `data` array. This operation will take time proportional to the number of succeeding records $(n - 1)$. Adding a record as the new first record gives the worst-case time, which is proportional to n. Inserting a new record using the list implementation, again assuming you have determined where it is to be inserted, takes a constant time—the time needed to change two pointers.

To delete one record, say the ith, using the sequential representation, requires that the succeeding $i - 1$ records be moved up. Thus the time required is proportional to $i - 1$. Using the list implementation requires a constant time for this deletion—the time needed to change one pointer. The time for deletion with a sequential implementation in the worst case is also proportional to n. It is obvious that insertion and deletion of one record can result in much greater execution time for the sequential implementation as compared to the list implementation.

The contrast is especially striking when record accesses, insertions, or deletions are performed on m records. The worst-case time to randomly access an entire collection of m records becomes proportional to m and m^2, for the sequential and list implementations, respectively. For random insertions and deletions, these are reversed in favor of lists. This means that if m is doubled or tripled, the respective times increase fourfold or ninefold instead of merely doubling or tripling.

When selecting an implementation, the basic considerations are comparative execution times and relative frequencies for random access, insertion, or deletion.

The list implementation will require at least as much memory as the sequential implementation. For instance, if each record requires one element for the information field, and the list implementation requires another element for the link field, then lists would require twice as much storage. It is possible that part of the storage used to implement a record would be left unused in any case, so that using it for the link field requires no extra storage.

3.9 Case Study: Merging and the Perfect Shuffle

Consider two sequences of numbers that are ordered, largest to smallest:

100 80 65 30 90 85 50 10

They may be merged to produce a new sequence containing all the numbers in order. For example, compare the two largest and place the larger one first in the final sequence. Continue comparing the two current largest and placing the larger in the next spot in the final sequence until all numbers have been placed. The result, of course, is

100 90 85 80 65 50 30 10

This merging algorithm takes $2n$ basic operations when there are n numbers in each original sequence. It is possible to merge the sequences using a different algorithm, which, when parallel processing is possible, can reduce the time to $O(\lg 2n)$ rather than $O(2n)$ when n is a power of 2. It is not obvious how to do this. The solution involves

1. A "perfect shuffle" operation, for which we next develop a program
2. A compare-and-exchange operation, which we will discuss after the perfect shuffle

3.9.1 The Perfect Shuffle

Using gambling terminology, a ***perfect shuffle*** of $2n$ cards occurs when the deck of cards is split into two halves and the shuffle interleafs the two halves perfectly. An original configuration of eight cards, with the configurations after two consecutive perfect shuffles, is shown in Figure 3.14. The cards are numbered one through eight. A third perfect shuffle would produce the original configuration.

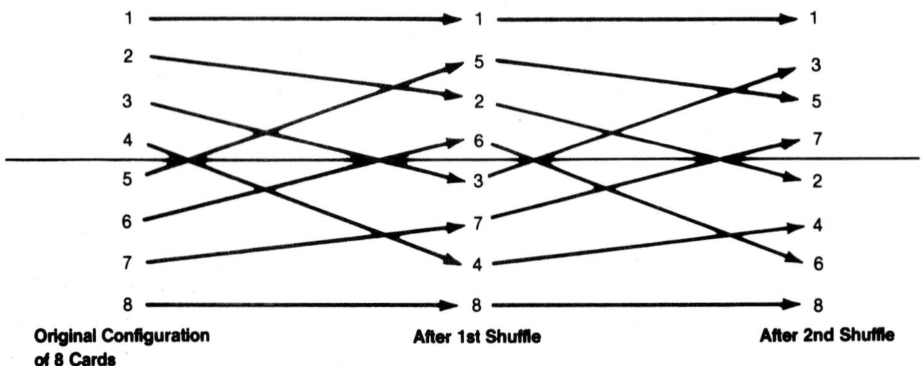

Figure 3.14 The Result of Two Perfect Shuffles

Suppose a sequence of perfect shuffles is made for $2n$ cards. Eventually the original configuration must reappear. How many shuffles will it take before this happens? One way to find out is to execute code that performs such a sequence of shuffles, keeping track of how many are made, and printing this total when the original configuration occurs again. A program segment to do this can be written as follows:

```
initial(configuration,n);
numbershuffles = 1;
perfectshuffle(configuration,n);
while(!original(configuration,n))
   {
      perfectshuffle(configuration,n);
      numbershuffles++;
   }
```

`Initial` initializes `configuration`. `Original` returns *true* if `configuration` is the original, and *false* otherwise. `Perfectshuffle` changes `configuration` so that it reflects the new configuration resulting from a perfect shuffle. As written, this code is independent of how the configuration is actually implemented.

3.9.2 Array Implementation of the Perfect Shuffle

Suppose we decide to implement `configuration` as an array and use `n` as a pointer to the card in position n. Then `initial` and `original` may be defined, respectively by

```
for(i=1;i<=(2*n);i++)                    ] initial
   configuration[i] = i;
```

and

```
temporiginal = TRUE;                     ] original
i = 1;
while((i<n+1)&&temporiginal)
   if(configuration[i] != i)
      temporiginal = FALSE;
   else
      i++;
original = temporiginal;
```

Perfectshuffle is somewhat more complex. The first and last cards, 1 and $2n$, never change position in **configuration**. After the shuffle, cards 1 and $n + 1$, 2 and $n + 2$, 3 and $n + 3$, . . . , **i** and n + **i** . . . , and n and $2n$ will appear in consecutive positions in the resultant configuration. An array, **result**, is used to hold the new configuration. In traversing the relevant n positions of **configuration** (the 0th is ignored), its **i**th entry is processed by copying **configuration[i]** and **configuration[i+n]** into their proper new consecutive positions in **result**. **I** serves as a pointer to the current entry of **configuration** being processed, and **newi** will point to the new position of that entry in **result**. The situation, when **n** is 6, is depicted in Figure 3.15(a) just before the fourth entry is to be processed.

If the following statements are executed

```
result[newi] = configuration[i];         ] process card i and i+n
result[newi+1] = configuration[i+n];       and update i and newi
i++;
newi = newi + 2;
```

then the program will have properly processed the **i**th and (**i+n**)th cards. It will also have updated **i** and **newi** so that they are pointing to the proper new positions, in **configuration** and **result**, respectively. The situation after the fourth element has been processed is as shown in Figure 3.15(b).

To complete the shuffle, **result** can be copied into **configuration**. A program segment for **perfectshuffle** might be as follows.

```
i = 1;                                   ] perfectshuffle
while(i < n)
   {
      result[newi] = configuration[i];
      result[newi+1] = configuration[i+n];
```

```
         i++;
         newi  =  newi + 2;
      }
   for(i=1;i<=(2*n);i++)
      configuration[i] = result[i];
```

Notice that the solution involves a number of array traversals, each traversal processing accessed elements in a different way.

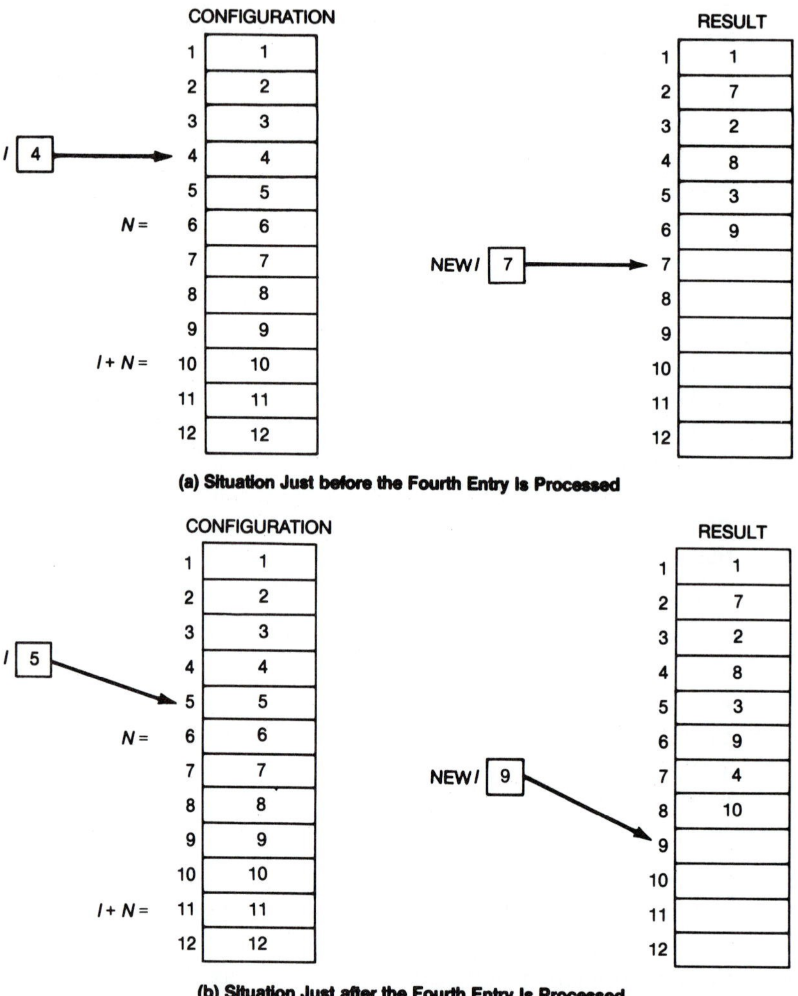

Figure 3.15 Two Arrays Used for a Perfect Shuffle of Six Elements

3.9.3 List Implementation of the Perfect Shuffle

Suppose you decided to implement `configuration` as a list of records stored in dynamic memory, and to use `n` as a pointer to the *n*th record of the `configuration` list. Figure 3.16 depicts these assumptions graphically for ten cards.

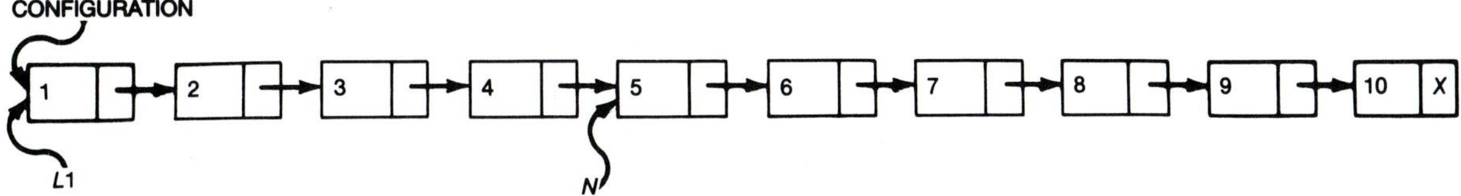

Figure 3.16 The List Implementation for CONFIGURATION

`Perfectshuffle` must, consecutively, move 6 before 2, 7 before 3, 8 before 4, and finally 9 before 5. Two pointers, `l1` and `n`, are shown in Figure 3.16. Traversing `configuration` and processing the records pointed to by `l1` and `n` will accomplish the movements, if the processing deletes the successor of the record pointed to by `n`, inserts this deleted record after the record pointed to by `l1`, and updates `l1` to point to it. `Move` carries out this processing task.

`Perfectshuffle` may now be implemented by

perfectshuffle

```
configurationpointer l1,newn;
l1 = configuration;
newn = l1;
while(l1 != n)
    {
        move(l1,n);
        l1 =l1->link;
        newn = newn->link;
    }
n = newn;
```

`Perfectshuffle` in this form is a refinement of `traverse`. `Move` plays the role of `process`. It uses local variables `hold1` and `hold2` to keep track of the successors needed:

move

```
move(pl1,n)
configurationpointer *pl1,n;
{
    configurationpointer hold1,hold2;
    hold1 = l1->link;
    hold2 = n->link;
    l1->link = hold2;
    n->link = hold2->link;
    hold2->link = hold1;
    l1 = l1->link;
}
```

Two complete programs that output the number of shuffles are presented at the end of this paragraph. The first is based on an array, and the second on a list implementation. In this case there is nothing to recommend the list implementation over the array implementation, since the configuration does not grow or shrink (except for the artificial limit on the array size that would be required by the array implementation). The two versions of **perfectshuffle** are both useful for the application to which we return in the section that follows the programs.

Array Implementation

```
#define TRUE 1
#define FALSE 0
typedef int arraytype[53];

main() /* Perfect shuffle using arrays */
/* Drives the perfectshuffle */
{
   arraytype configuration;
   int numbershuffles,n;
   printf("\n Enter an integer between 1 and 26 \n");
   scanf("%d",&n);
   initial(configuration,n);
   numbershuffles = 1;
   perfectshuffle(configuration,n);
   while(!original(configuration,n))
      {
         perfectshuffle(configuration,n);
         numbershuffles++;
      }
   printf("\n Number of shuffles = %d \n",numbershuffles);
}

initial(configuration,n)
/* Creates the initial configuration */
arraytype configuration;
int n;
{
   int i;
   for(i=1;i<=(2*n);i++)
      configuration[i] = i;
}

perfectshuffle(configuration,n)
/* Carries out a perfect shuffle */
arraytype configuration;
int n;
{
   arraytype result;
   int i,newi;
   i = 1;
   newi = 1;
   while(i < (n+1))
      {
         result[newi] = configuration[i];
         result[newi+1] = configuration[i+n];
```

the array must have 53 entries, since the 0th is not used

enter the number of cards in half a deck

first shuffle

shuffle until original configuration recurs, and keep count

traverses the configuration and processes each entry

does the processing of an entry

```
         i++;
         newi = newi + 2;
      }
   for(i=1;i<=(2*n);i++)
      configuration[i] = result[i];
}
```

updates

```
original(configuration,n)
/* Returns true if the original
   configuration has recurred
*/
arraytype configuration;
int n;
}
   int i,temporiginal;
   i = 1;
   temporiginal = TRUE;
   while((i < (n+1))&&temporiginal)
      if(configuration[i] != i)
         temporiginal = FALSE;
      else
         i++;
   return(temporiginal);
}
```

List Implementation

```
#define TRUE 1
#define FALSE 0
#define NULL 0
typedef struct configrec
{
   int info;
   struct configrec *link;
}configrecord,*configptr;
int num;
```

variables of type `configptr` *will point to a record of the list containing the configuration*

```
main() /* perfect shuffle using lists */
/* Drives the perfectshuffle */
{
   configptr configuration,n;
   int numbershuffles;
   printf("\n Enter an integer between 1 and 26\n");
   scanf("%d",&num);
   initial(&configuration,&n);
   numbershuffles = 1;
   perfectshuffle(configuration,&n);
   while(!original(configuration,n))
      {
         perfectshuffle(configuration,&n);
         numbershuffles++;
      }
```

enter the number of cards in half a deck

first shuffle

shuffle until the original configuration recurs, and keep count

```
   printf("\n The number of shuffles = %d\n",numbershuffles);
}

initial(pconfiguration,pn)
/* Creates the initial configuration */
configptr *pconfiguration,*pn;
{
   configptr p,q;
   int i;
   *pconfiguration = malloc(sizeof(configrecord));
   p = *pconfiguration;
   i = 1;
   while(i != (2*num+1))
      {
         p->info = i;
         if(i == num)
           *pn = p;
         i++;
         p->link = malloc(sizeof(configrecord));
         q = p;
         p = p->link;
      }
   q->link = NULL;
}

perfectshuffle(configuration,pn)
/* Carries out a perfect shuffle */
configptr configuration,*pn;
{
   configptr ll,newn;
   ll = configuration;
   newn = ll;
   while(ll != *pn)
      {
         move(&ll,*pn);

         ll = ll->link;
         newn = newn->link;
      }
   *pn = newn;
}

original(configuration,n)
/* Returns true if the original
   configuration has recurred
*/
configptr configuration,n;
{
   int temporiginal,i;
   configptr p;
   temporiginal = TRUE;
   i = 1;
```

traverses the configuration and processes each record

processes each record

updates

```
    p = configuration;
    while((p != n->link)&&temporiginal)
       if(p->info != i)
          temporiginal = FALSE;
       else
          {
             i++;
             p = p->link;
          }
    return(temporiginal);
}

move(pll,n)
/* Processes a record of configuration */
configptr *pll,n;
{
   configptr hold1,hold2;
   hold1 = (*pll)->link;
   hold2 = n->link;
   (*pll)->link = hold2;
   n->link = hold2->link;
   hold2->link = hold1;
   (*pll) = (*pll)->link;
}
```

3.9.4 Merging Sequences of Entries

Now that the perfect shuffle has been developed, let's return to the merging of two sequences. Set the first n entries of `configuration` to one of the sequences to be merged, and the second n entries of `configuration` to the other, but enter the second in reverse order.

Consider the following algorithm for merging two sequences of ordered (largest to smallest) entries, each of length n:

> Apply `perfectshuffle` and `compareexchange` to `configuration` a total of $2n$ times.

`Compareexchange` is a function that compares each of the n pairs of adjacent configuration entries and exchanges their values whenever the second is larger than the first. Table 3.3 shows the results obtained as this algorithm is applied to our sample sequences of length 4. Since $\lg 2n = \lg 8 = 3$, the algorithm terminates after the third perfect shuffle and compare-and-exchange operation. Notice that this results in `configuration` containing the correct merged sequence.

When $2n$ is a power of 2, say 2^k, then the k iterations always produce the correct merge. This is certainly not obvious, and it is not proven here, but one point is important. If this merge is implemented as a **for** loop and carried out conventionally (that is, sequentially), it will take time $O(n \lg n)$. The straightforward sequential merge discussed earlier takes only $O(n)$ time. However, if the n moves of `perfectshuffle` and the n pair comparisons and interchanges of

Table 3.3 The Result of Merging Two Sequences of Ordered Entries of Length 4

Initial Configuration	After First Perfect Shuffle	After First Compare Exchange	After Second Perfect Shuffle
100	100	100	100
80	10	10	85
65	80	80	10
30	50	50	65
10	65	85	80
50	85	65	90
85	30	90	50
90	90	30	30

After Second Compare Exchange	After Third Perfect Shuffle	After Third Compare Exchange
100	100	100
85	90	90
65	85	85
10	80	80
90	65	65
80	50	50
50	10	30
30	30	10

`compareexchange` are all done in parallel (at the same time), then the total time will be just $O(\lg n)$.

Parallel processing is beyond the scope of this text, but this application illustrates its power and some of the difficulties involved. Doing parallel processing correctly is tricky, since care must be taken to do the right thing at the right time. For instance, one could dress in parallel fashion, but certain constraints must be observed. Socks and shirt can be put on at the same time (a valet is needed of course, since a person has only two hands) followed by pants, with shoes and jacket next and in parallel. But shoes cannot go on before socks.

The perfect shuffle (and the topic of parallel processing) is pursued further in Stone [1971, 1980] and Ben-Ari [1982]. An application of these ideas to the stable marriage problem appears in Hull [1984].

■ Exercises

1. What record of a list has no pointer pointing to it from another list record? What record of a list has a null pointer in its link field?

2. If each record of a list has, in addition to its information and link fields, a "pred" field, then the list is called a *two-way list*. The pred field contains a pointer to the preceding record. The first record's pred field contains a null pointer. Write insertion and deletion functions corresponding to those of Section 3.3 for a two-way list.

3. A ***circular list*** is a list whose last record's link field contains a pointer to the first list record rather than a null pointer. Write insertion and deletion routines corresponding to those of Section 3.3 for a circular list.

4. Modify the solution to Example 3.1 so it is correct for
   a. A two-way list
   b. A circular list
5. Write a function to interchange the records of a list that are pointed to by `p1` and `p2`.
6. The solution developed for Example 3.1 essentially cycles pointers from one list record to the next. Instead, a solution could cycle information field values from one record to the next. Modify the solution so that it does this and compare the two execution times. What if the information field contains only a pointer to the actual information field value?
7. Consider the three arrays below—`data`, `p`, and `s`.

	DATA	P	S
0	1	−1	5
1	12	4	6
2	18	6	8
3	4	5	9
4	7	9	1
5	3	0	3
6	12	1	2
7	100	8	−1
8	20	2	7
9	5	3	4

An ordering of the integers in `data` is specified by `p` and by `s`. Arrays `p[i]` and `s[i]` point to the predecessor and successor of the integer stored in `data[i]`. A minus one indicates no predecessor or successor. Assume the first `i` elements of `data`, `p`, and `s` are properly set, as above, to reflect the usual ordering of integers. Suppose a new integer is placed into `data[i+1]`.

   a. If `i` is 10 and the new integer is 15, what will the new `p` and `s` arrays be after they are properly updated to reflect the correct ordering among the eleven integers? The `data` array, except for 15 being placed in position 10, is to be unchanged.
   b. Write a program segment to update `p` and `s` after a new integer is placed in `data`. You might want to assume that `first` and `last` point, respectively, to the element of `data` containing the first and last integers in the ordering.
8. a. What does `traverse` (Section 3.4) do when `process` interchanges the record that `recordpointer` points to with its successor record?
   b. Same as Exercise 8(a) except that, in addition, `process` then sets `recordpointer` to the link field value of the record to which it points.
9. Write a function to delete all the records from list `l1` that also appear on the list `l2`.

In Exercises 10–13 you must turn `traverse` of Section 3.4 into a solution to the exercise by defining its functions properly.

10. Write a function to delete all duplicate records from an alphabetical list such as that of Example 3.4.
11. Write a function to insert a new record in *front* of the record pointed to by `ptr`. You should not keep track of a predecessor nor traverse the list to find a predecessor. A "trick" is involved here (see Section 3.3.4).
12. This is the same as Example 3.4, but assume the list is implemented as a two-way list.
13. Create a new list that is the same as `l` except that each record has been duplicated, with the duplicate inserted as the new successor of the record it duplicates.

14. Create a list `l` that consists of all the records of the list `l1` followed by all the records of the list `l2`.
15. Write a function to print out the number of words for a list such as that of Example 3.2.
16. Write the required functions for `traverse` of Section 3.4 when list records are stored in dynamic memory and the list is implemented as

- **a.** A two-way list
- **b.** A circular list

17. A hospital has 100 beds. The array `records` contains records that represent, by floor and bed number, those beds that are not occupied. The first, second, and third elements of a record contain the floor number, bed number, and link value, respectively. How many beds are not occupied and what is the lowest floor with an available bed?

BEDS [ ]

	RECORDS		RECORDS
0	5	12	5
1	10	13	2
2	3	14	−1
3	7	15	2
4	10	16	5
5	12	17	21
6	3	18	5
7	6	19	10
8	3	20	1
9	7	21	7
10	3	22	1
11	15	23	0

18. Change the appropriate pointers for Exercise 17 so that the records are kept in order by floor and bed number.
19. Show what the arrays `floor`, `bed`, and `next` might have in their entries if the `beds` list of Exercise 17 were implemented using three corresponding words of these arrays.
20. How would the `records` array of Exercise 17 change if bed 2 on the fifth floor became occupied?
21. Suppose bed 10 on the sixth floor became empty. Assuming that the `records` array is used only for the `beds` list, what changes might be made to it to reflect this new information?
22. This is the same as Exercise 16 except that the list records are stored in an array `records`.
23. A ***palindrome*** is a sequence of characters that reads the same from front to back as from back to front. ABCDDCBA, ABCBA, and NOON are palindromes. Write a function `palindrome` to return the value *true* if the list it is called to check represents a palindrome, and the value *false* otherwise. The list records are stored in dynamic memory.
24. Suppose four records, 13, 7, 1, and 2, were deleted from lists whose records are stored in `records` of Figure 3.13. Then three records were inserted. If `reclaim` returns records at the front of `availist`, depict the `availist` and `records` after this processing.
25. Do the same as in Exercise 24, but assume that `reclaim` returns records at the rear of `availist`.
26. **a.** Why isn't it reasonable for `avail` to delete a record from anywhere on `availist` except the front or rear?
b. Why isn't it reasonable for `reclaim` to insert a record anywhere on `availist` except the front or rear?

27. Suppose a record is deleted from a list stored in `records`, but `reclaim` is not invoked to return it to `availist`. Is it ever possible to reuse the storage relinquished by that record?
28. Suppose records with different lengths are stored in `records` using the techniques of Chapter 2. The `availist` contains the available records in arbitrary order. Describe how `avail` and `reclaim` might be implemented.
29. This is the same as Exercise 28, except that the `availist` contains the available records ordered by length.
30. Write a function to create a list whose records are defined by

```
typedef struct node
{
   whatevertype info;
   struct node *linkptr;
   struct node *prevptr;
}listnode;
```

The input should consist of a sequence of information field values given in the order they should appear in the list. `Linkptr` points to the next record on the list, and `prevptr` points to the preceding record on the list.
31. Explain why pointer variables and the functions `malloc` and `free` remove the need for the programmer to manage storage for list records.
32. Both the sequential array and list representations for ordered records use arrays. Why are they different?
33. Suppose you are asked to store records that represent an inventory of books that are currently signed out from the library. Assume that frequent requests are made for output that includes the book title and the current borrower in alphabetical order by the borrower's name. Of course, books are frequently taken out and returned. Should a sequential array be used for the records or a list representation? Why?
34. Suppose records are stored using the sequential array implementation. Initially 1,000 records are stored. You are asked to delete every other record, starting with the first. After this deletion you must insert records before every third record, starting with the first record. Find an expression for the total number of shifts of records that must take place to accomplish these insertions and deletions.
35. Do Exercise 34, but instead of assuming a sequential implementation assume a list implementation.
36. Suppose you must access records in the order tenth, first, twelfth, thirtieth, and fiftieth. How much time will the five accesses take with a sequential representation, and how much time will they take with a list representation?
37. Describe a real-life situation in which the sequential array representation of ordered records is clearly more desirable, another in which the list representation is clearly favored, and a third situation that involves trade-offs between the two representations.
38. **a.** Write the `initial` and `original` routines for the array implementation of the perfect shuffle and for the list implementation of the perfect shuffle in Section 3.9.
b. Can `original` be reduced to checking only the nth card to see if it has returned to the initial configuration?

■ Suggested Assignments

1. Write and execute a program to input a series of lists, each of which contains a number of sentences. After inputting all the lists, the program should invoke functions `shorten` and `printlist` to work on each list. `Shorten` is to print each sentence of the list it is to deal with whose length exceeds 25, and delete such sentences from the list; `printlist` is to print the resultant list. You should write `shorten` by defining the functions of `traverse` so as to turn `traverse` into `shorten`. Use dynamic memory for record storage. Don't forget to echo print all input and annotate all output. Make up some fun sentences. Store one character in each list record, and, for simplicity, assume all sentences end with a period.

2. Modify your program (and run the new version) when three characters (instead of one) are stored per record. *Hint:* within a list, assume the first character of each sentence is stored in a new record rather than in the record containing the period of the previous sentence, even when it has the room.

Introduction to Recursion, Stacks, and Queues

Presents recursion as a special case of the top-down approach to problem solving
Explains recursive programs
  how to understand them
  how to simulate them
  how to write them
Shows how recursive programs may be translated by a compiler or written in a non-recursive language
Introduces two more data structures
  the stack
  the queue
Illustrates the use of a stack with operations
  setstack
  empty
  push
  pop
Case study—checking sequences for proper nesting
  uses the stack and treats it as a data abstraction

4.1 What Is Recursion?

People can't help but use themselves—their own life experiences—as a point of reference for understanding the world and the experiences of others. Definitions, algorithms, and programs may also refer to themselves, but for a different purpose: to express their meaning or intention more clearly and concisely. They are then said to be ***recursive.*** Languages such as C that allow functions to call themselves are called ***recursive languages.*** When no self-reference is allowed, languages are said to be *nonrecursive* or ***iterative.***

Self-reference is not without its pitfalls. You have most likely encountered the frustration of circular definitions in the dictionary, such as "Fashion pertains to style" and "Style pertains to fashion." From this you conclude that "Fashion pertains to fashion." This kind of self-reference conveys no information; it is to be avoided. "This sentence is false" is another type of self-reference to be avoided, for it tells us nothing. If true it must be false, and if false it must be true. Nevertheless, self-reference is an important technique in finding and expressing solutions to problems.

Recall that the top-down approach to problem solving entails breaking down an initial problem into smaller component problems. These components need not be related except in the sense that putting their solutions together yields a solution to the original problem. If any of these component problems is identical in structure to the initial problem, the solution is said to be recursive and the problem is said to be solved by recursion. If the solution and its components are functionally modularized, then the solution will refer to itself. Recursion is thus a special case of the top-down design methodology.

Suppose a traveler asks you, "How do I get there from here?" You might respond with a complete set of directions, but if the directions are too complex, or you are not sure, your response might be: "Go to the main street, turn left, continue for one mile, and then ask, "How do I get there from here?" This is an example of recursion. The traveler wanted directions to a destination. In solving the problem, you provided an initial small step leading toward the traveler's goal. After taking that step, the traveler will be confronted with a new version of the original problem. This new problem, while identical in form to the original, involves a new starting location closer to the destination.

Cursing is often used to belittle a problem; recursing has the same effect! Recursion, when appropriate, can give relatively easy-to-understand and concise descriptions for complex tasks. Still, care must be taken in its use, or else efficiency of storage and execution time will be sacrificed.

4.2 Using Recursion

Applying the recursive method is just like applying the top-down approach, but it can be tricky; it presents conceptual difficulties for many students. The purpose of this section is to show how to develop and understand recursive solutions. Some illustrative examples are provided to help you get the idea. Practice will help you become skilled in the use of recursion.

4.2.1 The Towers of Hanoi

A game called the Towers of Hanoi was purportedly played by priests in the Temple of Brahma, who believed that completion of the game's central task would coincide with the end of the world. The task involves three pegs. The version considered here has n disks initially mounted on peg 1 (the priests dealt with 64 disks). The n disks increase in size from top to bottom, the top disk being the smallest. The problem is to relocate the n disks to peg 3 by moving one at a time. Only the top disk on a peg can be moved. Each time a disk is moved it may be placed only on an empty peg or on top of a pile of disks of larger size. The task is to develop an algorithm specifying a solution to this problem, *no matter what the value of* n.

Consider the case when $n = 4$, shown in Figure 4.1(a). The following sequence of instructions provides a solution.

1. Move the top disk from peg 1 to peg 2.
2. Move the top disk from peg 1 to peg 3.
3. Move the top disk from peg 2 to peg 3.
4. Move the top disk from peg 1 to peg 2.
5. Move the top disk from peg 3 to peg 1.
6. Move the top disk from peg 3 to peg 2.
7. Move the top disk from peg 1 to peg 2.
8. Move the top disk from peg 1 to peg 3.

9. Move the top disk from peg 2 to peg 3.
10. Move the top disk from peg 2 to peg 1.
11. Move the top disk from peg 3 to peg 1.
12. Move the top disk from peg 2 to peg 3.
13. Move the top disk from peg 1 to peg 2.
14. Move the top disk from peg 1 to peg 3.
15. Move the top disk from peg 2 to peg 3.

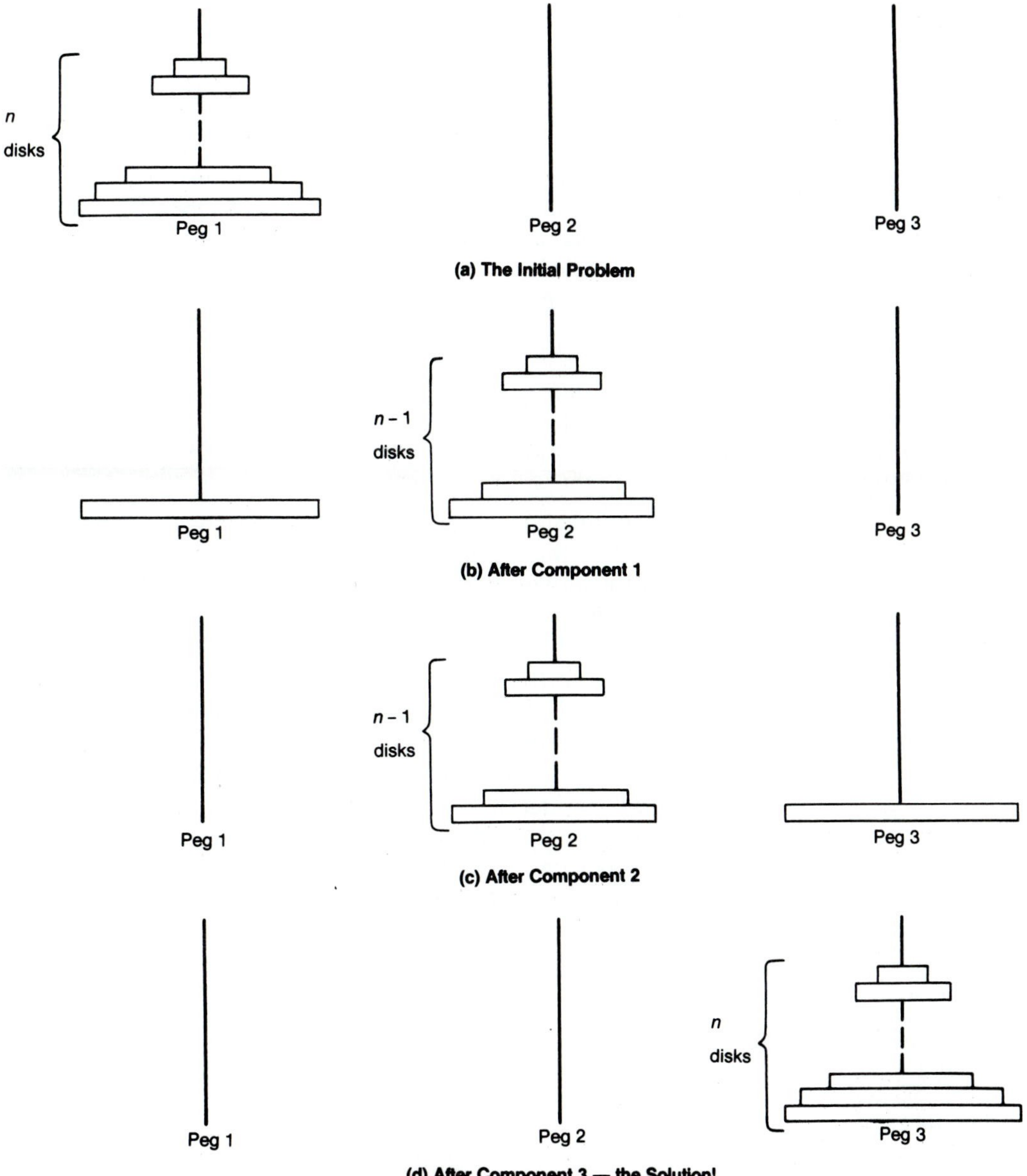

Figure 4.1 The Towers of Hanoi Problem

It is not difficult to arrive at such a solution for a specific small value of n. Try to find a solution for $n = 5$. You will find that, even though you succeed after some trial and error, creating a solution for $n = 25$ is indeed a formidable task. You may even be too old to care by the time you finish. If a particular value of n gives so much trouble, how does one specify a solution for *any* n, when one does not even know what value n will have?

One answer is to apply the technique of recursion. This means attempting to break down the problem into component problems that can be solved directly or that are identical to the original problem but involve a smaller number of disks. The three component problems below fit the requirements of this framework.

1. Move the top $n - 1$ disks from peg 1 to peg 2.
2. Move the top disk from peg 1 to peg 3.
3. Move the top $n - 1$ disks from peg 2 to peg 3.

If these three problems can be solved, and their solutions are applied in sequence to the initial situation, then the result is a solution to the original problem. This can be seen from parts (a)–(d) of Figure 4.1, which show the consecutive situations after each is applied.

We now generalize the original problem:

Move the top n disks from peg i to peg f.

i denotes the initial peg on which the top n disks to be relocated reside, and f denotes the final peg to which they are to be relocated. Let a denote the third available peg. Solving the original problem, which has *only* n disks, is equivalent to solving the generalized problem with i taken as 1 and f taken as 3. This is because the moves that accomplish its solution will also work for the generalized problem, since any disks below the top n are larger than they are, so their existence doesn't render any of the moves illegal. Solving the first component problem is equivalent to solving the generalized problem with n replaced by $n - 1$, i by 1, and f by 2. It is now apparent that the original problem, and the components 1, 2, and 3, have structure identical to the generalized problem, but the components involve fewer disks. They also involve different initial, available, and final pegs. This is why it was necessary to generalize the original problem.

Suppose you have found a solution to the generalization and denote it by `towers(n,i,a,f)`. Then, as just shown, the application of the solutions to components 1, 2, and 3, in sequence, will be a solution to the original problem. A recursive definition for `towers(n,i,a,f)` can now be expressed as follows. Note that moves in `towers(n,i,a,f)` are from peg `i` to peg `f`—that is, from the second parameter to the fourth parameter. The first parameter specifies the number of top disks, on the peg given by the second parameter, that are to be moved.

```
To obtain towers(n,i,a,f):                          moves top n disks from peg i to f
If n = 1, then
    move the top disk from peg i to peg f           special case n is 1
else
    apply towers(n - 1,i,f,a)                       moves top n - 1 disks from i to a
    move the top disk from peg i to peg f
    apply towers(n - 1,a,i,f).                      moves top n - 1 disks from a to f
```

This is the recursive algorithm for the Towers of Hanoi problem. Notice that the definition gives an explicit solution for the special case when n = 1 and an implicit solution for the case of n > 1.

To use the method of recursion we must recognize when it is applicable and find a correct way to generalize the original problem and then to break down the generalization. We have been successful and have found a recursive algorithm. Because no further refinement is needed, the corresponding recursive program can be written directly using functional modularization:

```
     towers(n,i,a,f)
     /* Moves the top n disks from peg i to peg f
     */
     int n,i,a,f;
     {
        if(n == 1)
           printf("\n %d -> %d\n",i,f);
        else
           {
              towers(n-1,i,f,a);
[1]           printf("\n %d -> %d\n",i,f);
              towers(n-1,a,i,f);
[2]        }
     }
```

The labels [1] and [2] are not part of the program but are used later as references when explaining the program. It is essential to see that this function has been written just like any other; whenever a component task is available as a function, we invoke it to carry out that task. The feature that distinguishes it and makes it a recursive function is that the required functions happen to be the function itself. The references within `towers` to itself are allowed in recursive languages.

Anytime a function calls itself during its execution, a ***recursive call*** has been made. The two invocations of `towers` within `towers` represent such recursive calls. In general, when a recursive program executes on a computer, or when its execution is simulated, many recursive calls will be made. Simulation of a program or function call means carrying out its instructions by hand and keeping track of the values of all its variables. These are referred to as the first, second, etc., recursive calls. The initial call to the function precedes the first recursive call.

4.2.2 Verifying and Simulating a Recursive Program

The verification of a recursive program can be done in two ways, as is true for a nonrecursive program. One is by formal proof, the other by checking all cases. With recursion, the cases given explicitly are checked first. A case is given explicitly when the action taken by the program in that case does not require a recursive call. Also, it is assumed that each function individually works correctly. For `towers(n,i,a,f)`, the only explicit case is when n = 1 and the function clearly outputs the proper result and terminates.

For the case when `n` exceeds 1, Figure 4.1 has already confirmed that as long as the three component functions work properly, then `towers(n,i,a,f)` will also. Note that these components correspond to smaller values of `n`. Mathematically inclined readers may recognize that this really amounts to a proof of correctness for `towers` using mathematical induction on `n`. One of the advantages of recursive programs is that they may be proven correct more easily in this way.

In order to understand how a recursive program actually executes, it is necessary to simulate its execution. Below are the first few steps of the simulation for a call to `towers(n,i,a,f)` with the values 4, 1, 2, 3—that is, `towers(4,1,2,3)`. It will soon become apparent that considerable bookkeeping is involved, requiring an organized way to do it.

Since `n` is greater than 1, the procedure requires the sequential execution of

```
towers(3,1,3,2)
printf("\n %d -> %d\n",1,3);
```

and

```
towers(3,2,1,3)
```

To do this requires suspending the execution of `towers(4,1,2,3)` at this point in order to simulate the first recursive call, `towers(3,1,3,2)`. Note that after this recursive call is completed, 1→3 is to be output. (1 → 3 means "Move the top disk from peg 1 to peg 3.") Then another recursive call must be simulated, `towers(3,2,1,3)`.

Dealing with `towers(3,1,3,2)`, since `n` > 1, the commands

```
towers(2,1,2,3)
printf("\n %d -> %d\n",1,2);
```

and

```
towers(2,3,1,2)
```

must be carried out sequentially. Now the execution of `towers(3,1,3,2)` must be suspended in order to simulate the second recursive call, `towers(2,1,2,3)`. Note that after this recursive call is completed, 1 → 2 is to be output, and then another recursive call must be simulated: `towers(2,3,1,2)`.

Dealing with `towers(2,1,2,3)`, since `n` > 1,

```
towers(1,1,3,2)
printf("\n %d -> %d\n",1,3);
```

and

```
towers(1,2,1,3)
```

must be carried out sequentially. These two calls to `towers` represent the third and fourth recursive calls. They both complete without generating any new recursive calls. The three statements result in the outputting of 1→ 2, 1→ 3, and 2→ 3, respectively. This completes the second recursive call (`towers(2,1,2,3)`) so we must pick up the simulation at the proper point, which is to output 1 → 2 and then make the fifth recursive call to simulate `towers(2,3,1,2)`.

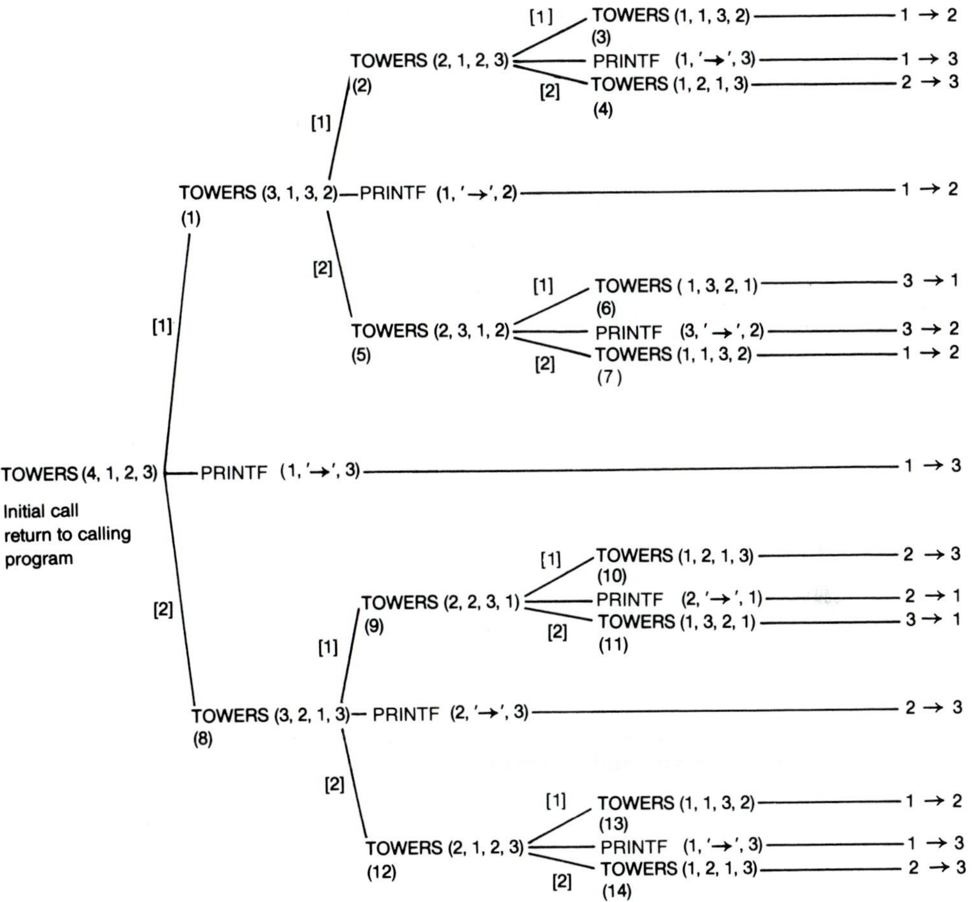

Figure 4.2 Bookkeeping for the Simulation of a Recursive Program

Enough is enough! At this point you may feel like a juggler with too few hands and too many recursive calls. Figure 4.2 represents a convenient way to keep track of the complete simulation; it may be generated as the simulation proceeds. The figure traces the recursive calls made to `towers` as the initial call to `towers(4,1,2,3)` is executed to completion. Each recursive call is numbered to show whether it is the first, second, . . . , or fourteenth. The bracketed return values indicate the labeled statement of procedure `towers` at which the preceding recursive call is to resume when the next call is completed. For example, when `towers(3,1,3,2)` is completed, `towers(4,1,2,3)` resumes at [1]. Our simulation stopped just as the fifth recursive call was to be carried out. The figure uses shorthand for the output. For example, 1 → 2 means, "move the top disk from peg 1 to peg 2." The solution is the same as our earlier one.

Figure 4.2 indicates very clearly what information must be available at each point in the simulation (or execution of the program) in order to carry it out. Specifically, it is necessary to know the following information:

- The four parameter values of the call currently being carried out
- Where to resume when the call currently being carried out is completed

For example, when the third recursive call is completed, resumption must be at the `printf` statement of the second recursive call; when the fifth recursive call is completed, resumption must be at the end of the first recursive call; and finally, after the initial recursive call is completed, resumption must be at the proper point in the program that called `towers` originally.

Notice that the last three parameters are never modified by `towers`, but the first parameter, which corresponds to the number of disks for the current problem, is modified. For instance, the first recursive call to `towers(3,1,3,2)` has modified the first parameter, making it 3 rather than 4 as it was initially. It is important that this modification be kept local to `towers(3,1,3,2)`, not reflected back to `towers(4,1,2,3)`, the initial call.

It is not always possible to find a recursive solution to a problem, nor is it always desirable to use one when available. Sometimes a recursive solution is the only one we can find. For the Towers of Hanoi problem it is difficult to find a nonrecursive solution, but a number are known. Recursive solutions normally make it easier to see why they are correct, probably because to achieve them requires that you make the structure inherent in the problem more explicit.

To make this point clearly, the recursive algorithm and a nonrecursive algorithm are repeated here. Convince yourself that the nonrecursive algorithm solves the Towers of Hanoi problem correctly (see Exercise 8). The nonrecursive program is taken from Walsh [1982]; another nonrecursive program appears in Buneman and Levy [1980].

A Recursive Solution for the Towers of Hanoi

To obtain `towers(n,i,a,f)`:
If `n` = 1, then
    move the top disk from `i` to `f`
else
    apply `towers(n - 1,i,f,a)`
    move the top disk from `i` to `f`
    apply `towers(n - 1,a,i,f)`.

A Nonrecursive Algorithm for the Towers of Hanoi

1. Label the disks 1, 2, . . . , `n` in increasing order of size.
2. Label the pegs `i`, `a`, and `f`, `n` + 1, `n` + 2, and `n` + 3, respectively.
3. Move the smallest disk onto another disk with an even label or onto an empty peg with an even label.
4. While all disks are not on the same peg
    a. move the second smallest top disk onto the peg not containing the smallest disk
    b. move the smallest disk onto another disk with an even label or onto an empty peg with an even label.

The Tower of Babel failed for lack of communication. The construction workers did not speak the same language. While recursion allows the solution to the Towers of Hanoi to be specified conveniently, it is execution time that causes trouble. The diagram of Figure 4.1 shows that the construction of the new tower of disks will take $2^4 - 1$ or fifteen moves. It is not difficult to generalize the diagram to n disks to conclude that $2^n - 1$ moves will be needed for n disks (see Exercise 7). Even with Olympic-caliber construction workers, it would take over one thousand years to complete the tower for 50 disks.

4.2.3 The Length of a List

We will now present a series of functions to further illustrate recursive programs. The functions

1. Determine the length of a list
2. Create a list that is a copy of another list
3. Count checkerboard placements
4. Generate all permutations of n integers and process each one. (This is applied to the stable marriage problem.)

In addition to providing repetition so that you can become more familiar with and understand recursion better, the examples provide a background to show how local and global variables and parameters are treated in recursive programs and why recursive solutions are not always the best. A list may be thought of as being either a null list or as one record followed by another list (the link field of the record plays the role of the head of this other list). This is nothing but a way to define a list recursively. Consider the recursive function defined by

```
length(listname)
/* Returns the number of records
   in the list pointed to by listname.
*/
listpointer listname;
{
   listpointer setnull(),next();
   if(listname == setnull())
      return(0);
   else
      return(1 + length(next(listname)));
}
```

returns zero for a null list

This function returns the length of the list, `listname`. To verify that this is correct we must check

1. The null list. It returns with `length` = 0.
2. A one-record list followed by another list. It returns `length` = 1 + the length of the list after the first record.

It is correct, since its value is correct for each case. Of course it is correct—after all, the length of a null list is zero, and the length of a list with at least one record is 1 for the record, plus the length of the rest of the list beyond the first record! This was how `length` was written in the first place.

4.2.4 Copying a List

Consider the function `copy`, which creates a list `second` that is a copy of a list `first`:

```
copy(first,psecond)
/* Creates a new list which is a copy
   of the list pointed to by first and
   whose head is second
*/
listpointer first,*psecond;
{
   listpointer null,rest,setnull(),avail(),next();
   null = setnull();
   if(first == null)
      *psecond = null;                 ] second should be set to null when first is null
   else
      {
         *psecond = avail();           ] sets second to storage for a copy of first's first
                                         record
         setinfo(*psecond,first);      ] copies its info field into that storage's info field
         copy(next(first),&rest);      ] creates a copy of the rest of first and makes rest
                                         its head
         setlink(*psecond,rest);       ] appends the list rest to the list second
      }
}
```

When `first` is the null list, `copy` faithfully terminates with the copy also a null list. When `first` is a one-record list, `copy` sets `second` to point to storage allocated for a record and sets the information field value of this record to the value of the information field in `first`'s first record. The recursive call to `copy (next(first),&rest)` is then an invocation of `copy` to copy the null list, since `next(first)` is null in this case. Assuming it performs its task correctly, `rest` will be null when it returns. The link field of the record pointed to by `second` is then set to the value of `rest` (the null pointer), and the initial call to `copy` terminates correctly.

Similarly, had there been more than one record in `first`'s list, the recursive call to `copy` would have returned with `rest` pointing to a correct copy of the list pointed to by `next(first)`. `Setlink` would correctly place a pointer to that correct copy into the link field of the record pointed to by `second`, and the initial call would terminate correctly. This verifies that `copy` is correct in all cases. Again, to copy the null list is easy. To copy a list with at least one record, simply copy that record, copy the rest of the list beyond the first record, and append that copy to the copy of the first record. This is how `copy` was written!

If you are confronted with a recursive program and want to understand it, approach it in the same way as you would a nonrecursive program. Assume that any functions that are called perform their functions correctly, and then attempt to see what the program itself does. Sometimes this will be apparent, as it was for `towers` and `copy`, and sometimes a simulation of the program helps to increase comprehension. Imagine, for example, that you were not told what `copy` did. It wouldn't have been so easy to find out without simulating some simple cases.

4.2.5 Local and Global Variables and Parameters

In order to understand what happens as a recursive program executes, it is necessary to review how local and global variables are treated, and also how parameters are treated. This must also be known to understand what happens when any program executes.

In nonrecursive programs, references to global and to static variables always refer to the current actual storage assigned to them. Hence any changes to their values during execution of the program will be reflected back in their values. Local automatic variables are treated differently. Local copies are made, and these are referred to during the execution of the function to which they are local. If the local variables are automatic, the storage for the local copies disappears when the function terminates or returns. If the local variables are static, the storage remains after the function is terminated, and the variable retains its value for the next time the function is called.

This situation holds for recursion also. Each recursive call to a function produces its own copies of automatic local variables. Thus there may be many different values for the same local variable—each applicable to its own invocation of the function. As with nonrecursion, there is only one storage allocation for a global or a static variable, and it holds the last value of the variable.

Parameters passed in the argument lists of functions are treated as variables local to the function. They are passed by value. New storage is established for each parameter. The storage is initially set to the value of the corresponding actual parameter when the function is invoked. In effect, this storage represents a *local copy* of the actual parameter. Any reference in the function is interpreted as a reference to the local copy only. This implies that any change to a parameter during the execution of the function will *not* be reflected back to the storage used for the actual parameter; it can not have its value changed by the function.

The only way to change the original value of a variable used as a parameter is to pass the *address* of the parameter instead of its value. This is done automatically in the case of arrays and character strings. When an array is passed as a parameter, the address of the first storage location in the array is passed. This negates the need to make local copies of all the values of the array in the function and thus waste memory. Addresses for parameters can also be passed as pointers. A copy is made in the function and is local to the function. Using the pointer, the value of the parameter can be changed.

Here is a simple example.

```
simple(x,py)
int x,*py;
{
    x = 1;
    *py = 2;
    *py = x + *py;
}
```

Suppose that `simple` is invoked with actual parameters `a` and `b`, containing 0 and 1 respectively. It is invoked by the statement, `simple(a,&b)`. Within the function, `x` initially has a copy of `a` as its value—0 in this case. `y` refers to the storage for `b`—that is, `y` is a pointer to the storage for `b`. The first statement of `simple` causes `x` to assume the value 1, the second statement causes the storage for `b` to contain 2, and the third statement sets the storage for `b` to 3. When the calling program continues, `a` will still be 0, but `b` will be 3.

Parameters of recursive programs are treated in just this way. Any time a recursive call is made within a recursive program, the recursive call acts just like a call to any function. The only difference is that, since a recursive function may generate many recursive calls during its execution, many local copies of its parameters may be produced. References to a parameter by value during the execution of each recursive call will then mean the current local copy of that parameter. Reference to a parameter passed by a pointer to it always means the same actual parameter.

In the recursive version of `copy`, note that

- `Null` and `rest` are local variables of the initial call to `copy` and remain local variables in all subsequent recursive calls. Local copies of `null` and `rest` are thus made on any call to `copy`.
- `First` is passed by value and `second` by pointer.
- Whenever `copy` is executing and generates a recursive call to `copy(next(first),&rest)`, the actual **first parameter** of `copy` is the current copy of `next(first)`—i.e., the copy associated with the currently executing call to `copy`. Any references to the **first parameter** during the generated recursive call refer to the new local copy associated with that call.

When `first` points to the list as shown in Figure 4.3, and `copy(first, second)` is executed, the sequence of events and memory configurations that will take place appear in Figure 4.4. `First0`, `first1`, `first2`, `first3` refer to the local copies of the actual **first parameter** associated with the initial, first, second, and third recursive calls to `copy`, respectively. Similarly for the other variables. A question mark indicates an as yet undefined value. Be sure you understand Figure 4.4 and how it represents the execution of `copy`.

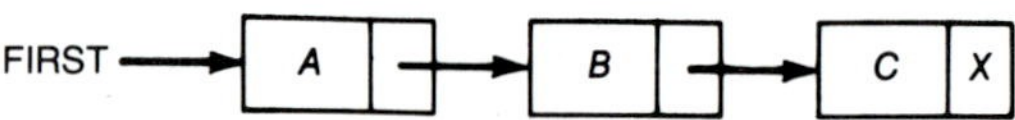

Figure 4.3 The List for COPY to Process

An alternative version of `copy` that returns a pointer to the copy of the list `first` would be as shown on page 160.

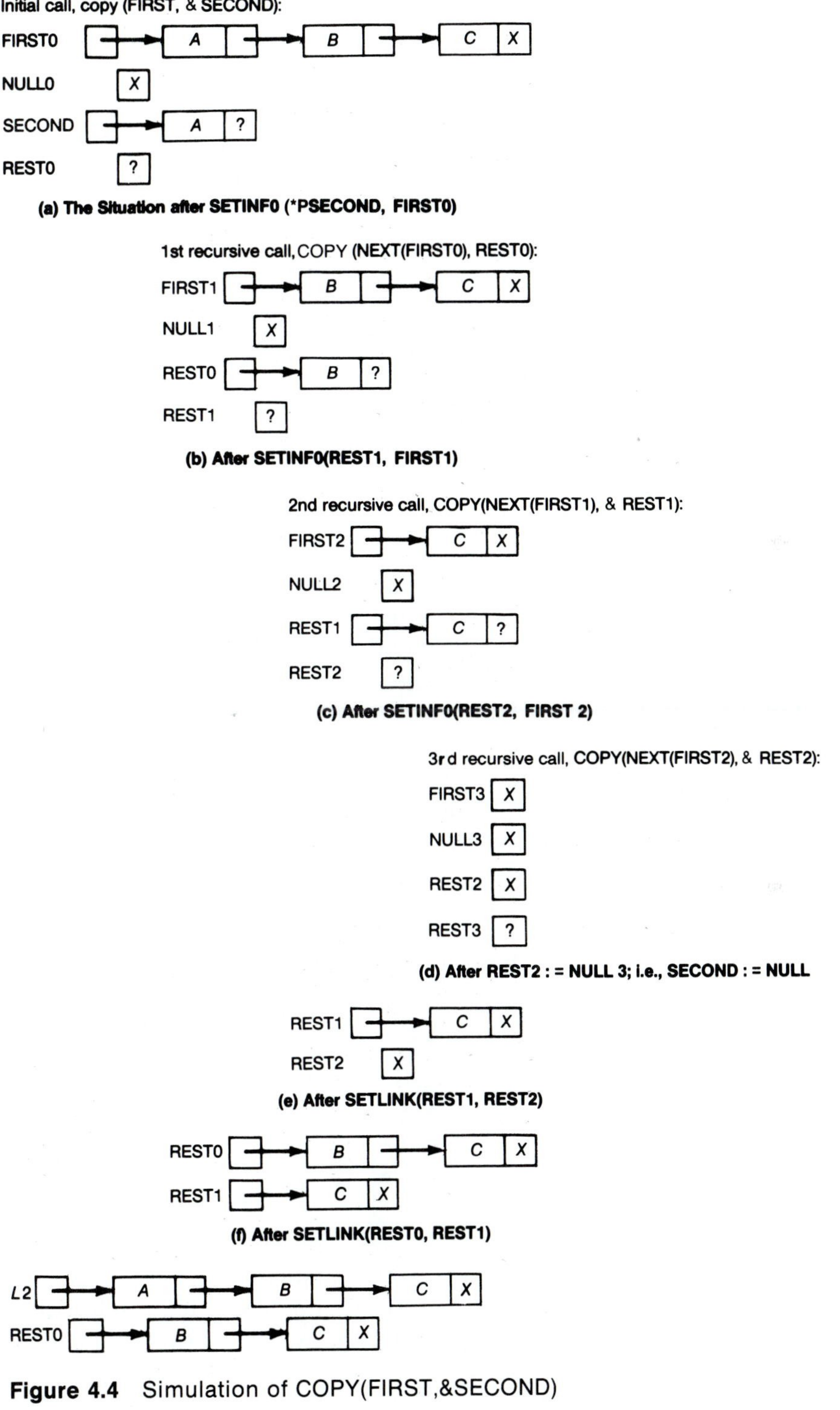

Figure 4.4 Simulation of COPY(FIRST,&SECOND)

```
listpointer copy(first)
/* Returns a pointer to the first record of a new list which is a
   copy of the list first.
*/
listpointer first;
{
   listpointer null,second,setnull(),avail(),next();
   null = setnull();
   if (first == null)
      second = null;
   else
      {
         second = avail();

         setinfo(second,first);

         setlink(second,copy(next(first)));
      }
      return(second);
}
```

- `first` *is null, so the returned pointer must be null*
- *sets* `second` *to storage for a copy of* `first's` *first record*
- *copies its info field into that storage's info field*
- `copy` *returns with a pointer to a copy to the rest of* `first`*, and* `setlink` *appends that copy to* `second`

This version differs from the original version in two ways. One, it has only one parameter, the list to be copied, and two, it returns a pointer to the new copy rather than setting a second parameter to point to the new copy.

4.2.6 Counting Squares

The third example relates to counting squares. Consider an $n \times n$ checkerboard and determine the number of ways a 4×4 checkerboard can be placed on it. For example, if $n = 5$, there are four ways to place a 4×4 checkerboard on the 5×5 board, as shown below.

```
|×|×|×|×| |        | |×|×|×|×|
|×|×|×|×| |        | |×|×|×|×|
|×|×|×|×| |        | |×|×|×|×|
|×|×|×|×| |        | |×|×|×|×|
| | | | | |        | | | | | |
     1                  2
| | | | | |        | | | | | |
|×|×|×|×| |        | |×|×|×|×|
|×|×|×|×| |        | |×|×|×|×|
|×|×|×|×| |        | |×|×|×|×|
|×|×|×|×| |        | |×|×|×|×|
     3                  4
```

For this particular example the solution is easy to see by inspection. However, how do you state an algorithm that produces the result in all cases? This can be done handily using recursion. Suppose you know the number of ways, $f(n - 1)$, in which the 4×4 board can be placed on an $(n - 1) \times (n - 1)$ board. An additional $(n - 3) + (n - 4)$ placements result from an $n \times n$ board, because of the n cells

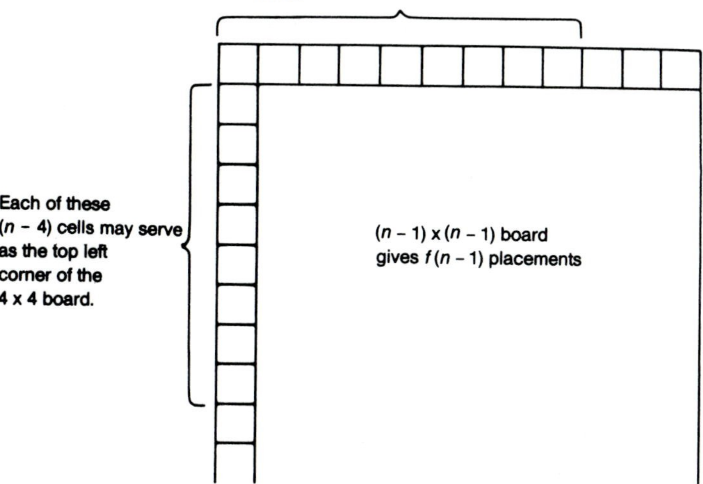

Figure 4.5 An $n \times n$ Checkerboard

added at the top and left sides of the $(n - 1) \times (n - 1)$ board, as shown in Figure 4.5. There are a total of $f(n) = f(n - 1) + (n - 3) + (n - 4)$ placements for the $n \times n$ board, when $n \geq 5$. If $n = 4$, $f(4) = 1$. So the following is true.

$f(n)$ is
  1 if $n = 4$
  $f(n - 1) + (n - 3) + (n - 4)$ if $n \geq 5$

It is easy to write a recursive function `f`, with parameter `n`, to return the correct result for any `n` ≥ 4.

```
f(n)
int n;
{
   if (n == 4)
      return(1);                          ] explicit case n = 1
   else
      return(f(n-1)+(n-3)+(n-4));         ] uses the result for an (n - 1) × (n - 1) board and adds
                                            the new possibilities due to another column and row
}
```

If `n` = 7, the program would execute as follows:

$f(7) = f(6) + (7 - 3) + (7 - 4)$] calls $f(n)$ with $n = 6$
$f(6) = f(5) + (6 - 3) + (6 - 4)$] calls $f(n)$ with $n = 5$
$f(5) = f(4) + (5 - 3) + (5 - 4)$] calls $f(n)$ with $n = 4$
$f(4) = 1$] evaluates $f(4)$ directly
$f(5) = 1 + 2 + 1 = 4$] evaluates $f(5)$ using $f(4)$

$f(6) = 4 + 3 + 2 = 9$] evaluates $f(6)$ using $f(5)$
$f(7) = 9 + 4 + 3 = 16$] evaluates $f(7)$ using $f(6)$

A simpler, more direct solution can be obtained by noticing that the top left corner of the 4×4 board can be placed in the first, second, . . . , $(n - 3)$th position of the top row of the $n \times n$ board, resulting in $(n - 3)$ different placements. The second row also allows $(n - 3)$ placements. In fact, each of the first $(n - 3)$ rows allows $(n - 3)$ placements, for a total of $(n - 3) \times (n - 3)$ distinct placements. Thus $f(n) = (n - 3) \times (n - 3)$ for $n \geq 4$. The program for this solution would be

```
f(n)
int n;
{
    return((n-3)*(n-3));
}
```

The recursive solution will take time and storage $O(n)$, whereas the nonrecursive solution requires constant time and storage. Obviously, this solution is better in every way than the recursive solution to this problem. Hence recursion does not always yield the best solution. Just as with any tool, it must be used judiciously. You wouldn't use a bulldozer to dig a two-foot hole in your yard.

4.2.7 Permutations

The final example returns to the stable marriage problem. Suppose you are asked to find a stable pairing for the n men and women of the stable marriage problem in Chapter 2, but you aren't aware of the algorithm discussed in Section 2.5. Probably the most straightforward approach is to search through all the possible pairings until a stable pairing is found. Each possible pairing may be thought of as a specific permutation of the n women. Thus the example pairing of Table 2.2 corresponds to the permutation (or listing) 4, 3, 1, 2, 5. In general there are $n!$ such permutations (where $n!$ means n factorial).

This approach yields a program that traverses the collection of permutations, processing each one and halting when a stable permutation is encountered. `Stable` may be conveniently invoked to check a permutation for stability. In contrast, the algorithm of Section 2.5 avoids such an exhaustive search by eliminating some permutations from consideration altogether. Still, many problems require just such an exhaustive search and contain a component to produce the permutations. The problem is to write a program to carry out the traversal. The function `permutations` does this:

```
permutations(n)
/* Generates and processes each
   permutation of the integers
   1 to n.
*/
int n;
```

```
{
    int done;
    done = FALSE;
    initialize(n);          ] creates the initial permutation
    while (!done)
        {
            process(n);     ] does the processing on the current permutation—for the stable marriage
                              problem this would be a stability check
            next(n,&done);  ] generates the next permutation
        }
}
```

where **next(n,&done)** must return, having updated the current permutation to the next permutation, unless the current permutation is the last one, when it simply sets done to *true*.

The problem is now to refine **next**. Suppose $n = 4$ and the first permutation is 3 2 1. Inserting 4 in all possible positions among 1, 2, and 3 gives the first four permutations of 1, 2, 3, and 4.

$\underline{4}$ 3 2 1
3 $\underline{4}$ 2 1
3 2 $\underline{4}$ 1
3 2 1 $\underline{4}$

Removing 4 leaves 3 2 1. The next four permutations for $n = 4$ can be obtained by first obtaining the next permutation after 3 2 1 for $n = 3$. But this next permutation for $n = 3$ can similarly be obtained by shifting 3 to the right one place, yielding 2 3 1. Then the next four permutations for $n = 4$ are

$\underline{4}$ 2 3 1
2 $\underline{4}$ 3 1
2 3 $\underline{4}$ 1
2 3 1 $\underline{4}$

Removing 4 leaves 2 3 1. Again, the next permutation after 2 3 1, 2 1 3, is obtained by shifting 3 right. The next four permutations for $n = 4$ are

$\underline{4}$ 2 1 3
2 $\underline{4}$ 1 3
2 1 $\underline{4}$ 3
2 1 3 $\underline{4}$

Continuing this process will produce, in turn,

$\underline{4}$ 3 1 2	$\underline{4}$ 1 3 2		$\underline{4}$ 1 2 3
3 $\underline{4}$ 1 2	1 $\underline{4}$ 3 2		1 $\underline{4}$ 2 3
3 1 $\underline{4}$ 2	1 3 $\underline{4}$ 2		1 2 $\underline{4}$ 3
3 1 2 $\underline{4}$	1 3 2 $\underline{4}$	and	1 2 3 $\underline{4}$

Generalizing, we see that, given a permutation of the n integers from 1 to n, the next permutation can be generated by shifting n to the right whenever possible. The only time this is not possible is if n is already at the right end. The next permutation must then be generated by removing n and replacing the leftmost $n - 1$ integers, which must be a permutation of the integers from 1 to $n - 1$, by their next permutation. If n is 1, then the last permutation has been produced. This provides a recursive definition for **next**.

```
next(n,pdone)
If n is not 1, then
    If n is not at the right end of the current permutation of 1, . . . , n then
        shift it right one position
    else
        remove "n" from the current permutation of 1, . . . , n
        next(n - 1,pdone)
        Insert "n" at the left end of the current permutation of 1, . . . , n - 1
else
    set done to true.
```

In order to proceed, a data structure to store the permutation must be chosen. To illustrate the effect of this selection, we will use two different structures—arrays and lists. We start by storing the permutation in an array `p`. Searching for the location of `n` in `p` will be avoided by keeping an array `l` of pointers. Both `p` and `l` are defined globally. `l[n]` points to the location of `n` in `p` when **`next(n, pdone)`** is invoked. **`Initialize`** must set `p[i]` to `n - i + 1` and `l[i]` to 1 for $1 \le$ `i` $\le$ `n`. **`Next`** may be defined as

```
next(n,pdone)
/* Generates the next permutation unless
   the current one is the last. In this case
   done is set to true.
*/
int n,*pdone;
{
   int i;
   if (n > 1)                          ] if there is another permutation
      if (l[n] < n)
         {
            p[l[n]] = p[l[n]+1];       ] the integer n is not at the right end, so shift it
            p[l[n]+1] = n;
            l[n] = l[n]+1;
         }
      else                             ] n is at the right end
         {
            next(n-1,pdone);           ] recursive call to get the next permutation of 1 to n-1
            for (i=n-1;i>=1;i--)       ] put n at the left end of that permutation
               p[i+1] = p[i];
```

```
            p[l] = n;                    ]
            l[n] = l;                    ]
         }
    else                                 ] no next permutation, so done
       *pdone = TRUE;                    ]
}
```

Figure 4.6(a) simulates the execution of `next(4,pdone)` when the current permutation is 2 1 3 4.

Now suppose `p` is implemented as a list whose records are stored in dynamic memory. We need the pointer arrays `ptr` and `pred`, which are defined globally, as is the record pointer `p`. When `next(n,pdone)` is invoked, `ptr[n]` will contain a pointer to the record containing `n` in its information field, and `pred[n]` will contain a pointer to the predecessor of that record in `p`. To simplify list shifts and the insertion of a record at the front of `p`, a dummy record is used as the first record of `p`. `Pred[k]` will initially contain a pointer to the dummy record, and `ptr[k]` will initially contain a pointer to the record of `p` that contains `k`, for 1 ≤ `k` ≤ `n`. Now `next` may be defined as follows:

```
next(n,pdone)
/* Generates the next permutation unless
   the current one is the last. In this case
   done is set to true.
*/
int n,*pdone;
{
   if (n > 1)                                    ] if there is another permutation
      if (ptr[n]->link != NULL)
         {
            pred[n]->link = ptr[n]->link;        ] the integer n is not at the right end, so
            pred[n] = pred[n]->link;             ] shift it
            ptr[n]->link = pred[n]->link;        ]
            pred[n]->link = ptr[n];              ]
         }
      else                                       ] n is at the right end
         {
            pred[n]->link = NULL;
            next(n-1,pdone);                     ] recursive call to get the next permutation
                                                   of 1 to n-1
            ptr[n]->link = p->link;              ] put n at the left end of that permutation
            p->link = ptr[n];                    ]
            pred[n] = p;                         ]
         }
      else                                       ] no next permutation, so done becomes
         *pdone = TRUE;                          ] true
}
```

Figure 4.6(b) simulates the execution of `next(4,pdone)` when the current permutation is 2 1 3 4.

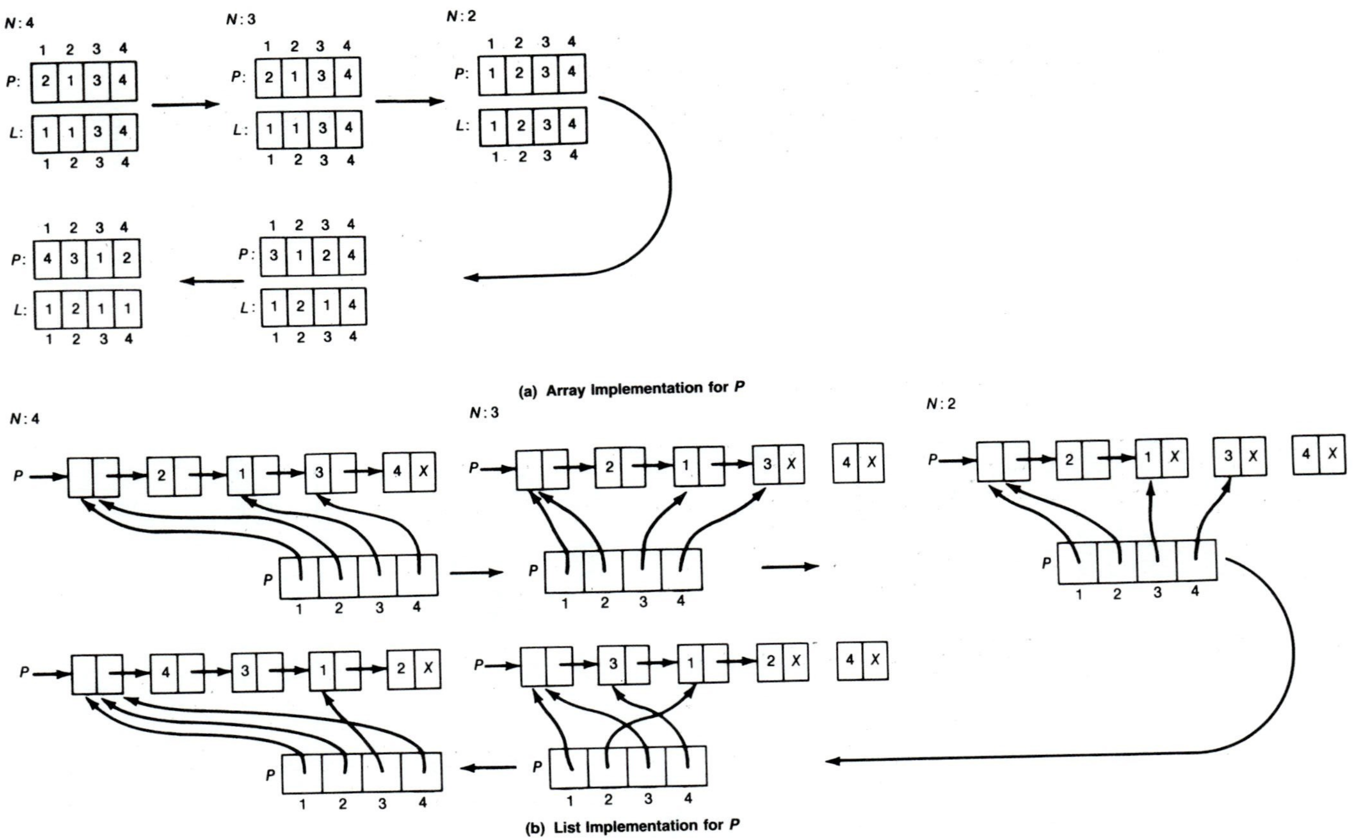

(a) Array Implementation for P

(b) List Implementation for P

Figure 4.6 Simulation of NEXT(4,&DONE) When *P* is 2134

In comparing the two implementations notice that the advantage of the list implementation is that the **for** loop required by the array implementation is no longer needed. Inserting `n` at the left end of the current permutation thus takes only two pointer changes rather than time proportional to n. Other permutation algorithms are explored in Sedgewick [1977].

To further illustrate the differences, two complete programs using function `permutations`, one for the array and one for the list implementation, are given below. The `process` function prints each permutation. To adapt these programs to obtain a solution for the stable marriage problem, the function `process` must test for stability. Another modification would be to abort the execution when a stable pairing is found. This requires that `process` be given access to `done` so that it can set `done` to *true* at that point.

Array Implementation

```
#include <stdio.h>
#define TRUE 1
#define FALSE 0
typedef int arraytype[21];              global definition of arraytype
arraytype p,l;                          arrays p and l declared globally

main()
/* Driver for permutations. */
{
   int n;
   printf("\n n = ?\n");
   scanf("%d",&n);
   permutations(n);
}

permutations(n)
/* Generates and processes each
   permutation of the integers
   1 to n.
*/
int n;
{
   int done;
   done = FALSE;
   initialize(n);                       creates initial permutation
   while (!done)
      {
         process(n);                    processes the current permutation
         next(n,&done);                 generates the next permutation
      }
}

initialize(n)
/* Creates initial permutation */
int n;
```

```
{
   int i;
   for (i=1;i<=n;i++)
      {
         p[i] = n - i + 1;
         l[i] = 1;
      }
}
```

traverses and fills the arrays `p` *and* `l`

```
process(n)
/* Prints the current permutation */
int n;
{
   int i;
   for (i=1;i<=n;i++)
      printf("\n%d\n",p[i]);
   printf("\n");
}
```

traverses the array `p`

```
next(n,pdone)
/* Generates the next permutation unless
   the current one is the last. In this case
   done is set to true.
*/
int n,*pdone;
{
   int i;
   if (n > 1)
      if (l[n] < n)
         {
            p[l[n]] = p[l[n]+1];
            p[l[n]+1] = n;
            l[n] = l[n]+1;
         }
      else
         {
            next(n-1,pdone);
            for (i=n-1;i>=1;i--)
               p[i+1] = p[i];
            p[1] = n;
            l[n] = 1;
         }
   else
      *pdone = TRUE;
}
```

List Implementation

```
#include <stdio.h>
#define TRUE 1
#define FALSE 0
#define NULL 0
typedef struct record
{
```

global definitions for `listrecord`, `listpointer`, `pointerarray` *types*

```
   int info;
   struct record *link;
}listrecord,*listpointer;
typedef listpointer pointerarray[21];
pointerarray ptr,pred;

listpointer p;


main()
/* Driver for permutations. */
{
   int n;
   printf("\n n = ?\n");
   scanf("%d",&n);
   permutations(n);
}


permutations(n)
/* Generates and processes each
   permutation of the integers 1 to n.
*/
int n;
{
   int done;
   done = FALSE;
   initialize(n);
   while (!done)
      {
         process(n);
         next(n,&done);
      }
}


initialize(n)
/* Creates initial permutation */
int n;
{
   int i;
   listpointer q;
   p = malloc(sizeof(listrecord));
   q = p;
   for (i=1;i<=n;i++)
      {
         q->link = malloc(sizeof(listrecord));
         q = q->link;
         q->info = n - i + 1;
         ptr[n-i+1] = q;
         pred[i] = p;
      }
   q->link = NULL;
}
```

pointer arrays `ptr` *and* `pred` *declared globally*

listpointer `p` *declared globally*

creates initial permutation

processes the current permutation

generates the next permutation

creates the list `p` *and fills pointer arrays* `ptr` *and* `pred`

```
process(n)
/* Prints the current permutation */
int n;
{
   listpointer q;
   q = p->link;
   while (q != NULL)                              traverses the permutation list
      {
         printf("\n%d\n",q->info);
         q = q->link;
      }
         printf("\n");
}

next(n,pdone)
/* Generates the next permutation unless
   the current one is the last. In this case
   done is set to true.
*/
int n,*pdone;
{
   if (n > 1)
      if (ptr[n]->link != NULL)
         {
            pred[n]->link = ptr[n]->link;
            pred[n] = pred[n]->link;
            ptr[n]->link = pred[n]->link;
            pred[n]->link = ptr[n];
         }
      else
         {
            pred[n]->link = NULL;
            next(n-1,pdone);
            ptr[n]->link = p->link;
            p->link = ptr[n];
            pred[n] = p;
         }
   else
      *pdone = TRUE;
}
```

4.3 A Close Look at the Execution of Recursive Programs

When any program invokes one of its functions, it is because the task performed by that component must now be carried out. Global variables and variables passed by address (pointers) specify storage that is not local to the component but that it may reference and change. It may also reference and change static variables. All such storage represents the *data* the component is to process. Any changes by the component to the data are reflected back in the data's storage.

Parameters passed to a function by value also specify storage that is not local to it, but these parameters are treated differently. When the component is invoked, their values are copied into storage that is local to the component. It is these local copies that are referenced, and perhaps changed, by the component as it executes, but such changes are not reflected back to the original values. In this way the information passed by value is made accessible to the component, which may even change the local copies, but such changes are kept local; the original nonlocal values are untouched.

In effect, these copies are treated as if they were additional local variables of the component. The actual local variables of the component represent temporary information that the component uses to do its job. Both the local copies and local variables disappear when the task is completed. This storage for local copies and local variables serves as a "scratchpad" for use by the component. The scratchpad contains information used temporarily by the component to perform its task on the data. This view of the data and scratchpad of a component is depicted in Figure 4.7.

The component may, in turn, invoke another component, which may invoke still another, and so on. Each time this is done, the calling component suspends its operation, so all components of the sequence, except the last, are waiting.

When the last component completes its task, the component that invoked it then continues. In order for this to happen, each component must remember from whence it was called. Also, upon return to the correct place, the scratchpad of the calling component must be the same as before the call. For nonrecursive programs, the important point is that each component must retain only one returning point, and the scratchpad of a component is automatically retained when it invokes another component.

With recursive programs the situation is considerably different, as evidenced

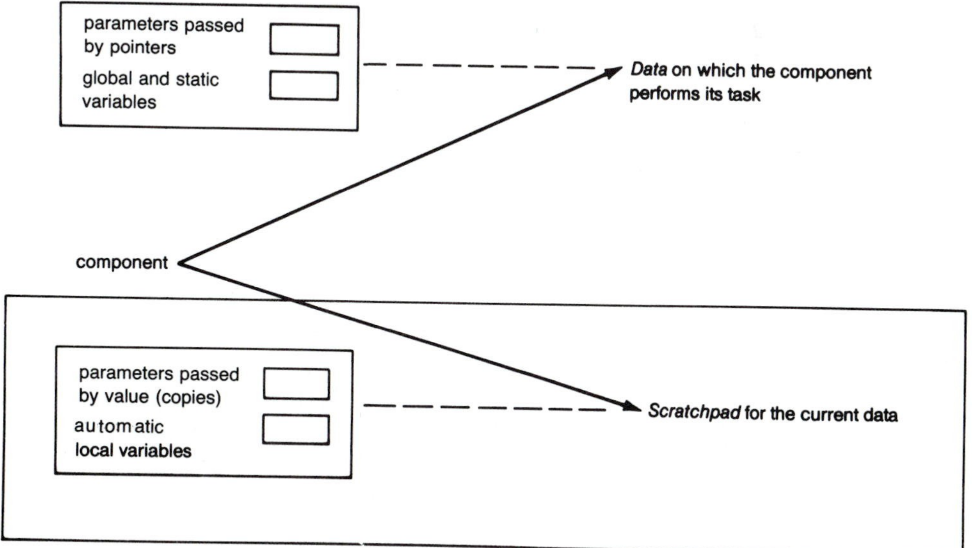

Figure 4.7 Data and Scratchpad for a Component

by Figures 4.2, 4.4, and 4.6. First, when a recursive function is invoked, this may be the initial, first, second, or *n*th recursive call to it. If it is the *n*th recursive call, there may be as many as (n + 1) returning places to be retained, not just one. Second, there may be (n + 1) scratchpads to be retained. How many there are is determined by the number of calls that are currently suspended.

Suppose that this number is *k*, that the return for the initial call is handled separately, and also that the scratchpad for the currently executing call is associated with the function. The number of sets of additional returns and scratchpads that must be retained is then *k*. The *depth* of a recursive program is given by the maximum value of *k*. It is the depth that determines the amount of storage required by the function. The following examples illustrate these ideas.

Example 4.1 In Figure 4.2, when the tenth recursive call ($k = 3$) is made to `towers`, there are three returns and three sets of scratchpads to remember in addition to the initial call's return.

[2] and `n` = 4, `i` = 1, `a` = 2, `f` = 3 for the initial call
[1] and `n` = 3, `i` = 2, `a` = 1, `f` = 3 for the eighth recursive call
[1] and `n` = 2, `i` = 2, `a` = 3, `f` = 1 for the ninth recursive call

`n` = 1, `i` = 2, `a` = 1, `f` = 3 for the tenth recursive call are stored, by our assumption, local to `towers`. In general, the depth of recursion will be $n - 1$. Using our terminology, there are no data. ■

Example 4.2 In Figure 4.4, when the third recursive call is made to `copy`, there are three returns and three sets of scratchpads to be retained beside the initial call's return:

`first0, null0, rest0` for the initial call
`first1, null1, rest1` for the first recursive call
`first2, null2, rest2` for the second recursive call

No returns are shown since they all return to the same place: the statement `setlink(*psecond, rest)`. The depth of the recursion is one less than the length of the list to be copied. The data for the initial call is `second`, while for the $(n + 1)$th recursive call it is `restn`. A change to `rest` in the $(n + 1)$th call is reflected in the scratchpad for the *n*th call. Storage could be saved by making `null` global to `copy`. ■

Example 4.3 In Figure 4.6 the situation corresponds to a point in the initial call when the second and then the third recursive calls to `next` are made. The local variable `i` is not shown, and the three scratchpad values are

`n` = 4 for the initial call
`n` = 3 for the second recursive call
`n` = 2 for the third recursive call

Again, the returns are all the same, to the statement following the recursive call to `next`, so they are not shown. The depth of the recursion is $n - 1$. The data consist of `p`, `ptr`, `pred`, and `done`. ■

It should by now be clear that the storage required by a recursive function is proportional to its depth. The execution time, on the other hand, has to do with the total number of recursive calls that are required to complete the initial call. This explains why the recursive solution to Counting Squares (Section 4.2.6) is so inefficient both in time and in storage.

4.4 Implementing Recursive Programs

Recursion is a powerful tool for the development of algorithms and leads to concise, clear recursive programs that can be easier to check for correctness. Complex algorithms may be expressed using relatively few program statements, which at the same time emphasize the structure of the algorithm. This will become even more apparent later in the text, as more difficult problems are solved.

A function that invokes itself is ***directly recursive.*** A function is ***indirectly recursive*** if any sequence of calls to other functions can lead to a call to the original function. Compilers for recursive languages must translate recursive as well as nonrecursive programs. It is not necessary to understand how a recursive program is translated (any more than it is necessary to know how a nonrecursive program is translated) in order to understand or to write the program itself. But it *is* necessary to know how the program will execute. This amounts to being able to simulate its execution.

The programmer constrained to a nonrecursive language can still use the power of recursion. This is done by writing a program as if the language allowed recursion, and then translating the program into an equivalent nonrecursive program. This is what compilers for recursive languages do and is one reason for spending time finding out how to translate (or implement) a recursive program.

As shown in the discussion of Counting Squares, some problems should not be solved using recursion under any circumstances. Sometimes, as in the Towers of Hanoi problem, we may only be able to think of a recursive solution. Often we can find both a recursive and a nonrecursive solution, which may be compared for trade-offs in clarity, conciseness, storage, and execution time.

Even though a recursive solution may not be best, it may suggest an approach to the problem that otherwise might have been missed and that may turn out to be the most desirable. In fact, the translated version of a recursive solution can often be helpful in finding desirable modifications. This is another reason for looking at the translation process.

Normally, if a recursive approach is right for a problem, and is applied intelligently, further refinements of the program do not improve its efficiency significantly. Breaking up a problem as required by the recursive approach does, however, create the possibility of doing certain tasks in parallel. For instance, the three components of the Towers of Hanoi solution may all be done at the same time with parallel processing. Languages and computer systems that allow concurrent processing will surely become more prevalent. When they do, recursive solutions will have another advantage.

If each successive call to a recursive function were implemented so that during execution a new copy of the function is created with its own storage for the return and its scratchpad values, then, in effect, the function could be treated like any function in a nonrecursive program. With the advent of cheaper and larger storage, this may well occur in the future, but until then, another means of managing the generated returns and scratchpad values is needed.

The essential difference between nonrecursive (or iterative) programs and recursive programs is the storage needed for the returns and scratchpad values of the latter. Figures 4.2, 4.4, and 4.6 actually represent the bookkeeping needed to simulate the execution of a recursive program. The basic idea in translating such programs is to implement this bookkeeping procedure as follows:

1. Each time a recursive call is made to the function,
   a. save the proper return place and the current scratchpad values,
   b. set the scratchpad values to their new values.
2. Each time a recursive call is completed,
   a. restore the current return and scratchpad values to those that were last saved (and save them no longer),
   b. return to the proper place in the recursive function, or to the original calling component if it is the initial call that has just finished.

This procedure does not apply to a function that returns a value, but it may be modified to do so. Or the function may be modified to return the value in an additional parameter passed by pointer. As an illustration of this, the first version of `copy` might be obtained by such a modification of the second.

Notice that the information to be retained (return and scratchpad values) must be recalled in the order opposite to the order in which it is generated. This is no different for nonrecursive programs, except that then the information is saved locally with each component. It is helpful to think of return and scratchpad values as the entries of a record. Then the collection of records corresponding to each suspended recursive call must be stored in some data structure. The data structure must retain not only these records, but also the correct order.

In step 1 above, the record to be saved must become the new first record in the order. In step 2, the current first record (the last saved) must be removed from the data structure. A data structure for storing information so that new information can be inserted, so that a deletion always removes the last piece of information inserted, and which can be tested to see if it is empty (contains no information) is called a ***stack.*** Stacks will be discussed in more detail later in the chapter; for now they will simply be used.

4.4.1 A Sample Implementation of Towers

The stack is the most convenient data abstraction to use for the bookkeeping recursion entails. To illustrate the translation, and the possibility of enhancing efficiency, the recursive functions `towers` and `next` will now be translated into nonrecursive functions.

In `towers` there are two recursive calls. The idea in implementing it is to write a nonrecursive program that executes just as the recursive program would, while managing the additional records generated by the recursion. This amounts to implementing the procedure described for simulating `towers`. Each recursive call will be replaced by code to insert the proper return indicator onto a stack, as well as the current scratchpad values. Whenever the end of a recursive call is reached, the proper return indicator and the scratchpad values last put on the stack will be removed and restored to the program's local storage. The earlier recursive version and its implementation as a nonrecursive function are as follows.

Recursive Version

```
towers(n,i,a,f)
/* Moves the top n disks
   from peg i to peg f
*/
int n,i,a,f;
{
   if(n == 1)
      printf("\n %d -> %d\n",i,f);
   else
      {
         towers(n-1,i,f,a);
         printf("\n %d -> %d\n",i,f)
         towers(n-1,a,i,f);
      }
}
```

- *in the nonrecursive version, a* `retrn` *value of 1 means this call has completed* (beside `towers(n-1,i,f,a);`)
- *in the nonrecursive version, a* `retrn` *value of 2 means this call has completed; in this version an "implicit" exit then occurs; this must be made explicit in the implementation* (beside `towers(n-1,a,i,f);`)

Nonrecursive Version

```
       towers(n,i,a,f)
       /* Moves the top n disks
          from peg i to peg f
       */
       int n,i,a,f;
       {
          int retrn;

          stack s;

          setstack(&s);
one:      if(n == 1)
             printf("\n %d -> %d\n",i,f);
          else
             {
                s_tack(1,n,i,a,f,&s);

                setvar1(&n,&i,&a,&f);

                goto one;
             }
```

- `retrn` *holds the place to continue after a recursive call completes*
- *storage allocated for the stack* `s`
- *initializes stack* `s` *to empty*
- *the start of* `towers`
- *saves the return and* `n`, `i`, `a` *and* `f` *on stack* `s`
- *sets scratchpad values:* `n` *to* `n-1`, *interchanges* `f` *and* `a`
- *makes a recursive call*

```
two:     if(!empty(&s))                          ] this is the start of the "ex-
           {                                       plicit" exit; when the stack is
                                                   empty, the original call to
                                                   towers is complete; other-
                                                   wise the return point must be
                                                   determined
              restore(&retrn,&n,&i,&a,&f,&s);    ] sets retrn and the scratchpad
              switch(retrn)                        to their proper values
                 {
                    case 1:                      ] after executing the printf
                       printf("\n %d -> %d\n",     statement, a recursive call must
                              i,f)                 be made, so return and n, i, a,
                       s_tack(2,n,i,a,f,&s);       f are saved on s and the
                       setvar2(&n,&i,&a,&f);       scratchpad values are set: n to
                       goto one;                   n-1, a and i are interchanged,
                                                   and the recursive call is made

                    case 2:                      ] a recursive call has completed;
                       goto two;                   the "explicit" exit must now be
                 }                                 made, so go to the "explicit"
           }                                       exit
}
```

S_tack is a routine that inserts its arguments, as fields of a record, onto the stack. The name **s_tack** is used to be sure the compiler can distinguish this routine from the type name **stack** that also appears in the function. **Setstack** ensures that the stack will initially contain zero entries; **empty** returns *true* if the stack contains no records and *false* otherwise. The **setvar** routines do the proper setting of the current scratchpad values for the ensuing recursive call. **Restore(&retrn,&n,&i,&a,&f,&s)** restores the proper scratchpad values when a return is to be made after completion of some recursive call.

`Setvar1(&n,&i,&a,&f)` sets `n` to `n - 1` and interchanges the values of `f` and `a`.
`Setvar2(&n,&i,&a,&f)` sets `n` to `n - 1` and interchanges the values of `a` and `i`.

The "implicit" exit of the recursive program (after the second recursive call) has been replaced in the implementation by a complex "explicit" sequence of statements. This is because the exit must, in effect, transfer control to the proper place in the calling program. If the stack itself is empty at this point, this means that it is the initial call to **towers** that has been completed. Return should then be to the calling program. Otherwise, it is some recursive call to **towers** that has been completed. At this point, the top stack record contains the four scratchpad values to be restored and the return location in **towers**.

You should simulate the execution of this implementation to see that it really works correctly. The statement labeled "one" corresponds to the first executable statement of the recursive program; this is the statement that is invoked in the implementation to represent a recursive call. It is only invoked, however, after the scratchpad values of the current call and proper return location have been saved on the stack, and the scratchpad values for the upcoming recursive call have been correctly set.

Notice that the implementation requires a stack that can hold the stored information for up to $n - 1$ recursive calls. The stack must be initialized to empty. Its contents must be preserved between calls. We will not dwell on its implementation details here, but a complete program to test this version is given in Section 4.5.1.

This example highlights the fact that considerable overhead is involved in executing recursive programs. Time is consumed because variables must be stacked and unstacked for each recursive call and its return. It is often possible to discover a more efficient nonrecursive algorithm for a problem, even though the recursive algorithm is evident, as was done in Counting Squares. Nonetheless, the recursive version is frequently clearer, easier to understand, and more concise, as well as easier to verify. Therefore some programmers prefer recursive solutions to problems, even if they are less efficient than the nonrecursive versions.

Another approach is to attempt to increase the efficiency of the iterative program (the implementation) that is translated from a recursive program. This attempt can be made whether or not there is a competing nonrecursive routine.

How can we create a more efficient version of a translated program such as **towers**? The reason for the stack in the first place is to save return codes and to save scratchpad values that are needed when the suspended call is ready to resume (after the saved values have been unstacked and restored, and the proper program segment is to be executed). If the programmer can determine where the return should be, or what the scratchpad values that are to be restored should be, then this information does not have to be stacked. It may not be necessary to save the values of some other variables. It may also be possible to eliminate some return codes. If no variables need to be saved, and there is only one return code, then the stack itself is not needed. Let us attempt to reach this goal for the implementation of the recursive **towers** routine.

Notice that in the case statement for **retrn** at 1, the call to **s_tack (2,n,i,a,f,&s)** saves the values of the current variables in the suspended call, in order to make the recursive call to **towers(n-1,a,i,f)**. When this new recursive call is completed, these current values will be restored, and the **retrn** will be 2. The statement labeled "two" will then be executed.

If the stack is empty, the initial call is complete. Otherwise **restore** will be called immediately and control transferred to the new value of **retrn**. The current values saved by **s_tack(2,n,i,a,f,&s)** will never be used, and so need not be saved at all. Thus the call to **s_tack(2,n,i,a,f,&s)** may be eliminated from the program. This means that the only return code appearing will be 1 in the call to **s_tack(1,n,i,a,f,&s)**. However, the value of **retrn** after **restore** is called will always be 1. Therefore, no return code needs to be stored on the stack; the case structure may be removed. **Retrn** is not needed at all. This new program then looks like the following.

Second Nonrecursive Version

```
towers(n,i,a,f)
/* Moves the top n disks
   from peg i to peg f
*/
int n,i,a,f;
```

```
           {
              stack s;
              setstack(&s);
one:          if(n == 1)
                 printf("\n %d -> %d\n",i,f);
              else
                 {
                    s_tack(n,i,a,f,&s);
                    setvar1(&n,&i,&a,&f);
                    goto one;
                 }
              if(!empty(&s))
                 {
                    restore(&n,&i,&a,&f,&s);
                    printf("\n %d -> %d\n",i,f);
                    setvar2(&n,&i,&a,&f);
                    goto one;
                 }
           }
```

retrn, the switch, and one call to s_tack have been eliminated; also, s_tack has one less parameter

Another improvement can be made by changing the **if–else** structure to a **while** loop. Doing so improves the clarity and eliminates the **goto:**

```
one: if(n == 1)
        printf("\n %d -> %d\n",i,f);
     else
        {
           s_tack(n,i,a,f,&s);
           setvar1(&n,&i,&a,&f);
           goto one;
        }
```

```
one: while(n > 1)
        {
           s_tack(n,i,a,f,&s);
           setvar1(&n,&i,&a,&f);
        }
     printf("\n %d -> %d\n",i,f);
```

This yields

Third Nonrecursive Version

```
           towers(n,i,a,f)
           /* Moves the top n disks
              from peg i to peg f
           */
           int n,i,a,f;
           {
              stack s;
one:          while(n > 1)
                 {
                    s_tack(n,i,a,f,&s);
                    setvar1(&n,&i,&a,&f);
                 }
```

***while** loop replaces **if–else** construct*

```
   printf("\n %d -> %d\n",i,f);
   if(!empty(&s))
      {
         restore(&n,&i,&a,&f,&s);
         printf("\n %d -> %d\n",i,f);
         setvar2(&n,&i,&a,&f);
         goto one;
      }
}
```

Finally, the function can be written in more structured form, as follows:

Final Nonrecursive Version

```
towers(n,i,a,f)
/* Moves the top n disks
   from peg i to peg f
*/
int n,i,a,f;
{
   stack s;
   int done
   done = FALSE;
   while(!done)
      {
         while(n > 1)
            {
               s_tack(n,i,a,f,&s);
               setvar1(&n,&i,&a,&f);
            }
   printf("\n %d -> %d\n",i,f);
   if(!empty(&s))
      {
         restore(&n,&i,&a,&f,&s);
         printf("\n %d -> %d\n",i,f);
         setvar2(&n,&i,&a,&f);
      }
   else
      done = TRUE;
}
```

This structured version is more efficient than the compilerlike direct translation because the number of stack operations has been reduced. It is also structured for clarity in reading. Both changes make it a better implementation.

4.4.2 A Sample Implementation for Permutations

The same approach can now be applied to develop a nonrecursive translation for `next`.

Nonrecursive Version

```
          next(n,pdone)
          /* Generates the next permutation unless
             the current one is the last. In this case
             done is set to true.
          */
          int n,*pdone;
          {
             int i,retrn;                              ] retrn holds the place to con-
                                                         tinue after a recursive call com-
                                                         pletes
             stack s;                                  ] storage allocated for the stack s
one:         if(n > 1)                                 ] the start of next
                if(l[n] < n)
                   {
                      p[l[n]] = p[l[n] + 1];
                      p[l[n] + 1] = n;
                      l[n] = l[n] + 1;
                   }
                else
                   {
                      s_tack(1,n,i,&s);                ] saves the return, n, and i on
                                                         stack s
                      setvar(&n,&i);                   ] sets scratchpad values: n to n-1
                      goto one;                        ] makes a recursive call
                   }
             else
                *pdone = TRUE;
two:         if(!empty(&s))                            ] this is the start of the "explicit"
                {                                        exit; when the stack is empty, the
                                                         original call to next is complete;
                                                         otherwise the return point must
                                                         be determined
                   restore(&retrn,&n,&i,&s);           ] sets retrn and the scratchpad
                   switch(retrn)                         to their proper values
                      {
                         case 1:                       ] after executing the for loop, a
                            {                            recursive call has completed;
                               for(i=n-1;i>=1;i--)       insert n at the left end, and the
                                  p[i+1] = p[i];         "explicit" exit must be made
                               p[1] = n;
                               l[n] = 1;
                               goto two;               ] go to the "explicit" exit
                            {
                      {
                {
          {
```

where `setvar(&n,&i)` simply sets `n` to `n-1`.

The same program can be written in a more structured way. First notice that the statement labeled "two" and the **goto** "two" statement create a **while** loop.

Introducing that **while** loop but retaining the structure of "one," the overall structure of the program becomes as follows

```
one:  if c1 then                                   ] c1 is (n > 1)
          if c2 then                               ] c2 is (l[n] < n)
              task c1 and c2 both true
          else
              task for c1 true but c2 false
              goto one
      else
          task for c1 false
      while not empty(&s)                          ] the new while loop
          loop task
```

Next, the structure of "one" can also be improved, as follows.

```
while (c1 and not c2)                              ] another loop
    task for c1 true but c2 false
if c1, then                                        ] a decision
    task for c1 and c2 both true
else
    task for c1 false
while not empty(&s)                                ] the new while loop
    loop task.
```

The logic of this version is much easier to follow. You can see at a glance that the segment control flows from the top down. It consists of a loop, followed by a decision, followed by a loop. The iterative version of `next`, translated from the recursive `next`, and using the improved structure, now becomes as follows:

Second Nonrecursive Version

this differs from the first version only in its structure, not in its operations

```
next(n,pdone)
/* Generates the next permutation unless
   the current one is the last. In this case
   done is set to true.
*/
int n,*pdone
{
   int i,retrn;
   stack s;
   while((n > 1) && !(l[n] < n))
      {
         s_tack(l,n,i,&s);
         setvar(&n,&i);
      }
   if(n > 1)
      {
         p[l[n]] = p[l[n] + 1];
         p[l[n] + 1] = n;
         l[n] = l[n] + 1;
      }
```

```
        else
            *pdone = TRUE;
        while(!empty(&s))
            {
                restore(&retrn,&n,&i,&s);
                switch(retrn)
                    {
                        case 1:
                            {
                                for(i=n-1;i>=1;i--)
                                    p[i+1] = p[i];
                                p[1] = n;
                                l[n] = 1;
                            }
                    }
            }
}
```

In general, when the value of a scratchpad variable does not change or does not need to be maintained between recursive calls, it need not be stacked. This is the case with the variable `i` of `next`. Also, when there is only one return place from a recursive call, there is no need to stack a return indicator. This is the situation with `next`. Finally, the value of `n` varies in a predictable fashion. Its restored value will always be 1 greater than its current value. Thus there is no need to stack `n`. Each time a recursive call returns, `n` may be correctly restored by adding 1 to its current value.

Therefore, the stack is unnecessary, since no information must be retained on it. The `s_tack` function can be removed, `setvar` can be replaced by the statement `n = n - 1`, and `restore` can be replaced by the statement `n = n + 1`. Still, the stack controls the second **while** loop in our translated version. Even though no information needs to be stacked, it is still necessary to know when the stack would have been empty so that the loop may be properly exited.

Notice that the first **while** loop decreases `n` by 1 every time a stack entry would have been made, and the second **while** increases `n` by 1 every time an entry would have been deleted from the stack. Hence, if an integer variable `s` is set to `n` initially, prior to the first **while** loop, the test to see if the stack is empty in the second **while** loop becomes `s = n`. The final version of `next` is an iterative program that has no stack. It is an example of the translated version giving us a better solution. This four-step solution is efficient and is also clear.

1. Set `s` to `n`.
2. Set `n` to the rightmost entry in the permutation that can still be shifted right.
3. If that entry is not 1, then
   Shift it right
   else
   Set `done` to *true*
4. Place the `s-n` entries that could not be moved to the right in the proper order at the left end of the permutation.

The final program is as follows:

Final Nonrecursive Version

```
   next(n,pdone)
   /* Generates the next permutation unless
      the current one is the last. In this case
      done is set to true.
   */
   int n,*pdone
   {
      int i,s;
1.    s = n;
2.    while((n > 1) && !(l[n] < n))
         n--;
3.    if(n > 1)
         {
            p[l[n]] = p[l[n] + 1];
            p[l[n] + 1] = n;
            l[n] = l[n] + 1;
         }
      else
         *pdone = TRUE;
4.    while(s > n)
         {
            n++
            for(i=n-1;i>=1;i--)
               p[i+1] = p[i];
            p[1] = n;
            l[n] = 1;
         }
   }
```

By translating the recursive solution and analyzing it, a highly efficient nonrecursive solution was built. A little insight can help a lot. For more on recursion, see Barron [1968] and Bird [1977a, 1977b]. It may now be time for you to make a recursive call on all preceding material!

4.5 Stacks

Earlier in this chapter the notion of a stack was introduced and used in the nonrecursive implementations of **towers** and **next**. Stacks are useful in situations requiring the retention and recall of information in a specific order—namely, when information is removed in a last-in, first-out order (LIFO for short). Removing tennis balls from a can is LIFO. In programming, stacks are useful when a program must postpone obligations, which must later be fulfilled in *reverse order* from that in which they were incurred.

Information is kept in order in a ***stack.*** Additional information may be inserted on the stack, but only at the front or top end. Thus the information at the top of the stack always corresponds to the most recently incurred obligation. Information may be recalled from the stack, but only by removing the current top piece of information. The stack acts like a pile of playing cards to which we can only add a card at the top and from which we can only remove the top card. Of course, this is not what is meant by a "stacked deck."

The stack, with the operations of front-end insertion and deletion, initialization, and an empty check, is a data abstraction. Stacks used to be called "pushdown stacks"; insertion of data onto the stack was referred to as "pushing" the stack, and deleting data was known as "popping" the stack. So far we have written programs that treat the stack with the four operations as a data abstraction. Stacks will be used frequently in algorithms developed throughout the rest of this book, and it is now time to consider this implementation. Of the many implementations possible for the stack, the following subsections illustrate the three most straightforward.

4.5.1 Array Implementation of a Stack

A stack may be implemented using arrays with the following declarations:

```
typedef struct
{
   whatever info;
}stackrecord;
typedef struct
{
   stackrecord stackarray[LIMIT];
   int top;
}stack;
stack s;
```

the type `stackrecord` *is a record with one member info of type* `whatever`

the type `stack` *is a record with members an array of type* `stackrecord` *and* `top` *of type* `int`

`s` *is an instance of type* `stack`*, and storage is allocated for it*

The definitions must be preceded by a typedef for "`whatever`." Let us assume `LIMIT` has been set in a define statement fixing the maximum number of items the stack can hold. Suppose 6, 45, 15, 32, and 18 were pushed onto the stack. Figure 4.8 illustrates the meaning attached to the declaration. Figure 4.8(a) is a conceptualization of the stack. Since 6 was the first entry on the stack, it is on the bottom. Likewise, 18 was the last entry, so it is on top. Figure 4.8(b) is the way the data is stored in the actual stack `s`. The `stackarray` holds the data and `top` contains an index to the current entry on the top of the stack. Although 6 is at the top of the array, it is the bottom stack entry; while 18 is at the bottom of the array, it is the top stack entry. Thus `top` has the value 4.

Addition or insertion of a new element to the stack will be accomplished by a function `push`. Removal or deletion of the current top stack element will be accomplished by a function `pop`. Executing `push(&newrecord,&s)` results in the contents of `newrecord` being placed on the stack as a new first element. A call to the function `pop(&s,&value)` causes the removal of the current top stack element, with `value` containing a copy of that value. A routine `setstack` sets the stack to empty so that it initially contains no entries.

Example 4.4 Suppose we execute

```
pop(&s,&y);
pop(&s,&z);
push(&newrecord,&s);   ] assume newrecord contains the number 5
```

If Figure 4.8 indicates the current stack, then Figure 4.9 shows the new situation after this execution. ■

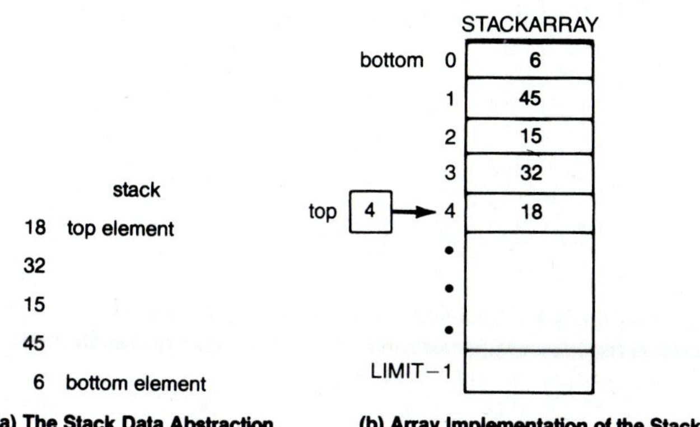

Figure 4.8 Stack before Insertion of a New Element

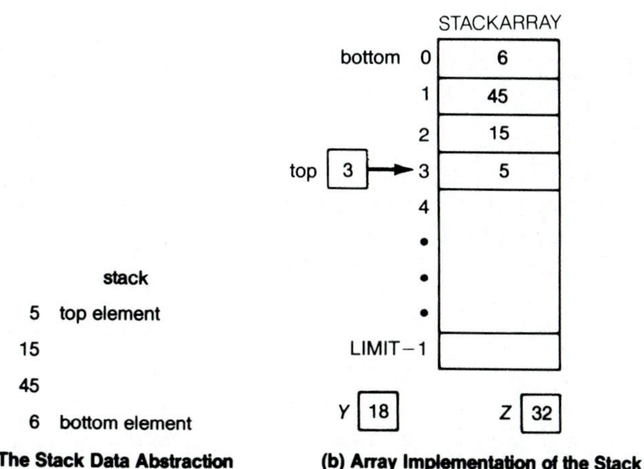

Figure 4.9 Stack after Insertion of a New Element

Stack underflow occurs when a program attempts to remove an element from an empty stack. It normally indicates either an error or the termination of a task. ***Stack overflow*** occurs when a program attempts to add an element to a full stack. Although, conceptually, the stack as a data structure has no limit, an actual implemented stack does have a limit. In the present implementation it is termed `LIMIT`. `Push` and `pop` should test, respectively, for stack overflow and underflow and take appropriate action whenever these conditions occur. Such precautionary measures are an example of defensive programming.

It is also necessary to test the stack to determine whether or not it is empty. This may be accomplished by invoking a function `empty`, which will return the value *true* when the stack is empty and *false* otherwise.

These routines may be implemented as follows:

```
setstack(ps)
/* Initializes the stack s to empty */
stack *ps;
{
   (*ps).top = -1;
}
```

sets `top` *to −1, to signify empty*

```
empty(ps)
/* Returns true only if the stack is empty */
stack *ps;
{
   return((*ps).top == -1);
}
```

`top` *= −1 signifies empty*

```
push(pnewrecord,ps)
/* Inserts the record newrecord
   at the top of the stack s
*/
stackrecord *pnewrecord;
stack *ps;
{
   if((*ps).top == (LIMIT - 1))
      overflow(ps);
   else
      {
         (*ps).top = (*ps).top + 1;
         (*ps).stackarray[(*ps).top].info =
                      (*pnewrecord).info;
      }
}
```

overflow test

no overflow, so updates `top` *and inserts the new record where* `top` *points*

```
pop(ps,pvalue)
/* Copies the contents of the top record
   of stack s into value and removes the
   record from the stack
*/
```

```
stack *ps;
stackrecord *pvalue;
{
   if(empty(ps))                                    ] underflow test
      underflow(ps);
   else
      {

         (*pvalue).info = (*ps).stackarray          ] no underflow, so copies the top
                               [(*ps).top].info;    ] record's contents into value and
         (*ps).top = (*ps).top - 1;                 ] updates top to reflect its removal
      }
}
```

The procedures **overflow** and **underflow** are assumed to take appropriate action when they are invoked. Notice that the elements of the stack will be of "**whatever**" type. We have taken the liberty here of assuming that the C compiler being used allows the contents of one structure to be assigned to another. Otherwise, for example, the assignment

```
(*ps).stackarray[(*ps).top].info =
                  (*pnewrecord).info;
```

that occurs in **push** could not be used. Instead, each field of info would have to be individually assigned.

The implementation discussed so far applies when *records* are to be stored on the stack. Instead, if only the contents of *simple variables* of type such as **int**, **float**, **char**, or **listpointer** are to be stored, then the declarations and definitions of **push** and **pop** may be simplified, as follows.

```
typedef struct                         ] the stackarray now no
{                                      ] longer holds records, just
   whatever stackarray[LIMIT];         ] simple variables of type
   int top;                            ] whatever
}stack;

push(value,ps)
/* Inserts the new value
   at the top of the stack s
*/
whatever value;
stack *ps;
{
   if((*ps).top == (LIMIT-1))
      overflow(ps);
```

```
    else
        {
            (*ps).top = (*ps).top + 1;
            (*ps).stackarray[(*ps).top] = value;
        }
}
```

now only a simple variable must be inserted

```
pop(ps,pvalue)
/* Copies the contents of the top entry
   of stack s into value and removes it
   from the stack
*/
stack *ps;
whatever *pvalue;
{
    if(empty(ps))
        underflow(ps);
    else
        {
            *pvalue = (*ps).stackarray[(*ps).top];
            (*ps).top = (*ps).top - 1;
        }
}
```

now only a simple variable must be copied

"`Whatever`" will, of course, be declared of type int, or float, etc. The same simplification can be made, when appropriate, to the implementations of Sections 4.5.2, 4.5.3, 4.7.1, 4.7.2, and 4.7.3.

The idea of functional modularity is to isolate or localize the code of a program that is invoked in a particular task, such as an operation on a data structure. The implementation of the stack data abstraction discussed so far has achieved this modularity, with respect to the `push`, `pop`, `setstack`, and `empty` operations on the stack, by embodying them in individual routines. Another kind of modularity may be achieved by placing the type definitions and the declarations of these operations together in one file. This will be discussed further in the next chapter.

An application of the stack to the nonrecursive `towers` of Section 4.4.1 follows. It illustrates the use of the stack and its treatment as a data abstraction.

```
#include <stdio.h>
#define LIMIT 50
typedef struct
{
    int n;
    int i;
    int a;
    int f;
}whatever;
```

Definitions of types and operations for the data abstraction stack: `whatever`, `stack-record`, `stack` *and* `set-stack`, `empty`, `push`, `pop`, `overflow`, *and* `underflow`

```
typedef struct
{
   whatever info;
}stackrecord;
typedef struct
{
   stackrecord stackarray[LIMIT];
   int top;
}stack;

setstack(ps)
/* Initializes the stack s to empty */
stack *ps;
{
   (*ps).top = -1;
}

empty(ps)
/* Returns true only if the stack s is empty */
stack *ps;
{
   return((*ps).top == -1);
}

push(pnewrecord,ps)
/* Inserts the record newrecord
   at the top of the stack s
*/
stackrecord *pnewrecord;
stack *ps;
{
   if ((*ps).top == (LIMIT-1))
      overflow(ps);
   else
      {
         (*ps).top = (*ps).top + 1;
         (*ps).stackarray[(*ps).top].info =
            (*pnewrecord).info;
      }
}

pop(ps,pvalue)
/* Copies the contents of the top record
   of stack s into value and removes the
   record from the stack
*/
stack *ps;
stackrecord *pvalue;
{
   if (empty(ps))
      underflow(ps);
```

```
    else
        {
            (*pvalue).info =
                (*ps).stackarray[(*ps).top].info;
            (*ps).top = (*ps).top - 1;
        }
}


overflow(ps);
/* Prints a message that the stack has overflowed */
stack *ps;
{
    printf(" The stack has overflowed \n");
}


underflow(ps);
/* Prints a message that the stack has underflowed */
stack *ps;
{
    printf(" The stack has underflowed \n");
}

main()
/* Driver for towers */
{
    int n;
    printf("\n enter a value for n\n");
    scanf("%d",&n);
    towers(n,1,2,3);
}


towers(n,i,a,f)
/* Moves the top n disks
    from peg i to peg f
*/
int n,i,a,f;
{
    stack s;
    int done;
    setstack(&s);
    done = FALSE;
    while(!done)
        {
            while (n > 1)
                {
                    s_tack(n,i,a,f,&s);
                    setvar1(&n,&i,&a,&f);
                }
```

final nonrecursive version

allocates storage for `s`*, an instance of type* `stack`

```
    printf("\n %d -> %d\n",i,f);
    if(!empty(&s))
        {
            restore(&n,&i,&a,&f,&s);
            printf("\n %d -> %d\n",i,f);
            setvar2(&n,&i,&a,&f);
        }
    else
        done = TRUE;
}

setvar1(pn,pi,pa,pf)
/* Sets n to n-1 and
   interchanges f and a
*/
int *pn,*pi,*pa,*pf;
{
    int t;
    *pn = *pn-1;
    t = *pf;
    *pf = *pa;
    *pa = t;
}

setvar2(pn,pi,pa,pf)
/* Sets n to n-1 and interchanges a and i
*/
int *pn,*pi,*pa,*pf;
{
    int t;
    *pn = *pn-1;
    t = *pa;
    *pa = *pi;
    *pi = t;
}

s_tack(n,i,a,f,ps)
/* Creates a record containing
   n,i,a, and f and inserts it
   on stack s
*/
int n,i,a,f;
stack *ps;
{
    stackrecord newrecord;
    newrecord.info.n = n;
    newrecord.info.i = i;
    newrecord.info.a = a;
    newrecord.info.f = f;
    push(&newrecord,ps);
}
```

depends on the implementation of the stack, only because it must know the structure of the stack records

allocates storage for `newrecord` *(an instance of type* `stackrecord`*), fills in its fields, and puts it on* `s`

```
restore(pn,pi,pa,pf,ps)
/* Removes the top record from
   stack s and copies its contents
   into n,i,a,f
*/
int *pn,*pi,*pa,*pf;
stack *ps;
{
   stackrecord value;
   pop(ps,&value);
   *pn = value.info.n;
   *pi = value.info.i;
   *pa = value.info.a;
   *pf = value.info.f;
}
```

depends on the implementation of the stack, only because it must know the structure of the stack records

In review of the program, notice that it treates the stack as a data abstraction. The type definitions and function definitions for the stack are placed at the top of the program. The functions **setvar**, **s_tack**, and **restore** are not basic stack operations; they are used by **towers**. Thus they have been placed after **towers**. Similarly, **towers** has been placed after **main**. Also, **s_tack** and **restore** are dependent on the stack implementation, since they must know the structure of a stack record, which is, in turn, determined by the needs of **towers** for its scratchpad.

4.5.2 List Implementation of the Stack with an Array of Records

In addition to the array implementation, a stack can be implemented as a list. Since we have discussed two ways to implement lists, we know two ways to implement stacks as lists. One is to store the stack records in an array; the other is to store them in dynamic memory. We have already given an implementation of a stack using an array of records in Chapter 3—where **availist** (Section 3.7) actually acts as a stack. When **avail** is invoked, it removes the top record from the **availist**, in addition to returning a pointer to the record. Thus it has effectively popped the record. Likewise, **reclaim** may return a record to the front of the **availist**. Doing so, **reclaim** is essentially pushing a new record onto the **availist**. **Availist** serves as the head of a list, which itself serves as a list implementation of a stack. Of course, appropriate overflow and underflow checking must be built into **avail** and **reclaim**, respectively.

4.5.3 List Implementation of the Stack with Records in Dynamic Memory

The third stack implementation is also as a list—one that involves dynamic storage allocation of the records. That is, the records are stored in the storage area set aside by C to store records referenced by pointer variables. First, the following declaration must be made.

```
typedef struct record
{
   struct whatever info;
   struct record *link;
}stackrecord,*stack;
```

the type `stackrecord` *is a record with members* `info` *of type* `whatever` *and* `link` *of type pointer to a stackrecord; the type* `stack` *is a pointer to a stackrecord*

If we then define `s` as type `stack`, code can be written that is independent of its implementation. `Setstack` must initialize the stack to empty. This means setting `s`, the head of the list implementing the stack, to null. `Push` must now use `malloc` to allocate storage for the entry to be pushed onto the stack before setting its `info` field and inserting that record as the new first record on the stack. `Pop` must copy the `info` field value of the top record into `value` and then delete that record from the stack.

These stack operations are implemented as follows.

```
setstack(ps)
/* Initializes the stack s to empty */
stack *ps;
{
   *ps = NULL;
}
```

a null pointer in `s` *now signifies an empty stack*

```
empty(ps)
/* Returns true only if the stack s is empty */
stack *ps;
{
   return(*ps == NULL);
}
```

the stack is empty if `s` *contains a null pointer*

```
push(pnewrecord,ps)
/* Inserts the record newrecord
   at the top of the stack s
*/
stackrecord *pnewrecord;
stack *ps;
{
   stackrecord *newentry;
   newentry = malloc(sizeof(stackrecord));
   newentry->info = pnewrecord->info;
   newentry->link = *ps;
   *ps = newentry;
}
```

puts a pointer to storage allocated for the new record into `newentry` *and inserts the new record on stack* `s`*; this version does not check for overflow but could do so (how to do it depends on what* `malloc` *does when it runs out of storage)*

```
pop(ps,pvalue)
/* Copies the contents of the top record
   of stack s into value and removes the
   record from the stack
*/
```

```
stack *ps;
stackrecord *pvalue;
{
   if(!empty(ps))
      {
         pvalue->info = (*ps)->info;
         *ps = (*ps)->link;
      }
   else
      underflow(ps);
}
```

tests for underflow

no underflow, so removes the top record on stack `s` *and copies its contents into* `value`

Notice that this implementation removes the artificial restriction imposed by **LIMIT** in the first implementation using an array. This is one of the advantages of using dynamic allocation by means of pointer variables.

It is very important to see that no matter what the implementation, as long as the stack is treated as a data abstraction when writing programs, the programs need not be changed, even if the programmer decides to change the implementation of the stack. Only the declarations and definitions related to the stack need be changed, as is evident in the following nonrecursive **towers** that uses the list implementation. It should be compared to the program of Section 4.5.1, in which the stack was implemented using an array.

```
#include <stdio.h>
#define NULL 0
typedef struct
{
   int n;
   int i;
   int a;
   int f;
}whatever;
typedef struct record
{
   whatever info;
   struct record *link;
}stackrecord, *stack;

setstack(ps)
/* Initializes the stack s to empty */
stack *ps;
{
   *ps = NULL;
}

empty(ps)
stack *ps;
```

definitions of types and operations for the data abstraction stack: `whatever`, `stackrecord`, `stack` *and* `setstack`, `empty`, `push`, `pop`, *and* `underflow`; *these differ from those in the corresponding program of Section 4.5.1*

```
{
   return(*ps == NULL);
}

push(pnewrecord,ps)
stackrecord *pnewrecord;
stack *ps;
{
   stackrecord *newentry;
   newentry = malloc(sizeof(stackrecord));
   newentry->info = pnewrecord->info;
   newentry->link = *ps;
   *ps = newentry;
}

pop(ps,pvalue)
/* Copies the contents of the top record
   of stack s into value and removes the
   record from the stack
*/
stack *ps;
stackrecord *pvalue;
{
   if(!empty(ps))
      {
         pvalue->info = (*ps)->info;
         *ps = (*ps)->link;
      }
   else
      underflow(ps);
}

overflow(ps);
/* Prints a message that the stack has overflowed */
stack *ps;
{
   printf(" The stack has overflowed \n");
}

underflow(ps);
/* Prints a message that the stack has underflowed */
stack *ps;
{
   printf(" The stack has underflowed \n");
}

main()
/* Driver for towers */
{
   int n;
   printf("\n enter a value for n \n");
   scanf("%d",&n);
   towers(n,1,2,3);
}
```

the rest of the program is exactly the same as the corresponding part of the program of Section 4.5.1

final nonrecursive version

allocates storage for `s` *(an instance of type* `stack`*)*

```
towers(n,i,a,f)
/* Moves the top n disks
   from peg i to peg f
*/
int n,i,a,f;
{
   stack s;
   int done
   setstack(&s);
   done = FALSE;
   while(!done)
      {
         while (n > 1)
            {
               s_tack(n,i,a,f,&s);
               setvar 1(&n,&i,&a,&f);
            }
   printf("\n %d -> %d\n",i,f);
   if(!empty(&s))
      {
         restore(&n,&i,&a,&f,&s);
         printf("\n %d -> %d\n",i,f);
         setvar2(&n,&i,&a,&f);
      }
   else
      done = TRUE;
}

setvar1(pn,pi,pa,pf)
/* Sets n to n - 1 and
   interchanges f and a
*/
int *pn,*pi,*pa,*pf;
{
   int t;
   *pn = *pn - 1;
   t = *pf;
   *pf = *pa;
   *pa = t;
}

setvar2(pn,pi,pa,pf)
/* Sets n to n - 1 and
   interchanges a and i
*/
int *pn,*pi,*pa,*pf;
{
   int t;
   *pn = *pn - 1;
   t = *pa;
```

```
        *pa = *pi;
        *pi = t;
}

s_tack(n,i,a,f,ps)
/* Creates a record containing
   n, i, a, and f and inserts it
   on stack s
*/
int n,i,a,f;
stack *ps;
{
   stackrecord newrecord;
   newrecord.info.n = n;
   newrecord.info.i = i;
   newrecord.info.a = a;
   newrecord.info.f = f;
   push(&newrecord,ps);
}

restore(pn,pi,pa,pf,ps)
/* Removes the top record from
   stack s and copies its contents
   into n,i,a,f
*/
int *pn,*pi,*pa,*pf;
stack *ps;
{
   stackrecord value;
   pop(ps,&value);
   *pn = value.info.n;
   *pi = value.info.i;
   *pa = value.info.a;
   *pf = value.info.f;
}
```

depends on the implementation of the stack, only because it must know the structure of the stack records

allocates storage for `newrecord`*, an instance of type* `stack-record`*, fills in its fields, and puts it on* `s`

depends on the implementation of the stack only because it must know the structure of the stack records

The problem of implementing many stacks simultaneously is introduced in the suggested assignment at the end of this chapter. More sophisticated algorithms for the management of the stacks are explored in Garwick [1964], Knuth [1973], and Korsh [1983].

4.6 Evaluation and Translation of Expressions

To illustrate the use of stacks, let us consider the problem of evaluating arithmetic expressions. People are accustomed to writing arithmetic expressions in ***infix notation,*** where an operator appears between its operands. Consequently, programming languages generally use infix notation to be "user friendly." Thus the programmer can write

$$(((a + (b/c * d)) + (a/w)) * b)/(((a * c) + d) + a)$$

Table 4.1 Notations for Two Arithmetic Expressions

	$a + (b * c)$	$(a + b) * c$
Prefix	$+ a * bc$	$* + abc$
Infix	$a + b * c$	$a + b * c$
Postfix	$abc * +$	$ab + c *$

Even humans must scan such an expression carefully, more than once, before discovering that its basis syntactic structure is (operand 1)/(operand 2). A serious problem for the compiler writers was how to translate such expressions without making many scans back and forth through them. The problem was compounded further because programmers were not required to write fully parenthesized expressions; this created the additional dilemma of how to resolve ambiguity. As will be shown below, ambiguity may be resolved by using a notation other than infix.

Consider the arithmetic expressions of Table 4.1. These arithmetic expressions are written in prefix, infix, and postfix notation. ***Prefix*** means that the operator appears to the left, before its operands, and ***postfix*** means that the operator appears to the right, after its operands. Although infix notation is what programmers normally use, there are contexts where prefix (or postfix) notation is used. For instance we write `sqrt(x)`, `f(x,y)`, and `minimum(x,y)`.

Note that the prefix and postfix expressions of the first column are equivalent ways to express the infix expression $a + (b * c)$, while the prefix and postfix expressions of the second column are equivalent to $(a + b) * c$. Unfortunately, the *infix* expressions of both columns are identical. This means that, unless parentheses are used, there is no way to distinguish between $a + (b * c)$ and $(a + b) * c$ using infix notation. Yet we *can* choose the proper prefix or postfix notation to make clear which of the two is intended, even though no parentheses (or special conventions) are used. This holds true in general for arithmetic expressions. For this reason, prefix and postfix notations are called ***parentheses-free*** notations. Compilers can easily process prefix and postfix expressions. Since postfix expressions are generally used, they are the main focus of the discussion that follows.

4.6.1 Postfix Expressions

Given an infix expression that is completely parenthesized, such as

$$((a + b) * (c/d))$$

you know how to evaluate it. This is because you have grown accustomed to the rules for its evaluation, although you might be hard pressed to state those rules completely and precisely. In any case, parentheses signal how the operators are to be applied to the operands, indicating that $(a + b)$ and (c/d) must be evaluated first before applying the * operator. Removing all parentheses yields

$$a + b * c/d$$

Unless conventions or rules are given, this expression is ambiguous. Its five distinct interpretations correspond to the ways in which parentheses may be placed:

$((a + b) * (c/d))$
$(((a + b) * c)/d)$
$((a + (b * c))/d)$
$(a + ((b * c)/d))$
$(a + (b * (c/d)))$

A postfix expression such as

$ab + cd/*$

makes little sense, for you are not used to it, having little experience in interpreting or evaluating it. The rule to be used is as follows:

1. Scan the postfix expression from left to right.
2. Whenever an operator is encountered,
   replace it, and the immediately preceding number of operands required by that operator, with the result of applying that operator to those operands.
3. Treat this replacement as an operand, and continue scanning from this point.

Thus the postfix expression is equivalent to the infix expression

$((a + b) * (c/d))$

The rule, in generating this expression, produces the two intermediate expressions: $(a + b)cd/*$, $(a + b)(c/d)*$.

The following list shows the five fully parenthesized infix expressions representing the interpretations of $a + b * c/d$ and their corresponding postfix expressions.

$((a + b) * (c/d))$ ···· $ab + cd/*$
$(((a + b) * c)/d)$ ···· $ab + c * d/$
$((a + (b * c))/d)$ ···· $abc* + d/$
$(a + ((b * c)/d))$ ···· $abc*d/+$
$(a + (b * (c/d)))$ ···· $abcd/*+$

These examples emphasize two points:

1. The rule for evaluating postfix expressions allows no ambiguity. It determines precisely the meaning or interpretation of the postfix expression.
2. An infix expression, unless fully parenthesized, may be ambiguous in its meaning or interpretation.

It is because of statement 1 that postfix notation, or postfix expressions, are called parentheses-free. A similar rule allows prefix notation, or prefix expression, to be parentheses-free.

Furthermore, evaluation of a postfix expression is easily accomplished by scanning the expression from left to right and using a stack to retain operands and

Table 4.2 Evaluation of a Postfix Expression

Input	Operand Stack
a	a
b	b
	a
c	c
	b
	a
*	$(b * c)$
	a
d	d
	$(b * c)$
	a
/	$((b * c)/d)$
	a
+	$(a + ((b * c)/d)$

results of intermediate evaluations. Any operand that is encountered is placed on an operand stack. When an operator is encountered, its operands are taken from the top of the stack, the operator is applied, and the result is put on the top of the stack. The process is illustrated in the following example.

Example 4.5 Table 4.2 shows the contents of the operand stack after each input is processed, simulating the procedure for evaluation of a postfix expression. The expression is ABC*D/+. ■

Since the procedure for the evaluation of an arithmetic expression using a stack is relatively straightforward and requires no parentheses, why don't programmers write arithmetic expressions in postfix notation only? It is because they are so used to infix notation that they don't want to change. As a result, high-level languages accept infix expressions rather than postfix. This leads back to the question of how infix expressions may be evaluated.

4.6.2 Infix Expressions

The rule to be used for a completely parenthesized infix expression is

1. Scan the infix expression from left to right.
2. When a "matched" pair of "left" and "right" parentheses is encountered, apply the operator to the operands enclosed within the pair of parentheses, and replace the paired parentheses and the contained operator and operands by the result. Continue scanning from this point.

One problem remains: How do we evaluate infix expressions that are *not* completely parenthesized? Recall that there are standard rules for interpreting infix expressions in this case. These rules are also incorporated in high-level languages. They are necessary because parentheses are not always available to signal what is to be done next. For example, if we evaluate

$$a + b * c/d$$

then when the * is encountered, the stacks appear as

Operand Stack	Operator Stack
b	+
a	

The operator * signals that, had the expressions been completely parenthesized, a *left* parenthesis would have occurred just *before* the *b*, or else a *right* parenthesis would have occurred just *after* the *b*. In other words, the appearance of the operator requires a decision as to whether *b* should be considered an operand of * or an operand of +. The standard rules resolve such ambiguities by assigning *priorities* or *precedence values* to operators, assuming a left-to-right scan of the expression. For the binary operators, +, −, *, /, and ** (for exponentiation), the priorities are as follows:

1. Exponentiation (**) has the highest priority.
2. Multiplication and division (*, /) have the same priority, which is higher than that of addition or subtraction (+, −).
3. Addition and subtraction (+, −) have the same priority.

A left parenthesis also needs a priority, the lowest.

Whether *b* is an operand of * or + can then be resolved by taking *b* as an operand of the highest priority operator (* in this case). Again, parentheses may be used to override priorities. For example, in

$$(a + b) * c/d$$

b is to be associated with the + operator.

Example 4.6 In order to see how *any* infix expression is evaluated using priorities, and to develop an algorithm for this evaluation, consider the expression,

$$a + (b * c/d ** e) * f \blacksquare$$

To evaluate it, when the first * is encountered the situation will be

Operand Stack	Operator Stack
b	(
a	+

In this case, since the left parenthesis is on top of the operator stack, the * should be placed on top of the operator stack, and scanning continued. After *c*, division (/) is encountered and the stacks become

Operand Stack	Operator Stack
c	*
b	(
a	+

At this point a decision must be made with respect to *c*: either it is to be associated with * (at the top of the stack) or with / (the current operator being processed). The standard rules associate *c* with the operator of highest priority. In this case, since * and / have equal priorities, associate *c* with the leftmost of the two operators in the input—that is, the top stack operator. Thus, the * must be popped, *c* and *b* must be popped, the * must be applied to *b* and *c*, and the result, (*b* * *c*), placed on top of the operand stack. Then the / must be placed on the operator stack. Had the current operator been of higher priority (say, **), then the current operator should simply be placed on the operator stack.

In the example, after / and *d* are processed, the stacks are as follows:

Operand Stack	Operator Stack
d	/
(*b* * *c*)	(
a	+

The ** becomes the current operator, and *d* must be associated with it or with /. Since ** has higher priority, place it on the operator stack; the result after processing *e* is

Operand Stack	Operator Stack
e	**
d	/
(*b* * *c*)	(
a	+

The current input character being scanned is now a right parenthesis. This "matches" the topmost left parenthesis on the stack. The next steps are to pop the operator stack; pop the operand stack to obtain the top two operands; apply ** to them, and place the result back on the top of the operand stack. Then pop the operator stack; pop the operand stack to obtain the top two operands; apply / to them and place the result back on top of the operand stack; pop the stack again; and notice that a left parenthesis has appeared, signaling completion of the process for the current input character. The result is

Operand Stack	Operator Stack
((*b* * *c*)/(*d* ** *e*))	+
a	

Finally, the last * is processed. It has higher priority than +, so it is placed on the operator stack. *f* is then processed and placed on the operand stack, yielding

Operand Stack	Operator Stack
f	*
((*b* * *c*)/(*d* ** *e*))	+
a	

Since the input is exhausted, the final steps are, for each remaining operator on the operator stack, to pop the operator stack, remove the required number of top operands from the operand stack, apply the operator, and place the result back on top of the operand stack. The final result appears at the top of the operand stack.

The algorithm for the evaluation of any infix expression can now be written. The algorithm, which follows, assumes that a character, when read, will be an entire operand or operator. This means, for example, that ** should be interpreted as a "character." The algorithm returns the value of the expression in **evaluate**.

```
1. Initialize the operand stack to empty.
2. Initialize the operator stack to empty.
3. While there is another input character,
       read the current character
       if the current character is "(", then
           push it on the operator stack;
       else if the current character is an operand, then
           push it on the operand stack;
       else if the current character is an operator, then
           if the operator stack is not empty, then
               if the current character does not have greater priority than the top
               operator stack character, then
                   pop the operator stack, remove the required number of operands
                   from the operand stack, apply the operator to them, and push the
                   result on the operand stack
           push the current character onto the operator stack
       else if the current character is ")", then
           pop the operator stack and set topchar to the popped value
           while topchar is not (
               remove the number of operands required by topchar from the operand
               stack, apply topchar to them, and
               push the result onto the operand stack
               pop the operator stack and set topchar to the popped value
4. While the operator stack is not empty,
       pop the operator stack, remove the required number of operands from the
       operand stack, apply the operator to them, and push the result on the operand
       stack
5. Pop the operand stack and set evaluate to the popped value
```

Notice that the evaluation of an infix expression requires two stacks rather than the one stack required for the evaluation of a postfix expression. Other operators may be introduced and given appropriate priorities. For example, the assignment operator, =, would be given a higher priority than **.

4.6.3 Translating Infix to Postfix

Suppose, rather than evaluating an infix expression, a programmer wished to translate it and produce the corresponding postfix expression as output. The reason is that postfix expressions can be executed directly, whereas infix expressions are tricky to evaluate. Moreover, if the translation can be done, then the postfix expression may easily be embellished to produce a machine language program for the evaluation of the original infix expression.

The following modification of the infix evaluation algorithm results in such a translation.

1. Eliminate the operand stack. Instead, any pushing onto the operand stack should be changed to outputting the same value.
2. Instead of applying operators to operands, simply output the operators.

4.7 Queues

The queue, like the stack, is a useful data abstraction for retaining information in a specific order. A ***queue*** is a data structure with restricted insertion and deletion operations. Information may be inserted on the queue, but only at the ***rear end,*** or ***bottom.*** Information may be removed from the queue, but only at the ***front end,*** or ***top.***

The queue acts like the pile of Community Chest cards in Monopoly. The top card is the only one that can be removed, and insertions to the pile can be made only at the bottom. If we think of the information stored as representing postponed obligations, then the queue gives access to the obligations in the order in which they were incurred. A popular mnemonic for helping to remember this characteristic is FIFO—first in, first out. Like LIFO, this is a common term in accounting and inventory control systems.

4.7.1 Array and Circular Array Implementation of the Queue

Queues can be implemented in the same basic ways as stacks—as an array of records, as a list with its records stored in an array, and as a list with its records stored in dynamic memory. As in the case of stacks, these implementations are discussed in that order.

A queue may be implemented using an array of records by first declaring

```
typedef struct
{
   whatever info;
}queuerecord;
typedef struct
{
   queuerecord queuearray[LIMIT];
   int front,rear;
}queue;
queue q;
```

the type `queuerecord` *is a record with one member* `info` *of type* `whatever`

the type `queue` *is a record with members an array of type* `queuerecord` *and* `front` *and* `rear` *of type* `int`

`q` *is an instance of type* `queue`*, and storage is allocated for it*

As with stacks, overflow and underflow should be checked in a general implementation. A typical queue situation is depicted in Figure 4.10(a) for the array implementation. Figure 4.10(b) shows the situation after 18, 32, and 15 have been removed and 17 and 20 have been inserted.

Storage for insertion of more records is available at the top of the **queuearray**, but not at the bottom. To ensure that all the relocated storage for **queue** is used before overflow occurs, programs "wrap around." That is, the queue is implemented so that the **queuearray** is viewed as a circle of records, with 0 following the **LIMIT**, 7. **Front** is used to point to the entry at the front of the queue, and **rear** is used to point to the array location in which the next

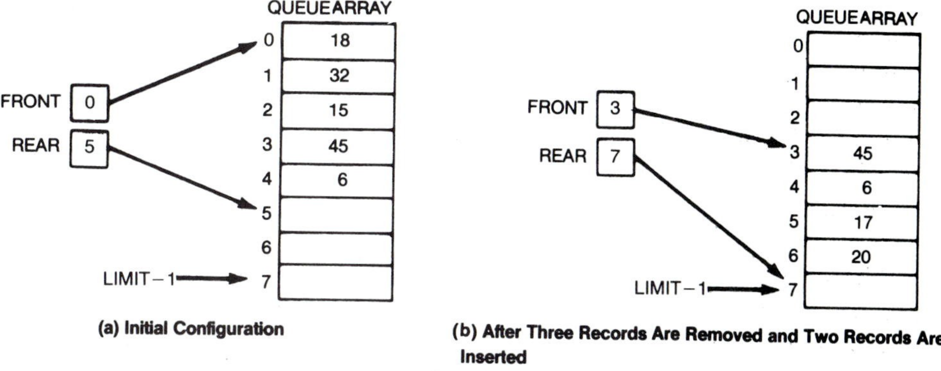

Figure 4.10 Typical Queue Configuration for an Array Implementation

inserted record is to be placed. As entries are inserted, `rear` moves down until it "falls off" the array, then it must be "wrapped around." As entries are deleted, `front` moves down until it "falls off" the array, then it must "wrap around."

The insertion operation may then be implemented as follows:

```
insert(pnewrecord,pq)
/* Inserts newrecord at the rear of queue q */
queuerecord *pnewrecord;
queue *pq;
{
   if ((*pq).front == -1)
      {
         (*pq).front = 0;
         (*pq).queuearray[0].info = (*pnewrecord).info;
         (*pq).rear = 1;
      }

   else

      if((*pq).rear == (*pq).front)
         printf("\n overflow \n");
      else
         {

            if((*pq).rear <= (LIMIT - 1))
               {

                  (*pq).queuearray[(*pq).rear].info =
                                 (*pnewrecord).info;
                  (*pq).rear = (*pq).rear + 1;
               }
            else
               {
```

`front` = `-1` signifies `queue` empty

empty, so update `front` to point to the start of the array, insert the new entry there and set rear to the next location

test for overflow which occurs when the queue is full, signified by `front` = `rear`

`rear` <= `LIMIT - 1` signifies that `rear` must wrap around

add new entry and move `rear` down

```
                    if((*pq).front == 0)
                        printf("\n overflow \n");
                    else
                        {
                            (*pq).queuearray[0].info =
                                (*pnewrecord).info;
                            (*pq).rear = 1;
                        }
                }
        }
}
```

`rear` *must now wrap around to the start of the array; if* `front` *= 0, then the array is full, so it cannot do so*

there is room to wrap around, so the new entry is inserted at the start of the array and `rear` *set to the next location*

`Setqueue` must set **`front`** and **`rear`** to minus one (−1). **`Empty`** will return the value *true* when **`front`** = −1, and *false* otherwise. The removal of a record can be implemented by a function **`remove`**, which returns in **`value`** the record that was deleted from the queue.

```
remove(pq,pvalue)
/* Deletes the front entry from
   queue q and copies its contents
   into value
*/
queue *pq;
queuerecord *pvalue;
{
    if(empty(pq))
        printf("\n underflow \n");
    else
        {
            (*pvalue).info = (*pq).queuearray
                                [(*pq).front].info;
            (*pq).front = (*pq).front + 1;
            if((*pq).front == (*pq).rear)
                setqueue(pq);
            if((*pq).front > (LIMIT - 1))
                (*pq).front = 0;
        }
}
```

underflow test

copies front record

deletes it by moving `front` *down*

if queue is empty, then reinitialize it

`front` > `LIMIT - 1` *signifies that it must wrap around*

4.7.2 List Implementation of the Queue with an Array of Records

Now we can turn to implementing a queue as a list with records stored in an array. The **`availist`** of Section 3.7 actually acts as a list implementation of a *queue* if **`reclaim`** returns a record to the *rear* of the **`availist`**. Thus queue can be implemented as a list of records stored in an array.

4.7.3 List Implementation of the Queue with Records in Dynamic Memory

The third queue implementation is also a list—one involving dynamic storage allocation of the records in dynamic memory. First, the following declaration must be made:

```
typedef struct record
{
   whatever info;
   struct record *link;
}queuerecord,*queue;
```

`Setqueue` must set `queue` to `null`. `Insert` will first request storage for the new record to be inserted by invoking `malloc`. It will then set its `info` data and insert it as the new last record in the queue. `Remove` must delete the first record of the queue and return its `info` data.

Your deck has now been "stacked," you've been "queued" into queues, and you mustn't postpone your obligation to use them!

4.8 Case Study: Checking Sequences for Proper Nesting

To bring together the major ideas of this chapter, a case study to check program structure for proper nesting is presented. Its main features are:

1. The top-down approach
2. Demonstration of the use of the stack, treating it as a data abstraction
3. Checking program structure for proper nesting by developing a nonrecursive and a recursive function
4. The different perspectives required to develop the two functions

Every computer programmer has at one time or another gotten error messages saying "incomplete loop structure" or "a missing parenthesis." You now have enough background to write a program that checks for such errors. Let's see how it can be done.

Arithmetic expressions, as well as a program text, consist of sequences of symbols. Complex arithmetic expressions may be composed by properly combining simpler arithmetic expressions, delineated by matching left and right parentheses. The simpler expressions are said to be *nested* within the more complex expressions that contain them. The complex expression $(a * (b + [c / d])) + b)$ contains two pairs of nested expressions. C programs contain compound statements delimited by matching { **(begin)** and } **(end)** pairs. Ignoring all other symbols, these matching pairs must satisfy rules of nesting to be syntactically correct.

Nesting means that one matching pair is wholly contained within another. When pairs are nested, they may not overlap, as do the two pairs in ([ )]. The rules of nesting are the same for any sequence that is built by combining simpler sequences. They require that the start and end of each component be specified. Checking complex sequences to determine that these **begin–end** pairs do not overlap is an important operation. It provides an interesting application of the stack data abstraction, as well as of recursion. An intimate connection exists among such sequences, stacks, recursions, and trees; it will be explored more fully in later chapters.

Two abstractions of this problem will be considered. The second is a generalization of the first. To begin, assume only one kind of left parenthesis and one kind of matching right parenthesis, and consider sequences composed of these. Thus, at first, expressions such as ([]) are not allowed, since they involve more than one kind of parenthesis.

Given a sequence of left and right parentheses, determine if they may be paired so that they satisfy two conditions:

- **i.** Each pair consists of a left and right parenthesis, with the left parenthesis preceding the right parenthesis.
- **ii.** Each parenthesis occurs in exactly one pair.

If a sequence has a pairing satisfying both of these conditions, the sequence and pairing are ***valid.*** The problem is to determine whether a given sequence is valid or not. No sequence starting with a right parenthesis, ")", can be valid, since there is no preceding left parenthesis, "(", to pair with it. Any valid sequence must therefore begin with some series of n "(" parentheses preceding the first appearance of a ")" parenthesis, such as Figure 4.11(a), for which n is 3. Suppose we remove this adjacent pair, the nth "(" parenthesis, and the immediately following first ")" parenthesis. This would be pair 1 in Figure 4.11(a). If the new sequence thus obtained is valid, then adding the removed pair to it results in a valid pairing. Thus the original sequence is valid.

Suppose you find that the resultant sequence is not valid. Can you conclude that the original sequence is not valid? In other words, has constraining one of the pairs to be the first adjacent "(" and ")" parentheses made a pairing of the original sequence satisfying (i) and (ii) impossible? The answer is no. To see this, assume that there *is* some valid pairing of the original sequence, in which the first ")" parenthesis is not paired with the immediately preceding "(" parenthesis, but there is *no* valid pairing in which it *is*. In general, the first ")" parenthesis must then be paired with an earlier "(" parenthesis, and the immediately preceding "(" parenthesis must have been paired with a later ")" parenthesis, as in Figure 4.11(b). These two pairs can then be rearranged by interchanging their "(" parentheses. The resultant pairing satisfies conditions (i) and (ii), yet it has the first adjacent "(" parenthesis paired with the immediately following ")" parenthesis, but this is the nesting constraint that has been specified. This contradicts the assumption that no valid pairing satisfies the constraint.

Consequently, the conclusion is that a solution to the problem is obtained as follows:

1. Pair the first adjacent left, "(", and right, ")", parentheses and remove the pair.
2. If the resultant sequence is valid, then so is the original sequence; otherwise the original sequence is not valid.

Think of a left parenthesis as denoting an incurred obligation, and a right parenthesis as the fulfilling of the most recently incurred obligation. This is the precise situation for which a stack is useful. As the program scans a sequence

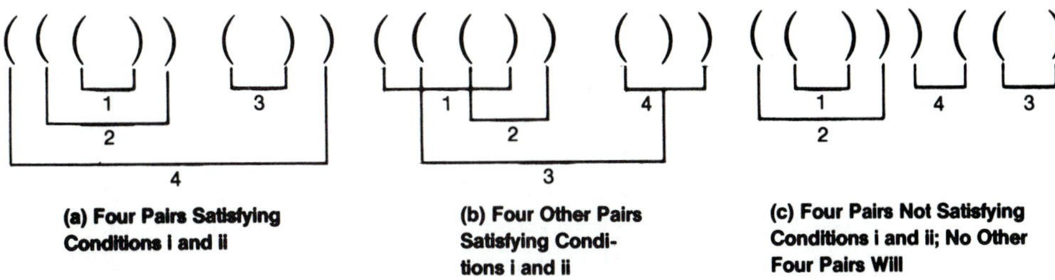

Figure 4.11 Valid and Invalid Nesting of Parentheses

from left to right, it pushes each "(" parenthesis onto a stack, representing an incurred obligation. Task 1 of the solution may then be carried out by popping the stack when the first ")" parenthesis is encountered, to fulfill the most recently incurred obligation.

Carrying out task 2 requires first determining if the resultant sequence is valid. Notice, however, that had the resultant sequence been processed in this same way, the contents of the stack would be *exactly* what they are now. Consequently, the program can continue to scan the original sequence (which is exactly what would be seen if it were scanning the resultant sequence), pushing whenever it encounters a "(" parenthesis, and popping whenever it comes to a ")" parenthesis. If the stack is empty when the entire scan is completed, then we have determined that the original sequence is valid; otherwise it is not. During the scan, any attempt to pop an empty stack means that no "(" parenthesis is available to be paired with the ")" parenthesis that caused the attempt (that is, the sequence is invalid).

This solution may be implemented as in the function `determine`, which follows this paragraph. Note that the stack is treated as a data abstraction. `Readchar` is a function that reads into its parameter the next character of the input sequence and returns *true*, unless the character read was a `specialchar` used as a sentinel, and then it returns *false*. When `determine` returns, the entire input sequence has been read. `Valid` will return *true* if a pairing satisfying (i) and (ii) exists, and *false* otherwise.

Nonrecursive Version

```
determine(pvalid)
/* Returns true in valid only if the
   input sequence is properly nested
*/
int *pvalid;
{
   char currentchar;
   struct
       {
          char topchar;
       }topcharacter;
```

```
    stack s;                                  ] s is an instance of type stack,
                                                and storage is allocated to it
    *pvalid = TRUE;
    setstack(&s);                             ] s initialized to empty
    while(readchar(&currentchar))             ] reads into and tests current-
                                                char
       if(leftparen(currentchar))             ] if a "(", then puts it on the
          push(&currentchar,&s);                stack
       else if(rightparen(currentchar))       ] if a ")" and if the stack is not
          if(!empty(&s))                        empty, then pops the stack into
             {                                  topcharacter; now two
                pop(&s,&topcharacter);          "adjacent" parentheses have
                                                been removed
                if(!match(topcharacter.topchar,  ] test for a match
                   currentchar))
                   *pvalid = FALSE;
             }
          else
             *pvalid = FALSE;
       else
          process(currentchar,&s);            ] do desired processing of the
                                                nonparenthesis
    if(!empty(&s))                            ] if s is not empty when all input
       *pvalid = FALSE;                         is complete, then unmatched
}                                               parentheses remain
```

Leftparen returns the value *true* if its parameter is a left parenthesis, and false otherwise. **Rightparen** is defined similarly. **Match** returns the value *true* if **topchar** and **currentchar** are left and right parentheses, respectively.

One of the aims of the text is to show how general functions can be adapted to solve particular problems. **Determine** is such a general function. It can be adapted to evaluate a completely parenthesized infix expression. We repeat the rule of Section 4.6.2 to be used to evaluate such an expression:

1. Scan the infix expression from left to right.
2. When a "matched" pair of "left" and "right" parentheses is encountered, apply the operator to the operands enclosed within the pair of parentheses, and replace the paired parentheses and the contained operator and operands by the result. Continue scanning from this point.

The matched pairs referred to in this rule are exactly the same as in this case study. Studying the rule, you can see that a right parenthesis signals that an operator and its operands are enclosed between the right parenthesis and its matching left parenthesis.

Determine may be modified to obtain a function **evaluate**, by defining the **process** routine as follows:

1. When an operand is encountered, place the operand on top of an operand stack.
2. When an operator is encountered, place the operator on top of the operator stack.

It is also necessary, when a "right" parenthesis is encountered, and the operator stack is not empty, to pop the operator stack, remove the required number of operands from the top of the operand stack, apply the operator to those operands, and place the result on the top of the operand stack. This must be done just before the `pop(&s,&topcharacter)` statement. `Determine`'s stack, `s`, plays the role of the operator stack. An operand stack must be introduced and must be available to both the `evaluate` and `process` functions.

The general function `determine` is actually more complex than need be for "paired parentheses." In fact, a stack is not even necessary. All that is really needed is to keep a tally of "(" parentheses, decreasing the tally by 1 every time a ")" parenthesis is read. If the tally ever becomes negative, then `determine` should, from that point, simply read in the rest of the input sequence and return *false*. Otherwise, if the tally is zero after the entire input sequence has been read, it should return true. `Determine` is implemented as shown in the nonrecursive function listed above because it will serve as the solution to the next problem, for which "paired parentheses" will be a special case.

Suppose, instead of containing only "(" and ")" parentheses, the input sequence could consist of any characters. Assume that each character could be either a left or a right character but not both, and also that each left character has a unique right character with which it matches. For instance, a, (, [, and l might be "left" characters and the unique "right" characters with which they match z,),], and r, respectively.

Given a sequence of left and right characters, determine if they may be paired so that

- **i.** Each pair consists of a left and a right matching character, with the left character preceding the right character.
- **ii.** Each character occurs in exactly one pair.
- **iii.** The sequence of characters between the left and right characters of each pair must also satisfy (i) and (ii).

If a sequence of left and right characters satisfies conditions (i), (ii), and (iii), the sequence and the pairing are *valid*. Condition (iii) then says that the sequence of characters between the left and right characters of each pair must be valid.

Let's see if this definition makes sense. Consider the above sample "matching" involving a, z, (,), [,], l, and r and the sequences of Figure 4.12.

Both the pairings of Figure 4.12(a) and those of Figure 4.12(b) satisfy (i) and (ii). However, only the pairing of (a) satisfies (iii). The pairing of (b) fails because the left and right characters of pair 3 are a and z, and the sequence of characters between them is])lr. This sequence does not satisfy conditions (i), (ii), and (iii), because none of the six possible ways to form two pairs will be valid. It is also apparent that the pairing of (b) fails, because the left and right characters of pair 2 are "[" and "]" and the sequence of characters between them, a, is not valid. One would have to be sure no other pairings for (b) are valid before concluding that (b) is not a valid sequence.

It is not immediately apparent that this problem generalizes the first problem, even if the characters are restricted to be just left and right parentheses. This

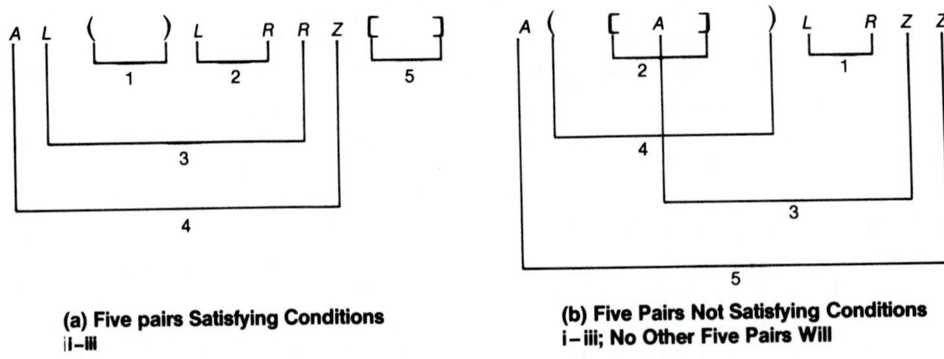

Figure 4.12 Valid and Invalid Nesting of Matched Characters

is because condition (iii) does not appear in the first problem. However, the reasoning used there shows that adding the condition does not change the problem. In fact, if the left and right matching characters are thought of as different kinds of parentheses, the same reasoning applied in the first problem can be applied to the present problem.

Again, any valid sequence must start with some series of $n > 0$ left parenthese preceding the first appearance of a right parenthesis. Suppose its matching left parenthesis does not immediately precede it. This is the situation, for example, in Figure 4.12(b), where there are four left parentheses, a, (, [, a, appearing before "]," the first right parenthesis. In order for this first right parenthesis to satisfy (i) and (ii), it must then be paired with a previous matching left parenthesis. But then the immediately preceding left parenthesis is the last character in the sequence between that pair of parentheses. In order to satisfy (iii), this sequence must be valid. *This* sequence cannot be valid since this last left parenthesis has no matching right parenthesis in *this* sequence, as indicated in Figure 4.13.

In conclusion, a solution may be obtained as follows:

1. Pair the first adjacent left and right parentheses that match, and remove the pair.
2. If the resultant sequence is valid, then so is the original sequence; otherwise the original sequence is not valid.

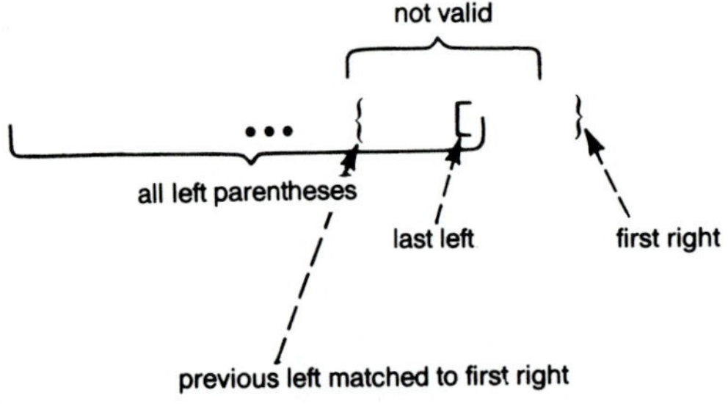

Figure 4.13 An Invalid Nesting Sequence

Function `determine` is also an implementation of this solution using a stack, assuming `leftparen`, `rightparen`, and `match` reflect the different left parentheses, right parentheses, and matched pairs, respectively. The stack is needed in order to implement this solution. It is no longer simply a question of increasing or decreasing a tally, depending on whether the program reads a "(" or a ")" parenthesis, and making sure it never goes below zero and ends at zero. It is not even enough to keep a distinct tally for each of the different kinds of "left" and "right" parentheses. This would not result in Figure 4.12(b), for example, being recognized as invalid, because each of the four numbers would satisfy the requirements just mentioned. It is condition (iii), and more than one kind of left and right parentheses, that makes the stack mandatory. Consider a pair satisfying conditions (i) and (ii). To satisfy condition (iii), the sequence of characters between the "left" and "right" parentheses of the pair must also be valid. In effect, a new set of tallies must be kept for that sequence, and they must satisfy the three conditions. The stack is actually holding *all* of these tallies. Each time a "left" parenthesis appears, it becomes a character in many sequences, in general, and the tally for it, associated with each of those sequences, must be increased by one. Pushing it onto the stack, in effect, increases all these tallies by one simultaneously. Similarly, popping the stack decreases them all simultaneously.

So far the solution has been nonrecursive and has required looking at the input as simply a sequence of parentheses satisfying certain local constraints; a left parenthesis must encounter a matching right parenthesis before any other right parenthesis appears. Any global structure inherent in the input has been ignored. Development of a recursive solution, however, requires that a valid input be defined recursively. The recursive definition of a valid sequence may be restated to show its structure more clearly.

A ***valid sequence*** is

- A null sequence
- A left and right matching pair of parentheses with a valid sequence between them
- A valid sequence followed by a valid sequence

In other words, a valid sequence is

- A null sequence,
- *One* valid sequence surrounded by a pair of matching parentheses, or
- A series of valid sequences, *each* surrounded by a pair of matching parentheses

The last case would appear as

(valid sequence)(valid sequence) · · · (valid sequence)

The following program is a recursive version of `determine` based on the recursive definition.

Recursive Version

```
determine(pvalid,last)
/* Returns true in valid only if the input
   sequence is properly nested; last must
   initially contain a special character
   used as the input terminator.
*/

int *pvalid;
char last;
{
   char currentchar;
   int done;
   static int more;
   done = FALSE;
   more = TRUE;
   while(!done && more)
      {
         more = readchar(&currentchar);
         if(leftparen(currentchar))
            determine(pvalid,currentchar);
         else if(rightparen(currentchar))

            if(!match(last,currentchar))
               *pvalid = FALSE;
            else
               {
                  done = TRUE;
                  last = SPECIALCHAR;
               }
         else
            process(last,currentchar);
      }
   if(last != SPECIALCHAR)
      *pvalid = FALSE;
}
```

- `static` *to retain its value between calls*
- *loops through each input character*
  - *reads into* `currentchar`, *updates* `more`
  - *determines if the input sequence between this left parenthesis and the matching "right parenthesis is valid; the left parenthesis is saved in* `last`
  - *test if the left parenthesis (in* `last`*) in fact matches the right parenthesis just read (which is now in* `currentchar`*)*
  - *set* `done` *to signify a match*
  - *reinitialize* `last`
  - *process nonparenthesis*
- `last != SPECIALCHAR` *means left parentheses remain unmatched*

Determine must be called initially with **last** set to **specialchar**. It is used as an input terminator and should not occur in the sequence being checked. When a valid sequence surrounded by a pair of matching parentheses has been encountered, the variable done is set to **true**. At that point the program continues looking for a next such sequence. However, **last** must be reinitialized to the **specialchar**. The variable **more** is used to signal whether or not more characters remain to be read in the input string. It is declared to be static because it must retain its value between any recursive calls to **determine**.

Both this recursive solution and the iterative solution work from the inside out. The iterative program looks for adjacent matching left and right parentheses in the interior of the sequence. The recursive program looks for a valid sequence surrounded by a matching pair of parentheses. Thus the iterative solution sees the input

```
[ ( [ ] ) ] ( ) { [ ] } #
```

as

```
[ ( [ 1 ] ) ] ( 4 ) { [ 5 ] } #        (6 pairs of matching parentheses)
  -   2   -         -   6   -
- -   3   - -
```

and the recursive solution sees it as

```
[ ( [ ] ) ] ( 2 ) { [ ] } #        (3 valid sequences each one surrounded by a pair of
- -   1 - -         - 3   -         matching parentheses)
```

where # denotes the `specialchar`.

Another recursive solution could be written to work from the outside in, looking for a rightmost mate to the first left parenthesis and then checking the sequence between them for validity. This would lead to a less efficient solution, because parentheses could be considered more than once. Recursion often involves this dual possibility, so both should be explored.

■ Exercises

1. Let i and j be two integers and define $q(i, j)$ by $q(i, j) = 0$ if $i < j$ and $q(i - j, j) + 1$ if $i \geq j$

a. What is the value of $q(7,2)$?

b. Can we determine $q(0,0)$?

c. Can we determine $q(-3,-4)$?

2. Let `a` be an array of type float and i and n be positive integers. The function `m(a,i,n)` is defined by

`m(a,i,n)` = `a[i]` if `i` = `n` and `max(m(a,i + 1,n),a[i])` if `i` < `n`

a. Find `m(a,i,n)` if `i` = 1, `n` = 6, and `a` is

0. 6.8
1. 3.2
2. −5.0
3. 14.6
4. 7.8
5. 9.6
6. 3.2
7. 4.0

b. What does `m(a,i,n)` do?

3. Let `a` be an array of type real, and i and n be positive integers. The function `m(a,i,n)` is defined by

$$\texttt{m(a,i,n)} = \begin{cases} \texttt{a[i]} \text{ if } \texttt{i} = \texttt{n} \\ \texttt{max(m(a,i,}\lfloor\texttt{(i + n)/2}\rfloor\texttt{),m(a,}\lfloor\texttt{(i + n)/2}\rfloor\texttt{+ 1,n))} \text{ if } \texttt{i} < \texttt{n} \end{cases}$$

$\lfloor$`(i + n)/2`$\rfloor$ means, "Do an integer divide of `(i + n)/2`."

a. Find `m(a,i,n)` for i = 1, n = 6, and `a` the array of Exercise 2.

b. What does `m(a,i,n)` do?

4. Let i be a nonnegative integer. Find $b(4)$ where

$$\begin{aligned} b(0) &= 1 \\ b(n) &= b(0) \times b(n-1) + b(1) \times b(n-2) \\ &\quad + b(2) \times b(n-3) + \cdots + b(n-1) \times b(0) \qquad n > 0 \end{aligned}$$

5. Write a recursive function `max` corresponding to Exercise 2.
6. Write a recursive function `max` corresponding to Exercise 3.
7. a. Why does the recursive solution to the Towers of Hanoi problem use the minimum number of moves?
b. What is the number of moves it uses?
8. Consider the following nonrecursive algorithm for the Towers of Hanoi problem.

1. Label the disks 1, 2, . . ., n in increasing order of size.
2. Label the pegs i, a, and f, respectively, $n + 1$, $n + 2$, and $n + 3$.
3. Move the smallest disk onto another disk with an even label or onto an empty peg with an even label.
4. If all disks are on the same peg, then terminate. Move the second smallest top disk onto the peg not containing the smallest disk. Go to 1.

a. Convince yourself that this correctly solves the Towers of Hanoi problem.
b. Is the recursive solution or this nonrecursive version easier to understand.
9. Suppose a fourth peg is added to the Towers of Hanoi problem.
a. Write a recursive solution for this problem.
b. Can you find a recursive solution that uses the minimum number of moves for this problem?
10. Mark any n distinct points on the circumference of a circle. How many triangles may be drawn whose vertexes lie on three of the n points?
11. How many ways may k distinct points be selected from the n points of Exercise 10?
12. Given a permutation of 1, 2, . . ., n, let n_i be the number of integers to the right of i which exceed i. For the permutation 2134, $n_1 = 2$, $n_2 = 3$, $n_3 = 1$, $n_4 = 4$. Write a `process` function that will turn `permutations` into a program that prints $n_1, n_2, \ldots, n_n$ for each permutation.
13. Suppose `l` is implemented as a two-way list. Write a recursive function to reverse `l`.
14. Implement the function of Exercise 5.
15. Implement the function of Exercise 6.
16. Compare the requirements for the stack storage required during execution for the implementations of Exercises 5 and 6.
17. Why are the more efficient versions of Section 4.4 more efficient?
18. The Fibonacci sequence is defined by

$$\begin{aligned} f(0) &= 0, f(1) = 1 \\ f(n) &= f(n-1) + f(n-2) \text{ for } n = 2,3,4 \ldots \end{aligned}$$

a. Write a recursive function `fibonacci(n)` to compute and print $f(n)$.
b. Analyze its time and storage requirements.
19. a. Translate the program of Exercise 18 and obtain as efficient a version as you can.
b. Analyze its time and storage requirements.
20. Write a nonrecursive program `fibonacci(n)`, which takes $O(n)$ time and uses only four local variables.
21. a. Write a function `element` with parameter k, which returns the value of the kth element on the stack of integers implemented as in Figure 4.8. For instance, if k is 1, it

returns the value of the current first element. It does not disturb the stack at all. Assume you do not have access to the stack directly, but only through the `push`, `pop`, and `empty` routines.

b. Same as Exercise 21(a), except assume you do have direct access to the stack.

22. Two stacks are implemented in one array of length 1,000 as shown. The tops of the stacks are pointed to by `top1` and `top2` and grow toward each other. Write a procedure `push` that pushes the contents of `v` onto the stack indicated by `s`. `s` will have a value of 1 or 2. If the stack to which `v` is to be added is full, then `push` should not add it, but should return with `s` set to 0.

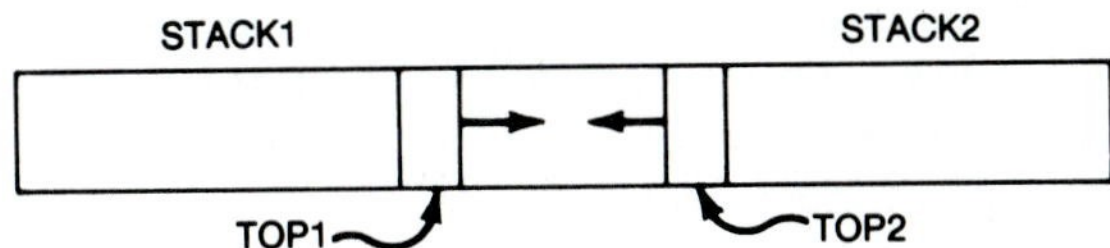

23. Write a function `maxstack` that returns in `m` the maximal element on a stack of integers implemented with pointer variables. `Maxstack` will return *true* when the stack is not empty, and *false* otherwise.

24. What does the following do?

```
pop(&s,&value);
push(&value,&s)
```

25. Why are parentheses not needed when prefix or postfix notation is used?

26. How do conventions eliminate ambiguity in infix notation?

27. Evaluate the postfix expression 3 6 + 6 2 / *8+.

28. Simulate the execution of the algorithm of Section 4.6.2 for evaluation of an infix expression on $(a * b/(c + d)) + e ** f$.

29. Simulate the execution of the translation algorithm of Section 4.6.3 on $(a * b/(c + d)) + e ** f$.

30. What priority must be given to the assignment operator, =, if the evaluation and translation algorithms for infix to postfix are to work on assignment statements as well as arithmetic expressions?

31. Write the function `evaluate`.

32. Describe how `evaluate` must be modified if arithmetic expressions are allowed to include function calls.

33. What will the pairing generated by the function `determine` be for the input sequence aa([[]()])zz?

34. Modify the function `determine` so that it outputs the pairs as follows:

```
   1 2 3 4 5 6 7 8
if ( ( ( ) ) ( ) ) is the input sequence,
then the output will be the pairs 3 4, 2 5, 6 7, 1 8.
```

35. Modify function `determine` so that it also outputs

```
( ( ( ) ) ( ) ),
4 2 1 1 2 3 3 4
```

for example, if the input is ((( )) ( )).

36. How must `determine` be modified if some left characters may also be right characters, and they will always match each other? For example, let the left characters be a, (, [, b, with the "right" characters being a,),], b. Here a is matched with a, b with b, "(" with ")," and "[" with "]." Then `a[a]` is not valid, but `a[CC](aa)a` and `ab()aab[]a` are.

37. Write the `remove` function for the array implementation of a queue.

38. Write the `insert` function for the pointer variable implementation of a queue.
39. Write the `remove` function for the pointer variable implementation of a queue.
40. Suppose function `buffer` has three parameters, `q` of type `queue`, `e` of type `whatever`, and `op` of type `character`. If `op` is r, then `buffer` returns after removing the top record of the queue and copying its value into `e`. If `op` is *n*, then `buffer` returns after inserting the value in `e` at the bottom of the queue. Write an implementation of `buffer`, assuming that access to the queue is only through the `empty`, `remove`, and `insert` routines.
41. A *deque* (pronounce like "deck") is a data abstraction that retains ordered information, but allows insertion and deletion at both its front and rear.
  a. Develop an array-based implementation of a deque and write corresponding `setdeque`, `insertf`, `insertr`, `removef`, `remover`, and `empty` routines.
  b. Do the same as in Exercise 41(a), except use pointer variables with dynamic storage allocation for the deque implementation.
42. Suppose there is a program to keep track of the current board configuration in a game of Monopoly by using a circular array of records, each record representing a board position (such as Boardwalk), and queues for Community Chest and Chance. Discuss how the records should be defined, what pointers to records will be convenient, and how these pointers and the circular array should be processed on each turn.

■ Suggested Assignments

1. Write and simulate a recursive program to reverse a list.
2. You might enjoy finding an algorithm for the following generalization of the Towers of Hanoi problem. The disks are each labelled with a positive integer. A configuration of disks on a peg is "legal" if each disk's integer is no larger than the sum of the integers on all disks below it, or there are no disks below it. How can the disks be moved so that any legal original configuration of *n* disks on peg 1 ends up on peg 3, with all intermediate configurations being legal?
3. Write the permutation program so it treats the permutation as a data abstraction.
4. In order to use storage efficiently when *n* stacks are needed during the execution of a program, it may be desirable to implement all the stacks in one array as shown here for $n = 4$.

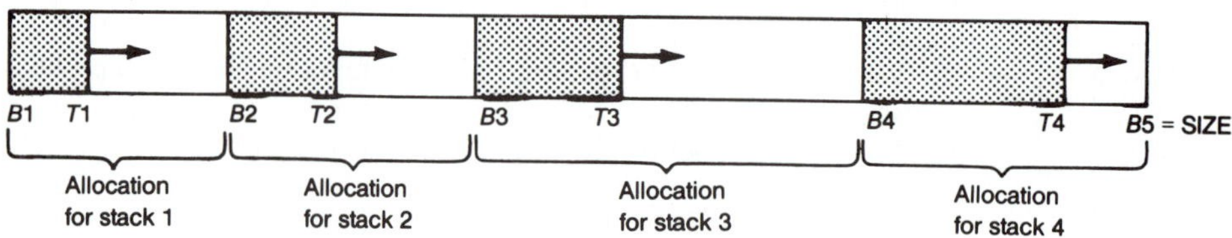

The *Bi*'s and *Ti*'s point to the bottoms and tops of the stacks, which grow to the right as indicated. Think of the total storage currently allocated to stack *i* as being from $B(i)$ to $B(i + 1)$. Stack *i* is actually using $T(i) - B(i + 1) + 1$ positions of the array. If $B1 = 1$, $B2 = 10$, $B3 = 15$, $B4 = 25$, $B5 =$ `size` of the array $= 35$, $T1 = 3$, $T2 = 12$, $T3 = 20$, and $T4 = 33$, then the stacks are using 3, 3, 6, and 9 entries, respectively, while they are allocated 9, 5, 10, and 10 entries.

When an entry is to be inserted into a stack that is currently using all its allocated storage, the stack is said to have overflowed. Stack *i* overflows if $Ti = B(i + 1) - 1$. Write a function to manage the storage provided by the array. Whenever a stack overflows, the function is to be invoked. If there is any unused space in the array, then the stack with an unused but allocated position which is "closest" to the overflow stack is to give up one of its unused positions. This position is then used by the overflow stack to accommodate its entry. This function must be written to shift stacks around. If no unused space exists in the array, then the procedure should print an "out of stack storage" message.

5 Packaging Data Abstractions

Introduces the concept of modules and file modularization to structure programs
With this type of program structure data abstractions are placed in files separate from the program file, and this
hides the details of the data abstraction from the programmer using them easing the programming task
increases efficiency as it enables the data abstractions to be compiled separately and stored in object code (separate compilation is possible)
To illustrate how programs are structured using modules and file modularization four examples, from previous chapters, are presented in detail
primes
stablemarriages
creation and printing of a list
nonrecursive Towers of Hanoi

5.1 Data Abstraction Revisited

The first step in creating a program is to develop the algorithm that will produce the solution. The algorithm must detail operations that will be performed on the given data. A decision must also be made about how the data will be organized. Typically data is best split into distinct groups, or collections, based on the basic operations required for each collection. The data structure utilized for each collection can be tailored to the specific operations to be performed on it. Each collection, with its operations, can then be treated individually as a data abstraction.

A *data abstraction* is a collection of data upon which only a set of specific operations are allowed. The technique of data abstraction has been used in this text as a tool in creating programs that are understandable and maintainable. Insight is required to determine the particular collection to use and the operations to act upon it. The same collection may be useful in a number of different problems. This may be so with the same set of allowable operations or with different sets of operations. As an example, recall that the stack data abstraction was used in both `towers` and `next` with the same operations.

Once the data abstractions to be used in a solution are determined, a decision must be made on how to implement them. This requires deciding what data structure is to be used to store the collection and how the operations on it will be defined. In this text each operation has been incorporated in a function using the tool of *functional modularization*. Treating the collection and its operations as a data abstraction means that the program can only process the collection using those functions. This guarantees that the collection is accessed only when one of the functions is invoked. Proper packaging of the data abstraction can thus ensure that it is used appropriately. How this packaging is done is the topic of this chapter.

The discussion is presented only now for several reasons. First, preceding chapters have introduced a number of data abstractions that can serve as vehicles to present different approaches to packaging. Next, packaging introduces another level of abstraction, which can complicate the understanding of the basic material. Time was needed to absorb the beginning concepts. Finally, packaging is language-dependent, and the aim of this book is to be as language-independent as possible yet still present programs in the C programming language. Given the language-dependence of packaging and the belief that students should first concentrate on basics, the topic is confined to this chapter. This does not mean it is unimportant—only that it might cloud the other concepts presented. Consequently the material in this chapter may be skipped or, alternatively, imposed on the programs in the later chapters. The C approaches to packaging are straightforward; should you desire, the programs can be readily modified to the style presented here.

5.2 The Prime Example

Consider the program below from Chapter 1 for calculating prime numbers.

```
#include <stdio.h>

main()
{
    int n;
    printf("\n n = ?\n");
    scanf("%d",&n);
    primes(n);
}

#define TRUE 1
#define FALSE 0
#define MAXN 500
typedef int collection[MAXN];

set(n,c)
/* Sets c to empty */
int n;
collection c;
{
    int i;
    for (i=1;i<=n;i++)
        c[i] = FALSE;
}

insert(i,c)
/* Inserts i in c */
int i;
```

reads in an integer `n` *and calls* `primes` *to print all prime numbers* ≤`n`

these definitions and functions give a specific implementation of a data abstraction: `collection` *with operations* `set`, `insert`, `omit`, *and* `belongs` *allowed. This is the* ***only*** *portion of the program that needs to be changed when the implementation of the data abstraction is changed.* `MAXN` *sets a limit on the size of arrays of type*

```
collection c;
{
   c[i] = TRUE;
}

omit(i,c)
/* Removes i from c */
int i;
collection c;
{
   c[i] = FALSE;
}

belongs(i,c)
/* Returns true only
   if i is in c
*/
int i;
collection c;
{
   return(c[i]);
}
```

`collection`, *so it sets a limit for* `n`.

```
primes(n)
/* Prints all prime numbers between 2 and n */
int n;
{
   collection candidates;
   create(n,candidates);
   remove(n,candidates);
   print(n,candidates);
}
```

this portion of the program is independent of the specific implementation of the data abstraction. It does not have to be changed if the implementation of the data abstraction changes. `Candidates` *is an instance of the data structure of type* `collection`.

```
create(n,c)
/* Creates a collection of integers between 2 and n */
int n;
collection c;
{
   int i;
   set(n,c);
   for (i=2;i<=n;i++)
      insert(i,c);
}
```

sets `c` *to empty*

inserts integers 2 to `n` *in* `c`

```
remove(n,c)
/* Removes all nonprimes from c */
int n;
collection c;
{
   int firstprime;
   int factor;
```

```
    firstprime = 2;
    factor = firstprime;
    while (nonprimes(factor,n))
        {
            delete(factor,n,c);
            factor++;
        }
}

nonprimes(factor,n)
/* Returns true only if non
   primes may remain in c
*/
int factor,n;
double sqrt();
{
   return(factor <= sqrt((double)n));
}

delete(factor,n,c)
/* Deletes multiples of factor from c */
int factor,n;
collection c;
{
   int nextmultiple;
   nextmultiple = 2 * factor;
   while (nextmultiple <= n)
       {
          omit(nextmultiple,c);
          nextmultiple = nextmultiple + factor;
       }
}

print(n,c)
/* Prints integers in c */
int n;
collection c;
{
   int i;
   for (i=2;i<=n;i++)
      if (belongs(i,c))
         printf("\n %d\n",i);
}
```

for all values of `factor` *from 2 to* `n`*, invokes* `delete` *to remove multiples of* `factor` *from* `c`

returns true as long as `factor` *is not larger than the square root of* `n`

invokes `omit` *to remove each nonprime from* `c` *that is a multiple of* `factor`

invokes `belongs` *for each integer from 2 to* `n`*, to determine if it is a prime, and if so prints it*

This program is structured with the data abstraction `collection` and its operations `set`, `insert`, `omit`, and `belongs` placed together. This facilitates finding its data structure and function declarations and definitions, whenever modifications are desired. Changes to **collection**, **set**, **insert**, **omit**, and **belongs** may be made, as long as they still do their tasks correctly *without* changing any other part of the program.

The program, however, is more cluttered and longer than necessary. It is burdened with exhibiting details of the data abstraction that are irrelevant to it. One way to avoid this is to use the *include* capability of C. Using C's **include** statement, we can

- Create a file called **collection** that contains all the statements specifying the data abstraction, and then
- Insert these into the program with one statement—the **include** statement

This is done in the following version of the program.

When this program is compiled, the C preprocessor will replace the **include** "collection" statement in the program file with the source code from the file collection. Thus the object code produced by the compiler for this version will be identical to that produced by the first version.

```
#include <stdio.h>

main()
{
   int n;
   printf("\n n = ?\n");
   scanf("%d",&n);
   primes(n);
}
```

reads in an integer n *and calls* primes *to print all prime numbers* ≤n

```
#include "collection"
```

replaced by the contents of the file collection

```
primes(n)
/* Prints all prime numbers between 2 and n */
int n;
{
   collection candidates;
   create(n,candidates);
   remove(n,candidates);
   print(n,candidates);
}

create(n,c)
/* Creates a collection of integers between 2 and n */
int n;
collection c;
{
   int i;
   set(n,c);
```

This portion of the program is independent of the specific implementation of the data abstraction. It does not have to be changed if the implementation of the data abstraction changes. Candidates *is an instance of the data structure of type* collection.

sets c *to empty*

```
   for (i=2;i<=n;i++)
      insert(i,c);
}

remove(n,c)
/* Removes all nonprimes from c */
int n;
collection c;
{
   int firstprime;
   int factor;
   firstprime = 2;
   factor = firstprime;
   while (nonprimes(factor,n))
      {
         delete(factor,n,c);
         factor++;
      }
}

nonprimes(factor,n)
/* Returns true only if non
   primes may remain in c
*/
int factor,n;
double sqrt();
{
   return(factor <= sqrt((double)n));
}

delete(factor,n,c)
/* Deletes multiples of factor from c */
int factor,n;
collection c;
{
   int nextmultiple;
   nextmultiple = 2 * factor;
   while (nextmultiple <= n)
      {
         omit(nextmultiple,c);
         nextmultiple = nextmultiple + factor;
      }
}

print(n,c)
/* Prints integers in c */
int n;
collection c;
{
   int i;
```

inserts integers 2 to `n` *in* `c`

for all values of `factor` *from 2 to* `n`, *invokes* `delete` *to remove multiples of* `factor` *from* `c`

returns true as long as `factor` *is not larger than the square root of* `n`

invokes `omit` *to remove each nonprime from* `c` *that is a multiple of* `factor`

```
   for (i=2;i<=n;i++)
      if (belongs(i,c))
         printf("\n %d\n",i);
}
```

invokes `belongs` *for each integer from 2 to* `n`, *to determine if it is a prime, and if so prints it*

The file collection, which can be stored separately, contains:

```
/* The data abstraction collection
   and its allowed operations */

#define TRUE 1
#define FALSE 0
#define MAXN 500
typedef int collection[MAXN];

set(n,c)
/* Sets c to empty */
int n;
collection c;
{
   int i;
   for (i=1;i<=n;i++)
      c[i] = FALSE;
}

insert(i,c)
/* Inserts i in c */
int i;
collection c;
{
   c[i] = TRUE;
}

omit(i,c)
/* Removes i from c */
int i;
collection c;
{
   c[i] = FALSE;
}

belongs(i,c)
```

These definitions and functions give a specific implementation of a data abstraction: `collection` *with operations* `set`, `insert`, `omit`, *and* `belongs` *allowed. This is the* ***only*** *portion of the program that needs to be changed when the implementation of the data abstraction is changed.* **`MAXN`** *sets a limit on the size of arrays of type* `collection` *so it sets a limit for* `n`.

```
/* Returns true only
   if i is in c
*/
int i;
collection c;
{
   return(c[i]);
}
```

So far, the programs in this text have been written so that they are compiled as a *single source code* file. This is still true for the two versions of **primes**. The first was written as a single source file. In the second, the **include** statement causes the precompiler to incorporate **collection** into the program file, producing a single source code file.

It is also possible in C to locate the functions of a program in more than one file. Each file of source code can be separately compiled, producing a corresponding file of *object code*. This ability to allocate the functions of a program to different files is a tool that can be used to achieve another kind of modularity besides functional modularity. This new modularity, which we call ***file modularity,*** allocates functions to files, whereas functional modularity allocates tasks to functions. In keeping with this definition of file modularity, the term ***module*** will be used to mean one or more files, to be separately compiled, used for the implementation of a data abstraction. Before compilation they are *source modules;* after compilation they are *object modules*.

To create a module for **collection**, two files in addition to the program file will be needed. They are called **collection.h** and **collection.c**. **Collection.h**, the header file, contains all definitions needed for **collection**'s data structure and all declarations for its functions. The header file must be included in any file using this data abstraction. **Collection.c**, which contains definitions of all the functions of the data abstraction that implement its operations, must also include the header file, as in the following example.

The two files are shown below. In **collection.h** a standard way of declaring a function is presented. It uses the **extern** declaration, as in the following example.

```
extern set(/* int,collection */);
```

The **extern** declaration informs the compiler that the function is defined elsewhere, in another file. The comment **/* int,collection */** identifies the parameters of the function—since it is a comment, it disappears in compilation.

With this version, the program file and collection are compiled separately into object modules. The *linker* must combine the two object modules to create an executable program.

The File `collection.h`

```
/* header for collection of integers */

#define TRUE 1
#define FALSE 0
#define MAXN 500
typedef int collection[MAXN];

extern set(/* int,collection */);
/* Sets collection to empty */

extern insert(/* int,collection */);
/* Adds int to collection */

extern omit(/*int,collection */);
/* Takes int out of collection */

extern belongs(/*int,collection */);
/* Returns true only if int is in collection */
```

The File `collection.c`

```
/* operations for collection of integers */

#include "collection.h"   ] replaced by the contents of the file collection.h

set(n,c)
/* Sets c to empty */
int n;
collection c;
{
   int i;
   for (i=1;i<=n;i++)
      c[i] = FALSE;
}

insert(i,c)
/* Inserts i in c */
int i;
collection c;
{
   c[i] = TRUE;
}

omit(i,c)
/* Removes i from c */
int i;
collection c;
{
   c[i] = FALSE;
}
```

```
belongs(i,c)
/* Returns true only
   if i is in c
*/
int i;
collection c;
{
   return(c[i]);
}
```

Final Version: The File `primestest.c`

```
#include <stdio.h>

main()
{
   int n;
   printf("\n n = ?\n");
   scanf("%d",&n);
   primes(n);
}
```

reads in an integer `n` *and calls* `primes` *to print all prime numbers* ≤`n`

```
#include "collection.h"
```

replaced by the contents of the file `collection.h`

```
primes(n)
/* Prints all prime numbers between 2 and n */
int n;
{
   collection candidates;
   create(n,candidates);
   remove(n,candidates);
   print(n,candidates);
}


create(n,c)
/* Creates a collection of integers between
   2 and n */
int n;
collection c;
{
   int i;
   set(n,c);
   for (i=2;i<=n;i++)
      insert(i,c);
}


remove(n,c)
/* Removes all nonprimes from c */
int n;
collection c;
```

This portion of the program is independent of the specific implementation of the data abstraction. It does not have to be changed if the implementation of the data abstraction changes. `Candidates` *is an instance of the data structure of type* `collection`.

sets `c` *to empty*

inserts integers 2 to `n` *in* `c`

```
{
   int firstprime;
   int factor;
   firstprime = 2;
   factor = firstprime;
   while (nonprimes(factor,n))
       {
          delete(factor,n,c);
          factor++;
       }
}

nonprimes(factor,n)
/* Returns true only if non
   primes may remain in c
*/
int factor,n;
double sqrt();
{
   return(factor <= sqrt((double)n));

}

delete(factor,n,c)
/* Deletes multiples of factor from c */
int factor,n;
collection c;
{
   int nextmultiple;
   nextmultiple = 2 * factor;
   while (nextmultiple <= n)
       {
          omit(nextmultiple,c);
          nextmultiple = nextmultiple + factor;
       }
}

print(n,c)
/* Prints integers in c */
int n;
collection c;
{
   int i;
   for (i=2;i<=n;i++)
       if (belongs(i,c))
          printf("\n %d\n",i);
}
```

for all values of `factor` *from 2 to* `n`*, invokes* `delete` *to remove multiples of* `factor` *from* `c`

returns true as long as `factor` *is not larger than the square root of* `n`

invokes `omit` *to remove each nonprime from* `c` *that is a multiple of* `factor`

invokes `belongs` *for each integer from 2 to* `n`*, to determine if it is a prime, and if so prints it*

Although this third version may seem similar to the second, it differs in an important way. Its functions are *distributed* among three files. Two of these, `collection.h` and `collection.c`, are used by the module for `collection`, the data abstraction. This allows the details of the implementation to be hidden, removes the need for the program itself to change whenever the data abstraction implementation is changed, and also shortens the program. The second version does all this as well, but the third version is even better. It allows `collection.c` to be compiled separately from file `primestest.c`, the file containing `main`, `primes`, `create`, and so on. More precisely, `primestest.c` must be compiled, and then the object code for `primestest.c`, along with the object code from the separately compiled file `collection.c`, can be linked by the linker. Finally, the resultant executable file produced by the linker can be run.

Once `collection.c` has been successfully compiled and verified, its object module can be stored in a library for use in the creation of programs such as `primes`. In this way C fosters the building up of programs by putting together previous solutions. In the creation or modification of large programs, the use of already compiled modules can significantly reduce time for compiling and program development.

Whenever the implementation of the data abstraction `collection` changes, changes may occur in the source code of `collection.h` or of `collection.c`. When they occur in `collection.h`, any file that includes it must be recompiled. In our example, this means that `collection.c` and `primestest.c` must be recompiled. To run `primestest.c`, its compiled version, along with the compiled version of the new `collection.c`, must be linked; then the resultant executable program file can be run. The new object code produced by compiling the new version of `collection.c` should replace the old version in the library. When the changes occur in `collection.c` only, it must be recompiled followed by relinking with the object code for `primestest.c` before the new executable program file can be run.

5.3 Stable Marriages

As a second example of file modularization, consider the stable marriage program of Section 2.5.2. That program is structured with the data abstractions `pairings`, with its operations `mate`, `read_mens_mates`, and `create_womens_mates` placed together, and `preferences`, with its operations `mostpreferred`, `nextpreferred`, `prefers`, `read_preferences`, and `create_priorities` also placed together. Grouping each data abstraction facilitates finding its data structures, function declarations, and definitions, whenever modifications to them are required. Such changes will not necessitate changing any other part of the program, since it was written treating pairings and preferences as data abstractions. Also, changes to one data abstraction do not require changes in the other. The program in Section 2.5.2 is written as a single source file. We now place the two data abstractions in modules. The modules and the program file structure of the program using file modularization are printed below. The headers, operations and program file are, respectively, `pairings.h`, `pairings.c`, `preferences.h`, `preferences.c`, and `stablemarriages.c`.

The File `pairings.h`

```
/* header for pairings */
#define MAXN 50
typedef int mates[MAXN];

extern mate(/* int,pairings */);
/* Returns the mate of person int */

extern read_mens_mates(/* int,pairings */);
/* Reads the mates of the men(int of them)
   into pairings
*/

extern create_womens_mates(/* int,pairings_1,pairings_2 */);
/* Creates the pairings_2 of the
   men(int of them), based on
   the mens' mates specified by
   pairings_1
*/
```

The File `pairings.c`

```
/* operations allowed on pairings */

#include "pairings.h"     ] replaced by the contents of file pairings.h

mate(person,pairs)
/* Returns persons mate
   as specified by pairs */
int person;
pairings pairs;
{
   return(pairs[person]);
}

read_mens_mates(n,pairs)
/* Reads the n wives into pairs */
int n;
pairings pairs;
{
   int i;
   printf("\n mpairs = ? \n");
   for (i=1;i<=n;i++)
      scanf("%d",&pairs[i]);
}

create_womens_mates(n,pairs1,pairs2)
/* Pairs 1 specifies the n wives, one
   for each man. Pairs2 is set to
   specify the n men, one for each woman.
```

```
*/
int n;
pairings pair;
{
   int i,j;
   for (i=1;i<=n;i++)
       {
          for (j=1;pairs1[j] != i;j++)
             ;
             pairs2[i] = j;
       }
}
```

The File `preferences.h`

```
/* header file for preferences */

#define MAXN 50
typedef int preferences[MAXN][MAXN];

extern mostpreferred(/* int,preferences */);
/* Returns the mate most preferred by
   person int as specified by pref */

extern nextpreferred(/* int_1,int_2,pref */);
/* Returns the mate preferred most, after
   the mate given by index int_2, by person
   int_1 as specified by pref
*/

extern prefers(/* int_1,int_2,int_3,pref */);
/* Returns true if individual int_1 prefers
   person int_2 to individualsmate int_3
   as specified by pref
*/

extern read_preferences(/* int,pref */);
/* Reads int number of rows of
   preferences into pref
*/

extern create_priorities(/* int,pref_1,pref_2 */);
/* Creates int number of individual
   priorities in pref_2 based on the
   individual preferences specified
   by pref_1
*/
```

The File `preferences.c`

```
/* operations allowed on preferences */

#include "preferences.h"  ] replaced by the contents of file preferences.h

mostpreferred(person,pref)
/* Returns the mate most preferred by
   person as specified by pref */
int person;
preferences pref;
{
   return(pref[person][1]);
}


nextpreferred(person,index,pref)
/* Returns the mate preferred most, after
   the mate given by index, by person
   as specified by pref
*/
int person,index;
preferences pref;
{
   return(pref[person][index]);
}


prefers(individual,person,individualsmate,priority)
/* Returns true if individual prefers person to
   individuals mate as specified by priority
*/
int individual,person,individualsmate;
preferences priority;
{
   return(priority[individual][person] <
      priority[individual] [individualsmate]);
}

read_preferences(n,pref)
/* Reads n rows of
   preferences into pref
*/
int n;
preferences pref;
{
   int i,j;
   for (i=1;i<=n;i++)
      for (j=1;j<=n;j++)
         scanf("%d",&pref[i][j]);
}
```

```
create_priorities(n,pref,priority)
/* Creates n individual priorities
   in priority based on the
   individual preferences specified
   by pref
*/
int n;
preferences pref,priority;
{
   int i,j;
   for (i=1,i<=n;i++)
      for (j=1;j<=n;j++)
         priority[i][pref[i][j]] = j;
}
```

The File `stablemarriages.c`

```
#include <stdio.h>
#include "pairings.h"       ] replaced by the contents of file pairings.h
#include "preferences.h"    ] replaced by the contents of file preferences.h

#define TRUE 1
#define FALSE 0

main()
{
   pairings mpairs,wpairs;
   preferences mpref,wpref,mpriority,wpriority;
   int i,j,n;
   printf("\n n = ?\n");
   scanf("%d",&n);
   read_mens_mates(n,mpairs);
   create_womens_mates(n,mpairs,wpairs);
   printf("\n Enter mens preferences \n");
   read_preferences(n,mpref);
   printf("\n Enter womens preferences \n");
   read_preferences(n,wpref);
   create_priorities(n,mpref,mpriority);
   create_priorities(n,wpref,wpriority);
   if (stabilitycheck(n,mpairs,wpairs,mpref,wpref,mpriority,
      wpriority))
      printf(" The pairings are stable \n");
   else
      printf(" The pairings are not stable \n");
   printf(" The pairings are: \n");
   printf(" man wife \n");
   for (i=1;i<=n;i++)
      printf(" %d  %d \n",i,mate(i,mpairs));
}
```

```
stabilitycheck(n,mpairs,wpairs,mpref,wpref,mpriority,wpriority)
int n;
pairings mpairs,wpairs
preferences mpref,wpref,mpriority,wpriority;
{
   int man,wife,individual,individualsmate,index,stable;
   stable = TRUE;
   for(man=1;(stable && man<=n);man++)
      {
         wife = mate(man,mpairs);
         individual = mostpreferred(man,mpref);
         index = 1;
         while (stable && (individual != wife))
            {
               individualsmate = mate(individual,wpairs);
               if(prefers(individual,man,individualsmate,
                          wpriority))
                  stable = FALSE;
               else
                  {
                     index++;
                     individual = nextpreferred(man,index,mpref);
                  }
            }
         individual = mostpreferred(wife,wpref);
         index = 1;
         while(stable && (individual != man))
            {
               individualsmate = mate(individual,mpairs);
               if(prefers(individual,wife,individualsmate,
                          mpriority))
                  stable = FALSE;
               else
                  {
                     index++;
                     individual = nextpreferred(wife,index,wpref);
                  }
            }
      }
   return(stable);
}
```

The `include "pairings.h"` and `include "preferences.h"` were put at the top of the program file because their contents are needed from that point on in the file. In the program file for `primestest.c`, the `include "collection.h"` appears just before the `primes` function, since its contents are only needed from that point on in the file.

The files `pairings.c`, `preferences.c`, and `stablemarriages.c` can be compiled separately. To run `stablemarriages.c`, they must first all be linked by the linker.

Any time changes are made in **pairings.h**, the files **pairings.c** and **stablemarriages.c** must be recompiled. Changes in **pairings.c** also require that **pairings.c** be recompiled. The same applies for **preferences.h** and **preferences.c**. However, changes to only one of **pairings.c**, **preferences.c**, or **stablemarriages.c** require only *its* individual recompilation. Relinking is always required before execution.

5.4 A List Example

Let us look at another example of file modularization of a program. Consider the program of Section 3.6.1 that reads in, creates, and prints the information fields of each record on a list of stock records. That version is in a single file and is functionally modularized. The data abstraction **list**, with its operations **next**, **setlink**, **setinfo**, **avail**, **getnextrecord**, **printrecord**, and **anotherrecord**, appear together.

The version of the program that follows uses a module for the list data abstraction with the header file, **list.h**, and the operations file, **list.c**. The file, **list.c**, and the program file, **listexample.c**, are compiled separately.

The file **list.h**:

The File list.h

```
/* header for list */

#define MAXSIZE 5
#define NULL 0
#define SENTINEL -1
typedef struct
{
   int month;
   int day;
   int year;
}date;
typedef struct
{
   char name[MAXSIZE];
   int shares;
   float value;
   date datebought;
}infofield;
typedef struct listrecord
{
   infofield info;
   struct listrecord *link;
}stockrecord,*listpointer;

extern listpointer next(/* listpointer */);
/* Returns a copy of listpointer in link field of
   record pointed to by listpointer */
```

```
extern listpointer setnull();
/* Returns a null listpointer value */

extern setlink(/* listpointer_1,listpointer_2 */);
/* Sets the link field of the record pointed to
   by listpointer_1 to the value of
   listpointer_2
*/

extern setinfo(/* listpointer_1,listpointer_2 */);
/* Sets the info field of the record pointed to
   by listpointer_1 to the contents of the
   info field of the record pointed to by
   listpointer_2
*/

extern listpointer avail();
/* Returns a pointer to storage for
   a record of type struct stockrecord */

extern listpointer getnextrecord();
/* Returns a pointer to a record
   containing the next input records'
   information, or a null pointer if
   the next input is the sentinel
*/

extern printrecord(/* listpointer */);
/* Prints the information in the record
   pointed to by listpointer */

extern anotherrecord(/* listpointer */);
/* Returns true if there are no
   more records and false otherwise */
```

The File `list.c`

```
/* operations allowed on a list */

#include "list.h"
```
replaced by the contents of file `list.h`

```
listpointer next(pointer)
/* Returns a copy of the
   link field in the record
   pointed to by pointer
*/
listpointer pointer;
{
   return(pointer->link);
}
```

```
listpointer setnull()
/* Returns a null pointer */
{
   return(NULL);
}


setlink(pointer1,pointer2)
/* Sets the link field of the
   record pointed to by pointer1
   to the contents of pointer2
*/
listpointer pointer1,pointer2;
{
   pointer1->link = pointer2;
}


setinfo(pointer1,pointer2)
/* Sets the infofield of the record
   pointed to by pointer1 to the
   infofield of the record
   pointed to by pointer2
*/
listpointer pointer1,pointer2;
{
   int i;
   for (i=0;i<MAXSIZE;i++)
      pointer1->info.name[i] = pointer2->info.name[i];
   pointer1->info.shares = pointer2->info.shares;
   pointer1->info.value = pointer2->info.value;
   pointer1->info.datebought.month = pointer2->info.datebought.
      month;
   pointer1->info.datebought.day = pointer2->info.datebought.day;
   pointer1->info.datebought.year = pointer2->info.datebought.year;
}


listpointer avail()
/* Returns a pointer to storage
   allocated for a record of type
   stockrecord
*/
{
   listpointer malloc();
   return(malloc(sizeof(stockrecord)));
}


anotherrecord(recordpointer)
/* Returns true if there is
   another record
*/
listpointer recordpointer;
```

```
{
   listpointer setnull();
   return(recordpointer != setnull());
}


listpointer getnextrecord()
/* Inputs the data for the new
   record and returns a pointer
   to a record containing the data
   in its infofield, or, if there
   are no new records, returns
   a null pointer
*/
{
   listpointer setnull();
   static stockrecord nextrecord;
   printf(" Enter number of shares \n");
   scanf("%d",&(nextrecord.info.shares));
   if(nextrecord.info.shares != SENTINEL)
      {
         printf(" Enter the stock name - less than %d characters\n",
                MAXSIZE);
         scanf("%s",nextrecord.info.name);
         printf(" Enter the price of one share of the stock \n");
         scanf("%f",&(nextrecord.info.value));
         printf(" Enter the month day year of the stock purchase
                \n");
         scanf("%d %d %d",&(nextrecord.info.datebought.month),
            &(nextrecord.info.datebought.day),
            &(nextrecord.info.datebought.year));
         return(&nextrecord);
      }
   else
      return(setnull());
}


printrecord(recordpointer)
/* Prints the contents of the infofield
   of the record pointed to by recordpointer
*/
listpointer recordpointer;
{
   printf(" The stock is %s \n",recordpointer->info.name);
   print(" The number of shares is %d \n",recordpointer->info.
         shares);
   printf(" The value of a share is %f\n",recordpointer->info.
          value);
```

```
    printf(" The date of purchase is %d %d %d\n\n",
          recordpointer->info.datebought.month,

    recordpointer->info.datebought.day,recordpointer->
                                   info.datebought.year);
}
```

Finally, here is the program file to create a list and print its contents. It treats the list as a data abstraction and uses file modularization for the data abstraction.

The File `listexample.c`

```
#include "list.h"

#include <stdio.h>
#define TRUE 1
#define FALSE 0


main()
/* Inputs a series of stockrecords,
   creates a list of the records, and
   prints the contents of each list
   record's infofield
*/
{
   listpointer stocks,recordpointer,next();
   int done;
   initialize(&stocks);
   recordpointer = stocks;
   done = FALSE;
   while(!done&&anotherrecord(recordpointer))
      {
         addrecord(&stocks,recordpointer,&done);
         recordpointer = next(recordpointer);
      }


   recordpointer=stocks;
   while (anotherrecord(recordpointer))
      {
         printrecord(recordpointer);
         recordpointer = next(recordpointer);
      }
}
```

replaced by the contents of file `list.h`

this portion of the program is independent of the list implementation

this is the traversal to input data and create the list

fills in the current record, allocates storage for the next and adds it to the list, and, if there is no data for the current record, terminates the list and sets `done` *to true*

this is the traversal to print the list

prints the record

```
initialize(plistname)
/* Allocates storage for the first record
   and sets listname to point to it
*/
listpointer *plistname;
{
   listpointer avail();
   *plistname = avail();
}

addrecord(plistname,recordpointer,pdone)
/* Fills in the current record's data, and
   allocates storage for the next record and
   adds it to the list. If there is no data for
   the current record it sets the link field of
   the last list record to null, or the list
   head, to null, and done to true.
*/
listpointer *plistname,recordpointer;
int *pdone;
{
   static listpointer predecessor;
   listpointer setnull(),avail(),
      getnextrecord(),pointer;
   pointer = getnextrecord();
   if (pointer != setnull())
      {
         setinfo(recordpointer,pointer);      ] there is data for the
         setlink(recordpointer,avail());        current record
         predecessor = recordpointer;
      }
   else if (*plistname != recordpointer)
      {
         setlink(predecessor,setnull());      ] there is no data for the
         *pdone = TRUE;                         current record, and the
      }                                         list is not null
   else
      {
         *plistname = setnull();              ] there is no data for the
         *pdone = TRUE;                         current record, and the
      }                                         list is null
}
```

The files `list.h` and `list.c` now embody the `list` data abstraction. Note that, should the format of the list change, these changes must be reflected in the header file and also in the operations file. In the later file, `list.c`, the changes would be localized to `setinfo`, `getnextrecord`, and `print-record`. Instead, were the format to remain the same but the records stored in an array of records rather than the dynamic memory, more extensive changes would be required in both `list.h` and `list.c`.

5.5 A Stack Example

This last example involves a stack and its application in the nonrecursive `towers` program of Section 4.5.3. The stack is implemented as a list. The program treats the stack as a data abstraction and is structured so the stack and its operations appear together.

We give the header file, `stack.h`, the operations file, `stack.c`, and the program file, `towerstest.c`, that can be used to achieve file modularization and separate compilation.

The File `stack.h`

```
/* header for stack */

#define NULL 0
typedef struct
{
   int n;
   int i;
   int a;
   int f;
}whatever;
typedef struct record
{
   whatever info;
   struct record *link;
}stackrecord,*stack;

extern setstack(/* pstack */);
/* Sets stack to empty */

extern empty(/* pstack */);
/* Returns true only if
   the stack is empty */

extern push(/* pstackrecord,pstack */);
/* Makes stackrecord the new
   top entry on stack*/

extern pop(/* pstack,pstackrecord */);
/* Removes the top entry from
   stack and returns with its
   contents in stackrecord
*/

extern overflow(/* pstack */);
/* Prints a warning when
   the stack overflows */

extern underflow(/* pstack */);
/* Prints a warning when the stack underflows */
```

The File `stack.c`

```
/* operations for the stack */

#include "stack.h"  ] replaced by the contents of file stack.h

setstack(ps)
/* Sets stack s to empty */
stack *ps;
{
   *ps = NULL;
}

empty(ps)
/* Returns true only if
   the stack s is empty */
stack *ps;
{
   return(*ps == NULL);
}

push(pnewrecord,ps)
/* Makes stackrecord the new
   top entry on stack s */
stackrecord *pnewrecord;
stack *ps;
{
   stackrecord *newentry;
   newentry = malloc(sizeof(stackrecord));
   newentry->info = pnewrecord->info;
   newentry->link = *ps;
   *ps = newentry;
}

pop(ps,pvalue)
/* Removes the top entry from
   stack s and returns with its
   contents in stackrecord
*/
stack *ps;
stackrecord *pvalue;
{
   if(!empty(ps))
      {
         pvalue->info = (*ps)->info;
         *ps = (*ps)->link;
      }
   else
      underflow(ps);
}
```

```
overflow(ps);
/* Prints a warning when
   the stack overflows */
stack *ps;
{
   printf (" The stack has overflowed /n");
}


underflow(ps);
/* Prints a warning when
   the stack underflows */
stack *ps;
{
   printf(" The stack has underflowed /n");
}
```

The File `towerstest.c`

```
#include <stdio.h>

main()
{
   int n;
   printf("\n enter a value for n \n");
   scanf("%d",&n);
   towers(n,1,2,3);
}


#include "stack.h"              ] replaced by the contents of file stack.h

towers(n,i,a,f)
/* Moves the top n disks
   from peg i to peg f
*/
int n,i,a,f;
{
   stack s;
   int done
   setstack(&s);
   done = FALSE;
   while(!done)
       {
           while(n > 1)
               {
                   s_tack(n,i,a,f,&s);
                   setvar 1(&n,&i,&a,&f);
               }
   printf("\n %d -> %d\n",i,f);
```

```
    if(!empty(&s))
        {
            restore(&n,&i,&a,&f,&s);
            printf("\n %d -> %d\n",i,f);
            setvar2(&n,&i,&a,&f);
        }
    else
        done = TRUE;
}

setvar1(pn,pi,pa,pf)
/* Sets n to n - 1 and
   interchanges f and a
*/
int *pn,*pi,*pa,*pf;
{
   int t;
   *pn = *pn - 1;
   t = *pf;
   *pf = *pa;
   *pa = t;
}

setvar2(pn,pi,pa,pf)
/* Sets n to n - 1 and
   interchanges a and i
*/
int *pn,*pi,*pa,*pf;
{
   int t;
   *pn = *pn - 1;
   t = *pa;
   *pa = *pi;
   *pi = t;
}

s_tack(n,i,a,f,ps)
/* Creates a record containing
   n, i, a, and f and inserts it
   on stack s
*/
int n,i,a,f;
stack *ps;
{
   stackrecord newrecord;
   newrecord.info.n = n;
   newrecord.info.i = i;
   newrecord.info.a = a;
   newrecord.info.f = f;
   push(&newrecord,ps);
}
```

```
restore(pn,pi,pa,pf,ps)
/* Removes the top record from
   stack s and copies its contents into n,i,a,f
*/
int *pn,*pi,*pa,*pf;
stack *ps;
{
   stackrecord value;
   pop(ps,&value);
   *pn = value.info.n;
   *pi = value.info.i;
   *pa = value.info.a;
   *pf = value.info.f;
}
```

Notice that the operations `push` and `pop` in `stack.c` have been written under the assumption that the C compiler allows the entire contents of one record to be copied into another record of the same type using just one assignment statement. In order to achieve greater portability, these operations could be written so that they do not depend on this assumption by using individual assignment statements for each field of the records. However, this can also be accomplished by restructuring the program. Moreover, restructuring can also achieve another level of data abstraction with respect to the stack records and their operations (in this example only one will be needed). This will require changes to `stack.h` and `stack.c` but will make the new stack module independent of the implementation of the stack records. The current stack module, consisting of the files `stack.h` and `stack.c`, must be changed and recompiled whenever the records being stacked have a different format from that which is represented by `whatever`. After the restructuring this will not be necessary. Any changes in the stack record format will be localized to the stack record module.

To do the restructuring, first create a module for the data abstraction `stackrecord` and its operations. The module consists of the files `stack_record.h` and `stack_record.c`.

The File `stack_record.h`

```
/* header for stackrecord */

typedef struct
{
   int n;
   int i;
   int a;
   int f;
}whatever;
typedef struct record
{
   whatever info;
   struct record *link;
}stackrecord,*stackrecordpointer;
```

```
extern setinfo(/* stackrecordpointer_1,stackrecordpointer_2 */);
/* Sets the info field of the record pointed to
   by stackrecordpointer_1 to the contents of the
   info field of the record pointed to by stackrecordpointer_2
*/
```

The File `stack_record.c`

```
/* operations for stackrecord */

#include "stack_record.h"   ] replaced by the contents of
                              file stack_record.h
setinfo(pointer1,pointer2)

/* Copies the contents of the record
   pointed to by pointer 1 into
   the record pointed to by pointer2
   */
stackrecordpointer pointer1,pointer2;
{
   pointer1->info.retrn = pointer2->info.retrn;
   pointer1->info.n = pointer2->info.n;
   pointer1->info.i = pointer2->info.i;
   pointer1->info.a = pointer2->info.a;
   pointer1->info.f = pointer2->info.f;
}
```

Here is the new stack module.

The File `stack.h`

```
/* header for stack */

#include "stack_record.h"        ] replaced by the contents of
                                   file stack_record.h
#define NULL 0
stackrecord *stack;

extern setstack(/* pstack */);
/* Sets stack to empty */

extern empty(/* pstack */);
/* Returns true only if the stack is empty */

extern push(/* pstackrecord,pstack */);
/* Makes stackrecord the new top entry on stack*/

extern pop(/* pstack,pstackrecord */);
/* Removes the top entry from
   stack and returns with its
   contents in stackrecord
*/
```

```
extern overflow(/* pstack */);
/* Prints a warning when
   the stack overflows */

extern underflow(/* pstack */);
/* Prints a warning when
   the stack underflows */
```

The File `stack.c`

```
/* operations for the stack */

#include "stack.h"                    ] replaced by the contents of file
                                        stack.h
setstack(ps)
/* Sets stack to empty */
stackrecordpointer *ps;
{
   *ps = NULL;
}

empty(ps)
/* Returns true only if
   the stack is empty */
stackrecordpointer *ps;
{
   return(*ps == NULL);
}

push(pnewrecord,ps)
/* Makes stackrecord the new
   top entry on stack*/
stackrecord *pnewrecord;
stackrecordpointer *ps;
{
   stackrecord *newentry;
   newentry = malloc(sizeof
                    (stackrecord));
   setinfo(newentry,pnewrecord);  ] new call to stack record operation
   newentry->link = *ps;
   *ps = newentry;
}

pop(ps,pvalue)
/* Removes the top entry from
   stack and returns with its
   contents in stackrecord
*/
stackrecordpointer *ps;
stackrecord *pvalue;
```

```
{
   if(!empty(ps))
      {
         setinfo(pvalue,(*ps));    ] new call to stack record operation
         *ps = (*ps)->link;
      }
   else
      underflow(ps);
}

overflow(ps);
/* Prints a warning when
   the stack overflows */
stackrecordpointer *ps;
{
   printf (" The stack has overflowed /n");
}

underflow(ps);
/* Prints a warning when
   the stack underflows */
stackrecordpointer *ps;
{
   printf (" The stack has underflowed /n");
}
```

As promised, the new stack modules are not dependent on the details of the stack records. The program file, `towerstest.c`, does not need to be changed from its original version. To run it, `stack_record.c` and `stack.c` must be compiled. Their object files, along with the previously generated object file for `towers-test.c`, can be linked, and then `towerstest.c` can be run. Any future changes in `stack_record.h` mean that `stack_record.c`, `stack.c`, and `towerstest.c` must be recompiled, but changes to only `stack_record.c` or `stack.c` will require just their recompilation. Similarly, changes to just `towerstest.c` require only its recompilation.

Using this technique it is possible, as demonstrated, to structure programs so that modules for data abstractions can be built using modules for other data abstractions. The examples presented, for the sake of simplicity, have dealt with small to moderate-sized programs. With programs of this size the overall impact of file modularity and modules may not appear to be great. The real power of the technique becomes quickly apparent when large programs are written by teams of programmers. The efficiency and control gained through modularity in such cases is significant.

5.6 Summary

Data abstraction and functional and file modularization are important concepts whose proper application to program development and program structure enhance program readability and maintainability. They aid the programmer in establishing libraries of useful functions that can be readily selected for use in creating new programs for new problems.

The ability to compile parts of a program separately can make debugging an easier task and can save time. In C this can be achieved by placing appropriate parts of a program in distinct files. When this is done it is necessary to keep track of which files must be compiled and linked in order to execute the program file.

■ Exercises

1. Why is it not necessary to place the `include "collection.h"` before the `primes` function in `primestest.c`?
2. Why is `primestest.c` independent of the implementation of `collection`?
3. Why must `primestest.c` and `collection.c` be recompiled when changes are made in `collection.h`?
4. Change `preferences.h` and `preferences.c` so that the preferences and priorities arrays are implemented using a pointer array pointing to their rows, which are stored as row records in dynamic memory (see Section 2.3.3).
5. Run `stablemarriages.c` with your solution to Exercise 4.
6. What must be changed in `list.h` and `list.c` if you want to add another field (say, dividends) to the list records?
7. Change the files of Section 5.4 so that the name field of the `stockrecords`, instead of being an array, is a list. Treat that list as a data abstraction.
8. Write and compile a module for the `queue` data abstraction using the circular array implementation of Section 4.6.1.
9. Write and compile a module for the `queue` data abstraction using the list implementation of Section 4.6.3.
10. Create a program file `ordlistexample.c`. The program is to do what `listexample.c` does, except the list that is created is to have the records appear in alphabetical order by name. The list is to be treated as a data abstraction using `list.h` and `list.c`.
11. Compile, link, and run your program created in Exercise 10.
12. Define file `list_record.h` and `list_record.c`, and modify `list.h` and `list.c` to reflect these changes. The result should make `list.h` and `list.c` independent of details of the listrecords (as was done with the stack in Section 5.5). To accomplish this, you will have to remove and modify some operations from `list.c`, placing their modified versions in `list_record.c`, and some declarations from `list.h`, placing their modified versions in `list_record.h`.
13. Create a module for a data abstraction list of stacks.

■ Suggested Assignments

1. Replace `collection.h` and `collection.c` with new files that implement collection as an array that contains the actual integers currently in the collection as its entries.
2. a. One of the two complete programs of Section 3.9.3 implements the configuration for the perfect shuffle as an array and the other implements it as a list. They do not treat the configuration as a data abstraction; write and run a single source file program that does.
b. Rewrite and run the program developed for (a) using file modularization to hide the details of the configuration's implementation and so that separate compilation can be done.

3. Change the stack implementation of Section 5.5 so that it is implemented as in Section 4.5.1. You can change only the files `stack.h` and `stack.c`; the program file, `towerstest.c`, cannot be changed.

4. Modify the implementation of the stack data abstraction in Section 5.5 so that instead of the stack containing records, it contains pointers to the records. Again, this should be achieved with changes only to `stack.h` and `stack.c`.

6 More Complex Lists

Considers lists of lists connected by pointers to
impose more structure on data
reduce search time
Emphasizes
list-structures, a special case of such lists
the traversal of list-structures as a general tool
the implementation of list-structures
Case study—information retrieval
illustrates the use and advantages of more complex lists

6.1 Imposing List Structure on Data

So far in this book, records in lists have had information members and link members. These are ***simple records.*** The lists themselves have looked like ***chains*** of records. Such lists may be used to store the records only or to store them and also impose an ordering on them. This chapter presents ***complex records,*** which contain members that are themselves names of lists. The members are called ***sublist members.*** Lists composed of such records have more complex structure than chains and are known as ***complex lists.*** Several such lists are depicted schematically in Figure 6.1. The following examples illustrate the use of complex lists and show how they provide one means of organizing data to capture certain inherent relations among the list records.

Example 6.1

The `accounts` list in Figure 6.1(a) consists of three records. The first two are complex, the third simple. The first record points to a sublist consisting of two records; the first of these is complex and the second is simple. `Accounts` might actually represent three companies' user accounts. The first user account is billed for two distinct computer services, $100 for last month's computing and $75 for this month's software consulting. The second user account owes $200 for the month's computing and $250 for the month's consulting. The third user account has a credit of $46. The *X* in the sublist member of the complex record "200" means its sublist is null. ■

Example 6.2

A programmer asked to simulate a card game with *n* players might choose to represent the current configuration of the *n* individual hands by using a list composed of complex records. A typical configuration is shown in Figure 6.1(b) for four poker players. The sublist that makes up each complex record

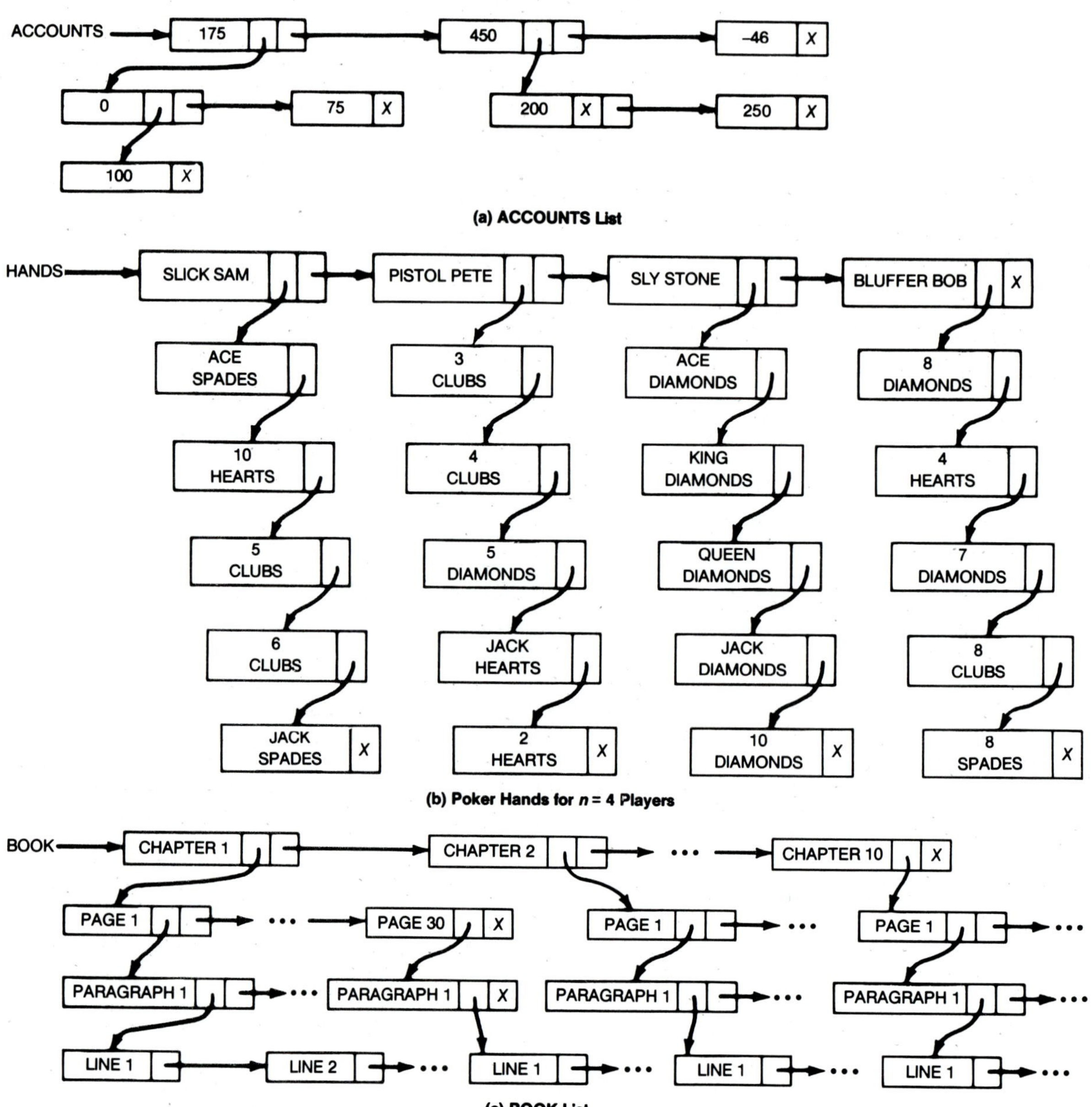

Figure 6.1 More Complex Lists

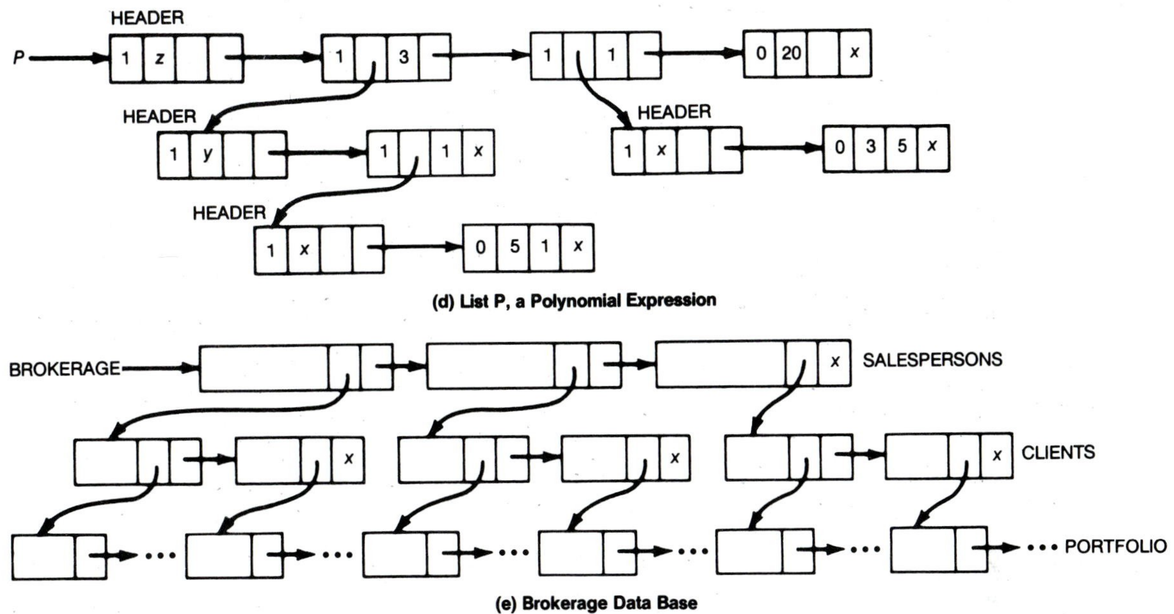

Figure 6.1 *(continued)*

contains all the cards of a particular player's hand, each card represented as a record. Insertions and deletions into an individual hand require insertions and deletions from the appropriate sublist. ■

Example 6.3 A book might be represented as the `book` list shown in Figure 6.1(c). Records for the individual lines of text would be simple; the records for paragraph, chapter, and page would be complex.

The data processing for word processing or text editing might involve inserting and deleting chapters, paragraphs, or lines. Creating an index for the book would require even more complex processing. This could be done by making a special "dictionary" that lists the key words relevant to the book's topic, then searching the text for all instances of key words. If the book were a computer science text, then the dictionary would include all key technical computer science words. The index could be created by accessing and processing each page. This processing would involve checking the page for occurrences of the key words and keeping track, for each such word in the dictionary, of the pages on which it occurred. (Unfortunately, such automatic indexing creates too large an index and one that may not be very useful, since not every mention of a key term is especially relevant.) ■

Example 6.4 A polynomial in x, y, and z may be represented using a list-structure. Suppose the polynomial $P(x, y, z)$ is $3zx^5 + 5z^3yx + 20$. We can write this as

$$P(x, y, z) = z^3(y(x(5))) + z(x^5(3)) + 20$$

This, in turn, can be represented as `p` of Figure 6.1(d).

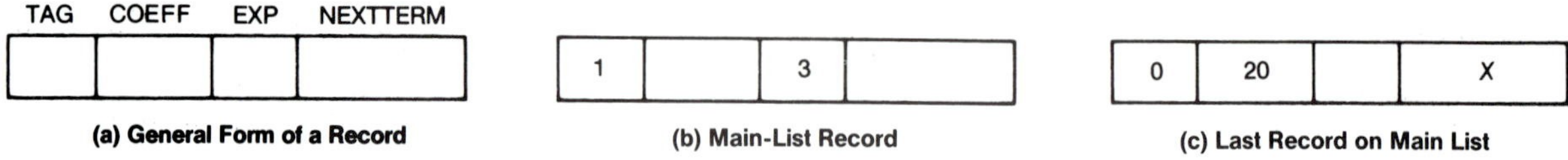

Figure 6.2 Records of the List-structure for a Polynomial

Each record of p has four fields, as shown in Figure 6.2(a). A `tag` field value of 1 indicates that the record is complex, while a `tag` field of 0 indicates that the record is simple.

Each sublist, including the main list, has a header record and represents a polynomial. The main list, for example, is a polynomial in z composed of three terms. The record (Figure 6.2(b)) on the main list indicates that this term contains z to the power 3 and a coefficient that is pointed to by the pointer in the `coeff` field. Its successor record is similarly expressed. The last record on the main list (Figure 6.2(c)) is simple, meaning that the value in the `coeff` field is to be interpreted as a constant. Sublists are interpreted in the same way. ■

Example 6.5 Each record on `brokerage`'s main list in Figure 6.1(e) represents a sales representative (a financial advisor) of a brokerage firm. The sublist of each salesperson contains information about each of his or her clients. Each client's sublist is the client's stock portfolio. ■

6.1.1 A Definition of List-structures

Each of the example lists organizes information by collecting related data on sublists. They are a step up in complexity from the chains of Chapter 3 but do not illustrate the most complex lists, which allow sharing of records and sublists. ***Sharing*** means that more than one record can point to another record or sublist. Records can also have additional pointer fields linking records to form intertwined lists. However, this chapter concentrates primarily on list-structures. They may be defined formally by either of two equivalent definitions:

> A ***list-structure*** is a collection of simple and complex records linked by pointers in the following way.
>
> The link and sublist fields of each record contain pointers to records of the collection.
>
> Each record of the collection has no more than one pointer to it from any record of the collection.

Or recursively:

> A ***list-structure*** is a list of simple and complex records whose complex record's sublist fields point to distinct list-structures called sublists. The predecessor of each record must be unique.

The first definition treats list-structures as a collection of linked records but does not convey their inherent structure. The recursive definition emphasizes this structure, making clear how a list-structure is itself built from other list-structures.

It is evident that each list of Figure 6.1 satisfies the first definition. To see

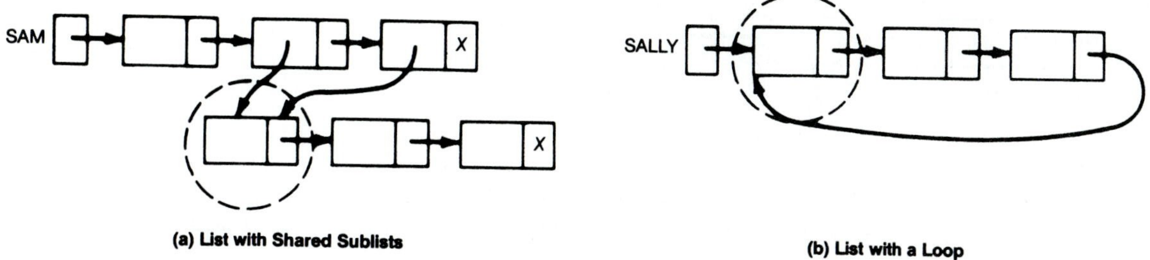

(a) List with Shared Sublists

(b) List with a Loop

Figure 6.3 Two Lists That Are *Not* List-structures

that they also satisfy the recursive definition, consider the `accounts` list. The main list consists of a list of simple and complex records, so it is necessary to check that the complex record's sublists are themselves list-structures. The first main-list record's sublist is a list-structure since the sublist's main list satisfies the definition and its complex record points to a list-structure, a single list record. The second main-list record's sublist is itself a list whose complex record's sublist is a list-structure, the null list-structure.

The lists `sam` and `sally` in Figure 6.3 are not list-structures, since they fail to satisfy the definitions. `Sam` has shared sublists; `sally` has a loop.

6.2 Traversal of List-structures

Inserting or deleting a record from a list-structure is done using the same procedures as in Chapter 3. Determining *where* to insert or delete involves a traversal through the records to locate the desired position. Unlike the chain, for which there is a natural order in which to traverse the records, list-structures have no simple natural order. Instead, the order in which records are to be accessed and processed is defined as follows:

> To **traverse a list-structure,**
> Access each record on the main list in order and
> 1. Process the record
> 2. If the record is complex, then
>   traverse the complex record's sublist.

Notice that the definition is actually recursive, since a complex record's sublist is itself a list-structure. To see how to apply it, consider `formula` in Figure 6.4. The records are numbered for ease of reference.

To determine the order in which records are accessed and processed in a traversal of the list-structure `formula`, apply the definition. It specifies that records 1 and 2 on the main list be accessed and processed in sequence. Since record 2 is complex, sublist 1 must be traversed. At the finish of traversal of sublist 1, it will be necessary to continue where processing left off on the main list. To know where to resume, save P1. To traverse sublist 1, apply the definition to it, and access and process records 3 and 4 in order. Since record 4 is complex, traverse sublist 2. Save P3 to know where to resume when its traversal is complete.

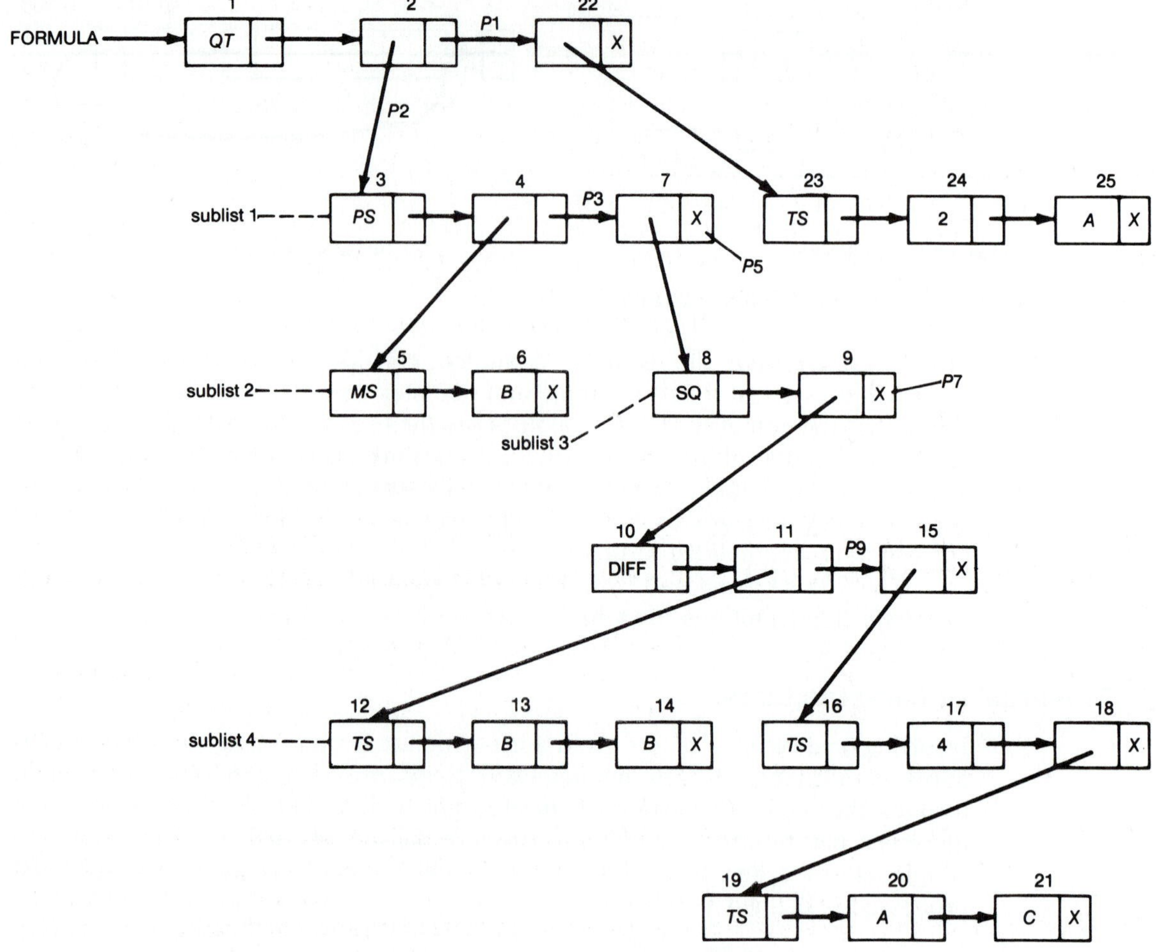

Figure 6.4 The List-structure FORMULA

To traverse sublist 2, apply the definition of traversal to it, and so access and process records 5 and 6. Since the link field of record 6 is null, no records remain on this sublist, so its traversal is complete.

Which task should be done now? Step 2 of the traversal definition has just been applied to sublist 2. The next record of some sublist must now be accessed. What record? It is the successor record of the complex record—record 4—whose sublist traversal was just completed. P3, which was saved for just this moment, points to record 7, so let the program follow it. Since P3 is no longer needed, discard it. Since record 7 is complex, traverse sublist 3. Continuing in this way, the program would access and process the records in the order in which they are numbered.

From this example it can be seen that whenever the link field of the record just accessed and processed is null, the traversal of some sublist has been completed and the program must determine where to go next. Each time the processing of a complex record was finished, the content of its link field was saved before traversing its sublist. In `formula`, this leads to saving P1, then P3. After record 6 comes a null link field signifying the completion of the traversal of sublist 2. P3 then tells the program where to go next. Once followed, it can be forgotten. P1 is still remembered, and P5, P7, and P9 need to be remembered in turn. After dealing with record 14, the program encounters its null link value, which signifies completion of sublist 4's traversal. Where does it go? It follows P9 and needs to remember only P7, P5, and P1, and so on.

Each pointer that is saved represents an obligation that must be postponed. It is the obligation to apply steps 1 and 2 of the definition of traversal of list-structures to successive records on the list pointed to by the pointer. The definition requires that the corresponding complex record's sublist be traversed immediately. In carrying out the traversal of that sublist, further obligations may be incurred and subsequently fulfilled. Each time step 2 is completed, the most recently saved pointer provides the information to determine what record to deal with next. When the record is selected for processing, the pointer is discarded. This implies that pointers saved during the complex records' traversal will be discarded when its traversal is complete. Consequently, the most recently saved pointer must point to the record to be processed each time step 2 is completed. If there is no remaining saved pointer, it means that the entire traversal is complete.

Traversing a list-structure thus requires retention, recall, and deletion of information in a specific order. The pointer information retained represents postponed obligations. These obligations must be fulfilled in reverse order from that in which they were incurred. This is the precise situation in which the stack data abstraction is very convenient. Notice how a stack can be used to store the pointers so that the list-structure can be traversed correctly. Each pointer saved is pushed on the stack and popped when needed. It is a typical LIFO situation.

It is important to recognize that the definition of a list-structure traversal does not merely explain how to traverse a *specific* list-structure, such as `formula`, but describes a procedure that may be applied to *any* list-structure. This is, of course, true for any algorithm or program. Programs and algorithms specify a procedure for any input, not just for a specific input. The definition of traversal of list-structures is really an algorithm, an initial description of a procedure for list-structure traversal.

6.2.1 An Iterative Function

We will now develop a program `traverse` to traverse a list-structure `ls`. In applying the definition it became clear that such a traversal may be described by the following algorithm.

1. Initialize the current record.
2. Initialize the stack of postponed obligations to "empty."
3. While there is a current record or a postponed obligation,
   if there is a current record, then
      a. process the current record, and
      b. update the current record to the next record to be processed
   else
      c. remove the top obligation from the stack and update the current record to it.

To update the current record, the loop task 3b needs to be specified in greater detail. If the record just processed was simple, then the next record to be processed is the successor of the current record. Otherwise—if the record just processed was complex—its successor record represents a postponed obligation that must be placed on the stack. In that case the next record to be processed is the first record on the current record's sublist. This gives a refinement for task 3b that is incorporated in the revised algorithm.

1. Initialize the current record.
2. Initialize the stack of postponed obligations to "empty."
3. While there is a current record or a postponed obligation,
    if there is a current record, then
        a. process the current record, and
        b. if the current record is complex, then
            i. save an obligation to its successor record on the stack
            ii. update the current record to the first record on its sublist,
          else
            update the current record to its successor record
    else
        c. remove the top obligation from the stack and update the current record to it.

A variable (call it **ptr**) is needed to contain a pointer to the current record. The stack can be treated as a data abstraction with the usual operations **setstack**, **empty**, **push**, and **pop** as was done in Chapters 4 and 5. The details for implementing the stack are built into the routines implementing these operations.

Assume that during the traverse each record is processed by calling a routine **process**. It will clearly need the pointer to the record to be processed, **ptr**. It will also need access to the list name **ls**. For example, if its task involves deleting the first record of **ls**, then it must be able to change the contents of **ls**. To treat the list-structure as a data abstraction, we need the basic functions **complex**, **next**, and **sublist**, each with **ptr** as a parameter. **Complex** returns a value *true* if the record to which **ptr** points is complex, the value *false* otherwise. **Next** and **sublist** return, respectively, a copy of the link and sublist field value of the record pointed to by **ptr**.

A more detailed refinement of the algorithm can now be written.

1. Set **ptr** to **ls**
2. **Setstack(s)**
3. While **ptr** is not null or not **empty(s)**
    if **ptr** is not null, then
        a. **Process(ls,ptr)**
        b. If **complex(ptr)**, then
            i. **Push(next(ptr),s)**
            ii. Set **ptr** to **sublist(ptr)**
          else
            Set **ptr** to **next(ptr)**
    else
        c. **Pop(s,ptr)**

Notice that if all records of `ls` are simple, then tasks (i), (ii), and (c) will never be invoked. This procedure is then essentially the same as the list traversal of Chapter 3, as it should be. As written, it does not provide for partial traversal (`done` is not involved in the loop control) but could be easily modified when necessary.

`Traverse` may be implemented as in the following iterative (nonrecursive) function. This implementation uses data abstraction and has been written using functional modularly.

Nonrecursive Version

```
traverse(pls)
/* Accesses and processes each record
   of the list-structure ls.
*/
liststructurepointer *pls;
{
   liststructurepointer ptr,null,setnull(),next(),sublist();
   stack s;                                  ] storage allocated for stack s
   null = setnull();
   ptr = *pls;                               ] current record pointer set to the first record
                                               of ls
   setstack(&s);                             ] initialize stack s
   while((ptr != null) || (!empty(&s)))      ] test for a current record to be processed or
                                               for more saved pointers
      if(ptr != null)                        ] ptr != null signifies there is a current
                                               record to be processed
         {
            process(pls,ptr);                ] process it
            if(complex(ptr))                 ] if current record is complex
               {
                  push(next(ptr),&s);        ] save pointer to its successor and update
                  ptr = sublist(ptr);        ] current record pointer to the first record of
                                               its sublist
               }
            else
               ptr = next(ptr);              ] update current record pointer to its successor
                                               record
         }
      else
         pop(&s,&ptr);                       ] the stack contains the pointer to the next
}                                              record to access, so set current record
                                               pointer to it and pop the stack
```

It is important to see that the program is functionally modular and independent of the implementation of the data abstractions to which it refers. Data abstractions for the stack with its operations, and for the list-structure and its operations (which must include `complex`, `next`, `sublist`, and `setnull`) are needed in order to use `traverse`. The programmer must either be given these or else must write them.

6.2.2 A Recursive Function

A recursive implementation can also be developed for `traverse`. Begin with a recursive algorithm for traversing a list-structure; this is obtained directly from the recursive definition of a list-structure traversal.

1. Initialize the current record.
2. While there is a current record,
   a. process the current record;
   b. if the current record is complex, then
      i. traverse the current record's sublist;
   c. update the current record to its successor record.

Once more we need the variable **ptr** to point to the current record, and the variable **nextsublist** to point to a sublist. Again, the list-structure is treated as a data abstraction. Also, to modularize functionally, assume that a function **traverse** is available to implement task (i). The algorithm can now be refined:

1. Set `ptr` to `ls`.
2. While `ptr` is not null,
   a. `Process(ls,ptr);`
   b. if `complex(ptr)`, then
      i. Set `nextsublist` to `sublist(ptr)`,
         `traverse(nextsublist);`
   c. Set `ptr` to `next(ptr)`.

This refinement is implemented in the following recursive procedure.

Recursive Version

```
traverse(pls)
/* Accesses and processes each record
   of the list-structure ls.
*/
liststructurepointer *pls;
{
   liststructurepointer ptr,nextsublist,null,
      setnull(),next(),sublist();
   null = setnull();
   ptr = *pls;                          ] current record pointer set to the first
                                          record of ls
   while(ptr != null)                   ] test for current record to be processed
      {
         process(pls,ptr);              ] process it
         if(complex(ptr))               ] if the current record has a sublist
            {
               nextsublist = sublist(ptr);  ] set nextsublist to it
               traverse(&nextsublist);      ] traverse it
            }
         ptr = next(ptr);               ] update current record pointer to its
      }                                   successor record
}
```

Notice that this program, at the point when it encounters a complex record and hence must traverse its sublist, does so by simply invoking a module that does that traversal—itself. After that traversal is complete, it merely resumes where it left off. In contrast, the nonrecursive version must perform its own bookkeeping to keep track of where to resume each time it encounters a complex record and then retrieve that information when it is needed.

A number of comments are in order about the two implementations of **traverse**. First, imagine that the recursive procedure **traverse** is presented to you with the statement that it is a refined version of the definition of traversal of a list-structure. It is easy to see that this is so. Contrast this with the effort involved in seeing that the nonrecursive version of **traverse** is also a refined version of the same defining algorithm. Second, the recursive version is more concise than the nonrecursive. Third, the recursive **traverse** is almost a direct translation of the defining algorithm. It required very little effort to achieve it in this case, because the definition is itself a recursive description.

These comments usually hold for algorithms that process data structures that can be defined recursively, such as list-structures. This is not an accident but can be expected when we deal with complex data structures. Recursive definitions allow concise descriptions of complex algorithms and data structures. Concise descriptions allow us to deal more easily with their complexity. In fact, it is difficult to develop a definition for a list-structure traversal that has *no* vagueness, is applicable to *any* list-structure, and does *not* involve recursion. Recursive definitions are especially useful to the programmer dealing with complex data structures, because they lead systematically and directly to recursive programs for their processing.

6.3 Using a Traverse Function for List-structures

Use of the general list-structure traversal functions just developed is illustrated in the following examples. The examples are intended to convey the flavor of list-structure applications and their processing.

Example 6.6 Print the information field of each stock record of the list-structure **brokerage** (shown in Figure 6.1(e)) which was bought prior to a specified date and which we store in **date**. A solution may be obtained by traversing **brokerage** and printing the relevant stock records. To do this requires only that we write the **process** function invoked by **traverse**. Either the recursive or the nonrecursive version may be used. The function **process** must be written to turn **traverse** into a solution to this problem.

The task is straightforward except for the determination, within **process**, of whether the record it is to process is currently a stock record. Since only stock records are simple, a test for complexity of the current record will provide this information. **Process** may be written as

```
process(pls,ptr)
/* Print the stock record of ls
   pointed to by ptr if it was
   bought prior to date
*/
liststructurepointer *pls,ptr;
{
   if(!complex(ptr) && prior(ptr,&date))
      printinfo(ptr);
}
```

current record not complex means it contains a stock record, so print its contents if bought early enough where `prior` returns *true* if `datebought` of the record pointed to by `ptr` is prior to `date`, and *false* otherwise, and `printinfo` prints the information field value of the record pointed to by `ptr`. ■

Example 6.7 Consider again the list-structure `brokerage` in Figure 6.1(e). The task now is to print, for each client, the total value of his or her portfolio. ■

In detail, what has to be done is

1. To traverse `brokerage`, and each time a client's record is encountered
2. Print the name
3. Then accumulate the total value of the portfolio as it is being traversed
4. Print this total when the portfolio has been completely traversed

While this seems straightforward and simple enough, some details require attention. We can apply the `traverse` function to this task. To do so, `process` must be written to turn `traverse` into a solution. Thus `process` must be able to recognize when the record it is to work on is a client's record. At this point, it must initialize the accumulated total to zero. For each ensuing record of the client's portfolio, it must then update the accumulated total by the value of that record's stock. Finally, `process` must recognize the end of the portfolio list and print the accumulated total.

If `total` is used to store the accumulated value, then it must be preserved between calls to `process`. This can be achieved by making `total` a static variable in `process` or by making `total` global. We choose the former. `Process` may be written as follows.

```
process(ptr)
/* If the current record points to a
   client's portfolio record that client's
   total portfolio value is updated.
   If the record is the last record on
   the client's portfolio list its total
   value is printed.
*/
liststructurepointer ptr;
{
   liststructurepointer null,setnull(),
      sublist(),next();
   float value();
   static float total;
   null = setnull();
   if(complex(ptr))
      if(sublist(ptr) != null)
         if(!complex(sublist(ptr)))
```

`total` *will retain its value between calls*

if the current record is complex, has a non-null sublist, and the first record of that sublist is not complex, then the current record must be a record of a client, so

```
                {
                   total = 0.0;                    ] total must be initialized
                   printname(ptr);                 ] the client's name printed
                }
    else                                           ] otherwise it must be a record on
       {                                             the client's portfolio list, so
          total = total + value(ptr);              ] total must be increased
          if(next(ptr) == null)                    ] if this is the last portfolio, print
             printf("\n Portfolio value is           the total
                     %12.2f \n",total);
       }
}
```

The **if** conditions are used to determine if this is the first call to `process` for a portfolio and, if so, to initialize and print the client's name or, after updating a client's total, to see if the record is the last of a portfolio. Assume `null` is nonlocal to `process`. `Process` will work with either version of `traverse`.

Example 6.8 Suppose `book`, the list-structure shown in Figure 6.1(c), stores the current version of a text that you wish to modify by replacing the current paragraph `p` of page `pg` of chapter `c` with a new paragraph. The new paragraph is stored as a list `newp`. To solve this problem we will write a new nonrecursive `traverse` function, called `paragraphinsert`, tailored to the situation. Since not all records of `book` need to be accessed, we do not want to traverse the entire list-structure as we have done in the previous two examples. Two versions of the function are presented. In both versions the idea is to

1. Traverse the main list searching for chapter `c`
2. Traverse that chapter's sublist searching for page `pg`
3. Traverse that page's sublist searching for paragraph `p`
4. Finally, replace that paragraph with `newp` ■

The first version assumes that records representing chapters, pages, or paragraphs have a number field. In the case of a chapter record the field contains the number of that chapter; for a page record it contains the number of that page; and for a paragraph it contains the number of that paragraph. These field values are shown in Figure 6.1(c). The program keeps track of whether it is currently looking for a chapter, a page, or a paragraph by using a variable `currentlist`. The value stored in `currentlist` will be `CH` (denoting that the search is now for a chapter), `PAGE` (denoting that the search is for a page), or `PAR` (denoting the search is for a paragraph). Similarly, a variable `currentnumber` will keep track of the particular chapter, page, or paragraph number currently being sought by the search. A variable `ptr` keeps track of the record currently being processed. Once the search for a chapter or a page is complete, **currentlist**, **currentnumber**, and **ptr** must be updated. Once the search for a paragraph has completed, the searching terminates and the new paragraph replaces the old.

Version 1

```
#define CH 1                      ] currentlist = 1 means the search is
                                    now for a chapter
#define PAGE 2                    ] currentlist = 2 means the search is
                                    now for a page
#define PAR 3                     ] currentlist = 3 means the search is
                                    now for a paragraph
#define TRUE 1
#define FALSE 0

paragraphinsert(book,newp,c,pg,p)
/* Replaces paragraph p of page pg
   of chapter c of book by the
   paragraph pointed to by newp.
   Assumes the records of book contain
   number fields.
*/
liststructurepointer book,newp;
int c,pg,p;
{
   int currentnumber,currentlist,found;
   liststructurepointer null,ptr,setnull(),next(),sublist();
   null = setnull();
   ptr = book;                    ] set ptr to the first chapter
   currentnumber = c;             ] set chapter searched for to c
   currentlist = CH;              ] indicate that the search is now for a
                                    chapter
   found = FALSE;
   while(!found && (ptr != null)) ] test for completion of present search or
                                    no more records of desired type
      {
         if(currentnumber != number(ptr))   ] if current record isn't the one being
            ptr = next(ptr);                  sought, update ptr
         else                               ] otherwise
            switch(currentlist)             ] determine what type is being sought
               {
                  case CH:                  ] chapter found, so update
                     currentlist = PAGE;    ] a page is to be found, its number is pg;
                     currentnumber = pg;      start looking in the chapter's sublist
                     ptr = sublist(ptr);
                     break;
                  case PAGE:                ] page found, so update
                     currentlist = PAR;     ] a paragraph is to be found, number p;
                     currentnumber = p;       start looking in the paragraph's sublist
                     ptr = sublist(ptr);
                     break;
                  case PAR:                 ] paragraph found, so search is finished
                     found = TRUE;            successfully; the traversal will be termi-
                                              nated
               }
      }
```

```
   if(found)
      setsublist(ptr,newp);                      if successful search
                                                 replace old paragraph with the new one
   else                                          otherwise
      printf("\n Paragraph not found \n");       print message
}
```

Setsublist sets the sublist field of the record pointed to by its first parameter to the value of its second parameter. Just before **setsublist** is invoked, code (not shown here) could be inserted to reclaim the storage used by the replaced paragraph. This is also true for the second version.

The second version assumes no number field, so the records are indistinguishable. Hence they must be kept in order—that is, chapters are in order on the main list, pages are in order on their lists, etc. Note that this ordering is not required by the first version. Now a count of list records must be maintained, to determine when the appropriate record number has been encountered. In the second version below only the differences between it and the first version have been annotated. Notice that this second program requires less storage for the list-structure (as the number fields are not needed), but it does somewhat more processing. Also, the sublists must be kept in order. This is another example of trading storage for time.

Version 2

```
#define CH 1
#define PAGE 2
#define PAR 3
#define TRUE 1
#define FALSE 0

paragraphinsert(book,newp,c,pg,p)
/* Replaces paragraph p of page pg
   of chapter c of book by the
   paragraph pointed to by newp.
   Assumes the sublists of book are
   in order.
*/
liststructurepointer book,newp;
int c,pg,p;
{
   int currentnumber,count,currentlist,found;
   liststructurepointer null,ptr,setnull(),next(),sublist();
   null = setnull();
   ptr = book;
   currentnumber = c;
   currentlist = CH;
   found = FALSE;
   count = 1;                                count initialized
   while(!found && (ptr != null))            count will contain the number of the
     {                                       current search type
```

```
        if(currentnumber != count)                    ] if the current record has the number
            {                                            sought
                count++;                              ] update count
                ptr = next(ptr);
            }
        else
            switch(currentlist)
                {
                    case CH:
                        currentlist = PAGE;
                        currentnumber = pg;
                        count = 1;                    ] chapter located, so reinitialize count
                        ptr = sublist(ptr);
                        break;
                    case PAGE:
                        currentlist = PAR:
                        currentnumber = p;
                        count = 1;                    ] page located, so reinitialize count
                        ptr = sublist(ptr);
                        break;
                    case PAR:
                        found = TRUE;
                }
        }
    if(found)
        setsublist(ptr,newp);
    else
        printf("\n Paragraph not found \n");
}
```

Example 6.9 Consider again the list-structure `formula` shown in Figure 6.4. It may be interpreted as representing the formula $(-b + \sqrt{(b^2 - 4ac)})/2a$. This happens to be the root of the quadratic equation $ax^2 + bx + c = 0$. In `formula` the symbols QT, PS, TS, MS, DIFF, and SQ stand for the operations of division, addition, multiplication, changing sign, taking the difference, and taking the square root, respectively. The square root and sign change operations apply to one operand. The others apply to two operands. The main list (and each sublist) represents an arithmetic expression. Their first records contain an arithmetic operator such as QT, PS, TS, MS, and DIFF. Their remaining list records represent the operand values of that arithmetic operator. The expression represented by such a list is to be evaluated by applying the operation to its operands. Thus sublist 4 would be evaluated by multiplying the operands in records 13 and 14 (b and b respectively), together. ■

Notice that each complex record's sublist is an arithmetic expression that must be evaluated. Thus the operand each represents must be obtained before the operator represented by the list on which it appears may be evaluated. For example, the sublists of complex records 2 and 22 must be evaluated before QT of record 1 can be applied to them.

The task is to write a function **evaluate** to return the value of an arithmetic expression represented by a list-structure. As with **formula**, the evaluation can be accomplished by traversing the expression's main list and, whenever a complex record is encountered, evaluating its sublist. When the last list record has been processed in this way, the operator and each of its operands are known. The final result is obtained by applying the operator to its known operands. Of course, in evaluating an operand, more complex records may be encountered, such as record 4, and they must then be evaluated before continuing. A **process** function can be written to turn either the recursive or the nonrecursive traversal program into **evaluate**.

One important detail remains: how to store the operands that are generated during the traversal so that they are available when needed. Suppose each operand encountered by **process** is stored in an operand stack, and each operator encountered is stored in an operator stack. If the current record being processed is the last record of a list (its link value is null), then the operator currently at the top of the stack will have its operands at the top of the operand stack. **Process** can then pop both these stacks, apply the operator to the operands, and place the result back onto the operand stack. If the record being processed represents the last record on the main list (the operator stack will then be empty), instead of placing the result on the operand stack it should copy it into **evaluate**.

A detailed description of **process** follows.

```
If next(ptr) is not null and the record pointed to by ptr is simple, then
    if it contains an operator, then
        place the operator on the operator stack
    else
        place the operand on the operand stack
    else
        pop the operator stack, remove the top k operands from the operand stack (k is
        the number of operands of the operator just popped), and apply the operator to
        the k operands.
        If the operator stack is not empty then
            push the result onto the operand stack
        else
            set evaluate to the result.
```

This solution may also be applied to the evaluation of logical or boolean expressions. In fact, it forms the basis of the interpretive language LISP.

We have now seen a number of applications of **traverse** to examples involving list-structures. The example, presented next, is not discussed in detail but points out another possible application.

Example 6.10 Suppose polynomials are represented as **p** is in Figure 6.1(d). It is then possible to write functions to perform important algebraic operations on polynomials such as the addition and multiplication of two polynomials. Even symbolic differentiation can be performed. Note that traversal of the list-structures representing the polynomials would form the heart of such functions. ■

6.4 Implementing List-structures

The graphic depictions of list-structures mirror the conceptual image of them. To implement list-structures in a language such as C, you may store their records in dynamic memory or in an array of records. Wherever the records are stored, it must be possible to distinguish simple records from complex ones. The main difference in the format of the records, compared to those of a chain, is that an additional field becomes necessary for the sublist pointer when the record is complex. We also assume that the record contains a field whose value will establish whether the record is simple or complex. The actual implementation of a list-structure record may be done in three ways:

1. Declare two types of records:
   one to be used for simple records
   another to be used for complex records
2. Declare one record type that consists of a fixed part and a union, which has
   one format for simple records
   another format for complex records
3. Declare one record type, used for both simple and complex records, but containing a `kind` or `tag` field to indicate whether the record stored is simple or complex

The first way is undesirable because it requires that a program deal with two distinct pointer types, one for simple records and another for complex records, so we dismiss it. The second method is feasible and also requires a `kind` field, which we can put in the fixed part. However, even though the two distinct union formats may have significant differences in the amount of storage they require, C will always allocate the larger amount. Thus this method does not save storage over the third way, which we now choose to use.

To implement the `accounts` list-structure of Figure 6.1(a), the following definitions could be used when the records are to be stored in dynamic memory.

```
typedef struct record
{
   int kind;
   int info;
   struct record *sublist;
   struct record *link;
}listrecord,*liststructurepointer;
```

implementation for `accounts` *records stored in dynamic memory*

When the records are to be stored in an array of records, the implementation should be changed to

```
typedef struct record
{
   int kind;
   int info;
   int sublist;
   int link;
}listrecord;
typedef int liststructurepointer;
```

implementation for `accounts` *records stored in an array of records of type* `listrecord`

`sublist` *now an array index*

`link` *now an array index*

`liststructurepointer` *now an array index*

This change is needed because now **listpointer**, **link**, and **sublistptr** will each be an integer index into the array of records rather than a pointer variable containing an absolute memory address.

As a second illustration, consider the records for the polynomials of Figure 6.1(e). Notice that a complex record in that list-structure has two possible formats, depending on whether the record is a header or not. If it is a header record, the second field contains a character; otherwise it contains a sublist pointer. Using a union, the polynomial records can be implemented as follows.

```
typedef union
{
   char unknown;
   polyrecord *sublist;
   int value;
}varying;

typedef struct record
{
   int tag;
   varying secondfield;
   int exponent;
   struct record *nextterm;
}polyrecord, *liststructurepointer;
```

implementation of polynomial records stored in dynamic memory

The **tag** field indicates whether the record is simple or complex. In this implementation the union allows the same storage to be used to hold the unknown (for a header record) or a sublist pointer. It was used here because a complex record has two distinct possible second fields and the union allows them to share the same storage. The alternative is to avoid the use of the union and keep separate fields for *both* the unknown and the sublist pointer in each record. This just wastes storage.

When the records are to be stored in an array of records, the implementation should be changed to

```
typedef union
{
   char unknown;
   int sublist;
   int value;
}varying;
```

implementation of polynomial records stored in an array of records of type `polyrecord`

`sublist` *is now an array index*

```
typedef struct
{
   int tag;
   varying secondfield;
   int exponent;
   int nextterm;                    ] nextterm is now an array index
}polyrecord;
typedef liststructurepointer;       ] liststructurepointer is now
                                      an array index
```

It is also possible to implement the main list and sublists of a list-structure as two-way lists. This is convenient, just as for chains, when it is necessary to go back and forth during the processing of a list-structure or to make the predecessor of any record easily accessible. In this case an additional field would be needed for the backward pointer.

The following program creates and prints the records of a list-structure to illustrate its implementation with records stored in dynamic memory. It also demonstrates two applications of the **traverse** function. The input consists, first, of an integer to indicate whether the list being created is null, and, second, a sequence of data for each record. This sequence is assumed to be in the order in which the records are accessed in a traversal of the liststructure. For example, input corresponding to **accounts** of Figure 6.1(a), would be as follows. (Program output is not shown, nor are program prompts for input.)

1 — *indicates a nonnull list-structure*

175 — *information field value*
1 — *indicates record is complex*
11 — *indicates the* **link** *and* **sublist** *fields are not null*

0 — *information field value*
1 — *indicates record is complex*
11 — *indicates the* **link** *and* **sublist** *fields are not null*

100 — *information field value*
0 — *indicates record is simple*
0 — *indicates the* **link** *field is null*

75 — *information field value*
0 — *indicates record is simple*
0 — *indicates the* **link** *field is null*

450 — *information field value*
1 — *indicates record is complex*
11 — *indicates the* **link** *and* **sublist** *fields are not null*

200 — *information field value*
1 — *indicates record is complex*
10 — *indicates the* **link** *field is not null but the* **sublist** *field is*

250 — *information field value*
0 — *indicates record is simple*
0 — *indicates the* `link` *field is null*

−46 — *information field value*
0 — *indicates record is simple*
0 — *indicates the* `link` *field is null*

The Program

```
Reads in list-structure records,
Creates the list-structure, and
Prints all its records.

#include <stdio.h>

typedef struct record
{
   int info;
   int kind;
   struct record *sublistptr;
   struct record *link;
}examplerecord,*liststructurepointer;
#define NULL 0

liststructurepointer next(p)
/* Returns a copy of the link field
   value of record pointed to by p.
*/
liststructurepointer p;
{
   return(p->link);
}

liststructurepointer sublist(p)
/* Returns a copy of the sublistpointer
   field value of record pointed to by p.
*/
liststructurepointer p;
{
   return(p->sublistptr);
}

liststructurepointer setnull()
/* Returns a null pointer */
{
   return(NULL);
}
```

definitions for the liststructure data abstraction

the null pointer will be 0

basic operations on liststructure

```
liststructurepointer avail()
/* Returns a pointer to storage allocated
   for a liststructure record of type
   examplerecord.
*/
{
   return(malloc(sizeof(examplerecord)));
}

complex(p)
/* Returns true only if the record pointed
   to by p is complex.
*/
liststructurepointer p;
{
   return(p->kind == 1);
}

createrecord(l,ptr)
/* Reads in the data for the current record
   and sets its fields appropriately.
*/
liststructurepointer l,ptr;
{
   int link,subptr,value,kind;
   liststructurepointer setnull(),avail();
   printf("\n enter info \n");
   scanf("%d",&value);
   printf("\n enter 0 for simple 1
          for complex \n");
   scanf("%d",&kind);

   if (kind == 0)
      {
         printf("\n enter link \n");
         scanf("%d",&link);
         if (link == 0)
            ptr->link = setnull();
         else
            ptr->link = avail();
      }

   else
      {
         printf("\n enter link & subptr \n");
         scanf("%d %d",&link,&subptr);

         if (link == 0)
            ptr->link = setnull();
         else
            ptr->link = avail();
```

] `kind` = `1` *will signify a complex record*

] *reads information to go in the* `info` *field*

] *reads the information to go in the* `kind` *field*

] *if a simple record*

] *read* `link` *data*

] *if* `link` *is null*

] *set it to null*

] *otherwise*

] *set it to storage allocated for the next record*

] *otherwise*

] *read* `link` *and* `sublist` *data*

] *if* `link` *is null*

] *set it to null*

] *otherwise*

] *set it to storage allocated for the next record*

```
        if (subptr == 0)

           ptr->sublistptr = setnull();
        else
           ptr->sublistptr = avail();
     }

     ptr->info = value;
     ptr->kind = kind:
  }

  printrecord(pls,ptr)
  /* Prints the contents of the info field
     of the record pointed to by ptr.
  */
  liststructurepointer *pls,ptr;
  {
     printf("\n %d  \n",ptr->info);
  }

  main()
  /* Reads in liststructure records, creates
     the liststructure, and prints all its records.
  */
  {
     int n;
     liststructurepointer l,avail();
     printf("\n enter liststructure: 0 for\
             null list 1 otherwise \n");
     scanf("%d",&n);
     printf("\n remember - the data for the\
             records must be in traversal order\
             \n");
     if (n == 0)
        l = NULL;
     else
        {
           l = avail()
           create(l);
        }
     traverse(&l);
     if (l == NULL)
        printf("\n The list is null \n");
  }

  #define LIMIT 50
  typedef liststructurepointer whatever;
  typedef struct
  {
     whatever stackarray[LIMIT];
     int top;
  }stack;
```

if `sublistptr` *is null*

set it to null

otherwise

set it to storage allocated for the first sublist record

set the `info` *field*

set the `kind` *field*

`l` *is the name of the liststructure created*

if liststructure input is null

set `l` *to null*

otherwise

set `l` *to allocated storage*

create `l`

this `traverse` *prints all records*

prints message to indicate that `l` *is the null liststructure*

definitions for the stack data abstraction—its entries will be pointers to liststructure records basic operations for the stack

```
setstack(ps)
/* Sets stack s to empty */
stack *ps;
{
   (*ps).top = -1;
}


empty(ps)
/* Returns true only if
   stack s is empty.
*/
stack *ps;
{
   return((*ps).top == -1);
}


push(value,ps)
/* Inserts contents of value as
   top entry of stack s.
*/
whatever value;
stack *ps;
{
   if ((*ps).top == (LIMIT - 1))
      overflow(ps);
   else
      {
         (*ps).top = (*ps).top + 1;
         (*ps).stackarray[(*ps).top] = value;
      }
}


pop(ps,pvalue)
/* Removes the top entry of stack s
   and places its contents in value.
*/
stack *ps;
whatever *pvalue;
{
   if (empty(ps))
      underflow(ps);
   else
      {
         *pvalue = (*ps).stackarray[(*ps).top];
         (*ps).top = (*ps).top - 1;
      }
}
```

```
overflow(ps)
/* Prints a message when
   the stack overflows.
*/
stack *ps;
{
   printf("\n stack overflow \n");
}

underflow(ps)
/* Prints a message when
   the stack underflows.
*/
stack *ps;
{
   printf("\n stack underflow \n");
}
```

this nonrecursive traversal uses a stack `s1`

```
traverse(pls)
/* Prints the info fields of all
   records of the liststructure l.
*/
liststructurepointer *pls;
{
   liststructurepointer ptr,null,setnull(),
      next(),sublist();
   stack s1;
   null = setnull();
   ptr = *pls;
   setstack(&s1);
   while ((ptr != null)||(!empty(&s1)))
      if (ptr != null)
         {
            printrecord(pls,ptr);
            if (complex(ptr))
               {
                  push(next(ptr),&s1);
                  ptr = sublist(ptr);
               }
            else
               ptr = next(ptr);
         }
      else
         pop(&s1,&ptr);
}
```

plays the role of `process` *for this traversal*

this nonrecursive traversal uses a stack `s2`

```
create(l)
/* Inputs records and creates the list l */
liststructurepointer l;
{
```

```
   liststructurepointer ptr,null,setnull(),
      next(),sublist();
   stack s2;
   null = setnull();
   ptr = l;
   setstack(&s2);
   while ((ptr != null)||(!empty(&s2)))
      if (ptr != null)
         {
            createrecord(l,ptr);      ] plays the role of process
            if (complex(ptr))           for this traversal
               {
                  push(next(ptr),&s2);
                  ptr = sublist(ptr);
               }
            else
               ptr = next(ptr);
         }
      else
         pop(&s2,&ptr);
}
```

Although the stacks have been given distinct names, since `s1` is local to **`create`** and `s2` is local to **`traverse`**, they could have both been named `s`. Note that either **`create`** or **`traverse`** could be replaced by recursive versions.

6.4.1 Sharing Storage

List-structures that share list records as well as sharing sublists are frequently needed to fit the demands of a problem. These structures are more complicated than those presented thus far and may require large amounts of storage for their implementation. A natural idea is to avoid the duplication of identical sublists or records. At times it is convenient to use additional fields linking records or sublists so that the resultant structure contains records with more than one pointer to them, and the structure may even contain loops. That is, by following pointers from a record we can arrive back at the record. You will see examples of this in the case study that follows. Whenever these possibilities occur, the structures created are still lists but are no longer list-structures. These more general lists provide extensive flexibility but lead to difficult storage management problems, which are considered later in the text.

6.5 Case Study: Information Retrieval

We now present a case study to illustrate the versatility of lists intertwined with pointers. When the name of a record or a pointer to it is known, retrieval of the record is simple. It may be directly accessed and processed to suit our needs. Slightly more difficult is the retrieval of a record that can be recognized when encountered but whose location is unknown. In order to retrieve it the records must be traversed until the desired one is encountered.

When large collections of records are involved, traversing all the records to find one is not feasible. The problem is not so much that retrieving one desired record takes too long but that many retrievals in rapid succession cause too much delay for the later retrievals. Imagine 1,000 computer terminals linked to a central computer. The banking terminals known as automatic tellers are an example. Suppose 200 requests occur in rapid succession for the retrieval of records. If 1 million records need to be traversed, the retrieval of an individual record could easily take a second, so the last of the 200 requests to be processed would be honored only after more than 3 minutes of elapsed time. No one wants to wait at a terminal for 3 minutes before each request is answered. In the meantime, even more requests become backlogged.

The basic technique to avoid traversing all stored records is to focus the search on a smaller group of records known to contain the desired one. This is the essence of most faster retrieval algorithms. In this case study, lists will be used to organize the data so that the search may be localized in this way. In Chapters 8 and 9 the search problem is presented in a more general context for information stored in random access internal memory, and in Chapter 10 for information stored in external memory.

6.5.1 Family Relationships

The central problem in this case study concerns information about a collection of individuals. The collection might represent everyone who graduated from a specific university, all registered voters in a given region, or all individuals known to have contracted a particular disease that is being researched.

The input information for each individual is given as a record with the individual's name, sex, birthdate, father's name, and mother's name as fields. Other relevant fields may be present but are ignored for our purposes here.

To simplify, assume that no duplicate records appear, no two individuals have exactly the same name, all siblings have the same parents, all parents are married, there are no divorces, and no one remarries. This is truly a noteworthy collection of people living in an idyllic world! The violation of these assumptions would create problems that could not be ignored. However, their consideration would detract from our immediate aims.

The task is to input a sequence of these records and represent the collection in memory so that questions involving certain relationships among individuals may be answered. Examples of possible questions are

How many children does John Smith have?

Who are the uncles of John Smith?

Who are the siblings of John Smith?

6.5.2 A First Solution

Perhaps the most straightforward approach to a solution for this information retrieval problem is to represent the collection of information by its image in memory as an array of records. To answer the question, "How many children does John Smith have?" requires a simple traversal of the records. Have a program look at the father's name field in each record and, whenever it comes to John Smith, increment a counter that represents the number of John Smith's children.

When the traversal is complete, the program would print the counter value. To answer the question, "Who are the uncles of John Smith?", the program must first traverse, looking at the name field of each record, to find John Smith. It would note the father's name, which is in the fathersname field of that record. Then it would traverse again, looking at the fathersname fields. Each time John Smith's father's name appears, and "male" is listed as the corresponding sex field value, the program must print the name that appears in the corresponding name field. The same sequence would be repeated for John Smith's mother.

The execution time for these traversals can be proportional to the total number of records. This makes the solution time proportional to the amount of information represented in the system. For large systems, this would be impractical, as noted earlier.

What is the least amount of time that could be taken by any solution for these kinds of questions? Clearly, identifying the brothers of John Smith requires printing the names of the brothers. To display who the uncles of John Smith are, the program must print the names of each of his uncles. The least amount of time required for any solution would thus be proportional to the length of the answer to any given question. Length in the case of the uncles is the number of uncles. In the next section, you will see that a different way of representing the information allows a solution that is closer in execution time to this length. This is much better than having it proportional to the entire amount of information stored.

6.5.3 A Better Solution

To find answers to relationship questions quickly, you must be able to localize the search and get to the relevant records without considering all of them. You can, if you somehow link records together in a meaningful way. The problem deals with family relationships. Suppose you set up a record in memory to correspond to each individual name in the system, each record having seven fields, five of the fields containing pointer information. The seven fields of each individual's record will be **nameptr**, **fnameptr**, **mnameptr**, **siblingptr**, **childrenlist**, **sex**, and **birthdate**.

You will also have a table of names, called **nametable**. Each record of **nametable** will have a name and a **recordptr** field. The **recordptr** field contains a pointer to the individual record of the person whose name appears in the name field. By searching the **nametable** for a name, we get the pointer to the corresponding individual's record. Following the trails (pointers) from the record, we can retrieve the data needed to answer questions.

Figure 6.5 depicts the form of the two kinds of records. In memory the collection of **nametable** records will be stored separately from the collection of individual records.

The memory would appear as shown in Figure 6.6, after the data has been input. The **childrenlist** field of a record **f** contains a pointer to the first record on the list of children of the individual represented by **f**. The **siblingptr** field plays the role of a link field for records on the list of siblings of **f**. The different lists are intertwined as shown in Figure 6.7.

In Figure 6.7 records **f** and **m** are husband and wife, so their **children-**

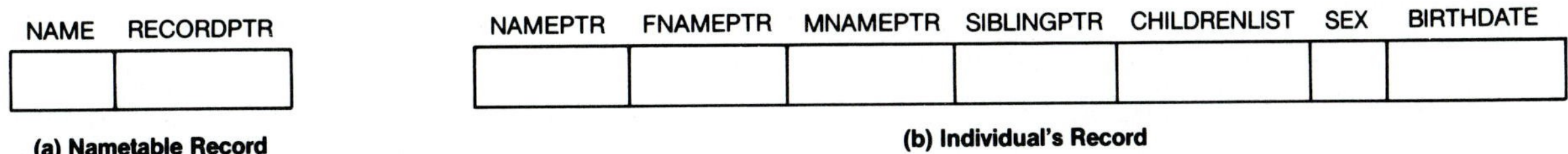

Figure 6.5 Format of the Nametable and Individual Records

`list` pointers are identical. It might be convenient to keep the lists of children in order by birthdate or to make them *circular,* so that the null pointer signifying the last record would instead point to the first record of the list.

If the assumptions about an "ideal" world were violated, it would be possible to have shared records, and loops could even appear. With the assumptions, the lists are list-structures. The main list of any sublist consists of siblings. All records are complex, with sublist fields (`childrenlist` fields) pointing to sublists representing children of the individual represented by the complex record. Sublist sharing, however, does occur because the fathers and mothers share the lists of children.

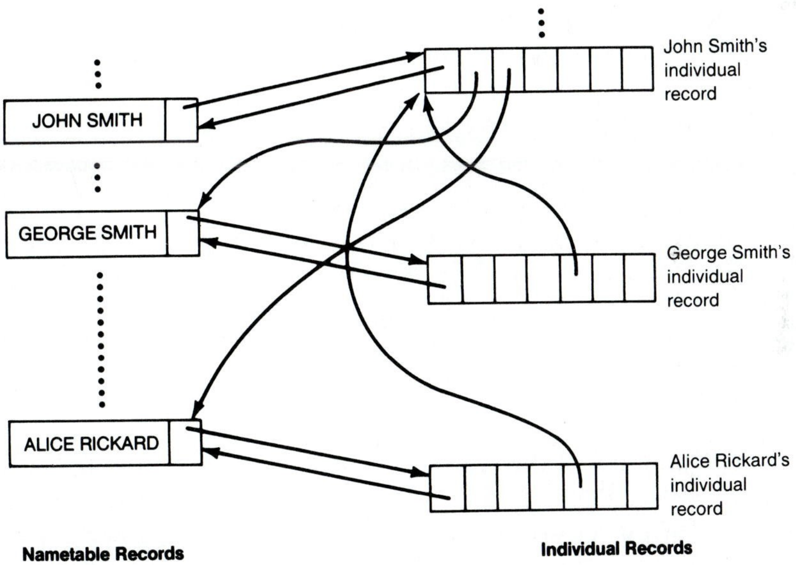

Figure 6.6 Memory in the Family Relationships Problem

6.5.4 Updating the System

How are the collections of individual records and of `nametable` records created originally? Suppose you have already dealt with the first hundred records and that the situation in memory accurately reflects all the information they contain. That is, the two collections are correct and as complete as possible, given this input. You now attempt to input the next record, the one hundred first. Recall that the

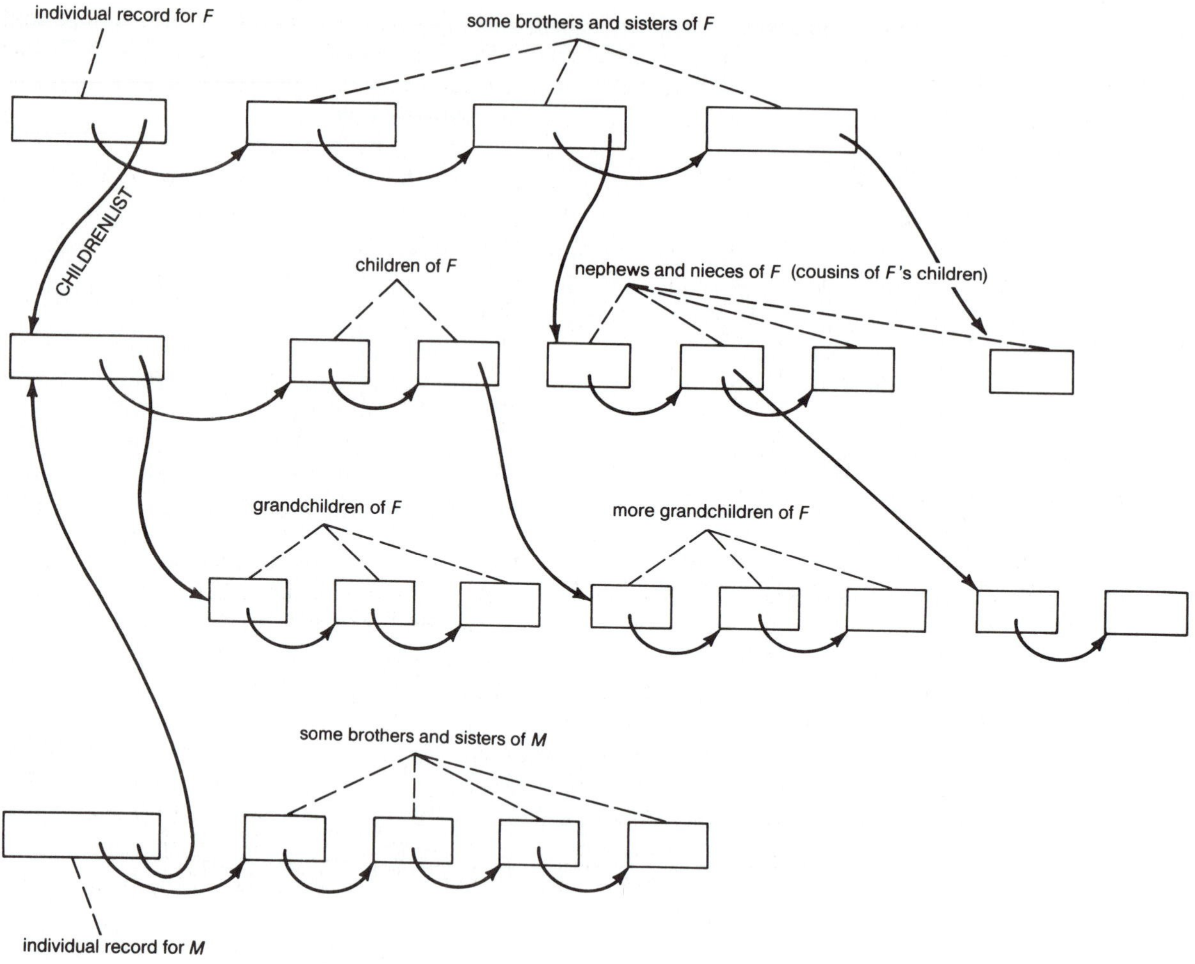

Figure 6.7 Typical Configuration of Individual Records

input consists of the individual's name, sex, birthdate, father's name, and mother's name. Input data for John Smith would appear as

```
JOHN SMITH  M  1/2/79  GEORGE SMITH  ALICE RICKARD
```

The program should check the record for validity (input validation). If valid, the two collections in memory must be updated to reflect the new information. Then the program should read the next record, and so on until there are no more to enter. An important component of the solution is an update function, which will create and add new records to the collections when necessary and enter new values into the proper fields. It must function as follows.

It is possible that one or more of the three names in the name fields of the newly input record are already in the `nametable`, with individual records having been created for them. For instance, the father's name might have been dealt with earlier when it appeared in the name field of another record. Assume first that each distinct name appearing in any field of the previously processed records has been entered into the `nametable` and has had an individual record created for it. Thus the `nametable` entry for each of these distinct names has the correct name in its name field, and a pointer in its `recordptr` field to its corresponding individual record. This individual record also has a pointer in its name field back to the record in the `nametable` it represents. Some fields of the individual record may not yet have been filled with appropriate information.

We cannot, however, assume that *any* name in the new input record has been seen before. Suppose John Smith is in the name field of the new record. Search the `nametable` to see if there is an entry for John Smith. If there is, remember where it is by placing a pointer to it in `nt_ptr` and then copy the pointer in the `recordptr` field into a variable `ir_nptr`. Then `ir_nptr` reveals where the individual record is that corresponds to John Smith. `Nt_ptr` is a pointer to John Smith's nametable record, and `ir_nptr` is a pointer to John Smith's individual record. `Ir_nptr` will be used later when we have to update John Smith's individual record. If there is no entry for John Smith in the nametable, you know that there is not yet an individual record created for John Smith. Create such a record, and also create an entry in the `nametable` corresponding to it. Store John Smith's name and a pointer to his corresponding record in the `recordptr` field of the nametable entry. Also place a copy of the pointer to this entry in the `nameptr` field of the individual record. Then copy the pointer to the individual record into `ir_nptr`.

At this point, whether or not information on John Smith was already in the system, both an entry in the nametable and an individual record for him exist. The nametable record is completely filled in, and the individual record has at least its `nameptr` field filled in. Also, `ir_nptr` points to the individual record.

We would follow the same process for John Smith's father and mother, creating the following four pointers.

`ir_fptr`
: A pointer to the individual record representing John Smith's father

`ir_mptr`
: A pointer to the individual record representing John Smith's mother

`nt_fptr`
: A pointer to the nametable entry for John Smith's father

`nt_mptr`
: A pointer to the nametable entry for John Smith's mother

How do we now complete the update properly? That is, which individual records and `nametable` entries must be modified, and how are the modifications done?

Consider the individual record for John Smith. The sex and birthdate fields can easily be filled in, as well as the `fnameptr` field, copying `nt_fptr` into it. The same can be done for `mnameptr`.

Now the individual record for the father of John Smith must be updated. Fill in the sex field (you know he is male). There is no additional information on his birthdate. (It may already be known. Why?) John Smith's record must be added to the list of children of his father. Assuming that the children are not kept in any special order, add his record at the front of the list. This requires copying the `childrenlist` pointer of his father's record into the `siblingptr` of John Smith's record, and then copying the pointer in `ir_nptr` into the `childrenlist` field of his father. This implies that whenever individual records are created, they must have their `childrenlist` and `siblingptr` fields set to null.

The mother's record can be treated similarly, except we may simply copy the father's `childrenlist` pointer (or `ir_nptr`) into her `childrenlist` field. This completes the update, which consisted of a search of the `nametable` and the updating of pointers in nine fields after the `nametable` entries and individual records were created. These nine fields were

> `fnameptr`, `mnameptr`, `sex`, `birthdate`, `siblingptr`—for the individual record of John Smith
>
> `sex`, `childrenlist`—for the individual record of George Smith and Alice Rickard, the father and mother

Example 6.11 Let us now trace this process with some data and show how the records would appear. Suppose the input data so far consisted of the information shown in Table 6.1, and suppose that we use different arrays to hold the individual records and the `nametable` entries. (Later, in Chapters 8 and 9, more appropriate implementations for collections such as `nametable` are introduced.) The situation in memory will then be as shown in Table 6.2. ■

The next input is

```
JOHN SMITH  M  1/2/79  GEORGE SMITH  ALICE RICKARD
```

Since none of these names appears in the `nametable`, an entry in the `nametable` and an individual record must be created for each of the names.

After this has been done, the new `nametable` entries, individual records,

Table 6.1 Input Data for Example 6.11

Name	Sex	Birthdate	Fathersname	Mothersname
Albert Einstein	M	3/14/1879	Hermann Einstein	Paulina Koch
Leo Tolstoy	M	9/9/1828	Nikolai Tolstoy	Marie Volkronskii
George Eliot	F	11/22/1819	Robert Evans	Christina Pearson
Margaret Truman	F	2/17/1924	Harry Truman	Bess Truman
Wilhelm Bach	M	11/22/1710	Johann S. Bach	Maria Bach
Jimmy Carter	M	10/1/1924	James Earl Carter	Lillian Carter
Sir Isaac Newton	M	12/25/1642	Isaac Newton	Hannah Newton
Harry Truman	M	5/8/1884	John Truman	Martha Young
Billy Carter	M	3/29/1937	James Earl Carter	Lillian Carter
Johann S. Bach	M	3/21/1685	Johann Ambrosius Bach	Elizabeth Lämmerhirt
Johann Gottfried Bach	M	5/11/1715	Johann S. Bach	Maria Bach

Table 6.2 The `nametable` and Individual Records (for Example 6.11) after Initial Input Data Are Processed

`Nametable` Records		Individual Records							
`Name`	`Recordptr`		`Nameptr`	`Fnameptr`	`Mnameptr`	`Siblingptr`	`Childrenlist`	`Sex`	`Birthdate`
1 Albert Einstein	1	1	1	2	3	0	0	M	03141879
2 Hermann Einstein	2	2	2			0	1	M	
3 Paulina Koch	3	3	3			0	1	F	
4 Leo Tolstoy	4	4	4	5	6	0	0	M	09091828
5 Nikolai Tolstoy	5	5	5			0	4	M	
6 Marie Volkronskii	6	6	6			0	4	F	
7 George Eliot	7	7	7	8	9	0	0	F	11221819
8 Robert Evans	8	8	8			0	7	M	
9 Christina Pearson	9	9	9			0	7	F	
10 Margaret Truman	10	10	10	11	12	0	0	F	02171924
11 Harry Truman	11	11	11			0	10	M	
12 Bess Truman	12	12	12			0	10	F	
13 Wilhelm Bach	13	13	13	14	15	0	0	M	11221710
14 Johann S. Bach	14	14	14	25	26	0	27	M	03211685
15 Maria Bach	15	15	15			0	27	F	
16 Jimmy Carter	16	16	16	17	18	0	0	M	10011924
17 James Earl Carter	17	17	17			0	16	M	
18 Lillian Carter	18	18	18			0	16	F	
19 Sir Isaac Newton	19	19	19	20	21	0	0	M	12251642
20 Isaac Newton	20	20	20			0	19	M	
21 Hannah Newton	21	21	21			0	19	F	
22 John Truman	22	22	22				11	M	
23 Martha Young	23	23	23				11	F	
24 Billy Carter	24	24	24	17	18	16	0	M	03291937
25 Johann Ambrosius Bach	25	25	25			0	14	M	
26 Elizabeth Lämmerhirt	26	26	26			0	14	F	
27 Johann Gottfried Bach	27	27	27	14	15	13	0	M	05111715

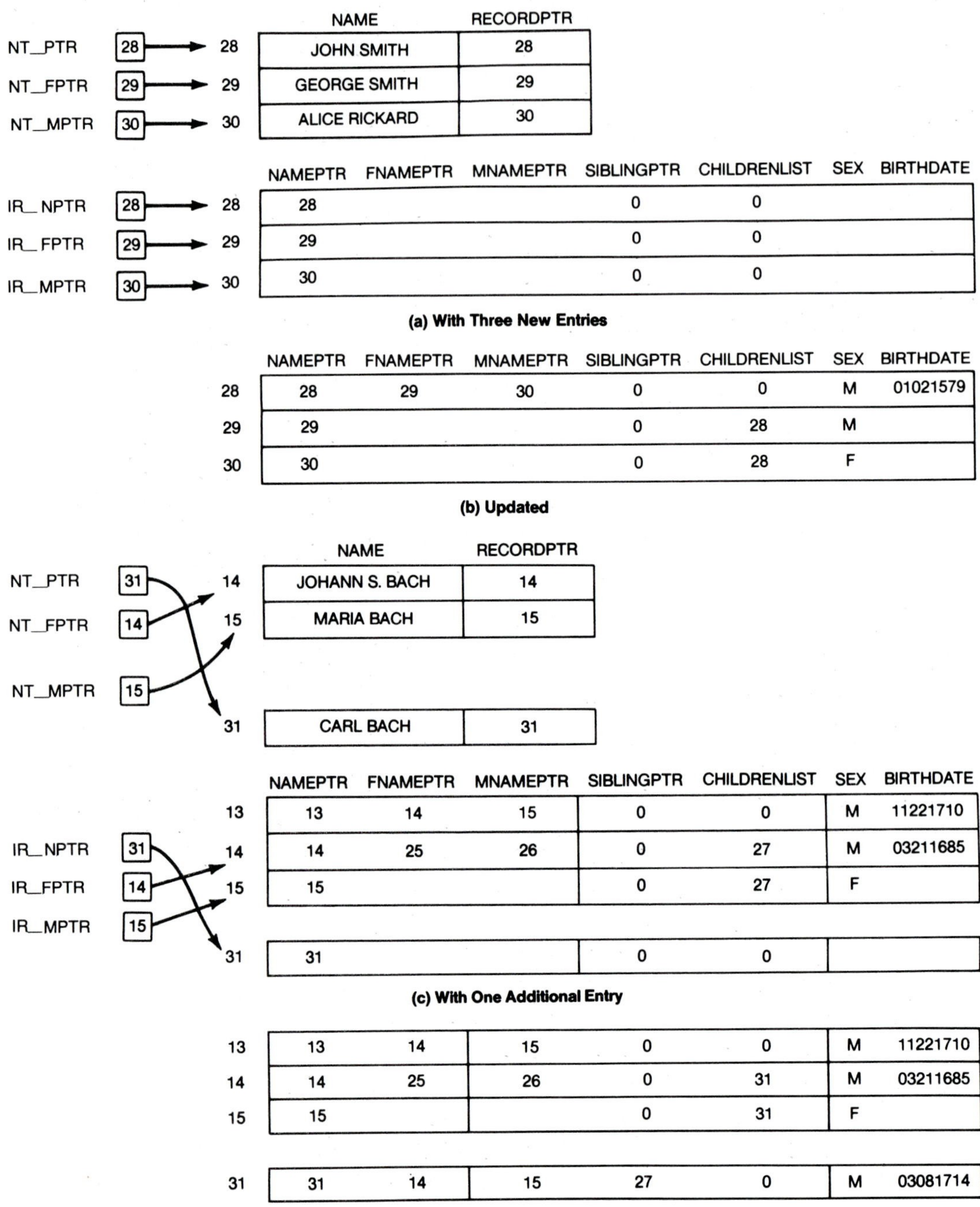

Figure 6.8 Nametable and Individual Records with Saved Pointers

and saved pointers will appear as shown in Figure 6.8(a). Updating the nine fields of the individual records yields the result shown in Figure 6.8(b).

The next input is

```
CARL BACH   M   3/8/1714   JOHANN S. BACH   MARIA BACH
```

Johann S. Bach and Maria Bach already appear in the `nametable` and have individual records. An entry in the `nametable` and an individual record must, however, be created for Carl Bach.

When this has been completed, the `nametable` entries, individual records, and saved pointers related to this input appear as in Figure 6.8(c). Updating the nine fields of the individual records yields the result shown in Figure 6.8(d). The time required to complete an update is the constant time for the pointer manipulations plus the time to search the `nametable`.

The following is an algorithm for updating the information base given another input record.

1. Search the `nametable`.
   a. Create entries in the `nametable` and create individual records for any of the three input names not present in `nametable`.
   b. Set their `recordptr` and `nameptr` fields.
   c. Set their `childrenlist` and `siblingptr` fields to null.
   d. Set `nt_ptr`, `nt_fptr`, `nt_mptr`, `ir_nptr`, `ir_fptr`, and `ir_mptr`.
2. Update the following fields of the individual record pointed to by `ir_nptr`:
   `sex` to input sex
   `birthdate` to input birthdate
   `fnameptr` to `nt_fptr`
   `mnameptr` to `nt_mptr`
3. Update:
   `sex.fptr` (the sex field of the record pointed to by `ir_fptr`) to `m`
   `siblingptr.ir_nptr` to `childrenlist.ir_fptr`
   `childrenlist.ir_fptr` to `ir_nptr`
   `sex.ir_mptr` to `f`
   `childrenlist.ir_mptr` to `ir_nptr`

6.5.5 Retrieving Information from the System

Now that we have built the collections, how do we answer questions about family relationships?

Example 6.12 How do we determine who the children of John Smith are? Search the `nametable` for John Smith. If the name is not there, print an appropriate message. If it is there, follow the pointer to John Smith's individual record. Traverse his list of children and count the number of records on it, or output the individual names. In any case, ignoring the search of `nametable`, the time required is proportional to the length of the answer—that is, it is proportional to the number of children of John Smith. ■

Example 6.13 How do we find all the uncles of John Smith? Search the `nametable`, and follow its pointer to the record for John Smith. Then, follow the `fnameptr` pointer to the entry in the `nametable` for his father and follow its `recordptr` back to the father's record. Do this again for the father to get to the grandfather's record. Once we have the grandfather's record we can traverse his children's list to find the uncles on John Smith's father's side. Repeat the process for John Smith's mother to find the uncles on her side. ■

Simply following the sibling pointer of the father's record doesn't work, because the traversal may have begun in the middle of this sibling list. To ensure starting at the beginning of the sibling list, it is best to use the children's list of the grandfather's record. If the sibling lists were circular, this would not be necessary; it would suffice to traverse the grandfather's list of children (John Smith's father's siblings) and then output the name of each male. The same processing must be done for John Smith's mother, to output all his uncles on his mother's side.

The total time, again ignoring the `nametable` search, is proportional to the answer, the number of uncles. Excluding the `nametable` search, this is certainly close to the minimal time that would be desirable. You will see in the chapters on searching and sorting how long it would take to search the `nametable`!

6.5.6 Other System Components

To complete design of the system, in addition to the `nametable` implementation and search function, components are needed for deletion of records. We will not pursue this topic here, but clearly the issues of storage reclamation and allocation would have to be considered.

Beyond this, there are some more basic unresolved problems. Exactly how are questions asked of the system?

One way is for anyone wanting answers to questions to bring them to the system's designers. The designers then write programs to output the solutions. This is feasible in certain situations; in fact, many organizations do information retrieval in this way. A related solution would be to give the data representation to questioners and have them write their own programs.

Another way is to design a simple "menu," or list, of questions that includes at least those most likely to be asked. Users could then "check off" their questions if they appear on the menu, and previously written programs could be run to answer them. This solution proves satisfactory as long as the questions people want answered are on the menu.

A more sophisticated scheme would be to design a general query language. Questioners could then ask their questions in this language. A built-in language translator would interpret the question and automatically produce a program to print the answer. Achieving this solution can be quite complex and might challenge the state of the art at the present time.

The issue of security has been ignored. It would be of major concern in any retrieval system. Users' access to specific information and ability to modify it would have to be limited.

6.5.7 Case Study Overview

This case study illustrates the use of many of the concepts this book has stressed. These include the basic concepts of top-down design, data abstraction, functional modularization, and the use of appropriate data structures to achieve clear, concise, and efficient programs.

It also shows the versatility of list-structures and the way in which pointers contribute to this versatility. List-structures provide a means of interconnecting data to cut retrieval time significantly. To do so, however, means that we have to organize the data to fit the desired retrievals. As usual, we are faced with higher costs to organize the data, that is, to build the links we will need, but gain reduced costs in search time for retrieving information. This is the classic trade-off.

■ Exercises

1. Draw a picture like Figure 6.1(b), corresponding to Example 6.2 for an actual configuration of hands for the game of poker with four players.

2. Draw pictures, similar to `p` of Figure 6.1(d), for the polynomials

$$z^2(y^2(x(8))) + z(y(3x)) + y(x) + 18 \quad \text{and} \quad x^3yz + 2xz + y^2xz^3$$

3. Give a recursive definition for a chain.

4. Why do the two definitions of list-structures not allow more than one pointer to a record, or loops, to occur in a list-structure?

5. Why does a null `ptr` and an empty stack indicate the end of the traversal of a list-structure?

6. What will be in the stack when record 20 of `formula` (Figure 6.4) is accessed?

7. Simulate the execution of the iterative implementation of `traverse` on `p` of Figure 6.1(d).

8. Simulate the execution of the recursive implementation of `traverse` on `p` of Figure 6.1(d).

9. Give an example of a list containing loops for which the traversal functions fail because they do not terminate.

10. a. Write a `process` function to turn the iterative traversal into a program that prints the number of sublists of a list-structure.

b. Will your solution also work for the recursive traversal?

11. a. Write a function to return a pointer to the record of a list-structure that has the maximum information field value.

b. Modify your solution to return a pointer to a list. The list should contain pointers to all records whose information field value coincides with the maximum value.

12. Give an algorithm to determine whether two list-structures whose records have the same format are identical.

13. Modify your solution to Exercise 12 so that the algorithm determines whether the two list-structures have the same "structure," independent of the information values stored.

14. Each complex record of a list-structure has a field pointing to the record's sublist. The sublist is composed of a main list (composed of the chain of records linked by their link fields). Suppose each complex record of a list-structure also has a field called `number` that contains the number of records on the complex records sublist. Write a `process` function to turn the `traverse` functions into a program to insert a record after the record whose information field value is `value`. The program must, of course, also correctly update the number field for the appropriate sublist.

15. Write a function to implement `evaluate` (Example 6.9).

16. Modify your solution to Exercise 15 so that it outputs the evaluation of each operation as it occurs.

17. Modify your solution to Exercise 16 so that it prints out an appropriate message, such as "too many operands for operator PS of the sublist of record 7" or "missing operands for the operator PS of the sublist of record 7,'' whenever the list-structure does not represent a valid arithmetic expression.

18. Assume that `p` points to a record of Example 6.9 containing an operator or operand. Suppose `ptr` points to a record of a sublist after which the record pointed to by `p` is to be inserted. It is to be inserted as the first record of a sublist if it is an operator, and as the next record on the sublist if it is an operand. Write an `insertion` function to accomplish this. For example, suppose the list-structure, `ls`, is currently:

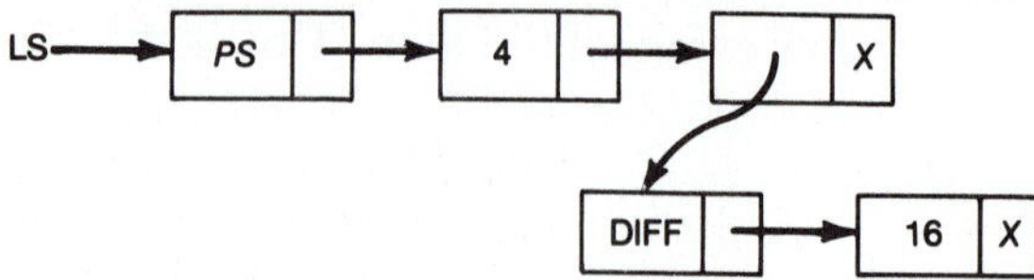

If `ptr` points to DIFF, and the record pointed to by `p` contains PS, then after insertion `ls` will be

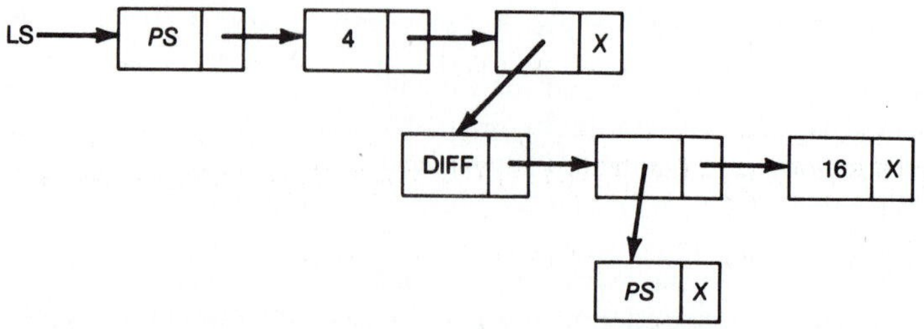

If the record pointed to by `p` contained 432.713, then after insertion `ls` would have been

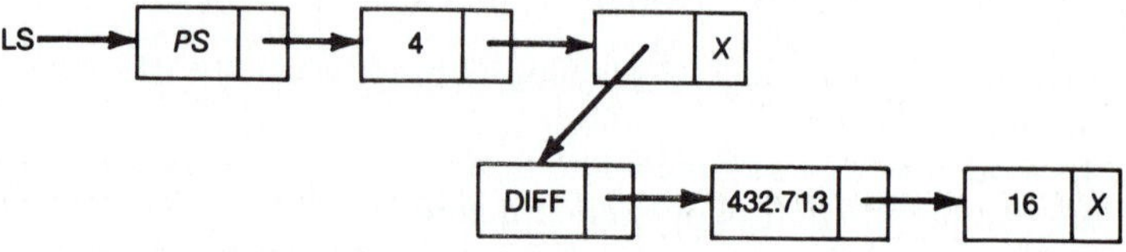

19. Insertion and deletion of records in list-structures is similar to their insertion and deletion in chains. However, the deletion of a sublist has ramifications for the `reclaim` function of Chapter 3. Discuss these, and explain how they might be resolved by modifying the definition of `reclaim` or by increasing the responsibility of the programmer. In either case, the idea is to be sure all unused records are returned to `availist`.

20. Modify `paragraphinsert` (Example 6.8) so that all deleted records are returned to the `availist`.

21. Let `ptr` and `pv` point, respectively, to a record of a list-structure and to its preceding record. Write a function to delete the record pointed to by `ptr` if it is simple, and to replace it with the list-structure to which it points if it is complex. For example, consider the following list-structure.

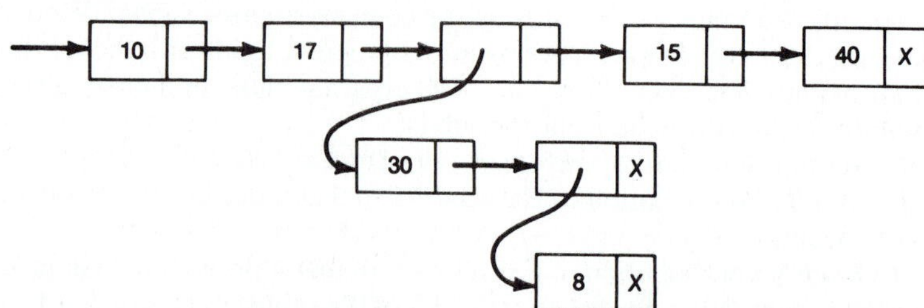

If `ptr` points to 17, then the function produces

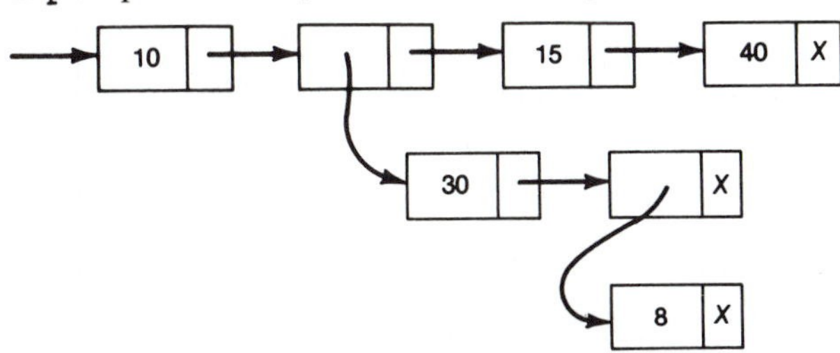

If `ptr` points to the complex record following 17, then the function produces

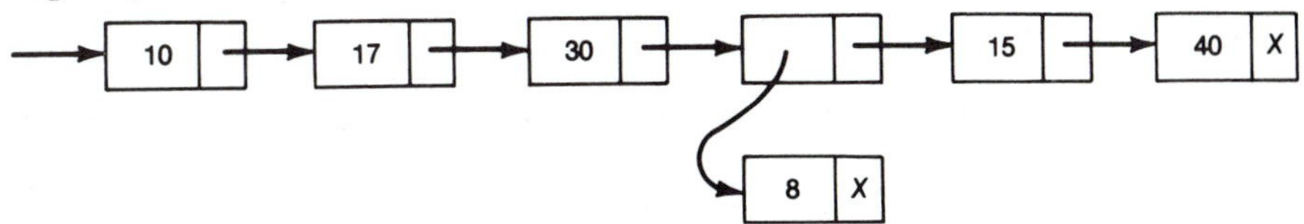

22. Give an implementation of **`next`** and **`sublist`** of the function **`traverse`** (Section 6.2.1) for each declaration of the polynomial `p`.

23. Give a declaration for the records of Example 6.8 using dynamic memory and write implementations for all the functions of **`traverse`** and **`process`** that depend on this implementation.

24. Draw a picture, corresponding to Table 6.2, for the complete input data (31 names) of Example 6.11.

25. Modify the answer to Exercise 24 to reflect the lists of children being kept as circular lists.

26. Show the complete situation in the arrays of your solution to Exercise 24 after the input below is processed.

```
JOHANN AMBROSIUS BACH M 2/22/1695 CHRISTOPH BACH
MARIA MAGDALENA GRABLER
```

27. Show the complete situation after the input of Exercise 26 is processed, when circular lists are used for the lists of children.

28. Suppose the records of Example 6.11 were to be kept in alphabetical order by the name in the name field. What would the arrays look like after all the input data were processed?

29. How does the algorithm for updating the information base given another input record (p. 287) have to be modified if inputs are allowed for which one or more field values are unknown?

30. Write two functions for Example 6.11, **`children(person)`** and **`brothers(person)`**. They should print out the names of all children and all brothers of **`person`**, respectively. Simulate the behavior of the functions on the data of the example.

31. Modify your solutions to Exercise 30 so that the functions will work on circular lists of children.

32. Suppose the **`nametable`** is implemented as a list. How will your solutions to Exercises 30 and 31 be modified?

33. Write an algorithm to print out the names of individuals who were born before 1900. How much time will your algorithm take?

34. Can you find a way to implement the information system so that a faster solution can be obtained for Exercise 33? If you find a faster solution, then determine how its update time will compare to that for Exercise 33.

35. Write a detailed description for a routine that will delete an individual record and its **`nametable`** entry from the system. This implies that all relevant pointers will be properly modified and that storage will be reclaimed.

■ Suggested Assignment

Consider the following list-structure for a book. `Book` might represent the current structure of a textbook. Suppose we want to print this information as a table of contents. It would appear as follows:

```
CHAPTER 1
    1.1 ARRAYS
    1.2 RECORDS
        1.2.1 POINTERS
        1.2.2 EXAMPLE
    1.3 SUMMARY
CHAPTER 2
    2.1 LISTS
    2.2 USES
CHAPTER 3
    3.1 APPLICATIONS
        3.1.1 BACKGROUND
        3.1.2 RANKINGS
              3.1.2.1 FLOWCHART
```

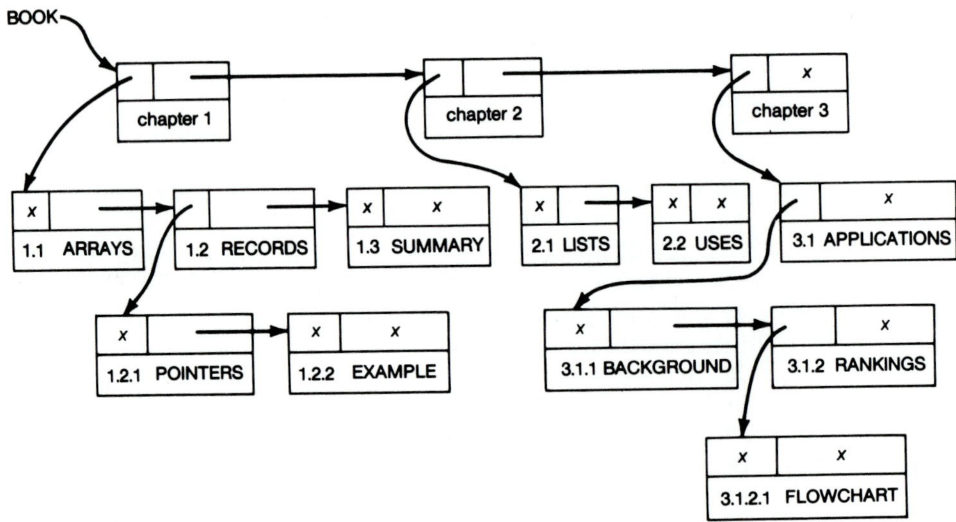

This problem can be abstracted to the printing out of a "picture" of a list-structure. Assume all records are declared as

```
typedef struct listrecord
{
   whatever info;
   int recordtype;
   struct listrecord *link,*sublist;
}bookrecord,*liststructurepointer;
```

Write a function `printlist` that will print out a "picture" of the list-structure pointed to by `ls`. Consider, for example, the list-structure `accounts` of Section 6.1. The list-structure is

```
INFO    = 175
RECORDTYPE = COMPLEX
        INFO    = 0
        RECORDTYPE = COMPLEX
                INFO    = 100
                RECORDTYPE = SIMPLE
        INFO    = 75
        RECORDTYPE = SIMPLE
INFO    = 450
RECORDTYPE = COMPLEX
        INFO    = 200
        RECORDTYPE = COMPLEX
        INFO    = 250
        RECORDTYPE = SIMPLE
INFO    = -46
RECORDTYPE = SIMPLE
```

Your program should read in and echo print three list-structures. One should be null. It should then call on `printlist` to print out the "picture" for each of the three list-structures.

The input data for `accounts` might be

```
1       indicates a nonnull list-structure; 0 would indicate a null list structure
175  CMPLX
1    1       indicates the link and sublist fields of "175" are not null
0    CMPLX
1    1
100  SMPL
0       indicates the link field of "100" is null; it is thus the last record of a sublist
75   SMPL
0
450  CMPLX
1    1
200  CMPLX
1    0       indicates the link field of "200" is not null, but its sublist field is null
250  SMPL
0
-46    SMPL
0
```

Notice that the input is given in traversal order.

The `printlist` function is to have almost exactly the same detailed refinement as either the iterative `traverse` (Section 6.2.1) or the recursive `traverse` (Section 6.2.2). You must write the proper `process` routine, say `process2`, to turn `traverse` into `printlist`. You may add parameters to `process2` if necessary.

For extra credit, do the reading in and echo printing of the three list-structures in the program by calling a function `readechoprint`. It must also be obtained by writing the proper `process` routine, say `process1`, to turn `traverse` into a function for `readechoprint`.

Of course, it will be necessary for you also to write the stack operation routines `setstack`, `push`, `pop`, and `empty`, as well as `next`, `sublist`, and `complex`.

7 Trees

8 9 10 11 12 13 1 2 3 4 5 6

Introduces three new data structures
- *binary trees*
- *trees*
- *ordered trees*

Shows
- *how to apply them to store data*
- *that they are useful as conceptual aids to problem solving and uses them in the* n*-queens problem*
- *how to implement them*

Emphasizes the basic operations for
- *binary trees*
  - *preorder, inorder, and postorder traversals*
- *trees*
  - *preorder and postorder traversals*
  - *backtracking*
  - *depth-first and breadth-first traversals*

Clarifies the relation between recursion, trees, and stacks

Discusses recursive solutions to show
- *when they are efficient*
- *how to improve them*

7.1 Branching Out

All data structures provide a way to organize data. Different structures serve different purposes. Complex lists, as shown by the information retrieval case study of Chapter 6, can result in considerable intertwining and sharing of lists and data. Everyone is familiar with the concept of a family tree. In fact, a nice exercise would be to print the family tree for an individual whose family history is stored in the data base of that case study. The family tree is actually embedded within the lists containing the family history. Trees may be viewed as a special case of lists in which no intertwining or sharing takes place. They are the basis for structures and operations used in all aspects of programming, from the structure of programs for compilers, to work in data processing, information retrieval, and artificial intelligence. Trees are ubiquitous; they seem to sprout everywhere—even in the field of computer science!

Formally, ***trees*** are collections of nodes. Trees derive both their appearance and their name from the lines, known as ***branches,*** that connect the nodes. Understanding how to represent trees, and how to perform certain operations on them, opens the door to an appreciation of many elegant algorithms and useful techniques in computer science.

Trees play a significant role in the organization of data for efficient information retrieval and are ideal candidates for fast searches, insertions, deletions, and sequential access. Efficiency and speed are possible because trees "spread out" the data they store, so that different paths in the tree lead quickly to the relevant data. They are also convenient for conceptualizing algorithms.

Many problems can be solved by imagining all the possible answers, represented as a tree. The algorithm or program is then viewed as a traversal through the tree. The general procedure for a traversal through a tree, which will be developed in this chapter, can then be adapted and used as the basis for the program. This often results in easily created and efficient programs. In such cases the tree itself serves as a conceptual aid and need not actually be "grown" or stored in memory. Nevertheless, it provides the framework for obtaining the algorithm.

The mathematics of trees has always been of interest and is discussed quite thoroughly by Knuth [1973a]. In this chapter we consider fundamentals and introduce special trees as they are needed in subsequent chapters.

As indicated in Figure 7.1, there are many ways to depict *inclusion* or

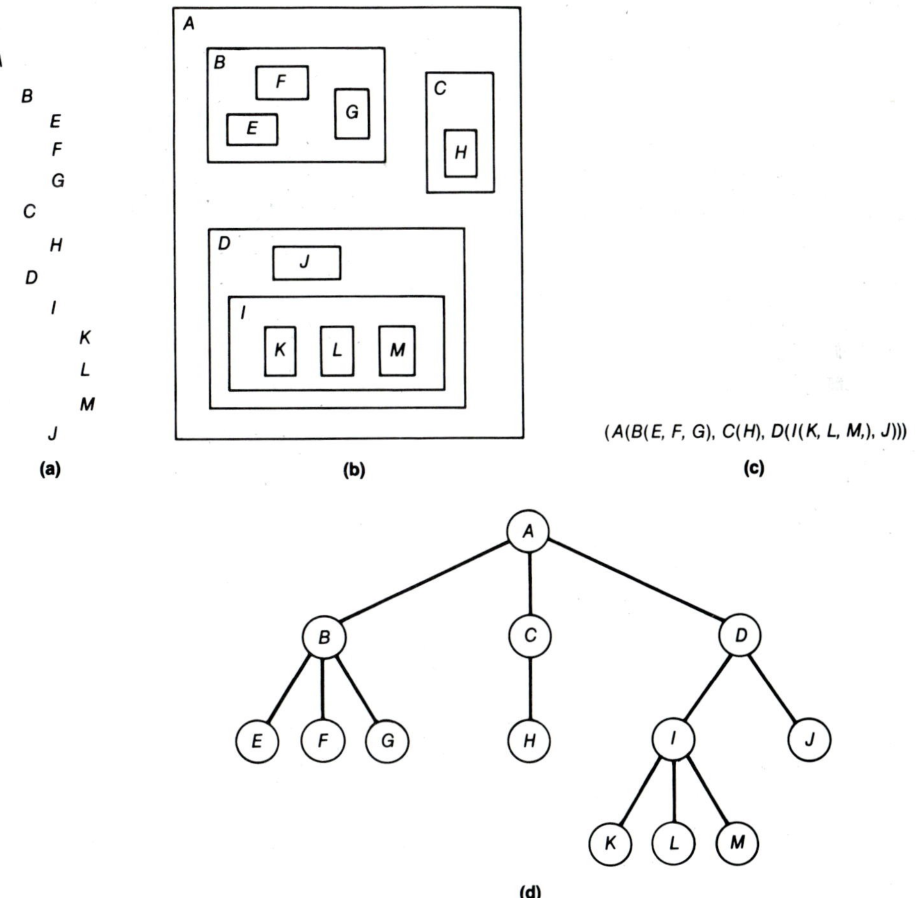

Figure 7.1 Capturing Inclusion Relationships

hierarchical relationships. Each part of the figure conveys the same information about the relations between objects *A* to *J*. Figure 7.1(a) uses indentation reminiscent of program structure, or Pascal, COBOL, and C record structure, to convey inclusion. Figure 7.1(b) uses nested blocks or sets, while Figure 7.1(c) has nested parentheses. The last, Figure 7.1(d), uses lines that branch out like a tree turned upside down. This is how the data structure that is the topic of this chapter, the tree, is depicted.

If Figure 7.1(a) is being used to represent the structure of a C record, then the structure shows that record *A* includes three fields, *B*, *C*, and *D*, or that *D* includes two subfields, *I* and *J*. The *tree* of Figure 7.1(d) captures this inclusion information. To a C compiler, it is also important that field *B* comes before *C* and that *C* precedes *D*. When such ordering information is needed, we use ***ordered trees.*** To capture order, as well as inclusion information, Figure 7.1(d) must be an *ordered tree*.

Much of the terminology for the tree data structure is taken from botany and is therefore familiar and colorful. For instance, *A* of the tree in Figure 7.1(d) is at the ***root*** of the tree. The tree consists of three ***subtrees,*** whose roots contain *B*, *C*, and *D*. The entries in the tree, *A* to *J*, are each stored at a ***node*** of the tree, connected by lines called ***branches.*** The tree is ordered if each node has a specified first, second, or *n*th subtree. The order itself may be specified in many ways. In this example, the order is specified by taking the subtrees in alphabetical order, determined by their root entries. Rearranging the order of the subtrees in Figure 7.1(d) results in the same tree but not the same ordered tree, if we assume the ordering is specified for each node from left to right by the way the tree is pictured. A distinction will be made between *ordered trees* and *trees* throughout this text. Keep in mind that these terms refer to two distinct kinds of structures.

Besides these two kinds of trees, there are binary trees. A ***binary tree*** is either

- The null binary tree, or
- A root node and its left and right subtrees, which are themselves binary trees with no common nodes

This recursive definition emphasizes the fact that binary trees with at least one node are composed of a root and two other binary trees, called the left and right subtrees, respectively. These subtrees, in turn, have the same structure. All binary trees consist of nodes, except for the null binary tree, which has no nodes. The null binary tree, just like the null list, cannot be "drawn." Both are used to make definitions more uniform and easier, and both represent the smallest data structure of their kind. There is exactly one binary tree with one node, its root. This tree has null left and right subtrees. The two binary trees with exactly two nodes are pictured as in Figure 7.2. One has a root and a nonnull left subtree, the other a root and a nonnull right subtree. Figure 7.3 pictures a larger binary tree.

The lines used to indicate a left and right subtree are called *branches*. Branches show the relationship between nodes and their subtrees. In Figure 7.3 the nodes are numbered 1 to 20 for easy reference. Node 5 has a ***predecessor*** (node 2), a ***left successor*** (node 10), and a ***right successor*** (node 11). Every node has at most two successors, and every node except the node labeled *root* has exactly one

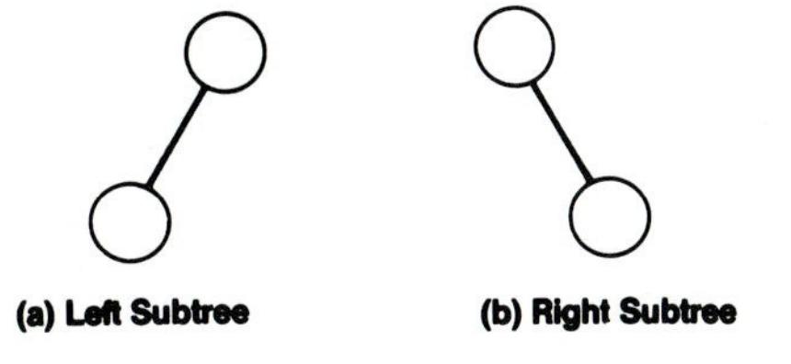

Figure 7.2 Two Two-Node Binary Trees

predecessor. Predecessors are also known as "parents," successors can be called "children," and nodes with the same parent are (what else?) "siblings." As far as is known, trees do not exhibit sibling rivalry.

Notice that, starting from any node in the tree, there is exactly one path from the node back to the root. This path is traveled by following the sequence of predecessors of the original node until the root is reached. For node 18, the sequence of predecessors is 9, 4, 2, and 1. There is always exactly one path from the root to any node.

Follow the branch from node 1 to node 2 or 3 and you come to the left or right subtree of node 1. Its right subtree is shown in Figure 7.4. Similarly, each node has a left and a right subtree. Nodes with at least one successor are called ***internal*** nodes. Those with no successors are called ***terminal*** nodes (also known as "external" nodes or "leaf" nodes). The left and right subtrees of a terminal node are always null binary trees.

By definition, the root of a binary tree is at ***depth*** 1. A node whose path to the root contains exactly $d - 1$ predecessor nodes has depth d. For example, node 10 in Figure 7.3 is at depth 4. This is the ***path length*** of the node. The longest path length is called the ***depth of the binary tree;*** it is 5 for the tree of Figure 7.3. For

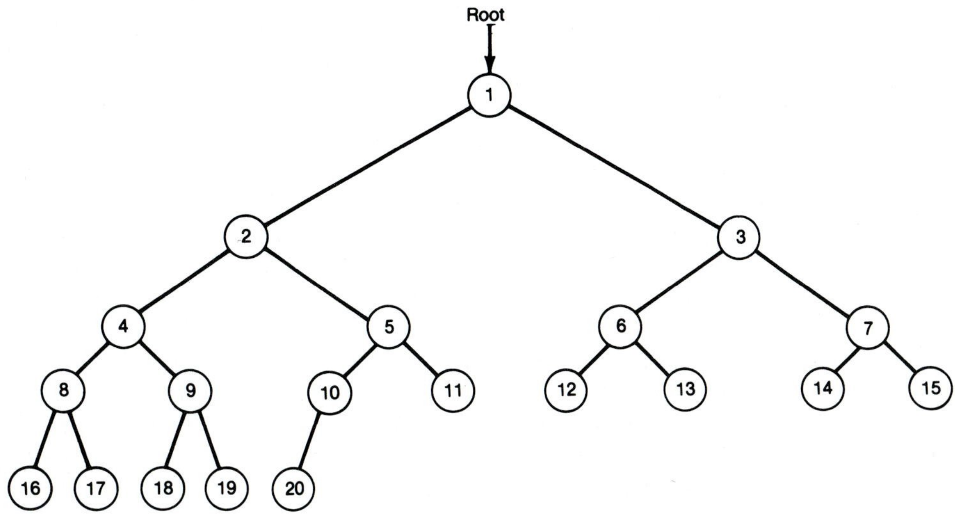

Figure 7.3 A Binary Tree

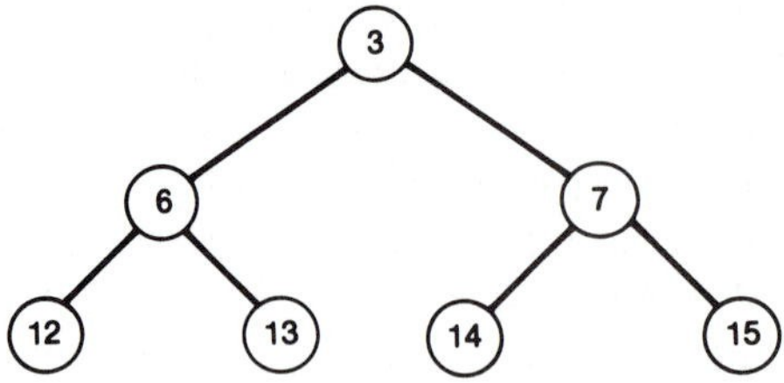

Figure 7.4 The Right Subtree of the Root of Figure 7.3

many applications it is the depth of a binary tree, like the depth of a list-structure, that determines the required storage and execution time.

Suppose your program must count the number of occurrences of each integer appearing in an input sequence of integers known to be between zero and 100. This is easy. Store the count for each integer of the allowed range in an array and increment the appropriate entry by 1 for each integer as it is input. The code would be `array[i]++`, where `i` is the variable containing the integer just read. Note that the efficiency of this solution derives from the selection operation for an entry, which is supported by the array data structure.

What if the range of the integers was not known? Sufficient storage is not available for an array to store counts for all possible integers. What is required is a data structure that can be dynamically extended to accommodate each new integer and its count as the integer is encountered in the input. This data structure must be searched to see if the new integer already appears. If it does, its count is increased by 1. Should the integer not appear, it must be inserted with its count set

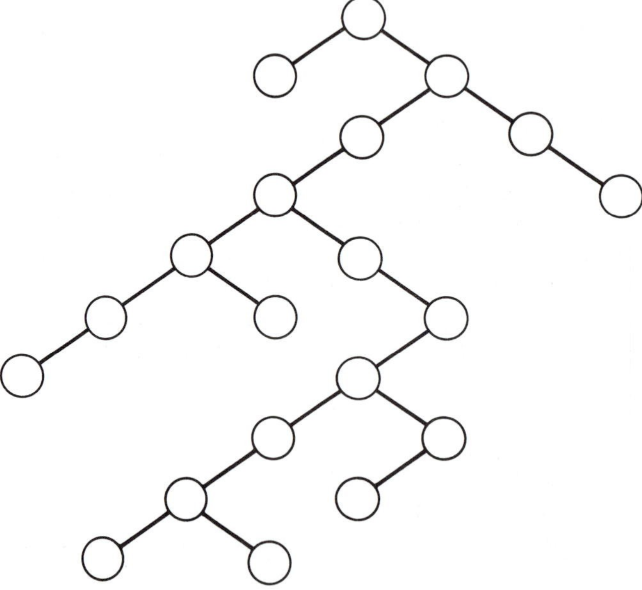

Figure 7.5 A Sparse Binary Tree

to 1. A special tree, a binary search tree introduced in Chapter 9, is convenient to use for this data structure. This tree allows the search for an integer to consider only nodes along a particular path. At worst, this path must be followed from the root to a terminal node. Thus the longest search time will be determined by the depth of the tree. The same data structure and the depth measure are important for the related problem, "Produce an index for a book." Now, instead of storing integer counts, the position of each occurrence of a word must be retained. Do you see the possibility of storing dictionaries of modest size in binary search trees?

Binary trees need not have such a compact look as that of Figure 7.3 but can appear sparse, as in Figure 7.5. A compact binary tree like Figure 7.3 is called a *complete* binary tree. To be more precise, a binary tree of depth d is a ***complete*** binary tree when it has terminal nodes only at the two greatest depths, d and $d - 1$. Further, any nodes at the greatest depth occur to the left, and any nodes at depth less than $d - 1$ have two successors. In Figure 7.3, nodes 16 to 20 are the nodes at greatest depth; they occur to the left. The sparse tree has the same number of nodes but twice the depth.

7.1.1 Depth versus Capacity*

Let us take a moment here to derive two important relations between the depth, d and the number of nodes, n, in a binary tree. First note that in any binary tree there is at most one node at depth 1, at most two nodes at depth 2, and, in general, at most 2^{k-1} nodes at depth k, since a node can give rise to at most two nodes at the next depth. The total number of nodes, n, is then at most $1 + 2^1 + 2^2 + \cdots + 2^{d-1}$. This sum is $2^d - 1$. So

$$n \leq 2^d - 1$$

The minimum possible depth, $d_{\min}$, for a binary tree with n nodes will be given by

$$d_{\min} = \lceil \lg (n + 1) \rceil$$

where $\lceil x \rceil$ indicates the smallest integer that equals or exceeds x. If $n = 20$, then $d_{\min} = \lceil \lg 21 \rceil = \lceil 4.39 \rceil = 5$; and if $n = 31$, then $d_{\min} = \lceil \lg 32 \rceil = 5$. The binary tree corresponding to $d_{\min}$ may always be taken as a *complete* binary tree. Consequently, the depth of a complete binary tree will never exceed $(\lg n) + 1$. This contrasts sharply with the depth of the sparsest binary tree with n nodes, which is n. For instance, if n is 1,000, the complete binary tree has a depth of only 10, while the sparsest has depth 1,000. This has important implications for how trees are constructed and for information retrieval, as shown in Chapter 9.

7.2 Trees of Records

The nodes of binary trees may be used to store information. For example, the nametable of Section 6.5 could be implemented by storing each of its records at a node of a binary tree. Just as lists are referred to by name, the tree can be named,

---

* This section can be omitted on first reading.

say `nametable`. Obviously, `nametable` must have records inserted into it, deleted from it, and searched for in it. Insertion, deletion, search, and traversal are the basic tree operations.

Balanced trees and binary search trees (Chapter 9) and heaps (Chapter 8) are all binary trees with special properties that make them useful for storage of information. The properties that make them useful favor efficient searching, inserting, and deleting. Each of these types of binary tree requires its own algorithms for these operations, in order to take advantage of or to preserve their characteristics. For now, to get the flavor of these operations, consider some simple examples.

7.2.1 Insertion and Deletion of Records in Binary Trees

Assume that each node of a binary tree is represented by a record containing an information field, a left pointer field, and a right pointer field. The notation `node.p` stands for the record or node pointed to by the variable `p`.

To accomplish an insertion, storage must first be allocated for a new record. Next, its fields must be set correctly; this includes entering data into the record and setting its pointers to the succeeding left and right nodes, or to null if it is a leaf. Finally the proper pointer adjustments must be made in the tree to the predecessor of the new entry. Consider Figure 7.6, which shows a binary tree `t` before and after the insertion of a new entry C, which replaces `predecessor` O's null right subtree. The information for the new record is assumed to reside in `value`, so C is stored in `value`. Thus the new record must have its information field set to `value` and its left and right pointer fields set to null. The predecessor's right pointer field must be set to point to the new record. This is accomplished by the following.

```
p = avail();                   set p to allocated storage
setinfo(p,&value);             set the new info field
setleft(p,null);               set the left pointer
setright(p,null);              set the right pointer
setright(predecessor,p);       set the predecessor's pointer (the right pointer in
                               this case)
```

`Setinfo` copies the contents of the storage pointed to by its second parameter into the info field of the record pointed to by its first parameter. Note that it is

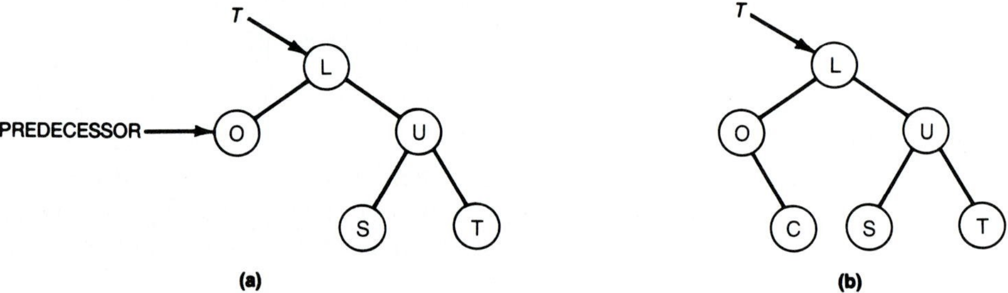

Figure 7.6 A Binary Tree *T* before and after the Insertion of C

defined somewhat differently from the `setinfo` used in previous chapters. `Setleft` and `setright` copy the contents of their second parameter into the proper field of the record pointed to by their first parameter. Notice that `setleft` is used to set the left pointer of the new record; similarly for `setright`. However, `setright` is also used to change the right pointer of the predecessor record so that it points to the new record, which is now its right node. Thus `setleft` and `setright` can be used to set pointers for any node in the tree. Together with `setinfo` and `avail`, these functions reflect the binary tree's implementation details. The code for the insertion itself is independent of the implementation.

If a new record is to replace a nonnull subtree (say, if C were to replace U in `t`), then the new record's left and right pointer fields would have to be adjusted accordingly. The left and right pointers from U would have to be copied into the new record's (C's) pointer fields. Furthermore, the storage for the replaced record U might be reclaimable. If so, care is required to save the pointer to it in its predecessor's left or right field so that its storage can be reclaimed. In this example, after saving the pointer to U, the right pointer of U's predecessor, L, would be replaced by a pointer to C, its new right node. Then U's storage can be reclaimed. The code below does this correctly, assuming `predecessor` points to a record whose nonnull right subtree is to be replaced.

```
q = right(predecessor);          ] saves the pointer to the old node
p = avail();                     ] sets p to storage for the new node
setinfo(p,&value);               ] sets the info field of the new node
setleft(p,left(q));              ] copies the left pointer of the old node into the
                                   left pointer of the new
setright(p,right(q));            ] copies the right pointer of the old node into the
                                   right pointer of the new
setright(predecessor,p);         ] sets the right pointer of the new node's predeces-
                                   sor to point to the new node
reclaim(q);                      ] reclaims the old node's storage
```

`Right` returns a copy of the right pointer field value of the record pointed to by its parameter. This code is for illustrative purposes. If the record is really reclaimable, it would be more efficient simply to replace its `info` field by the new `info` value. The statement `setinfo(q,&value)` would suffice. However, if the replaced record were needed for another purpose, say for insertion in another binary tree, then this would not work.

The deletion of a terminal node pointed to by `p`, whose predecessor is pointed to by `predecessor`, may be accomplished by the following.

```
if(left(predecessor) == p)          ] if the deleted node is a left successor
   setleft(predecessor,null);       ] set its predecessor's left pointer
                                      to null
else                                ] otherwise
   setright(predecessor,null);      ] set its predecessor's right pointer to
                                      null
```

`Left` is analogous to `right`. The decision is required in order to know whether it is `predecessor`'s left or right successor that is to be deleted. Again, if the deleted node's storage may be reclaimed, care must be taken not to lose the pointer to it. Deletion of an internal node must take into account what is to be done with the node's subtrees.

The wary reader may have qualms about the code developed for insertion and deletion. *Remember*—special cases must always be checked. When insertion or deletion occurs at the root node, indicated by a null value in `predecessor`, it is the name of the tree whose pointer must be adjusted. The illustrative code fails in this case. You should modify the program segments so that they also account for this special case.

7.2.2 Climbing Binary Trees

We have seen examples whose solution includes a traversal through a collection of records in an array or a list. A traversal through a collection of records stored in a binary tree is also the basis for the solution to many problems. We will consider three distinct ways to traverse a binary tree: (1) preorder, (2) inorder, and (3)post-order.

Pre-, in-, and postorder traversals are often referred to mnemonically as root-left-right, left-root-right, and left-right-root traversals. The prefixes *pre, in,* and *post* refer to whether the root is accessed prior to, in between, or after the corresponding traversals of the left and right subtrees. In all cases, the left subtree is traversed before the right subtree. When nodes are listed in the order in which they are processed, all nodes in the left subtree appear before all nodes in the right subtree, no matter which traversal is used. However, the type of traversal determines where the root appears. Since we defined binary trees recursively, it is convenient to give recursive definitions for these traversals.

To preorder traverse a binary tree:

if the binary tree is not the null binary tree, then
1. access and process its root
2. traverse its left subtree in preorder
3. traverse its right subtree in preorder

To inorder traverse a binary tree:

if the binary tree is not the null binary tree, then
1. traverse its left subtree in inorder
2. access and process its root
3. traverse its right subtree in inorder

To postorder traverse a binary tree:

if the binary tree is not the null binary tree, then
1. traverse its left subtree in postorder
2. traverse its right subtree in postorder
3. access and process its root

Let's apply these definitions to Figure 7.6(b).

To do a preorder traversal of `t`, since it is not null, requires that its root, L, be accessed and processed first. Next, the left subtree of `t` must be preorder traversed. Applying the definition to it, its root, O, is accessed and processed. Since O's left subtree is null, its right subtree is traversed next in preorder. This results in C being accessed and processed, terminating the preorder traversal of O's right subtree and also of `t`'s left subtree. Completing `t`'s traversal requires a preorder traversal of its right subtree, resulting in U, S, and T being accessed and processed in turn.

An inorder traversal of `t` requires its left subtree to be inorder traversed first. Applying the definition to this left subtree requires its null left subtree to be inorder traversed (note how easy that is), its root O to be accessed and processed next, and then its right subtree to be inorder traversed, which results in C being accessed and processed. This terminates the inorder traversal of `t`'s left subtree. `T`'s root, L, must then be accessed and processed, followed by an inorder traversal of `t`'s right subtree. This causes S, U, and T to be accessed and processed in turn, completing the inorder traversal of `t`.

Try applying the postorder traversal definition to `t` yourself. The sequences below represent the order in which the records stored at the nodes of `t` are accessed and processed for each of the traversals.

```
locust  ] preorder
oclsut  ] inorder
costul  ] postorder
```

Notice that the terminal nodes C, S, and T are dealt with in the same order for all three traversals. This is not just a coincidence but will always happen.

The trees of Figure 7.7 represent a table of contents, an arithmetic expression, and a program that invokes functions that, in turn, invoke other functions. Traversing these trees, respectively, in pre-, in-, and postorder results in the order of access to nodes shown in Figure 7.7(d–f). Each is a natural application of one of the three traversals: a listing of the table of contents, an arithmetic expression in the usual notation, and a listing of the order in which the functions are needed to test another function (for example, P1 and P2 are needed to test P3).

Not all data structures need to be traversed. For example, stacks, queues, heaps, and the hash tables to be introduced in Chapter 9 are not normally traversed. Just as applications of arrays and, even more so, lists often reduce to traversals, applications of binary trees often do as well. Therefore procedures for their traversal merit study.

7.2.3 Three Preorder Traversals of a Binary Tree

Writing a recursive function to traverse a binary tree based on the recursive definition for preorder traversal is straightforward. The same is true for an inorder and postorder traversal.

Recursive Version

```
preorder(ptree)
/* Preorder traverses the
   binary tree tree.
*/
binarytreepointer *ptree;
```

```
{
   binarytreepointer l,r,setnull(),left(),right();
   if(*ptree != setnull())
     {
       process(ptree);          ] process the root node of tree
       l = left(*ptree);        ] set l to tree's left subtree
       preorder(&l);            ] call preorder to traverse tree's left sub-
       r = right(*ptree);       ] tree; similarly for tree's right subtree
       preorder(&r);            ]
     }
}
```

To convince yourself it works, simulate it on the tree of Figure 7.6(b).

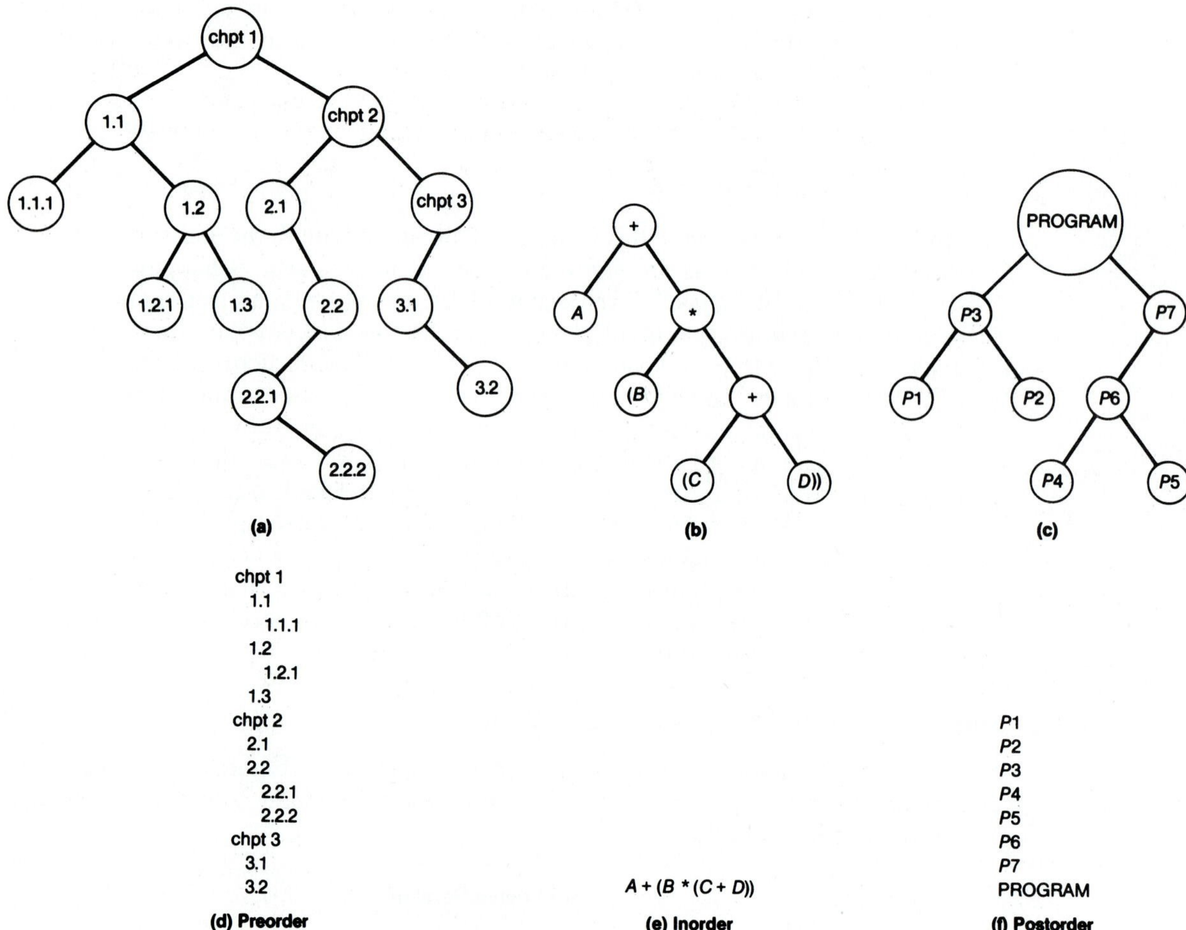

Figure 7.7 Trees for (a) a Table of Contents, (b) an Arithmetic Expression, and (c) Components of a Program. Order of Access to Nodes is (d) for Preorder Traversal of (a), (e) for Inorder Traversal of (b), and (f) for Postorder Traversal of (c)

We will now develop an iterative procedure for contrast with the recursive one. It will also be useful if the programming language you are using is not recursive. Recall that the application of the definition of preorder traversal to Figure 7.6(b) required keeping track of the left subtree about to be traversed and remembering at which node to resume when that left subtree traversal terminated. For example, in Figure 7.6(b), after node L is processed, its left subtree must be preorder traversed. We must remember, after that traversal is complete, to resume the traversal by traversing L's right subtree. Put another way, it was necessary to suspend the current traversal, incurring its completion as a postponed obligation, and begin a traversal of the proper left subtree. These postponed obligations must be recalled and resumed in reverse order to the order in which they were incurred. That is, in a last-in first-out fashion. Obviously, the ubiquitous stack is called for. It seems to pop up everywhere.

To accomplish this let `p` point to the root of the subtree about to be traversed. After the processing of `node.p`, a pointer to its right subtree can be pushed onto the stack before traversal of its left subtree. At the time that `node.p`'s right subtree is to be processed (when its left subtree traversal terminates), the stack will contain pointers to all right subtrees whose traversals have been postponed (right subtrees of nodes already accessed), but the top stack entry will point to `node.p`'s right subtree. Thus popping the stack and setting `p` to the popped value correctly updates `p` to point to the correct next record to be accessed.

Nonrecursive Version Saving Right Pointers on a Stack

```
preorder(ptree)
/* Preorder traverses the
   binary tree tree.
*/
binarytreepointer *ptree;
{
   binarytreepointer p,null,setnull(),left(),right();
   stack s;                                    ] storage allocated for stack s
   null = setnull();                           ] null set to null pointer value
   setstack(&s);                               ] s initialized to empty
   p = *ptree;                                 ] current node pointer set to tree
   while ((p != null) || !empty(&s))           ] test for completion
      if(p != null)                            ] if there is a current node
         {
            process(ptree,p);                  ] process it
            push(right(p),&s);                 ] save the pointer to its right subtree on stack s
            p = left(p);                       ] set current node pointer to its left subtree root
         }
      else                                     ] otherwise
         pop(&s,&p);                           ] since the stack s cannot be empty, pop it, updat-
}                                                ing the current node pointer
```

The **while** loop condition is true whenever the traversal is not yet completed. A nonnull `p` means that a record is pointed to by `p` and is the next one to be accessed and processed. A null p value means no record is pointed to by p, and some left subtree traversal must have just been completed. If, at that point, the stack is not empty, then more needs to be done; but if it is empty, then no right subtrees remain to be traversed, and the traversal is done. Again, to convince yourself the program works, simulate it on the tree of Figure 7.6(b).

The recursive procedure reflects the structure of binary trees and emphasizes that they are made up of a root with binary trees as subtrees. It sees the special cases, such as a null tree, and the substructures of the recursive definition, such as left and right subtrees. In order to develop the nonrecursive version, it is necessary to think of the binary tree as a collection of individual records. Writing the function then involves providing for the correct next record to be accessed and processed within the **while** loop. This is a general strategy for attempting to find nonrecursive solutions. The nonrecursive version requires that the structure be viewed as a collection of its individual parts, with each part treated appropriately and in the correct order. This explains why recursive versions are clearer.

An alternative nonrecursive function is based on saving on a stack the path from the root to the predecessor of the node currently being processed. It is useful if the processing of a node requires accessing its predecessor node. This alternative approach guarantees that at the time the node is processed its predecessor is at the top of the stack. However, this algorithm requires some searching to find the proper right subtree to traverse next when a subtree traversal has terminated. Such a termination is indicated by p being null. Figure 7.8 shows a situation when such a termination has occurred. P is null, having been set to the null right pointer value of node 10 after node 10's left subtree has been traversed. Looking back along the path from node 10 to the root, we find the path nodes 8, 6, 5, 1. It is not difficult to see that node 5's right subtree is where the traversal must resume. Precisely this path back toward the root must be followed until a node on this return path (node 6) is the left successor of its predecessor. P must then be set to the right subtree of that node (node 12) and the traversal resumed. If no node which is the left successor of its predecessor is found on the return path, the entire tree has been traversed.

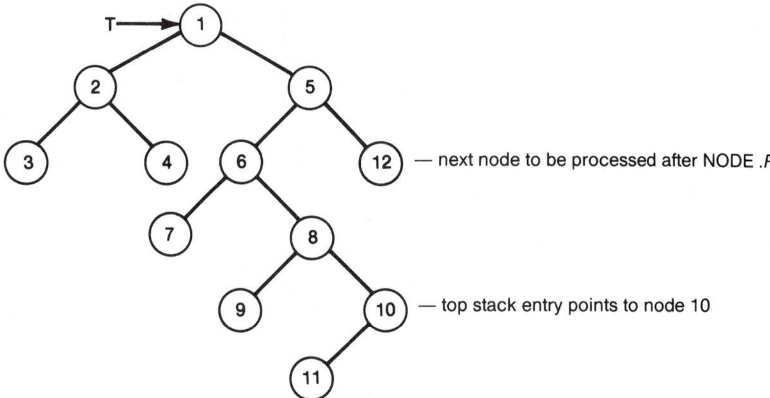

Figure 7.8 Node 5's Left Subtree Has Just Been Traversed

The following function is a nonrecursive preorder traversal that saves the path to the root on a stack. **Item** returns a copy of the pointer at the top of the stack without disturbing the stack.

Nonrecursive Version Saving the Path to the Root on a Stack

```
preorder(ptree)
/* Preorder traverses the
   binary tree tree.
*/
binarytreepointer *ptree;
{
   binarytreepointer null,p,q,rightpointer;
   binarytreepointer setnull(),left(),right(),item();
   stack s;                                          ] storage allocated
                                                       for stack s
   null = setnull();                                 ] null set to null
                                                       pointer value
   setstack(&s);                                     ] s initialized to
                                                       empty
   p = *ptree;                                       ] current node pointer
                                                       set to tree
   while((p != null) || !empty(&s))                  ] test for completion
      if(p != null)                                  ] if there is a current
         {                                             node
            process(ptree,p);                        ] process it
            if(left(p) != null)                      ] if there is a left
               {                                       subtree
                  push(p,&s);                        ] save a pointer to
                                                       the current node on
                                                       the stack s
                  p = left(p);                       ] update the current
               }                                       node pointer to the
                                                       left subtree root
            else                                     ] otherwise
               {
                  push(p,&s);                        ] save a pointer to
                                                       the current node on
                                                       the stack s
                  p = right(p);                      ] update the current
               }                                       node pointer to the
         }                                             right subtree root
      else                                           ] otherwise
         {
            do                                       | search along the
            {                                        | return path for the
                                                     | next right subtree at
                                                     | which the traversal
                                                     | is to resume
            pop(&s,&q);                              |  ] pop the stack
                                                     |    and set q to the
                                                     |    popped node
```

```
        if(!empty(&s))                        if the popped
                                              node is not the
                                              root of tree
            rightpointer = right(item(&s));   set right-
                                              pointer to its
                                              predecessor's
                                              right successor
        else                                  otherwise
            rightpointer = null;              set it to null
    }while(!empty(&s)&&(q==rightpointer));    test for comple-
                                              tion of traversal
                                              or for q contain-
                                              ing a pointer to
                                              the right subtree
                                              to be traversed
                                              next; note that p
                                              will be null if the
                                              traversal is done
    if(q != rightpointer)                     if not done then
        p = rightpointer;                     update the current
                                              node pointer to the
                                              correct next right
  }                                           subtree
}
```

Notice that the first two versions of the preorder traversal do not retain information about the depth of a node or about a node's predecessor, although they could be modified to do so. The third version retains this information, since the depth of the current node is equal to the number of stack entries plus one, and the top stack entry always points to the current node's predecessor. When this information is needed, the last version provides it directly, especially if a basic stack operation that returns the size of the stack is available.

Each of the three traversal functions can be modified to be a partial traversal when required, by including a variable **done** to signal termination, just as was done for the list traversals. This would be the case, for example, if you were traversing only to find a desired record. Similar functions can be written for the inorder and postorder traversals.

7.3 Using the Traverse Functions for Binary Trees

In this section a number of examples are presented to show how the traverse functions developed thus far can be applied to develop solutions to programming problems.

Example 7.1 Print the number of terminal nodes in a binary tree **tree**. ■

The nonrecursive preorder traversal that saves right subtree pointers on a stack will be used to perform this task. The other versions could have been adapted as readily. The approach taken is to leave the traverse function as it is and write **process** to turn **preorder** into a solution to the problem.

To accomplish this, process must test each node it deals with to see if it is a terminal node. If so a counter, tncount, should be increased by 1. Making tncount a static variable in process allows its values to be preserved between calls to process. The first time process is called during the traversal it must initialize tncount to zero, and the last time it is called, in addition to updating tncount, process must print its final value.

If p points to the current record to be processed, then when p points to the root of the traversed tree tree, process has been called for the first time, so it must set tncount to zero. But how can process recognize when p points to the last node so that tncount can be printed? To do this, process must have access to the stack s. When s contains no nonnull pointers and node.p is a terminal node, then node.p is the last node. Assume that a function last returns *true* if s contains no nonnull pointers and *false* otherwise. Consequently s must be a parameter of, or global to, process. Finally, we must assume that only nonnull binary trees are to be considered since process is invoked by preorder only when tree is not null. Process may now be defined as follows.

```
process(ptree,p,ps)
/* Prints the number of terminal nodes in
   binary tree tree when p points to the last
   node in a preorder traverse of tree which
   saves right pointers on stack s.
*/
binarytreepointer *ptree,p;
stack *ps;
{
   binarytreepointer null,setnull(),left(),right();
   static int tncount;
   null = setnull();
   if(p == *ptree)                               ] if first time called
      tncount = 0;                               ] set tncount to zero
   if((left(p) == null)&&(right(p) == null))     ] if terminal node
      {
        tncount++;                               ] update tncount
        if(last(ps))                             ] test for last node
           printf("\n The number of terminal nodes is %d",tncount);
      }
}
```

It would certainly be more efficient to make null global so that setnull would not be invoked for each node. Similarly, setting tncount to zero in preorder could remove the need for the (p == *ptree) test for each node. In fact, it would be easier to take a second approach to finding a solution. Namely, modify preorder so that it sets tncount to zero initially, and after its **while** loop is exited, simply print tncount. This second solution is considerably more efficient, because the test performed by last is not needed. The second approach is more efficient, but it involves changing a traversal, which may be already compiled. Which approach to use depends on what alternatives are available and just how important the extra efficiency is.

Example 7.2 The second example concerns the problem of inserting a new node in the binary tree `tree` in place of the first terminal node encountered in a preorder traversal of `tree`. The information field value of the new node is to be copied from that of the record `value`. ■

In this case `process` will be written to make a solution out of the nonrecursive version of `preorder` that stores the path from the root to the node being processed. This is convenient, since the predecessor of the node to be processed is required by `process` when the insertion is made, and it will be the top stack entry at that time.

```
process(ptree,p,null,ps,value)
/* If p points to the first terminal node, encountered
   in a preorder traversal of binary tree tree that saves
   the path to the root on stack s, then replaces that node by
   a new node whose info field is set to the contents of value.
*/
binarytreepointer *ptree,p,null;
stack *ps;
int value;
{
   binarytreepointer q,ptr,avail(),
                     left(),right();
   if((left(p) == null)&&(right(p) == null))   /* if terminal node, then, for the new node: */
      {
         ptr = avail();                         /* allocate storage */
         setinfo(ptr,&value);                   /* set the info field */
         setleft(ptr,null);                     /* set the left pointer */
         setright(ptr,null);                    /* set the right pointer */
         if(p != *ptree)                        /* if the replacement is not for the root node */
            {
               q = item(ps);                    /* get its predecessor */
               if(left(q) == p)                 /* determine if the predecessor's left or */
                  setleft(q,ptr);               /* right pointer is to point to the new */
               else                             /* node and set it */
                  setright(q,ptr);
            }
         else                                   /* otherwise */
            *ptree = ptr;                       /* set tree to point to the new node */
         setstack(ps);                          /* setting the stack to empty will cause
                                                   the traversal to terminate */
      }
}
```

When `process` is called, it tests whether the node is a terminal node. Since it will cause the traversal to be terminated after the replacement, this must be the *first* terminal node. Storage is then obtained for the new record and its fields filled in properly. Since it will be a terminal node, its pointer fields are set to null. To insert the new record, the predecessor of the terminal node must have one of its pointer fields set to point to the new record. The correct one is determined by whether the replaced record was its left or right successor. The special case of the insertion occurring at the root requires only that `tree` be set to point to the new record. Finally, setting the stack to empty ensures that the traversal will be aborted.

`Value` is passed by `preorder` to `process`. `Item` simply returns a copy of the top stack entry.

Example 7.3 The final example involves writing a function `depth` to return the depth of a binary tree as its value. ■

The nonrecursive version of `preorder` that saves the path to the root on the stack can be turned into such a function. When a node is being processed, its depth is one more than the number of stack entries at that moment. To determine the depth, initialize a variable `d` to 1 and `size` to zero before the **while** loop, increase `size` by 1 after `push`, and decrease it by 1 after `pop`. Give `process` access to `d` and `size`. `Process` must simply compare `size+1` to `d`, and when greater, set `d` to `size+1`. After termination of the traversal, `depth` must return `d`.

Another solution for `depth` can be obtained by recursion. This requires a way to express the depth recursively. The ***depth of a binary tree*** `t` is

- Zero if `t` is null, else
- One more than the maximum of the depths of `t`'s left and right subtrees

Now the function can be written directly as follows:

```
depth(tree)
/* Returns the depth of
   the binary tree tree.
*/
binarytreepointer tree;
{
   binarytreepointer setnull(),left(),right();
   if(tree == setnull())
      return(0);
   else
      return(1 + max(depth(left(tree)),
               depth(right(tree))));
}
```

if the binary tree is null
its depth is zero
otherwise
use `depth` *to find the depth of its left and right subtrees; its depth is then one plus their maximum*

where `max` returns the maximum of its parameters as its value.

7.4 Implementing Binary Trees

This section introduces three ways to implement a binary tree.

1. Using an array of records with just an information field
2. Using records with an information field and left and right pointer fields linked together via their pointer fields
3. Using a list-structure

Chapter 8 contains an application of the first implementation. A program using the second implementation, with the records stored in dynamic memory, is included. The program specifies the details of this important representation and illustrates how to create and process binary trees and how to test functions developed in the earlier examples.

7.4.1 Sequential Representation

The sequential representation uses an array to store information corresponding to each node of a tree. Consider the binary tree shown in Figure 7.9. Its depth is 5 and it has fourteen nodes. The nodes are numbered in a special way. This numbering may be obtained by preorder traversing the tree and, as each node is accessed,

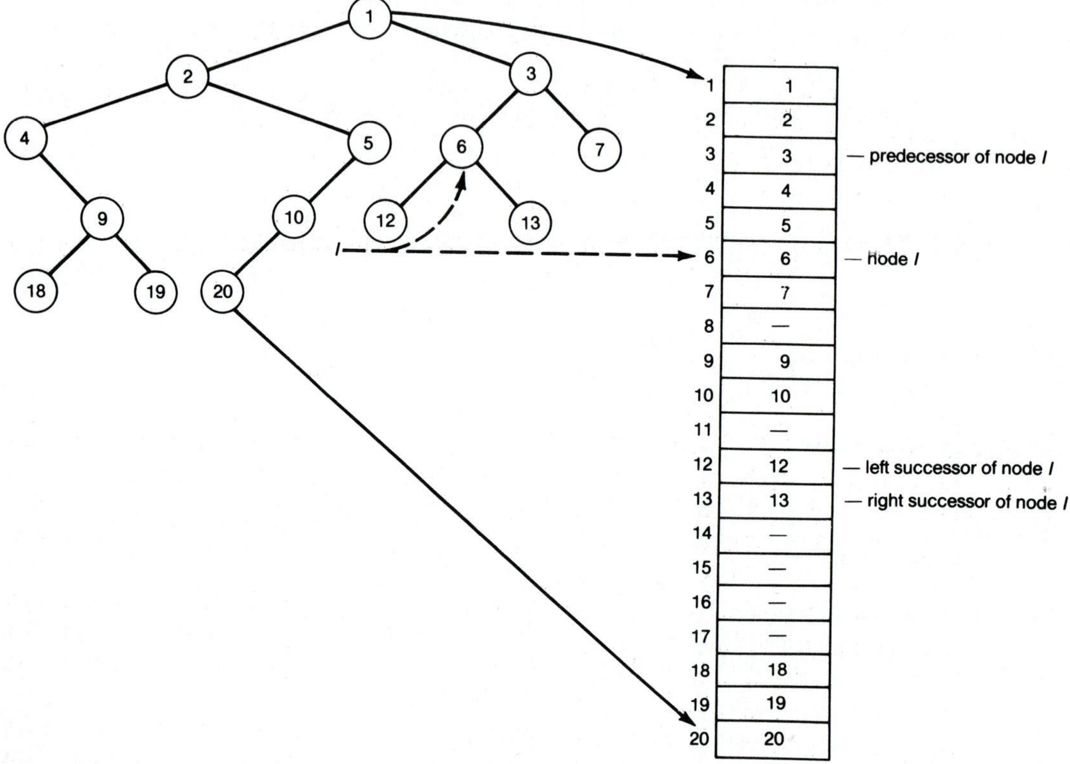

Figure 7.9 Sequential Representation of a Binary Tree

assigning it a node number. The root is assigned 1, each left successor of a node is assigned twice the number of its predecessor, and each right successor is assigned one more than twice the number of its predecessor. With nodes numbered in this way, the predecessor of node `i` is numbered `i/2` (integer divide), its left successor is numbered `2*i`, and its right successor `2*i+1`.

The ***sequential representation*** of a binary tree is obtained by storing the record corresponding to node `i` of the tree as the *i*th record in an array of records, as shown in Figure 7.9. A node not in the tree can be recognized by a special value in its corresponding array position (such as node 8, which has − as its value) or by a node number (like 24) that exceeds the highest node number in the tree (20 in this example). Given a pointer `p` to a node in the array, it is easy to determine the position of its predecessor (`p/2`), its left successor (`2*p`), and its right successor (`2*p+1`).

A binary tree with n nodes will require an array length between n and $2^n - 1$. The smallest length (n) is sufficient when the binary tree is complete, and the greatest length ($2^n - 1$) corresponds to the case of an extremely skewed binary tree whose nodes have only right successors. No space in the array is unused for a complete binary tree, and the array length is proportional to the number of nodes in the tree. However, a sparse tree can waste a great deal of array space. The worst case requires $2^n - 1$ positions but uses only n. Thus the sequential representation is convenient for dealing with complete static binary trees. Such trees arise, for example, when you must put student records in alphabetical order by student name. How to do such ordering is considered in the next chapter (Section 8.4). For cases when the tree may change size or shape drastically, the sequential representation is not appropriate. An example of this situation is found in the integer or word counting problem of Section 7.1.

7.4.2 Linked Representation

A binary tree data structure can also be implemented by representing each node of the tree as a record with three fields:

1. A left pointer field,
2. An information field
3. A right pointer field

(called here the `leftptr`, `info`, and `rightptr` fields). This is the most common representation. The left and right pointer fields link records of the tree, just as the link and sublist fields of lists link their records. In effect, the pointer fields specify a node's left and right subtrees, just as the sublist field of a list specifies its sublist. The `leftptr` and `rightptr` fields of a node point to the record that represents, respectively, the root of the node's left and right subtree. The `info` field contains the information stored at the node. A variable referred to as the name of the tree points to the record representing the root of the tree, and a null pointer in the name denotes the null tree.

We can store each record of a binary tree using an array of records as shown in Figure 7.10, just as was done for the records of lists. The binary tree `fred`, for example, has its root stored in position 5 of the array, while the root of `t` is in

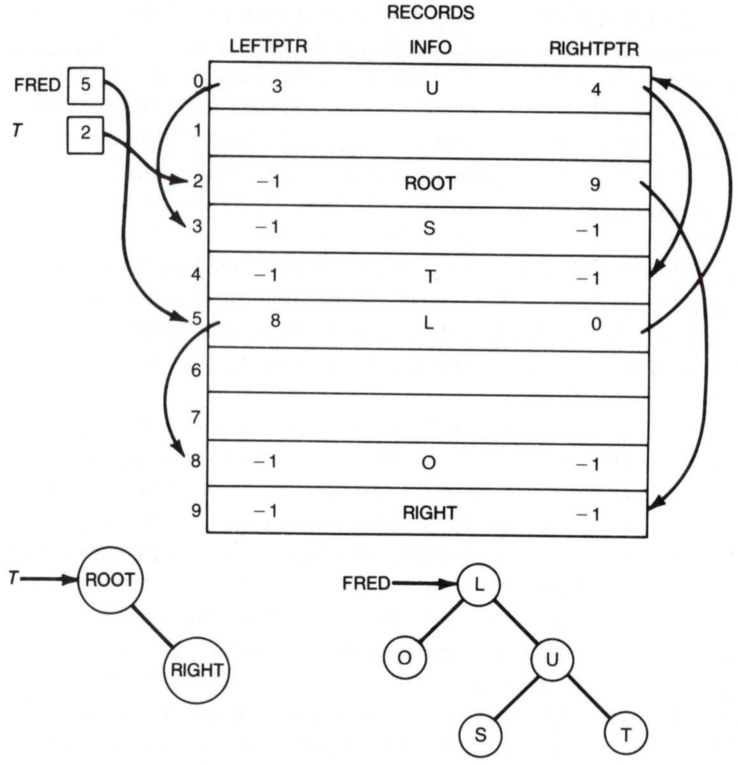

Figure 7.10 Linked Representation for Binary Trees with Records Stored in an Array

position 2. The left successor of **fred**'s root is stored in position 8, and its right successor in position 0. A minus one is used as the null pointer.

The definitions for the records and the array declaration are as follows.

```
typedef struct                                  a binary tree record type
{
   whatever info;
   int leftptr;
   int rightptr;
}binarytreenode;
typedef int binarytreepointer;                  pointers will be array indices

#define MAX 50                                  the array can hold 50 records
typedef binarytreenode recordsarray[MAX];       the array type
recordsarray records;                           storage is allocated for the array records
                                                that will hold the binary trees
```

Instead of using an array and array indices, we may store the records of the tree in dynamic memory and use pointers. The record declarations then become

```
typedef struct treenode                  a binary tree record type
{
   whatever info;
   struct treenode *leftptr;
   struct treenode *rightptr;
}binarytreenode,*binarytreepointer;      pointers point to records stored in dynamic
                                         memory
```

Such linked representations require storage proportional to the number of nodes of the binary tree represented, no matter what the shape of the binary tree. Contrast this with the sequential representation of binary trees. If a linked representation uses three elements per record, whereas a sequential representation uses one element per record, then for *complete* binary trees three times as much storage is used in a linked representation as in a sequential one. If the binary tree is not complete, then the sequential representation may require storage proportional to $2^d - 1$, where d is the depth of the binary tree. This could result in significant amounts of wasted space; there may not even be enough storage. Consequently, the sequential representation is more practical only when dealing with complete or nonsparse binary trees.

Using the linked representation, it is obviously possible to insert or delete records, once we know where to do so, by making changes in only a few pointer fields.

The following program illustrates the binary tree implementation with records stored in dynamic memory. It is a program that could be used to test all the functions of Section 7.3 (although they have been renamed). The names are self-explanatory. The input consists of

An integer to indicate whether the binary tree being created is null,

A *sequence* of data for each record

A value for the info field of a new node

The sequence is assumed to be in the order in which the records are accessed in a preorder traversal of the binary tree being input. For example, if the input corresponded to the right subtree of Figure 7.9 and the new value replacing the first terminal node were 50, then the input would be as follows. (Program output and prompts are not shown.)

Typical Input

1	*indicates nonnull binary tree*
3	*data for the root;*
11	*both its subtrees are nonnull*
6	*data for the next record in preorder;*
11	*both its subtrees are nonnull*
12	*data for the next record in preorder;*
00	*both its subtrees are null*
13	*data for the next record in preorder;*

00	*both its subtrees are null*
7	*data for the next record in preorder;*
00	*both its subtrees are null*
50	*the new value*

The Program

```
Reads the data for nodes of a binary tree, creates
the tree and prints how many terminal nodes it
has and its depth, reads the value for the new node,
replaces the first terminal node in preorder access
by the new node, and then prints all the final binary
tree's nodes, its terminal count, and its depth.

#include <stdio.h>

typedef struct treerecord
{
   int info;
   struct treerecord *leftptr;
   struct treerecord *rightptr;
}binarytreerecord,*binarytreepointer;
#define NULL 0

binarytreepointer left(p)
/* Returns a copy of the left
   pointer of the node p points to.
*/
binarytreepointer p;
{
   return(p->leftptr);
}

binarytreepointer right(p)
/* Returns a copy of the right
   pointer of the node p points to.
*/
binarytreepointer p;
{
   return(p->rightptr);
}

binarytreepointer setnull()
/* Returns a null pointer */
{
   return(NULL);
}
```

the binary tree data abstraction

```
binarytreepointer avail()
/* Returns a pointer to storage
   allocated for a new node.
*/
{
   return(malloc(sizeof(binarytreerecord)));
}

setinfo(p,pvalue)
/* Copies the contents of value
   into the record p points to.
*/
binarytreepointer p;
int *pvalue;
{
   p->info = *pvalue;
}

setleft(p,q)
/* Copies q into the left pointer
   of the record p points to.
*/
binarytreepointer p,q;
{
   p->leftptr = q;
}

setright(p,q)
/* Copies q into the right pointer
   of the record p points to.
*/
binarytreepointer p,q;
{
   p->rightptr = q;
}

printnode(pl,ptr)
/* Prints the info field of the
   record ptr points to.
*/
binarytreepointer *pl,ptr;
{
   printf("\n %d",ptr->info);
}

main()
/* Reads the data for nodes of a binary tree, creates
   the tree and prints how many terminal nodes it
   has and its depth, reads the value for the new node,
   replaces the first terminal node in preorder access
```

from here on the program is independent of the binary tree implementation

```
   by the new node, and then prints all the final
   binary tree's nodes, its terminal count, and its
   depth.
*/
{
   int n,value;
   binarytreepointer t,setnull(),avail();
   printf("\n enter binarytree 0 for null tree 1\
         otherwise \n");
   scanf("%d",&n);
   if (n == 0)
      t = setnull();              a zero indicates that the input is a null
                                  binary tree, so t is set to null
   else
      {
            t = avail();          the input is not a null binary tree, so
            createtree(&t);       allocate storage for t and create the binary tree t
      }

   printtree(&t);                 print all the tree's nodes

   terminalcount(&t);             print the number of terminal nodes

   printf("\n The depth is %d",depth(t));   print t's depth
   printf("\n enter value ");
   scanf("%d",&value);            read the new value

   replacefirstterminal(&t,value);   replace the first terminal node

   printtree(&t);                 print all the tree's nodes

   terminalcount(&t);             print the number of terminal nodes

   printf("\n The depth is %d",depth(t));   print t's depth
}

createtree(ptree)                 this is a recursive preorder traversal
/* Read the data and create the binary tree tree. */
binarytreepointer *ptree;
{
   binarytreepointer l,r,setnull(),left(),right();   allocates storage for l & r,
   if (*ptree != setnull())
      {
```

```
            createnode(ptree);
            l = left(*ptree);

            createtree(&l);
            r = right(*ptree);

            createtree(&r);
        }
}


createnode(pptr)
/* Reads the data, and fills in the fields
   of the node pointed to by ptr.
*/
binarytreepointer *pptr;
{
   int leftlink,rightlink,value;
   binarytreepointer setnull(),avail();
   printf("\n enter info \n");
   scanf("%d",&value);

   setinfo(*pptr,&value);

   printf("\n enter enter left & right ptrs \n");
   scanf("%d %d",&leftlink,&rightlink);

   if (leftlink == 0)
      setleft(*pptr,setnull());
   else
      setleft(*pptr,avail());
   if (rightlink == 0)
      setright(*pptr,setnull();
   else
      setright(*pptr,avail());
}

#define LIMIT 50


typedef binarytreepointer whatever;
typedef struct
{
   whatever stackarray[LIMIT];
   int top;
}stack;
#define TRUE 1
#define FALSE 0
```

the left and right subtrees

fills the root node's fields

creates the left subtree

creates the right subtree

reads the `info` *value*

sets the `info` *field*

reads left and right pointer data

sets the left and right pointers properly

the `stack` *data abstraction*

the stack will contain pointers to nodes of a binary tree

```
setstack(ps)
/* Sets the stack s to empty. */
stack *ps;
{
   (*ps).top = -1;
}

empty(ps)
/* Returns true only if stack s is empty. */
stack *ps;
{
   return((*ps).top == -1);
}

push(value,ps)
/* Inserts value at the top of stack s. */
whatever value;
stack *ps;
{
   if ((*ps).top == (LIMIT - 1))
      overflow(ps);
   else
      {
         (*ps).top = (*ps).top + 1;
         (*ps).stackarray[(*ps).top] = value;
      }
}

pop(ps,pvalue)
/* Removes the top entry of stack s
   and copies its contents into value.
*/
stack *ps;
whatever *pvalue;
{
   if (empty(ps))
      underflow(ps);
   else
      {
         *pvalue = (*ps).stackarray[(*ps).top];
         (*ps).top = (*ps).top - 1;
      }
}

whatever item(ps)
/* Returns a copy of the top entry on stack s. */
stack *ps;
{
   return((*ps).stackarray[(*ps).top]);
}
```

```
last(ps)
/* Returns true only if stack s
   contains no non null pointers.
*/
stack *ps;
{
   int i,temp;
   binarytreepointer null,setnull();
   null = setnull();
   temp = TRUE;
   for (i=0;i<=(*ps).top;i++)
      if ((*ps).stackarray[i] != null)
         temp = FALSE;
   return(temp);
}

overflow(ps)
/* Prints a message if the stack overflows. */
stack *ps;
{
   printf("\n stack overflow ");
}

underflow(ps)
/* Prints a message if the stack underflows. */
stack *ps;
{
   printf("\n stack underflow ");
}
```

from here on the program is independent of both the binary tree and the `stack` *implementation*

this is the nonrecursive traversal that saves the path to the root

```
printtree(ptree)
/* Prints the info field values of all
   nodes of the binary tree tree.
*/
binarytreepointer *ptree;
{
   binarytreepointer null,p,q,rightpointer;
   binarytreepointer setnull(),left(),right(),item();
   stack s1;
   null = setnull();
   setstack(&s1);
   p = *ptree;
   while ((p != null) || !empty(&s1))
      if (p != null)
         {
```

```
            printnode(ptree,p);
            if (left(p) != null)
               {
                  push(p,&s1);
                  p = left(p);
               }
            else
               {
                  push(p,&s1);
                  p = right(p);
               }
         }
      else
         {
            do
            {
               pop(&s1,&q);
               if (!empty(&s1))
                  rightpointer = right(item(&s1));
               else
                  rightpointer = null;
            }while(!empty(&s1) &&
               (q == rightpointer));
            if (q != rightpointer)
               p = rightpointer;
         }
}

terminalcount(ptree)
/* Prints the number of terminal nodes
   in the binary tree tree.
*/
binarytreepointer *ptree;
{
   binarytreepointer p,null,setnull(),left(),right();
   stack s2;
   null = setnull();
   setstack(&s2);
   p = *ptree;
   while ((p != null) || !empty(&s2))
      if (p != null)
         {
            updatetncount(ptree,p,&s2);
            push(right(p),&s2);
            p = left(p);
         }
      else
         pop(&s2,&p);
}
```

prints the `info` *field of the node* `p` *points to*

this is a nonrecursive traversal that saves right pointers

updates the terminal count appropriately and prints it after the last node

```
updatetncount(pt,p,ps)
/* Prints the number of terminal nodes in
   binary tree tree when p points to the last
   node in a preorder traverse of tree which
   saves right pointers on stack s.
*/
binarytreepointer *pt,p;
stack *ps;
{
   binarytreepointer null,setnull(),left(),right();
   static int tncount;
   null = setnull();
   if (p == *pt)
      tncount = 0;
   if ((left(p) == null) && (right(p) == null))
      {
         tncount++;
         if (last(ps))
            printf("\n The number of terminal nodes\
                  is %d",tncount);
      }
}

replacefirstterminal(ptree,value)
/* Replaces the first terminal node, encountered
   in a preorder traversal of binary tree tree, by a
   new node with its info field set to the contents
   of value.
*/
binarytreepointer *ptree;
int value;
{
   binarytreepointer null,p,q,rightpointer;
   binarytreepointer setnull(),left(),right(),item();
   stack s3;
   null = setnull();
   setstack(&s3);
   p = *ptree;
   while ((p != null) || !empty(&s3))
      if (p != null)
         {
            replacenode(ptree,p,null,&s3,value);
            if (left(p) != null)
               {
                  push(p,&s3);
                  p = left(p);
               }
            else
               {
                  push(p,&s3);
                  p = right(p);
               }
         }
```

this is a nonrecursive traversal that saves the path to the root

```
      else
         {
            do
            {
               pop(&s3,&q);
               if (!empty(&s3))
                  rightpointer = right(item(&s3));
               else
                  rightpointer = null;
            }while(!empty(&s3) &&
               (q == rightpointer));
            if (q != rightpointer)
               p = rightpointer;
         }
}

replacenode(ptree,p,null,ps,value)
/* If p points to the first terminal node, encountered
   in a preorder traversal of binary tree tree that
   saves the path to the root on stack s, then
   replaces that node by a new node whose info field is
   set to the contents of value.
*/
binarytreepointer *ptree,p,null;
stack *ps;
int value;
{
   binarytreepointer q,ptr,avail(),left(),right();
   if ((left(p) == null) && (right(p) == null))
      {
         ptr = avail();
         setinfo(ptr,&value);
         setleft(ptr,null);
         setright(ptr,null);
         if (p != *ptree)
            {
               q = item(ps);
               if (left(q) == p)
                  setleft(q,ptr);
               else
                  setright(q,ptr);
            }
         else
            *ptree = ptr;
         setstack(ps);
      }
}

depth(tree)
/* Returns the depth of the binary tree tree. */
binarytreepointer tree;
```

```
{
   binarytreepointer setnull(),left(),right();
   if (tree == setnull())
      return(0);
   else
      return(1 + max(depth(left(tree)),
               depth(right(tree))));
}

max(i,j)
/* Returns the maximum of i and j. */
int i,j;
{
   if (i >= j)
      return(i);
   else
      return(j);
}
```

7.4.3 List-structure Representation

Another way to represent a binary tree is indicated in Figure 7.11. Each node's record is made complex. A complex record's sublist points to the representation of the node's left subtree. The result is that `btree` is implemented as the list structure `lstree`. Abstractly, binary trees are a special case of list-structures, but there are list-structures that do not correspond to binary trees. However, in computer science the term *tree* usually implies zero or restricted sharing of storage, whereas the term *list-structure* or *list* implies the possibility of more general sharing of storage.

7.5 Trees

So far we have considered only binary trees, but trees may have nodes with more than two successors. This is the case in the tree of Figure 7.1, where the nodes have up to three successors. It would be natural to assume that binary trees are a special case of trees, but the tree literature does not treat them this way. The formal definition of a *tree,* as opposed to a binary tree, is as follows: A ***tree*** is a root node with subtrees $t_1, t_2, \ldots, t_n$ that are themselves trees and have no nodes in common.

Formally there are no null trees (although there are null binary trees), so each tree has at least one node, its root. It is convenient nonetheless to refer to null trees, so the terminology applied to binary trees also applies to trees. The important distinction is that no order is imposed on the subtrees of a tree, whereas for binary trees there is a distinct left and right subtree. Consequently, when trees are depicted, it makes no difference in what order subtrees are drawn; any order represents the same tree. When order among the subtrees is to be imposed, they are called *ordered trees*. For example the structures in Figure 7.12, when viewed as binary trees, represent two distinct binary trees, since their left and right subtrees differ, but they represent the same tree when viewed as trees.

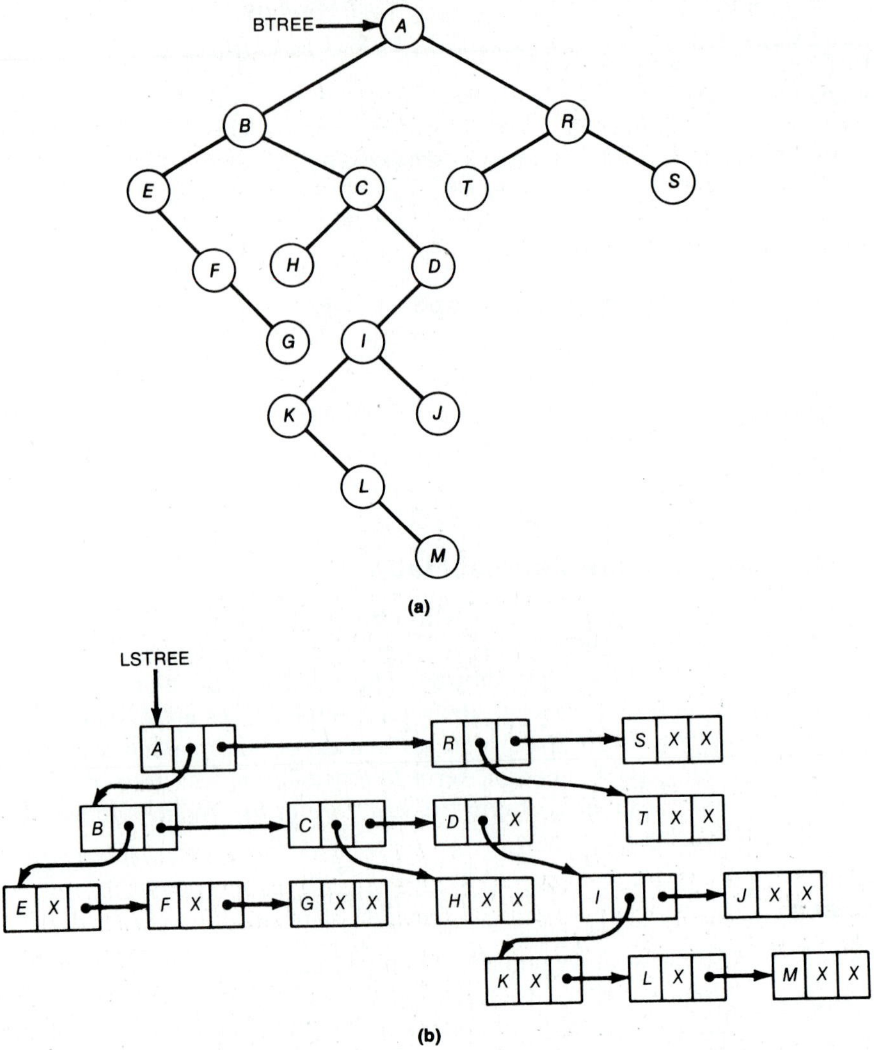

(a)

(b)

Figure 7.11 (a) List-structure Representation of (b) a Binary Tree

Figure 7.12 Two Distinct Binary Trees or One General Tree

7.5.1 Implementing Trees as Binary Trees

When a constraint is imposed limiting the number of successors of any node to at most k, the tree is called a ***k-ary*** tree. Such trees may be implemented by generalizing the sequential representation for binary trees. The nodes are numbered as before, except the jth successor of the node numbered i is now assigned node number $k \times (i - 1) + (j + 1)$. Thus, when $k = 5$, the fourth successor ($j = 4$) of the node numbered i ($i = 3$) is assigned the number $5*(3 - 1) + (4 + 1) = 15$. A 5-ary tree with nodes numbered in this way is

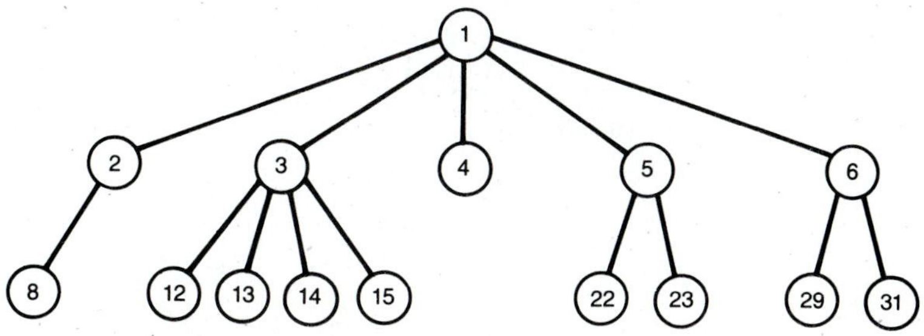

This implementation will not be pursued further but is similar in character to the sequential implementation for binary trees. This means that formulas can be derived to compute the array position of a node's predecessor and successors, which are important requirements for tree processing. Also, this representation is convenient for essentially static, healthy-looking (nonsparse) trees.

Another representation is based on a natural generalization of the linked representation for binary trees. Simply expand each record so that it has as many pointer fields as it has subtrees. However, this leads to variable-length records, which are usually not desirable. The variable-length records occur because nodes need not all have the same number of successors. Further, it may not even be possible to predict in advance what the greatest number of successors will be. When it is known that the tree will be a k-ary tree, then all records could be made the same length, large enough to accommodate k subtree pointers. This gives a fixed record size but can result in considerable wasted storage for unused pointer fields within records. This is particularly true for sparse trees.

Surprisingly, there is a way to represent a tree as a binary tree, which then allows all records to be of fixed length. This is an important result. Since any tree can be represented by a binary tree, studying only binary trees is really no restriction at all.

Example 7.4 Let us now look at how to represent a specific tree as a binary tree. Consider the tree of Figure 7.13(a). How can this tree be represented as a binary tree? ■

The binary tree is obtained as follows: First, create a root A of the binary tree to correspond to the root A of the tree. Next, pick any successor of A in the tree—say, B—and create a node B in the binary tree as A's left successor. Then take the remaining siblings of B, which are C and D in this case, and let C be B's right successor and D be C's right successor, in the binary tree. So far this yields the binary tree shown in Figure 7.13(b). If we view this procedure as the process-

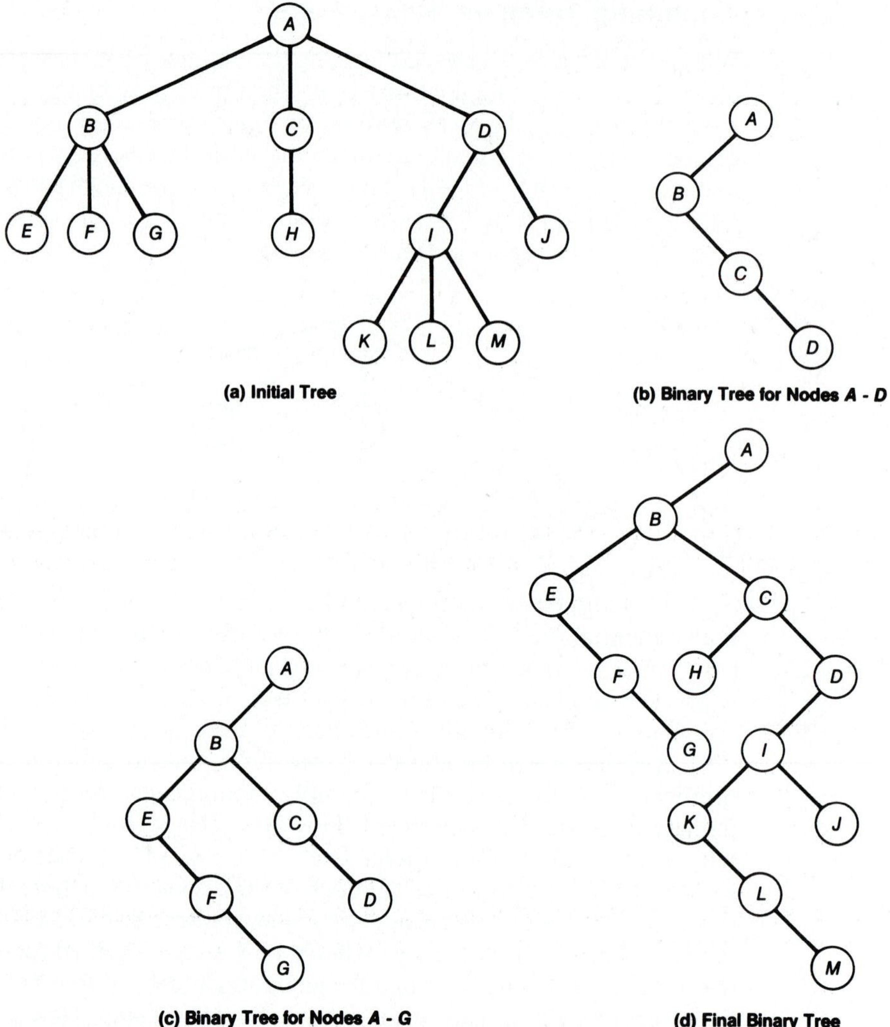

Figure 7.13 Representation of a General Tree as a Binary Tree

ing of node A of the tree, then the binary tree is completed by repeating this procedure for every other node of the tree. For example, after node B is processed (that is, its successors have been added to the binary tree), the result is Figure 7.13(c). The final binary tree created using this procedure appears in Figure 7.13(d).

Applying this procedure, given any tree, a corresponding binary tree can be constructed. The specific binary tree generated will depend on the order in which successors are taken in the tree. For instance, had C been selected initially as the first successor of A, then the resultant binary tree would be different. If the ordering of each node's successors is specified and they are taken in the specified order, then the construction creates a unique binary tree for each tree. In any case, a tree with *n* nodes will correspond to a binary tree with *n* nodes. It is not difficult to find an algorithm that, given a binary tree with no right subtree, can reverse the construction and generate the tree it represents. This means that when the tree is ordered, there is a *unique* binary tree that can be constructed to represent it. Conversely, given a binary tree with no right subtree, there is a unique tree that it represents, which can also be constructed. Hence there are exactly as many trees with n nodes as there are binary trees with n nodes and no right subtrees.

If we define an ***ordered forest*** as an ordered collection of ordered trees, then each tree has its unique binary tree representation. Can you see how to append these binary trees to the binary tree representing the first ordered tree of the ordered forest to obtain a binary tree representing the forest? (*Hint:* Use the fact that the binary trees have no right subtrees.) For those of you who wish to count trees, pursuing this should lead to the conclusion that there are exactly as many ordered forests as there are binary trees.

7.6 Traversals of Trees

In this section algorithms are developed for traversing trees and are applied to two examples. The second example should be studied carefully, because it illustrates an important modified traversal of trees that has many applications. Assuming the trees are ordered, it makes sense to refer to a tree's *first* subtree, *second* subtree, and so on. If an order is not given, the programmer can impose one.

When trees are used to store data at their nodes, then tree traversals give a means to access all the data. However, a tree might be used to represent a maze or all routes from Philadelphia to San Francisco. Traversal of the tree then provides the means to find exits from the maze or the shortest route across the country. The maze and the routes must not intersect. When they do, a more general data structure, a *graph,* is needed for their representation. Unlike trees, a ***graph*** allows more than one path between its nodes.* Should a tree contain family relationships by storing an individual's record at a node, a traversal allows the parent (predecessor) or the children (successors) of an individual to be found.

The preorder and postorder traversals of binary trees generalize quite naturally to ordered trees.

To preorder traverse an ordered tree:

1. Access and process its root, then
2. Preorder traverse its subtrees in order.

To postorder traverse an ordered tree:

1. Postorder traverse its subtrees in order, then
2. Access and process its root.

There is no natural inorder traversal of trees. Preorder and postorder traversals of a tree correspond, respectively, to preorder and inorder traversals of its corresponding binary tree. The preorder and postorder access sequences for the tree of Figure 7.13(a) are ABEFGCHDIKLMJ and EFGBHCKLMIJDA. You should confirm that a preorder and an inorder traversal of the binary tree of Figure 7.13 result in these respective access sequences. A preorder traversal is also called a ***depth-first*** traversal.

---

* It is not difficult to generalize tree traversal algorithms to obtain graph traversal algorithms.

7.6.1 Obtaining the Binary Tree for a Tree

It should now be clear that confining attention to binary trees, their representation, and operations on them is not actually a restriction. That is, since trees can be represented as binary trees, any operations can be performed on them by performing equivalent operations on their binary tree representations. In this sense no generality is lost in dealing with binary trees.

Example 7.5 Let the task for this example be the development of an algorithm to generate the binary tree corresponding to a general tree. ■

In order to do this we must be able to traverse a general tree. As it is traversed, we can generate the binary tree by properly processing each node as it is accessed. A nonrecursive algorithm to preorder traverse a tree `t` follows.

Nonrecursive Tree Preorder Traversal

```
1. Set p to t
2. Setstack_t(ts)
3. While p is not null or not empty_t(ts),
       if p is not null, then
           process(t,p)
           For each successor pointer ps of node.p,
           except next(p),
               push_t(ps,ts)
           Update p to next(p)
       else
           pop_t(ts,p)
```

This algorithm is a generalization of the nonrecursive preorder traversal of a binary tree that saves right pointers. In the binary tree case, the next subtree is the left subtree, and only one successor of the node just processed must be saved—the right successor. The difference is that now *all* the subtree pointers of the node just processed, except for the next one, must be saved.

Now that we have a general tree traversal, it will be adapted to our task. Let `bt` point to the binary tree to be generated by the algorithm. Recall the list-structure representation of a binary tree. Think of the leftpointer field of each node of `bt` as pointing to a sublist. This sublist contains all the successors of the corresponding node in `t`. Thus, in Figure 7.13(d), node A of the binary tree representation has a leftpointer field pointing to the sublist consisting of nodes B, C, and D. These are the successors of A in the general tree, Figure 7.13(a). Similarly, D has a leftpointer field pointing to the sublist consisting of I and J, the successors of D in the general tree.

Consequently, to produce `bt`, when a node of `t` is processed we must

Create a sublist consisting of all its successors

Set the leftpointer field of the corresponding node in `bt` to point to this sublist

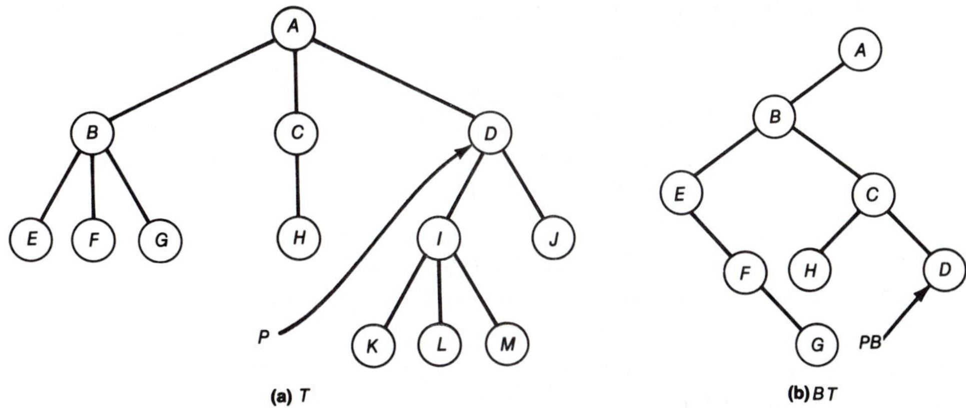

Figure 7.14 Binary Tree *BT* Generated from General Tree *T*

Copy the `info` field of the node in `t` into the `info` field of the corresponding node in `bt`

The rightpointer fields of these nodes in `bt` serve as the link fields of the sublist.

Recall that, as we preorder traverse a general tree `t`, we are preorder traversing its corresponding binary tree, `bt`. That is, the order in which the nodes of `t` are accessed is exactly the same as the order in which the corresponding nodes of `bt` are accessed. Thus we can achieve a solution by preorder traversing *both* `t` and `bt` at the same time, and processing the corresponding nodes as described above. For example, if this were carried out on the general and final binary tree of Figure 7.13, and nodes A, B, E, F, G, and C had been processed, we would have generated the binary tree shown as Figure 7.14(b).

Suppose `p` points to the node currently being processed in `t`. Let `pb` point to the corresponding node in `bt`. In the example, `p` would now point to D of `t` and `pb` to D of `bt`.

After processing the node to which `p` points, we can update `p` to point to one of its successors, `next(p)`, and stack on `ts` all pointers to the remaining successors. These pointers represent the latest postponed obligations for the preorder traversal of `t`. `Next(p)` is a function returning a pointer to the successor of `p` that is not stacked, or a null pointer if there are no successors. At the same time, to keep track of the postponed obligations for `bt`'s preorder traversal, we will keep a parallel stack, `bts`. Only nonnull pointers will be pushed onto `bts`. When the top pointer in stack `ts` is popped, the top pointer in `bts` will also be popped. These pointers will then point to *corresponding* nodes—one in `t`, the other in `bt`. Storage can be created for the nodes of `bt` as the traversal proceeds by using `avail` to return a pointer to the available storage for a node, since a pointer variable implementation is used for the binary tree.

One last detail remains. In order to do the processing required on `node.p` and `node.pb`, `process` will be invoked. As already noted, `process` must create a sublist consisting of new nodes corresponding to the successors of `node.p` in `t`, set `leftptr.pb` to point to that sublist, and copy `info.p` into info.pb. We assume that a procedure create, given p, creates the required sublist, and returns with first pointing to the first node of that sublist. The preorder traversal algorithm to create the binary tree corresponding to a general tree is as follows:

Nonrecursive Algorithm to Generate a Binary Tree Corresponding to a General Tree

```
1. Set p to t
        If p is null
            Set bt to null
        else
            bt = avail()
            Set pb to bt
2. Setstack_t(ts)
   Setstack_bt(bts)
3. While p is not null or not empty_t(ts),
        if p is not null, then
            process(t,bt,p,pb).
            For each successor pointer ps of node.p, except next(p),
                push_t(ps,ts)
            If right(pb) is not null
                push_bt(right(pb),bts)
            p = next(p)
            pb = left(pb)
        else
            pop_t(ts,p)
            pop_bt(bts,pb).
```

The process algorithm to be used in the preorder traversal is:

```
Create(p,first)
Set leftptr.pb to first
Set info.pb to info.p
```

Notice that the traversal of the binary tree bt is embedded in the traversal of the general tree t. Also, suffixes have been used to distinguish the stack storing pointers to nodes of the general tree from the stack storing pointers to nodes of the binary tree. Finally, since the tree t is not ordered, the function next is free to pick any successor. The order in which the rest of the successors are placed on the stack is arbitrary but must determine the order in which create places them on the sublist. You should simulate this algorithm on the tree of Figure 7.13(a) to see how it works.

The correspondence between an ordered tree and its binary tree can now be defined more formally. In this case the binary tree corresponding to a tree is unique. An ordered tree t may be represented by a binary tree bt as follows:

```
Each node of t corresponds to a node of bt,
If node n of t corresponds to node nb of bt, then
    the leftmost successor of n in t corresponds to the left successor of nb in bt;
```

All other siblings of `n` in `t` form a right chain from the node in `bt` corresponding to the leftmost successor of `n` in `t`.

We may now give a recursive definition specifying an algorithm for generating the binary tree `bt` representing the general ordered tree `t`.

To generate a binary tree corresponding to an ordered tree:

If `t` is null
    Set `bt` to null
else
    Create the root node of `bt` corresponding to the root of `t`.
    If `t` has a subtree, then
        generate the binary tree `bt.left` corresponding to the leftmost subtree of `t`, `t.leftmost`, and
        make the generated binary tree the left subtree of `bt`.
For every other subtree of `t`, in order,
    generate the binary tree corresponding to the subtree, and
    insert it at the end of the right chain of `bt.left`.

For illustration this algorithm is applied to the ordered tree in `t` in Figure 7.15(a).

First create the root of BT corresponding to the root of `t` shown in Figure 7.15(b). To carry out statement 2, note that `t` has three subtrees with B at the root of its leftmost subtree. We must thus generate `bt.left` to correspond to Figure 7.15(c). To do this, apply the definition to this tree and obtain Figure 7.15(d) as its

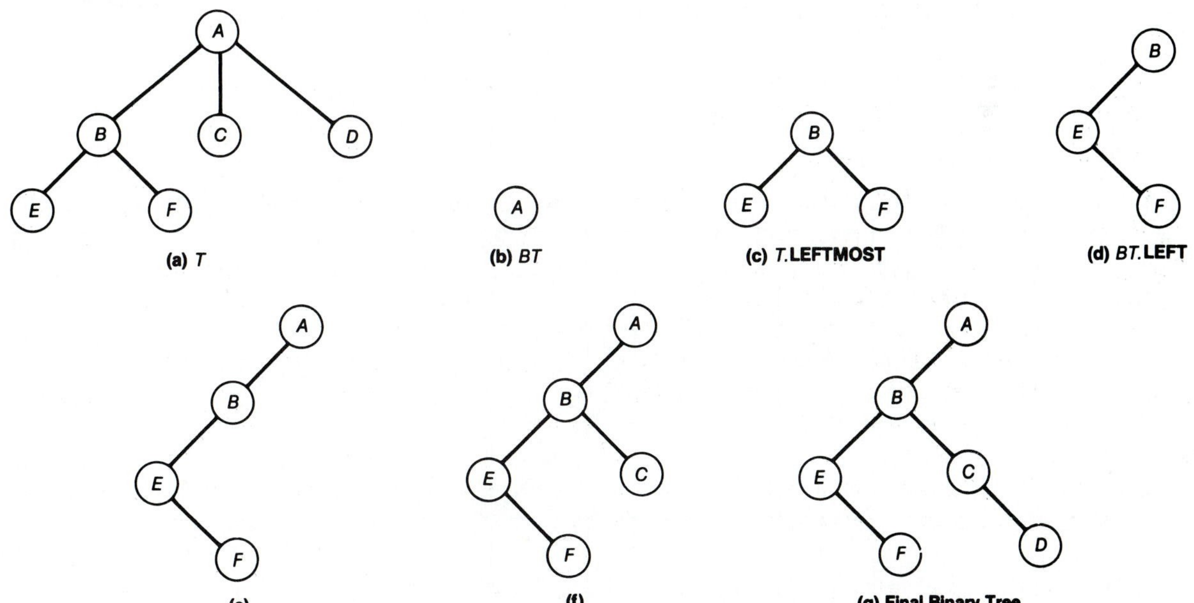

Figure 7.15 Generation of Binary Tree *BT* from an Ordered Tree *T*

corresponding binary tree. Completing the first part of statement 2 for `t` yields the binary tree shown in Figure 7.15(e).

To complete the second part of statement 2, generate the binary tree for the next subtree of `t`, with C at its root, and then insert it at the end of the right chain of B to obtain Figure 7.15(f). Finally, do the same for the last subtree of A, with D at its root, and complete the application to `t`, to obtain the result shown in Figure 7.15(g).

This is another example for which we found a recursive solution. Compare the clarity and conciseness of the recursive solution with that of the nonrecursive solution.

7.6.2 Backtracking: The *n*-queens Problem

In the last section a tree traversal was developed and used to generate a binary tree. Here and in the following two sections we will develop a modified tree traversal that employs backtracking. *Backtracking* is a useful technique in solving many problems. First we apply it to the *n*-queens problem.

Chess is played on a square board with eight rows and eight columns, just like a checkerboard. We can think of the board as a two-dimensional array, `board` (Figure 7.16).

A queen located in the *j*th row and *k*th column may move to a new position in one of the following ways:

- To the right, or left, along its row
- Up, or down, in its column

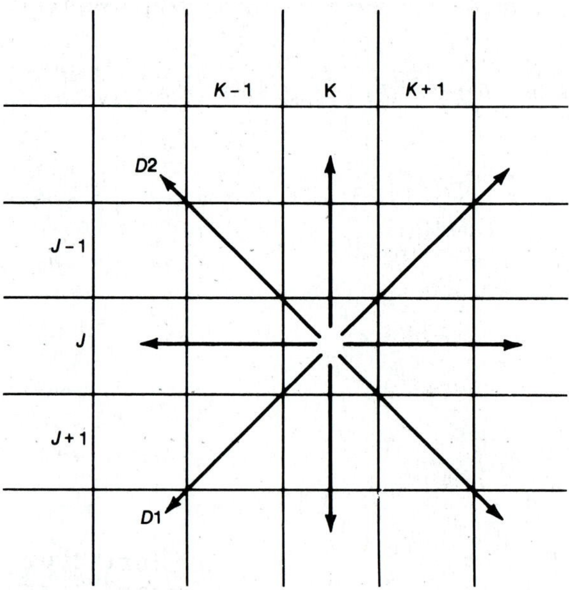

Figure 7.16 A Partial Chessboard Represented as a Two-Dimensional Array, BOARD

- Up, or down, along its $d1$ diagonal
- Up, or down, along its $d2$ diagonal

The *n*-queens problem is to find *all* ways to place n queens on an $n \times n$ checkerboard so that no queen may take another. As an example, the eight-queens problem is to find *all* ways to place eight queens on the chessboard so that no queen may take any other—that is, move into a position on its next move that is occupied by any other queen.

The question is how to solve the *n*-queens problem. At first glance this problem has little relation to trees, but let us see. It is not even clear that a solution exists for all n.

Since a queen can be moved along one of its rows, columns, or diagonals, a solution clearly is achieved by specifying how to place the n queens so that *exactly* one queen appears in each row and column, and no more than one queen appears on any diagonal of the board. One could attempt to find a solution by searching through all possible placements of the n queens satisfying these restrictions. There are, however, $n!$ such placements. Even for a moderate n, this is obviously not a practical solution. Instead we must construct a solution. The idea behind the construction is to determine if the placements obtained for the first i queens can lead to a solution. If they cannot, abandon that construction and try another, since placing the remaining $n - i$ queens will not be fruitful. This *may* avoid the need to consider all possible constructions.

To construct a solution involves testing a partial construction to determine whether or not it can lead to a solution or must be abandoned as a dead end. This testing is the next question.

Consider a general tree, with each of its nodes representing a sequence of decisions on the placement of queens. Take the root to represent the initial situation, in which no decisions have yet been made. The root will have n successors. Each successor corresponds to a choice of row for the placement of the first queen. Each of these successor nodes, in turn, has n successors, corresponding to a choice of row for the placement of the second queen, and so on. The tree for the four-queens problem is shown in Figure 7.17.

Since exactly one queen must appear in each column in *any* solution, assume the ith queen is placed in column i. Hence, each path, from the root to a node at depth i in the tree, specifies a partial construction in which the first i queens have been placed on the board. The path indicated in the four-queens tree specifies a partial construction in which the first, second, and third queens have been placed in rows 2, 4, and 1 (and columns 1, 2, and 3), respectively. The tree helps us visualize all possible solutions and provides a framework in which to view what we are doing.

Suppose a path has been found to a node at depth k. The path is *feasible* if none of the k queens whose positions are specified by the path can take any other. If the node at depth k is a terminal node, and the path is feasible, then a solution has been found and may be printed. If the node at depth k is not terminal, and the path is feasible, we want to extend the path to a node at depth $k + 1$. Let `p` point to such a node. Then `node.p` must be a successor of the node on the path at depth k.

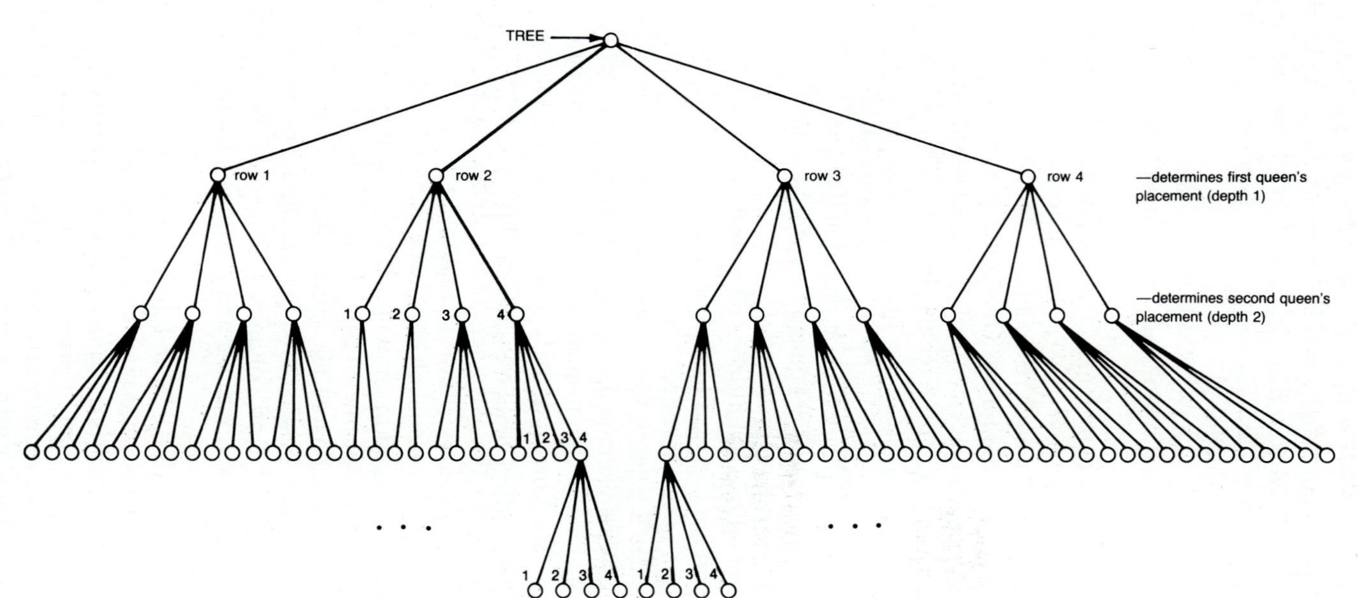

Figure 7.17 Tree for the Four-queens Problem

`p` *is feasible* if the position that `node.p` specifies for the $(k + 1)$th queen does not allow it to take any of the other k queens. If `p` is feasible, the path can be extended downward in the tree to include `node.p`, so there is now a feasible path of depth $k + 1$. If `p` is *not* feasible, then another successor of the node at depth k must be tried until a feasible one is found to extend the path, or until all have been tried and none is feasible. In the latter case, the choice of node at depth k cannot be extended to a solution, and the computer backs up in the tree to a node representing a shorter path that has not yet been explored. This procedure to extend the new path is repeated until a solution is found or until all possibilities have been tried.

The procedure described amounts to a modified general tree traversal called ***backtracking.*** A different approach would be to create an algorithm for the problem by applying a general tree preorder traversal that uses a process routine. The process routine would check each node to be processed to see whether the node is terminal and represents a feasible path. If so, it prints the solution. This approach amounts to an exhaustive search of all $n!$ possibilities, since the preorder traversal backs up only when the preorder traversal of a subtree has been completed—that is, after a *terminal* node has been processed. The backtracking traversal need not access and process all nodes. It backs up when the traversal of a subtree has been completed or when it becomes known that no path involving the root of a subtree can be extended to a solution. The backtracking procedure generates only *feasible* paths—not *all* paths. In effect, it prunes the tree by ignoring all nodes that cannot lead to a solution.

7.6.3 Depth-first

A backtracking algorithm can be derived by modifying the general tree preorder traversal algorithm. The "`p` not null" test in the loop body of the preorder traversal algorithm must be replaced by two tests. One to see if `p` points to an existing node and another "`p` feasible" test to prune the tree. How this feasibility test is implemented is what determines the amount of pruning that occurs and hence the efficiency of the solution. The `process` routine called in the loop body must determine if `node.p` is terminal, and, if so, print the solution. If these were the only changes made, then nothing at all would be printed when no solution exists.

You, as the programmer, do not know whether a solution exists for every n. Therefore, initialize a flag, `found`, to *false,* and have `process` set `found` to *true* if it finds a solution. Upon exiting from the loop body, test `found`, and if it is *false* print "No solution." The resultant algorithm for a backtracking preorder traversal is as follows:

Backtracking Preorder Tree Traversal

1. Set `p` to the root of `t`.
2. Set `found` to false.
3. Set the stack to empty.

4. While `p` is not null or the stack is not empty,
   - if `p` is not null, then
     - if `p` is feasible, then
       - `process(p)`,
       - push all successors of `node.p` onto the stack except `next(p)`,
       - move down in `t` by setting `p` to `next(p)`,
     - else
       - backtrack in `t` by popping the stack and setting `p` to the popped value,
   - else
     - backtrack in `t` by popping the stack and setting `p` to the popped value;

   if not `found` then
   - print `no solutions`.

The function `next(p)` is assumed to return a null value if `node.p` has no successors. If only one solution is to be found and printed, only the test of the **while** loop must be changed. It should become "(`p` not null or stack not empty) and (not `found`)." The `process` algorithm to be used with the backtracking preorder traversal is as follows:

If `node.p` is a terminal node, then
1. Print the solution, and
2. Set `found` to *true*.

The algorithms developed in this section are quite general. They are applicable to any problem that can be reduced to a backtracking traversal (like the *n*-queens problem). They should be viewed as general tools for problem solving. We must now specialize them to the *n*-queens problem so that they are detailed enough to implement as a function. Data structure decisions, specifically the implementation of the current board configuration, must be made along the way.

The tree is not actually stored in memory; it was used as a conceptual aid in formulating the problem abstractly. As a result, the problem has been recognized as one that may be solved by a general tree backtracking procedure. It is not necessary to refer to the tree at all, but we have done so here to place the problem in this more general context, and we continue with this approach.

Suppose `p` points to a node at depth k. The depth of the node specifies the placement for the kth queen, column k. `P` itself determines the choice of row. In this way `p` corresponds to a particular `row` and `col` pair and vice versa. A nonnull value for `p` corresponds to a column and row value $<n + 1$. Initializing `p` to the first successor of the root corresponds to setting `row` to 1 and `col` to 1.

`Next` must have `row` and `col` as parameters; it simply increases `col` by 1 and sets `row` to 1. As the traversal proceeds, `row` and `col` vary in a regular way. This can be used to advantage. Instead of pushing all successors of `node.p` onto the stack, which would involve $n - 1$ entries, simply push the current value of `row`. Then the backtracking task can be carried out by adding 1 to the current value of `row` when this value is less than n. If it equals n, the stack must be popped, `row` set to the popped value plus 1, and `col` set to `col-1`.

To implement the crucial test, "`p` feasible," we use a function `feasible` to return the value *true* when `p` is feasible and *false* otherwise. `Feasible` must have `row` and `col` as parameters and must have access to information about the current board configuration. It must determine if placing a queen in the position specified by `row` and `col` will allow it to "take" one of the currently placed queens. If a queen may be taken, it must return "false," otherwise "true."

We could use an $n \times n$ two-dimensional array `board` to keep track of the current board configuration. If we did this, `feasible` would have to traverse through the row, column, and diagonals specified by `row` and `col` in order to determine what value to return. This checking must involve all entries in many rows and columns. Since `feasible` is invoked in the loop body of the backtracking preorder traversal algorithm, it is executed once for every node of the tree that is accessed. Operations that appear in loop bodies should be done efficiently since they have a significant effect on the overall efficiency of the implementation.

To do its job, `feasible` must know whether or not the `row`, `col`, and the diagonals specified by `row` and `col` are occupied. If this information can be efficiently extracted and made available, `feasible` will be more efficient. We now see exactly what information is required and proceed to the details involved in efficiently extracting it.

Consider Figure 7.16. Notice that entries $[j, k]$, $[j + 1, k - 1]$, and $[j - 1, k + 1]$ all lie along the d1 diagonal. Notice also that $j + k = (j + 1) + (k - 1) = (j - 1) + (k + 1)$. This means that all entries on the diagonal d1, determined by j and k, have the same row + col sum: $j + k$. The same is true of differences along d2. That is, all entries on the diagonal d2, determined by j and k, have the same row minus col difference: $j - k$. Suppose we keep information about the current board configuration as follows:

`r`$[j]$
: Is *true* if the current board configuration has no queen in the jth row, and is *false* otherwise.

`d1`$[j + k]$
: Is *true* if the current board configuration has no queen along the diagonal `d1` with row + col sum $j + k$, and *false* otherwise.

`d2`$[j - k]$
: Is *true* if the current board configuration has no queen along the diagonal `d2` with row − col sum $j - k$, and *false* otherwise.

`Feasible` can now simply return the value of (`r`$[j]$ and `d1`$[j + k]$ and `d2`$[j - k]$). The arrays `r`, `d1`, and `d2` require storage for n, $2(n - 1)$, and $2(n - 1)$ entries, respectively, and must be properly initialized, but `feasible` now takes constant time to execute. Also, when `row` and `col` are changed, these changes must be reflected in `r`, `d1`, and `d2`. What we have done amounts to finding a way to store the current board configuration so that the operations performed on it by the algorithm are done efficiently. `R`, `d1`, and `d2` have indices that range from 1 to n, 2 to $2n$, and $-(n - 1)$ to $(n - 1)$, respectively. Since C does not allow such array indices, it is necessary to refer in the program below to corresponding entries in arrays whose indices will range from 0 to $n - 1$, 0 to $2(n - 1)$, and 0 to $2(n - 1)$, respectively.

Finally, we must implement the printing of a solution in `process`. This can be done by printing the sequence of values stored on the stack. They specify the rows in which queens 1 to n were placed. To do this we will need a stack operation `item`. It returns a copy of the `i`th stack entry, which represents the row in which the (`i+1`)th placed queen (the queen in column `i`) appears. When `i` is zero, it returns a copy of the top entry.

The backtracking traversal algorithm that was developed and applied to this problem is a general tool for problem solving. It may be adapted, for example, to solving a maze, finding good game-playing strategies, and translating high-level language programs.

The nonrecursive solution may be written as follows.

Nonrecursive *n*-queens Program

```
#include <stdio.h>

main()
/* Reads in n and prints all solutions
   to the n-queens problem.
*/
{
   int n;
   printf("\n n = ?");
   scanf("%d",&n);
   queens(n);
}

#define NLIMIT 20
typedef int rowcheck[NLIMIT];
typedef int diagonalcheck1[2*NLIMIT-1];
typedef int diagonalcheck2[2*NLIMIT-1];
```

definitions for types used to store the board configuration

```
#define SLIMIT 20
typedef int whatever;
typedef struct
{
   whatever stackarray[SLIMIT-1];
   int top;
}stack;

setstack(ps)
/* Sets stack s to empty. */
stack *ps;
{
   (*ps).top = -1;
}

empty(ps)
/* Returns true only if stack s is empty. */
stack *ps;
{
   return((*ps).top == -1);
}
```

the **stack** *data abstraction*

```
push(value,ps)
/* Inserts contents of value as
   the top entry on stack s.
*/
whatever value;
stack *ps;
{
   if((*ps).top == (SLIMIT-1))
      overflow(ps);
   else
      {
         (*ps).top = (*ps).top + 1;
         (*ps).stackarray[(*ps).top] = value;
      }
}

pop(ps,pvalue)
/* Removes the top entry of stack s
   and copies its contents into value.
*/
stack *ps;
whatever *pvalue;
{
   if(empty(ps))
      underflow(ps);
   else
      {
         *pvalue = (*ps).stackarray[(*ps).top];
         (*ps).top = (*ps).top - 1;
      }
}

whatever item(i,ps)
/* Returns a copy of the ith
   entry in stack s. When i is
   zero it returns a copy of
   the top entry.
*/
stack *ps;
{
   return((*ps).stackarray[(*ps).top-i]);
}

overflow(ps)
/* Prints a message if the stack overflows. */
stack *ps;
{
   printf("\n stack overflow ");
}

underflow(ps)
/* Prints a message if the stack underflows. */
stack *ps;
```

```
{
   printf("\n stack underflow ");
}

queens(n)
/* Prints all solutions to the n-queens problem */
int n;
{
   stack s;
   #define TRUE 1
   #define FALSE 0
   int i,row,col,found;
   rowcheck r;
   diagonalcheck1 d1;
   diagonalcheck2 d2;
   col = 1;
   row = 1;

   for(i=0;i<=n-1;i++)
      r[i] = TRUE;
   for(i=0;i<=2*n-2;i++)
      d1[i] = TRUE;
   for(i=0;i<=2*n-2;i++)
      d2[i] = TRUE;
   found = FALSE;
   setstack(&s);
   while(((col < n+1)&&(row < n+1)) || !empty(&s))
      if((col < n+1)&&(row < n+1))

         if(feasible(row,col,r,d1,d2,n))
            {
               process(row,col,&found,&s,n);


               push(row,&s);

               r[row-1] = FALSE;
               d1[row+col-2] = FALSE;
               d2[row-col+n-1] = FALSE;
               col = col + 1;
               row = 1;
            }
         else
            row = row + 1;
      else
         {
            pop(&s,&row);
            col = col - 1;
            r[row-1] = TRUE;
            d1[row+col-2] = TRUE;
            d2[row-col+n-1] = TRUE;
```

a backtracking preorder traversal (queens(n))

`r`, `d1`, *and* `d2` *will contain the board configuration*

`col` *and* `row` *determine the next placement attempt*

initialization of the board; no queens have been placed

test for completion (while)

if `col`, `row` *position is on the board*

if potential partial solution

if the partial solution is complete, it is printed and `found` *set to* true

stores the row position of the queen just placed

updates the board configuration

moves the `col` *over*

sets `row` *back to 1, its first possible value*

otherwise

try the next row

otherwise

backtrack to the last `col` *and* `row` *placement*

update the board configuration

```
            row = row + 1;                                    try the next row
        }
    if(!found)
        printf("\n NO SOLUTIONS");
}

feasible(row,col,r,d1,d2,n)
/* Returns true only if the placement of the
   next queen in position col,row does not
   allow any queen to take another under
   the current board configuration given
   by r,d1,d2.
*/
int row,col,n;
rowcheck r;
diagonalcheck1 d1;
diagonalcheck2 d2;
{
    return(r[row-1]&&d1[row+col-2]&&d2[row-col+n-1]);
}

process(row,col,pfound,ps,n)
/* If the partial solution is a complete
   solution then it is printed and
   found is set to true.
*/
int row,col,*pfound,n;
stack *ps;
{
    int i;
    whatever item();
    if(col == n)
        {
            for(i=n-1;i>=1;i--)
                printf("\n COL %d ROW is %d----",         the rows for the queens
                        n-1,item(i-1,ps));                are on the stack; the row
                                                          for col n-1 is at the top
            printf("\n COL %d ROW is %d----\n",           the row position of the
                    n,row);                               queen in col n was not
            *pfound = TRUE;                               stacked
        }
}
```

You may be tempted to try a more analytic approach to this problem so as to eliminate the need for all this searching. Be forewarned that famous mathematicians also attempted to analyze this problem but had difficulty solving it other than by backtracking! Actually, there are no solutions for $n = 1$, 2, and 3, and at least one solution for all $n \geq 4$. For the curious, the number of solutions for n up to 15 are:

N	4	5	6	7	8	9	10
Solutions	2	10	4	40	92	352	724

N	11	12	13	14	15
Solutions	2,680	14,200	73,712	365,596	2,279,184

7.6.4 Breadth-first

One final point about the backtracking traversal algorithm. Suppose the **while** loop task is replaced by the task:

```
if p is not null, then
    if p is feasible, then
        process(p)
        push all successors of node.p onto the stack
    pop(sp)
else
    pop(s,p).
```

This implementation also represents a preorder tree traversal. The stack is used to store and recall postponed obligations. It can be further modified by changing the stack to a queue and replacing `empty`, `push`, and `pop` by the corresponding queue operations. `Pop` must return null if called when the queue is empty. The result is another modified general tree traversal, a *backtracking breadth-first* traversal. It accesses the nodes in *level* order. In contrast, the backtracking preorder traversal presented earlier might be called a *backtracking depth-first* traversal. Removing the "`p` is feasible" test of the backtracking breadth-first traversal turns it into a *breadth-first* traversal. You should convince yourself that this version leads to the nodes of Figure 7.13(a) being accessed and processed in the order A, B, C, D, E, F, G, H, I, J, K, L, M. Keep in mind that in this application the root node was never considered. The difference between a backtracking traversal and a traversal is that backtracking tests for feasibility. This allows tree paths to be ignored when it can be determined that they cannot lead to a solution.

7.6.5 Branch and Bound

There is another type of modified tree traversal which is often found useful. It is called a ***branch and bound traversal.*** An algorithm for this traversal is as follows:

Nonrecursive Branch and Bound Traversal

```
1. Set p to t.
2. Set bag to empty.
3. While p is not null
       if p is feasible, then
           i. process(t,p), and
```

ii. add each successor pointer of `p` to the `bag`;
Select a pointer from the `bag` and set `p` to it.

This algorithm uses a data abstraction consisting of a **bag** data structure and operations on the **bag** that set it to empty, test it for emptiness, select (and remove) a pointer from it, and add a pointer to it. The idea is to define the select operation so that it removes the pointer from the **bag** that points to the node most likely to lead to a solution. The execution time required by the branch and bound traversal is directly related to how well the **select** function does the job of picking the next node to process and how well the **feasible** function does its job of pruning the tree. The better the selection and pruning the better the execution time. The **select** function should return null if the **bag** is empty.

If the **select** function always selects the node most recently added to the **bag**, then the data abstraction becomes a stack, and the algorithm is turned into a backtracking depth-first traversal. If the **select** function always selects the node that was added earliest to the **bag**, then the data abstraction becomes a queue, and the algorithm is turned into a backtracking breadth-first traversal. Thus backtracking may be viewed as a special case of branch and bound.

Horowitz and Sakni [1978] contains extensive discussions of backtracking and branch and bound traversals, with many applications worked out in detail. Also see Golomb and Baumert [1965]. Wirth [1976] deals with these techniques for problem solving; in particular, the stable marriage problem and the eight-queens problems are solved recursively.

7.7 More on Recursion, Trees, and Stacks

Now that we are steeped in trees, we can look back at Figures 4.2 and 4.4 and notice that they are pictures of trees. We shall call them the *execution trees* of their corresponding recursive programs. In fact, any recursive program can be viewed as generating such a tree as it executes. The recursive program can be thought of as executing by traversing its corresponding execution tree. The processing done at each node in the course of this traversal is the carrying out of the program's task on a specific problem specified by its data and current scratchpad. Now that you know a good deal about tree traversals, is it any wonder that the stack appears in the translation of a recursive program? It is clearly the number of nodes in the tree that determines the execution time of the algorithm, and it is the depth of the tree that determines the storage requirements. This point can become somewhat muddled when recursion is applied to trees themselves, but you should realize that this is the case even when no trees are apparent in the nature of the problem, as in the Towers of Hanoi problem in Chapter 4.

Further, we can now see that recursion clarifies because it hides the bookkeeping required by the tree traversal and because it elucidates the structure that must be inherent in the problem in order for a recursive solution to be found in the first place. Although it is an extremely powerful tool for these reasons, it must be applied with care. The purpose of this section is to provide some insight into the nature of those problems where a more skeptical approach is wise.

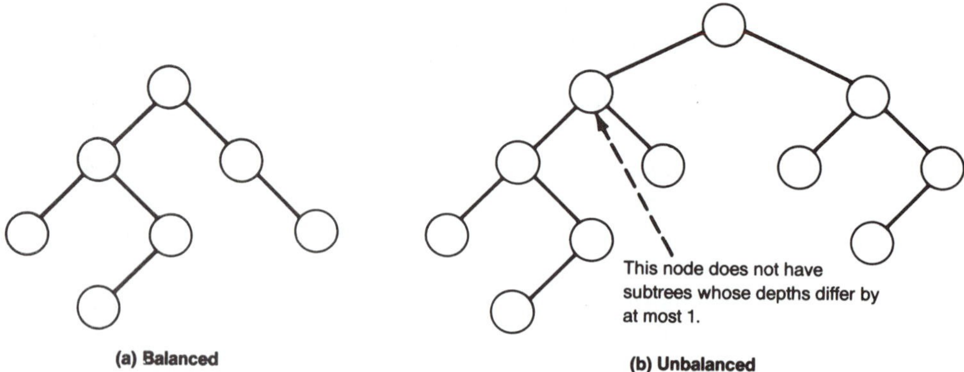

Figure 7.18 Balanced and Unbalanced Binary Trees

7.7.1 Balanced Binary Trees

In a ***balanced*** binary tree, no matter what node of the tree is considered, the left and right subtrees of that node have depths that differ by at most 1.

The binary tree of Figure 7.18(a) is balanced; the binary tree of (b) is not. Balanced trees are important in information retrieval applications; they will be discussed fully in Chapter 9. In information retrieval, the data are stored at the tree's nodes. The depth of the tree determines the search times for retrieval and, with balanced trees, the tree's depth is controllable and can be limited, as will be shown in Chapter 9. Here we consider the "worst case" of such trees.

A binary tree is a ***Fibonacci tree*** if it is balanced and has the minimum number of nodes among all balanced binary trees with its depth. Fibonacci trees represent the worst case for balanced trees, since they contain the fewest nodes (and hence the least storage capacity) among all balanced trees with a specified depth. The binary tree in Figure 7.19 is a Fibonacci tree of depth 4. This is a Fibonacci tree because it is balanced, and no balanced binary tree with a depth of 4 has fewer than 7 nodes. Any complete binary tree of depth 4, for example, will not be a Fibonacci tree because, although balanced, it will have more than the minimum number of nodes (7) for this depth.

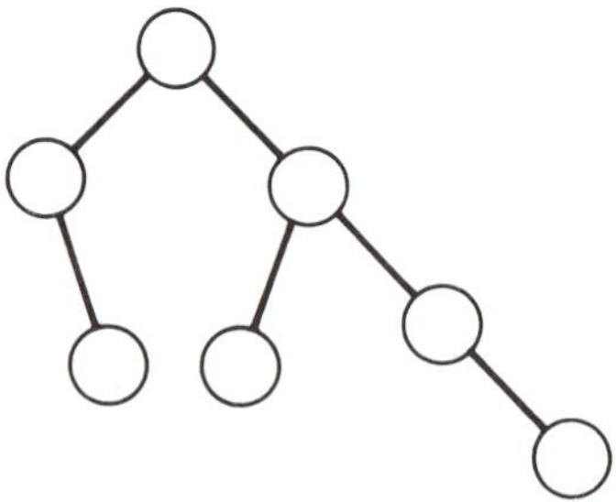

Figure 7.19 A Fibonacci Tree of Depth 4

The Fibonacci numbers are a well-known sequence of integers defined by the following recursive definition:

$$F_0 = 0, \qquad F_1 = 1,$$
$$F_n = F_{n-1} + F_{n-2} \qquad \text{for } n > 1$$

The first few are 0, 1, 1, 2, 3, 5, 8, 13, 21, 34, ... These numbers seem to appear in the most unexpected places. In computer science they often arise in the analysis of algorithms. The number of nodes in a Fibonacci tree of depth d can be shown to be $F_{d+2} - 1$ (see Exercise 34b). For example, if d is 4, then $F_{d+2} - 1 = F_6 - 1 = 8 - 1 = 7$.

Example 7.6 The task now is to develop an algorithm to generate a Fibonacci tree of depth d. If possible, apply the method of recursion to find a recursive definition of the solution. ■

Clearly, if $d = 0$, there is only one Fibonacci tree of depth d, the null binary tree. If $d = 1$, there is only one Fibonacci tree of depth d, the tree with one node—its root.

Any subtree of a balanced binary tree must also be balanced, or else the tree itself would not be balanced. *Any* subtree of a Fibonacci tree must therefore be balanced and must also be a Fibonacci tree. Otherwise it could be replaced by a Fibonacci tree of that depth with fewer nodes. This is the key to the recursive solution. We can now construct a Fibonacci tree of depth $d > 1$ as follows: Since $d > 1$, the Fibonacci tree must have a root, and its two subtrees must be Fibonacci trees. One (say, the right) must have depth $d - 1$ (so the tree itself has depth d). The other, the left subtree, must be a Fibonacci tree and must differ in depth from $d - 1$ by at most 1. Hence it must have depth $d - 2$ or $d - 1$. It has just been demonstrated that a Fibonacci tree of depth $d - 1$ has at least one subtree of depth $d - 2$. Hence the Fibonacci tree of depth $d - 1$ has more nodes than the Fibonacci tree of depth $d - 2$. Thus the left subtree of the Fibonacci tree being constructed must have depth $d - 2$. (Why?) This gives the complete recursive solution.

To construct a Fibonacci tree of depth *d*:

1. If $d = 0$, then
   construct the null tree,
2. else if $d = 1$, then
   construct the tree with one node, its root,
3. else if $d > 1$, then
   a. construct a root,
   b. construct a Fibonacci tree of depth $d - 2$ and make it the left subtree of the root, and
   c. construct a Fibonacci tree of depth $d - 1$ and make it the right subtree of the root.

The explicit constructions are given by the algorithm's statements 1 and 2 for $d = 0$ and $d = 1$. Statement 3 gives the implicit construction for $d > 1$. You should apply this definition to the case $d = 4$, and confirm that it constructs the example given earlier of a Fibonacci tree of depth 4. It should also be clear that other Fibonacci trees of depth 4 exist.

The recursive program can be written directly from the definition.

Recursive Version 1—Linked Representation with Records Stored in an Array

```
fibonaccitree(d,ptree)
/* Creates a Fibonacci tree, tree, of depth d. */
int d;
binarytreepointer *ptree;
{
   binarytreepointer tl,tr,avail();
   *ptree = avail();                          ] allocates storage for tree
   if(d == 0)
      *ptree = NULL;                          ] tree must be null
   else if(d == 1)
      {
         records[*ptree].leftptr = NULL;      ] tree has only a root node
         records[*ptree].rightptr = NULL;     ]
      }
   else
      {
         fibonaccitree(d-2,&tl);              ] tree is constructed by creating its left
         records[*ptree].leftptr = tl;        ] and right subtrees as proper Fibonacci
         fibonaccitree(d-1,&tr);              ] trees
         records[*ptree].rightptr = tr;       ]
      }
}
```

For concreteness, we have chosen to implement the constructed tree using a linked representation. The tree itself will be stored in the **records** array (Section 7.4.2) with the fields of a record being **info**, **leftptr**, and **rightptr**. **Records** is assumed to be a global variable. When the routine returns, **tree** will point to its root record in the array representation.

Using implementation with pointer variables for the binary tree, the procedure becomes the following.

Recursive Version 2—Linked Representation with Records Stored in Dynamic Memory

```
fibonaccitree(d,ptree)
/* Creates a Fibonacci tree, tree, of depth d. */
int d;
binarytreepointer *ptree;
{
   binarytreepointer tl,tr;
   *ptree = malloc(sizeof(binarytreerecord));   ] allocates storage for tree
   if(d == 0)
      *ptree = NULL;                             ] tree must be null
```

```
    else if(d == 1)
        {
            (*ptree)->leftptr = NULL;          ] tree has only a root node
            (*ptree)->rightptr = NULL;
        }
    else
        {
            fibonaccitree(d-2,&tl);            ] tree is constructed by creating
            (*ptree)->leftptr = tl;              its left and right subtrees as
            fibonaccitree(d-1,&tr);              proper Fibonacci trees
            (*ptree)->rightptr = tr;
        }
}
```

Finally, for contrast, the function may be written treating the tree as a data abstraction, as follows.

Recursive Version 3—The Tree Is Treated as a Data Abstraction

```
fibonaccitree(d,ptree)
/* Creates a Fibonacci tree, tree, of depth d. */
int d;
binarytreepointer *ptree;
{
   binarytreepointer null,tl,tr,avail(),setnull();
   null = setnull();
   *ptree = avail();
   if(d == 0)
      *ptree = null;                   ] tree must be null
   else if(d == 1)
      {
         setleft(*ptree,null);         ] tree has only a root node
         setright(*ptree,null);
      }
   else
      {
         fibonaccitree(d-2,&tl);       ] tree is constructed by creating its left and right subtrees
         setleft(*ptree,tl);             as proper Fibonacci trees
         fibonaccitree(d-1,&tr);
         setleft(*ptree,tr);
      }
}
```

7.7.2 Trading Storage for Time

Consider the execution tree for these functions when $d = 6$, which is given in Figure 7.20. Each node of the tree represents a call to the recursive function `Fibonaccitree`. Nodes with the same d-value thus correspond to requests of the recursive function to carry out identical tasks, that is, to create identical trees.

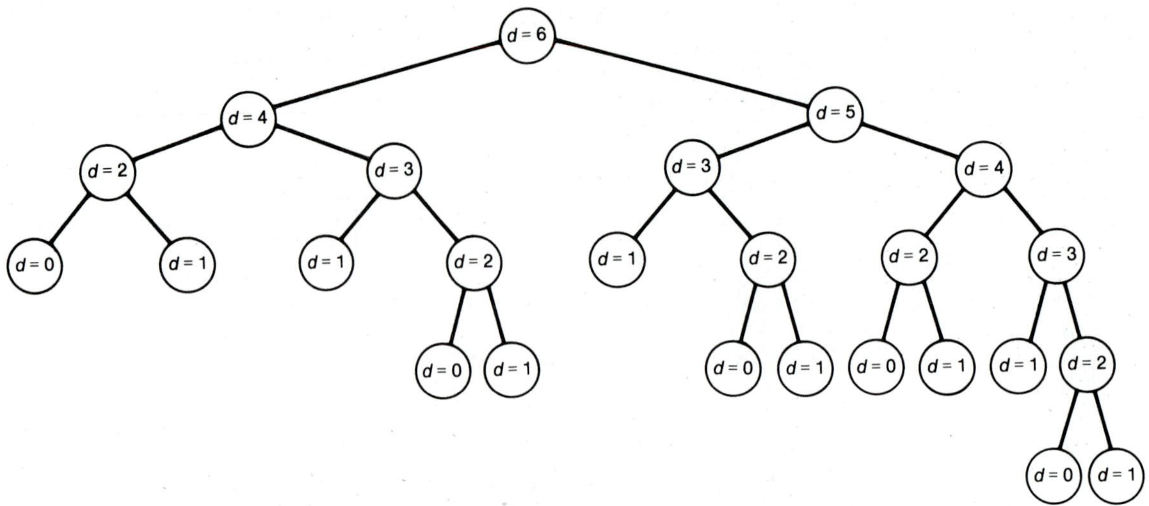

Figure 7.20 Execution Tree for Depth $d = 6$

Figure 7.20 shows a rather healthy-looking (nonsparse) tree with depth $d = 6$. This holds true for any value of d and means that while the storage is not excessive, the number of nodes in the tree will be $O(\phi^d)$, where $\phi = (1 + \sqrt{5})/2$.* This is because

> The execution tree for **`Fibonaccitree`** will always "resemble" the tree it is constructing.
>
> The depth of an execution tree determines the size of the underlying stack needed for the program to execute properly.
>
> The number of nodes in a Fibonacci tree of depth d is $F_{d+2} - 1$.

Hence the execution time will increase exponentially with d. A close inspection reveals that many identical tasks or problems are solved repeatedly during its execution. For example, $d = 0, 1, 2, 3$, and 4 are solved 5, 8, 5, 3, and 2 times, respectively. This is what causes the excessive execution time and illustrates the situation to be wary of. When the same problems occur repeatedly, the efficiency can be increased if the algorithm can be modified to save the results for these problems so they may be used directly when needed instead of being regenerated by recursive calls. Of course, if this requires excessive storage, then such an approach won't do. Excessive storage is needed when an excessive number of *distinct* problems must be solved and their results saved. Still, this represents a viable strategy when applicable, as is the case here.

Notice that a Fibonacci tree of depth $d \geq 2$ can be constructed even if only Fibonacci trees of depth $d - 2$ and $d - 1$ are known. All that is necessary is to create a root node and append the tree of depth $d - 2$ as its left subtree and the tree of depth $d - 1$ as its right subtree. Consequently, the Fibonacci tree of depth d can be obtained by constructing the trees for depth $0, 1, 2, \ldots, d$ in turn, while retaining only the lastest two. This gives the nonrecursive solution:

* In fact, the number of nodes will be $2F_{d+1} - 1$.

An Efficient Nonrecursive Version

If $d = 0$, then
    set `t` to null;
else if $d = 1$, then
    a. create a root node
    b. set `t` to point to the root node;
else
    c. set `tl` to null,
    d. create a root node,
    e. set `tr` to point to the root node, and
    f. for k from 2 to d,
        i. create a root node with `tl` its left subtree and `tr` its right subtree
        ii. set `t` to point to the root node
        iii. set `tl` to `tr` and `tr` to `t`.

This solution is efficient in both execution time and storage (see Exercises 16 and 17 of Chapter 4 for a related example).

Although it was possible to cut down drastically on the number of Fibonacci trees retained in this solution, such a saving is not always possible. Sometimes solutions to *all* the problems generated by recursive calls will need to be retained. Even so, when this number is not excessive and an appropriate data structure can be found in which to store and efficiently access a solution when needed, then execution time can be improved. This is another instance of what we have frequently seen: time may be traded for storage.

It is hoped that you do not feel we have been barking up the wrong trees! Perhaps you even agree with the humorist Ogden Nash:

I think that I shall never see
A billboard lovely as a tree.
Indeed, unless the billboards fall
I'll never see a tree at all.

■ Exercises

1. a. What is the minimum number of nodes that a binary tree of depth d can have?
b. What is the maximum number of nodes that a binary tree of depth d can have?

2. Suppose `t` is a binary tree with n internal nodes and m terminal nodes. `T` is a ***full binary tree*** if each of its nodes has zero or two successors. What is the relation between m and n when `t` is a full binary tree?

3. There are 0, 1, 2, and 5 distinct binary trees with, respectively, 0, 1, 2, and 3 nodes.
a. How many distinct binary trees are there with 4 nodes?
b. Can you find a formula for the number of distinct binary trees with n nodes? This formula `bt`(n) may be expressed in terms of `bt`(k) for $k < n$.

4. Modify the program segments of Section 7.2.1 so that they work correctly in all cases.

5. a. Suppose the binary tree that follows is preorder, inorder, and postorder traversed. List the order in which the nodes will be accessed for each.
b. Do you notice anything striking about the inorder listing?

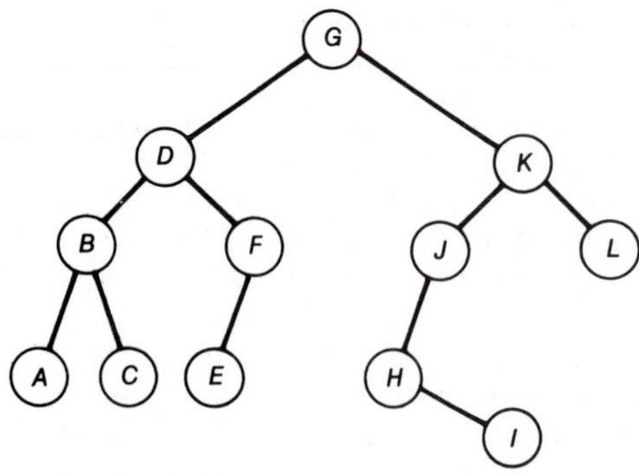

6. Prove that all terminal nodes will always be accessed in the same relative order for all three traversals.

7. a. Suppose the stack used in a pre-, in-, or postorder traversal is implemented as an array. What is the requirement for `limit` in terms of the depth of the binary tree, to guarantee that the stack is large enough for the traversal to work?

b. What is the necessary value for `limit` in order to guarantee that the traversal will work with the stack, for any binary tree with n nodes?

8. Suppose the following two binary trees are preorder and postorder traversed. The preorder and postorder listings are given for each tree.

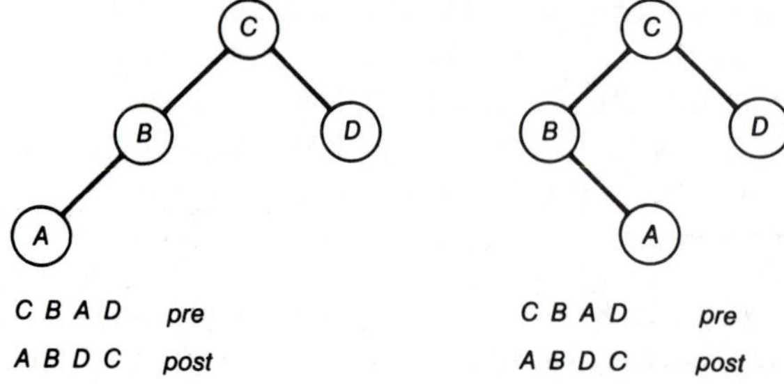

Both binary trees have identical listings. This cannot happen with preorder and inorder listings. That is, we cannot find two distinct binary trees that have identical preorder and inorder listings. The same is true for postorder and inorder listings. Find an algorithm that will create the unique binary tree that is thus determined by its preorder and inorder listings.

9. a. Can you find a way to use the left and right pointer fields of terminal and internal nodes that contain null pointers in a binary tree to create "threaded binary trees" so that they can be traversed without using a stack? (*Hint:* Consider pointers that point to the predecessor and successor of a terminal node in an inorder traversal.)

b. What about for inorder and postorder traversals?

10. Write inorder and postorder traversal routines (nonrecursive and recursive).

11. a. Suppose you wish to use a linked representation for binary trees with an array implementation as in Figure 7.10. Suppose that input is given as a name value followed by a sequence of records, each record representing a node of a binary tree. For the binary tree `fred` of Figure 7.10, the input would be

```
 5
 8   L   0
-1   O  -1
```

3	U	4
−1	S	−1
−1	T	−1

Three records appear in the input in the order in which they would be accessed by a preorder traversal. Assume the head value is read into `fred`, and `preorder traverse` is called. Write a `process` routine that will turn `preorder traverse` into a routine that reads the records of the binary tree into the `leftptr`, `info`, and `rightptr` fields properly.

b. Same as Exercise 11(a), but assume the records are given in the order in which they would be accessed in a postorder traversal.

12. The binary tree `sample` is stored using a linked representation. List the order in which its nodes will be accessed in a preorder traversal.

		leftptr	info	rightptr
	1	0	R	0
	2	3	W	4
	3	5	R	0
`sample` 7	4	0	C	0
	5	4	E	6
	6	0	T	0
	7	10	C	3
	8	6	A	3
	9	1	B	4
	10	1	O	0

13. What will be in the stack during a preorder traversal of `sample` in Exercise 12 when its rightmost node is accessed? What about when it is inorder and postorder traversed?

14. **a.** Suppose every subtree of `sample` of Exercise 12 is interchanged with its right subtree. What will `leftptr`, `info`, and `rightptr` look like?

b. What would `leftptr`, `info`, and `rightptr` look like if all the terminal nodes of `sample` were deleted in Exercise 12?

15. Suppose a binary tree is stored using the `records` array implementation as in Figure 7.10. If `tree` points to its root node, write a function to print out the sequence of pointers that specify the path in the tree to the right most node in `tree`. For example, in Figure 7.10 the rightmost node of `fred` is `1`, and the sequence of pointers to be printed out for `fred` would be 6, 1, 5.

16. **a.** If the binary tree of Figure 7.5 were represented sequentially, what numbers would be assigned to its nodes?

b. What binary tree with n nodes will require the largest array for its sequential representation?

17. When dealing with *arbitrary* binary trees, would you use linked or sequential representation? Why?

18. **a.** Write a function that will return, given a binary tree `t`, with a pointer to a terminal node of `t` containing the largest value in its information field.

b. Write a function that, given a binary tree `t` and two pointers `p` and `q` to nodes of `t`, returns a value *true* if `node.q` is a successor of `node.p` and a value *false* otherwise.

c. Write a function that does the same thing as Exercise 18(b), except that the function returns a value *true* if `node.q` is in the subtree of `node.p` and a value *false* otherwise.

19. Consider the binary tree that was produced by the transformation from a general tree to a binary tree as a general tree, and find the binary tree produced by its transformation.

20. Consider again the solution to the information retrieval problem of Chapter 6. Suppose you create a record, `r`, in memory. `R` will have a pointer field pointing to the record for a father. You can then think of `r` as a record representing the node of a binary tree.

a. Describe this binary tree.

b. What general tree would have `r` as its binary tree under the transformation of Section 7.5.1?

21. **a.** Write a function to append a binary tree `t1` to a binary tree `t2` by replacing some terminal node in `t2` at least depth by the whole tree `t1`. For example, see the figure. Use a linked representation with pointer variables.

b. What does your function do if `t1` and `t2` are the same tree?

c. How will your solution change if a sequential representation is used?

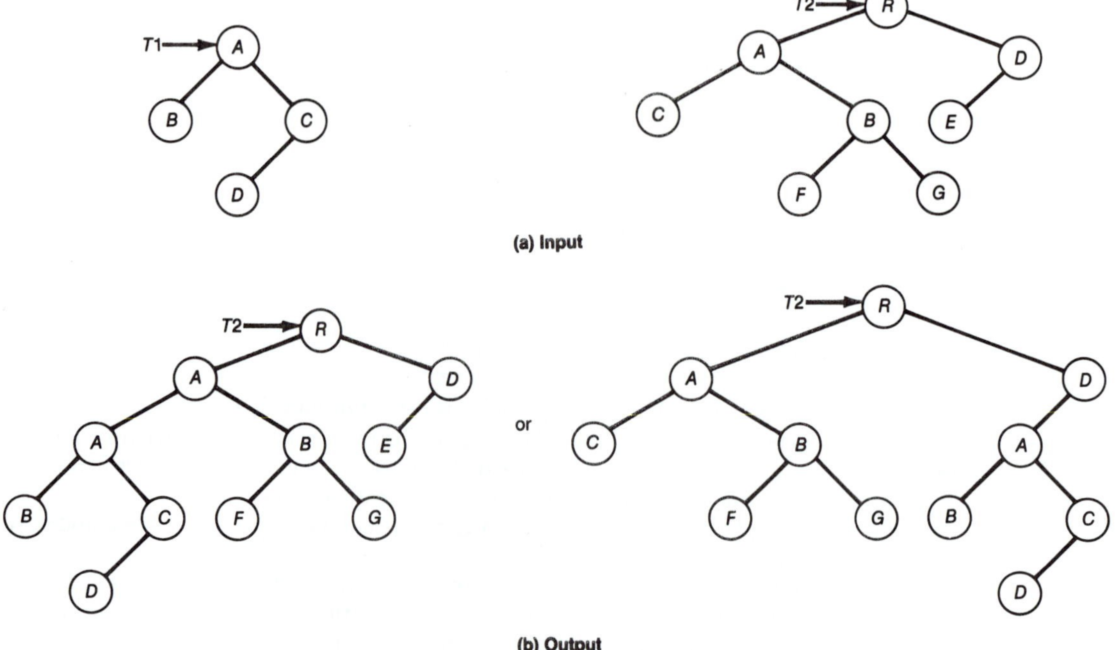

(b) Output

22. **a.** Write a routine that deletes all the terminal nodes of a binary tree.

b. Write a routine that deletes `node.q` if it is a successor of `node.p` in a binary tree.

23. **a.** Write a function to interchange all left and right subtrees of a binary tree.

b. Create a function to interchange *all* left and right subtrees, except that the interchanged version of the original tree will be created as a new tree, leaving the original tree unchanged. Assume pointer variables are used for its implementation.

24. **a.** Modify the `preorder` traversal so that it returns, in a variable `identical`, a value *true* if `t1` and `t2` point to identical trees, and a value *false* otherwise. That is, the value is *true* if the two trees have the same structure and the same information field values.

b. Do the same task, except that the binary trees need have only the same structure.

25. **a.** Suppose you are given a maze with the structure of a binary tree. The maze has a starting point and an exit. A node is associated with the starting point, with the exit, and with every point in the maze where one of two paths must be taken. The maze is given as a two-dimensional array `a`. `A[i,j]` is 1 if there is a path from node `i` to node `j` in the maze, and is 0 otherwise. There are n points in the maze. Adapt the `preorder` traversal to achieve an algorithm for solving the maze—that is, for printing out the path from the starting node to the exit node. Your solution should be detailed enough to write a function corresponding to it directly.

b. If the maze has loops, what modifications must be made in your solution so that the algorithm works correctly?

26. **a.** Modify the preorder traversal algorithm for creating a binary tree from a general tree (p. 332) and the `process` algorithm so the preorder traversal returns, in the variable `transform`, a value "true" only if a binary tree `bt` is the transformed version of a general tree `t`.

b. Modify the preorder traversal algorithm so that it produces the transformed tree by processing the nodes of `t` in breadth-first order. (*Hint:* Consider the queue.)

27. Write the function `create` used in the `process` algorithm.

28. Modify the backtracking preorder traversal algorithm so that it does a backtracking *breadth-first* traversal.

29. Suppose you are given a "map" of n cities and the distances between them. Can you find a way to modify the preorder traversal algorithm to determine the shortest distance between two cities? What is a feasible test to use to allow `feasible` to limit the execution time of the solution?

30. **a.** Suppose a general tree is given as follows:

(A(B(E, F, G), C(H), D(I(K, L, M), J)))

This corresponds to the general tree:

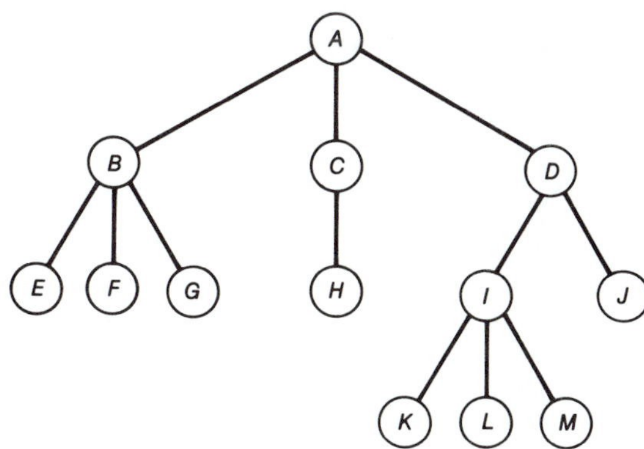

Suppose that input is given by such a parenthesized expression. Can you find an algorithm that will create the general tree from it? Assume that the general tree will be represented in memory as a collection of lists of successors, with one successor list for each node.

b. What is the connection between parenthesized expressions and a listing of nodes in the order in which they are accessed by a preorder traversal?

31. T is a binary tree. `Result(t)` is defined by

$$\texttt{result(t)} = \begin{cases} 0 & \text{if } \texttt{t} \text{ is null} \\ 1 + \texttt{result(left(t))} + \texttt{result(right(t))} & \text{otherwise} \end{cases}$$

`Left(t)` and `right(t)` are, respectively, the left and right subtrees of `t`.

a. If `t` is the binary tree that follows, then what is `result(t)`?

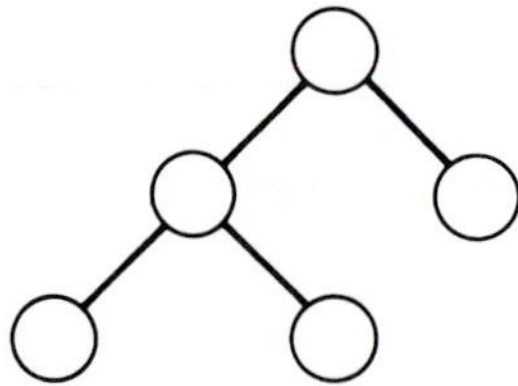

b. What does `result` do?

32. `T1` and `t2` point to binary trees represented using pointer variables.

```
check(t1,t2)
binarytreepointer t1,t2;
{
   binarytreepointer null,setnull();
   null = setnull();
   if(((t1 == null) && (t2 == null)) || ((t1 != null)
      && (t2 != null)))
      return(check(t1->leftptr,t2->leftptr)
              && check(t1->rightptr,t2->rightptr));
   else
      return(FALSE);
}
```

a. Find the function value if it is invoked for trees `t1` and `t2`.

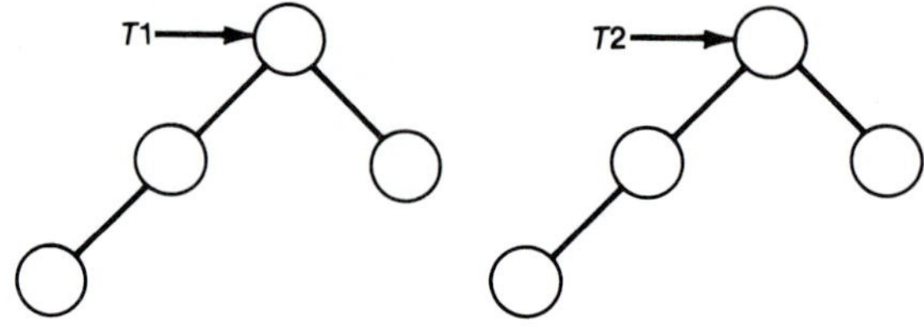

b. What does `check` do?

33. a. Find $b(4)$ where

$$b(0) = 1$$
$$b(n) = b(0) \times b(n-1) + b(1) \times b(n-2) + b(2)b(n-3) + \cdots + b(n-1) \times b(0) \qquad n > 0$$

b. Find a connection between the number of distinct binary trees with n nodes and $b(n)$.

34. a. Give a recursive definition of balanced binary trees.

b. Find a recursive definition for $F(d)$, the number of nodes of a Fibonacci tree of depth d.

35. Write a recursive function `result` corresponding to Exercise 31.

36. a. Write a recursive function `count` to return the number of terminal nodes of a binary tree.

b. Write a recursive function `terminal` to delete all terminal nodes of a binary tree using pointer variables.

37. Write a recursive routine `partialexchange` to interchange all subtrees of a binary tree whose left subtree `info` field value exceeds the right subtree value. Assume the binary tree is represented using pointer variables.
38. Write a recursive function using pointers to transform a general tree into its binary tree representation.
39. Write a recursive program that produces a solution, if one exists, to the n-queens problem.
40. Write a recursive function to produce a copy of a binary tree. Both trees should be implemented using pointers.

■ Suggested Assignments

1. Write a function to print the family tree for an individual whose family history is stored in the data base of the case study of Chapter 6. The individual is at the root of the family tree, and its subtrees are the family trees of all the individual's children. Print the tree using indentation as in Figure 7.1(a). Assume individual records are stored in dynamic memory and that the appropriate functions are available for searching and accessing the nametables. If this function is to also be executed, then this would be a good assignment for a group project.

Also discuss the connection between the lists used in the case study and the binary tree representation of a general tree.
2. Consider the problem of finding a stable pairing, given preferences, as discussed in Chapter 2. Describe a tree that represents all possible pairings, and write a backtracking traversal function to produce all stable pairings. Base your solution on the backtracking preorder traversal algorithm given in the text. Compare this solution with the solution given in Chapter 2.
3. Formulate a solution to the stable pairing problem as a traversal through all permutations of the men. Use the permutation traversal program of Chapter 4 as the basis for your algorithm. Compare this solution to your solution to Assignment 2 and also to the solution given in Chapter 2.
4. Write an efficient recursive function `fibonaccicheck(t,d,flag)`, which is to return in `d` the depth of the binary tree `t`, and with flag *true* if `t` is a Fibonacci tree and *false* otherwise.

8 Introduction to Searching and Sorting

Considers how collections of information may be stored to allow
- *efficient searches*
- *efficient traversals*

Develops efficient in-memory sorting algorithms
- *to illustrate the principles of good design in algorithm development*
- *to show how sorting is used to facilitate searching*

Worst-case and average times are developed for
- *linear search*
- *binary search*
- *maximum entry sort*
- *bubble sort*
- *insertion sort*
- *heapsort*
- *quicksort*

Illustrates the use of simulation in analyzing the execution time of a program

8.1 Overview

So far in this book, arrays, lists, binary trees, and trees—the basic data structures—have been introduced and applied to a variety of problems. Selecting the appropriate data structure requires knowing what operations are to be performed on it. The frequency with which these operations are to be performed, the characteristics of the data to be stored, and the average and worst-case time and storage requirements all combine to determine this choice. Other considerations, such as clarity and adaptability, may also serve as criteria for deciding which data structures to use. It is rarely possible to pick a data structure that is best for all criteria. Instead, trade-offs must be made.

In the case study of family relationships in Section 6.5, one of the important operations was a search of the nametable data base. At that time no decisions were made as to how the nametable data base would be structured to facilitate the search. This chapter and the next will show that many implementations are possible and that the appropriate choice is determined by the kinds of operations to be performed on the data base. Nametable might be organized in many ways. It can be implemented as an array, a list, a binary search tree, a balanced binary search tree, or a hash table. The techniques used to create and search these structures are introduced in this and the next chapter.

Searching and sorting masses of data to retrieve specific information and organize it for manipulation and presentation are nothing new. These basic operations were performed and studied before the advent of computers. Volumes have been written on these topics, yet they are still being researched. Even the general public and the press are evidently interested in searching, as you can see from the following letter and response:

> Dear Ann Landers:
>
> Why is it that whenever I lose anything, it is always in the last place I look?
>
> —*Dizzy Lizzy*
>
> Dear Liz:
> Because when you find it you stop looking—and that's the last place you looked.

Although searching and sorting may appear mundane, the speed with which they can be carried out largely determines whether a particular application of the computer is practical (and "cost-effective") or not. Estimates indicate that about one-fourth of the processing time in computer centers is spent just sorting. The relation between sorting and searching will become apparent in this chapter. If one can be done faster, so can the other. The choice of data structures is always important in algorithm design and is the key to the evolution of good (that is, efficient) searching and sorting procedures. The basic data structures studied in the preceding chapters (arrays, lists, and binary trees) are used in the design of efficient procedures.

Normally, the objects stored, searched for, and sorted are records. In sorting, one field of the records, called the ***sort key,*** is chosen as the basis for the sort. Thus, in a payroll application, an employee name field might be the key for an alphabetical ordering, while a salary field might serve as the basis for a sort to determine an ordering by amount of earnings. At times the sort key can be a combination of fields. As an example, we may desire to sort with name as the primary key and zip code as the secondary key. For simplicity it will be assumed in this chapter that the objects being sorted are integer numbers. However, any variable type could have been assumed. For sorting purposes, the only requirement is that, given any two objects, it is possible to tell which precedes the other.

Searching normally involves comparing records to a given ***search key*** value. The goal is to determine whether there exists among the records of the data base a record with key equal to that of the search key. If the key value can be matched, then a pointer to the record with the matching value must be returned. The basic principle for shortening search times is to organize the data base so that the search can be focused quickly on the part of the data base that will contain the desired record, if it is present.

The chapter first explores simple *linear, binary,* and *interpolation searches* and a number of elementary sorting algorithms, such as the *bubble sort* and the *insertion sort*. These lead to more advanced methods for sorting based on a special binary tree called a *heap*. Next, an application of recursion yields another fast sort, *quicksort*.

Some of the algorithms developed in the text are fairly complex and difficult, if not impossible, to analyze mathematically. For this reason the last topic considered in the chapter is the use of simulation as a tool in discovering the behavior and efficiency of such complex algorithms.

The chapter concludes with a summary of the strengths and weaknesses of each approach introduced. Knuth [1973b] and Wirth [1976] discuss many searching and sorting algorithms that are not dealt with in this text. Knuth also contains mathematical analyses of many of these algorithms.

8.2 Elementary Searches

Three simple searches are applicable when records are stored in arrays: (1) linear search, (2) binary search, and (3) interpolation search. You probably have all used these methods in everyday activities. Understanding their limitations and how they work will help you see the need for the more complex structures and algorithms of later sections.

8.2.1 Linear Search

A ***linear search*** is so named because it proceeds in sequence, linearly through an array. Suppose `data` in Figure 8.1 is an array of integers.* The task is to determine

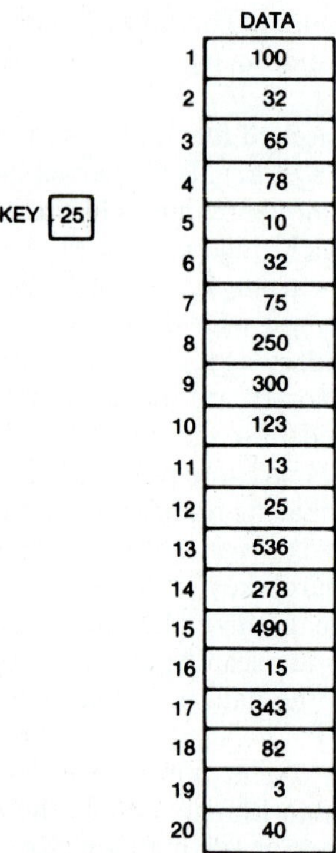

Figure 8.1 An Array of Integers to Be Searched for the Key Value 25

* To simplify the explanation in this chapter, the 0th array position will be ignored, and data stored in arrays will start in position 1 unless otherwise noted.

whether the number stored in the variable **key** is in the array, and if so, what its index is.

One obvious method would be to traverse the **data** array, checking each element of **data** to see if it contains the same value as **key**. If an element currently being processed did contain the same value as **key**, its index would simply be returned, and the search would be complete. Arriving at the end of **data** without having found the **key** value would mean that no element with that value is stored in the array. This procedure is easily implemented using a loop structure (as in the following function). The worst-case time required for its execution will be of the order n, written $O(n)$, where n is the length of the **data** array. In particular, if the value being sought is in element i of the array, it will take $O(i)$ time to find it. The linear search is implemented as follows:

```
#define MAX 100
typedef struct
{
   int key;
}record;
typedef record recordarray[MAX];

linearsearch(data,n,key,pfound,ploc)
/* Searches the n records stored in
   the array data for the search key.
   Found will be true only if a record
   is present with key field equal to
   the search key value and then loc
   will contain its array index.
*/
recordarray data;
int n,key,*pfound,*ploc;
{
   *ploc = 1;

   while ((*ploc <= n) && (data[*ploc].key != key))
      (*ploc)++;


   *pfound = (*ploc < n + 1);
}
```

traverses through the `n` *records in the data array*

sets `loc` *to index the first record*

tests for another record to be searched and if so, whether that record has the search key value

`found` *should be true only if* `loc` $<$ `n` + *1*

A special but common case is when the search is always for a key known to be stored in the array, and each key stored is distinct and equally likely to be the search key. This is like standing in front of a locked door with a bunch of keys. You need to find the key that opens the door from among n keys in arbitrary order on your key-ring. The average time for such a search would be $O(n/2)$. That is, on the average, you would look at half the keys, or half the elements of the array, before finding the right one.

Thus the procedure called *linear search* is so named, not only because it proceeds linearly through an array, but also because its processing time increases linearly with n; when n is doubled, the time required to complete the search is doubled.

8.2.2 Saving Time: A Neat Trick

Occasionally programming tricks can be used to enhance efficiency. In this case paying attention to some details produces a trick that can pay off by saving processing time. The straightforward implementation of the linear search requires a test (`loc` $\leq n$) for the end of the array before checking the next element. This is true whether the implementation is a **for** loop or a **while** loop. However, it is possible to avoid performing this test.

Place the search key in element $n + 1$ of `data`. Then, in implementing the linear search, there is no need to test for the end of the array before checking the next element. Since the array is now considered to be $(n + 1)$ elements in length, we are certain to find the search key before we "fall off the end." After the loop is exited, note the element in which `key` was found, and test to see if it was the $(n + 1)$th element, which means that the search was unsuccessful. Thus only one test (`data[loc].key != key`) must be performed. This saves n tests in unsuccessful searches, and `i` tests in successful searches, when the search key appears in element `i` of `data`. This simple modification of the basic linear search can easily produce significant time savings (20 to 50 percent). In general, whenever loops are modified to reduce the tests or processing they perform, execution time is saved *each* time through the loop. The more efficient linear search implementation appears as follows:

```
#define MAX 100
typedef struct
{
   int key;
}record;
typedef record recordarray[MAX];

linearsearch(data,n,key,pfound,ploc)        ] faster traversal
/* Searches the n records stored in
   the array data for the search key.
   Found will be true only if a record
   is present with key field equal to
   the search key value and then loc
   will contain its array index.
*/
recordarray data;
int n,key,*pfound,*ploc;
{
   *ploc = 1;
   data[n + 1].key = key;                   ] stores the search key as a "last" record in
                                              data
   while (data[*ploc].key != key)           ] no need to test for another record
      (*ploc)++;
   *pfound = (*ploc < n + 1);
}
```

Another way to save time in a linear search is to order the records in the array. One way to do this is to store them in decreasing order of key value. The linear search can then be modified by terminating the search as soon as a record is reached whose key value is less than the search key. The desired record cannot be in the array past that point. Although this results in extra comparisons for successful searches, time is saved overall when unsuccessful searches occur frequently enough.

It is also possible, if the frequency with which records will be retrieved is known, to store the records in decreasing order of retrieval frequency. The most frequently retrieved record will then be at the top of the array. This approach significantly improves search efficiency when the desired record is likely to be near the top of the array. In fact, if the frequencies decrease rapidly enough, the average search time for the linear search will be a small constant.

8.2.3 Binary Search

Certainly no one does a linear search to look for a phone number in the telephone directory. Imagine trying to do so in the directory for New York City or any other large city! But there are ways to carry out the search so that the name is found in a few seconds, even from among a few million names. The structure of the telephone directory is the clue to the solution, which takes advantage of the alphabetical ordering of the entries in the phone book.

Assume that the numbers stored in `data` are arranged in decreasing order, as in Figure 8.2. They are said to be ***sorted*** in decreasing order. Since a telephone book is sorted in alphabetical order, one of the things most people do by habit when using the telephone directory is to flip the directory open toward the front, middle, or back depending on the location in the alphabet of the name being sought. If the page opened to has names farther down in the alphabet, the search name cannot be on that page or anywhere in the directory to its right. It can only be to the left of the selected page. This process of elimination is behind the search technique called *binary search*. It is not difficult to see why this search technique is called ***binary***. Every time a test is made in the search, there are two choices. In the telephone book example, search either half of the remaining pages for the name.

A binary search is also a good strategy for winning the game of twenty questions, which requires guessing the identity of an object after finding out if it is in the animal, the mineral, or the vegetable category. Twenty questions with "yes" or "no" answers are allowed. Selecting each question so that about half the remaining possibilities are eliminated, no matter what the answer, is best. (For example, given the animal category, "Is the object male or female?") In this way 2^{20}, or over a million, objects can be distinguished.

In twenty questions it is difficult to select a question that makes close to a 50-50 split of the remaining possibilities. However, if you are asked to determine a number known to lie between 1 and 1024 by asking yes-no questions, it is easy to do so. Ask, "Is it greater than 512?" and continue splitting the remaining possibilities in half. No more than 10 such questions are needed to find the number from among the 2^{10} (1024) initial possibilities. Similarly, when searching for a specific key value among 2^n records, at most n key comparisons are needed to determine

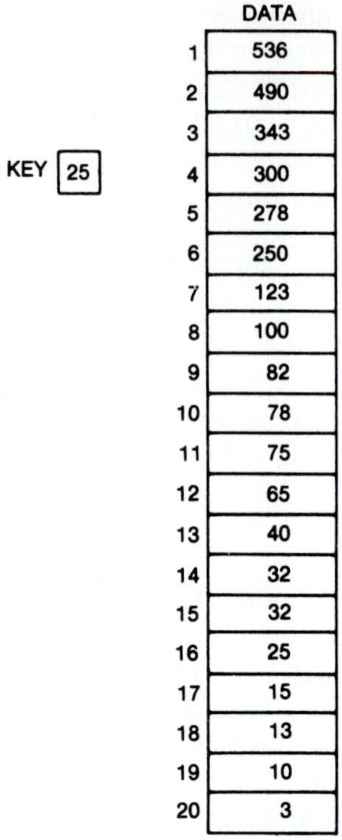

KEY 25

	DATA
1	536
2	490
3	343
4	300
5	278
6	250
7	123
8	100
9	82
10	78
11	75
12	65
13	40
14	32
15	32
16	25
17	15
18	13
19	10
20	3

Figure 8.2 Array of Integers Sorted in Decreasing Order

whether it is present, as long as each comparison splits the remaining collection of records into two parts that differ in size by at most one.

When searching data stored in arbitrary order in an array, there is no reason to expect the search key to be in any particular region of the array. However, when the data have been stored in *sorted* order, the situation is different. It is possible to check the middle element to see if the search key is there. If it is, the program would note its location and terminate the search. If the key is not there, then if the search key is greater than the key in the middle element, eliminate the middle element and all elements below it from consideration. If the desired record is in `data` at all, it must be above the middle element. Similarly, if the search key is less than the key in the middle element, eliminate the middle element and all elements above it. In any event, at most half the elements remain to be considered, and the same procedure can then be applied to the appropriate half: either elements 1 to `[mid-1]` or elements `[mid+1]` to `n`. `Mid` is a variable that points to the middle element.

For example, if `mid` is 10, then the search key value, 25, is not greater than `data[mid]`, 78. Hence, if it is in `data` at all, it must be between positions `mid+1` and `n`—11 and 20. Taking 15 as the middle element of these, the new `mid` value is 15. `Key` is less than `data[mid]`, 32. Hence we need to search between `mid+1` and 20—16 and 20. With a new `mid` value of 18, `key` is greater than `data[mid]`, 13. Now search only between 16 and 17. The next `mid` value is 16, and the `key` is found.

The basic structure of the binary search algorithm is a *loop,* as shown in the following function.

```
#define TRUE 1
#define FALSE 0
#define MAX 100
typedef struct
{
   int key;
}record;
typedef record recordarray[MAX];

binarysearch(data,n,key,pfound,ploc)
/* Searches the n records stored in order by
   key field value(largest first) in the array
   data for the search key. Found will be true
   only if a record is present with key field
   equal to the search key value and then loc
   will contain its array index.
*/
recordarray data;
int n,key,*pfound,*ploc;
{
   int top,mid,bottom;
   top = 1;                                   ] top and bottom initialized
   bottom = n;
   *pfound = FALSE;
   *ploc = 0;
   while ((top <= bottom) && !(*pfound))      ] test for more records to be
      {                                         searched and search key not yet
                                                found
         mid = (top + bottom)/2;              ] update mid
         if (data[mid].key == key)            ] if search key found
            {
              *pfound = TRUE;                 ] set found
              *ploc = mid;                    ] set loc
            }
         else if (data[mid].key < key)        ] else if entry pointed to by mid is
            bottom = mid - 1;                   less than search key,
                                                move bottom up to eliminate
                                                lower half from consideration
         else                                 ] else move top down to eliminate
            top = mid + 1;                      upper half from consideration
      }
}
```

`Mid` is initialized to the middle element of `data`, `top` to 1, and `bottom` to `n`. `Top` and `bottom` are variables that point to the top and bottom elements of the consecutive elements left to be searched, all others having been eliminated from consideration. In the loop body, test for `key` equal to `data[mid]`. If the equality is true, the program exits the loop and the search is done, since `key` has been found at element `mid`. If not, `top` and `bottom` must be updated to reflect the new sequence of elements that are to be searched. This updating must set `bottom` to `mid` whenever `key` is greater than `data[mid]`, and `top` to `mid + 1` otherwise. The test for continuing the loop involves checking whether `key` was found, and whether any elements are left to be searched between `top` and `bottom`. The search is terminated as soon as the desired entry is found or as soon as it is concluded that the entry is not present. `Loc` will be zero if the key value was not found and will index its location in `data` if found.

8.2.4 Timing the Binary Search

How much time is required by the binary search algorithm in the worst case? Each pass through the loop requires at most a constant amount of work. The time to execute the algorithm will then be determined by the number of passes through the loop, plus, of course, a constant time for initialization and finalization. What is the greatest number of loop iterations executed?

In each pass through the loop, the search involves at most half the elements that were under consideration during the preceding pass through the loop. Starting with n elements, after one pass through the loop at most $1/2n$ elements are left, after two passes through the loop at most $1/2(1/2)n$ elements, after three passes at most $1/2(1/2)^2n$ elements, and after k passes at most $1/2(1/2)^{k-1}n$ or $1/2^k n$ elements. This number, $1/2^k n$, is less than 1 when $-k + \lg n < 0$ or when $k > \lg n$. This means that the loop cannot be executed more than $\lceil \lg n \rceil$ times. If n is 20, for example, then $\lg 20 = 4.32$, and $\lceil 4.32 \rceil$ is 5. Thus in the worst case, the binary search is $O(\lg n)$. If each record stored is searched with equal frequency, then the average time to find a stored record is actually about $(\lg n) - 1$. (The proof is not given here.)

8.2.5 Interpolation Search

Sometimes, telephone directories, like dictionaries and encyclopedias, have tabs so that users can flip open the book to the beginning of the section containing entries with a specific first letter and gauge whether to search toward the front, middle, or back pages of the section. The tabs have been inserted or interpolated within the data to guide the search. This represents a generalization of the binary search called the ***interpolation search.*** The topic will not be pursued in detail, but note that this technique allows the elimination of greater fractions of the remaining names than does a binary search. Not surprisingly, this tends to reduce the execution time.

8.2.6 Efficiency Comparisons

When n is large, the binary search takes much less time, in the worst case, than the linear search. This is because it makes $\lg n$ rather than n comparisons, going through its loop body $\lg n$ rather than n times. However, the steps performed in the loop body of the binary search are more complex and more time-consuming than the steps performed in the loop body for the linear search. Hence it is possible, for smaller values of n, that the linear search will be faster. Similarly, the interpolation search will need to perform more complex steps in its loop body, even though it may need to loop fewer times than the binary search.

Of course the binary and extrapolation searches require sorted data. When only a few searches are to be made or when n is small, it may not pay to spend time to sort the data first. For repeated searching or large n, the efficiencies of the binary and extrapolation searches easily overcome the cost of sorting.

8.3 Elementary Sorts

We now turn our attention to three simple sorting methods applicable to records stored in arrays: (1) maximum entry sort, (2) bubble sort, and (3) insertion sort. They are also applicable to records stored in lists. Understanding their limitations and how they work sets the stage for the more complex structures and algorithms of the next section.

8.3.1 Maximum Entry Sort

Perhaps the most straightforward way to sort numbers in an array into decreasing* order is to begin by placing the largest number in element 1. The next largest number is then placed into element 2, and so on. The ***maximum entry sort*** repeatedly finds the next largest array entry and places it in its proper position in the array. Suppose the point has been reached in this procedure where the k largest numbers have been properly placed into the first k elements of the array `data`. Assume a variable `next` points to the element of data into which the next largest element is to be placed. `Next` must now be updated to `next + 1` so that it contains the value $k + 1$, as indicated in Figure 8.3.

Assume that a function `maxloc` exists, with parameters `data`, `next`, and `n`, the array length. `Maxloc` returns with its value indexing the largest element between the `next`th and the `n`th elements of `data`. The sort may then be obtained by a loop in which `maxloc` is invoked ($n - 1$ times, with `next` taking on values 1, 2, . . . , $n - 1$, respectively, on each call. Within the loop, when each call to `maxloc` is made, an exchange between `data[next]` and `data[maxloc]` occurs.

`Maxloc` might be implemented by traversing the elements `next` to `n` of `data`. Each time a new element is accessed, it is compared to a variable, `largest`, containing the largest entry seen so far in this traversal. If the new element is greater than `largest`, `largest` is set to the new element value, and `maxloc` is set to point to the location of the new element in `data`.

This algorithm is probably similar to what most peole do instinctively when confronted with a small sorting problem. It may be implemented as in the procedure `maxentrysort`.

---

* The sorting programs assume that decreasing order is desired. They can easily be modified to sort in increasing order.

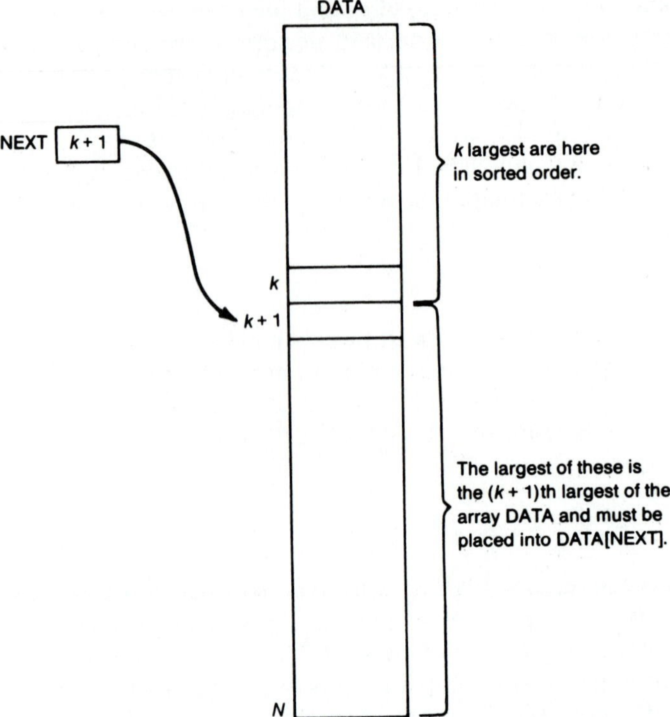

Figure 8.3 Ready to Determine the Next Largest

```
#define MAX 100
typedef struct
{
   int key;
}record;
typedef record recordarray[MAX];

maxloc(data,next,n)
/* Returns the array index of the
   largest entry in data between the
   entries indexed by next and n.
*/
recordarray data;
int next,n;
{
   int largest,i,tmaxloc;
   tmaxloc = next;
   largest = data[next].key;
   for (i = next + 1; i <= n; i++)
      if (data[i].key > largest)          ] comparison
         {
            tmaxloc = i;
            largest = data[i].key;
```

```
            return(tmaxloc);
        }
}

maxentrysort(data,n)
/* Sorts the n records stored in array data
   in descending order.
*/
recordarray data;
int n;
{
   int next,loc;
   for (next=1; next<=n - 1; next++)
      {
         loc = maxloc(data,next,n);
         interchange(data,next,loc);
      }
}
```

interchange

For the simple record used here for illustration, the interchange function is as follows.

```
interchange(data,i,j)
/* Interchanges the entries of
   array data indexed by i and j.
*/
recordarray data;
int i,j;
{
   record tempdata;
   tempdata.key = data[i].key;
   data[i].key = data[j].key;
   data[j].key = tempdata.key;
}
```

How much time does this implementation of the maximum entry sort take? One interchange is made on each call to **maxloc** for a total of $n - 1$ interchanges. The number of comparisons is $(n - k)$ on the call to **maxloc**, when **next** has the value k. The total number of comparisons is $(n - 1) + (n - 2) + \cdots + 2 + 1$, which sums to $[n(n - 1)]/2$. Thus the time is determined by the time of the $(n - 1)$ interchanges plus the time of the $[n(n - 1)]/2$ comparisons. Each interchange takes a constant amount of time, and each comparison takes, at most, a constant amount of time. The result is $O(n^2)$ time. This means that if n is doubled or tripled, the time will increase by a factor of about 2^2, or 4, and 3^2, or 9, respectively, when n is large. For $n = 10^5$, the time is roughly proportional to $1/2\ 10^{10}$, which is within a factor of 100 of 10^{13}, the guide for feasibility presented in Chapter 1. Quicker algorithms are obviously needed for large n, and even perhaps for small n. The next elementary sort technique offers some improvement.

8.3.2 Bubble Sort

The ***bubble sort*** gets its name from the way smaller entries "sink" to the bottom of the array during the sort while larger entries "bubble up" to the top. To carry out the bubble sort on the array shown in Figure 8.4(a), traverse the array, comparing two adjacent elements, starting with the first two, and ending with the last two. If the $[i + 1]$th element value exceeds the ith, interchange the two element values. When a traversal is completed, it is called a ***pass*** through the array. Continue making passes until a pass occurs in which no interchanges are required.

In the example, after pass 1, the array looks like Figure 8.4(b). Since at least one interchange was made, another pass is made, yielding Figure 8.4(c). Again, at least one interchange was made, so the program must make another pass.

Will this process continue forever making passes, or eventually stop? Clearly, once it stops since no interchanges were made on the last pass, the array is sorted. If any number were out of order, at least one interchange would have been made during that pass.

Notice that after the first pass the smallest entry, 3, was at the bottom of the array. After the second pass the two smallest entries, 10 and 3, were in order at the bottom of the array. This was not accidental. Notice that the two smallest entries will never be moved, and the third smallest element (13 in this case) will be

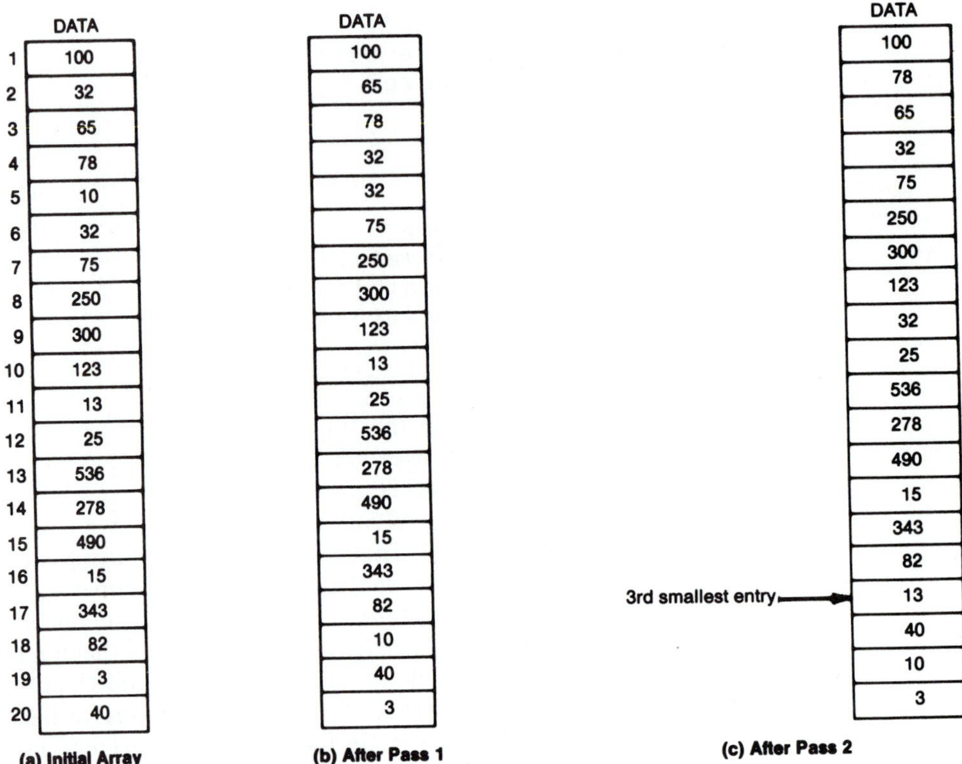

Figure 8.4 Bubble Sort

encountered on the next pass. Once it is encountered, it will always be interchanged with the adjacent lower record to which it is compared. It will eventually come to rest just above the second smallest entry.

In general, after the kth pass, the k smallest entries will be in order in the bottom k elements of the array. Of course, more than the k smallest may be in order at this point, but only k can be guaranteed. Hence the array will be in sorted order after at most $n - 1$ passes. The procedure can therefore be modified to compare down to only the $[n - k]$th element on the kth pass. The bubble sort is implemented with the following function.

```
#define TRUE 1
#define FALSE 0
#define MAX 100
typedef struct
{
   int key;
}record;
typedef record recordarray[MAX];

bubblesort(data,n)
/* Sorts the n records stored in array data
   in descending order.
*/
recordarray data;
int n;
{
   int i,done;
   done = FALSE;
   while (!done)
      {
         done = TRUE;
         for (i=1;i<=n-1;i++)
            if (data[i + 1].key > data[i].key)
               {
                  interchange(data,i,i + 1);
                  done = FALSE;
               }
      }
}
```

8.3.3 Timing the Bubble Sort

If the array were initially given in sorted order, only one pass would be required, and the time would be proportional to n. If the array were initially given in *reverse* sorted order, then $n - 1$ passes would be required, with $(n - 1 - k)$ interchanges and comparisons. This is the worst case, and takes time determined by the $\Sigma_{k=1}^{n-1} (n - k)$ interchanges and comparisons. This sum is $(n - 1) + (n - 2) + \cdot\ \cdot\ \cdot + 1$ or $[n(n - 1)]/2$ interchanges and comparisons. The worst-case time for the bubble sort is $O(n^2)$, just as for the maximum entry sort. However, the maximum entry sort will always take time $O(n^2)$, since the number of comparisons it makes is not dependent on the data. The time taken by the bubble sort thus varies from $O(n)$ for sorted data to $O(n^2)$ for reverse sorted data. The more ordered the initial data, the shorter the time.

8.3.4 Insertion Sort

The next sort to be considered is insertion sort. An ***insertion sort*** works by assuming that all entries in the array are already in sorted order and inserting the next entry in its proper place in the order. Figure 8.5 presents an example of an insertion sort.

In this example the same array, `data`, is used as for the bubble sort. Each record is processed in turn, starting from the second. Figure 8.5(a) represents the situation after processing of the first six records. The seventh is yet to be processed. It is processed, as are all the other records, by assuming the preceding records are already in sorted order. Notice that records 1–6 are in order. To insert the seventh record, 75, into its proper place among the first seven records, compare record 7 with its predecessor, record 6. Since 75 exceeds 10, it should go somewhere higher up in the array, so compare it to the predecessor of record 6, record 5. Since 75 exceeds 32, compare it to the predecessor of record 5, record 4.

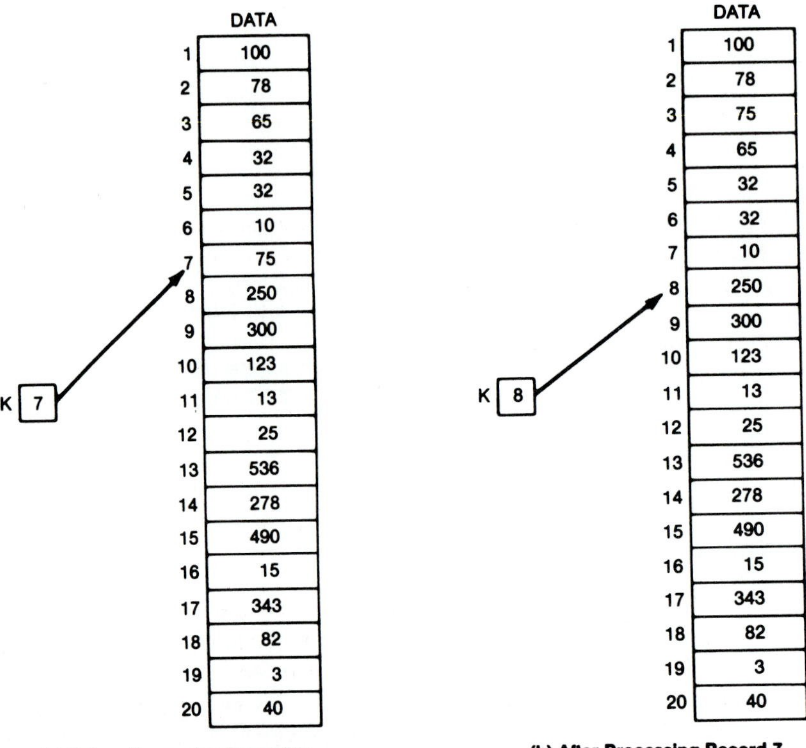

(a) Before Processing Record 7

(b) After Processing Record 7

Figure 8.5 Insertion Sort

Again, 75 exceeds that element's value of 32, so compare it to its predecessor's value, 65. The last comparison is with 78. Since 75 does not exceed 78, record 7 must be inserted between record 2, where 78 is now, and record 3. To do this, move records 3 to 6 down one element, respectively, and place 75 in record 3. The result is Figure 8.5(b).

`K` has been updated by 1, so it points to the next record to be inserted. This algorithm for an insertion sort can be described by a loop structure in which `k` varies from 2 to `n`, as in the following function.

```
#define TRUE 1
#define FALSE 0
#define MAX 100
typedef struct
{
   int key;
}record;
typedef record recordarray[MAX];

insertionsort(data,n)
/* Sorts the n records stored in array data
   in descending order.
*/
recordarray data;
int n;
{
   int k,i,inserted;
   for (k=2;k<=n; k++)
      {
         i = k;
         inserted = FALSE;
         while ((i > 1) && !inserted)
         if (data[i - 1].key < data[i].key)
            {
               interchange(data,i,i - 1);
               i--;
            }
         else
            inserted = TRUE;
      }
}
```

traversal to "insert" the `k`*th record*

Within the loop, process the `k`th record by inserting it properly among the top `k` elements. This may be accomplished by another loop, in which record `k` is compared to each consecutive predecessor until it does not exceed the current predecessor record. It is inserted at that point in the array. As an exercise, you should modify the **`insertionsort`** program to incorporate the programming trick of Section 8.2.2. In Table 8.1 (see Section 8.7), this is referred to as the *modified* insertion sort.

8.3.5 Timing the Insertion Sort

If the initial array were given in sorted order, the insertion of the kth record would require one comparison and no insertions. The total time would be $O(n - 1)$. If the initial array were given in reverse sorted order, the insertion of the kth record would require $(k - 1)$ comparisons, and the kth record would have to be inserted at the top of the array. To accomplish this, each of the $(k - 1)$ records must be moved down one element. The total time will be the time for the $1 + 2 + \cdots + (n - 1)$ comparisons, plus the time for the $1 + 2 + \cdots + (n - 1)$ shifts down. Consequently, the total time is $O(n^2)$. This represents the worst case. Again we see that the time can vary with n^2 for large n. The insertion sort, like the bubble sort, performs better the closer the initial data is to being sorted. If each of the $n!$ possible initial orderings of the array with n distinct entries is equally likely to occur, then the average time for all three of the sorts considered so far is also $O(n^2)$.

In the three implementations for the sorting algorithms, it was assumed that the interchanges taking place were actually interchanges of records. When records are large, it takes appreciably more time to move a record than it does to move a single pointer to the record. Consequently significant amounts of time can be saved by keeping an array, `p`, of indexes or pointers to the records. The entries of this array can then be kept in order, so that `p[i]` indexes or points to the `i`th record in sorted order. Interchanging indexes or pointers takes less time than for records but uses more memory (which is an added expense). This is another example of trading time for storage. In the procedures shown for maximum entry sort, bubble sort, and insertion sort, the interchange operations would then apply to the array `p`, and the comparison operations would apply to the actual records indexed or pointed to by `i`.

8.3.6 Attempted Improvements

The next question is, can we improve the insertion sort? We could try to improve it by changing how the search is done for the correct location of the kth entry. In effect, the insertion sort traversed *linearly* through records $[k - 1]$ to 1 to insert the kth record. Instead, we could do a *binary search* of the consecutive elements 1 to $[k - 1]$. We will then know where to insert the kth record. This will reduce the $1 + 2 + \cdots + (n - 1)$ comparisons to $\lg 2 + \lg 3 + \cdots + \lg (n - 1)$, which is about $n \lg n$. It does not, however, alleviate the need for the $1 + 2 + \cdots + (n - 1)$ shifts due to the insertions, so the time is still $O(n^2)$.

What else can be tried to improve the insertion sort? Aha, lists! Recall that lists are convenient for insertions, so simply represent the records in a list rather than an array. Then, once you know where to insert a record, merely change two pointers. Thus the $1 + 2 + \cdots + (n - 1)$ or $[n(n - 1)]1/2$ insertion time is reduced to time $O(n)$. The list, coupled with the binary search reduction in comparison time to $n \lg n$, seems to give a new implementation of the insertion sort with worst-case time $n \lg n$. The fly in this ointment is that the ability to do a binary search has disappeared. It is no longer possible to locate the middle record by selection, which is what makes the binary search with sorted arrays so fast. Just the first record's location is known; the middle record can be found only by traversing the list and counting records until the middle one is reached.

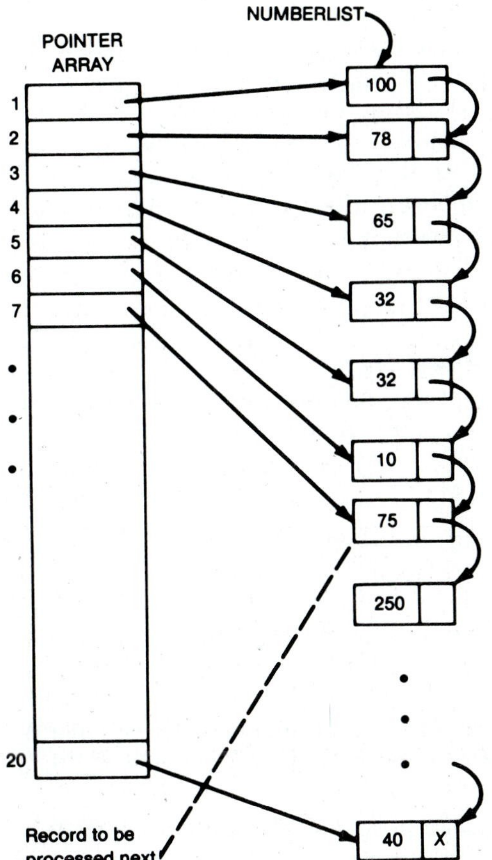

Figure 8.6 Selection of Records by Means of a Pointer Array

Wait! We are not yet defeated in our quest for a faster insertion sort. Use a pointer array, assuming enough storage is available, to tell where all the records are on the list. This allows selection of the list records as in Chapter 2. The situation is then as shown in Figure 8.6.

`Numberlist` is the head of the list of records in the illustration. Suppose the first six records have been properly processed as in the insertion sort, and the seventh is to be processed next. A binary search can now be done, since the middle record, among 1 to 6, will be indexed by the middle entry of elements 1 to 6 of the pointer array. Thus it is possible, in lg 6 time, to determine where the seventh record is to be inserted. The insertion will require the changing of two pointers. But here's the rub! To maintain the pointer array, it must have its seventh element inserted in the corresponding position of the pointer array. We have merely succeeded in transferring the insertion problem to the pointer array; we have not eliminated it!

Although these attempts to find a faster sorting algorithm have so far not been successful, they provide insight into the binary search and sorting problems. First, notice that except for the binary search, all the searching and sorting algorithms so far considered may be applied to records stored in lists as well as in arrays. Observe that to achieve both a search in binary search time (lg n) and fast insertions and deletions, a linked type structure is needed, as well as some way to eliminate from consideration a significant fraction of the records. A second observation is that the original insertion sort would be faster if the length of the array in which each insertion is made were shorter. We must somehow break up the array of records to be sorted, so that the individual insertions do not involve *all* of the previous records. These observations lead to the ideas behind heapsort and quicksort, two faster sorting algorithms.

8.4 Heapsort: A Faster Sort

In this section and the next, two less obvious but faster sorts are considered. These two sorts, heapsort and quicksort, were developed from different points of view and as a result have different advantages.

8.4.1 Heapsorts

Heapsorts use the concept of a heap. A ***heap*** is a binary tree with the property that all records stored in nodes are in sorted order along the path from each node back to the root. The tree of Figure 8.7 is not a heap. Its records are *not* in sorted order along the path from each node to the root. For example, the path from node 10 (where 123 is stored) to the root is not in sorted order. That path has records 123, 10, 32 and 100. (The nodes in this chapter are numbered like the nodes on trees in Chapter 7 and are referred to by their number.) Notice that the tree has the same information as the `data` array, but the information has been spread out along different paths.

Figure 8.8(a) is a heap storing the same information. It is one of many heaps that can be created to store the information. Since the path from every node to the root is in sorted order, the record at the root of a heap must be at least as great as any other record in the tree. The same holds for all subtrees. The record at the

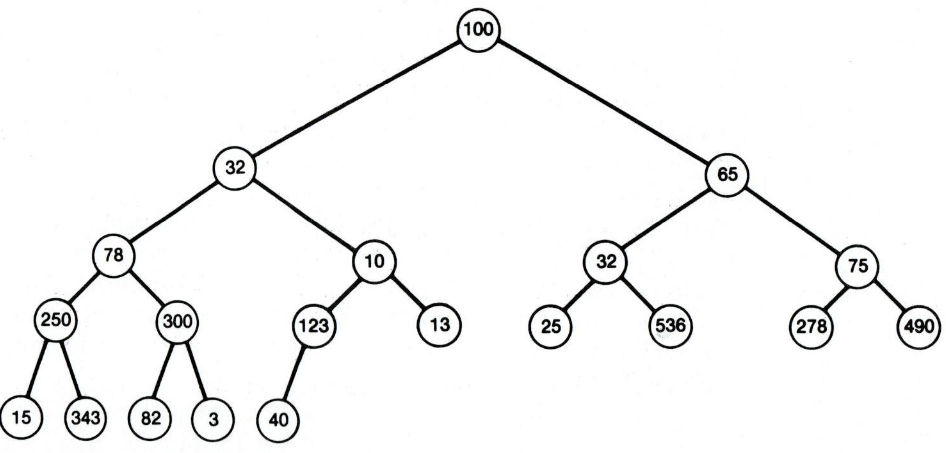

Figure 8.7 Not a Heap

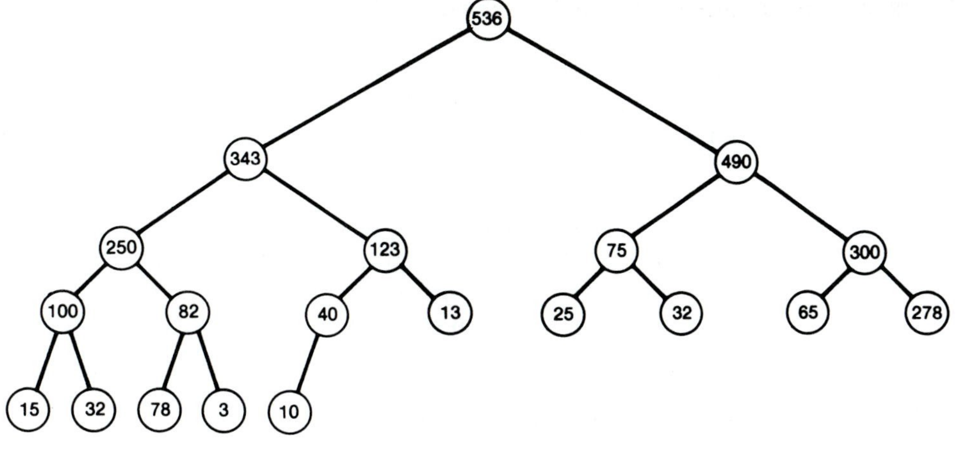

(a) A heap

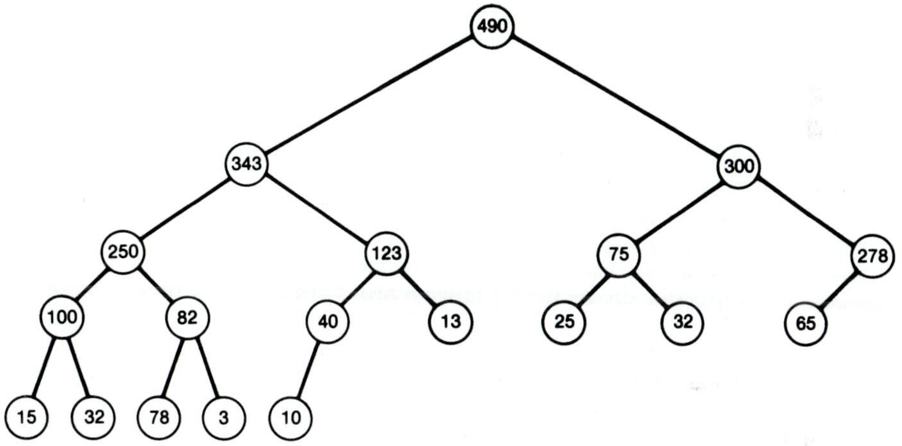

(b) After Removing 536 and Reheaping

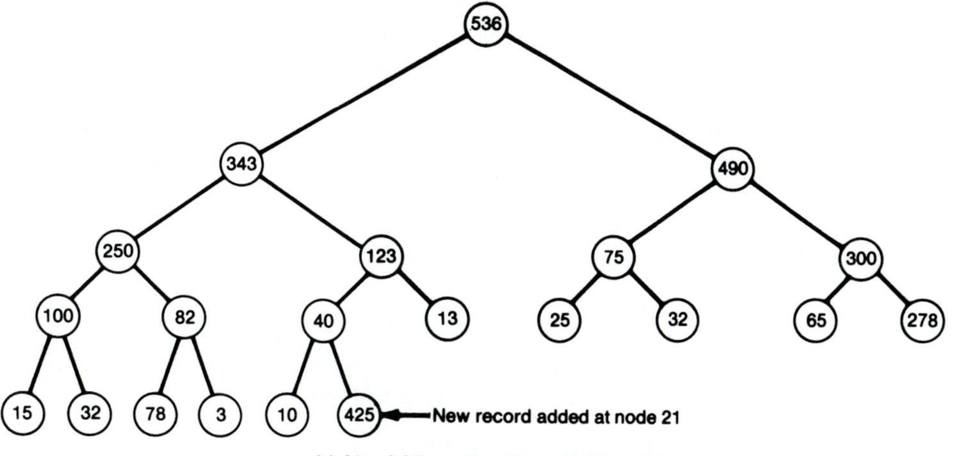

(c) After Adding a New Record to Heap (a)

Figure 8.8 Heaps

root of any subtree must be at least as great as any other record in the subtree. The root record may then be taken as the first record in a sorted output of the information stored in the tree.

To sort, output 536 first, and then remove it from the tree. Now suppose that somehow the records can be rearranged in the tree to create a new heap—a process called ***reheaping.*** The result might look like Figure 8.8(b). This tree has one less node than the original. Clearly, this process of removing the root can be repeated, outputting it next in the sorted output, and reheaping. When all the records have been output in sorted order, the remaining tree will be the null binary tree (the heap will be empty), and a sort will have been obtained. The algorithm is stated simply:

To perform a heapsort:

1. Create a heap.
2. While the heap is not empty
   a. output the record at the root of the heap,
   b. remove it from the heap, and
   c. reheap.

As stated, the algorithm is not detailed enough. It does not specify how to create a heap (step 1) or how to reheap (step 2).

8.4.2 Creating a Heap

Consider the heap of Figure 8.8(a) with one new record as in Figure 8.8(c). Notice that all paths are in order, except for the path from the new record at node 21 to the root. This prevents this tree from being a heap. To make it a heap, the insertion sort idea may be useful. Insert the new record at its proper place along the already sorted path from its predecessor node to the root, and allow 425 to work its way up along the path as far as it can go the reach its proper place. This can be done by comparing 425 to its predecessor and interchanging if it exceeds its predecessor's value. In this case, it does exceed that value, so interchange to obtain the tree shown in Figure 8.9(a).

All other paths remain sorted, as before. Now compare 425 at node 10 with its predecessor. Since it exceeds 123, interchange again to obtain Figure 8.9(b). Finally, compare 425 with its predecessor's value, and interchange to obtain Figure 8.9(c).

At this point, when 425 is compared to its predecessor's value, the 425 has reached its proper place. All paths must now be in order, since the path from node 10 to the root is in order, and the interchanges have not disturbed the order along any other path.

This gives us the means ***to create a heap:***

Start with records stored in the complete binary tree and process each node in turn, starting with node 2 and ending with node n.

The processing of the ith node is exactly the same processing as was done on the new record 425. Since nodes 1 to $i - 1$ will already have been processed prior to processing node i, the binary tree consisting of nodes 1 to $i - 1$ will already be a

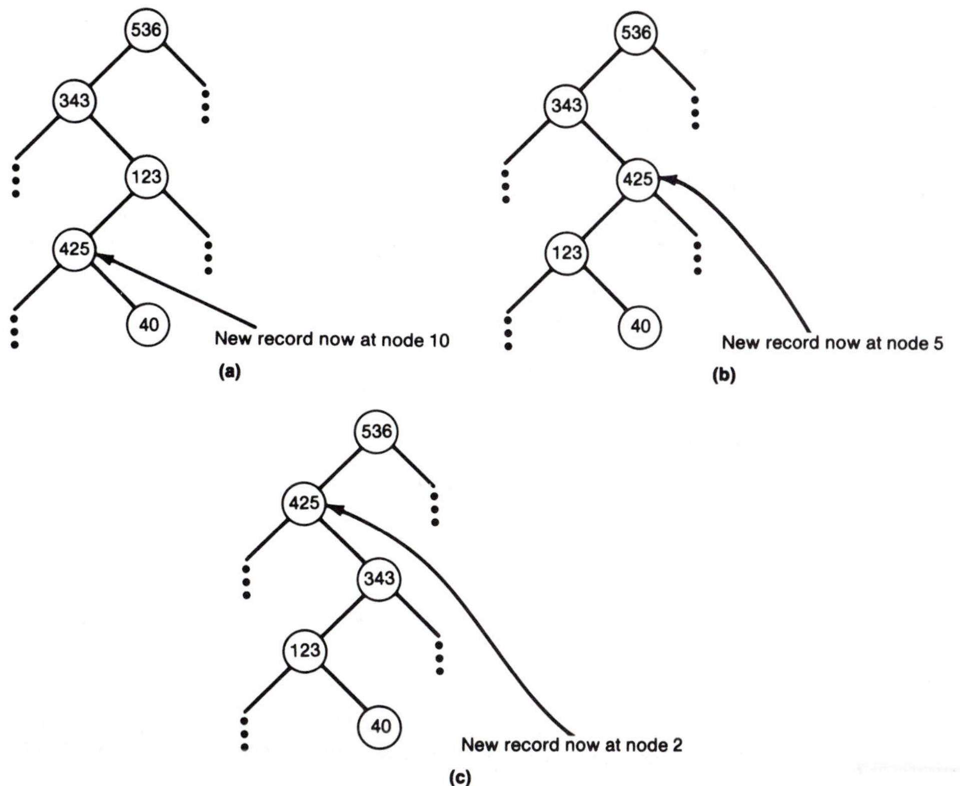

Figure 8.9 Heap Creation

heap. Processing node i then, in effect, treats the record at node i as a new record and creates a new heap. For the example of twenty records, this procedure leads to the heap of Figure 8.8(a).

8.4.3 Timing the Heap Creation

In order to analyze the time required, recall that the number of nodes n and the depth of a complete binary tree are related by

$$d = \lceil \lg_2(n + 1) \rceil$$

This is important. Since the heaps dealt with initially in our heapsort algorithm are complete, their depth is $O(\lg(n))$.

We now analyze the time required to create a heap by this algorithm. Starting from a complete binary tree is important. For instance, if we started with the binary tree shown in Figure 8.10, this algorithm would be equivalent to the original insertion sort of Section 8.3.4.

The heap creation algorithm does a total amount of work determined by the sum of the number of comparisons and interchanges needed in processing each node. A node at depth k cannot require more than k comparisons and k interchanges in its processing. The worst-case time will be achieved for any initial tree

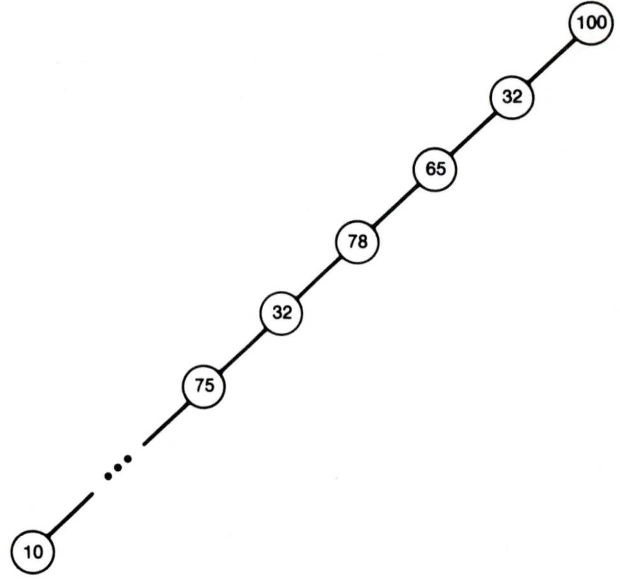

Figure 8.10 An Incomplete Binary Tree

in which the numbers stored at nodes 1, 2, 3, . . . , n form an increasing sequence. For instance, if the integer i is stored at node i, for i = 1, 2, . . . , n, we obtain such an increasing sequence. If n is 15, the tree will be as shown in Figure 8.11.

It can be shown that the total time for such a tree to be turned into a heap by the algorithm is proportional to $\Sigma_{k=0}^{d} kn_k$, where n is the number of nodes at depth k, d is the depth, and k is the number of comparisons and interchanges required for each node at depth k. This is because every record will work its way to the root of the tree when it is processed. Since $n_k = 2^{k-1}$, this sum will be proportional to n lg n. The efficiency of this method can be increased somewhat by first determining where a record to be processed will end up along its path to the root, and then shifting everything down before inserting it. This efficiency could also have been achieved with the insertion sort.

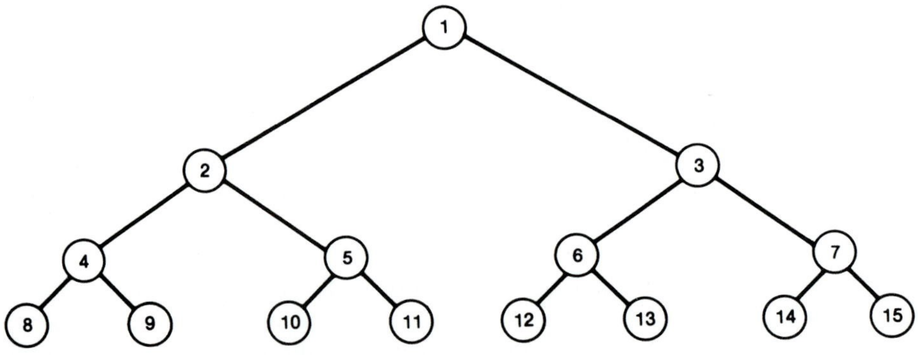

Figure 8.11 Binary Tree with Numbers Forming an Increasing Sequence

8.4.4 Better Heap Creation

For a tree of depth d, a better procedure for creating a heap is to start at node number $2^{d-1} - 1$, the rightmost node at depth $d - 1$. Even better, start at $\lfloor n/2 \rfloor$, the integer part of $n/2$, the first nonterminal node at depth $d - 1$. Process each node in turn, from node $\lfloor n/2 \rfloor$ to node 1. The processing at each node i is to turn the tree with node i as its root into a heap. This can be done, assuming that its left and right subtrees are already heaps, as in the following example.

Consider the initial complete binary tree in Figure 8.12(a). Start at node 5 ($= \lfloor 11/2 \rfloor$) (83 is stored there) and compare its successors 94 and 7, determining that 94 is the larger. Compare 94 with 83; since 94 exceeds 83, interchange 94 and 83 to obtain Figure 8.12(b).

The subtree with node 5 (94) as root is now a heap. Move to node 4, and the similar comparisons reveal that it is already a heap. Move to node 3, compare its successors 29 and 30, and then compare the larger to 16. Since 30 exceeds 16, interchange 30 and 16 to obtain Figure 8.12(c).

The subtree of node 3 is a heap, so move to node 2. Compare its successors 57 and 94, and then compare the larger to 14. Interchange 94 and 14 to obtain Figure 8.12(d).

At this point, notice that all nodes processed so far must be the roots of subtrees that remain heaps, except perhaps for the root of the subtree, where 14

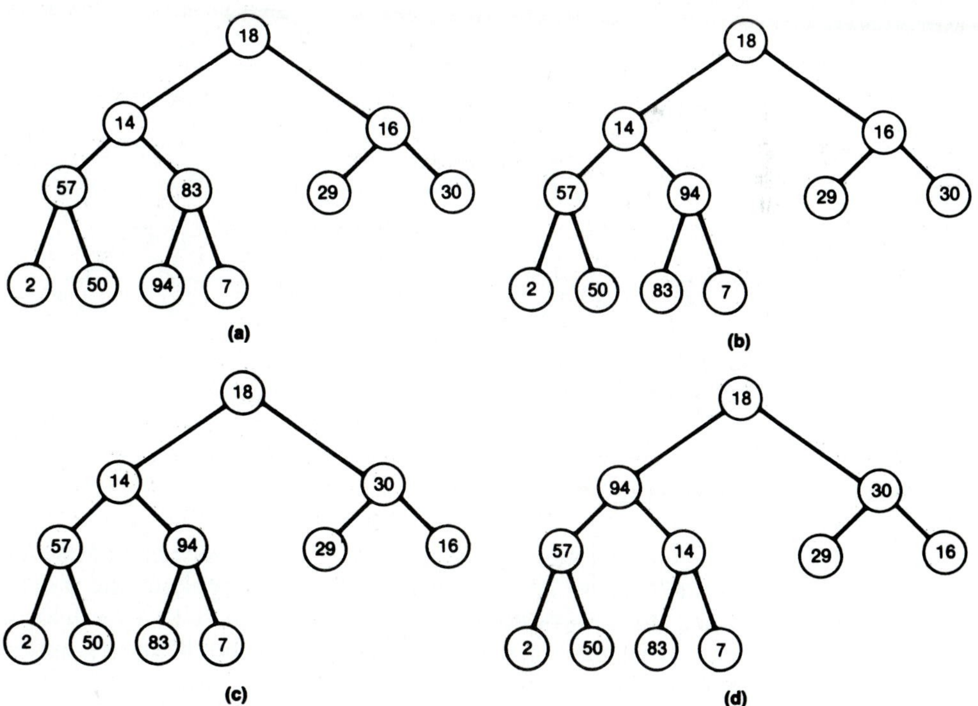

Figure 8.12 A Fast Heap Creation

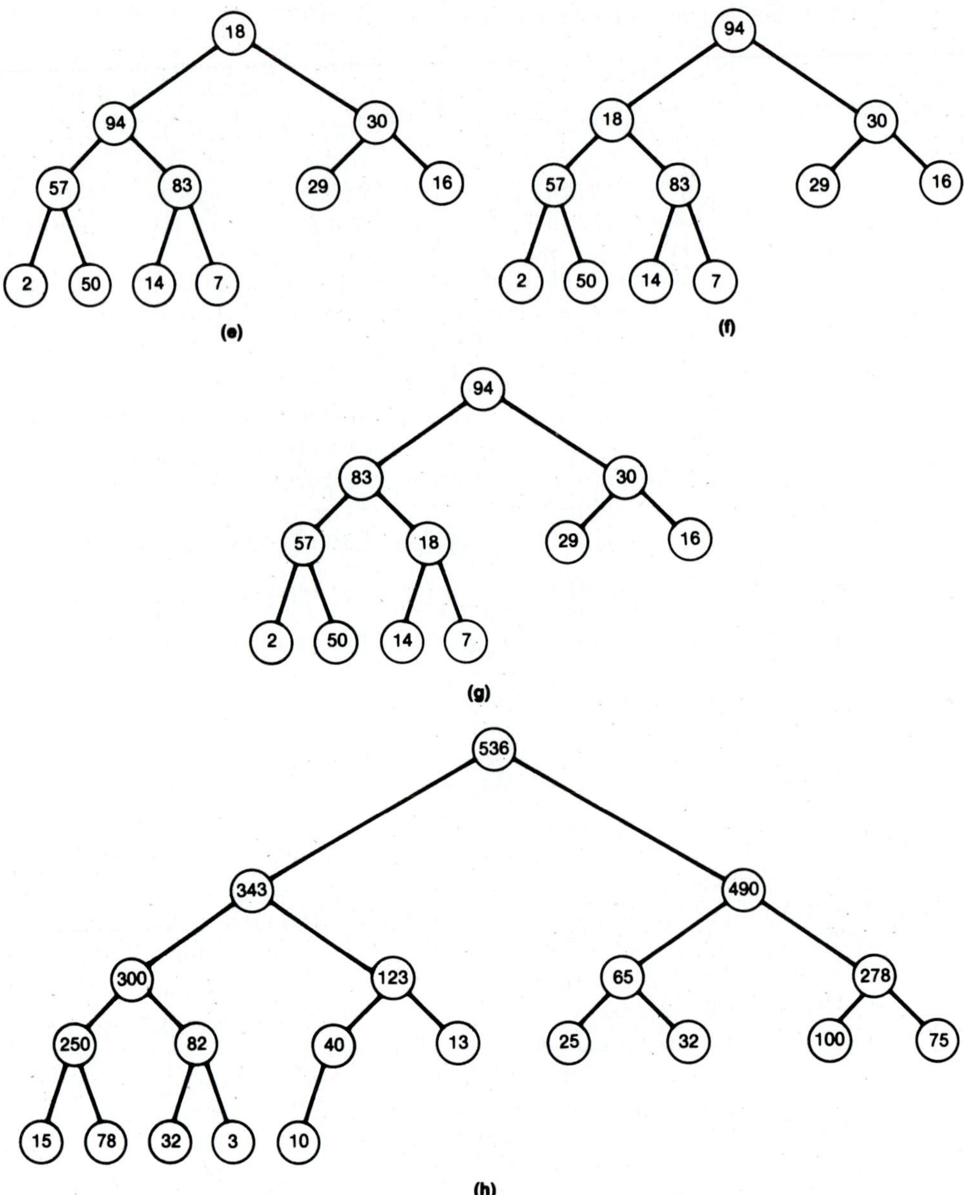

Figure 8.12 *(continued)*

now appears after the interchange. This subtree need not be a heap and, in fact, is not in this case. You can make it a heap by applying the same process to the node where 14 is currently stored, node 5. Compare its two successors and then compare the larger of those with 14. Then interchange 14 and 83 to obtain Figure 8.12(e).

The subtree with root node 2 is now a heap, and the processing of node 2 is complete. Notice that all nodes processed so far are roots of subtrees that are heaps. The last node to be processed is now node 1. Compare its successors, 94 and 30. Since the larger, 94, exceeds 18, interchange to obtain Figure 8.12(f).

The 18 from the node being processed, node 1, has now moved down to node 2. Hence its subtree may no longer be a heap. Apply the process to node 2. The 18 can move down again and will continue to move down until it either becomes situated at a terminal node or becomes the root of a subtree that remains a heap. In this case, it should be compared with 83, the larger of its two successors, and interchanged to get Figure 8.12(g).

At this point, you can see that 18 is the root of a heap by comparing it to the larger of its two successors. Processing of node 1 has been completed, and the heap has been created. The heap obtained from the original example with this algorithm is Figure 8.12(h). Notice that this heap differs from that in Figure 8.8(a). As mentioned earlier, more than one heap can be constructed to store the same data.

Without analyzing this heap creation algorithm in detail, the result can be stated. This procedure is actually only $O(n)$. This heap creation algorithm is faster than that of the last section because few nodes must move down long paths. In the other algorithm, many nodes may move up long paths. A use for this linear time heap creation algorithm will be demonstrated in another context in Section 9.2, Priority Queues.

8.4.5 Some Details of Heap Implementation

One way to implement the heap creation algorithm is to make use of a function, or routine, that works on a binary tree whose left and right subtrees are already heaps. The function does the ''shifting'' down of the root record until it becomes the root of a subtree that remains a heap, or until it reaches a terminal node. This ''shift'' routine need not do the interchanging along the way. Instead it can determine the final position of the root being shifted down, moving each record along that path to its predecessor, finally placing the root where it belongs.

Notice that the first heap creation algorithm requires testing the record being inserted along a path to the root against its current predecessor. Before this can be done, the program must test for whether or not there is a predecessor—that is, whether the record has already reached the root. This test must precede every comparison. Similarly, in the second heap creation algorithm, the record being shifted down must be tested against its successors. Before doing this, it is necessary to test whether there are successors.

These tests can be avoided by always putting ''plus infinity'' at the root of the initial complete binary tree for the first algorithm, and ''negative infinity'' at the subtrees of all terminal nodes for the second algorithm. This is similar in effect to adding the search key to the end of the array in the linear search algorithm. ***Plus infinity*** and ***negative infinity*** stand for, respectively, any number larger or smaller than the numbers appearing in the binary tree. In this way, a record being inserted along a path in the first algorithm will never reach the root (so it will always have a predecessor with which it may be compared), and a record being shifted down in the second algorithm will always have successor nodes (since it will never become a terminal node).

8.4.6 Reheaping

Think of step 1 of the heap sorting algorithm as phase I, in which a heap is created. The execution of step 2 until the records are sorted is phase II. In phase II, the root element of the heap is removed and output. The program must then reheap. This may be done in two ways.

One is to allow the "gap" created at the root by removal of its record to shift down by comparing its two successors and interchanging the larger of the two successors with the gap, then repeating this process until the gap is at a terminal node. A convenient way to do this is to replace the record removed from the root by a "negative infinity" and invoke the shift down function referred to earlier for the second algorithm.

A second way to reheap is to replace the gap with the rightmost record at greatest depth. (Actually, any record with no successors will do.) The same shift function may be invoked to reheap.

Since the length of the longest path in a complete binary tree is $O(\lg n)$, the reheaping after each record is removed can take time at most $O(\lg n)$. Because n records will ultimately be removed, the total time required for phase II will be at most $O(n \lg n)$. For either implementation of phase I, the total heapsort time is $O(n \lg n)$. This was achieved by "spreading out" the records along paths of a complete binary tree, and, in effect, doing insertions only along the path from a record to the root.

We have been dealing with a ***max heap,*** in which the largest record is at the top. A ***min heap,*** with the smallest record at the top, is dealt with similarly. The only difference is that interchanging occurs when a successor's key is smaller, rather than larger.

8.4.7 An Implementation for Heapsort

A detailed version of the heapsort algorithm can now be developed. You have now seen a number of ways to create a heap and to reheap. We will use the second heap creation algorithm for phase I and the second reheaping algorithm for phase II. Both algorithms use the shift function.

To proceed we must decide on an implementation of the binary tree data structure. The binary tree used in heapsort is initially complete. The required processing involves predecessors and successors of nodes. Sequential representation for the binary tree is ideal, so we use it. The binary tree is stored in the `data` array and consists of n records.

Storage is needed for the sorted version of `data`. Although another array may seem necessary for this purpose, we will use only the `data` array. The algorithm, after creating a heap (in `data`), continually takes the root record as the next record in the sorted output and then reheaps. Before reheaping, the rightmost record at the lowest level of the heap is placed at the root. The storage vacated by that rightmost record will no longer be needed. We choose to store the output record there. You should convince yourself that this will result in the records appearing in `data` in *reverse* sorted order upon termination. To remedy this, we write `shift` so that it produces min heaps. The records will then appear in correct sorted order upon termination.

`Shift` has parameters `data`, `root`, and `last`. `Root` points to the root of a subtree, and `last` points to the node of the original heap that is currently the rightmost node at greatest depth. The nodes `last+1` to `n` are currently storing the already sorted `n-last` output records. Whenever `shift` is invoked, the left and right subtrees of `root` (excluding nodes `last+1` to `n`) are assumed to be heaps. `Shift` returns after reheaping, by allowing the `root` record to move down to its final position. This is done by first storing the key value and record of the initial `root` record in `keyvalue` and `recordvalue`, respectively. `Ptr` points to the node currently being considered as the final position for the initial `root` record. This will be the final position if either of the following two conditions is met.

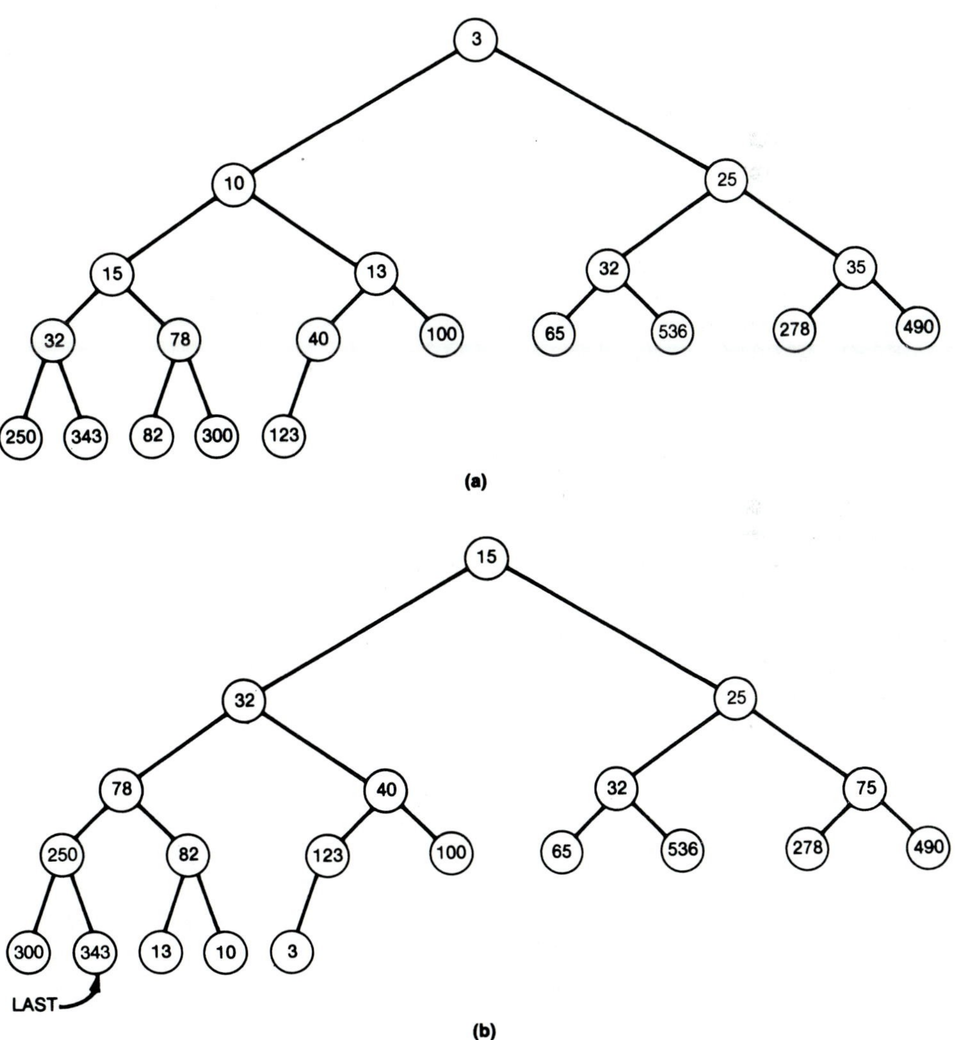

Figure 8.13 (a) Initial Heap and (b) Heap after First Three Entries Have Been Output

1. The successor record of `ptr` with minimum key value has a key value greater than or equal to `keyvalue`, or
2. `Ptr` points to a terminal node or to a node whose successors are nodes among `last+1` to `n`.

Condition 2 can be recognized by the test (`succ<=last`), where `succ` points to the left successor node of `ptr`. Condition 1 requires finding the minimum key value for the successors of `ptr`. `Ptr` may not have a right successor, or that successor may represent an output record. This can be tested for by the test (`succ<last`).

`Copy` copies the contents of the record pointed to by its second parameter into the record pointed to by its first parameter. When `shift` determines that `ptr` is not the final position, it moves the record at `ptr` to its predecessor node. This is why the original record at `root` is saved. When the final position is found, the saved record is placed there. The initial heap and the situation after the first three entries have been output are shown in Figure 8.13 for the tree of Figure 8.7.

The implementation for heapsort follows.

```
#define MAX 100
typedef struct
{
   int key;
}record;
typedef record recordarray[MAX];

heapsort(data,n)
/* Sorts the n records stored in array data
   in descending order.
*/
recordarray data;
int n;
{
   int root,last;
   root = n/2;                              create the heap
   last = n;
   while (root > 0)
      {
         shift(data,root,last);             make the subtree of
         root--;                            root a heap and
      }                                     update root
   root = 1;
   while (last > 1)
      {
         interchange(data,1,last);          output and
         last--;                            reheap
         shift(data,root,last);
      }
}
```

```
shift(data,root,last)
/* Makes the subtree of root into
   a heap(min heap). The left and
   right subtrees of root must be
   heaps. All subtrees are stored
   in array data in sequential
   representation. Only the nodes
   between root and last are
   considered to be in the subtrees.
*/
recordarray data;
int root,last;
{
   int ptr,succ;                      ] ptr keeps track of the location of
   int keyvalue;                        the root entry as it shifts down
   record recordvalue;
   ptr = root;                        ] initialize ptr to the root
   succ = 2 * ptr;                    ] set succ to ptr's left successor
   if (succ < last)                   ] if the node indexed by ptr has a right
      if (data[succ + 1].key < data[succ].key)   successor and it is less than
                                        ptr's left successor
         succ++;                      ] set succ to it
```

at this point, `succ` *points to the smallest of* `ptr`*'s successors*

```
   keyvalue = data[root].key;         ] save the root key value
   copy(&recordvalue,&data[root]);    ] save the root record
```

*the purpose of the **while** loop is to determine the proper place for the original root record;* `ptr` *will point to that location when the loop is exited*

```
   while((succ <= last) && (data[succ].key < keyvalue))   ] test for ptr at a
      {                                 terminal node and, if not, whether ptr
                                        must be shifted down
         copy(&data[ptr],&data[succ]);  ] move succ's record up to ptr's location
         ptr = succ;                    ] update ptr to succ, moving it down
         succ = 2 * ptr;                ] set succ, as
```

```
        if (succ < last)
           if (data[succ + 1].key < data[succ].key)
              succ++;
     }
   copy(&data[ptr],&recordvalue);
}
```

above, to the smallest successor of `ptr`

insert the original root record where it belongs

8.4.8 Heapsort is Uniformly Fast

As presented, heapsort is efficient. Unlike the other sorts considered, which are array- or list-oriented, it is tree-oriented. They are $O(n^2)$ in the worst case, whereas heapsort is $O(n \lg n)$. Moreover, we shall see in Section 8.7 that it gives uniformly good sort times, no matter how ordered or unordered the original data. Although times are somewhat faster when the data is initially either fairly well ordered or reverse ordered, the range of these times is small compared to the other sorts. This is to be expected, since the construction of the heap takes little time and the reheaping tends to destroy any order present in the data. In effect it appears to be in random order. Actually, during reheaping, when `shift` works on larger entries at the root, it takes $O(\lg n)$ time, since they tend toward the bottom of the tree, while the opposite is true for smaller entries. Because most entries are near the bottom of the tree and are larger, their shifting makes up the bulk of the sorting time. Thus this time should be relatively insensitive to initial order in the data. This uniformity of sort times is one of its main virtues, since it eliminates the great variation in time from $O(n)$ to $O(n^2)$ of the other sorts. In addition, it is fast.

8.5 Quicksort: Another Fast Sort

As a final example of a sorting method, we consider an algorithm called ***quicksort.*** This algorithm is appropriately named, since its average execution is very quick. Its worst-case execution time is slow, but the worst case should occur rarely.

One way to develop quicksort is to attempt a recursive solution to the problem of sorting an array `data` of n records. The general recursive method immediately prescribes guidelines—break up the original problem into smaller versions of the original problem and then achieve the solution from their solutions. Here, this dictates that the original array be broken down into component arrays, which can be sorted independently and from which the final sorted array can be derived.

Thus `data` is to be separated into two components to be sorted, an upper array and a lower array. We then have two options for proceeding. One is to *combine* or *merge* the resultant two sorted component arrays to achieve a final sorted solution. This method is the ***merge sort,*** which is not pursued here but is applied to the sorting of files in Chapter 11. The second approach, which is taken here, is to ensure that the resultant two sorted component arrays require *no further processing,* but yield the final sorted solution directly.

Merely splitting `data` into two components and then sorting each component independently is not sufficient to guarantee that the resultant array is sorted,

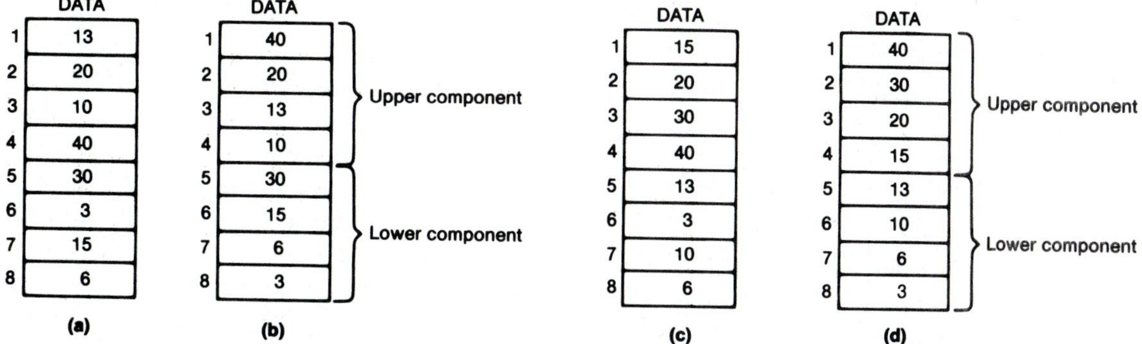

Figure 8.14 Sorting an Array by Component

with no further processing required. This is because some entries in the upper component may be smaller than some entries in the lower component. For example, suppose the initial array is `data`, shown in Figure 8.14(a), and the upper and lower components consist, respectively, of entries 1 to 4 and 5 to 8. Sorting these components independently yields Figure 8.14(b), which is clearly not sorted.

Notice, however, that if all entries in the upper component were no less than *all* entries in the lower component, then sorting each component independently would always lead to a result that is sorted. For example, suppose the initial array is Figure 8.14(c). Taking the upper and lower components as entries 1 to 4, and 5 to 8, respectively, and independently sorting them produces Figure 8.14(d). This array is now sorted.

Note that the fifth entry, 13, occupies the same position in the sorted array as in the initial array. This is because all entries in the upper component are no less, and all entries in the lower component are no greater, than 13. The key value 13 actually occupied its proper position in the sorted version of `data` before the two components were sorted. Hence it need not be included in either component and may serve as a separator or ***partitioning entry*** between the two components to be sorted.

To carry out this procedure for an arbitrary array requires finding a partitioning entry. Normally a partitioning entry, such as 13 in position 5, will not occur in the initial array to be sorted. For example, no such partitioning entry (separating larger entries above from smaller entries below) occurs in Figure 8.14(a). This means that the initial array must be rearranged so that a partitioning entry may be found and subsequently used to separate the components.

In keeping with the top-down approach, assume that this task (rearranging the initial array and determining a partitioning entry) is carried out by the function `partition(i,j)`. The arguments `i` and `j` contain pointers to entries of the array, as shown in Figure 8.15. `Partition(i,j)` returns an index pointer to a partitioning entry of the array consisting of all entries between `i` and `j`. Thus, if `partition(i,j)` returns a value `p`, then all entries between `i` and `p-1` are at least as great as `data[p].key`, and all entries between `p+1` and `j` are no greater than `data[p].key`. The pointer `p` separates the upper and lower components of `i,j`.

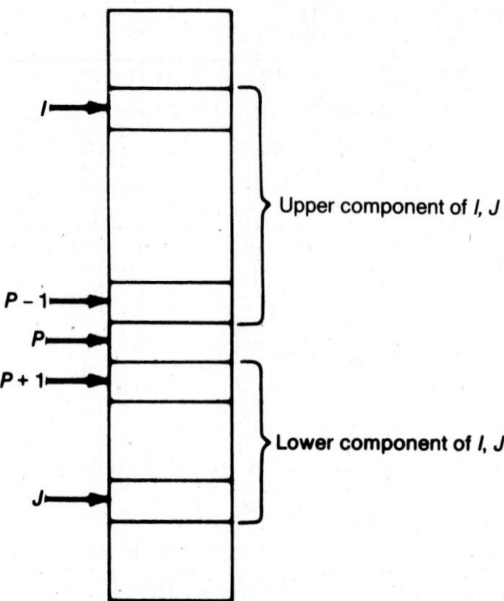

Figure 8.15 Array with a Partitioning Entry *P* Separating Upper and Lower Components

8.5.1 Two Quicksort Procedures

The procedure `quicksort` may now be written, recursively, as follows.

Recursive Version

```
quicksort(i,j)
/* Sorts the records stored in array data
   between positions indexed by i and j in
   descending order.
*/
int i,j;
{
   int p;
   if(i < j)
      {
         p = partition(i,j);     ] when partition returns, all entries above the pth entry are
                                   larger than it, and those below are smaller
         quicksort(i,p-1);       ] sorts entries above the pth
         quicksort(p+1,j);       ] sorts entries below the pth
      }
}
```

To sort a global array of `n` records, `quicksort(1,n)` is invoked. The crux of the algorithm is the `partition` function, which will be discussed shortly.

Every time a call is made to `quicksort`, two new obligations are incurred, and a current obligation is postponed. For instance, the initial call to `quicksort` generates the initial obligation: sort the n entries of data. During the execution of this call, partition determines a partitioning entry, and two new obligations are incurred. These are represented by the two recursive calls to quicksort, one for each component. The current obligation must then be postponed to carry out these new obligations. Each recursive call also generates two new obligations, requiring the execution of the current recursive call to be postponed.

As we have seen previously, what can be done recursively can also be done iteratively. Quicksort can be written nonrecursively by using a stack to store one of the new obligations, while the other can be processed immediately. It turns out that the choice of which of the two obligations to stack, and which to deal with immediately, is critical to the algorithm's storage requirements. The partition function does not necessarily split an array into two equal parts, as evidenced by our earlier example. Selecting the larger of the two components to stack results in a worst-case stack depth of $O(\lg n)$. An arbitrary choice instead leads to a worst-case stack depth of $O(n)$. The difference in storage needed for the stack can be significant.

The structure of the nonrecursive algorithm amounts to a loop in which the smaller of the two new component arrays is processed and the larger is stacked. The procedure may be written as follows:

Nonrecursive Version

```
quicksort(i,j)
/* Sorts the records stored in array data
   between positions indexed by i and j in
   descending order.
*/
int i,j;
{
   int p,top,bottom;
   stack s;
   setstack(&s);                          ] initializes stack s to empty
   push(j,&s);                            ] stores the original task on stack s
   push(i,&s);
   while(!empty(&s))                      ] test for remaining tasks
      {
         pop(&s,&top);                    ] removes the top task from stack s
         pop(&s,&bottom);
         while(top < bottom)
            {
               p = partition(top,bottom);      ] generates two new tasks
               if((p - top) > (bottom - p))    ] puts the larger of the two tasks on
                  {                              stack s and updates top or bottom
                     push(p-1,&s);
                     push(top,&s);
                     top = p + 1
                  }
               else
```

```
                {
                    push(bottom,&s);
                    push(p+1,&s);
                    bottom = p - 1;
                }
            }
        }
}
```

8.5.2 The Partition Function

We must now return to the partitioning task on which the efficiency of both versions of **quicksort** depends. To determine a partitioning entry, and a corresponding rearrangement, the first array entry is selected as a basis. This is a somewhat arbitrary selection and will be discussed more fully later. In general, this first array entry will not be in its proper sorted position. It will need to be shifted, and the array rearranged, so that all larger entries appear in the upper component and all smaller entries appear in the lower component.

A clever way to do this requires two pointers, **upper** and **lower**. Initially, **upper** is set to **i**, the first array index, and **lower** to **j**, the last array index. The initial situation is shown in Figure 8.16(a).

Lower is now moved upward until an entry larger than **data[upper].key** is encountered. In this case, 15 will be that entry. It is then inter-

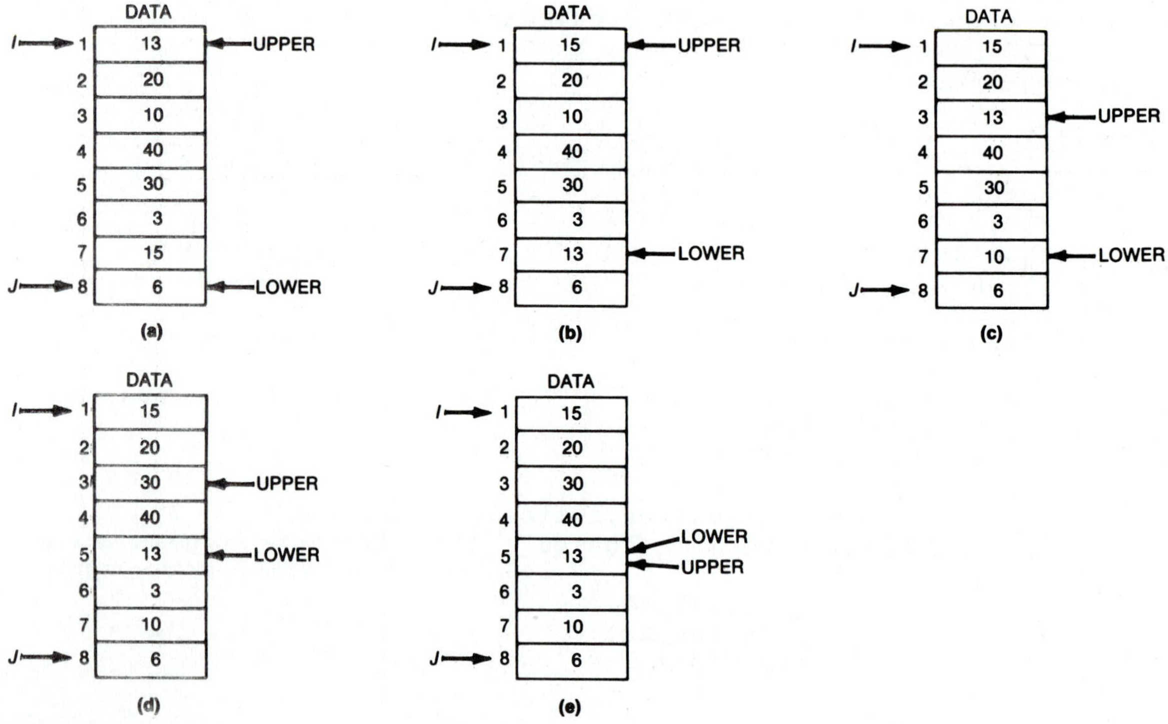

Figure 8.16 Sorting an Array by Means of a Partitioning Function

changed with `data[upper]`; see Figure 8.16(b). At this point, attention is shifted to `upper`, which is moved downward until an entry smaller than `data[lower].key` is encountered. This entry will be 10, and it is interchanged with `data[lower]`, yielding Figure 8.16(c).

Attention now shifts back to `lower`, which is again moved upward until an entry greater than `data[upper].key` is encountered. This will be 30, and it is interchanged with `data[upper]`, resulting in Figure 8.16(d).

`Upper` is then moved downward until an entry smaller than `data[lower].key` is encountered. In this case no such entry appears, and when upper reaches `lower`, no such entry *can* appear. This is so because, at all times, any entries above `upper` are greater than the original first entry (13 in the example), and any entries below `lower` are less than the original first entry. Hence, whichever pointer is being moved, only entries between `upper` and `lower` can result in an interchange. When `upper` and `lower` coincide, no entries are left to interchange. Furthermore, when `upper` and `lower` coincide, they must be pointing to the original first entry or basis, since at all times at least one of them points to it. The final situation, then, is as shown in Figure 8.16(e).

This procedure clearly carries out the task of `partition(i,j)`, which is to return the value of `upper` (or `lower`). Notice that, whether `upper` or `lower`

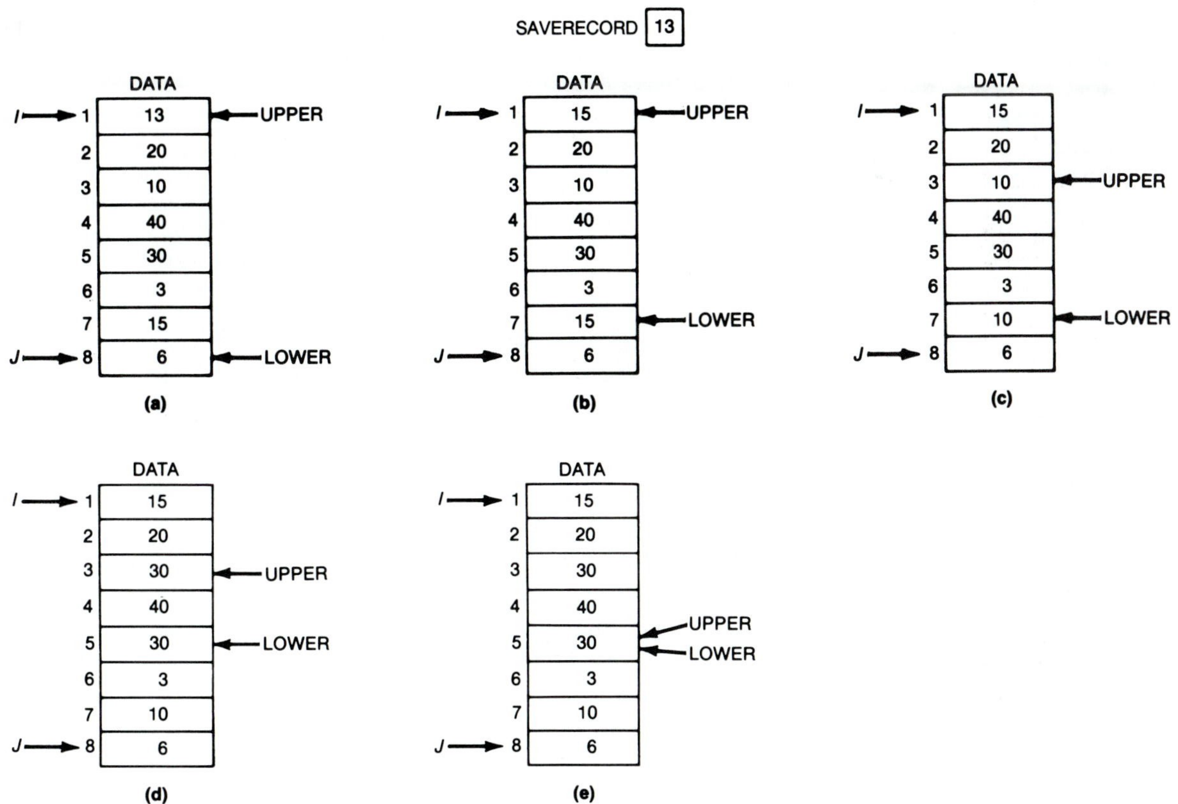

Figure 8.17 Partitioning an Array by Means of a Temporary Variable, SAVERECORD

is the focus of attention, it is always the original first entry (13 here) that is the basis for comparison.

A slight modification makes partition more efficient. Instead of *interchanging* the basis with the larger or smaller entry that has been found, simply *move* the larger or smaller entry to the position pointed to by the current stationary pointer. This is the position that would have been occupied by the basis (13 in the example). However, the basis does not now appear in the array but is saved in a temporary variable, `saverecord`. For the example, this would generate the sequence shown in Figure 8.17. When `upper` and `lower` meet, the record stored in `saverecord` must be copied into `data[upper]`. This version of `partition` is faster because a move is carried out much faster than an interchange, and many such operations are required as the algorithm executes. It is therefore the algorithm implemented below.

```
partition(i,j)
/* Rearranges the entries in array
   data between positions indexed by
   i and j and returns an array index
   which guarantees that all entries
   above it are larger than the entry
   it indexes, and all entries below it
   are smaller.
*/
int i,j;
{
   int upper,lower;
   record saverecord;
   upper = i;                                               initialize upper
   lower = j;                                               and lower
   copy(&saverecord,&data[i]);                              save the basis,
                                                            data[i]
   while(upper != lower)                                    test for completion
      {
         while((upper < lower) && (saverecord.key >=        move lower up,
                                   data[lower].key))        looking for a record
            lower--;                                        whose key exceeds
         if(upper != lower)                                 the basis key
            copy(&data[upper],&data[lower]);                copy the basis into
                                                            lower's position
         while((upper < lower) && (saverecord.key <=        move upper down,
                                   data[upper].key))        looking for a record
            upper++;                                        whose key is less
         if(upper != lower)                                 than the basis
            copy(&data[lower],&data[upper]);                copy the basis into
      }                                                     upper's position
   copy(&data[upper],&saverecord);                          copy the basis into
                                                            its final position
      return(upper);                                        return the index of
}                                                           the basis
```

It is important to recognize that whenever `partition(i,j)` is invoked, it processes only entries between `i` and `j` of the `data` array and deals with each of these entries exactly once. Each entry is compared with `saverecord`, and perhaps copied into `data[upper]` or `data[lower]`. Consequently, a call to `partition(i,j)` takes time $O(j - i + 1)$, since there are $j - i + 1$ entries between `i` and `j`.

8.5.3 Analyzing Iterative Quicksort

We now want to analyze the nonrecursive version of quicksort to determine its time and storage requirements. To provide some insight into its behavior, we will simulate its application to our initial array, focusing on the changes that occur in this array and in the stack during execution.

Initially, the stack is empty, and the array is as shown in Figure 8.18(a). When `quicksort(1,8)` is invoked, it calls `partition(1,8)`, which returns with `p` pointing to the partitioning entry and the rearranged array of Figure 8.18(b).

The upper component array is the larger, so (1,4) is placed on the stack, and the lower component array is processed. This leads to a call to `partition(6,8)`. When `partition` returns, the situation is Figure 8.18(c).

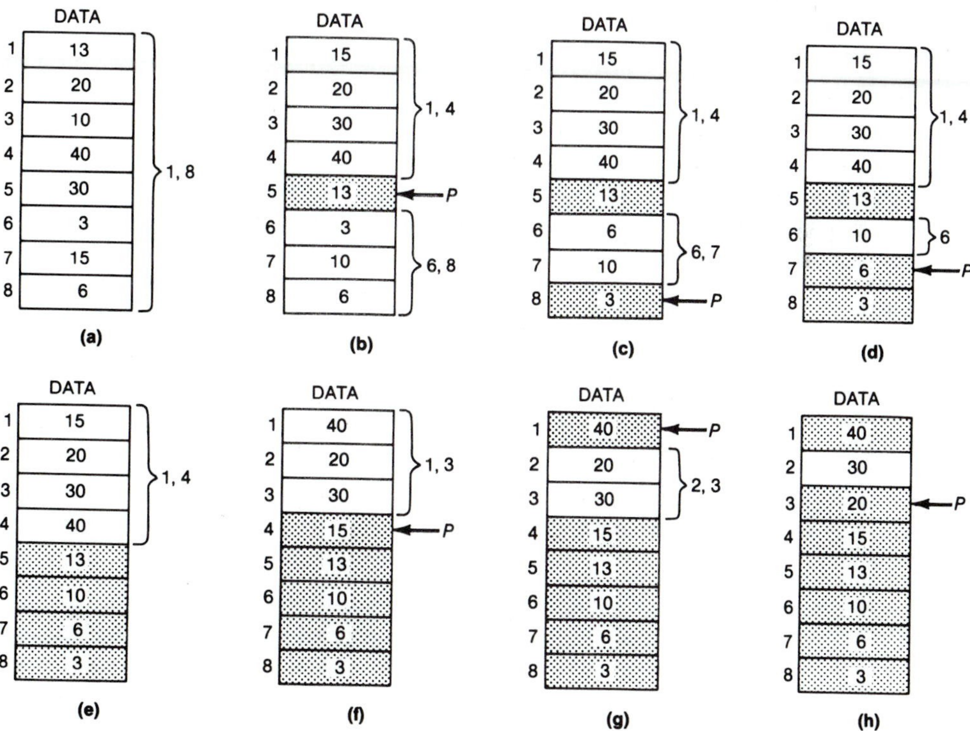

Figure 8.18 Iterative Quicksort

The *current* upper component array is larger, so (6,7) is placed on the stack, and the lower component array is processed. Since the lower component contains no entries, (6,7) is removed from the stack and `partition(6,7)` is invoked, returning the situation depicted in Figure 8.18(d).

Now (6,6) is placed on the stack, and the lower component is processed. Again, this component has no entries, so (6,6) is removed from the stack. Since `top` (= 6) is not less than `bottom` (= 6), the outer **while** loop body is now executed, causing (1,4) to be removed from the stack. At this time the stack is empty, and the array is as shown in Figure 8.18(e). `Partition(1,4)` is now invoked, and returns, yielding Figure 8.18(f).

Now (1,3) is placed on the stack. The lower component again contains no entries, so (1,3) is removed from the stack, and `partition(1,3)` is invoked. The result is Figure 8.18(g).

At this point (2,3) is placed on the stack. Since the upper component contains no entries, (2,3) is removed from the stack, and `partition(2,3)` is invoked. It returns with Figure 8.18(h).

Now (2,2) is placed on the stack. The lower component has no entries, so (2,2) is removed from the stack. Since `top` (= 2) and `bottom` (= 2), the outer **while** loop tests for an empty stack. As the stack is empty, `quicksort` terminates.

It should not be clear that each time the inner loop body of `quicksort` is executed, and `top` < `bottom`, `p` is set to point to an entry of the array that has been correctly placed in its final sorted position. If `top` = `bottom`, then the one entry is already in its proper sorted position. The inner loop body is thus executed at most n times. Ignoring the time taken by `partition`, the inner loop body takes a constant time to execute. Each time the inner loop body executes, it generates one new problem that is placed on the stack and another new problem that is processed immediately. As soon as this latter problem has fewer than two entries (`top` ≥ `bottom`), the inner loop is exited. Unless the stack is empty, the outer loop removes the next problem from the stack, and the inner loop then functions again. Consequently, each entry that is placed in its proper position requires, at most, an execution of the inner loop body or an execution of the inner loop body plus the additional constant time required by the outer loop test plus removal of a problem from the stack. This means that the total time is, at most, $c_1 + c_2 \times n$ plus the total time taken by `partition`, for some constants c_1 and c_2.

8.5.4 The Worst and Best Cases

To analyze the total time of `partition`, recall that each execution takes time O(length of the component array it is called to work on). Since the length of a component is at most n, with `partition` being invoked at most n times, total time is at most $O(n^2)$. Hence `quicksort` has a worst-case time $O(n^2)$. You should convince yourself that the worst case occurs whenever the initial array is in sorted or reverse sorted order.

The best case (fastest execution) actually occurs when the partitioning entry returned by `partition` splits the array in half. In this case, `partition` is called to work on one component array of length n, two component arrays of length $n/2$, four component arrays of length $n/4$, . . . , 2^k component arrays of length $n/2^k$, etc. By an argument similar to the worst-case analysis of the binary search, about lg n such calls will be made to `partition`. Its total time will then be $O(n \lg n)$.

While the worst-case time for `quicksort` is poor, its best-case time is fast—in fact, better than `heapsort`. The average time for `quicksort` is also $O(n \lg n)$. This assumes that each ordering of the n entries is equally likely to appear in the initial array. Evidently, cases differing significantly from the best occur rarely, and this is why `quicksort` is aptly named.

The storage requirements for `quicksort`, beyond the initial array, are a few variables plus the stack depth. Since the larger of each generated component array problem is stacked, the next problem to be stacked must have length at most one-half the current top stack entry length. For example, in the preceding section, note that when (6,7) was placed on the stack, its length was no greater than half the length of the preceding stack component (1,4). Again, by an argument similar to the worst-case binary search analysis, at most $O(\lg n)$ such problems can appear on the stack at any time, so the storage requirements for quicksort are $O(\lg n)$. Thus, quicksort, while faster on the average than heapsort, does not have the guaranteed worst-case $O(n \lg n)$ time of heapsort. Moreover, quicksort requires additional storage $O(\lg n)$ to achieve its faster average time.

For smaller values of n, the simpler sorts, like the insertion sort, will be even faster than quicksort. Of course, if the initial array is known to be nearly sorted, the insertion sort will be faster anyway. Clearly, one way to speed up quicksort is to modify it by using a faster sort, such as insertion sort, when small component arrays are encountered. It is also possible to enhance the performance of quicksort by taking more care in the selection of the entry to be used as a basis by `partition`. Instead of taking the first entry of a component as the basis, the median of three entries may be selected, or an entry may be selected at random.

8.5.5 Distributive Partitioning

Although sorting has been extensively researched, a new generalization of the quicksort, *distributive partitioning,* has recently been discovered [Dobosiewicz, 1976]. It appears to be even faster than quicksort. Recall that the quicksort was based on the idea of rearranging the initial array so that it could be split into two component arrays to be sorted independently. Each of these arrays was then recursively sorted in the same way. ***Distributive partitioning*** carries this idea to its logical limit, by splitting the initial array into n component arrays, to be sorted independently and recursively. The price paid by this new algorithm is that additional storage of size $O(n \lg n)$ is required. Note that all the sorting algorithms considered sort in place, except the quicksort and distributive partitioning. Quicksort and distributive partitioning require additional storage, limiting their use for large n. Since quicksort's additional storage increases $1/n$th as fast as that of distributive partitioning, it will not be as severely limited.

8.6 Simulation of an Algorithm

It is often difficult, if not impossible, to analyze an algorithm mathematically and determine its time and storage requirements. Simulation is a useful basic tool for determining the behavior of an algorithm for this purpose. To illustrate, an algorithm for a simulation of the heapsort is constructed in this section.

The storage required by the heapsort algorithm in the implementation is $O(n)$. A reasonable measure for the time required is given by the number of interchanges and comparisons necessary to produce a sort. Assume that a procedure `treesort` has been written that is one of the detailed implementations discussed previously for heapsort. It has parameters `n`, `a`, `sa`, `int1`, `int2`, `comp1`, and `comp2`. These represent, respectively, the number of records, the input array of records to be sorted, the output array of sorted records, the number of interchanges required in phases I and II, and the number of comparisons required in phases I and II.

The simulation program to be written must explore the time requirements, as measured by `int1`, `int2`, `comp1`, and `comp2`, for various values of n, such as 20, 40, 60, 80, and 100. This will suggest how the execution time depends on n. Alternatively, the actual execution times could be measured. Intuitively, the algorithm will have fastest execution time when the input is nearly sorted, the slowest time when the input is nearly reverse sorted. For random initial orderings, the time can be expected to fall between these two extremes. This may not be the case but seems likely a priori. Consequently, we want to generate a number of samples from each of these three distinct classes of input, execute the `treesort` routine for each sample, and collect statistics on the numbers of interchanges and comparisons based on the samples taken.

We will choose twenty-five samples of each type of input, for a total number of executions of `treesort` of (twenty-five samples for each input class and value of n) $\times$ 3 input classes $\times$ 5 values of n, or 375 runs. One way to see if twenty-five samples is enough to achieve good statistics is to run an additional twenty-five. If the results do not vary significantly, then the twenty-five samples, or perhaps even fewer, are sufficient. If necessary, we can use a larger number of samples. Re-

		$n = 40$		
Input Class		Min	Ave	Max
"Nearly sorted"	`int1`	*	*	*
	`int2`	*	*	*
	`comp1`	*	*	*
	`comp2`	*	*	*
"Random"	`int1`	*	*	*
	`int2`	*	*	*
	`comp1`	*	*	*
	`comp2`	*	*	*
"Nearly reverse sorted"	`int1`	*	*	*
	`int2`	*	*	*
	`comp1`	*	*	*
	`comp2`	*	*	*

member, the twenty-five samples are taken from a possible number of $n!$ samples. It may seem the height of foolishness to base estimates on such a ridiculously small fraction of the possibilities. Thank goodness for statistics (when properly applied).

For each of the twenty-five samples for a given input class, the task is to find the following statistics for `int1`, `int2`, `comp1`, and `comp2`: their minimum, average, and maximum over all twenty-five sample values. Other statistics, such as the range and standard deviation, could be calculated if needed. We will have the simulation program print this information for each value of n, as indicated for $n = 40$ in the chart on the previous page. The *'s represent actual numeric values that will be output. A total of thirty-six values will be printed for each n; $5 \times 36 = 180$ statistics.

The program will keep statistics tables, one table for each input class for the current value of n. An algorithm for the simulation program is as follows:

1. Set `n` to 20.
2. While `n` ≤ 100
   a. Set `ns` to 1.
   b. Initialize statistics tables.
   c. While `ns` ≤ 25,
      i. Generate a sample from each input class, call `treesort` to work on each input, and then update the appropriate statistics tables.
      Set `ns` to `ns+1`.
   d. Output the statistics tables for the current value of `n` and for each input class.
   e. Set `n` to `n+20`.

Task (i) may be carried out as follows:

a. Generate a "random" sample for `a` of size `n` and call `treesort(n, a, sa, int1, int2, comp1, comp2)`.
b. Update the statistics table for "random" input.
c. Generate a "nearly sorted" input for `a` of size `n` by making 20 percent of `n` random interchanges on `sa`. Copy `sa` into `a`.
d. Generate a "nearly reverse sorted" input for `a` of size `n` by copying `sa` in reverse order in `ra`. Call `treesort(n, a, sa, int1, int2, comp1, comp2)`.
e. Update the statistics tables for "nearly sorted" input.
f. Call `treesort(n, ra, sa, int1, int2, comp1, comp2)`.
g. Update the statistics table for "nearly reverse sorted" input.
h. Set `ns` to `ns+1`.

At this point we can explain in more detail what is meant by the three classes of input. Assume that all input arrays, `a`, will contain integers between 1 and 1,000. Random inputs for `a` of size `n` are generated by placing the n integers into `a` in such a way that all orderings of the n numbers are equally likely. Consider the two arrays shown in Figure 8.19.

Array (b) has been obtained from array (a), which is sorted, by making two interchanges. These were interchanging `a1[2]` with `a1[6]`, and interchanging `a1[4]` with `a1[9]`. These two interchanges represent 20 percent of `n` interchanges, since `n` is 10. A *nearly sorted* input for `a` of size `n` is obtained by making 20 percent of `n` such interchanges in an initially sorted array. The interchanges are to be selected at random. This means that each interchange is obtained by picking

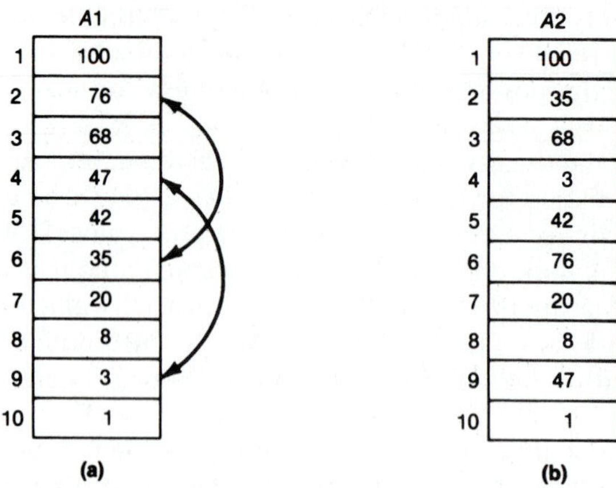

Figure 8.19 Array (b) Obtained from Sorted Array (a) by Two Interchanges

a value for `i` at random, so that each of the locations 1 to `n` of `sa` is equally likely to be selected. An integer `j` may be similarly obtained. Then `sa[i]` and `sa[j]` are interchanged. The only details still left to implement in the simulation algorithm are how to generate the required random integers to be placed in `a` and used for interchange locations, how to update the statistics tables, and how to finalize the tables before printing them.

Assume that a function `rng` is available that returns a real number as its value. This real number will be greater than 0.0 and less than 1.0. Whenever a sequence of these numbers is generated by consecutive calls to `rng`, the numbers appear, from a statistical point of view, to have been selected independently. Also assume that the returned value will lie in a segment of length l between 0 and 1, with probability l. For example, if l is of length 0.25, then the returned value will lie in that interval (say, between 0.33 and 0.58) 25 percent of the time. The random number generator `ranf` of FORTRAN is an example of such a function.

To generate an integer between 1 and 1,000, take the value `rng` returns, multiply it by 1,000, take the integer part of the result, and add 1 to it. For example, if the value returned is 0.2134, multiplying by 1,000 gives 213.4. Its integer part is 213; adding 1 yields 214. In fact, if any number strictly between 0.213 and 0.214 had been returned, 214 would have been generated. Hence 214 would be generated with probability 1/1,000, the length of the interval from 0.213 to 0.214. The same is true for each integer between 1 and 1,000. Carrying out this procedure n times will fill the array `a` to generate a "random" input (See Exercise 23 for a more exact approach). An alternative method in C to generate an integer at random between integers `low` and `high` uses the library function `rand`. Evaluating `rand()%(high-low+1) + low` yields the desired integer between `low` and `high`.

To generate a *nearly sorted* or *nearly reverse sorted* input, select each of the 20 percent of `n` interchanges as follows. Call `rng` twice. Multiply the two returned values by `n`, take the integer part, and add 1. Or evaluate `rand()%(high-low+1) + low` twice with `high` set to `n` and `low` set to 1. Either method gives two integers, `i` and `j`, between 1 and `n`. Interchange `sa[i]` with `sa[j]`.

The statistics tables can keep current running minimums, maximums, and the accumulated sum of the appropriate statistic. When each call to `treesort` returns, the minimum, maximum, and accumulated sum may be updated for each statistic, `int1`, `int2`, `comp1`, and `comp2`. When the inner loop of the algorithm is exited, and task *d* is to be carried out, the statistics tables are ready to be printed, except for the twelve averages. They must be finalized in task *d* by dividing the accumulated sums by 25.

The algorithm presented in this section can be used directly to obtain simulation results for `treesort`. Simply replacing the call to `treesort` in task (i) by a call to suitably modified versions of the other sort programs will produce their simulation results as well. To use simulation in the analysis of other programs, not necessarily sorts, requires some insight into what input is appropriate to generate and what statistics are meaningful to collect. This is not always so straightforward as in our example, but the general procedure and goal for the simulation of an algorithm should now be clear.

8.7 Simulation Results for the Sorts

Table 8.1 gives simulation results (in actual execution time measured in 1/1000 second intervals). It should be carefully studied. Note that the $O(n)$ and $O(n \lg n)$ sorts may be easily identified. The best and worst input cases are also evident, as well as the relatively uniform behavior of heapsort.

Each entry in the table is the average of 20 runs on a VAX 730 under VMS Version 4.0. For each n the five values correspond to input that is sorted, half sorted—half random, random, half reverse sorted—half random, and reverse sorted. If the entries for heapsort seem counter to your intuition, remember that its implementation sees sorted input as reverse sorted and reverse sorted input as sorted. This is because it uses a min heap to produce descending order.

8.8 Synopsis of Search and Sort Efficiencies

We have consistently viewed the record as the basic unit of data. Collections of records usually appear in problems, and their processing typically reduces to traversing through the records of the collection, inserting or deleting records, randomly accessing records, accessing records in sorted order, or searching the collection for a given record. The basic data structures are available for storage of the collection, and each supports some operations well at the expense of others. Arrays are excellent for random access and traversal but poor for general insertions and deletions. Lists support traversal, insertions, and deletions well but are poor for random access.

Linear searches of arrays and binary searches of sorted arrays can be performed, respectively, in $O(n)$ and $O(\lg n)$ time. Under special conditions, linear searches can be fast.

Simple sorting algorithms such as the bubble and insertion sort have worst-case time $O(n^2)$ but are $O(n)$ when dealing with almost sorted data. Quicksort gives very fast average times and heapsort does sorting in worst-case time $O(n \lg n)$.

Table 8.1 Simulation Results in Actual Execution Time (milliseconds)*

n	Bubble Sort					Insertion Sort					Modified Insertion Sort				
10	1	2	6	8	9	1	2	5	7	7	0	2	4	6	9
20	1	8	23	33	36	1	5	16	28	30	1	6	17	25	30
40	2	31	101	138	148	2	16	67	110	121	5	16	65	107	120
100	4	217	646	863	923	7	89	412	678	761	6	87	402	660	744
200	8	966	2653	3463	3724	12	364	1657	2706	3058	11	354	1612	2639	2993
400	17	3933	11277	14732	15858	24	1583	7645	12489	14595	20	1373	6352	10581	12157
	srt'd	half srt'd half rnd'm	rnd'm	half rev srt'd half rnd'm	rev srt'd	srt'd	half srt'd half rnd'm	rnd'm	half rev srt'd half rnd'm	rev srt'd	srt'd	half srt'd half rnd'm	rnd'm	half rev srt'd half rnd'm	rev srt'd

n	Heapsort					Iterative Quicksort					Recursive Quicksort				
10	9	9	8	8	7	10	9	9	8	10	5	5	3	3	4
20	18	19	18	18	15	21	19	15	17	23	13	11	10	11	14
40	43	43	41	40	37	51	47	33	38	55	35	31	21	25	36
100	130	126	122	119	115	196	171	94	106	202	156	133	65	74	158
200	291	282	277	264	256	626	521	202	231	633	581	484	149	169	602
400	640	624	610	587	572	2175	1750	432	492	2195	2042	1644	318	372	2056
	srt'd	half srt'd half rnd'm	rnd'm	half rev srt'd half rnd'm	rev srt'd	srt'd	half srt'd half rnd'm	rnd'm	half rev srt'd half rnd'm	rev srt'd	srt'd	half srt'd half rnd'm	rnd'm	half rev srt'd half rnd'm	rev srt'd

* These results were produced by Sharon Doherty.

It is important to recognize that in this chapter we have been considering *comparative* searches and sorts. This means that we have assumed no special knowledge of the key values involved and have used only comparisons between key values in each search or sort algorithm. It is possible to prove that such searches and sorts have worst-case times $O(\lg n)$ and $O(n \lg n)$, respectively.

Other kinds of search and sort algorithms are possible. Some may take significantly less time. For example, suppose you must sort n distinct keys whose values are known to be integers between 1 and 1,000. Simply store the record with key value i as the ith record in an array of records. This places the records in the array in (decreasing) sorted order and takes $O(n)$ time. Sorts that place records in groups, depending on their *actual* key values, and then attempt to sort further within the groups, are called *distributive sorts*. These are not considered in this text. We will, however, consider a very important noncomparative search in Section 9.3.

Simulation is a basic tool for the analysis of the storage and timing requirements of algorithms although we have used it only for analyzing sorts.

As searching as this chapter may have been, it is hoped that it didn't leave you out of sorts!

■ Exercises

1. a. If all comparisons and assignment statements take the same amount of time to execute, then compare the execution times of the first linear search procedure and the procedure revised for greater efficiency.

b. For what values of n will the binary search be faster than the linear search of the improved procedure in the worst case?

2. When you look up a book by author in the library, what kind of a search are you doing?

3. In a ***ternary search*** of a sorted array, the array is divided into three "nearly" equal parts and searched. Key values are examined "near" 1/3 and "near" 2/3 and compared with the search key to determine in which third to search further. Determine the worst-case time for this search and compare it to the worst-case time for a binary search.

4. Suppose a sorted array stores 1,000 integers between 0 and 1,000,000. A pointer array indicates where the least integer greater than 1,000 × (`i` − 1) but not greater than 1,000 × `i` appears in the array. `P[i]` contains that pointer for `i` = 1, 2, . . . , 1,000. If no such integer is in the array, then `p[i]` = 0. Write a function to do an interpolation search, coupled with a binary search.

5. Assuming all comparisons and assignments take the same time to execute, do the following.

a. Determine the worst-case times for the sorts of the procedures given in the text for the maximum entry sort, the bubble sort, and the insertion sort.

b. For each value of n, determine which of the three sorts has least worst-case time.

6. What input order produces the worst case time for

a. The bubble sort?

b. The insertion sort?

7. Write a function to carry out the bubble sort when the integers are stored in a chain.

8. Write a function to carry out the insertion sort when the integers are stored in a chain.

9. Modify the `insertionsort` function so that it does a binary search for the proper insertion position, and then does the insertion.

10. Modify the function so that it does not deal with the last `i` elements after the `i`th pass.

11. Suppose input is given in the order

16, 18, 22, 15, 4, 50, 17, 31, 4, 90, 6, 25

Create the heap produced by

a. The first heap creation algorithm of Section 8.4.

b. The second heap creation algorithm of Section 8.4.

c. How many comparisons and interchanges were required in Exercise 11(a) and Exercise 11(b)?

12. For each heap of Exercise 11(a) and 11(b), produce

a. The reheaped heap after the root element is removed using the first reheaping algorithm of Section 8.4.

b. The reheaped heap after the root element is removed using the second reheaping algorithm of Section 8.4.

c. How many comparisons and interchanges were required in Exercises 12(a) and 12(b)?

13. Why does the pointer array of Section 8.3.6 fail to help?

14. Show the entries of the `data` array, for the input of Exercise 11, when the `heapsort` function is applied after the first three elements have been output.

15. Modify the `heapsort` function so that it counts the number of interchanges and comparisons in each phase and returns their values as parameters.

16. Modify the `heapsort` function so it sorts a `data` array of pointers to records instead of records themselves.

17. What input sequence will cause the second heap creation algorithm to take worst-case time? Calculate the number of comparisons and interchanges it requires.

18. Determine the number of comparisons and copies required by `quicksort` for an array of n records, which is (a) in sorted order; (b) in reverse sorted order; (c) in order so that `partition` always produces two component arrays whose lengths differ by at most 1.

19. Modify `partition` so that it selects an entry at random to be used as the basis entry.

20. Modify `partition` so that it selects the median of the first, middle, and last entries as a basis entry.

21. Explain why the implementation given for `quicksort` requires a stack depth $O(\lg n)$.

22. Modify `quicksort` so that it sorts all component arrays of length at most 20 by using `insertionsort`.

23. Generation of n integers to fill the array `a` in Section 8.6 randomly was really only an approximation of a random input. This is because duplicate values might occur. While the effect of this duplication may be negligible for the simulation results, a "true" random input can be generated. You can fill array `a` as follows: For `i` from 1 to `n`, set `a[i]` to `i`. Then, for `i` from 1 to `n`, pick an integer `int` at random between `i` and `n`, and interchange `a[i]` and `a[int]`.

a. Convince yourself that this will generate a "true" random input.

b. Write a procedure to generate this "true" random input.

24. Consider the "perfect shuffle" example of Chapter 3. When $2n - 1$ is a prime number p, then the number of shuffles required is $p - 1$. The initial configuration is in sorted order, and so is the final configuration after $p - 1$ shuffles. The configurations produced along the way represent different permutations of the initial input. With successive reshufflings, the configurations seem more and more like a "random" arrangement, and then less and less like a "random" arrangement. Take $p = 101$ and use the one hundred configurations, produced by the hundred shuffles required to reproduce the original, as inputs to the heapsort algorithm. Output the statistics table based on one hundred samples of an input of size 101.

Suggested Assignments

1. Write and run the `heapsort` function of Section 8.4.7. A main program should read in examples for the input array `a`. For each example, `n` and the array `a` should be printed, and `heapsort` should be called to sort `a`. When `heapsort` returns, the output array, `sa`, should be printed along with the values for `int1`, `int2`, `comp1`, and `comp2`. At least two examples for small `n` should be worked through by hand to test the correctness of `heapsort`.

2. Write an efficient recursive function `minheaps(t,count,flag)` to return in `count` the number of subtrees of the binary tree pointed to by `t` that are minheaps, and to return in `flag` *true* if `t` points to a minheap and *false* otherwise.

10 11 12 13 1 2 3 4 5 6 7 8

9 More Searching: Insertion and Deletion

Deals with dynamic data structures, which
- *can grow and contract in size*
- *support efficient searches*

The data structures are
- *priority queues, which*
  - *support insertions and deletions*
- *hash tables, which*
  - *support insertions and deletions*
  - *have excellent average search time*
  - *do not support ordered traversals*
- *binary search trees, which*
  - *support searching, inserting, and deleting*
  - *have good average times for these operations*
  - *support ordered traversing*
- *balanced binary search trees, which*
  - *support all the operations of binary search trees*
  - *also support fast access to information in an arbitrary position in a sorted ordering of the information stored*
  - *have good worst-case time for all the operations*

Worst-case and average times are given for the operations on each data structure

9.1 Overview

In the previous chapter, techniques were presented for ordering and storing data so that it could be efficiently *searched* and traversed when desired. Those methods work well as long as the collection of data is essentially *static*—meaning that relatively few insertions and deletions are required. This is a general characteristic of arrays, which were the basis for the faster binary search: they support efficient search but not efficient insertion and deletion. Lists can be used for more efficient insertion and deletion, but then a binary search is not possible.

In this chapter the focus is on achieving efficient search *and* efficient insertions and deletion. Sometimes traversals through the data in sorted order by key value are also desirable. Four data structures that are appropriate for dealing with dynamic data are presented. First, *priority queues* are discussed. They provide the means to deal with a special case of insertion and deletion, as well as serving as an application of heaps. Next, *hash tables* are considered. Hash tables are important data structures that have excellent average search, insertion, and deletion times. Finally, *binary search trees* and *AVL trees* are introduced. These data structures support all the operations—search, insertion, deletion, and traversal—quite well.

9.2 Priority Queues

It often happens that there are a number of tasks, n, each with an associated priority. The n tasks are to be carried out in order of priority. When studying for examinations, most students review and prepare in an order of priority determined by the date of the exam. Most people read the chapters of a book in order, with priority determined by chapter numbering. In this case the situation is static, since the number of chapters does not change. Computer centers process submitted programs by attaching a priority to each and processing them in order of priority. Here the number of programs does change. This represents the usual case, where it is necessary to add new tasks with their priorities to the current collection. The general situation is covered by a *priority queue*.

A ***priority queue*** is a data structure with objects, their priorities, and two operations, insertion and deletion. ***Insertion in a priority queue*** means that an object with its priority is added to the collection of objects. ***Deletion from a priority queue*** means that an object with highest priority is deleted from the collection. A ***stack*** may be thought of as a priority queue with the highest priority object the one most recently added. A ***queue*** may be thought of as a priority queue with the highest priority object the earliest added.

High-level programming languages do not have priority queues directly available in their memories. It is important to be able to implement such queues, because they are of use in their own right and (as will be shown later) often appear as components of algorithms.

9.2.1 Simple Implementations

To implement a priority queue, first represent its objects and priorities as records with priority fields. Two ways to store the records come immediately to mind. The records can be stored in an array or in a list. In either case, the programmer may choose to store the records in arbitrary order or in order of priority. Table 9.1 gives the worst-case insertion and deletion times for each of the four resultant implementations, when n records are present in the priority queue. For example, when using the ordered array implementation, the top array record will have highest priority; thus deletion can be performed in constant time by using a pointer `top` to the current top record. Insertion of a record requires a search of the array to find its proper position. A binary search will allow this position to be found quickly, but to insert it requires $O(n)$ time, because all records below it must be shifted down.

Table 9.1 Worst-Case Insertion and Deletion Times for the Priority Queue

	Implementation	Insertion	Deletion
Unordered	Array	Constant	$O(n)$
	List	Constant	$O(n)$
Ordered	Array	$O(n)$	Constant
	List	$O(n)$	Constant

The table shows that if insertions are more frequent than deletions, it is better to use unordered records. In addition to considering the time for insertion and deletion, the amount of storage required for the list and array implementations must be evaluated. Arrays take less storage.

9.2.2 Using a Heap

Another way to implement a priority queue is to use a heap. You have seen how to build a heap efficiently so that storage is minimal, heap creation takes at most $O(n)$ time, and reheaping takes at most $O(\lg n)$ time. To use a heap for the priority queue, the records are stored at the nodes of a heap that is ordered by priority field values. To insert a new record, place it as a new rightmost entry at the greatest depth of the heap. Then let it work its way up in the heap as in the first heap creation algorithm. Adding the new record in this way will take time at most $O(\lg n)$. To delete a record, simply delete the record at the root of the heap, and then reheap by invoking `shift`. This takes time at most $O(\lg n)$. The time to create the heap initially will be at most $O(n)$ if the second heap creation algorithm is used. This is also the time that would be required to create an initial unordered array or unordered list of records. To create sorted arrays or lists takes time at most $O(n \lg n)$. Referring to Table 9.1, you can see that the heap implementation affords a compromise solution. With arrays and lists, one operation can be done quickly (in constant time) and the other in $O(n)$ time. With the heap, both operations can be done in at most $O(\lg n)$ time.

9.2.3 Using Leftist Trees

Still another way to implement a priority queue is as a ***leftist tree,*** which is a null binary tree or a binary tree with the following properties:

1. It is a heap.
2. Its left and right subtrees are leftist trees.
3. The path that is obtained by starting from the root and branching to the right until a node with no right successor is reached is the shortest path from the root to any node with at most one successor.

For example, the tree (a) of Figure 9.1 violates condition 3, while the trees (b) and (c) are leftist trees.

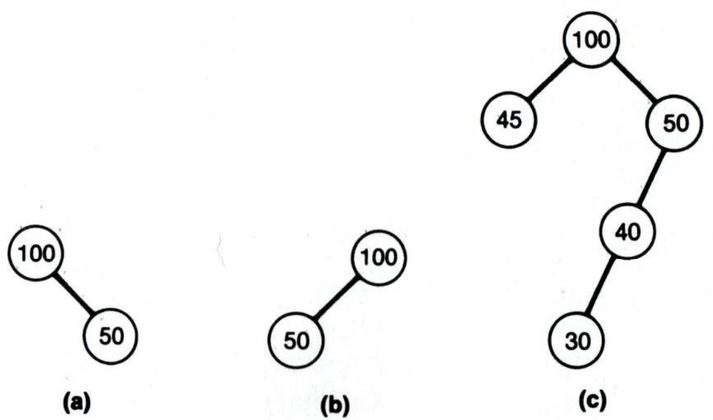

Figure 9.1 One Nonleftist and Two Leftist Trees

As an exercise, you should prove by induction on the number of nodes, n, in a leftist tree, that the shortest path in the tree, from the root to a node with at most one successor, contains at most $\lfloor \lg (n + 1) \rfloor$ nodes. Such a shortest path can always be obtained by traversing the right chain from the root.

Leftist trees are implemented using a linked representation. (See Figure 9.2) Each node's record has an additional field, the distance field, containing the number of nodes along the right chain.

A leftist tree implementation of a priority queue has a number of pluses. Both additions and deletions can be done in constant time when the priority queue is acting as a stack. The time for these operations is $O(\lg n)$ for the general case.

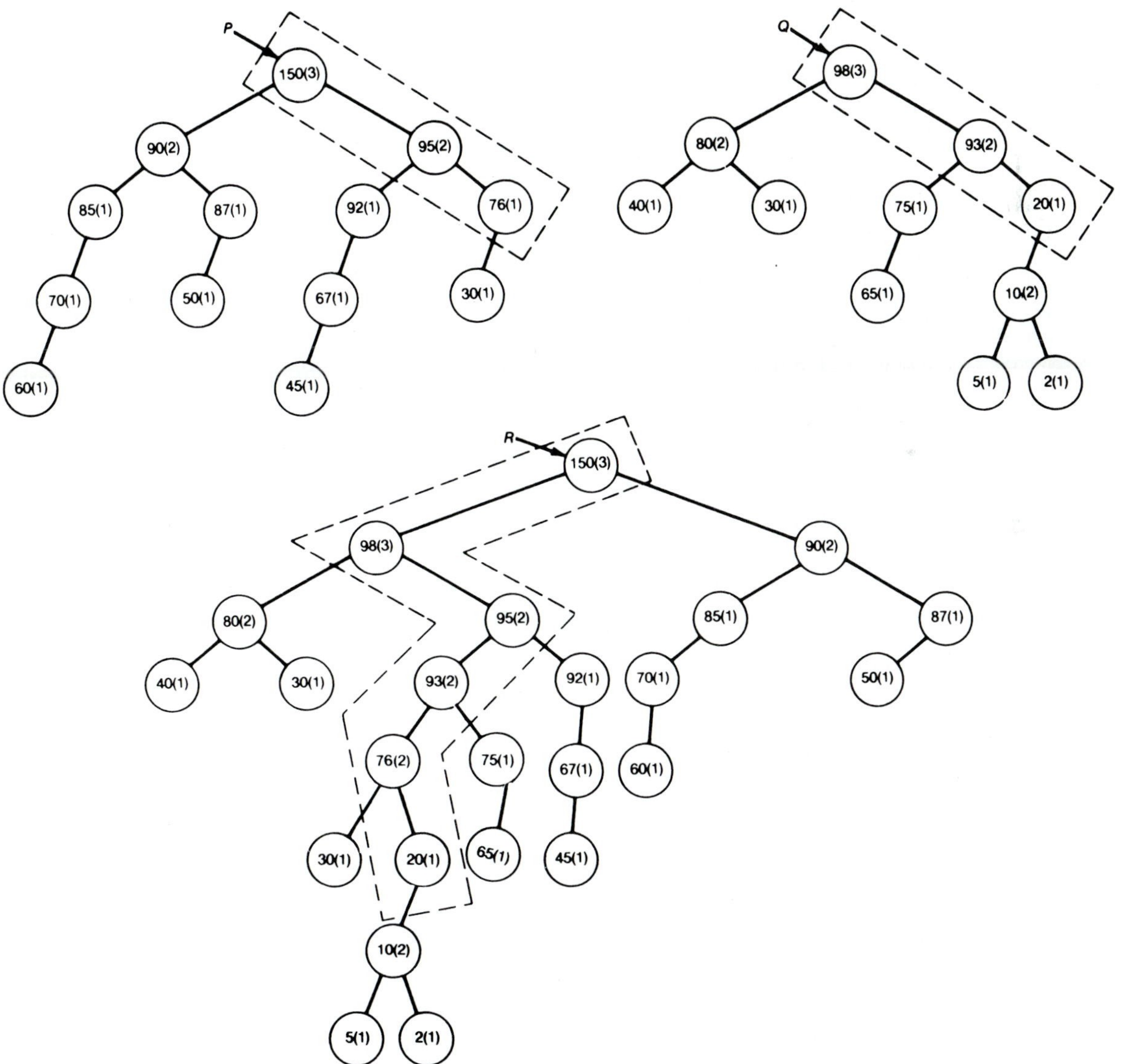

Figure 9.2 The Merging of Leftist Trees Implemented in Linked Representation

Also, two priority queues can be merged into one in $O(\lg n)$ time, where n is the total number of entries in the two priority queues to be merged. This is significantly faster merging than can be done with any of the previous methods, except for unordered lists. Crane [1972] introduced *leftist trees* as a data structure that can be used to implement priority queues. (See Knuth [1973b] for more details.)

The algorithm for merging two priority queues represented as leftist trees in $O(\lg n)$ time is as follows:

1. Make `node.p` the root of the merged tree, and merge `q` with `p`'s right subtree.
2. Update the distance field of `node.p`.
3. If the distance of the root of the left subtree is not at least as great as the distance of the root of its right subtree, then interchange the two subtrees.

`P` is assumed to point to that root of the two leftist trees to be merged which contains the maximum key value, and `q` points to the other root. The result of merging the two trees `p` and `q` is shown as the tree `r`. The distance field values appear in parentheses. Notice in Figure 9.2 that, in effect, the two right chains of `p` and `q` are merged, with the other subtrees coming along for the ride. It is because only these two shortest paths participate in the algorithm that the time is $O(\lg n)$.

9.3 Hash Tables

The next data structure we consider is the *hash table*. A hash table is a data structure for the storage of records. It provides a means for rapid searching for a record with a given key value and adapts well to the insertion and deletion of records. Many compilers, for example, use hash tables to implement their symbol tables. They are also used extensively in systems where the primary objective is information retrieval. Thus `nametable` of Chapter 6 or a dictionary of words might be implemented in a hash table.

To illustrate the need for hash tables, suppose we want to store 1,000 records representing 1,000 customer accounts. Assume that each record has an account number as its key and, since we control account numbers, they range from 1 to 1,000. The solution is simple. Store the record with key value `i` in element `i` of an array `data`. Then, given a key value to search for (say, 836), go directly to element 836 of `data` to find it. What could be a quicker search? We are given a record and know immediately where to go to find it. The search time is a constant, independent of the number of records stored. However, this kind of search requires the ability to assign key values so that all keys are within a range of array indices (1 to 1,000 in this case). It also requires that we have enough storage to accommodate all records.

Now suppose we are dealing with records representing information about our employees, and that the keys are social security numbers. Even with only 1,000 employees, there are 10^9 possible social security numbers. It is not possible to know in advance which of the 10^9 social security numbers our 1,000 employees will actually have. If we were to allocate storage using social security numbers as addresses, we would run into two problems. First, there would not be enough storage. Second, if we did have sufficient storage, 999,999,000 ($10^9 - 10^3$) storage elements would be wasted! Nonetheless, it is extremely attractive to be able to look at the search key value and to know where to find it. This is the goal of hash tables and hash searching—to find a record directly, given its key value.

9.3.1 Building a Hash Table

This section deals with a scaled-down version of the social security example. There are eighteen records, each with a key value that is a three-digit number. The records and their key values will be given in some order, normally unpredictable. We are to build a table, implemented in an array, in which the eighteen key values will be stored, so that searching can be done efficiently. One way to do this is to build a special kind of table—a ***hash table.*** This table will then be searched for given key values. To build a hash table requires a hashing function and a collision resolution policy. A ***hashing function*** is a method of calculating an array or table address for any key. To be useful, the address must be quickly calculable.

The hash function should have other properties, as will become evident. The hash function used here assigns to any key the remainder after division of the key by the table size. If the table size is m and the key value is k, then k mod m denotes this remainder. The starting table or array size is 23.* The eighteen key values and their order are given in Table 9.2, along with the hashing function values assigned to each.

Table 9.2 Hash Addresses

Key Value		Hashing Address	Key Value		Hashing Address
019	→	19	468	→	08
392	→	01	814	→	09
179	→	18	720	→	07
359	→	14	260	→	07
663	→	19	802	→	20
262	→	09	364	→	19
639	→	18	976	→	10
321	→	22	774	→	15
097	→	05	566	→	14

The hashing address for 019 is found, for example, by dividing 019 by the table size 23, to obtain $019 = 0 \times 23 + 19$. The remainder, 19, is the assigned hashing address. As each key value is input, its hashing address is calculated, and the key value is placed into that element of the table. After the first four key values are entered, the table is as shown in Figure 9.3(a).

When the fifth key value, 663, is input, its hashing address is 19, but element 19 of the table is already occupied by another key value. This event is called a ***collision.*** The ***collision resolution policy*** is the method used to determine where to store a value that has undergone collision. The most straightforward policy for

* With division-type hashing functions, the divisor, or table size, is usually a prime number greater than the number of entries to be placed in the table. We have taken this prime to be 23.

	HASH TABLE (a)	HASH TABLE (b)
0		802
1	392	392
2		364
3		
4		
5		097
6		
7		720
8		468
9		262
10		814
11		260
12		976
13		
14	359	359
15		774
16		566
17		
18	179	179
19	019	019
20		663
21		639
22		321

Figure 9.3 Hash Table (a) after Four Entries and (b) Finally

resolving the conflict is called ***linear probing.*** It entails proceeding through the table from the collision element and placing 663, the colliding entry, into the first unoccupied element found. The hash table is assumed to have been initialized, so that each element was "unoccupied" or "empty." If the search for an empty element reaches the end of the table, it circles to the top of the table. In this case, 663 is entered at element 20. The final table is shown in Figure 9.3(b). A total of eight initial collisions occurred in building it.

Each time a location of the table is accessed in an attempt to insert a key value, ***one probe*** has been made. To enter the first key value required one probe; to enter the fifth key value required two probes. To enter keys 1 through 15 required, respectively, 1, 1, 1, 1, 2, 1, 4, 1, 1, 1, 2, 1, 5, 4, 7, 3, 1, 3 probes. You can build the table and confirm these probe numbers.

9.3.2 Searching a Hash Table

How would you search a hash table when asked to find a given key, such as 642? If the key were stored in the table, it would either be found at its hashing address or at the end of a linear probe. If its hashing address were empty, or if the search came to an empty element in the linear probe before finding the key, you might conclude that it was not stored in the table. In this case, the hash address of 642 is 21. Element 21 is not empty but does not have 642 as its value. If you do a linear probe, you will eventually come to element 3, which is empty, without finding 642; thus you would conclude that 642 is not in the table.

If the key searched for were 802, you could go to its hash address (20), find that element occupied with a different key, and start the linear probe, finding 802 at element 0.

Notice that if the search key value is present in the table, the search will require exactly as many probes to find it as were required to enter it into the table. The search traces out the same path. Instead, if the search is for a key value that is not present, the search will take exactly as many probes as would be required to enter it into the current table.

A search that finds a key value is called *successful,* and one that fails to find a key value is *unsuccessful*. Theoretically, one can calculate the number of probes required for every possible key value. Knowing the frequency with which each possible key value (there are 1,000 in our example) will be searched for, one can determine the average number of probes required to search the table. The maximum number of probes can always be determined given the table. In the example, a successful search would require at most seven probes, while an unsuccessful search (for example, for key value 248) could require nine probes. If one never had to search for a key not stored, and all stored keys were searched for with equal frequency, the average number of probes would be

$$\begin{aligned} &1/18 \times 1 + 1/18 \times 1 + 1/18 \times 1 + 1/18 \times 1 + 1/18 \times 2 + 1/18 \times 1 \\ &+ 1/18 \times 4 + 1/18 \times 1 + 1/18 \times 1 + 1/18 \times 1 + 1/18 \times 2 + 1/18 \times 1 \\ &+ 1/18 \times 5 + 1/18 \times 4 + 1/18 \times 7 + 1/18 \times 3 + 1/18 \times 1 + 1/18 \times 3 \end{aligned}$$

or $40/18 = 2.22$ probes. This calculation involves multiplying the frequency of search for each record by the number of probes required to enter it, and then adding all these products. In this case, each frequency was 1/18, and the required probes were noted when the hash table was built.

If no collisions occurred in building the table, every successful search would take exactly one probe. If the hash function actually assigned every key value not stored in the table to an empty address, exactly one probe would be required for any search. This would be the ideal situation. It is apparent now that a desirable hashing function will "scatter" or distribute the key values throughout the table, so that relatively few collisions ensue.

The hash table was of length 23 and stored eighteen key values. Its usage ratio is 18/23; the table is 78 percent full. Intuitively, the lower this ratio, the greater the storage wasted, but the lower the likelihood of a collision. Appropriate hashing functions must be selected with care in real applications, but it is possible to achieve very quick searches using hash tables.

9.3.3 Random Hashing

A great deal of literature in computer science is devoted to the selection of hashing functions and collision resolution policies. To give some idea of what can be achieved, this section states results for an idealized scheme that assumes the hashing function to be perfectly random. Given any key value, the scheme assigns an address to that key value by picking randomly from among all the addresses of the table. This random selection is made so that each of the m addresses in a table of size m is equally likely to be selected. The table is built by inserting, in turn, each given key value. A key value is stored by determining its hash address. If that address is empty, the key value is stored there. If that address is occupied, the collision resolution policy works as follows. Another random hash function again selects an address at random. If that address is empty, the key value is stored there. If it is occupied, this procedure is repeated until the key value is finally entered. Thus an insertion of a key value may require the generation of a sequence of hash addresses ending with the actual final storage address.

After the table is built, searches are performed as follows. Trace the sequence of hash addresses that were generated to store the search key (if it is in the table) or that would have been generated (had the key been stored). The basic assumption made here is that the hash functions generate precisely the same sequence of hash addresses for the search as for building the table. This may seem like a strange way for *random* hash functions to work, but it is our assumption nevertheless. Table 9.3 shows the theoretical results for such a scheme, when n keys are stored in the table of size m.

The successful and unsuccessful search columns are given approximately by the functions $(1/\alpha)\ln 1/(1-\alpha)$ and $1/(1-\alpha)$ where $\alpha = n/m$. The remarkable fact is that the *average* search time does not depend on n, the number of records stored in the table, but only on the usage ratio, n/m. Thus storage can be traded for speed in hash table searches. For example, if n is 10,000 and m is 11,112, α is about 0.90, and an average of only 2.56 probes will be required for a successful search. Contrast this with the 5,000 comparisons or probes needed for the linear search in the random case, or the 12.29 comparisons or probes needed for a binary search. Actual hashing functions and collision resolution policies can come close to achieving this kind of average behavior. The worst-case times for hash table searching can, however, be quite large.

Hash tables are not a searching panacea. A major disadvantage is that entries will not be in order by key. The only way to access the records in sorted order is to sort them. However, if this isn't important, hashing is often a good approach.

Table 9.3 Average Number of Probes for Searches

Usage Ratio n/m	Successful Search	Unsuccessful Search
.25	1.15	1.33
.50	1.39	2.00
.75	1.85	4.00
.80	2.01	5.00
.90	2.56	10.00
.95	3.15	20.00

9.3.4 Other Collision Resolution Policies: Open Addressing and Chaining

The linear probing collision resolution policy is a special case of ***open addressing***. The idea of open addressing is to resolve collisions by following a specific *probe sequence* whenever a collision occurs, in order to determine the insertion location for a new key. To be specific, let k_i denote the key stored in the ith location of a hash table of size m. Assume that at least one table location is unoccupied and set all unoccupied locations to the "null" key value. This prevents "falling off" the table when searching for a key and reduces the search time, because an end-of-table search test need not be made.

Let $h(k)$ denote the hash function value for search key k. The sequence of indexes determined by

$$[h(k) + i \times p(k)]\text{mod } m^* \qquad \text{for} \quad i = 0, 1, 2, \ldots, m - 1$$

is a probe sequence if the indexes are all distinct. This implies that, as i goes from 0 to $m - 1$, the generated indexes form a permutation of the indexes $0, 1, 2, \ldots, m - 1$. Consequently, in attempting a new key insertion, all locations of the hash table will be accessed in some order before deciding that the key cannot be inserted. It also ensures that, in attempting to search for a key, all locations of the table will be accessed in some order before concluding that the search key is not in the table, or until a null key is encountered.

Linear probing is the special case obtained by taking $p(k) = 1$ for all keys k. In general, a key is inserted by accessing the table locations given by its probe sequence, determined by $[h(k) + i \times p(k)]\text{mod } m$ as i goes from 0 to $m - 1$, until a null key is encountered. The key is then inserted in place of that null key. A search is done the same way. The algorithm for a hash table search using a probe sequence is as follows:

1. Set i to $h(k)$
2. While k_i is not the search key k and k_i is not the null key
   set i to $[i + p(k)]\text{mod } m$.
3. If $k_i = k$, then
   set `found` to *true*
   else
   set `found` to *false*.

Notice that $p(k)$ represents a displacement from the current probe address.

With linear probing, large clusters of keys stored in adjacent locations of the hash table tend to get larger as insertions are made. This is because large clusters have a greater probability of the new keys' hash address falling within the cluster, assuming a "random" hash function and "random" keys. A cluster gets larger when a new key is inserted at either end of the cluster, or when two separated clusters become connected because of the new key insertion. Both of these events occurred in the scaled-down social security number example. This phenomenon is called ***primary clustering***. As the table usage ratio increases, primary clustering

* The formula states that the ith index in the probe sequence is found by calculating $[i + p(k)]\text{mod } m$. However, if the previous index, the $(i - 1)$th, is known, then simply adding $p(k)$ to it and taking the result mod m will also yield the ith index.

leads to greater search and insertion times. This is clearly undesirable. It happens because the large clusters must be traversed, with the average time being proportional to half the cluster length when keys are searched with equal frequency. Thus the insertion, or search for a key, begins to look like a linear search through a cluster.

To avoid primary clustering, try taking the next probe to be in a position removed from the current one instead of being adjacent to it. This is open addressing with ***displaced linear probing.*** Taking $p(k) = \alpha$ for some integer α that is not a factor of m will give such a probe sequence. To see this, take $m = 13$ and $\alpha = 5$. The probe sequence is then generated by $[h(k) + i \times 5]$ mod 13 for $i = 0, 1, 2, \ldots, 12$. If $h(k) = 7$, this gives the probe sequence

7, 12, 4, 9, 1, 6, <u>11</u>, 8, 0, 5, 10, 2

Note that any key k whose hash address is 7 will have *exactly* the same probe sequence. Even worse, suppose a key's hash address is 11, and 11 is occupied upon its insertion. The next probe for this key will be in location $[11 + 1 \times 5]$ mod 13, which is location 3. A collision at 3 will result in a further probe at $[3 + 1 \times 5]$ mod 13 or 8, then 0, 5, etc. Thus the key that originally hashed to address 11 picks up at the intersection of 11 with the probe sequence for any key hashing to 7, and follows that same probe sequence from 11 onward. Similarly, any key that collides, upon insertion, with a key already occupying its hash address, will continue along this exact probe sequence from its point of entry.

In effect, there is exactly one probe sequence for all keys; they just enter, or merge into it, at different positions specified by their hash addresses. This means that, as a "cluster" builds up along this probe sequence (say, at 11, 3, 8, 0, and 5, as they become occupied), it has the same tendency to grow as a cluster of physically adjacent occupied addresses did with linear probing. This is just primary clustering, although the clusters do not appear in adjacent locations.

We need effective techniques for dealing with this problem. Figure 9.4 gives the hash tables that result from their application to our example. The hash tables produced by linear probing, and the displaced linear probing just discussed, appear in tables (a) and (b) of the figure, corresponding to $\alpha = 1$ and $\alpha = 4$, respectively. In addition, the number of probes required for the insertion of each key is indicated for each table. You should create these tables yourself to confirm their correctness and to aid in understanding the discussion.

The average number of probes for a successful search of this table is $1/18 \times (11 \times 1 + 5 \times 2 + 1 \times 3 + 1 \times 12) = 36/18$ or 2.00, which is an improvement over linear probing for this example. However, for the reasons stated previously, the theoretical average number of probes in a successful search will be the same as for linear probing.

How can we eliminate or break up large clusters to improve these results? It can be done using open addressing with ***secondary clustering.*** Consider the following analogy. Suppose there are m stores, each selling a certain specialty item, and each with exactly one such item in stock. Assume n people decide to buy that item the same day, and they, in turn, each select one of the m stores at random. If a customer finds the item in stock at the shop of his or her choice, he or she buys it. However, if someone has already bought the item, it will be out of stock, and the

Keys	Hash Address
019	19
392	01
179	18
359	14
663	19
262	09
639	18
321	22
097	05
468	08
814	09
720	07
260	07
802	20
364	19
976	10
774	15
566	14

	Hash Table (a)	Hash Table (b)	Hash Table (c)	Hash Table (d)	Hash Table (e)
0	802 (4)	663 (2)	364 (5)	364 (4)	392 (1)
1	392 (1)	392 (1)	392 (1)	392 (1)	
2	364 (7)				
3		321 (2)			
4		364 (3)	566 (3)		
5	097 (1)	097 (1)	097 (1)	097 (1)	097 (1)
6			720 (3)	260 (3)	663 (3)
7	720 (1)	720 (1)	639 (2)	720 (1)	720 (1)
8	468 (1)	468 (1)	468 (1)	468 (1)	468 (1)
9	262 (1)	262 (1)	262 (1)	262 (1)	262 (1)
10	814 (2)	976 (1)	976 (1)	814 (2)	976 (1)
11	260 (5)	260 (2)		976 (2)	364 (2)
12	976 (3)	566 (12)	814 (3)		321 (2)
13		814 (2)		566 (3)	
14	359 (1)	359 (1)	359 (1)	359 (1)	359 (1)
15	774 (1)	774 (1)	774 (1)	774 (1)	774 (1)
16	566 (3)				566 (3)
17			260 (4)	639 (3)	260 (4)
18	179 (1)	179 (1)	179 (1)	179 (1)	179 (1)
19	019 (1)	019 (1)	019 (1)	019 (1)	019 (1)
20	663 (2)	802 (1)	663 (2)	663 (2)	806 (1)
21	639 (4)		802 (2)	802 (2)	814 (2)
22	321 (1)	639 (2)	321 (1)	321 (1)	639 (2)
	linear probing	displaced linear probing	secondary clustering	quadratic residue	double hashing
Average number of probes for a successful search	2.22	2.00	1.89	1.72	1.61

Figure 9.4 Typical Hash Tables for the Five Open-Addressing Techniques Considered (Usage Ratio 78 Percent)

person may ask the store manager for directions to another store. Let the stores be numbered from 0 to $m - 1$. Whenever this occurs, suppose the manager of the ith shop sends the customer to the $(i + 1)$th shop. Of course, the manager of the $(m - 1)$th store refers people to the 0th store. The result of all this feverish activity is that *all* customers arriving at a particular out-of-stock store are sent to the same next store. Again, at that store, they are *all* sent to the same next store whenever the item has been sold. It seems clear that this results in *primary clusters* of customers being formed. The physical locations of the stores is irrelevant to this process.

Suppose each store manager, instead of giving identical directions to each would-be purchaser, sends customers to another store depending on which store they tried originally and on the number of stores they have already been to. The effect will be to disperse the unhappy customers. Rather than *all* these people being sent on to the same sequence of shops, only those with the same initial shop and the same number of previous attempts at buying are given identical directions. Clusters should still appear, but they should tend to be smaller than the primary clusters. This is, in fact, what happens, and the clusters that appear after such dispersion are called ***secondary clusters.***

Translating this remedy to the problem involves choosing $p(k)$ so that it becomes a function of $h(k)$, the initial hash address of key k. This implies that only keys hashing to the same address will follow identical probe sequences. Unlike linear or displaced linear probing, keys whose probe sequences intersect do not merge into the same probe sequence at intersection. They go their separate ways. Again, to ensure that $p[h(k)]$ generates a probe sequence, it is necessary to choose it carefully. As long as $p[h(k)]$ is not a factor of m, for each key k, a probe sequence will result. If m is a prime number, this will always be the case when $p[h(k)]$ is between 0 and $m - 1$.

As an example, take

$$p(k) = \begin{cases} [h(k) + 4] \bmod m & \text{if it is not zero} \\ 1 \text{ otherwise} \end{cases}$$

Using our $h(k) = k \bmod m$ and $m = 13$, any key with hash address 7 (say, key 137) has the probe sequence

7, 5, 3, 1, 12, 10, 8, 6, 4, 2, 0, $\underline{11}$, 9

Any key hashing to 11 now (say, key 258) has the probe sequence

11, 0, 2, 4, 6, 8, 10, 12, 1, 3, 5, 7, 9

Notice that a collision at 11, for such a key, does not result in the probe sequence for keys with hash address 7 being followed from its intersection with 11. It follows the sequence 11, 0, 2, . . . instead of 11, 9, 7, 5, ...

The hash table for this secondary clustering remedy is hash table (c) of Figure 9.4. The average number of probes for a successful search in this table is $1/18 \times [(11 \times 1) + (3 \times 2) + (3 \times 3) + (1 \times 5)] = 31/18$ or 1.72. This gives an improvement over hash tables (a) and (b), as expected. It occurs because the secondary clusters tend to be shorter than the primary clusters. Notice that the "physically adjacent" clusters in the table are deceiving; they are not relevant. It is the clustering along the probe sequences that is important. In linear and displaced linear probing there is, in effect, only one probe sequence. With the secondary clustering techniques, there is a distinct probe sequence for each distinct hash address.

Open addressing with the ***quadratic residue*** technique attempts to break up primary clusters in a similar way, although it generates a probe sequence somewhat differently. The probe sequence for key k starts with $h(k)$ and follows with

$$[h(k) + i^2] \bmod m, [h(k) - i^2] \bmod m \qquad \text{for } i = 1, 2, \ldots, (m - 1)/2$$

Again, to ensure that m distinct indexes are generated, care must be taken in the choice of m. If m is prime and of the form $(4 \times j) + 3$, then m distinct indexes are guaranteed. Since $m = 23$ in our example, $j = 5$ and $(m - 1)/2 = 11$. The probe sequence for key k is then

$$h(k),$$
$$[h(k) + 1^2] \bmod 23, [h(k) - 1^2] \bmod 23,$$
$$[h(k) + 2^2] \bmod 23, [h(k) - 2^2] \bmod 23, \ldots,$$
$$[h(k) + 11^2] \bmod 23, [h(k) - 11^2] \bmod 23$$

If k is 364, $h(k) = 19$, and the probe sequence is

19, 20, 18, 0, 15, 5, 10, 12, 3, 21, 17, 9, 6, 22, 16, 12, 1, 8, 7, 4, 11, 2, 13

This is really a secondary clustering technique, since keys that hash to the same address will still have identical probe sequences. The hash table for this technique appears as hash table (d) of Figure 9.4, which gives an average number of probes of $1/18 \times [(10 \times 1) + (4 \times 2) + (3 \times 3) + (1 \times 4)] = 31/18$ or 1.72 for a successful search. When a key is inserted with these secondary clustering techniques, the result may be the lengthening or connecting of two clusters. These events may occur simultaneously along more than one probe sequence when the key is inserted.

Returning to the example of the out-of-stock specialty item, we might look for a remedy that avoids even these secondary clusters, since they also tend to increase search and insertion times. It seems reasonable to try to disperse these secondary clusters by giving each would-be customer a separate set of directions. This may be done by having store managers randomly select the next store for a customer to try. This idea is known as open addressing with ***double hashing.*** The technique uses a second hash function for $p(k)$. To be most effective, this should be as "random" as the initial hash function and should assign a value to key k by selecting this value independently of the value assigned to key k by the initial hash function.

The theoretical analysis for this technique has not been carried out as fully as for other methods, but the results indicate that double hashing gives the best results among the open addressing techniques. Empirically, it gives results that are the same as those for "random" hashing (see Table 9.3). This is somewhat surprising, since random hashing corresponds to our store remedy. Double hashing, instead of picking a store randomly, over and over again, until a customer is satisfied, merely picks an individual displacement at random for each key. This displacement then determines the probe sequence for a given hash address.

Care must be exercised in the selection of the second hash function so that a desirable probe sequence is generated. If m is a prime, then one possibility that ensures the generation of such a probe sequence is

$$p(k) = \begin{cases} q \bmod m & \text{where } q \times m + r = k, \quad r \text{ is } k \bmod m, \quad \text{and } q \bmod m > 0 \\ 1 \text{ if } q \bmod m = 0 \end{cases}$$

For instance, $p(657) = 11$, since $657 = 50 \times 13 + 7$ when $m = 13$. Hence the probe sequence for 657 is

7, 5, 3, 1, 12, 10, 8, 6, 4, 2, 0, 11, 9

Key 137 also has hash address 7, but $p(137) = 10$, since $137 = 10 \times 13 + 7$. Its probe sequence, however, is distinct from 657's:

7, 4, 1, 11, 8, 5, 2, 12, 9, 6, 3, 0, 10

Now, even keys with the same hash address are unlikely to have the same probe sequence. The idea is that, statistically, probe sequences should appear to be approximately independently and randomly generated for two distinct keys. The hash table produced by this technique is given as hash table (e) of Figure 9.4, and the average number of successful probes is $1/18 \times [(11 \times 1) + (4 \times 2) + (2 \times 3) + (1 \times 4)] = 29/18$ or 1.61.

As a further illustration, suppose key 582 is to be inserted in the hash tables of Figure 9.4. Its hash address, 582 mod 23, is 7, since $582 = 25 \times 23 + 7$. The sequence of probed locations and the number of probes required for each table are given below.

Linear probing	7, 8, 9, 10, 11, 12	(7)
Displaced linear probing	7, 11, 15, 19, 0, 4, 8, 12, 16	(9)
Secondary clustering	7, 18, 6, 17, 5, 16	(6)
Quadratic residue	7, 8, 6, 11, 3	(5)
Double hashing	7, 9, 11, 13	(4)

It is interesting that the average number of probes required to make an insertion is the same as the average number of probes required to carry out an unsuccessful search. This fact is useful in the analysis of hashing. The results of the example are typical of the behavior of open addressing techniques. As the usage ratio of the table increases, the secondary clustering and quadratic residue methods provide considerable improvement over the primary clustering methods. The double hashing techniques improve the results even more. For lower usage ratios, the improvements are much less noticeable. These improvements in average numbers of *probes* do not translate directly into similar improvements in average *times,* which depend on implementation details.

Chaining is another method of collision resolution. The idea is to link together all records that collide at a hash address. These may be kept separately or within the hash table itself. ***Separate chaining*** treats each location of the hash table as the head of a list—the list of all keys that collide at that location. Separate storage is used to store records of the list, which consist of key values and link pointer values. When a collision occurs, an insertion is made at the front of the corresponding list. Using this technique for our example yields the hash table shown in Figure 9.5 with corresponding numbers of probes (key comparisons). The table's average number of probes for a successful search is $1/18 \times [(12 \times 1) + (5 \times 2) + (1 \times 3)] = 25/18$ or 1.39.

In contrast to open addressing, separate chaining allows clusters to form only when keys hash to the same address. Hence the lengths of the lists should be similar to the lengths of clusters formed with secondary clustering techniques. A

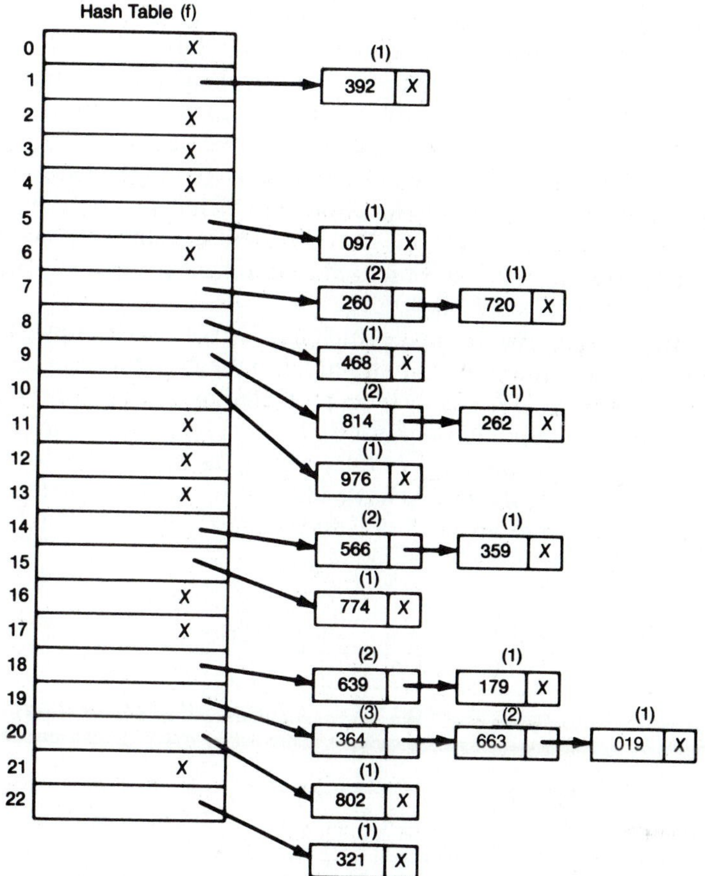

Figure 9.5 Hash Table for Separate Chaining

comparison of the 1.39 probes to the 1.89 or 1.72 probes with secondary clustering is somewhat unfair, since the hash table with separate chaining really uses additional storage. The actual amount of additional storage depends on the record lengths. When they are small, and storage that would otherwise be unused is available for the link pointer values, then the usage ratio should more properly be measured as $n/(n + m)$. This is 18/41, or 44 percent, in the example. When the link field takes up the same amount of storage as a record, then the usage ratio should more properly be measured as $n/(2n + m)$. This is 18/59, or 31 percent, in the example.

Coalesced chaining maintains lists of records whose keys hash to the same address. These lists are stored within the hash table itself. Whenever two such lists "intersect," they coalesce. This is analogous to two separated clusters becoming connected when a new key is inserted in the location that separated them. Each hash table entry is now a record containing a key value and a link value to the next record on its associated list.

A key is inserted into the table by going to its hash address and traversing its list until a null key is found, the key itself is found, or no records remain on the list. If the null key is found, the new key is inserted in the record stored at that location, and its link field is set to null. If the key itself is found, no insertion is necessary. If no records remain on the list, then an unoccupied location must be found, the new key inserted there, and its link field set to null. This new record must then be appended at the end of the traversed list.

In order to create this new record to be appended, a pointer **p** is kept updated. Initially, **p** points to location *m* (which is just off the table). Whenever a new record must be found, **p** is decremented by 1 until the location it points to is unoccupied. If **p** "falls off" the table (becomes less than 0), then the table is full and no insertion is possible.

Figure 9.6 illustrates coalesced chaining for the example. **P** is initially 23 and the first four keys are inserted directly into their hash addresses. Key 663 collides at its hash address, 19. **P** is then decremented by 1 and, since location 22 is empty, 663 and a null next pointer are inserted there. This new record is then appended at the end of the list beginning in 19, by setting the link field of location 19 to 22. Key 262 is inserted directly into its hash address, 09. The next entry is 639, but its hash address, 18, contains an entry. **P** is then decremented by 1, and since location 21 is

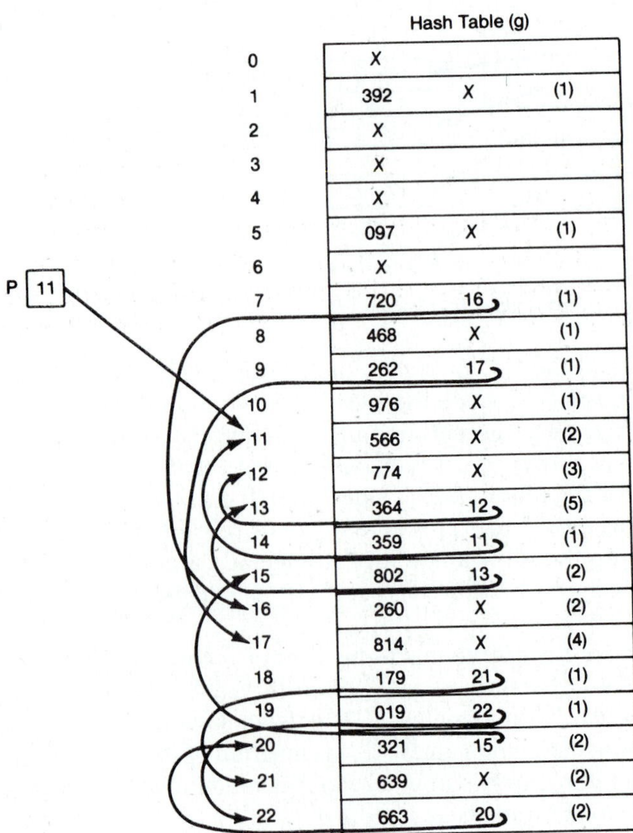

Figure 9.6 Hash Table for Coalesced Chaining

empty, 639 and a null link value is inserted there. This record is then appended at the end of the list beginning in 18 by setting the link field of location 18 to 21.

Figure 9.6 shows the resultant hash table, the number of probes for each key insertion, and the value of p after all eighteen keys are entered. The average number of probes for a successful search of this table is $1/18 \times [(9 \times 1) + (6 \times 2) + (1 \times 3) + (1 \times 4) + (1 \times 5)] = 33/18$ or 1.81. If extra storage is available for the link fields, then n/m is a reasonable measure of the table usage here. These 1.81 probes are not as good as the 1.61 or 1.72 probes resulting from double hashing and quadratic residues in the example. Theoretical results, however, show that coalesced chaining does yield better average results than "random" hashing when storage is available for link pointer fields. You may expect coalesced chaining to give results that are not as good as separate chaining, better than linear or displaced linear probing, not as good as "random" or double hashing, but perhaps comparable to the secondary clustering techniques. If the link fields take additional storage, it should be taken into account in the usage factors for comparison. Note that coalesced chaining generally yields more but shorter lists (or clusters) than linear or displaced probing, because connecting or coalescing of clusters occurs to a lesser extent with coalesced chaining.

A third method of collision resolution will be discussed in Chapter 10 in connection with external memory, or secondary storage, where it is especially appropriate and useful.

9.3.5 Searching in Ordered Hash Tables

If keys are entered into a hash table in sorted order, open-addressing and chaining techniques will always result in searches along a probe sequence or along a list, in which the keys appear in the same or reverse order, respectively. In both cases, the search algorithm may be easily modified so that whenever a key is encountered that precedes the search key in the relevant ordering, the search is immediately terminated unsuccessfully. This can significantly decrease search times for unsuccessful searches but will not affect successful search times. You can generate the new hash tables (a) through (g) of Figures 9.4 to 9.6 to see the effect on the tables of the keys appearing in sorted order.

Of course, one cannot normally control the order in which keys to be inserted appear. It is not difficult, however, to modify the insertion algorithms so that the resultant hash table is exactly the same as the hash table resulting when keys are given in sorted order. The idea of the algorithm is clever and simple. For open addressing, simply insert a key as usual unless, in following a probe sequence, a key is encountered that precedes the new key in the ordering. Then the search key is inserted in *that* position, and the insertion proceeds as though the replaced key were being inserted using the displaced key instead of the new key. For separate chaining, it is necessary to traverse the list at which a collision occurs, and insert the new key in its proper position of the list.

This technique does not work directly for coalesced chaining, because the insertion of a new key in a list may start from the interior of the list when a collision occurs. In order to keep coalesced lists in order, it is necessary to find the first list record or be able to traverse the list in either direction. To achieve this, the lists might be implemented as circular lists or two-way lists. Circular lists take more traversal time but less storage than two-way lists.

Keeping ordered hash tables yields significant improvements in the average number of probes required for unsuccessful searches with open addressing. These improvements are especially striking for high usage ratios.

9.3.6 Deletion from Hash Tables

Deletion in hash tables using separate chaining is straightforward, since it amounts to the deletion of a record from a list. With open-addressing and coalesced chaining, the deletion of a key is not so straightforward, since a key of the table will be needed to reach another key when it is on that key's probe sequence or list. Deleting it would break this path. One solution to this problem is to mark a deleted key location as "deleted," so that the path is not broken. When a significant fraction of keys has been deleted, the actual usage ratio of the resultant table is low, but search times will still reflect the original higher usage ratio. New insertions, when encountering a "deleted" location, may recapture this wasted storage by occupying such "deleted" locations. However, if "deleted" locations build up, without being recaptured by insertions, search times deteriorate to a linear search for unsuccessful searches and are larger than necessary for successful searches. The only remedy is to rebuild the hash table. Although the algorithm is not given here, this may be done in place, by using only storage allocated to the table in order to carry out the creation of a new table. Hash tables can also be expanded or decreased in size, and recreated. Again, this can be done in place.

9.3.7 Hashing Overview

Let us review the advantages and disadvantages of hashing. First, note that some estimate is needed in advance for the maximum number of entries to be stored in a hash table, since its size must be declared. This is important; too high an estimate wastes space, and too low an estimate means a large usage ratio and poorer performance. Second, the hash function must be carefully chosen so that it can be computed quickly and generates relatively few collisions.

The main characteristic of hashing is its excellent average search, insertion, and deletion time. However, when deletions are frequent, care is required in deciding which collision resolution policy to use. The major disadvantages of hashing are the possibility of large worst-case times and the lack of support for traversal through the records in sorted order. Also, the only information obtained from an unsuccessful search is that the record isn't in the table. In the data structure considered next, more information may be obtained.

Choosing the appropriate hashing technique involves consideration of time and storage as well as the relative frequency with which successful searches, unsuccessful searches, and deletions will occur. However, some generalizations can be made.

Using open addressing to resolve collisions can be quite efficient for moderate usage ratios. Although the average times for successful searches depend on whether simple linear probing or more complex probing such as double hashing is used, the differences are small. These differences are more significant for unsuccessful searches, so more complex probing is desirable when they will occur frequently. Ordered hash tables can significantly reduce the search times in this case. For larger usage ratios the chaining methods have superior search times.

With open addressing, when deletions are frequent, the table can actually be storing relatively few entries, with many table positions simply marking deleted entries. Thus the table performance is governed by a usage ratio that does not reflect the actual, much smaller, number of positions used to store records. Separate chaining uses storage more efficiently in this case, and deletion is easy. Separate chaining also has better average time behavior than the other methods.

When records are small, the links required by chaining take significant extra storage compared to open addressing, whereas the opposite is true when records are large. When record size is moderate, the extra storage for links using separate chaining must be weighed against the reduced usage ratio that could be obtained if this storage were used in open addressing.

9.4 Binary Search Trees

We turn now to the next data structure: binary search trees. A ***binary search tree*** is a binary tree with the property that its left subtree contains records no larger than the root record, its right subtree contains records no smaller than the root record, and its left and right subtrees are also binary search trees. This is a recursive definition.

A binary tree fails to be a binary search tree if even one node contains a record in its left subtree or its right subtree that is, respectively, larger or smaller than the record stored at the node. Figure 9.7 has three examples of binary search trees containing the same fifteen records.

Note that a binary search tree need not be a heap, and that a heap need not be a binary search tree. In general, they are different kinds of binary trees. There are many binary trees that can store the same records. Any binary tree with n nodes can store n records in such a way that the tree is a binary search tree. (Just do an inorder traversal of the binary tree and insert the records in sorted order.)

9.4.1 Searching the Search Trees

In Chapter 7, three important traversals through the nodes of any binary tree were defined: 1) preorder, 2) inorder, and 3) postorder. In order to search a binary tree to determine if a particular key value is stored, any one of those traversals could be used to gain access to each node in turn, and the node tested to see if the search key value is there. This would be equivalent to a linear search.

Instead, the special nature of binary *search* trees facilitates highly efficient search. We simply compare the search key with the root key. If they match, the search is complete. If not, determine whether the search key is smaller than the key at the root. If so, then if it is in the tree at all, it must be in the left subtree. If it is larger than the root key, it must be in the right subtree if it is in the tree at all. Thus either the left or right subtree is eliminated from consideration. This procedure is repeated for the subtree not eliminated. Eventually, the procedure finds the key in the tree or comes to a null subtree and concludes that the key is not stored in the tree.

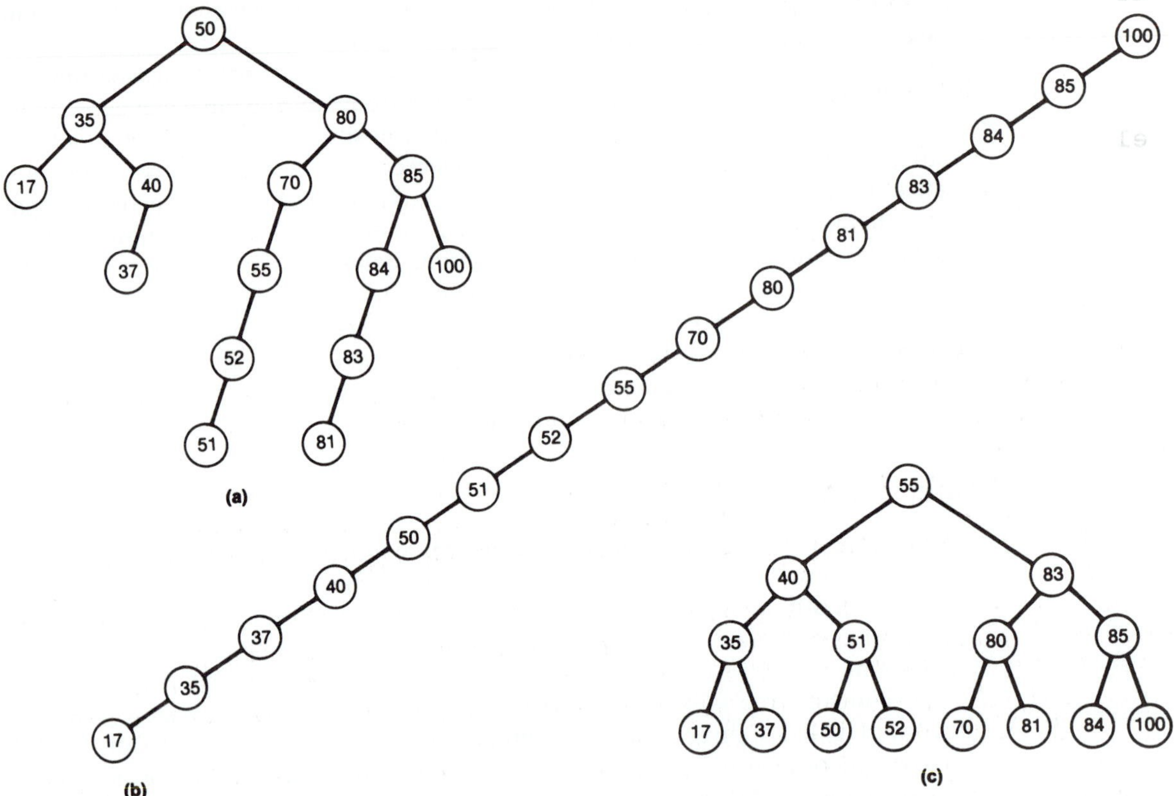

Figure 9.7 Three Binary Search Trees Containing the Same Data

Assume that nodes of the binary search tree are represented as follows.

```
typedef struct treenode
{
   whatever info;
   struct treenode *leftptr;
   struct treenode *rightptr;
}binarytreenode,*binarytreepointer;
```

This special search may be implemented as follows:

```
found = FALSE;
p = t;
pred = NULL;
while ((p != NULL) && (!found))
   if (keyvalue == p->key)
      found = TRUE;
```

This code sets `found` *to* true *only if a record whose key is equal to* `keyvalue` *is in the binary search tree* `t`*. If* `found` *is* true*, then* `pred` *contains a pointer to the predecessor of that record, and* `p` *contains a pointer to that record. If found is* false*, then* `pred` *points to the node that would have been its predecessor had it been in the tree.*

```
else if (keyvalue < p->key)
   {
      pred = p;
      p = p->leftptr;
   }
else
   {
      pred = p;
      p = p->rightptr:
   }
```

Found indicates whether the search key value was present in the tree. If so, **p** points to the node in which the search key was found, and **pred** points to its predecessor. If the search key was not found, then **pred** points to the node that would have been its predecessor had it been in the tree. Note that this allows additional information to be obtained, if desired, beyond the fact that the search key was not found. The key less than the search key and the key greater than the search key can easily be determined, so that records closest to the desired one are known.

Notice that when (b) of Figure 9.7 is searched in this way, the search is equivalent to a linear search of an array in which the records are stored in sorted order. This search algorithm, applied to (c), would be equivalent to a binary search of an array in which the records are stored in sorted order. A search of (a) would fall somewhere between these two extremes.

What allows the search of Figure 9.7(c) to be equivalent to a binary search? It is the fact that the tree is ''scrunched up'' or near minimum possible depth, and not as straggly (unnecessarily deep) as the others. It has an intuitive kind of ''balance,'' so that we eliminate from consideration about half the records each time we make a comparison. We are back to the game of ''twenty questions.''

9.4.2 Growing the Search Tree ''Simply''

This section develops an algorithm for creating or growing a binary search tree that stores records at its nodes. Imagine that you have already processed some records and created a binary search tree for them. Given the next input record, search the current tree for its key value. Assume no duplicates will occur in the tree, although this need not create any real problem, since a node can contain a pointer to a list, stored separately, of records with identical key values. Eventually, since the new record is not in the tree, a null subtree will be reached. However, if this null subtree is replaced by a node that stores this record, the resultant tree will still be a binary search tree. For instance, inserting 45 by this procedure in Figure 9.7(c) produces Figure 9.8. This gives an algorithm for growing a binary search tree. Start with the first input record at the root. For each additional input, search the tree. The search will reach a node whose left or right successor must be followed, but the successor is null. The record replaces that null subtree.

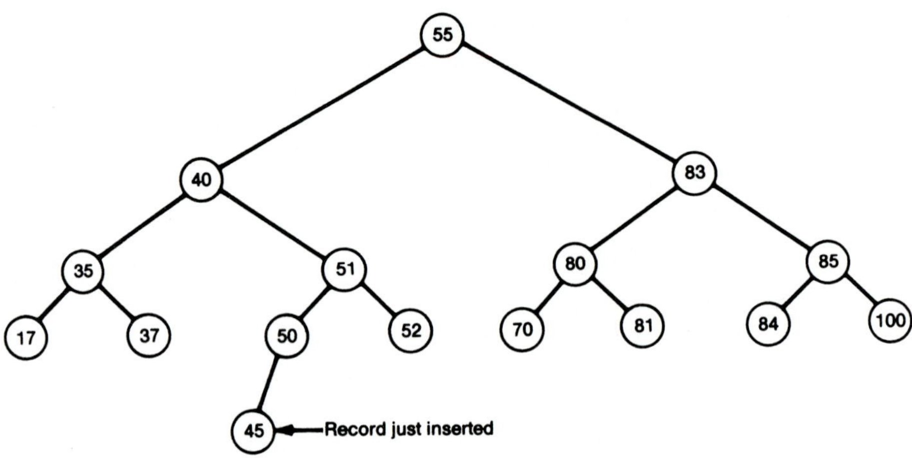

Figure 9.8 Binary Search Tree Created from Figure 9.7

This can be accomplished by using `pred` from the search implementation, and then invoking the following.

```
p = malloc(sizeof(binarytreenode));
p->key = keyvalue;
p->leftptr = NULL;
p->rightptr = NULL;
if (keyvalue < pred->key)
   pred->leftptr = p;
else
   pred->rightptr = p;
```

This code creates and inserts a new record with key equal to `keyvalue` *as the successor of the record pointed to by* `pred`. *It replaces the correct null subtree of* `pred` *by the new record, which becomes a terminal node.*

We now have algorithms for growing, searching, and inserting records into a binary search tree.

9.4.3 The Shape of Simple Binary Search Trees

The binary search tree grown by the algorithm of the preceding section will have its shape determined by the input order of the records to be stored. If they are input in sorted order or reverse sorted order, the result is Figure 9.7(b) or its mirror image. If they are input in the order 55, 40, 83, 35, 51, 80, 85, 17, 37, 50, 52, 70, 81, 84, 100, the result is Figure 9.7(c). There are $n!$ possible input orderings of n distinct keys. Some of these may give rise to the same binary search tree. Recall that the tree grown cannot have depth greater than n nor less than $\lceil \lg(n + 1) \rceil$. Suppose the input is selected so that each of the $n!$ possible orderings is equally likely to occur. This would be the case if the first input record is selected at random from among the n records, the second is selected at random from among the remaining $n - 1$ records, and so on. What will be the *average* depth of trees grown by the algorithm in this case? To calculate the average depth directly would mean to generate, for each of the $n!$ orderings of input records, the binary search tree grown and note its depth. Then add up the $n!$ depths and divide by $n!$ to obtain the average depth.

It is difficult to analyze this problem using probability theory. However, the average depth has been shown to be $O(c \lg n)$, where c is about 4. The ***average search time*** can be calculated for a randomly grown binary search tree. It is the average time required to search for a record stored in the binary search tree, assuming each record is equally likely to be searched. This average search time is $O(1.39 \lg n)$. In the case of random input, the average search of the binary search tree grown by the algorithm will be only 39 percent more than the smallest possible average search time! Moreover, the algorithm for growing the tree will take an average time at most $O(n\lg n)$. If the records are given in sorted order instead of in random order, it will take the algorithm $O(n^2)$ time to grow the tree.

It is possible to grow "balanced" binary search trees, also called AVL trees (after the discoverers of these trees, Adelson-Velskii and Landis [1962]). The algorithm for growing AVL trees is slower and more complex, as is the insertion and deletion of records. However, they are guaranteed to have depth no greater than about $1.44 \lg n$. This is the *worst-case* depth. Consequently, AVL trees may be searched in time at most $O(1.44 \lg n)$. Such trees appear quite healthy and are never sparse. However it takes great care to grow healthy trees, as will be seen later.

9.4.4 Deleting a Record "Simply"

At this point all the important operations on binary search trees have been considered except deletion. The purpose of this section is to derive an algorithm for deleting a record from a binary search tree so that the remaining tree is still a binary search tree. To delete a terminal record, simply replace it by a null tree. To delete a record with only one successor, simply insert the successor's subtree at the position occupied by the deleted node. For instance, in the tree shown in Figure 9.9(a), deleting 51 and 71 yields the tree shown in Figure 9.9(b).

Consider Figure 9.9 again. A difficulty occurs if you wish to delete 80, a record with two successors. The node 80 must be replaced by a record that will allow the tree to retain its binary search tree property. This means that the record replacing 80 must be at least as large as any record in the left subtree of 80, and no larger than any record in the right subtree of 80. There are two choices: replace 80 with the largest record in its left subtree or the smallest record in its right subtree.

Notice that the largest record in any binary search tree is always found by going to its root and following right successors until a null tree is reached. The smallest record is found by going to its root and following left successors until a null tree is reached. Thus, in the example, we may take either 77's or 81's record to replace 80's record. The record selected, say 77, must then be inserted in place of 80's record, which is then effectively deleted. Taking 77 requires that 74's record replace it. The result is Figure 9.9(c). It should be clear that searching, inserting, or deleting, using the procedures in a search tree of depth d, will take worst-case time proportional to d.

Binary search trees are treated in this chapter as abstract objects. A sequential representation for deep but sparse trees requires array lengths proportional to

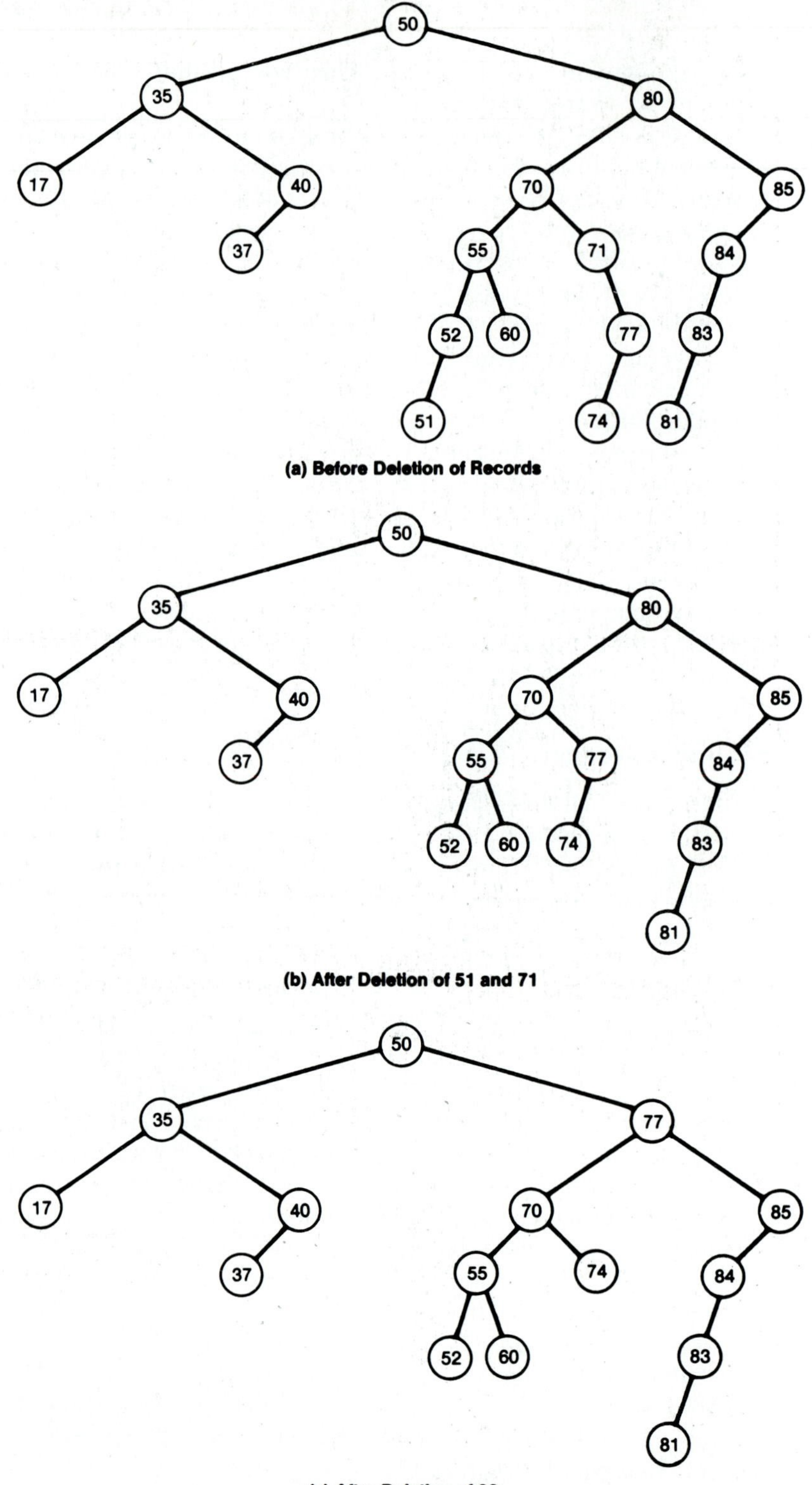

(a) Before Deletion of Records

(b) After Deletion of 51 and 71

(c) After Deletion of 80

Figure 9.9 A Binary Search Tree before and after Deletion of Records

$2^d - 1$. Deletions for this representation require a great deal of shifting of records. For instance, to delete 85 requires shifting 84, 83, and 81. To save storage, and to achieve faster insertions and deletions, requires using a linked representation.

9.4.5 A Balancing Act

The "simple" algorithms for growing binary search trees and inserting and deleting records within them are relatively simple and have excellent time and storage requirements—on the average—when randomly done. These randomly grown trees can be fine for compiler symbol tables or for small data base applications such as dictionaries, but there are situations where good average behavior is not enough. Suppose your rocket ship's computer must search a binary search tree for retro-rocket firing instructions and must complete the search within a specific interval. This is not the time to find that the tree is out of shape and that a much longer than average time will ensue.

One answer is the AVL tree, which is discussed in this section. An ***AVL tree*** is a balanced binary tree that is also a binary search tree. (*Balanced binary trees* were defined in Chapter 7 in the discussion of Fibonacci trees.)

AVL trees have excellent worst-case time and storage requirements and allow access to the ith record to be performed quickly. The algorithms for the growth of such trees and insertion and deletion within them are considerably more complex than for "simple" binary search trees. Balanced trees are very useful whenever all four operations—searching, inserting, deleting, and accessing the ith record—are needed and worst-case rather than average time is important.

Because we want to use AVL trees to store records, it is desirable for an AVL tree to have as small a depth as possible and as many nodes (in which to store records) as possible for that depth. The "best" AVL tree of depth d is thus complete and has $2^d - 1$ nodes. A balanced binary search tree (AVL tree) of depth d, which has the *least* number of nodes among all AVL trees of depth d, represents the "worst" AVL tree of depth d. Such a tree will be a Fibonacci tree that is also a binary search tree. These trees represent the worst-case AVL trees. A Fibonacci AVL tree of depth d will store the minimum possible number of records.

Suppose n_d represents the number of nodes of such a tree. Then any AVL tree with depth d must have a number of nodes n that is at least n_d. It is possible to prove that n_d is related to the $(d + 2)$th Fibonacci number, F_{d+2}. In fact, $n_d = F_{d+2} - 1$. A great deal is known about the Fibonacci numbers. In particular, $F_{d+2} > (\phi^{d+2}/\sqrt{5}) - 1$, where $\phi = (1 + \sqrt{5})/2$. It follows from this that $n \geq n_d > (\phi^{d+2}/\sqrt{5}) - 2$. Also, from Chapter 7, $n \leq 2^d - 1$. After some manipulations we may conclude that

$$d < 1.44 \lg (n + 2) - 0.328$$

This means that the depth of any AVL tree with n nodes is never greater than 1.44 $\lg (n + 2)$. In other words, an AVL tree storing n records has a worst-case depth $O(\lg n)$. Since the best possible depth of a binary tree storing n records is $\lceil \lg (n + 1) \rceil$, the *worst depth* of an AVL tree storing n records is at most 44 percent more than the best achievable. Contrast this with the "simple" binary search tree for which the *average* depth is at least 39 percent more than the best achievable; it is clearly very desirable to be able to create and use AVL trees.

9.4.6 Maintaining Balance

Consider the AVL tree of Figure 9.10(a). To insert a new record into this tree, let us first do a "simple" insertion. The dashed branches indicate the sixteen possible insertion positions for a new node. You should confirm that, of these, only an insertion of a new node as a successor of 45, 53, 81, or 100 will cause the new tree to fail to remain an AVL tree. An insertion at node 45 causes the subtrees with roots 55, 40, and 70 to become unbalanced. For example, the subtree with root 40 would have a left subtree of depth 3, while its right subtree would have depth 5. These differ by more than 1. Notice that 55, 40, and 70 lie along the search path from the root to the new node inserted as a successor of 45. If 43 were inserted, then the result would be the tree of Figure 9.10(b). Thus the "simple" insertion discussed earlier will not retain the balance of a search tree.

This imbalance is remedied by rearranging the subtree with root 55 as shown in Figure 9.10(c). Notice that the subtrees with roots 40 and 70 are no longer out of balance. In fact, the tree of Figure 9.10(c) is now an AVL tree. Notice also that the subtree in Figure 9.10(c) replacing the subtree of 55 in Figure 9.10(b) has exactly the same depth as the original subtree of 55 in Figure 9.10(a). If any of the other insertions that would have produced an imbalance in Figure 9.10(a) had occurred, they could have been remedied by similar rearrangements. You should confirm this by trying them all and finding the suitable rearrangements. Remember, the rearrangements must not only rebalance but also preserve the binary search tree property.

It is possible to analyze the general situation to determine exactly when an insertion will cause an imbalance and what its remedy will be. An insertion into an AVL tree with zero or one node cannot cause an imbalance. When the tree has more than one node, the types of imbalance, and their corresponding remedies, reduce to the four indicated in Figures 9.11 and 9.12.

Each rectangle in Figures 9.11 and 9.12 represents an AVL tree. Any of these may be null. An *X* represents the position of the inserted new record that has caused imbalance. Three *X*'s appear in imbalances *LR* and *RL*, actually representing three possibilities, although only one will have taken place. The *LR* and *RL* imbalances are meant to include the special case where *B* is actually the inserted node. This is why the *X* appears next to node *B*. Subtrees 1, 2, 3, and 4 must then be null. This fact is noted here, since it is not clear from the figures. In cases *LL* and *RR*, the subtree with root *B* represents the node closest to the inserted node, along the path from the inserted node to the root, where an imbalance occurs. In cases *LR* and *RL* the subtree with root *C* represents this node. In all remedies, the subtrees represented by the rectangles retain their relative positions. Note that all remedies preserve the binary *search* tree property. It is very important to see that, in each case, the depth of the remedy is exactly the same as the depth of the original subtree before the new insertion was made. Consequently, no nodes on the path from the subtree root, *B* in cases *LL* and *RR*, and *C* in cases *LR* and *RL*, imbalanced by the new insertion, will be imbalanced after the remedy is applied. It

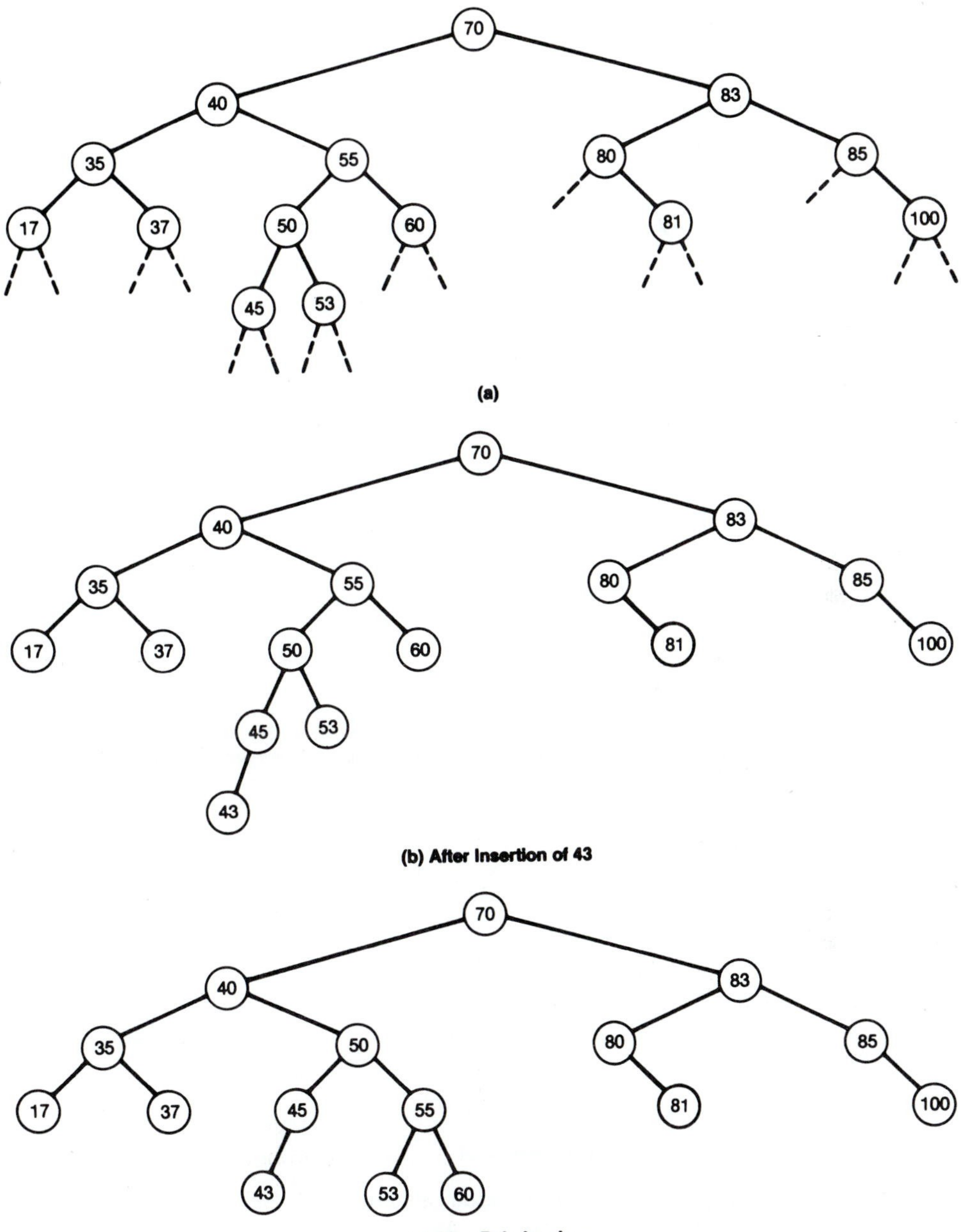

Figure 9.10 An AVL Tree before and after Insertion

is also important to see that these remedies are applied *locally;* they do not involve the creation of a new AVL tree in its entirety.

In Figure 9.11, when 43 was inserted, case *LL* occurred. The roles of *B* and *A* were taken by 55 and 50, respectively. The three rectangles, 1, 2, 3 of Figure 9.11 (a and b), represented, respectively, the subtrees shown in Figure 9.13. The *X* represented 43.

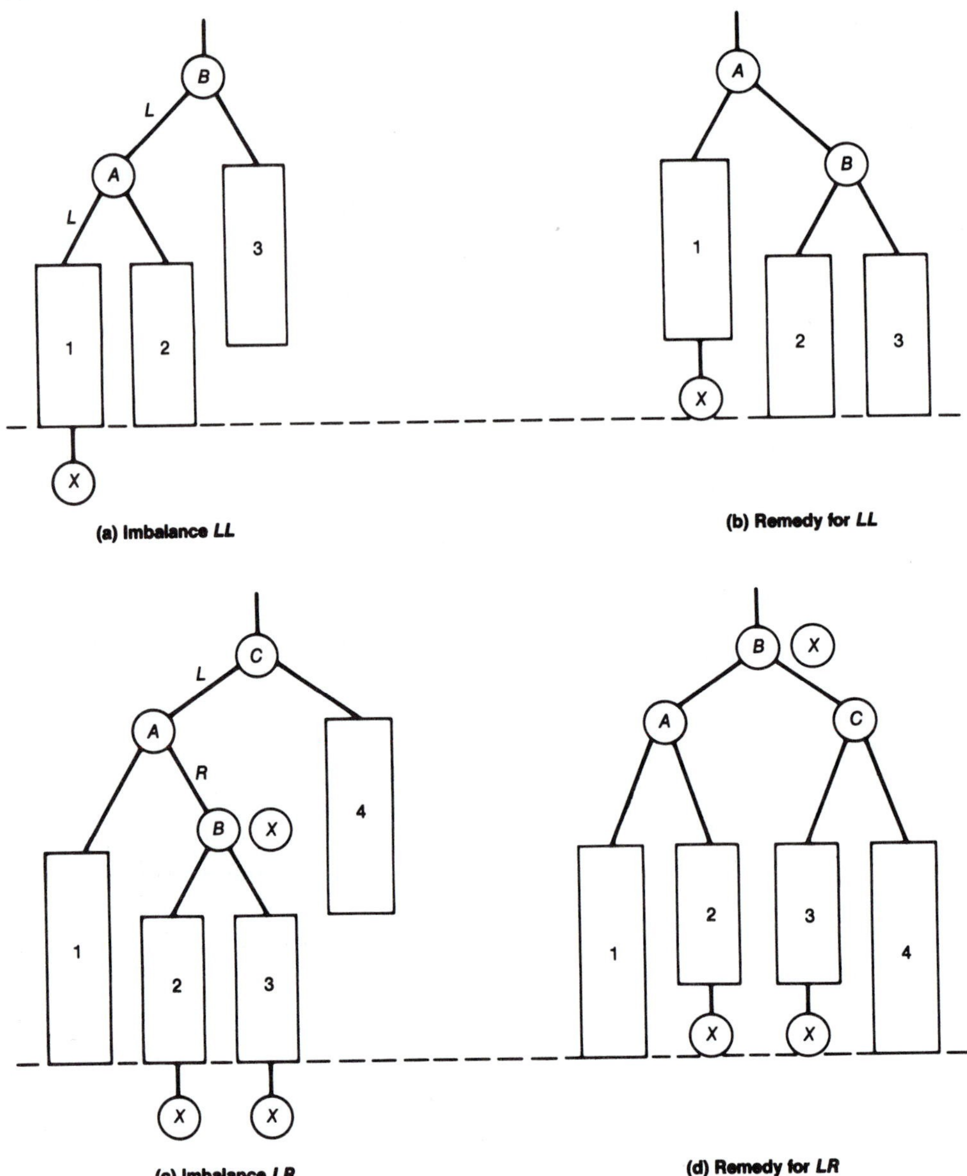

Figure 9.11 Two Imbalances and Their Remedies

Consider imbalance *LL*. The remedy looks as though *A* has moved up to the root and *B* has moved to the right. This is called a *rotation to the right of the subtree with* B *at its root*. The remedy for imbalance *RR* would be described as a *rotation to the left of the subtree with* B *at its root*. To rectify imbalance *LR*, perform a rotation to the left of the subtree with root *A* to obtain Figure 9.14(a). A further rotation to the right of the subtree rooted at *C* produces (b) of Figure 9.14. Assume that rotations are accomplished by the procedures `rotateleft` and

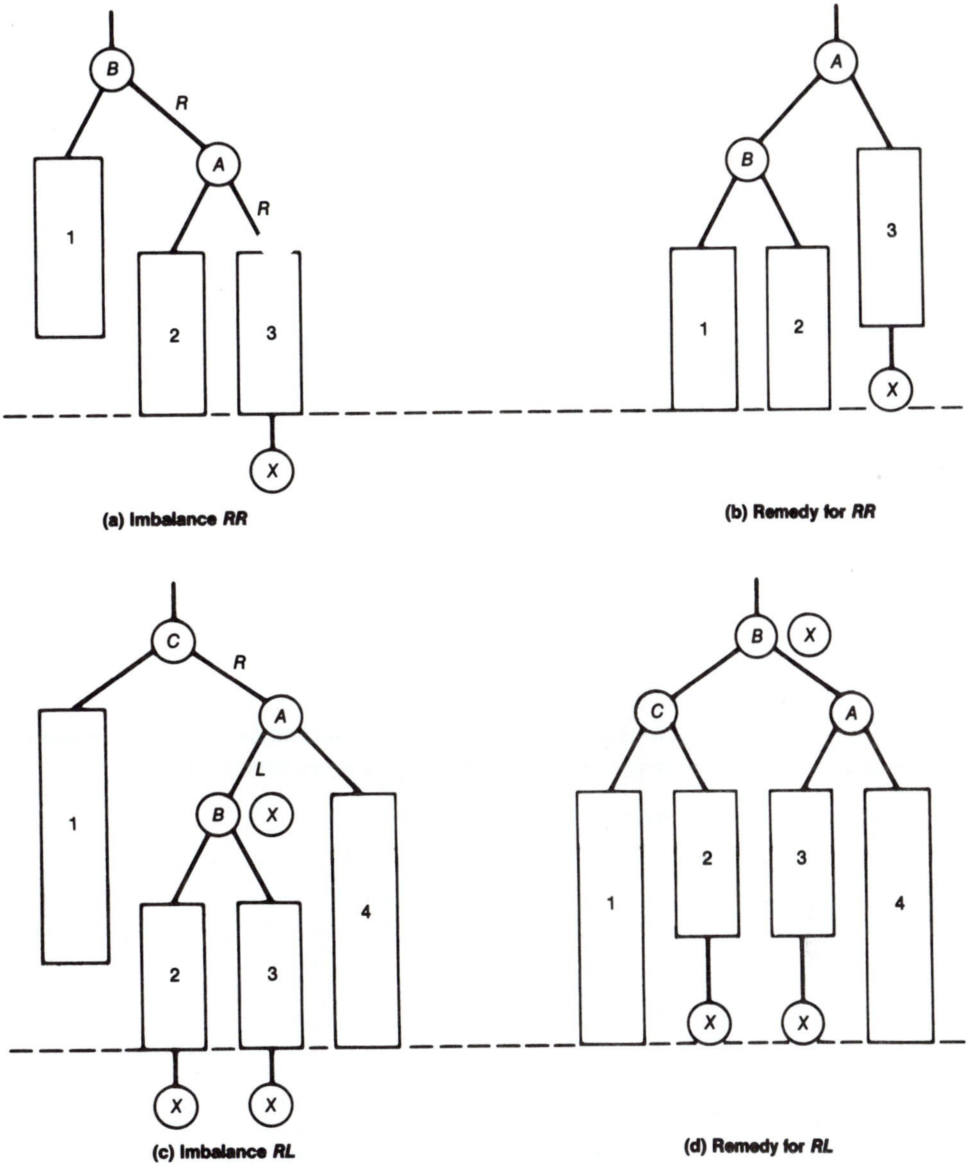

(a) Imbalance RR
(b) Remedy for RR
(c) Imbalance RL
(d) Remedy for RL

Figure 9.12 Two More Imbalances and Their Remedies

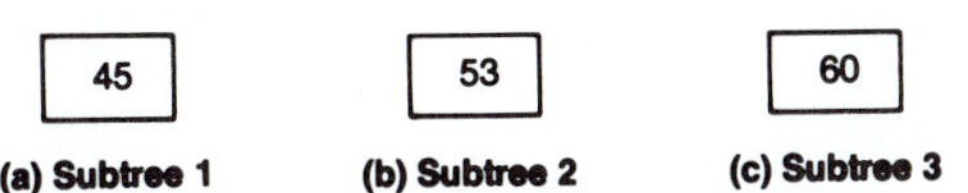

45
53
60
(a) Subtree 1
(b) Subtree 2
(c) Subtree 3

Figure 9.13 Rectangles 1–3 of Figure 9.12(a) and 9.12(b)

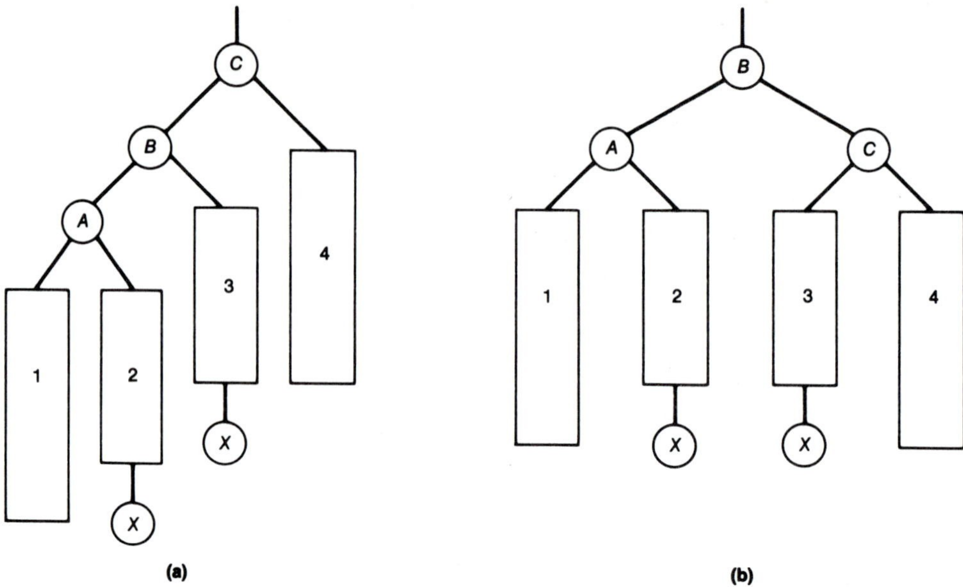

Figure 9.14 The Double Rotation Producing Remedy *LR*

`rotateright`, each with a parameter that points to the root of the subtree to be rotated. Then the remedies for each imbalance may be obtained by

LL:	`rotateright(plast)`	where `last` points to *B*
RR:	`rotateleft(plast)`	where `last` points to *B*
LR:	`rotateleft(p(last.leftptr))` `rotateright(plast)`	where `last` points to *C*
RL:	`rotateright(p(last.rightptr))` `rotateleft(plast)`	where `last` points to *C*

The procedure for `rotateright`, for example, might be as follows:

```
rotateright(plocalroot)
/* Performs a rotation to the right
   of the subtree whose root is
   pointed to by localroot.
*/
binarytreepointer *plocalroot;
{
   binarytreepointer q;
   q = (*plocalroot).leftptr;
   (*plocalroot).leftptr = q->rightptr;
   q->rightptr = *plocalroot;
   *plocalroot = q;
}
```

Note that the procedure also changes the pointer in `localroot`, so it points to the root of the new subtree. It is assumed that nodes of the AVL tree are represented as follows:

```
typedef struct treenode
{
   whatever key;
   struct treenode *leftptr;
   struct treenode *rightptr;
   int balance;
}binarytreenode,*binarytreepointer;
```

The **balance** field stores the node's right subtree depth minus the node's left subtree depth. In an AVL tree it will have values −1, 0, or +1.

Consider the binary tree shown in Figure 9.15(a), which was balanced until the new node, marked by *X*, was inserted. The initial **balance** values are also shown. Because of the insertion, the **root** node and node *C* have become unbalanced. Since node *C* is closest to the inserted node, we remedy this imbalance by applying the remedy for *RL* to obtain Figure 9.15(b). The tree itself is now balanced, but the balances of nodes *A*, *B*, and *C* are now incorrect, as are the balances of the three nodes between *X* and *A*. The last node, however, does have the correct balance value.

In general, after rebalancing, one of the nodes involved in the remedy will be the new root of the subtree that was rebalanced (*B* in the example). If the remedy was *LL* or *RR*, all nodes along the path from this node to the inserted node, starting with its successor, need their balances reset. If the remedy was *LR* or *RL*, then all nodes along this path, starting with its successor's successor (the successor of *A* in the example), need their balances reset. The node not on this path involved in the remedy (*C* in the example) must have its balance reset, and, finally, the new root of the rebalanced subtree must have its balance set to 0. The special case when the inserted node is at *B* requires only that *C*'s balance be set to 0. All nodes *above* this new root need not be reset; they retain their original values. Any time the root node is involved, special processing is required, since the head of the tree must be modified rather than a left or right subtree pointer of a node.

The algorithm for ***inserting a node into an AVL tree*** can now be written.

1. Search for the `keyvalue`.
2. If it is not found, then
   a. Create a new node for it and set its field values.
   b. Insert the new node into the tree.
   c. If the tree has more than one node, then
      If it is not necessary to rebalance, then
         reset `last`'s balance and the balances of nodes on the search path between `last` and the new node.
      If it is necessary to rebalance, then
         i. apply the appropriate remedy to rebalance, reset the balance of the node involved in the remedy but not on the new search path,

reset the proper new search path balances, set the balance of the root of the subtree at which rebalancing occurred to 0.

ii. If this root was the root of the tree itself, then
    set the head of the tree to this root;
  otherwise
    set its predecessor to this root;

else
  reset the balance of the predecessor of the inserted node.

It has already been noted that, when rebalancing is necessary, once the subtree whose root is nearest the newly inserted node has been rebalanced with the correct remedy, all other subtrees along the path to the root of the entire tree will also be back in balance. Again, this is because the smallest subtree causing the

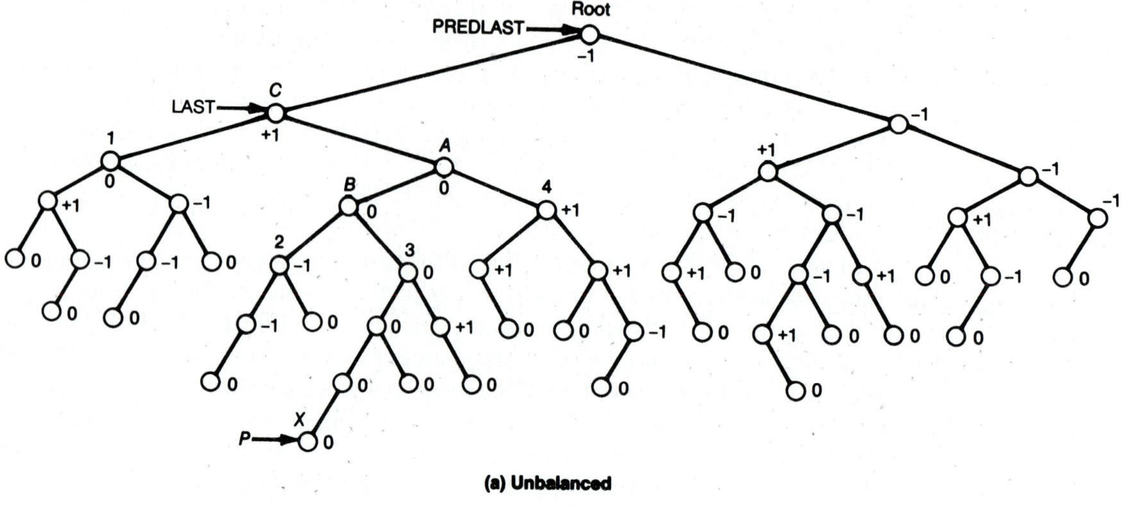

(a) Unbalanced

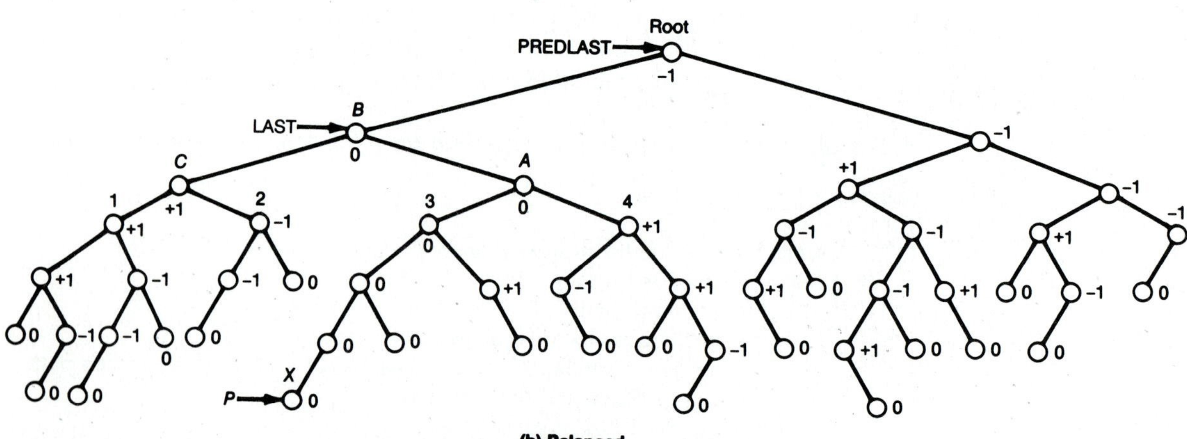

(b) Balanced

Figure 9.15 Rebalancing a Binary Tree

imbalance has been modified by the remedy to have its original depth. All the subtrees were originally balanced when it had that depth, so they must be balanced now. During the search in step 1 for the insertion key, suppose you keep a pointer **last**. **Last** is updated to point to the node that may become imbalanced on the search path nearest the insertion node. Only nodes with balance values of +1 or −1 may become imbalanced due to the insertion. It is necessary to rebalance only if **last.balance** was −1 and the search path went left at **last**, or **last.balance** was +1 and the search path went right at **last**, and **p** is not **t**, and **pred.balance** = 0. Only nodes on the search path, between the inserted node and **last**, will need to have their balance fields updated.

During the search, an updated pointer to the predecessor node of **last** should be kept in **predlast**. **P** will point to the node whose key field is currently being compared with the search key, and **predp** points to its predecessor. An implementation of the AVL tree insertion is given in the **insertavl** function. For clarity, the procedures **createnode** and **search** are then given separately, followed by procedures **insertnode** and **resetpathbalances**.

Nonrecursive AVL Insertion

```
#define TRUE 1
#define FALSE 0
#define NULL 0

insertavl(keyvalue,pt)
/* Inserts a new record with key equal to
   keyvalue in the AVL tree t, if a record
   with this keyvalue is not present in t.
   After insertion t will still be an AVL tree.
*/
whatever keyvalue;
binarytreepointer *pt;
{
   binarytreepointer p,predp,last,predlast,q;
   int found;
   search(keyvalue,*pt,&p,&predp,
          &last,&predlast,&found);
   if(!found)
      {
         createnode(keyvalue,&p);
         insertnode(keyvalue,p,predp,pt);
         if(p != *pt)
            if(predp->balance == 0)
               if(keyvalue < last->key)
                  if(last->balance == 0)
                     {
                        last->balance = -1;
                        resetpathbalances(keyvalue,
                           last->leftptr,p);
                     }
```

searches for **keyvalue**

if not in the tree

create a new node

inserts it

if **t** *has more than one node*

no need to rebalance, so reset **last**'s *and appropriate path balances*

```
        else if(last->balance == +1)
          {
            last->balance = 0;                    ] no need to rebal-
            resetpathbalances(keyvalue,           ] ance, so reset
               last->leftptr,p);                  ] last's and appro-
          }                                       ] priate path bal-
                                                  ] ances
        else
          {                                       ] need to rebalance
            q = last->leftptr;                    ]  ] task (i) of the
            if(keyvalue < q->key)                 ]  ] algorithm
               ll(keyvalue,&last,p);              ]  ]
            else                                  ]  ]
               lr(keyvalue,&last,&q,p);           ]  ]
            last->balance = 0;                    ]  ] task (ii) of the
            if(predlast == NULL)                  ]  ] algorithm
               *pt = last;                        ]  ]
            else if(keyvalue < predlast->key)     ]  ]
               predlast->leftptr = last;          ]  ]
            else                                  ]  ]
               predlast->rightptr = last;         ]  ]
          }                                       ]
    else
       if(last->balance == 0)
          {
            last->balance = +1;                   ] no need to rebal-
            resetpathbalances(keyvalue,           ] ance, so reset
               last->rightptr,p);                 ] last's and appro-
          }                                       ] priate path bal-
                                                  ] ances
       else if(last->balance == -1)
          {
            last->balance = 0;                    ] no need to rebal-
            resetpathbalances(keyvalue,           ] ance, so reset
               last->rightptr,p);                 ] last's and appro-
          }                                       ] priate path bal-
                                                  ] ances
       else
          {                                       ] need to rebalance
            q = last->rightptr;                   ]  ] task (i) of the
            if(keyvalue < q->key)                 ]  ] algorithm
               rr(keyvalue,&last,p);              ]  ]
            else                                  ]  ]
               rl(keyvalue,&last,&q,p);           ]  ]
            last->balance = 0;                    ]  ] task (ii) of the
            if(predlast == NULL)                  ]  ] algorithm
               *pt = last;                        ]  ]
            else if(keyvalue < predlast->key)     ]  ]
               predlast->leftptr = last;          ]  ]
            else                                  ]  ]
               predlast->rightptr = last;         ]  ]
          }                                       ]
```

```
            else
               predp->balance = 0;
         }
}

ll(keyvalue,plast,p)
/* Applies remedy ll, resets the balance of the node
   involved in the remedy but not on the new search
   path, and resets the proper new search path balances.
*/
whatever keyvalue;
binarytreepointer *plast,p;
{
   rotateright(plast);
   ((*plast)->rightptr)->balance = 0;
   resetpathbalances(keyvalue,(*plast)->leftptr,p);
}

lr(keyvalue,plast,pq,p)
/* Applies remedy lr, resets the balance of the node
   involved in the remedy but not on the new search
   path, and resets the proper new search path balances.
*/
whatever keyvalue;
binarytreepointer *plast,*pq,p;
{
   rotateleft(&((*plast)->leftptr));
   rotateright(plast);
   if(keyvalue < (*plast)->key)
      {
         (*pq).balance = 0;
         ((*plast)->rightptr)->balance = +1;
         resetpathbalances(keyvalue,
                           ((*plast)->leftptr)->rightptr,p);
      }
   else if(keyvalue > (*plast)->key)
      {
         (*pq)->balance = -1;
         ((*plast)->rightptr)->balance = 0;
         resetpathbalances(keyvalue,
                           ((*plast)->rightptr)->leftptr,p);
      }
   else
      ((*plast)->rightptr)->balance = 0;
}

rr(keyvalue,plast,p)
/* Applies remedy rr, resets the balance
   of the node involved in the remedy but
```

reset the balance of the inserted node's predecessor

```
    not on the new search path, and resets
    the proper new search path balances.
*/
whatever keyvalue;
binarytreepointer *plast,p;
{
   rotateleft(plast);
   ((*plast)->leftptr)->balance = 0;
   resetpathbalances(keyvalue,(*plast)->rightptr,p);
}

rl(keyvalue,plast,pq,p)
/* Applies remedy rl, resets the balance
   of the node involved in the remedy but
   not on the new search path, and resets
   the proper new search path balances.
*/
whatever keyvalue;
binarytreepointer *plast,*pq,p;
{
   rotateright(&((*plast)->rightptr));
   rotateleft(plast);
   if(keyvalue > (*plast)->key)
      {
         (*pq)->balance = 0;
         ((*plast)->leftptr)->balance = -1;
         resetpathbalances(keyvalue,((*plast)->rightptr)->leftptr,p);
      }
   else if(keyvalue < (*plast)->key)
      {
         (*pq)->balance = +1;
         ((*plast)->leftptr)->balance = 0;
         resetpathbalances(keyvalue,((*plast)->leftptr)->rightptr,p);
      }
   else
      ((*plast)->leftptr)->balance = 0;
}

rotateright(plocalroot)
/* Performs a rotation to the right
   of the subtree whose root is
   pointed to by localroot.
*/
binarytreepointer *plocalroot;
{
   binarytreepointer q;
   q = (*plocalroot)->leftptr;
   (*plocalroot)->leftptr = q->rightptr;
   q->rightptr = *plocalroot;
   *plocalroot = q;
}
```

```
rotateleft(plocalroot)
/* Performs a rotation to the left
   of the subtree whose root is
   pointed to by localroot.
*/
binarytreepointer *plocalroot;
{
   binarytreepointer q;
   q = (*plocalroot)->rightptr;
   (*plocalroot)->rightptr = q->leftptr;
   q->leftptr = *plocalroot;
   *plocalroot = q;
}

resetpathbalances(keyvalue,start,p)
/* Resets the balances of all nodes on
   search path between the nodes
   pointed to by start and p.
*/
whatever keyvalue;
binarytreepointer start,p;
{
   binarytreepointer q;
   q = start;
   while(q !=p)
      if(keyvalue < q->key)
         {
            q->balance = -1;
            q = q->leftptr;
         }
      else
         {
            q->balance = +1;
            q = q->rightptr;
         }
}

createnode(keyvalue,pp)
/* Returns with p pointing to a new node
   record with key equal to keyvalue,
   left and right pointer fields null, and
   balance field zero.
*/
whatever keyvalue;
binarytreepointer *pp;
{
   *pp = malloc(sizeof(binarytreenode));
   (*pp)->key = keyvalue;
   (*pp)->leftptr = NULL;
   (*pp)->rightptr = NULL;
```

```
   (*pp)->balance = 0;
}

search(keyvalue,t,pp,ppredp,plast,ppredlast,pfound)
/* Returns with found true only if the binary search
   tree t has a node with its key equal to keyvalue.
   If found is true
      p and predp point respectively, to
      the found node and its predecessor,
   else
      predp, and last, will point, respectively,
      to the node that will be the new node's
      predecessor, and the node along the search
      path closest to the new node's insertion point
      that may become unbalanced.
*/
whatever keyvalue;
binarytreepointer t,*pp,*ppredp,*plast,*ppredlast;
int *pfound;
{
   *pfound = FALSE;
   *pp = t;
   *plast = t;
   *ppredp = NULL;
   *ppredlast = NULL;
   while((*pp != NULL) && (!*pfound))
   if(keyvalue < (*pp)->key)
      {
         if((*pp)->balance != 0)
            {
               *ppredlast = *ppredp;
               *plast = *pp;
            }
         *ppredp = *pp;
         *pp = (*pp)->leftptr;
      }
   else if(keyvalue > (*pp)->key)
      {
         if((*pp)->balance != 0)
            {
               *ppredlast = *ppredp;
               *plast = *pp;
            }
         *ppredp = *pp;
         *pp = (*pp)->rightptr;
      }
   else
      *pfound = TRUE;
}

insertnode(keyvalue,p,predp,pt)
/* Inserts the new node, pointed to
```

```
   by p, as the proper successor
   of predp.
*/
whatever keyvalue;
binarytreepointer p,predp,*pt;
{
   if(predp == NULL)
      *pt = p;
   else
      if(predp == *pt)
         if(keyvalue < (*pt)->key)
            (*pt)->leftptr = p;
         else
            (*pt)->rightptr = p;
      else
         if(keyvalue < predp->key)
            predp->leftptr = p;
         else
            predp->rightptr = p;
}
```

As another illustration of recursion, a recursive version is presented next. It is based on the following formulation.

To insert a node in t:

If t is null then
    create the new node, set its field values and set t to it
else
    if keyvalue < t.key, then
        insert the node in t.leftptr
        if t is balanced, then
            reset its balance
        else
            rebalance t and reset the balances of the nodes involved in the remedy
    else if keyvalue > t.key then
        insert the node in t.rightptr
        if t is balanced, then
            reset its balance
        else
            rebalance t and reset the balances of the nodes involved in the remedy.

The recursive insertavl procedure is as follows:

Recursive AVL Insertion

```
#define TRUE 1
#define FALSE 0
#define NULL 0

insertavl(keyvalue,pt,pincrease)
/* Inserts a new record with key value to
```

```
   keyvalue in the AVL tree t, if a record
   with this keyvalue is not present in t.
   After insertion t will still be an AVL tree.
   Increase must be zero when the function is invoked.
*/
whatever keyvalue;
binarytreepointer *pt;
int *pincrease;
{
   binarytreepointer q;
   if(*pt == NULL)                                      ] if t is null
      {
         createnode(keyvalue,pt);                       ] create and make
                                                          the new node t's
                                                          root
         *pincrease = 1;                                ] t's depth has
      }                                                   increased
   else if(keyvalue < (*pt)->key)                       ] else if the new
      {                                                   node is to be
                                                          inserted in t's left
                                                          subtree
         insertavl(keyvalue,                            ] insert it there
                  &((*pt)->leftptr),pincrease);
         if(*pincrease) == 1)                           ] if the left subtree
            if((*pt)->balance == 0)                       depth increased
               (*pt)->balance = -1;                     ] reset t's balance
            else if((*pt)->balance == +1)
               {
                  (*pt)->balance = 0;                   ] reset t's balance
                  *pincrease = 0;                       ] t's depth did not
               }                                          increase
            else
               {
                  q = (*pt)->leftptr;                   ] rebalance t and
                  if(keyvalue < q->key)                   reset the balances
                     ll(pt);                              of nodes involved
                  else                                    in the remedy
                     lr(pt,q);
                  (*pt)->balance = 0;                   ] set t's balance to
                                                          zero
                  *pincrease = 0;                       ] t's depth did not
               }                                          increase
      }

    else if(keyvalue > (*pt)->key)                      ] else if the new
      {                                                   node is to be
                                                          inserted in t's
                                                          right subtree
          insertavl(keyvalue,                           ] insert it there
                   &((*pt)->rightptr),pincrease);
          if(*pincrease == 1)                           ] if the right sub-
             if((*pt)->balance == 0)                      tree depth in-
                                                          creased
                (*pt)->balance = +1;                    ] reset t's balance
```

```
            else if((*pt)->balance == -1)
                {
                    (*pt)->balance = 0;              ] reset t's balance
                    *pincrease = 0;                  ] t's depth did not
                                                       increase
                }
            else
                {
                    q = (*pt)->rightptr;             ] rebalance t and
                    if(keyvalue > q->key)            | reset the balances
                        rr(pt);                      | of nodes involved
                    else                             | in the remedy
                        rl(pt,q);                    ]
                    (*pt)->balance = 0;              ] set t's balance to
                                                       zero
                    *pincrease = 0;                  ] t's depth did not
                                                       increase
                }
        }
}

ll(pt)
/* Apply remedy ll and reset the
   balance of the node involved in
   the remedy.
*/
binarytreepointer *pt;
{
   rotateright(pt);
   reset1balance((*pt)->rightptr);
}

lr(pt,q)
/* Apply remedy lr and reset the balances
   of the two nodes involved in
   the remedy.
*/
binarytreepointer *pt,q;
{
   rotateleft(&((*pt)->leftptr));
   rotateright(pt);
   reset2balances(q,*pt,(*pt)->rightptr);
}

rr(pt)
/* Apply remedy rr and reset the
   balance of the node involved in
   the remedy.
*/
binarytreepointer *pt;
{
   rotateleft(pt);
   reset1balance((*pt)->leftptr);
}
```

```
rl(pt,q)
/* Apply remedy rl and reset the balances
   of the two nodes involved in the remedy.
*/
binarytreepointer *pt,q;
{
   rotateright(&((*pt)->rightptr));
   rotateleft(pt);
   reset2balances(q,*pt,(*pt)->leftptr);
}

rotateright(plocalroot)
/* Performs a rotation to the right
   of the subtree whose root is
   pointed to by localroot.
*/
binarytreepointer *plocalroot;
{
   binarytreepointer q;
   q = (*plocalroot)->leftptr;
   (*plocalroot)->leftptr = q->rightptr;
   q->rightptr = *plocalroot;
   *plocalroot = q;
}

rotateleft(plocalroot)
/* Performs a rotation to the left
   of the subtree whose root is
   pointed to by localroot.
*/
binarytreepointer *plocalroot;
{
   binarytreepointer q;
   q = (*plocalroot)->rightptr;
   (*plocalroot)->rightptr = q->leftptr;
   q->leftptr = *plocalroot;
   *plocalroot = q;
}

createnode(keyvalue,pp)
/* Returns with p pointing to a new node
   record with key equal to keyvalue,
   left and right pointer fields null, and balance field zero.
*/
whatever keyvalue;
binarytreepointer *pp;
{
   *pp = malloc(sizeof(binarytreenode));
   (*pp)->key = keyvalue;
   (*pp)->leftptr = NULL;
   (*pp)->rightptr = NULL;
   (*pp)->balance = 0;
}
```

In order to determine the balance of `t` upon return from the recursive calls (these are underlined in the algorithm), we will need to know if the subtree in which the node was inserted has increased in depth. A flag `increase`, with values 1 or 0, indicates an increase. `Increase` may be nonlocal to, or a parameter of, the function, but it must be initialized to 0 before the function is invoked. We make it a parameter.

The functions for resetting balances are

```
reset1balance(q)
/* Sets the balance of node
   q to zero.
*/
binarytreepointer q;
{
   q->balance = 0;
}

reset2balances(q,t,p)
/* Resets the balance of nodes
   p and q determined by the
   balance of t.
*/
binarytreepointer q,t,p;
{
   if(t->balance == -1)
      p->balance = +1;
   else
      p->balance = 0;
   if(t->balance == +1)
      q->balance = -1;
   else
      q->balance = 0;
}
```

Suppose you wanted to create an AVL tree by reading a sequence of key values and to test the AVL insertion. The code below, when `insertavl` and the functions it invokes are included, creates the AVL tree using the recursive version of `insertavl`. It prints the key field values of the resultant tree nodes in preorder access order as the tree is created, and prints both the key and balance values in preorder access order for the final tree. The `preorder` traversal routine calls a `process` routine, as in Chapter 7, that prints out the `key` and `balance` field values of a node it is called to work on.

```
#include <stdio.h>

#define NULL 0
typedef int whatever;
```

```
typedef struct treenode
{
   whatever key;
   struct treenode *leftptr;
   struct treenode *rightptr;
   int balance;
}binarytreenode,*binarytreepointer;

binarytreepointer left(p)
/* Returns a copy of the left pointer
   of the node pointed to by p.
*/
binarytreepointer p;
{
   return(p->leftptr);
}

binarytreepointer right(p)
/* Returns a copy of the right pointer
   of the node pointed to by p.
*/
binarytreepointer p;
{
   return(p->rightptr);
}

info(l)
/* Returns the key field value of
   the node pointed to by l.
*/
binarytreepointer l;
{
   return(l->key);
}

bal(l)
/* Returns the balance field value of
   the node pointed to by l.
*/
binarytreepointer l;
{
   return(l->balance);
}

binarytreepointer setnull()
/* Returns a null pointer. */
{
   return(NULL);
}
```

The function `insertavl` *and all its invoked functions should go here, since they depend on the tree's implementation.*

```
#define SENTINEL -1

main()
/* Reads record information, creates an AVL tree
   storing the records, prints the key field values
   of the tree records in preorder access order
   after each record is inserted in the tree, and
   prints the key & balance field values of the
   final tree in preorder access order.
*/
{
   binarytreepointer t,setnull();
   int keyvalue,increase;
   t = setnull();
   printf(\" enter keyvalue or sentinel \n");
   scanf("%d",&keyvalue);
   while(keyvalue != SENTINEL)
      {
         increase = 0;
         insertavl(keyvalue,&t,&increase);
         printf("\n enter keyvalue or sentinel \n");
         scanf("%d",&keyvalue);

         printtree(t);
      }
   preorder(t);
}
```

sets the tree `t` *to null*

inputs first record's key

inserts the record into `t`

inputs next record's key

prints `t`*'s keys in preorder access order*

prints the final tree's keys and balances in preorder access order

```
printtree(t)
/* Prints the keys of t in
   preorder access order.
*/
binarytreepointer t,left(),right();
{
   printf("\n %d \n",info(1));
   printtree(left(t));
   printtree(right(t));
}

preorder(t)
/* Prints the keys & balances of
   t in preorder access order.
*/
binarytreepointer t,left(),right(),setnull();
{
   if(t == setnull())
      printf("\n The tree is null \n");
   else
      {
         process(t);
```

```
            preorder(left(t));
            preorder(right(t));
        }
}

process(t)
/* Prints the key and balance fields of
   the node pointed to by t.
*/
binarytreepointer t;
{
   printf("\n key:%d balance:%d \n",info(t),bal(t));
}
```

Notice that all components of the program except **insertavl** and its associated functions are written treating the binary tree as a data abstraction.

Deletion procedures for AVL trees are not developed in detail here, but the basic ideas will be illustrated. Consider the AVL tree of Figure 9.16(a). The tree is a Fibonacci tree of depth 5. Suppose the rightmost node of its right subtree, 12, is deleted, as in a simple binary search tree. The result is Figure 9.16(b).

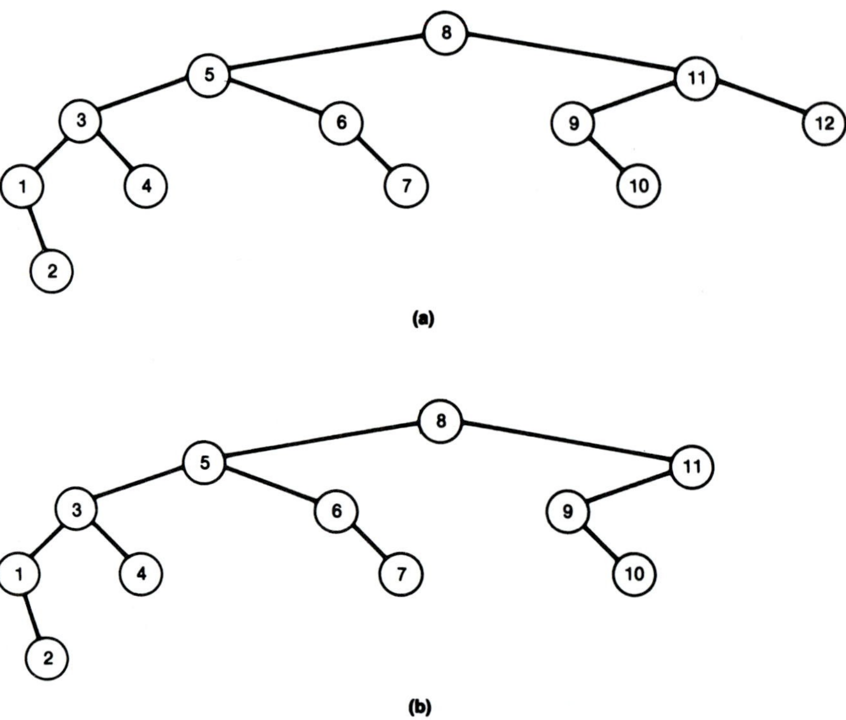

Figure 9.16 A Fibonacci Tree of Depth 5 and Deletion

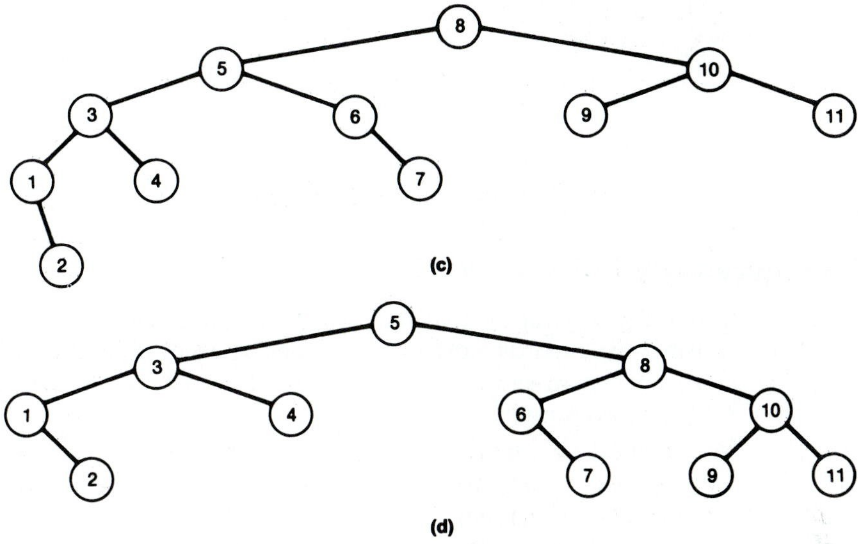

Figure 9.16 *(continued)*

Node 11, the predecessor of 12, is now unbalanced. Rebalancing can be achieved by applying remedy *LR* at node 11 to obtain Figure 9.16(c). Node 8, the predecessor of 11 before rebalancing, is now unbalanced. Rebalancing can be done by applying remedy *LL* at node 8 to obtain Figure 9.16(d).

This tree is finally an AVL tree. Deleting the rightmost node from any such Fibonacci tree will always lead to a rebalancing at every node along the search path.

The basic algorithm for deletion of a node from an AVL tree is first to delete, as in a simple binary tree. Then the search path must be retraced, from the deleted node back to the root. If an imbalance occurs, it must be remedied. Deletion can require $O(\lg n)$ rebalances, while insertion can require at most one rebalance.

A recursive deletion algorithm is sketched below.

```
To delete a node from t:
    If t is not null, then
        if keyvalue<t.key, then
            delete the node from t.leftptr
            ____________________________
            if t is balanced, then
                reset its balance
            else
                rebalance t and reset balances
        else if keyvalue>t.key, then
            delete the node from t.rightptr
            _____________________________
            if t is balanced, then
                reset its balance
            else
                rebalance t and reset balances
```

```
else
    delete the node with the largest key value in t.leftptr
    replace the root of t by that deleted node
    if t is balanced, then
        reset its balance
    else
        rebalance t and reset balances.
```

9.4.7 Access By Order in AVL Trees

Given a key value to find, it is easy to search the AVL tree for it. However, consider the records stored at the nodes as ordered by their processing positions in an inorder traversal of the AVL tree. For instance, in the AVL tree of Figure 9.10, the ordering is

1. 17	**9.** 60
2. 35	**10.** 70
3. 37	**11.** 80
4. 40	**12.** 81
5. 45	**13.** 83
6. 50	**14.** 85
7. 53	**15.** 100
8. 55	

By *access by order to a node* is meant that, given an index (say, 10) produce the tenth record (key value 70 above). The difficulty is that it is not immediately apparent where node 10 is nor what its key value is. One way to access this node is simply to inorder traverse the tree, counting nodes. Arriving at the tenth node, produce it. This will take time $O(i)$ if the index is i. In the worst case this is $O(n)$, if n nodes are stored in the tree. Since AVL trees with n nodes have maximum depth 1.44 lg n, any key search, insertion, or deletion can be done in at most $O(\lg n)$ time. There is also a simple way to access by order, or index, in at most $O(\lg n)$ time. To accomplish this, add an **`index`** field to each node. It will contain an integer that is 1 plus the number of nodes in its left subtree. The **`index`** field thus contains the nodes' index. For example, the **`index`** field value of 70 would be 10. It is then possible to search the tree for an index value, much as it is searched for a key value. The index search thus takes time at most $O(\lg n)$. Of course, the insertion and deletion algorithms must be modified to keep the **`index`** fields updated correctly.

Creating an AVL tree is done by growing it as was done for the simple binary search tree: start with a null tree and insert each input record, one at a time. The difference is that a "simple" insertion is used to grow the simple binary search tree, whereas the **`insertavl`** procedure is used to grow an AVL tree. The AVL tree may be grown in $O(n \lg n)$ time. Also, since it may then be inorder traversed in $O(n)$ time, we have another way to sort in $O(n \lg n)$ time.

9.4.8 Binary Search Tree Overview

Easily constructed binary search trees allow efficient insertion and deletion and can also be searched in *average time* $O(\lg n)$. More complex construction, insertion, and deletion algorithms for balanced binary search trees guarantee search, insertion, and deletion in *worst-case time* $O(\lg n)$. Binary search trees allow easy access to records in sorted order, and balanced binary search trees also allow $O(\lg i)$ access to the ith record in sorted order. It is not necessary to estimate in advance how many entries will be made in a binary search tree, as it is for hash tables. Hash tables can be searched very quickly, on the average, when properly constructed, but they do not allow records to be easily enumerated in sorted order.

9.5 A Brief Review

This chapter and the last have provided examples of the effective use of appropriate data structures with their appropriate implementations. These include the use of a heap for priority queues, the use of a binary tree for a heap, the use of a heap for sorting, and the use of hash tables and binary search trees for searching. Previously we found that trees find numerous applications, ranging from storing data to aiding in the conceptualization of algorithms. Binary trees are not only useful themselves but can serve as the representation for general trees. You have seen that stacks and queues underlie the important tree traversal operations. The virtues and shortcomings of arrays and lists have also been explored.

With respect to problem solving methodology, the top-down approach, with recursion as a special case, has been consistently adhered to. A number of basic strategies have also been illustrated repeatedly. These included searching through the collection of all possible solutions, constructing a solution, and adapting a previously written algorithm to a new but related problem. The rest of this book deals with the same concepts but applies them to more advanced problems.

■ Exercises

1. Justify all the entries of Table 9.1 for the priority queue implementations.

2. Write two functions to insert and delete, respectively, records from a priority queue implemented as a heap.

3. a. Build a hash table for the twenty-seven names of the `nametable` of Chapter 6. Do not store duplicates. The table will be of size 31. Assign to each letter of this alphabet the integer corresponding to its position in the alphabet. For example A is assigned 1, E is assigned 5. Add the integers corresponding to every letter of a name and divide the sum by 31. The remainder is then the hash address of the name. For example, Jimmy Carter has the sum $(10 + 9 + 13 + 13 + 25 + 3 + 1 + 18 + 20 + 5 + 18) = 135$. Its hash address is 11. Use linear probing when a collision occurs.

b. How many probes were needed to insert each name?

4. Criticize the choice of hash function in Exercise 3.

5. Search the hash table of Exercise 3 for John Smith, and write down the probe addresses needed.

6. Show the state of hash tables (a) through (g) of Section 9.3 when key 019 is deleted.

7. Suppose that the eighteen keys are entered into the hash table of Section 9.3 in order, from largest to smallest. As you search for a key, you conclude that it is not in the table whenever you encounter a key value smaller than the search key as you trace out the linear probe path. Convince yourself that this is true, and that it will result in fewer probes for an unsuccessful search.

8. Write a function to build a hash table for each of the open-addressing and chaining techniques of Section 9.3.
9. Run each function of Exercise 8 with the input data and hash function of Exercise 3.
10. What is the maximum number of probes for an unsuccessful search of each of the hash tables (a)–(g) of Figures 9.4, 9.5, and 9.6?
11. Can you find a way to build a hash table as in Exercise 7 so that the sorted search can be done even if the input was not actually in sorted order?
12. How might the average number of probes be studied for a given hash function as in Exercise 3?
13. For $m = 107$, generate n random key values between 000 and 999 and build (by executing a program) hash tables (a) to (g) of Figures 9.4, 9.5, and 9.6 for these keys. Do this twenty-five times for each n and output the average number of probes to insert the n keys over the twenty-five samples. Do this repeatedly for a series of n values corresponding to usage ratios of approximately 0.50, 0.55, 0.60, . . . , 0.90. 0.95. Compare results of this simulation to your expectations.
14. Take the `nametable` names of Chapter 6 and grow a simple binary search tree (as in Section 9.4) when the names are input in the order in which they appear in that figure. The order is determined alphabetically by last name, first name, and then middle initial. Thus Robert Evans precedes Harry Truman. If a duplicate name occurs, do not enter it again in the tree.
15. Delete Paulina Koch from the binary search tree of Exercise 14, using the simple deletion algorithm of Section 9.4.
16. Discuss the advantages and disadvantages of storing the `nametable` entries of Chapter 6 in a sorted array, sorted chain, binary search tree, AVL tree, and hash table.
17. Write a function, `search`, with parameters `keyvalue`, `p`, and `t`, a pointer to the root node of a binary search tree. `Search` is to return with `p` pointing to the node of `t` in which `keyvalue` equals `p→key`. If no such node exists, `p` should return with its value `null`.
18. Write a function, `insertbst`, with parameters `keyvalue` and `t`. It is to insert a node with `keyvalue` into the simple binary search tree `t` if no node exists with that `key`.
19. Write a function, `deletebst`, with parameters `keyvalue` and `t`. It is to delete a node whose `key` equals `keyvalue` in the simple binary search tree `t`, if such a node exists.
20. Should a linked or sequential implementation be used for binary search trees grown "simply" when they will contain fifty integers picked at random from the first 1,000 integers? Why?
21. What is the minimum depth of a binary search tree storing 137 entries, and how may it be constructed in time $O(n)$ for n entries?
22. Should a linked or sequential implementation be used for a binary search tree grown as an AVL tree when it will contain 50 integers picked at random from the first 1,000 integers? Why? (Cf. Exercise 20.)
23. Follow the same directions as in Exercise 14, but grow a binary search tree that is an AVL tree. It should be the same AVL tree that would result if it were grown by invoking `insertavl` of Section 9.4.6 for each input name.
24. Create a binary search tree, with the names of Exercise 23 in it, which has minimum possible depth.
25. Delete the rightmost node of the AVL tree grown in Exercise 23, using the recursive deletion algorithm of Section 9.4.6.
26. Modify the nonrecursive function `insertavl` so that indexing can be done as described in Section 9.4.6.
27. Modify the recursive function `insertavl` so that indexing can be done as described in Section 9.4.6.

28. Why does growing and then inorder traversing an AVL tree correspond to an $O(n \lg n)$ sort?
29. Write a function `search`, with parameters `indexvalue`, `p`, and `t`. It is to return with `p` pointing to the node, if it exists, in the AVL tree `t`, whose `index` field is equal to `indexvalue`. `P` should be `null` if there is no such node.
30. How might we estimate the relation between the average depth of a simple binary search tree grown randomly and n, the number of inputs?
31. Suppose AVL trees are grown randomly. That is, each of the $n!$ arrangements of n distinct inputs is equally likely to occur. Starting with the null tree, `insertavl` is invoked for each input. How might the average depth of such AVL trees be estimated as a function of n?

■ Suggested Assignments

1. This is the same as the suggested assignment 2 of Chapter 2, except the integers for part (a) and the records for parts (b) and (c) are to be stored in a binary search tree.
2. Design the nametable for the case study of Chapter 6. Discuss the relative merits of arrays, lists, binary search trees, AVL trees, and hash tables for its implementation.
3. Write an efficient `check(t,d,flag)` to return in `d` the depth of the binary tree pointed to by `t`, and to return in `flag` *true* if `t` points to a balanced binary tree and *false* otherwise.

10 Files

Introduces the file data structure
- *treats communication with the outside world*
  - *input, output, and secondary storage*

Discusses sorting of files using
- *straight merge*
- *natural merge*
- *replacement selection*
- *polyphase sort*

Considers file organization to support sequential and random access

Explains the physical basis for the file organizations using
- *direct access*
- *indexed sequential access*
- *B-trees*

Illustrates how the basic operations on B-trees are done and what their time requirements are
- *creating*
- *inserting*
- *deleting*
- *searching*
- *traversing*

10.1 The File Data Structure

A file is a collection of records. This is a loose definition of a file. Almost all of the data structures discussed in the preceding chapters satisfy it. The term *file,* however, is usually reserved for large collections of information stored on devices outside the computer's internal memory. It usually implies that the records are stored in secondary storage in the computer's external memory, on tapes or disks. As a result, the ways in which the file must be organized so that operations on it can be carried out efficiently are dependent on the characteristics of the secondary storage devices used to implement the file. The basic operations on a file are to insert and delete records, process or update records, and search for or retrieve records. These operations are the same as the basic operations on arrays, lists, trees, list-structures, and more complex lists, which are stored in the computer's internal memory. In designing algorithms that use files stored in external memory, programmers must weigh the trade-offs between the time and the storage required to support these operations. They must do this just as they would for data structures stored in internal memory. Time spent in organizing information results in faster operations, but this efficiency must be weighed against the increased care required to nurture and maintain the better-organized data structure. For example, balanced trees are faster to use in the worst case but harder to grow. Similar effects pertain to file manipulations.

10.2 Internal and External Memory

Computer memories are normally thought of as falling into two basic categories, internal and external. Which memory is used to store data depends on the tradeoff of efficiency of access to data versus the cost of that efficiency.

The data structures and algorithms considered thus far are all appropriate to the ***internal memory*** of a computer. This memory is also referred to as ***main*** memory or ***random access*** memory. A program can process only information stored in its internal memory. If the program is to process information stored in external memory, that information must first be read into its internal memory. Except for the instructions involved in this transfer of information, all program instructions refer to variables that name internal memory locations.

By means of random access, it is possible to access *any* individual internal memory element in exactly the same length of time—typically one-millionth of a second or less. This access time is independent of the past history of accessed elements. However, random access memory is expensive and, although available in increasingly larger sizes, is still relatively small in size compared to the storage needs of many applications.

External memory, also referred to as ***secondary storage,*** is so called because it is physically outside the computer itself. It is relatively inexpensive and is available in very large amounts, but access to an arbitrary record is slow compared to internal memory. ***Magnetic tapes, floppy disks,*** and ***magnetic disks*** (also known as ***hard disks***) are the usual devices for external storage of data. The characteristics of these devices that are essential for efficient use of data structures are discussed in this chapter. Since the characteristics of secondary storage devices are different from those of internal memory, the data structures and algorithms required to process the data they store are distinct from those for internal memory. However, many of the same concepts and techniques of good design and implementation of algorithms are still applicable and form the basis for representing and operating on information stored in external memory.

10.2.1 Operating Systems

Programming languages such as C do not ordinarily allow direct manipulation of external storage elements. Instead, as with internal storage, they provide commands that allow programmers to deal with external memory conceptually. C provides very limited kinds of operations to be performed on its conceptual external memory, whereas COBOL provides very extensive operations. FORTRAN falls between these extremes. Whatever high-level language is used, the operating system of a computer installation provides commands to make files available for processing by a program. Operating systems allow permanent storage of files generated by a program during its execution. The stored files can then be retrieved for later use.

You may have used the DOS, MVS, VM, or NOS operating system on a mainframe computer; RT-11, RSTS, RSX, TSX, VAX/VMS, or UNIX on a minicomputer; or MS-DOS, PC-DOS, UNIX, or CP/M on a micro- or personal computer. In effect, operating systems provide repositories of files that may be added to, or referenced by, programs. Such files are used to store data or information to be processed. They are also used to store algorithms (such as programs to be executed), data base management systems to organize and maintain large data bases, compilers to be invoked, or even other operating systems to be used when needed. Thus operating systems support the development of libraries of data and algorithms that programmers use, add to, or delete from. They support the general programming strategy recommended and demonstrated in this book; in solving a problem, the programmer begins by attempting to apply an already known algorithm, either directly or after appropriate modification.

10.2.2 Filters

Frequently, a solution to a problem is readily found by starting with one or more files of data and repeatedly applying available programs to these files. These programs, in turn, produce output data in the form of files, which then become the input files for other programs. The basic idea behind this kind of solution is a ***filter***—a program whose input is one file and whose output is another file. A solution to a problem may often be found by starting with an input file and applying a sequence of filters. Each filter takes as its input the output file of the preceding filter. System commands allow this ***composition*** of filters, so that complex programs can be generated with few commands.

Example 10.1 Suppose an input file contained the roll scores for the bowling problem of Chapter 1. The problem is to structure the solution so that processing this file produces an output file of statistics. ■

Suppose `gamescores` is a filter that takes the input file and produces an output file of game scores. Once the game scores are available, a statistical package in the computer's operating system library might be used to process the game scores as an input file (as data), producing appropriate statistics. Applying this program, or filter, to the game scores file would result in an output file containing the required information. This file could be stored for future use or processed by a printing routine, producing printed output directly.

The two filters, `gamescores` and `statistics`, applied sequentially, produce the desired output file. Note that this solution is written so that the calculation of the game scores is done first, independently of the calculations producing the statistics. In the solution of Chapter 1 these tasks were intertwined.

The idea behind filters is to allow the construction of complex programs by sequencing simpler but powerful programs. The next example illustrates this more forcefully.

Example 10.2 Use filters to produce a simplified index for a book. The index should consist of the important words of the book in alphabetical order and the pages on which they appear. ■

One way to achieve a solution is to apply the following filters in sequence.

1. `Word-count references`
2. `Truncate`
3. `Sort`

The first takes a file consisting of the book text (organized as a sequence of pages) and produces an output file of records. Each record contains a word or sequence of words, the number of pages on which it appears, and the pages on which it appears. `Truncate` takes a file of records as its input and outputs a file that is identical to its input file, except that all records with a designated key field value greater than *n* are deleted. The key field contains the number of pages on which the word or sequence appears. A reasonable value for *n* might be 10. This should eliminate frequently occurring but not relevant words such as "the," "a," "and," and so on. `Sort` takes an input file of records and creates an output file in which the records appear in sorted order by designated key field value—in this case, the word field. The sequencing of these three relatively simple filters provides a quick and effective solution.

Using these system capabilities to store and access files of data or programs provides a framework in which to approach the entire task of problem solving. In effect, a computer installation provides a ***programming environment*** that determines the tools available for program construction. Such tools include text editors, data base management systems, file management utilities, ways to create a new program from existing programs already stored as files, and debugging aids. The enhancement of such programming environments is currently one of the major research and development areas of computer science. The ***command languages,*** also known as ***job control languages,*** provided by operating systems are used to operate on general files.

10.3 Organization of Files

During the execution of high-level language programs, operations typically deal only with files treated as data. Operations include traversing and processing all the records of a file, randomly accessing and processing individual records selected in random order, or some combination of these two modes. The basic function of a file system, in addition to providing storage facilities, is to allow files to be searched efficiently and conveniently, so that records of an entire file may be sequentially retrieved or a portion of the file's records (perhaps only one record) may be randomly retrieved. In Example 10.1, after the bowling game scores file has been obtained, one may want to retrieve the scores of a particular game or individual.

This chapter briefly discusses the file processing facilities provided by C. It shows a number of ways in which more flexible and powerful file processing may be implemented. The literature on files would itself require a large file for its storage, and file storage and manipulation is currently an active area of research. This book considers a very small portion of that activity. The discussion deals only with the case of fixed-length records that are to be retrieved on the basis of a single field value, the *primary key field.* A primary key uniquely identifies a record. It is the field normally used as the search key, and the key by which records are sorted.

Just as with data structures that are stored in internal memory, the programmer must take great care to keep related records of files stored in external memory physically contiguous or linked by pointers. In internal memory, the time requirement of an algorithm is measured by the number of operations performed. These might be arithmetic operations or assignments, comparisons between two records (keys), or comparisons between two variables. When dealing with external memory, the time requirements are measured by the number of accesses to secondary storage.

10.3.1 Sequential Files

C has no built-in ability to perform input/output. Input/output is done by using the standard C library <`stdio`> or by developing a user library. The **`printf`** and **`scanf`** functions used in the programs of the book are in this standard library. The <`stdio`> library contains a number of other functions that also perform input/output.

C input/output is character-oriented. All reads or writes to or from keyboards, screens, tapes, or disks are character-oriented. C reads or writes in bytes. The functions that read or write numbers or strings in turn use calls to the basic character-oriented input/output functions.

There are two ways to read or write files in C. They are termed *high-level* and *low-level* input/output. In high-level input/output, reading and writing is done a character at a time. The input/output is buffered, and the programmer does not have to consider buffer sizes or other characteristics of the operating system. The buffers, however, are not available to the programmer. In low-level input/output, which is essentially UNIX-type input/output to provide a UNIX interface, the buffers are not provided; the programmer must provide buffers and pointers to control the input/output process. In the following discussion only high-level input/output will be considered.

The simplest organization for a file is sequential. A ***sequential file*** is a sequence of records. The records may or may not be kept in sorted order in the sequence. In standard C input/output all files are sequential files. A record of a file is not necessarily declared to be of type structure. Although file records are typically of type structure, a file record may also be declared to be of type **`integer`**, **`float`**, **`character`**, or any other C type. All records of a file need not be the same type.

Example 10.3 To illustrate how records composed of structures are treated, suppose you are asked to keep a master file, **`bookinventory`**, consisting of records representing all books currently in stock in a book store. Each record is to contain a title, author, publisher, price, and currentstock field. These declarations may be used:

```
typedef struct
{
   char title[MAXTITLE];
   char author[MAXAUTHOR];
   char publisher[MAXPUBLISHER];
   float price;
   int currentstock;
}bookrecords;
bookrecords bookinventory; ■
```

The name of a file is a variable within a C program. Unlike other variables, it represents stored information that may have been available before the execution

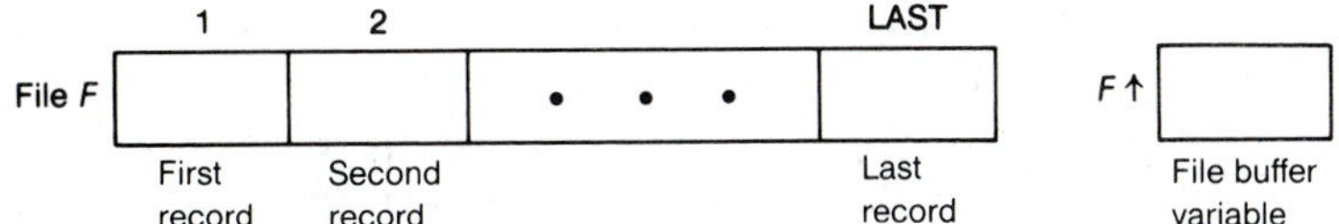

Figure 10.1 File *F* and *F*↑

of the program or that may be available after the execution of the program. A file named **f** is depicted in Figure 10.1.

Associated with each file is a ***file pointer,*** which always points to a record or is positioned prior to the first record or after the last record. File pointers must be declared and are of type **FILE**. For example,

```
FILE *f_ptr;
```

declares **f_ptr** as a file pointer.

A record may be read from a file or written to a file. A read or write statement refers to the record indicated by the current position of the file pointer. Each file also has a portion of main memory, called the ***buffer,*** associated with it. When the file pointer is pointing to a file record, the file buffer contains a copy of that record's contents.

To attach a file to a program, it is necessary to execute an open statement. For reading the records in the file containing the **bookinventory** records, the following code is used.

```
f_ptr = fopen("bookinventory","r");
if(f_ptr == NULL)
   printf("Can not open the file");
```

opens the file for reading and returns a pointer to the first file record unless an error has occurred, when it returns a null pointer

F_ptr is the pointer to the file **bookinventory**. The **r** signifies that the file will be opened for reading only and that the file is already in existence.

Executing the first statement causes the file pointer **f_ptr** to be positioned to the first record. If any error occurs and the file can not be opened, the file pointer will returns a **NULL** value. For this reason, it is a wise policy always to test for the **NULL** pointer when opening a file, as was done above.

If the open is executed with a **w** (instead of an **r**) it opens the file for writing. If no file by the name used exists, it creates a new file and places the file pointer at the beginning of the file. If a file already exists, it places the file pointer at the beginning of the file, in effect erasing or truncating the file. If a file is opened with an **a**, it creates a new file or, if one already exists, positions the pointer at the end of the file for appending items. A similar set of values, **r+**, **w+**, and **a+** is used to open files for both reading and writing.

To read a single record or numbers of records from a file the **fread()** function is used. The general form is

fread(pointer to the location of the memory in which the records read are to be placed , size of record to be read , number of records to be read , pointer to the file to be read)

For example, to read a single record from the opened file:

```
fread(&bookinventory,sizeof(bookrecords),1,f_ptr);
```

Executing this statement will cause the value of the record pointed to by the file pointer to be copied into memory starting at the memory location pointed to by `&bookinventory`. Also, `fread` returns the number of records read, or zero when the end of file is reached.

To write a record to a file that is open for writing:

```
fwrite(&bookinventory,sizeof(bookrecords),1,f_ptr);
```

Executing this statement will cause the value of the record starting at the location pointed to by `&bookinventory` to be copied into the storage pointed to by the file pointer, and the file pointer moved to point to the storage to be used for the next record.

Reading from a file thus causes information in secondary storage (the file) to be transferred to variables whose values are stored in internal memory. Writing to a file causes the information stored in internal memory to be transferred to secondary storage.

Example 10.4 To illustrate how files composed of single variables such as integers are treated and the effect of the file operations, consider the following program. The file `prime` will be created initially to consist of the first 10 primes. Note that the reading and writing are done with `fscanf` and `fprintf`. They are like `scanf` and `printf` except that they work on files of individual variables. In contrast, `fread` and `fwrite` work on files of records. Also, `fscanf` returns `EOF` when the end of the file is reached or an error occurs. ■

```
#define NULL 0
#include <stdio>

main()
/* Creates a file consisting of the first 10 prime
   numbers, and a file containing these primes in
   reversed order, and prints the contents of both
   the files.
*/
{
   /* This section creates file prime and
      stores the first ten primes in it.
   */
   int a[20],i,dummy;
   FILE *f_ptr,*fr_ptr,*fopen();
   f_ptr = fopen("prime","w");          ] open prime for writing
   fprintf(f_ptr,"%d",2);               ] write the first 10 primes
   fprintf(f_ptr,"%d",3);
   fprintf(f_ptr,"%d",5);
   fprintf(f_ptr,"%d",7);
   fprintf(f_ptr,"%d",11);
```

```
    fprintf(f_ptr,"%d",13);
    fprintf(f_ptr,"%d",17);
    fprintf(f_ptr,"%d",19);
    fprintf(f_ptr,"%d",23);
    fprintf(f_ptr,"%d",29);
    fclose(f_ptr);                                  close prime


    /* This section reads from the prime file,
       fills a with its contents, and creates
       reversedprime which will contain
       the contents of a in reversed order.
    */
    i = 0;
(1) f_ptr = fopen("prime","r");                     open prime for reading
    if(f_ptr == NULL)                               if an error has occurred, take
       {                                            proper action
          printf("Can not open");
          exit(-1);
       }
    while(fscanf(f_ptr,"%d",&dummy) != EOF)         read and test the next file
       {                                            entry
          a[i] = dummy;                             store it in a[i] and update
          i++;                                      array index i
       }
    i--;                                            decrease i so it points to the
                                                    last prime read
(2) fr_ptr = fopen("reversedprime","w");            open reversedprime for
                                                    writing
    if(fr_ptr == NULL)                              if an error has occurred, take
       {                                            proper action
          printf("Can not open");
          exit(-1);
       }
    while(i >= 0)                                   while array a contains more
       {                                            primes
          fprintf(fr_ptr,"%d",a[i]);                write the next prime to the file
          i--;                                      and update array index i
       }
    fclose(f_ptr);                                  close the prime file
    fclose(fr_ptr);                                 close the reversedprime
                                                    file
    /* This section prints, at the terminal,
       the contents of prime and then of
       reversedprime.
    */
    f_ptr = fopen("prime","r");                     open file prime for reading
    while(fscanf(f_ptr,"%d",&dummy) != EOF)         read and test each file entry
       printf("\n %d\n",dummy);                     and print it
    fr_ptr = fopen("reversedprime","r");            open file reversedprime
                                                    for reading
```

```
    while(fscanf(fr_ptr,"%d",&dummy) != EOF)      ] read and test each file entry
       printf("\n %d\n",dummy);                   ] and print it
    fclose(f_ptr);                                ] close file prime
    fclose(fr_ptr);                               ] close file reversedprime
}
```

Prime and **reversedprime** are files of integers and **a** is an array of integers.

After (1) **fopen** is executed, the file called **prime** and its file pointer can be depicted as in Figure 10.2(a). After nine executions of the first **while** loop body, the situation will be as shown in Figure 10.2(b).

The tenth execution sets **a[9]** to 29 and moves the file pointer beyond the last file record. The **EOF** test yields the value *true,* so the loop is exited with **i** set at 10.

After (2) **fopen** is executed, **reversedprime** appears as in Figure 10.3(a). After the second **while** loop body has been executed nine times, **reversedprime** looks like Figure 10.3(b). The last execution yields the file shown in Figure 10.3(c).

The standard function, **exit**, closes any open files, flushes any buffered output, signals what has happened, and terminates program execution. A zero parameter value, by convention, signals that all is well, while other values may have different meanings. The -1 is used here to signal that a file could not be opened. Files can also be closed by simply invoking the function **fclose**, whose parameter is the file pointer of the file to be closed. It is important to close all files appropriately.

Suppose you wished to append the eleventh prime, 31, to **prime**, after 29. This can be done directly in C by opening the file **prime** to its end so that items can be appended. To do this, as noted earlier, the file need only be opened with the **a** to position the file pointer

```
f_ptr = fopen("prime","a");
fprintf(f_ptr,"%d",31);
```

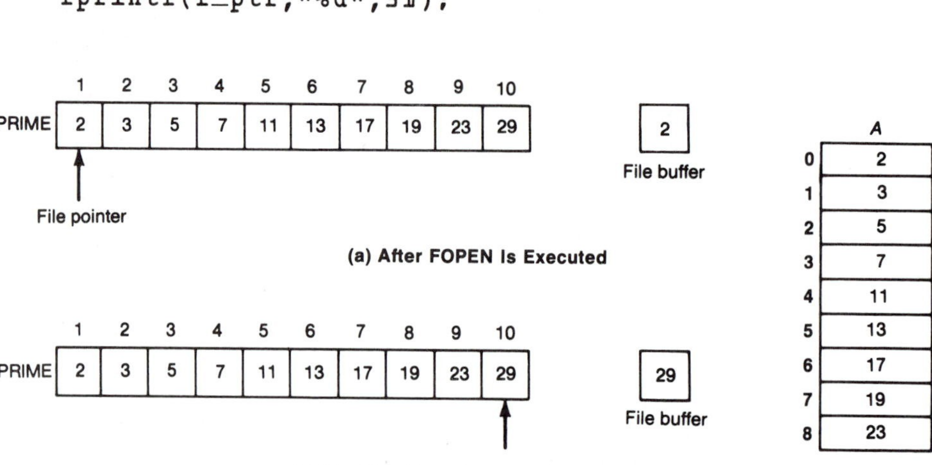

Figure 10.2 File PRIME

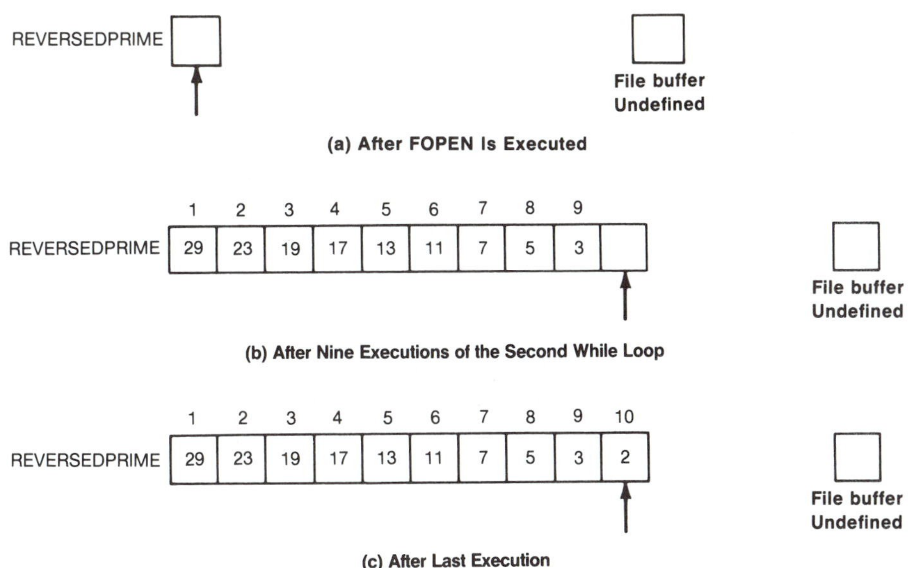

Figure 10.3 File REVERSEDPRIME

Example 10.5 Suppose there are two files with records of the same type in sorted order based on key value. Merge the two files. ■

Producing a new file consisting of all the records of the two files in sorted order is called ***merging*** the two files. The merging of two files is a basic component of efficient methods of external sorting. The task in Example 10.5 is to write a function to produce a merged file assuming records are ordered with the smallest key value appearing in the first record.

The basic idea is straightforward. Read a record from each sorted file, and append the record with the smaller key value to the merged file. Read the next record of the file that had the record with the smaller key value. Compare it with the record that has not yet been appended. Append the record with the smaller key value to the merged file. Repeat this process of reading and comparing records from the two files until one of the files becomes empty. Then append the records on the remaining file to the merged file.

Assume that the files to be merged are not empty and have been opened with filepointers `f1_ptr`, `f2_ptr`, and `f3_ptr`. Filepointers `f1_ptr` and `f2_ptr` point to the input files to be merged. Filepointer `f3_ptr` points to the resultant merged file. The files are made up of records of `typedef filerecords`, with key the field of `filerecords` on which merging is to be based. The merge may be written as follows:

```
merge(f1_ptr,f2_ptr,f3_prt)
/* Merges the files pointed to by f1_ptr
   and f2_ptr. The merged file is pointed
   to by f3_prt. The files must be opened before the merge is invoked.
*/
```

```
FILE *f1_ptr,*f2_ptr,*f3_ptr;
{
   struct filerecords record1,record2;
   int flag,length;
   flag = 0;
   length = sizeof(filerecords);
   fread(&record1,length,1,f1_ptr);                   read the first record
   fread(&record2,length,1,f2_ptr);                   from each input file
   while(flag == 0)                                   test for nonempty
                                                      input files
      if(record1.key < record2.key)                   if file f1 record has
         {                                            the smaller key value
            fwrite(&record1,length,1,f3_ptr);         append it to f3
            if(fread(&record1,length,1,f1_ptr) == 0)  read into record1
               {                                      from f1; if f1 empty,
                  flag = 1;                           signify by setting flag
                                                      to 1
                  fwrite(&record2,length,1,f3_ptr);   append record2 to
               }                                      f3
         }
      else                                            otherwise
         {
            fwrite(&record2,length,1,f3_ptr);         append record2 to
                                                      f3
            if(fread(&record2,length,1,f2_ptr) == 0)  read into record2
               {                                      from f2; if f2 empty,
                  flag = 2;                           signify by setting
                                                      flag to 2
                  fwrite(&record1,length,1,f3_ptr);   append record1 to
               }                                      f3
         }
   if(flag == 1)                                      if f1 empty
      while(fread(&record2,length,1,f2_ptr) != 0)     append the rest of f2
         fwrite(&record2,length,1,f3_ptr);            to f3
   else                                               otherwise
      while(fread(&record1,length,1,f1_ptr) != 0)     append the rest of f1
         fwrite(&record1,length,1,f3_ptr);            to f3
}
```

The files must be opened before the merge is invoked.

The following program, when the merge is included, merges two files and prints the resultant file.

```
#define NULL 0
#include <stdio>
typedef struct
{
   int key;
}filerecords;
```

```
main()
/* Merges two files and prints the merged file.
*/
{
   filerecords record;
   FILE *f1_ptr,*f2_ptr,*f3_ptr;
   f1_ptr = fopen("prime","r");
   if(f1_ptr == NULL)
      {
         printf("Can not open file1");
         exit(-1);
      }
   f2_ptr = fopen("other","r");
   if(f2_ptr == NULL)
      {
         printf("Can not open file2");
         exit(-1);
      }
   f3_ptr = fopen("result","w");
   if(f3_ptr == NULL)
      {
         printf("Can not open file3");
         exit(-1);
      }
   merge(f1_ptr,f2_ptr,f3_ptr);


   fclose(f1_ptr);
   fclose(f2_ptr);
   fclose(f3_ptr);
   f3_ptr = fopen("result","r");

   while(fread(&record,sizeof(filerecords),1,f3_ptr) != 0)
      printf("\n %d\n",record.key);

   fclose(f3_ptr);
}
```

opens and tests the input files for reading and the output file for writing

invokes `merge` *to produce the output file*

closes the files

opens the merged file for reading

reads and prints the merged file

closes the merged file

10.4 Sequential Access in External Memory

A range of devices is now available for use as secondary storage, the most common being magnetic tapes and disks. Tape cassettes like those used with stereo equipment are prototypical of the magnetic tape used for secondary storage. If a song is being played on such a tape, the time required to access another song on the tape depends on how far away from the current position that song is. This accessibility is the same for magnetic tapes used as secondary storage. Such a tape can be pictured as containing a sequence of fixed-length *blocks* (Figure 10.4).

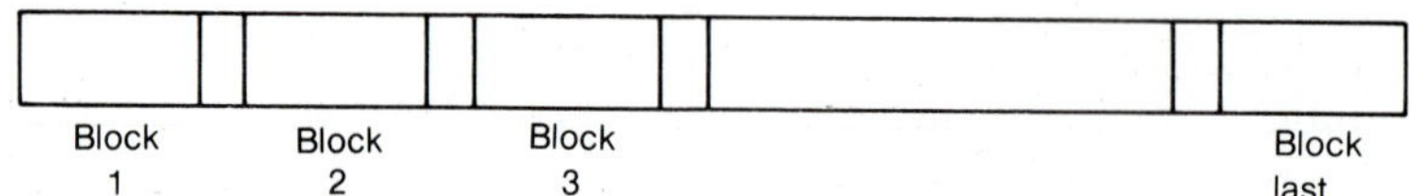

Figure 10.4 Sequential Access on Magnetic Tape

Each block contains a fixed number of records of a file (say, n per block). One or more ***input buffer areas*** (reserved storage areas) are set aside in internal memory, each large enough to hold one block of records. These buffers are required in order to allow for efficient reading and writing of files.

Suppose one buffer is set aside. To read a block of records into the buffer, the tape must be moved at sufficient speed past a read head. This speed determines the rate at which data are transferred to the buffer. If a sequential file is stored on magnetic tape, executing the open statement causes the buffer storage to be allocated, the tape to be rewound so that the first block may be read, and the first block to be read into the buffer. After these operations have occurred, the buffer and the file pointer can be visualized as in Figure 10.5.

If a read is executed, the first record is copied from the buffer into its memory location, and the file pointer is advanced to the next buffer position. Consecutive executions of a read for this file cause similar actions. Finally, when n such reads have occurred, the next block of records from the tape is placed into the buffer, the file pointer is automatically repositioned at the first record of the buffer, and the process is repeated. Had two buffers been set aside, as the current buffer is being read the other would be filled with the next block of file records. A similar procedure takes place for the writes with respect to an output buffer for the file. In this way the buffer is being filled, when reading from a file (or emptied, when writing to a file), at the same time that the computer is carrying out other commands of a program. Record blocking is done because n records can be read or written as a block much faster than individually, since it reduces tape starts and stops. Today's computers, whether mainframe or personal, can execute on the order of 100,000 commands in the time it takes for a block to be read into or written from the buffers. A program may actually process n records of the file while the next block is being transferred to the buffer. For example, the records may be sorted or individually processed during this transfer time. In this case, the time required to process the entire file is determined by the time required to scan

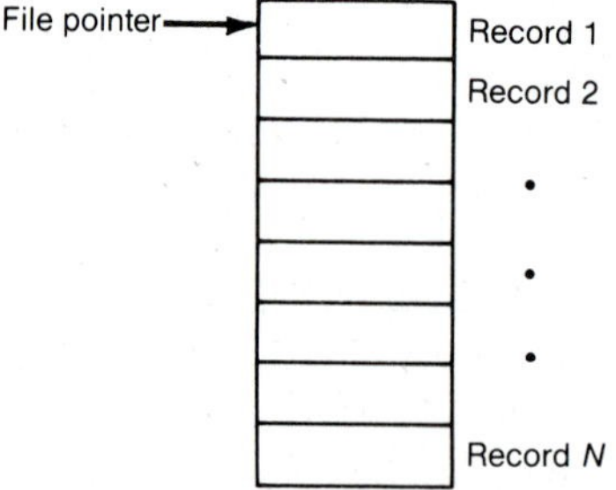

Figure 10.5 Input Buffer for the File

the file in this fashion. Thus the number of accesses to secondary storage determines the execution time of the program. This may take minutes, which is a very long time in computer terms.

It should now be clear why sequential files should not be used when records must be accessed in an order other than the order in which they appear on the file. Attempting to access the records in random order may mean spending great amounts of computer time, since minutes may be required for each access. Instead, the typical use for sequential files is when records are to be processed in turn, starting from the first record. In other words, when the processing to be done can be accomplished by a traversal through the records of the file, then sequential files are appropriate. This is typical of external sorting, copying, updating, and printing (such as end-of-the-month billings).

As a practical example, suppose you are given the master file, `bookinventory`, of Example 10.3, and another transaction file, `booktransactions`. `Booktransactions` consists of records representing the arrival of new books for inventory and the sales of books in the last week. If both files are sorted on the same key (say, title), it is possible to traverse each of the files once and update each master file record to reflect new arrivals and sales. A new file must be created for this updated master file. This step would actually be advantageous for security purposes, since the old master file and `booktransactions` file could be saved. If anything were to happen to the new master file, the procedure could be repeated and the file reconstructed.

10.5 Sorting Tape Files

Once again, one picture—or in this case, a good example—is worth a thousand words. The different merging techniques demonstrated for the following example illustrate some of the complexities of sorting files stored on magnetic tape, when all records of the file cannot fit into internal memory at the same time. Tape sorts are used here, since they highlight the concepts of sorting, but these concepts are also applicable to disk sorts. Detailed analysis of the sorting algorithms discussed here, and others, may be found in Knuth [1973b]. We begin with an extreme case.

Example 10.6 Sort an original file of twenty-one records that are stored sequentially on a tape file. The records have integer key values. Assume that only two records can be kept in internal memory at any one time. Storage for the two records is in addition to input and output buffers. ■

Suppose the sequence of records in the original file is as follows:

2 12 17 16 14 30 17 2 50 65 20 32 48 58 16 20 15 10 30 45 16

It is not possible simply to read all the records into internal memory and then apply one of the internal sort algorithms of Chapter 8, since available internal storage is assumed to be only enough to hold two records. Instead, the general strategy, given that two sorted files can always be merged as shown in Section 10.3, is to create sorted subfiles repeatedly and merge them repeatedly until a final merged file containing all the original records is produced. The literature contains many ingenious algorithms for external sorting. This chapter gives only the flavor of the solutions. One major constraint on a solution is the number of tapes available for use in the sort. Assume three available tapes.

10.5.1 Straight Merge

Perhaps the most straightforward sorting technique is the straight merge. The ***straight merge*** distributes the initial records onto two tapes, *a* and *b*, so that they contain the same number of records, or so that one tape contains only one more record than the other. If this is done for the original file in Example 10.5, then the configuration of tapes a and b will appear as the *initial distribution*.

a 2|17|14|17|50|20|48|16|15|30|16
b 12|16|30| 2|65|32|58|20|10|45|

Now *a* and *b* can be thought of as being composed of subfiles, each of which is sorted and of length 1. A subfile is ***a run of length* r** if it consists of *r* records sorted in order. Here, *a* contains eleven subfiles, or runs, of length 1, and *b* contains ten runs of length 1.

Apply a merge procedure to each pair of runs, each pair containing a run from tape *a* and the corresponding run from tape *b*. Thus

2 17 14
12 16 30, etc.

are "paired." The merge procedure consecutively merges each pair (consisting of a sorted subfile of length 1 from *a*, and a corresponding sorted subfile of length 1 from *b*). The resultant merged files are written consecutively to tape *c*. The result of the *first merge of* a *and* b *to* c is

c 2 12|16 17|14 30|2 17|50 65|20 32|48 58|16 20|10 15|30 45|16

Think of *c* as containing ten subfiles or runs of length 2 and one run of length 1 and distribute these to *a* and *b* equally to obtain the *second distribution*.

a 2 12|14 30|50 65|48 58|10 15|16
b 16 17| 2 17|20 32|16 20|30 45|

By now there are five paired runs of length 2 and one run of length 1. These may again be consecutively merged, and written to *c* to obtain the *second merge of* a *and* b *to* c.

c 2 12 16 17|2 14 17 30|20 32 50 65|16 20 48 58|10 15 30 45|16

Another distribution to *a* and *b* yields the *third distribution*.

a 2 12 16 17|20 32 50 65|10 15 30 45
b 2 14 17 30|16 20 48 58|16

These pairs of length 4 can now be merged to obtain the *third merge of* a *and* b *to* c.

c 2 2 12 14 16 17 17 30|16 20 20 32 48 50 58 65|10 15 16 30 45

It takes two more distributions and merges to complete the sort. The *fourth distribution*

a 2 2 12 14 16 17 17 30|10 15 16 30 45
b 16 20 20 32 48 50 58 65|

is followed by the *fourth merge*.

c 2 2 12 14 16 16 17 17 20 20 30 32 48 50 58 65|10 15 16 30 45

The *fifth distribution* is next. It is followed by the *fifth merge*.

a 2 2 12 14 16 16 17 17 20 20 30 32 48 50 58 65
b 10 15 16 30 45
c 2 2 10 12 14 15 16 16 16 17 17 20 20 30 32 45 48 50 58 65

This completes the sort, which has taken five distributions and five merges. The sort is described as a *five-pass* sort, with five distribution phases and five merge phases, using three tapes. Programming this process is not a trivial task. Ignoring details, the basic time requirements can be seen to be determined by the number of times files must be rewound or rewritten and the number of records that must be accessed from secondary storage (tapes). This assumes that the internal memory processing will be done so quickly that it does not add to the total time for the sort. Before the original file, *c*, can be distributed (rewritten) to tapes *a* and *b*, those tapes must be rewound and the original file must be rewound. Before *a* and *b* can be merged (and written) to *c*, they must be rewound, and *c* must be rewound. Also, in each phase, whether distribution or merge, each record must be accessed from secondary storage. Thus the total time is proportional to the number of passes (five here). If the access time of a record is T_a, and the rewind time T_r, then the total time is $5 \times (2 \times 21 \times T_a + 3 \times T_r)$. Note the factor of 2 associated with the twenty-one records and the access time. The factor is 2 because there are two phases, distribution and merge.

10.5.2 Natural Merge

The straight merge sort does not take advantage of any natural ordering that may exist in the original file. Even if that file were given in sorted order, the straight merge would proceed as before. A ***natural merge sort*** distributes the records of the original file to *a* and *b*, so that sorted subfiles or runs are preserved and treated as a unit. Such a distribution would assign 2 12 17 to *a*, since they form a run. The 16 terminates this run and goes to *b*. The 14 terminates this run and goes to *a* as the beginning of its second run, followed by 30. So far the result is

a 2 12 17|14 30
b 16

The 17 now terminates the 14 30 run and goes to *b*. Note that this extends the first run of *b* to 16 17. At this point, 2 terminates this run with the following result.

a 2 12 17|14 30
b 16 17

If ***balance*** is to be maintained, each file must end up with a number of runs differing by no more than 1 from the other files. Therefore the next run (starting with 2) must go to *b*. Subtleties of this kind must be carefully monitored in the actual implementation of merge sorting algorithms. The resultant distribution will be the *initial distribution*.

a 2 12 17|14 30 |20 32 48 58|15 16
b 16 17 | 2 50 65|16 20 |10 30 45

Merging these pairs of runs and writing the merged results to *c* yields the *first merge*.

c 2 12 16 17 17|2 14 30 50 65|16 20 20 32 48 58|10 15 16 30 45

Another distribution and merge gives the *second distribution,*

a 2 12 16 17 17|16 20 20 32 48 48
b 2 14 30 50 65|10 15 16 30 45

which is followed by the *second merge*.

c 2 2 12 14 16 17 17 30 50 65|10 15 16 16 20 20 30 32 45 48 58

A third and final distribution and merge complete the sort. The *third distribution* yields

a 2 2 12 14 16 17 17 30 50 65
b 10 15 16 16 20 20 30 32 45 48 58

The result of the *third merge* is as follows:

c 2 2 10 12 14 15 16 16 16 17 17 20 20 30 30 32 45 48 50 58 65

This is a three-pass, two-phase sort, using three tapes. The total time is $3 \times (2 \times 21 \times T_a + 3 \times T_r)$. Any inherent ordering of the initial data allows the number of passes to be reduced, as compared to the straight merge sort.

Note that to merge runs embedded in a file, the procedure of Section 10.3.1 requires modification.

10.5.3 Replacement-Selection

Since there is typically room for a reasonable number of records in internal memory, both the straight and natural merge sorts can be speeded up. For instance, if *m* records can be sorted in internal memory, the straight merge sort can start with the distribution of runs of length *m* on each of the tapes a and b.

There is a clever way to produce runs for distribution (for example, with the natural merge sort) without actually storing the *m* records. This is the ***replacement-selection sort,*** which uses a heap of size *m* and works as follows. Start with the first *m* keys of the original file of Example 10.6 in internal memory and create a heap to obtain Figure 10.6(a) ($m = 7$).

Remove the root key from the heap and output it to an output file. The next input file key, 2, is inserted at the root of the heap, and the heap is reheaped, giving Figure 10.6(b).

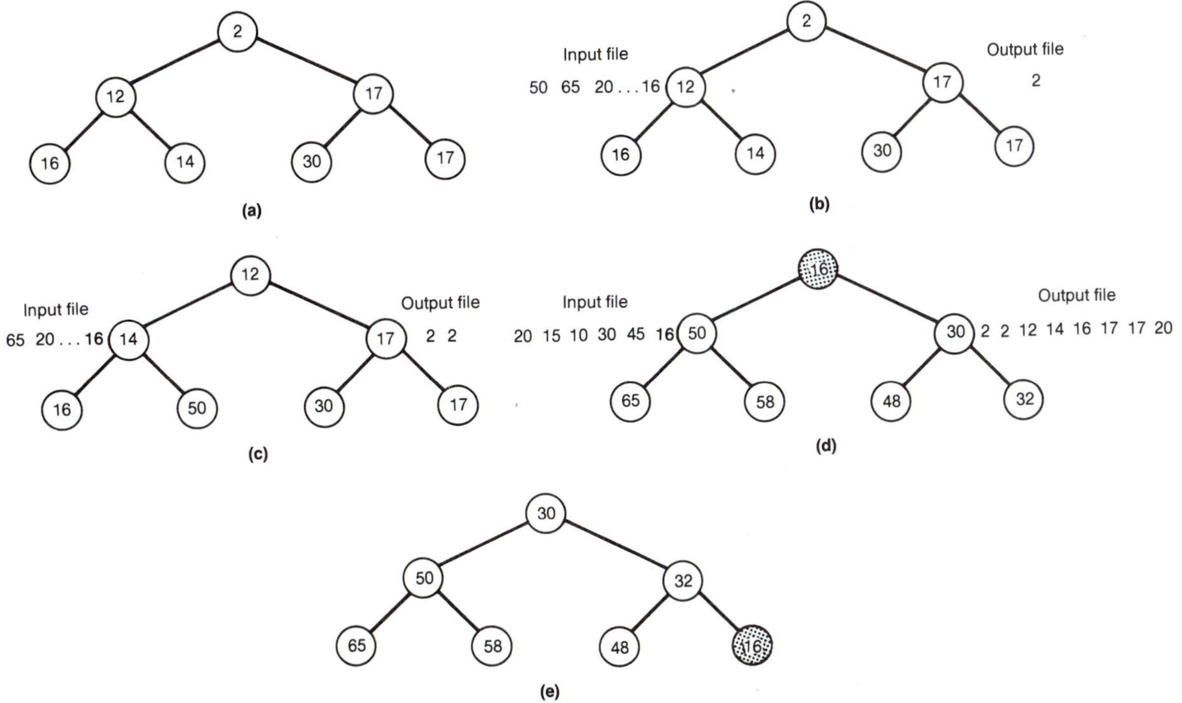

Figure 10.6 Replacement-Selection Sort

Again, the root key is removed and written to the output file. The next record key of the input file, 50, is inserted at the root and reheaping occurs. Figure 10.6(c) results.

Continuing in this way generates a run on the output file of length 8, which would be terminated when 16 from the input file is inserted at the root of the heap. The situation at that point is shown in Figure 10.6(d). Instead of terminating the run at length 8, treat 16 as associated with the next run, since 16 is less than the last output value, 20. This means that 16 must be distinguished from the heap entries for the current run; it is shaded in Figure 10.6(d). In reheaping, current run entries are considered smaller than next run entries. Figure 10.6(e) shows the heap after reheaping. Each input smaller than the last output is handled in this way. Eventually the heap becomes filled with entries of the next run, and the process repeats.

Notice that the length of the output run will always be at least m (with the possible exception of the last run generated). Continuing this process, called *replacement-selection,* we obtain the output file,

2 2 12 14 16 17 17 20 30 32 48 50 58 65|10 15 16 16 20 30 45

The original file consisted of ten runs; the output file after replacement-selection consists of two runs. With randomly ordered input files, this replacement-selection generates runs whose average length is $2m$. The example exhibits this behavior in an exemplary fashion.

Notice that both the straight and natural merges spend half their time accessing records for the distribution phase. Spending this time can be avoided by using another tape. By this technique, each time two runs are merged, they can be written, alternately, to tapes *a* and *b*. This eliminates the need for extra, basically unproductive, time spent in distribution from tape *c*.

10.5.4 Polyphase Sort

Rather than using more tapes, it is possible to incorporate the distribution phase (except for the initial distribution) into the merge phase. Such a sort is called a ***polyphase sort.*** In this type of sort, the tapes being merged, and the tape to which the merged subfiles are written, vary continuously throughout the sort. In this technique, the concept of a pass through records is not as clear-cut as in the straight or the natural merge. A distribution, a merge, and a pass all blend together. This might have more properly been called an *amorphous* sort, except that it has considerable character and is one of the better sorts.

The polyphase sort starts with an initial distribution of runs on tapes a and b. The initial distribution is critical to its proper execution. For the case of the original file of twenty-one records in Example 10.6, the initial distribution should be thirteen runs to tape *a*, and 8 runs to tape *b*, each of length 1. It is the *number,* not the length, of the runs on each tape that is critical. The number of records for the example is twenty-one because the first few Fibonacci numbers are 0, 1, 1, 2, 3, 5, 8, 13, 21. The Fibonacci numbers are crucial to the polyphase sort because the number of records must be a Fibonacci number to make the polyphase sort work.

When a three-tape polyphase sort is used, the original number of runs should be a Fibonacci number, with the distribution of runs between tapes *a* and *b* the two preceding Fibonacci numbers, which add to the original number of runs. In the present case, 8 + 13 = 21. When more tapes are used, *generalized* Fibonacci numbers, which specify the required number of records, become the basis for the initial run distribution among the tapes. No programs will be shown for the implementation of the details of the external sorting algorithms discussed in this section. Therefore it is unnecessary to resolve in detail the question of how to proceed when the actual number of runs is not a Fibonacci number. The remedy, though, involves adding an appropriate number of "dummy" runs [Knuth, 1973b].

Getting back to the workings of the polyphase sort, the initial situation after distribution will be an *initial distribution.*

a	2|12|17|16|14|30|17| 2|50|65|20|32|48	13 runs of length 1
b	58|16|20|15|10|30|45|16|	8 runs of length 1
c		

This distribution required twenty-one record accesses.

We now proceed by merging the first eight runs of *a* and the eight runs of *b* to *c* to obtain the *merge of the first eight runs of* a *and* b *to* c.

a	50|65|20|32|48	5 runs
b		
c	2 58|12 16|17 20|15 16|10 14|30 30|17 45|2 16	8 runs

Notice that b is now empty, a total of 8 + 8 = 16 records have been accessed, and a and c contain 5 + 8 = 13 runs. All three tapes had to be rewound before the initial distribution, but only b need be rewound now. It is possible to continue merging the first five runs of c and the five runs of a to b. This results in a *merge of the first five runs of* a *and* c *to* b.

a		
b	2 50 58|12 16 65|17 20 20|15 16 32|10 14 48	5 runs
c	30 30|17 45 | 2 16 |	3 runs

Notice that a is empty, a total of 5 + 5 × 2 = 15 records have been accessed, and b and c contain 5 + 3 = 8 runs. Tape a is now rewound, and the first three runs of b are merged with the three runs of c. The result is the *merge of the first three runs of* b *and* c *to* a.

a	2 30 50 58|12 16 17 45 65|2 16 17 20 20	3 runs
b	15 16 32|10 14 48	2 runs
c		

Tape c is now empty and must be rewound. A total of (3 × 3) + (3 × 2) = 15 records were accessed, and a total of 2 + 3 = 5 runs remain. Merging the first two runs of a and b to c yields

a	2 16 17 20 20	1 run
b		
c	2 15 16 30 30 32 50 58|10 12 14 16 17 45 48 65	2 runs

This leaves b empty, so we rewind it. A total of (2 × 3) + (2 × 5) = 16 records were accessed, and 1 + 2 = 3 runs remain. Merging the run of a and the first run of c to b yields.

a		
b	2 2 15 16 16 17 20 20 30 30 32 50 58	1 run
c	10 12 14 16 17 45 48 65	1 run

A total of (1 × 5) + (1 × 8) = 13 record accesses occurred, and 1 + 1 = 2 runs are left. Tape a is rewound. Then a final merge produces

a	2 2 10 12 14 15 16 16 16 17 17 20 20 30 30 32 45 48 50 58 65
b	
c	

This final merge of b and c to a took 13 + 8 = 21 record accesses. A total of 117 (= 21 + 16 + 15 + 15 + 16 + 13 + 21) record accesses is required. These 117 record accesses represent an effective 117/21, or 5 4/7, passes. The total time for this algorithm is $117 \times T_a + 8 \times T_r$. The straight merge sort and the natural merge sort required $210 \times T_a + 15 \times T_r$ and $126 \times T_a + 9 \times T_r$ time, respectively.

The polyphase sort, until completion, results in exactly one empty tape, so that the remaining tapes may be partially merged to it. After each merge, the distribution of runs is made up of two consecutive Fibonacci numbers (13 + 8, 8 + 5, 5 + 3, 3 + 2, 2 + 1, 1 + 1, 1 + 0). With more tapes, this is also true, but generalized Fibonacci numbers appear.

10.6 Direct Access in External Memory

Accessing a song on a phonograph record is different from accessing a song on a tape cassette. Think of the songs as stored along the grooves of a record rather than along the tape of a cassette. Instead of going through each song between the current arm position and the location of the desired song (and scratching the record!), the arm is moved directly to the proper groove. Once the arm is placed, it is necessary to wait until the record revolves, so the beginning of the song appears under the arm. The movable arm eliminates the need to pass through all songs that intervene between its current and desired positions. The magnetic disk works the same way. It is the reading head that moves to the desired storage location, thus saving access time compared to the magnetic tape.

Magnetic disks and disk packs are examples of *direct access* devices used for secondary storage. In this context, ***direct access*** means that a program can go straight to desired information stored on a given surface and cylinder. This access time is not constant. It is slower than random access in internal memory, but generally much faster than the sequential access time for tapes. A floppy disk has similar access capability but is slower and has much less storage capacity. Thus in terms of access time, direct access storage devices fall between sequential access devices, such as magnetic tapes, and random access memory. Hard disks are generally used with mainframes and minicomputers, whereas microcomputers or personal computers vary from no disks through floppy disks to hard disks.

A random access memory allows very fast access to any element of the memory. The access time is the same for all stored elements, no matter which element was last accessed. Sequential devices allow fast access "locally," but all elements between the currently accessed element and the next desired element must be passed through before the next element may be accessed. Consequently, the time to access the next desired element is proportional to its distance from the currently accessed element. Direct access devices are intermediate between these two extremes. They act like sequential devices with tabs. Just as using the alphabetical tabs in a dictionary allows a person seeking a word to find it quickly, so do "tabs" allow one to close in, relatively quickly, on the desired area of the sequential storage. In direct access devices, the "tabs" are the movable read/write heads.

Sequential devices are convenient for tasks that may be accomplished by traversing records. However, when the order in which the records must be processed cannot be predicted, sequential access devices are not efficient. Tasks requiring random access to records cannot be accomplished efficiently using sequential memory devices. The introduction of economical direct access devices made random access feasible. As a result, airline reservation systems, interactive computing, and instant updating of bank accounts have become commonplace. This was made possible by the development of appropriate technology for direct access memory.

A ***magnetic disk*** is a flat, circular platter on whose surfaces information can be stored and accessed. It can be pictured as a phonograph tone arm and record, with its concentric *tracks* corresponding to the grooves of the phonograph record and its ***movable read/write head*** corresponding to the tone arm. A ***disk pack***

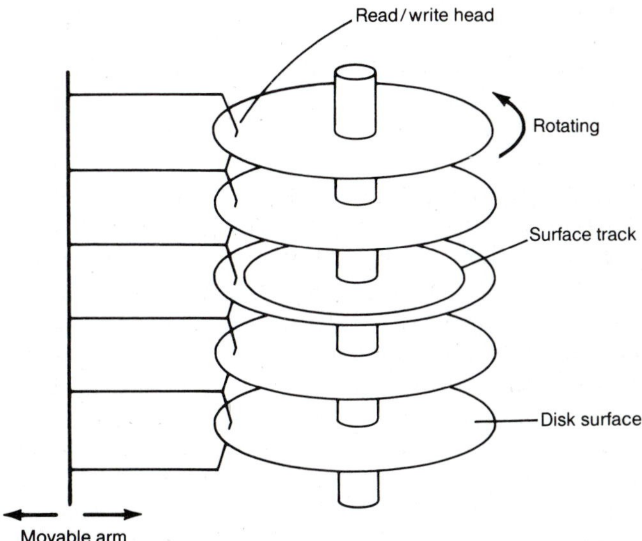

Figure 10.7 A Disk Pack

consists of a pile of such magnetic disks and a read/write head for each record surface—that is, one head for each side of a record (see Figure 10.7). The read/write heads are typically coupled so that they all move at the same time. They are positioned over the same track on their respective surfaces, although only one head is actually reading or writing at any moment. There may be twenty magnetic disks and a hundred tracks on each disk.

Each track of a surface in a disk pack stores records in blocks, similar to the blocking of records on magnetic tapes. Each track behaves as a sequential access device, like a magnetic tape. That is, each block must be passed through, as the disks rotate, before another block farther along the track can be accessed by the surface read/write head.

If we focus on the same track on each surface, then the pile of tracks forms a conceptual *cylinder* in space, as shown in Figure 10.8. Assuming tracks are numbered (say, from 1 to 100), a cylinder consists of all tracks with the same number. Thus the disk pack can be viewed as composed of one hundred concentric cylinders.

A cylinder is important because it allows any block of records stored on a surface of the cylinder to be accessed without moving the read/write heads. Accessing a block stored on a different cylinder (or track) requires moving the read/write heads. The time required to move the heads from one cylinder to another is called ***seek time;*** it is proportional to the distance between the cylinders. This time typically takes a significant fraction of a second (1/10th to 1/20th). It is the dominant factor in dealing with time requirements for accessing blocks on magnetic disks.

Once the read/write heads are positioned over the desired cylinder, the time required for the desired block to rotate under the heads is called ***latency time.*** It can be on the order of one hundredth of a second.

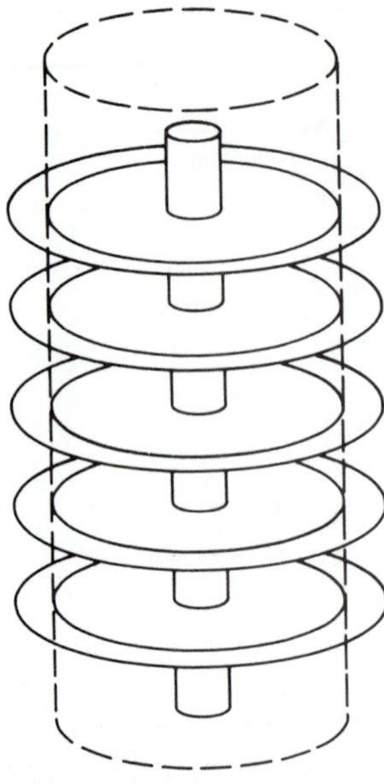

Figure 10.8 Conceptual Cylinder

10.7 Sequential and Random Access of Disk Files

Often large amounts of information, too much to fit into internal memory, must be organized so that random requests for specific pieces of information can be readily satisfied. The methods of organization that are useful in internal memory are not adequate for data stored on disks in external memory.

10.7.1 Sequential Access

There is a natural way to store records sequentially on magnetic disk to minimize total seek time for a traversal through the records. This storage technique is based on the cylinder concept. It starts by filling blocks of the top surface track of the outermost cylinder with records. The records are in sequence within the blocks. When the track is full, the same process is repeated with the track of the next surface, and the next, and the next, until the lowest surface track is filled. At that time the outermost cylinder has been filled. Continuing in the same way, records are stored on each of the inner cylinders, starting with the next adjacent cylinder. This is similar to storing records sequentially on magnetic tape. In fact, we can picture the surfaces and cylinders laid out linearly as in Figure 10.9. This arrangement has all the inherent drawbacks of magnetic tape, whenever random accessing of records is required.

We can adapt disk storage to random accessing by taking advantage of the tab feature of the disk, which allows the head to go directly to any cylinder and surface. The problem is how to determine exactly where to go. If one knew that the record to be retrieved were the *i*th record, then it would be easy to calculate on which cylinder and surface it would be located. This is not often the case, since the search is conducted by means of key value, not by order in the sequence.

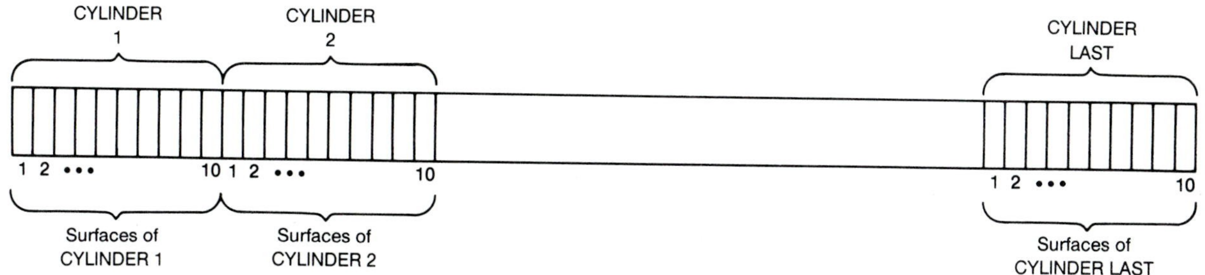

Figure 10.9 Sequential Access on a Magnetic Disk Pack

A linear search of the file could be done but might take $O(n)$ time, when n records are stored in the file. This could take minutes. If the records are stored in sorted order by key value, a binary search of the file might be done. The difficulty here is that lg n accesses are required. A million-record file would require twenty accesses, and each access might require a seek. While the binary search is better, it still might take seconds. This is reasonable for isolated requests, but during this time there may be many requests for desired retrievals. Waiting requests may build up interminally, with unlimited waiting time before all are processed. The need to insert or delete records further compounds the problem.

Just as in the case of internal memory, keeping records in blocks with pointers to succeeding blocks is a possibility, based on the concept of lists. This may avoid insertion and deletion difficulties, but it does not alleviate the problem of searching. We encountered this same problem with lists in internal memory. What about binary search trees? Even if balanced, a million records may need as much as $20 \times c$ seeks, where c is a small constant.

10.7.2 Random Access

We still have hash tables in our arsenal. Using hash tables in secondary storage requires some accommodation to its access capabilities. ***Buckets,*** an extension of the chaining policy for collision resolution with internal memory, are appropriate. The idea is to create a hash table based on key values. The hash table will contain pointers to lists. Each list, referred to as a *bucket,* contains all records that hash to the same hash table address. The lists are stored in blocks on the disk, each block holding a fixed number of records and a pointer to the next block containing other records on the list. When a key is inserted into the hash table, the program determines its hash address and then inserts the key into the bucket pointed to by that address. The key may be inserted into the bucket by traversing the list of linked blocks until a block is encountered with room for the record. If no such block is found, a new block is appended to the list, and the record is inserted in that block. Care must be taken to avoid wasting seek time (and latency time) when these lists are being traversed. This means that the blocks of a bucket should be on the same cylinder. Searching for a key is similar to making an insertion. Deletion involves the usual deletion from a list, with care taken to release unneeded blocks when possible. When small enough, the hash table itself is kept in internal memory to avoid one disk access.

In practice, such hash tables can be devised so that one or two disk accesses are required for either successful or unsuccessful searches. This is accomplished by selecting a good hash function, an appropriate fixed number of records per block, and an appropriate number of buckets. The usage factor of such a hash table is given by n/bk, where n is the number of records stored, b is the number of buckets, and k the fixed number of records per bucket. If the performance of the table degrades as insertions are made, the table may be reorganized.

Other interesting and important external hashing methods are presented in Larson [1976], Litwin [1960], and Fagin, Nievergelt, Pippenger, and Strong [1979].

10.7.3 Indexed Sequential Access

While the hash table solution may yield fast average access times, there is no guarantee for the worst case, nor any convenient way to access records in sorted order by key value. To achieve the ability to access records in random order or in sorted order, as necessary, we must incorporate an old idea familiar to all. Suppose a visitor from outer space wanted to find the location of a particular street, say Bond Street in London. The visitor might go to a world atlas and determine first where London's country, England, is situated. The intergalactic traveler might then find a map of the country, and locate London. Finally, a city map of London gives the creature the exact location of the street. On a more mundane level, suppose a student wants to locate a particular book in the university library. The student would go to the file cabinet of authors and find the drawer that contains authors' last names with the appropriate beginning initial. She would then search for the card with the correct author and title, which gives a library call number. Next she would consult a library directory to learn the floor location of those call numbers. Finally, she would go to that location and search for the book with that particular call number. The critical concept in such searches is the availability of one or more *directories,* to be used to determine quickly the location of the particular item desired.

The magnetic disk supports the use of such a directory to focus the search. It can be used to find a particular cylinder and surface relatively quickly, eliminating the need for traversing sequentially through intervening records. Until recently, when B-trees (see next section) were introduced, the most popular method of creating and maintaining such a directory used the natural sequential storage of records, so that they appear in sorted order by key value. This is known as the ***indexed sequential access method (ISAM);*** it may be implemented in various ways, typically using three or four levels of directories. A first directory, known as the ***master index,*** may be searched to determine the cylinder on which a particular search key appears. If a disk pack has two hundred cylinders (tracks), then the master index has two hundred entries, one for each cylinder. The entry for the ith track gives the highest key value appearing on that track. A search of the master index then readily determines the cylinder on which a search key may reside. That cylinder is accessed; it contains a *cylinder index* directory. If a disk pack has ten surfaces, the cylinder index has ten entries, one for each surface. The entry for the ith surface gives the highest key value appearing on that surface. A search of the cylinder index determines the surface on which a search key may reside. Finally, the track of the cylinder on that surface may be searched sequentially for the desired key, resulting in a successful or unsuccessful search. With such an implementation, unused storage is initially left in blocks so that the insertion of new records may be more easily accommodated. If a block is full, records can be shifted to the right to other blocks, so that the new record is inserted in proper order.

Overflow areas must also be available and maintained on disk, in case the track storage is exhausted due to insertions. Tracks and cylinders are set aside for this purpose. Insertions may require the master or cylinder index to be updated. Similarly, deletions of records, leaving vacated storage to be reclaimed, may require updating of directories and shifting of records. Deletions may also be treated simply by marking a record as deleted, but this may eventually lead to the need for reclamation of this storage, degrading the efficiency of the implementation. Because of overflow from insertions, performance may degrade, necessitating reorganization, allocation of more disk storage, and reconstitution of the file.

The overflow areas may be maintained as lists of records in sorted order, linked by pointers. When the proper cylinder index is searched, the pointer to be followed may point to an overflow area, in which case the search amounts to a traversal of a list of records. Otherwise, the record is said to reside in the *prime area,* and the search amounts to a sequential traversal of records on a track. The ***prime area*** consists of reserved tracks on cylinders designated as prime cylinders.

For a given number of records to be stored, there is no guarantee that overflow will not degrade the system, unless a high price is paid by dedicating large amounts of track storage to reduce this possibility.

Each cylinder index actually has additional entries giving the highest key value in its overflow area for each surface and a pointer to the first record of the overflow list for the surface. Conceptually, we may visualize the organization of such implementations as shown in Figure 10.10.

10.7.4 B-trees for Sequential and Random Access

A more recent method allows for achieving both the random access of records and a traversal through the records in sorted order. This method allows a more flexible use of the disk and guarantees excellent worst-case performance for a given number of records, with an acceptable amount of dedicated disk storage. It is known as the ***virtual sequential access method (VSAM).*** To see how it might be implemented, we study its basis *B-trees*. VSAM and many data base management systems use modified B-trees in their implementation. The basic reference for B-trees is the classic paper by Bayer and McCreight [1972]. Hash trees are an alternative to B-trees for the organization of large files of data. They are discussed and compared to B-trees by Bell and Deen [1984]. Tremblay and Sorenson [1984] discuss many file structure organizations. See Ullman [1982] for more on data base systems.

Figure 10.10 shows that the directories (the master index and the cylinder indexes) form a tree structure that guides the search for a record. Programmers try to find specialized trees leading to efficient searches, efficient use of storage, and

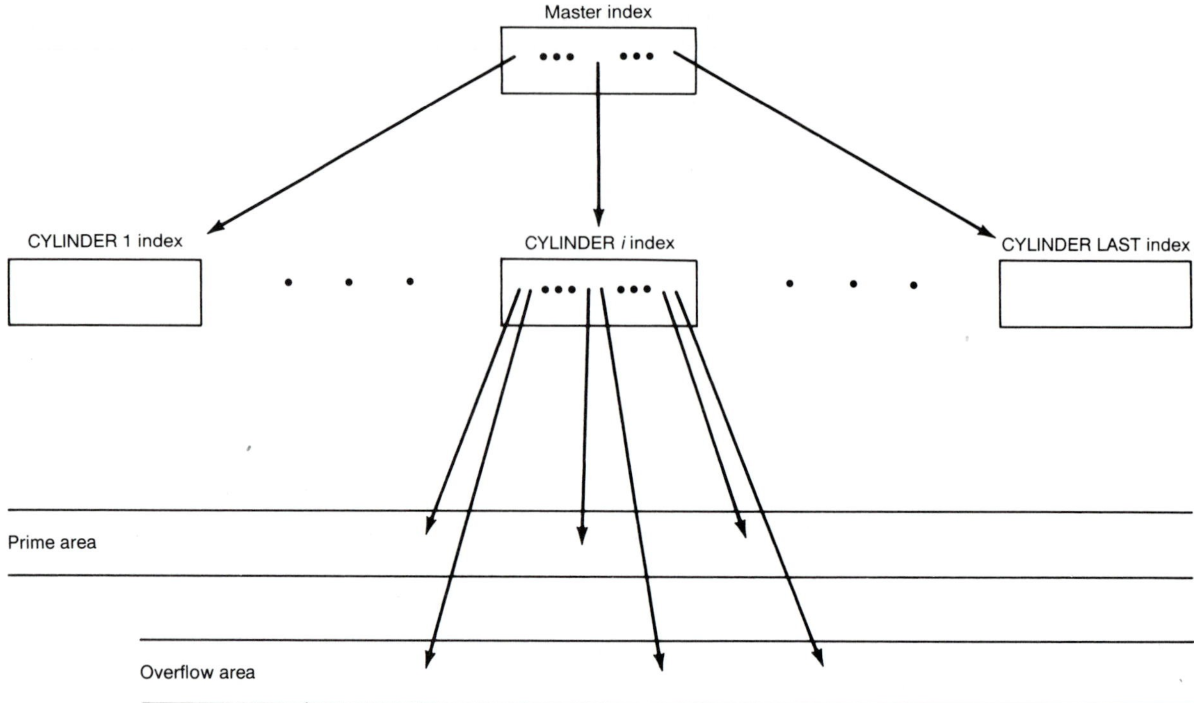

Figure 10.10 Organization of Indexed Sequential Files

relatively easy maintenance. Since the depth of the tree determines the worst-case search times, the goal is to find trees with short paths to terminal nodes. This implies that the nodes of the tree generally will have many successors. B-trees satisfy these requirements.

A ***B-tree of order* m** has the following four properties:

1. Every node of the tree, except the root and terminal nodes, has at least $\lceil 1/2\ m \rceil$ subtrees.
2. Every terminal node has the same depth.
3. The root node has at least two subtrees, unless it is a terminal node.
4. No node has more than m subtrees.

Each node of a B-tree will have the form shown in Figure 10.11. This represents storage for $m - 1$ keys and m pointers, although the storage may not all be used at a given time. If n is less than m, not all m keys are present in the node. Each pointer P_i points to a subtree of the node. The keys $K_1, K_2, \ldots, K_n$ are kept in sorted order, so $K_1 < K_2 < \cdots < K_n$ within the node. The subtree pointed to by P_{i+1} contains all records of the file whose key values are less than K_{i+1} and greater

P_1	K_1	P_2	K_2	•••	P_i	K_i	P_{i+1}	K_{i+1}	•••	P_n	K_n	P_{n+1}	•••		

Figure 10.11 Form of Each Node on a B-Tree

than or equal to K_i. P_1 and P_{n+1} point to subtrees containing records with key values less than K_1 and greater than or equal to K_n, respectively. For example, if the keys are

1,3,5,6,7,8,13,20,21,23,24,30,37,40,56,60,62,63,70,80,83

then the tree of Figure 10.12(a) is a B-tree of order 4 storing these keys and their records.

The terminal nodes of the B-tree in Figure 10.12 are not shown. Instead, the pointers to them have been replaced by null pointers. This reflects the way the tree might be represented in external storage. Notice that, in general, null pointers will appear at the same depth in the tree—depth one less than the terminal nodes. A generalized inorder traversal (see Chapter 7) of the B-tree accesses the keys in sorted order. Associate with each null pointer the key value accessed immediately after the pointer is considered in such a traversal. A unique key is then associated with every null pointer except the last, and each key has a unique null pointer associated with it. For example, the first three null pointers have keys 1, 3, and 5 associated with them. The fourth null pointer (to the right of 5) has key 6 associated with it. Consequently, the number of null pointers, and the number of terminal nodes, is exactly one greater than the number of keys stored in the tree.

Any B-tree has a root node with at least two successors. Each successor has at least $\lceil 1/2\ m \rceil$ successors. Thus there are at least $2\lceil 1/2\ m \rceil^{d-2}$ nodes at depth $d \geq 3$ of any B-tree. A B-tree of depth $d \geq 3$ has at least $2\lceil 1/2\ m \rceil^{d-2}$ terminal nodes, so

$$n + 1 \geq 2\lceil 1/2\ m \rceil^{d-2}$$

This implies that $d \leq 2 + \lg_x\lceil (n + 1)/2 \rceil$, where $\lg_x$ denotes logarithm with base x and $x = \lceil 1/2\ m \rceil$. If $n = 2^{24} - 1 = 16{,}777{,}215$ and $m = 2 \times 2^8 = 512$, then $(n + 1)/2 = 2^{23}$, and $\lg_x[(n + 1)/2] = \lg_{256}(2^{23}) < 3$.

A B-tree storing 16,777,215 records will therefore have depth ≤ 4. We shall see that $d - 1$ is the maximum number of nodes that must be accessed when searching a B-tree for a search key. Thus we are guaranteed that no more than three node accesses are required to search for a key in the B-tree with 16,777,215 records!

A B-tree may be viewed as a generalization of a binary search tree, with a special imposed balance requirement to ensure against too great a depth. To search a B-tree for a search key value (say, 22) entails accessing its root node and traversing the node's keys until 22 is encountered, a key that exceeds 22 is reached, or the last key stored in the node is passed. If 22 is found, the search is complete. In Figure 10.12(a) the key value 40 is reached. The pointer to its left points to a subtree that must contain the search key, if it is in the tree at all. That subtree is then searched in the same way. Its root node is accessed, and 30 is reached. Following its left pointer, the final subtree root is accessed. Its key value, 23, is reached. Its left pointer is null, which means that the search terminates unsuccessfully.

Property 1 ensures that, except for the root and terminal nodes (which don't appear anyway), every node of a B-tree will be at least half full. Property 2 ensures that the B-tree will not be scraggly. All paths to terminal nodes must have

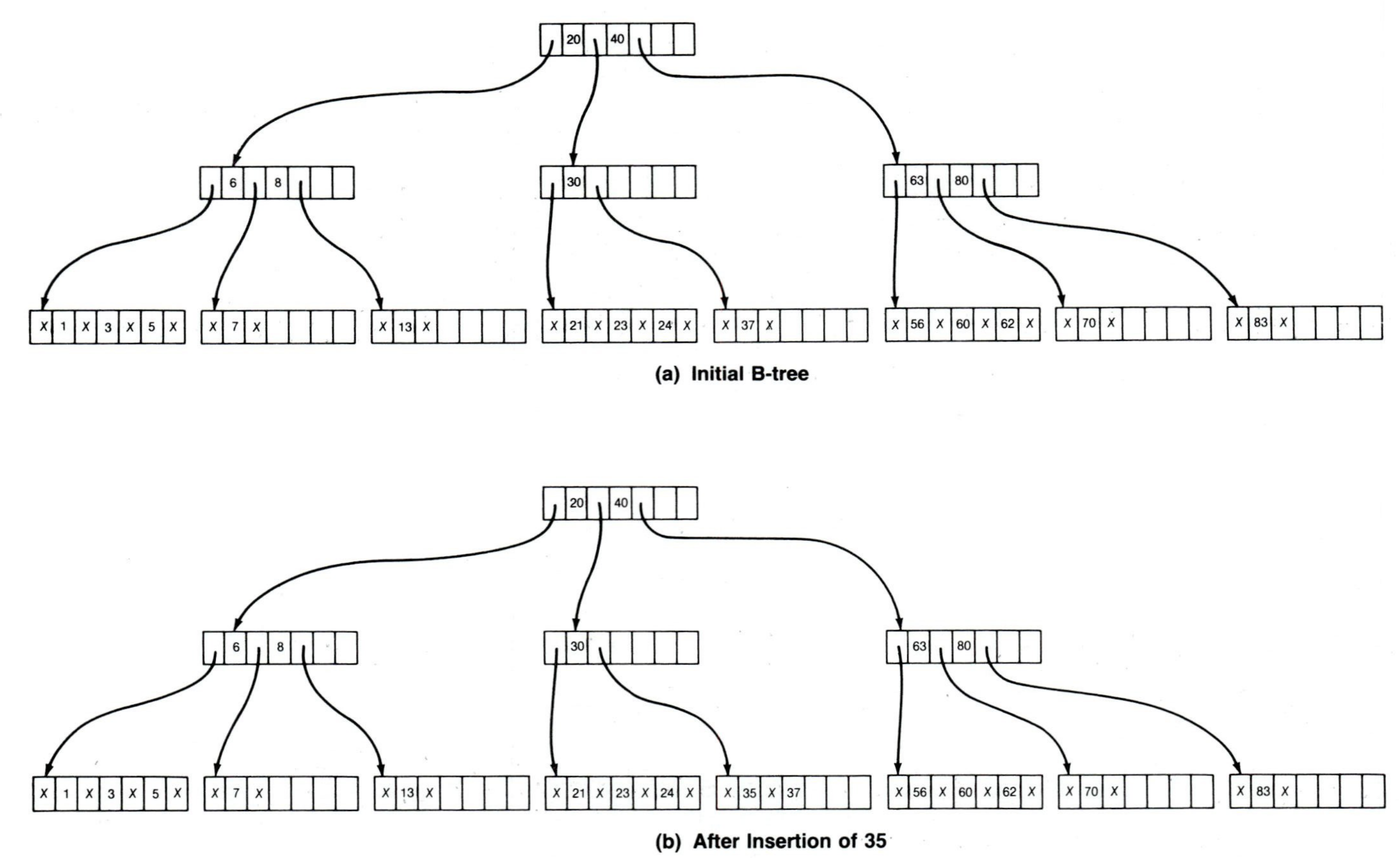

(a) Initial B-tree

(b) After Insertion of 35

Figure 10.12 A B-Tree of Order 4 with Twenty-one Records

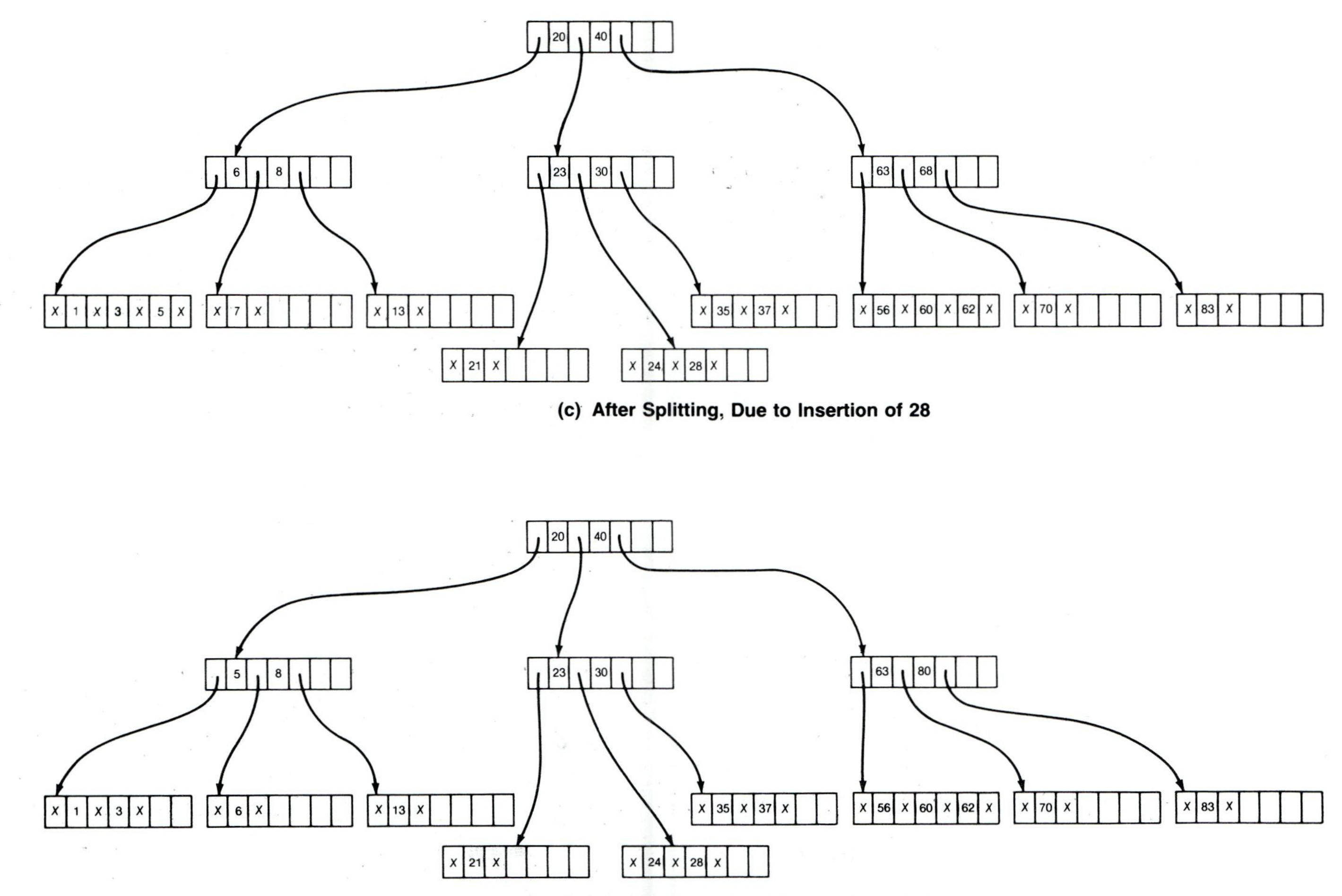

(c) After Splitting, Due to Insertion of 28

(d) After 7 is Deleted and 5 is Borrowed

Figure 10.12 *(continued)*

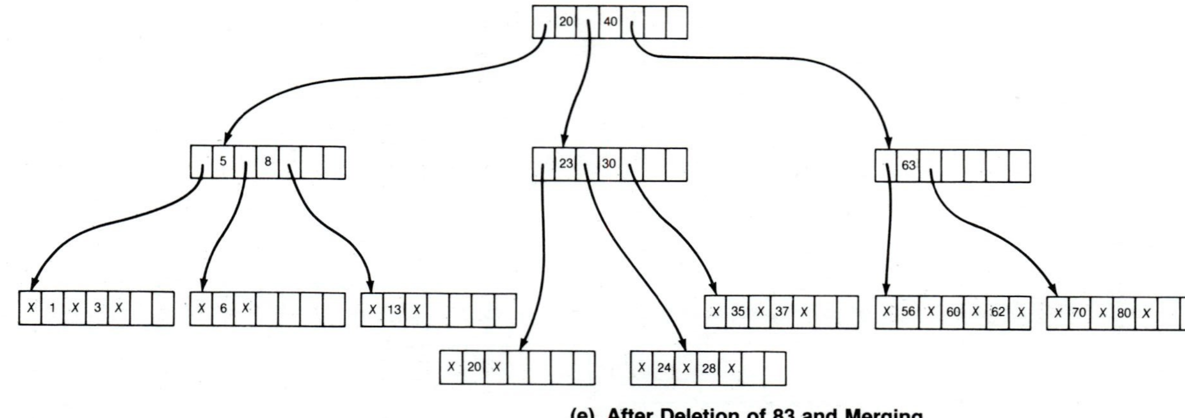

(e) **After Deletion of 83 and Merging**

Figure 10.12 (*continued*)

the same length. The idea is to store information of a node on blocks of a cylinder on the disk, so that accessing a node requires one seek time and all keys of the node may be read into internal memory. The search through the keys of a node, to determine the next node to access, then takes place rapidly in internal memory, using an appropriate search technique.

After an insertion or deletion, of course, the tree must be maintained as a B-tree. This may be done making *local* modifications that are simpler than those required for AVL trees. For insertion, the key to be inserted is searched until a null pointer is to be followed. This assumes that only one record with a given key value appears in the tree and that it is similar to the initial insertion in AVL trees. If the node containing the null pointer has unused storage, then the key is simply inserted at the proper place in this node. This may require the shifting of keys in the node, but it is accomplished quickly in internal memory. For example, if key 35 is inserted in the tree of Figure 10.12(a), the result is the tree of Figure 10.12(b).

All insertions will be made in this way, in nodes at the lowest level, until the node becomes full. For example, if 28 is to be inserted next in the tree of Figure 10.12(b), no room exists in the node × 21 × 23 × 24 ×. The $m + 1$ key values (the m old keys and the 1 new key) can be split by leaving $\lceil m/2 \rceil - 1$ in the old node and moving the remaining records, except the middle one, the $\lceil 1/2m \rceil$th, to a newly created node. The middle record is inserted in the predecessor (parent) of the old node. The result is the B-tree of Figure 10.12(c).

Had the predecessor been full, it would have been split in the same way in turn. Splitting may be necessary at every node of the search path, back to and including the root. If this occurs, the depth of the resultant B-tree is one greater than the original B-tree.

Deletion is done similarly. A key is simply deleted from a lowest-level node, and the keys shifted over, if the resultant number of keys satisfies the constraint that the node contain at least $\lceil m/2 \rceil - 1$ keys. If the constraint is violated, a key can be borrowed from a "neighbor" node, provided this may be done without violating the constraint for that node. In this case, the predecessor or successor key of the borrowed key moves into the deletion node, and the borrowed key takes its place in the predecessor node. For example, if key 7 is deleted from the tree of Figure 10.12(b), key 5 is borrowed from its neighbor (13 cannot be borrowed). The result is Figure 10.12(d).

If no neighbor can spare a key, the total number of keys between a neighbor and the deletion node will be less than m. These nodes may then be merged, along with a key from their predecessor. In the tree of Figure 10.12(d), if 83 is to be deleted, this situation will occur. The result is Figure 10.12(e).

It is possible for the predecessor to become too sparse, although this did not happen in our example. It is then treated as though its key were deleted, and so on, until the entire process is complete. This may go all the way to the root, in which case the root disappears and the depth of the tree decreases by 1.

If the key to be deleted were not in a lowest-level node, it would be replaced by its successor and the successor node treated as if the successor were being deleted.

These insertion and deletion procedures preserve the B-tree properties. The B-tree is an external memory data structure that plays the same role as AVL trees in internal memory. In practice, a modification of the basic B-tree is used to ensure better storage utilization and to increase the efficiency of traversal through the records in sorted order for VSAM. With B-trees the generalized inorder traversal must be used for sequential access. This is time-consuming and requires stack storage. Instead of storing some key records in higher-level nodes, the idea is to store all records only in lowest-level nodes and chain the lowest-level nodes by pointers. For example, in Figure 10.12(a) all nodes at depth 3 could be linked in a chain, with the leftmost node first and the rightmost node last on the list. A traversal then amounts to a traversal of this chain.

It is clear that storage management is needed for external memory, just as for internal memory. This problem is not discussed here, but the internal memory techniques are applicable, when properly modified to take into account the structure of the disks.

10.8 Summary

Files are stored in secondary storage and provide powerful facilities for the temporary and permanent storage of large amounts of data. Magnetic tapes and magnetic disks are two important devices on which to store files. These are typical of sequential and direct access devices, respectively.

Because of the structure and resultant access capabilities of these devices, internal memory techniques must be modified in order to deal efficiently and conveniently with files stored on them. It is possible to sort efficiently, even with sequential files, by using external sorting techniques. Primarily, these are merge sorts, such as straight, natural, and polyphase sorts. Other merge sorts may also decrease sorting time. In general, sequential files are suitable for tasks that can be accomplished by traversing the records of the file. These tasks include sorting and updating master files.

It is possible to achieve efficient random accessing of records with direct access devices when access is by a specific key. Hash tables are useful for this purpose. To achieve a combined capability of random plus sequential access in sorted order by a specific key requires considerable file organization. This organization involves the creation of a file directory, which may consist of a number of levels. The directory guides the search efficiently to the desired record with specific key value. A number of directory implementations are possible; directories based on B-trees are becoming increasingly popular. Such directories may be searched relatively quickly, allowing efficient insertions and deletions while utilizing storage well.

At this point, you should have filed away the substance of this book. It is hoped that you have done so to allow quick retrieval, while maintaining room for insertions. Deletions may be necessary but should be minimal.

■ Exercises

1. Suppose a function reads in each record of Example 10.4 and creates a file consisting of every other prime number on the file. Show the state of the input and output files and their file pointers after the fourth record of the output file has been written.

2. Write a function to create the output file of Exercise 1.

3. Write a function to create `reversedprime` of Example 10.4, assuming the array `a` may only be of length 10 while `reversedprime` may contain many more entries.

4. How many writes and reads will be executed by the function `merge` if file 1 and file 2 are, respectively,

1 2 8 10 13 15 40
3 7 10 12 17 20 45 50 60

5. Write a function to create a sequential file that is the same as file 1, except that all records on file 1 that are also on file 2 do not appear.

a. Assume file 1 and file 2 records appear in sorted order based on the key field.

b. Assume file 1 and file 2 are not sorted, and you do not know how to sort a file.

6. Write a function to produce a new file that is the same as an input file except that all blanks have been deleted from it.

7. Write a function that takes two sequential files and appends the second file to the first.

8. Why are the sort procedures of Chapter 8 inappropriate for files?

9. Why does the number of passes required by a straight sort not depend on any initial ordering among records?

10. Write a function for the straight merge.

11. Modify the merge function of Section 10.3 so that it merges two runs embedded in files.

12. Write a function to distribute records as required by the natural merge.

13. Write a function for the natural merge.

14. Simulate the behavior of replacement-selection to verify that the average length run produced is $2m$.

15. Why must Fibbonacci numbers govern the number of initial runs for three tapes in the polyphase sort?

16. **a.** If four tapes are used in a polyphase sort, what is the relation determining the initial distribution of runs?

b. Can you generalize to n tapes?

17. Write a function for the polyphase sort using three tapes.

18. Why do the movable read/write heads and surfaces act as tabs for a disk?

19. Suppose the master index of Section 10.7.3 does not fit on one cylinder. How may another directory level be created to serve as an index to the master index?

20. Why do B-trees allow more flexible use of a disk than directories implemented using prime and overflow areas?

21. Create a B-tree of order 4 to store the nametable records of Chapter 6. The records are to be ordered alphabetically so that the B-tree can be searched with the name field as key.

22. Write a function to insert a record into a B-tree of order m that is stored in internal memory.

23. Can you write the function of Exercise 22 so that it is independent of whether the B-tree is stored in internal or external memory? If so, write it. If not, explain why not.

24. Write a function to delete a record from a B-tree of order m that is stored in internal memory.

25. Why does the chaining of lowest-level nodes discussed in Section 10.7.4 allow more efficient traversal through a file?

26. Write a function to create a B-tree stored in internal memory.

27. Suppose we want to store variable length records in a B-tree. How may this be done?

28. Why is it not feasible to store all records in the root node of a B-tree so that only one seek is required?

29. A B-tree of order 3 is called a ***2-3 tree,*** since each node has two or three successors. Although not useful for external storage, such a tree may rival AVL trees for an internal memory structure in which to store records. Compare its search, insertion, and deletion algorithms and its time requirements with those for AVL trees.

30. Write a search function for a B-tree of order *m*.

31. Write a function to traverse through the records of a B-tree in order by key value.

32. Suppose the individual records of Figure 6.5 are to be stored on a disk with the `recordptr` field of the `nametable` pointing to the address of an individual record on the disk. The address is a cylinder and surface specification. What is a reasonable way to allocate disk storage to the individual records?

33. Suppose records of a file were stored in a hash table, with buckets for random access by key, and linked in sequential order by pointers for sequential access. Compare the insertion and retrieval times of such an implementation with the use of B-trees.

■ Suggested Assignment

This assignment is appropriate for a group of students to do together. It involves a task of reasonable size, which must be partitioned so that each member of the group knows just what to do and so that, when all parts are put together, the final solution works correctly. The idea is to produce an "index" for a book. This involves

1. The creation of files, using the seqential files available in C.
2. The creation of appropriate functions that will allow the records of a file to be accessed randomly, or in sequential order, by key.

One file, the book file, is to consist of records that represent the pages of a book. Each page contains one hundred lines, and each line consists of one hundred characters. The key consists of a page number and a line number. A second file, the dictionary file, is to consist of records representing words to appear in an index for the book represented on the book file. When the solution is run, it should use a scaled-down version of the book file, which will consist of a few pages of ten lines and twenty characters each, with the dictionary containing relatively few words (say, twenty-five).

The dictionary file is to be a sequential file, with the file implemented using B-trees. Instead of a disk, assume that enough internal memory exists to store the book file. The index for the book should be output so that the words of the index appear in alphabetical order, followed by the page and line numbers on which the word appears in the book. Also, an input file consisting of page and line numbers appearing in random order should result in an output consisting of the text for each record of this input file.

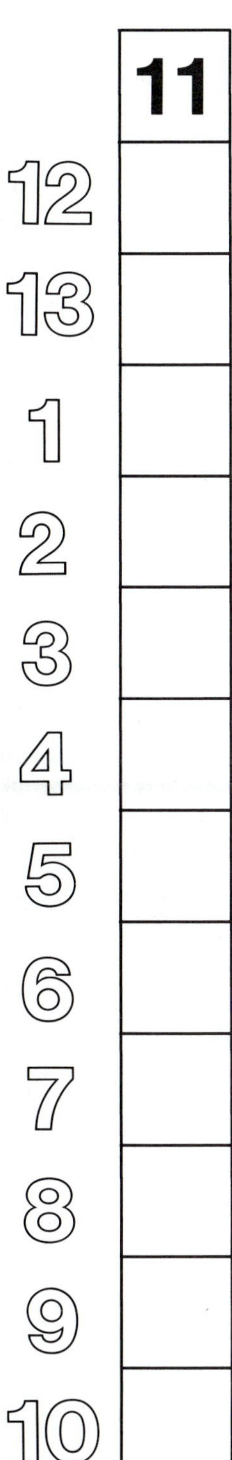

11 Topological Sorting: An Archetypal Solution

Introduces topological sorting
as an example of the application of the problem solving methodology and programming style presented in this text
background for the problem is given first
each step and decision is explained as the solution evolves
Emphasis is on
top-down design
data abstraction
functional modularization
intelligent choice of information to store and data structure in which to store it

11.1 Background

Topological sorting requires ranking a set of objects subject to constraints on the resultant topology—that is, on the placement of the objects. It occurs in many practical situations. For example, textbooks are often written so that each chapter builds on material covered earlier and cannot be understood without this base of information. Determining the order in which to present topics to ensure that all prerequisite material has been covered reduces to finding a topological sort of the topics. Other examples involving topological sorting are presented later.

The approach to the topological sorting problem presented in this chapter and the characteristics of the final program are intended to serve as prototypes. The problem is substantial and the algorithm developed important, but it is the process by which it is achieved that is most important. Developing an efficient topological sorting program is a complex process and demonstrates the general problem solving methodology used in this text. It requires the application of structured programming concepts, during which the selection of data structures plays a significant role.

The resultant topological sorting program is a model solution, representing nearly the best programmers can hope to achieve. Few solutions to problems have all its characteristics. It is concise and clear; correctness is easy to determine; and the storage and execution time requirements can be analyzed. Invalid input data are not difficult to deal with. What more can we ask?

The following are some examples of problems whose solutions require topological sorting.

Example 11.1 A large skyscraper is to be constructed. Imagine that you must write a program to prescribe the order in which all the tasks are to be performed. The tasks include T_3—install windows; T_{50}—install floors; T_8—install window sashes; T_{1000}—clear the ground; T_7—build the foundation; T_9—install doors. For any two tasks, it is possible to specify whether one should be done before the other. Clearly, T_8 must be done before T_3, and T_{1000} must be done before T_7, while it makes no difference whether or not T_3 is done before T_9. The constraint that T_i be done before T_j is represented as the pair (i, j). ■

Example 11.2 Imagine that you want to write a book on data structures. All technical words used must be defined. First write down all the relevant words. If word w_j uses w_i in its definition, represent this constraint by the pair (i, j). ■

Example 11.3 As a student you must take a number of courses to graduate. Represent the fact that course c_j has course c_i as a prerequisite by the pair (i, j). ■

Example 11.4 A number of books must be read for a course you are taking. Represent the fact that you prefer to read book i before book j by the pair (i, j). ■

Suppose that an order is given in which the construction tasks of Example 11.1 are to be carried out. If you proceed to carry out the tasks, you may not be able to do the next task, since tasks that must precede it have not yet been finished. The same situation can arise in Examples 11.2, 11.3, and 11.4, when an order is specified in which words are to be defined, courses to be taken, and books to be read, respectively. This is because words used in the next word's definition have not yet been defined, all prerequisites for the next course may not have been taken, or you will not read the next available book because you want to honor your preferences. A topological sort gives an order in which to proceed so that such difficulties will never be encountered.

11.1.1 Binary Relations and Partial Orders

Some mathematical concepts and terminology must be defined before the topological sorting problem can be stated and solved in abstract terms. As with the solution to any problem, stating this solution abstractly is desirable so that it will not be tied to a particular application.

You readily understand what is meant by the statements: "Fred *is related to* Sam"; "John *is taller than* Sue"; "3 *is the square root of* 9." The phrases each specify a connection or *relation* between two objects. In the first two cases the relations refer to two people. In the third case the relation refers to numbers. Each is a binary relation on a set of objects.

Mathematics abstracts from such examples to define a ***binary relation* R *on a set* S.** S is taken as the set or collection of objects referred to by the relation. R contains information, for any two of these objects, on whether or not they are related. R is a set of pairs of objects (a, b), where a and b belong to S. If the pair (a, b) belongs to R, then this is interpreted to mean that a is related to b. This is written as aRb. If (a, b) does not belong to R, then a is not related to b. This is written as $a\not{R}b$.

For instance, specify S to be the set of integers between 2 and 10, so $S = \{2, 3, \ldots, 10\}$; and take $R = \{(4, 2), (6, 2), (8, 2), (8, 4), (9, 3), (10, 2), (6, 3), (10, 5)\}$. Then R captures the "is divided evenly by but is not equal to" relation on S, since a pair (a, b) will belong to R only if a "is divided evenly by but is not equal to" b. By looking at R, we can determine if aRb or $a\not{R}b$ for any a and b in S.

Of particular interest are the kinds of binary relations called *partial orders*. A binary relation R on S is called ***a partial order on* S** if it has the following properties:

- ***Irreflexivity*** For any a in S, $a\not{R}a$
- ***Asymmetry*** For any two distinct a and b in S, aRb implies $b\not{R}a$
- ***Transitivity*** For any three distinct a, b, and c in S, aRb and bRc implies aRc

These properties specify that whenever certain pairs are in R, then other pairs must necessarily be included in R or excluded from R. The "is divided evenly by but is not equal to" relation on S in the preceding paragraph fulfills all three properties of a partial order.

It is irreflexive, since a is divided evenly by but is equal to a for all a in S.

It is asymmetric, since if a "is divided evenly by" b, then b cannot be divided evenly by a when a is not equal to b.

It is transitive, since whenever a is divided evenly by b and b is divided evenly by c, then a must also be divided evenly by c.

To show that a relation does not have a property requires only one counterexample.

Two extreme binary relations on a set S are the null relation, which contains no pairs at all, and the universal relation, which contains all possible pairs. The null relation is a partial order. This is because no counterexamples can be found. The universal relation will never be irreflexive (unless S has no objects in it) or asymmetric (unless S has only one object), but it will always be transitive.

11.1.2 Graphic Representation of Partial Orders

One can represent any binary relation R on a set of n objects graphically, as in Figure 11.1. Let S consist of ten objects, the integers $1, 2, 3, \ldots, 10$. Take R to contain the pairs (1, 2), (8, 3), (7, 6), (2, 7), (5, 4), (7, 8), (2, 4), (4, 7), (2, 8), (8, 5). Create a node for each object in S and draw arrows between two nodes for each pair in R. For example, an arrow will appear from 7 to 8 for the pair (7, 8).

Any such diagram can be interpreted as representing a binary relation on a set S. For such a diagram to represent a partial order requires that

- No arrows appear from any node to itself (irreflexivity)
- No arrows appear from any node i to another node j and back from j to i (asymmetry)
- If arrows appear from i to j and from j to k, then an arrow must appear from i to k (transitivity)

In depicting partial orders, it is unnecessary to draw all the arrows needed to represent transitivity, because they are always assumed. With this understanding,

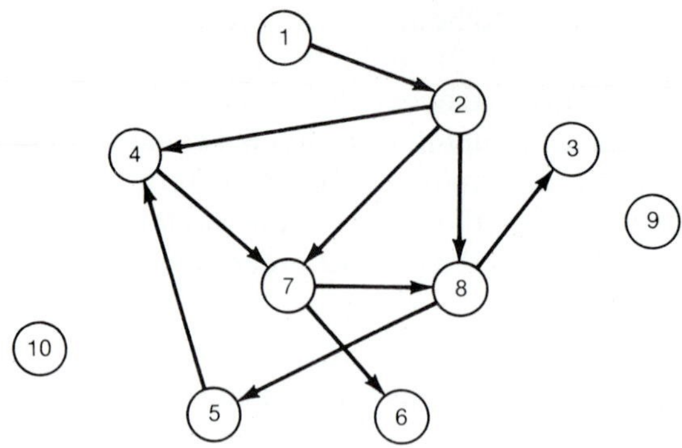

Figure 11.1 Binary Relation R on a Set of $n = 10$ Objects

it is not difficult to see that a diagram represents a partial order if and only if it contains no loops. This means that no node can be found such that one can follow a series of arrows starting from that node and ending at that node. In Figure 11.1, there is a loop involving nodes 5, 4, 7, and 8. Hence the diagram does not represent a partial order. Note that if one starts with a diagram representing a partial order (no loops), erasing a node and all arrows emanating from it results in a diagram that represents a new partial order on the set of remaining nodes.

11.1.3 Topological Sorts: Consistent Rankings

Partial orders are important. They are meant to capture abstractly any concrete example in which the pairs of R (or arrows of the diagram) mean "is greater than," "precedes," "is ranked higher than," or "comes before." A special case of a partial order is one whose diagram looks like the following:

$$3 \rightarrow 5 \rightarrow 1 \rightarrow 2 \rightarrow 4 \rightarrow 6 \rightarrow 8 \rightarrow 7$$

For such a diagram, it seems clear what would be meant by a listing or ranking of the eight objects that is consistent with the given partial order. Such a ranking would be 3, 5, 1, 2, 4, 6, 8, 7. No other ranking would be consistent with the given partial order. This can be generalized to any partial order by interpreting the arrows as constraints on the ordering of objects in a ranking. For example, an arrow from 3 to 5 would mean that 3 must be ranked higher than 5. Then, a ranking consistent with a partial order would mean a ranking of the n objects that violates no constraints (that is, a ranking that violates no arrows or pairs).

Example 11.5 Consider the partial order on the set of nine integers represented by Figure 11.2. ■

The ranking 2, 3, 4, 5, 6, 7, 8, 9, 10 would not be consistent with this partial order, because it violates at least one of the constraints—namely, that 6 be ranked higher than 3, or that 10 be ranked higher than 2. This diagram actually represents the "is divided evenly by but is not equal to" relation introduced earlier.

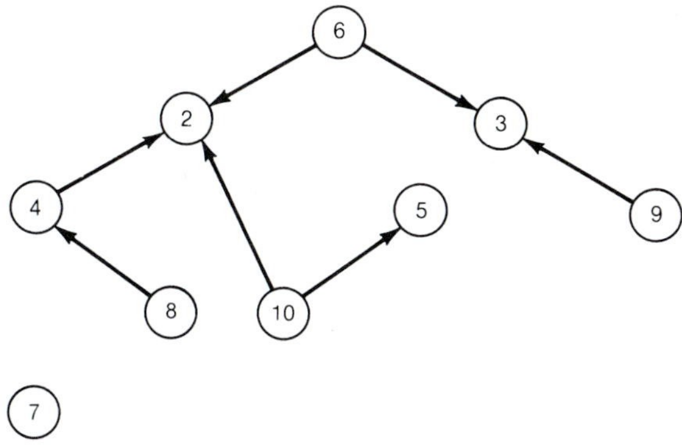

Figure 11.2 A Partial Order on the Integers 2, . . . , 9

The definition of topological sorting can now be stated more formally than at the outset of the chapter. A ***topological sort*** is a ranking of the n objects of S that is consistent with the given partial order. Let us try to solve the following ***topological sorting problem.***

Example 11.6 Given a partial order on a set S of n objects, produce a topological sort of the n objects, if one exists. If no such ranking exists, then print out a message saying that none exists.* ■

For simplicity assume that S is always the set of the first n integers 1, 2, 3, . . . , n, and that the partial order is given as m pairs of integers representing arrows in the corresponding diagram. Assume no pairs are replicated. For concreteness, take the input to have the following form:

```
10        value of n
7 3
5 3
2 10
6 8
5 6       m = 9 pairs
4 8
7 1
4 2
7 6
```

This particular instance of the topological sorting problem will be referred to repeatedly throughout the chapter. Is there an obvious algorithm for this problem? Try to think of one before continuing.

---

* If a relation is asymmetric and transitive but not irreflexive, then one can eliminate all pairs of the form (x, x) from the relation or, equivalently, erase all self-loops from its diagram. The resulting relation is a partial order, and it still makes sense to find a topological sort with respect to it. The topological sort then satisfies the constraints of the original relation involving distinct objects.

11.2 A Searching Solution

Consider the specific ranking 4, 8, 1, 2, 7, 10, 9, 5, 3, 6 of the 10 objects of the example. It is easy to determine whether or not this ranking violates any constraints of the partial order by checking each one. Since this ranking violates two of the nine constraints, $6 \rightarrow 8$ and $7 \rightarrow 1$, it is not a topological sort. Any ranking may be checked in this way. This leads to an obvious algorithm based on the generation of all rankings of the n objects.

A search-based algorithm:

> If a ranking is found which violates no constraints, then the ranking is a topological sort, print it and stop. If all possible rankings have been tried and no topological sort found, then print out the message that none exists, and stop.

To implement this algorithm in a programming language requires finding a way to generate the rankings so that all the distinct rankings are eventually generated. The procedure `permutations` of Chapter 4 does this. Any implementation of the algorithm could take time proportional at least to the number of distinct rankings of n objects. A particular ranking can be constructed by selecting any one of the n objects to be first in the ranking, then selecting any one of the remaining $n - 1$ objects to be second in the ranking, and so on. Thus there are $n \times (n - 1) \times (n - 2) x \cdot \cdot \cdot \times 2 \times 1$ distinct rankings of n objects. This product is n factorial. Consequently this solution can deal with values of n no greater than 16.* For larger n, an algorithm must be found that need not consider all rankings.

11.3 A Constructed Solution

The first solution to Example 11.6 searched through all possible rankings. Another approach is to attempt the construction of the required ranking. To this end consider a ranking, $obj_1, obj_2, \ldots, obj_n$, of the n objects that is a topological sort with respect to a given diagram. What can be said about obj_1, the highest-ranked object? Clearly there must be no objects that are constrained by the diagram to appear higher in the ranking than obj_1. Otherwise, those constraints would be violated, and the ranking would not be a topological sort. In terms of the diagram, this means that no arrows must point to obj_1. We describe this by saying that obj_1 must have no predecessors.

Now suppose the node corresponding to obj_1 is erased, as well as all the arrows emanating from obj_1. As noted earlier, this results in a new diagram that represents a new partial order on the remaining $n - 1$ objects. Consider the ranking of these $n - 1$ objects obtained by taking the original topological sort of the n objects and removing obj_1. That is, consider $obj_2, obj_3, \ldots, obj_n$. It must be a topological sort of the remaining $n - 1$ objects in the new diagram with respect to the new partial order. This is because any constraint in the new diagram that is violated by this ranking would have been violated in the original ranking of the n objects. Note that if any topological sort of the remaining $n - 1$ objects were taken with respect to the new partial order, and obj_1 were placed in front of it, the

---

* See Section 1.8.2.

ranking of n objects thus obtained would be a topological sort with respect to the original partial order. Placing obj_1 first in this ranking cannot violate any of the original constraints because they did not require that any object precede obj_1.

We have just discovered how to construct a topological sort:

A construction-based algorithm:

While S is not empty
1. Select any object with no predecessors.
2. Place it in the next position of the output ranking.
3. Remove that object from S, and
4. Remove its arrows from the partial order.

The output ranking produced will always be a topological sort.

11.3.1 Correctness

One difficulty remains. How can the programmer be certain the algorithm can actually be carried out? It may be impossible to carry out because at some point there may be no objects with zero predecessors. That this is indeed an algorithm requires showing that there always is at least one object with no predecessors.

One method of proof for any proposition is to assume it is not true and then show that this assumption leads to a contradiction. This method of proof is applied here. The goal is to prove that every time the loop task is to be carried out, at least one object with no predecessors can be found among those remaining. To assume that this is not true means that at some point the task cannot be carried out because *every* object left has at least one predecessor. Recall that the original diagram, representing a partial order, had no loops. It will be shown that the assumption implies a loop in the diagram. This will be the contradiction.

Suppose i_1 is one of the remaining objects. Under the assumption, every object has at least one predecessor, so i_1 has a predecessor (say, i_2). Note that i_2 cannot be the same object as i_1, or the irreflexivity property would not hold. Again, i_2 must have a predecessor (say, i_3). The object i_3 cannot be i_1 or i_2. If it were i_1 or i_2, then a loop involving i_2 and i_1 or a loop with just i_2 would exist. Continuing with this argument, $i_1, i_2, i_3, i_4, \ldots$ must all be distinct objects. But since there are only n objects in total, eventually an object must repeat. This implies that the repeated object is the starting and ending object of a loop. The conclusion is that the assumption was false. Therefore what we wanted to prove must be true, and we never get bogged down—there will always be an object with no predecessors.

This algorithm yields additional insight into the topological sorting problem. Since it is clear that the loop can always be carried out to completion, it will *always* produce a topological sort of the n objects. In other words, a topological sort always exists. This was certainly not obvious before.

To be sure the algorithm is understood, it is applied next to Example 11.6, depicted again in Figure 11.3. Initially (see Figure 11.3(a)), 4, 7, 5, and 9 have zero predecessors.

The first step is to select and remove 5 (either 4, 7, or 9 could also have been removed) and its successor arrows, to obtain Figure 11.3(b). S is not empty, so the loop must be repeated. Now, 4, 7, and 9 have no predecessors. Select and remove

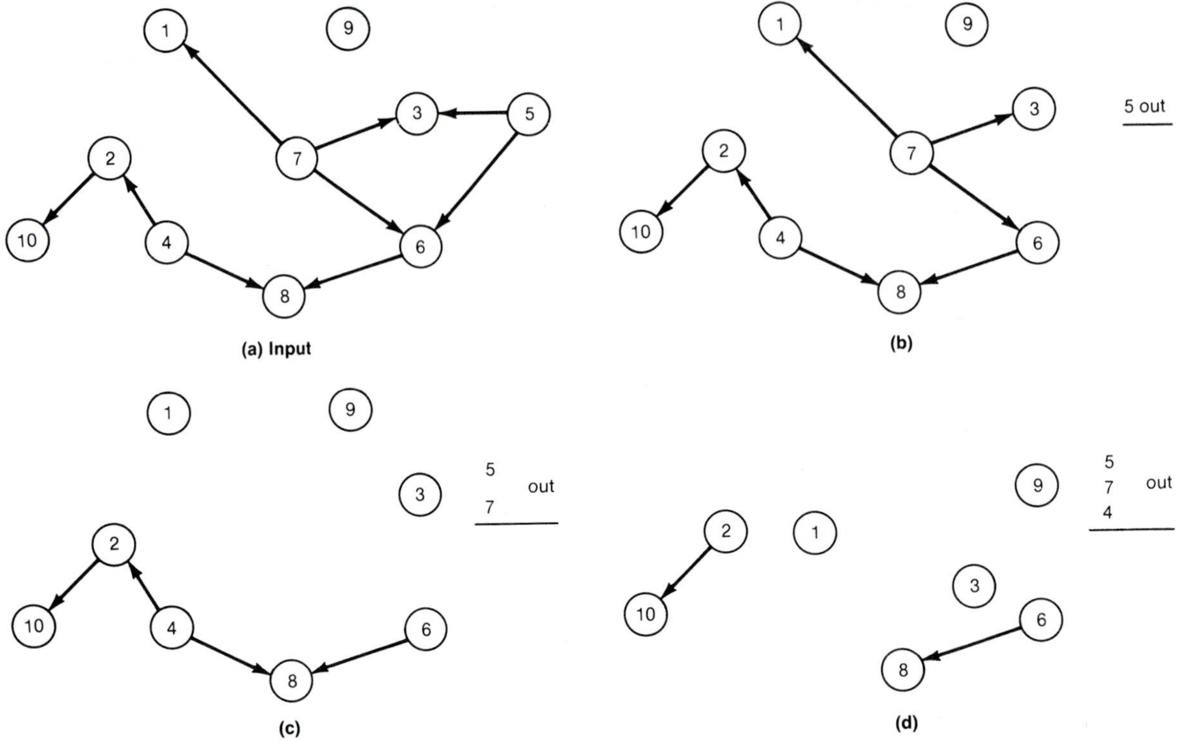

Figure 11.3 Graphic Depiction of Example 11.6

7 and its successor arrows, and obtain Figure 11.3(c). S is still not empty, and now 4, 9, 1, 3, and 6 have no predecessors. Select 4. Updating produces Figure 11.3(d).

S is still not empty, but 9, 1, 3, 6, and 2 now have zero predecessors. Continuing in this way, removing 1, 3, 6, 8, 9, 2, and finally 10 in succeeding iterations yields the final ranking: 5, 7, 4, 1, 3, 6, 8, 9, 2, 10.

Notice that every time an object is selected and removed, the diagram is updated to reflect the new S and the new partial order. As a result, some additional objects may end up with zero predecessors. Once an object has zero predecessors, it will remain in each succeeding diagram, always with zero predecessors, until it is removed.

The *first refinement* describes an implementation of the algorithm.

First refinement:

1. Read n.
2. Initialize for phase I.
3. While there is another input pair,
   a. record the information in the pair i, j — phase I

---

4. Initialize for phase II. — phase II
5. While the set S is not empty,
   a. select an object with no predecessors, and output it as the next object in the output ranking;
   b. update the records to reflect the removal of the output objects.

Phase I reads into memory the information about the number of objects and the partial order. Every time an *i*, *j* pair is read in, the new information that this represents must be incorporated into a representation in memory. The "record the information" of task 3a refers to the modification of this representation to reflect the new arrow, $i \rightarrow j$.

Phase II describes the processing required by our algorithm. Task 5a involves the selection, removal, and outputting of an object. Task 5b involves modifying the partial order representation and *S*, to reflect the removal of an object and its arrows, and outputting it in the ranking. After task 5b is carried out, that representation should reflect the new set *S* and the new partial order resulting from the object's removal.

11.3.2 An Initial Implementation

A straightforward representation of the partial order would be to keep an image in memory of all input arrows. We might use two arrays, `first` and `second`, for this purpose. `First` would contain the first integer, and `second` would contain the second integer of an input pair. The "record the information" task would then involve putting *i* and *j* into the next available locations of `first` and `second`, respectively. For Example 11.6, after phase I was executed, the result would be the arrays shown in Figure 11.4.

Suppose the **while** loop of phase II is being executed, and task 5a is to be carried out. An object with no predecessors must be selected. How is such an object found? Any object that has no predecessors will not appear in the `second` array. Somehow the `second` array must be searched to select an object with no predecessors. This can be accomplished by using an array *S*, traversing `second`, and marking location *i* of *S* when object *i* appears in `second`. Any location in *S* left unmarked corresponds to an object with no predecessors.

Suppose this is done, and object 5 is selected. Object 5 can then be output to the next place in the ranking. To accomplish task 5b, the "updating of the records," then requires that the array `first` be traversed. As it is traversed, each time a 5 is encountered, the program must mark the location of `first` in which it appears, and the corresponding location of `second`. The mark signifies that the corresponding arrow emanating from 5 has been removed from the representa-

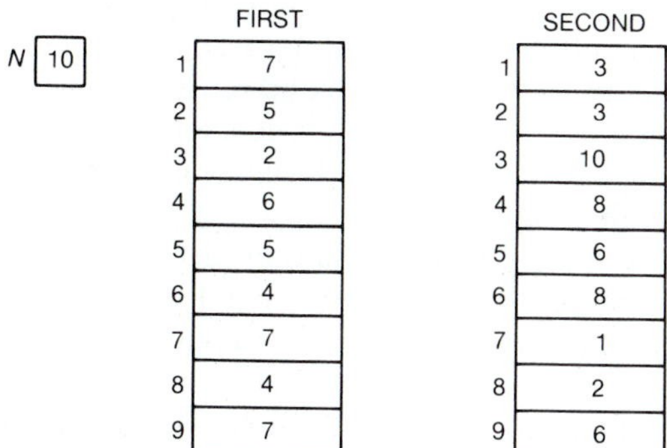

Figure 11.4 Result of Phase I of the First Refinement

tion. This completes one execution of the loop. This same processing must be repeated for each repetition of that loop. The loop will be repeated n times, once for each of the n objects. The `first` and `second` arrays must be traversed each time. This will take time proportional to their length, which, in general, will be m. Hence this implementation of the algorithm will take time proportional to $n \times m$. The storage required is roughly $2m$ locations for `first` and `second`, and n locations for S.

11.3.3 A Better Implementation

It is apparent that a lot of time is spent finding the information needed to carry out the processing in phase II. Efficiency can be improved by focusing on the following important question. *Precisely* what information is needed to carry out the processing?

Notice that each time through the loop, the program must *select an object with no predecessors*. To do this requires knowing which of the objects left in S have zero predecessors. Suppose that it is known, before and after each execution of the loop body, exactly how many predecessors each remaining object has. With this knowledge, an object with zero predecessor count can be selected. Once an object becomes eligible to be selected (has zero predecessors), it remains eligible until it is actually selected. Why not collect all those initially eligible in the initialization for phase II? The program could then select among them arbitrarily. Think of this collection as kept in a bag from which the object selected for output is pulled.

As the rest of the loop body is executed, *the records must be updated to reflect the removal of this object and its arrows*. Removing its arrows amounts to reducing the predecessor count of each successor of the object removed. Whenever the predecessor count of one of these successors becomes zero, that successor becomes eligible for selection on the next repetition of the loop. That successor is immediately added to the bag. Consequently, at the start of each loop repetition, the bag will contain exactly those objects eligible for selection, thus eliminating the need to search for them. In fact, the "S not empty" test is now equivalent to asking if the "bag is not empty." Keeping track of the successors of each object eliminates the need to search for them when that object is output. Incidently, we now know two operations that will be needed on the count collection, `decrease(i,count)` and `iszero(i,count)`. The first reduces the count of the `i`th object by one, and the second returns *true* only if the count of the `i`th object is zero. The precise information needed for processing has now been isolated. What must be known are the predecessor counts and successors for each object, and what's in the bag.

The loop body of phase I must update predecessor counts and successors. The input pair `i, j` contains the information that `j` has one more predecessor than currently reflected in `j`'s predecessor count, and that `i` has one more successor, `j`, than currently reflected by `i`'s successors. The loop body of phase II must update the predecessor counts of all successors of the removed object. It must also update the bag. We have developed the following *better refinement* of the algorithm.

A better refinement:

1. Read n.
2. Initialize
   a. Initialize the predecessor counts for each of the n objects to zero.
   b. Initialize current successors for each of the n objects to zero.
3. While there is another input pair,
   a. increase the predecessor count of j by 1;
   b. add j to the current successors of i.
4. Place all objects with zero predecessor count into the bag.
5. While the bag is not empty,
   a. remove an object from the bag and output it in the output ranking;
   b. for each successor of the output object, decrease its predecessor count by 1; if the predecessor count becomes zero, add the successor to the bag.

The implementation treats the predecessor counts, the collections of successor counts, the bag, and the output ranking as data abstractions. In order to refine the solution further, we must decide how to store the *predecessor counts, the successors of each object, the bag, and the output ranking*. These are data structure decisions. They should be based on the kinds of operations to be performed in tasks 1 through 5. First we functionally modularize the solution.

```
1. read(n);
2. a. predinitialization(n,count);
   b. succinitialization(n,successor);
3. while nextpair(i,j)
   a. increase(j,count);
   b. insert(i,j,successor)
4. baginitialization(bag,n,count);
5. while not emptybag(bag)
   a. remove(bag,obj);
   b. update(successor,obj,bag,count)
```

Every operation performed in tasks 1 through 5 that involves the bag, any of the n predecessor counts or collections of successors, or the output ranking has been implemented by a corresponding function. Note the use of a prefix to designate the structure involved in some of these operations. When written in this form, the program is independent of the specific details of implementation of each of these structures. This means that even if changes in the data structure implementations are ultimately adopted, this version of the solution will never need to be modified.

The next step is to decide on specific data structures for implementation of the data abstractions. This choice must be based on the functions that operate on the data structures. These functions include `predinitialization`, `succinitialization`, `increase`, `decrease`, `iszero`, `insert`, `baginitialization`, `emptybag`, and `remove`.

At some future time a decision may be made to change the implementation of any data abstraction. This requires finding *all* declarations and definitions of the data structures and functions involved and replacing them with the new versions. This modification may be made more easily and more reliably when the originals have been localized in the program. Such localization is called ***encapsulation.*** Not all high-level languages provide appropriate tools for achieving the same degree of encapsulation. In the ideal final program the data abstractions are defined in precisely one place; even more important, no operations are allowed on the corresponding data structures except those specified by the functions of the data abstraction. In the implementation above, this means, for example, that for the bag only the `baginitialization`, `emptybag`, `remove`, plus any other operations we take as basic to the bag will appear together. This makes it easier to determine which operations may be affected by a new implementation of the bag. The greater the encapsulation and modularization, the more expeditious the process of achieving correct modifications and adaptations. How to do this in C was discussed in Chapter 5.

We are actually in a position now to make a decision on the implementations for `count`, `successor`, and `bag`. The programmer does not know, in advance, the order in which objects will be output. In task 5b of the better refinement, after an object is output, its successors must be accessed and their predecessor counts updated. This means that the *predecessor counts and the collections of successors must be accessed in arbitrary order*. Because arrays support random access to their entries, we choose to store the predecessor counts in an array `count` and pointers to each collection of successors in an array `succ`. `Count[i]` and `succ[i]` will then contain, respectively, the predecessor count and a pointer to the successors of object `i`. This allows the predecessor count and collection of successors of any object to be selected, taking constant time. Since we shall need to access the collection of successors of objects, we define `access_succ(i, succ)` as a basic operation that returns a pointer to the collection of successors of object `i`.

There are *n* collections of successors, one for each object. These may be stored separately or may share storage. This choice has important ramifications, which will be discussed later. For now, it is best to share storage and to implement each collection of successors as a list of records. The records consist of two integer fields, `succobj`, containing a successor object, and `link`, containing a pointer to the next list record. Either dynamic memory or an array may be used to store the records. Selecting the array for storage means the programmer must manage its allocation himself or herself. Dynamic memory is probably a more natural choice, but an array of records is used to illustrate its simple management in this case and to make the later discussion comparing shared or separate storage for the list records more concrete. `Lists` will be the array for record storage, and a variable `t` will keep track of the next available record in `lists` for task 3b. Since only insertions will be made into the lists, the entries of `lists` will be allocated one after another as needed, starting with the first. Thus `t` must be initialized correctly.

The apparent choice for the output ranking is an integer array `rank`, with a variable `next` specifying where the next output object is to be placed in the `rank` array. For convenience, we use the record `ranking` with the two fields `rank` and `next`.

The bag could be implemented similarly, in an array with `bag` pointing to the next available element for a new bag entry. When an object is to be removed from

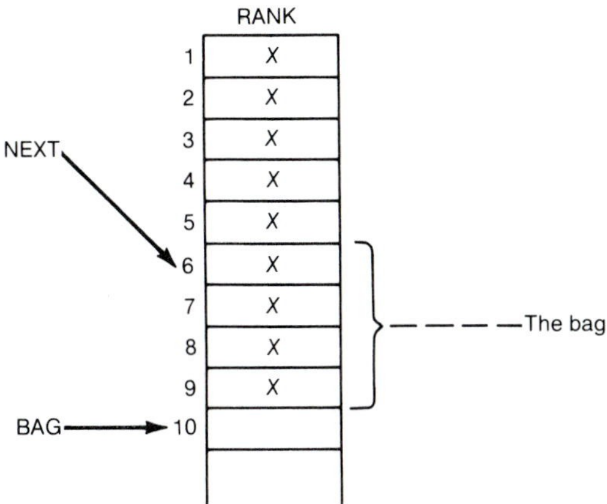

Figure 11.5 Data Structure Implementation of Bag and Output-Ranking Data Abstractions

the bag, we can store its value in `obj` and then decrease `bag` by 1. Thus an object can be added or removed from the bag in constant time. This implementation is permissible because objects may be selected from the bag in any order. However, implementing the bag as in Figure 11.5 affords an advantage. By allowing the bag and the output ranking to share storage, it saves time. However, this selection is made primarily to emphasize a point to be made later about the independence of modules. In order to simplify the example, only the array entries starting with 1 are used. As you know, in C they start with zero; 0th array positions will not be used in this example so that ranking and array positions will be identical.

The X's represent nine objects placed in the rank array. `Next`, pointing to position 6, indicates that the next object to be selected from the bag will be the one in `rank[next]`,`rank[6]` in this case. `Bag`, pointing to 10, indicates that when a successor is to be added to the bag, it should be placed in `rank-[bag]`,`rank[10]` in this case. In other words, the bag contains all objects in `rank` between `next` and `bag-1`.

The bag is initialized by traversing the `count` array and placing any object with zero count into the location of the `rank` array to which `bag` points. `Bag`, of course, must then be updated by 1 to move its pointer down. `Bag` must initially be 1, and `next` must initially be 1. Objects are then output in the order in which they are placed into the bag, easing processing and keeping the time constant for addition or removal of an object. Each time an object is selected, `next` must be increased by 1 to move it down. The bag is empty when `next` equals `bag`.

Before proceeding, phase I is illustrated by applying it to Example 11.6. For this example, `count`, `succ`,`t`, and `list` would appear as in Figure 11.6, after the first eight pairs have been input. Figure 11.7 graphically depicts the successor lists.

At the start of phase I, no information was processed yet on predecessors or successors for any object. The first pair, 7 3, contains the information that 3 has one more predecessor than was known, and that 7 has one more successor than

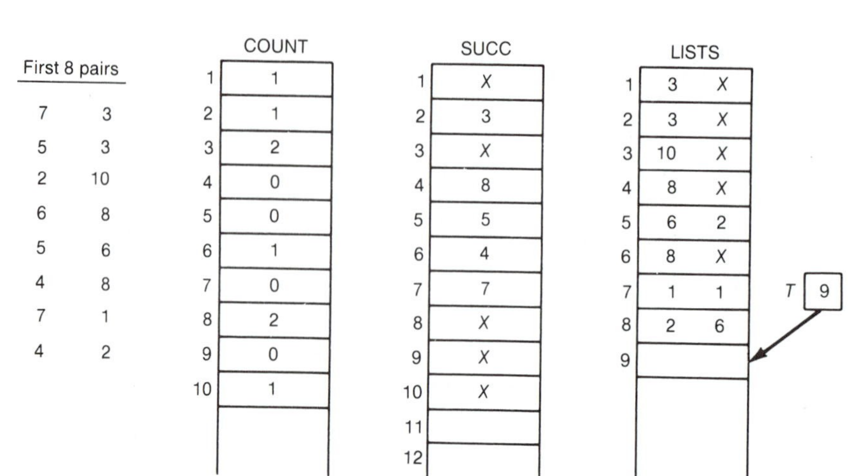

Figure 11.6 Data Structures Involved in Phase I after Input of First Eight Pairs

was known, namely 3. One must be added to the `count` for 3, and 3 to the list of successors of 7, and so on for the other seven pairs.

The detailed processing of an input pair is illustrated for the last pair of this example. It is the ninth pair, 7 6. To update the `count` for 6, add 1 to `count[6]`. To create a record to contain the successor 6, place 6 into `lists[9].succobj` and add this new record to the current successor list for 7 by changing two pointers. First, copy the pointer from `succ[7]`, the head of the list to which the

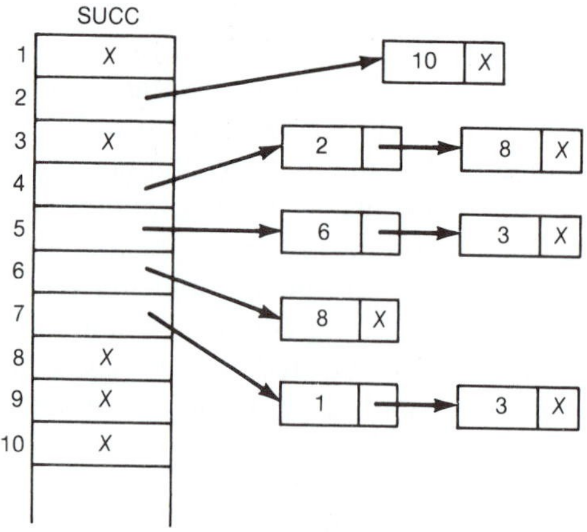

Figure 11.7 Graphic Depiction of Successor Lists

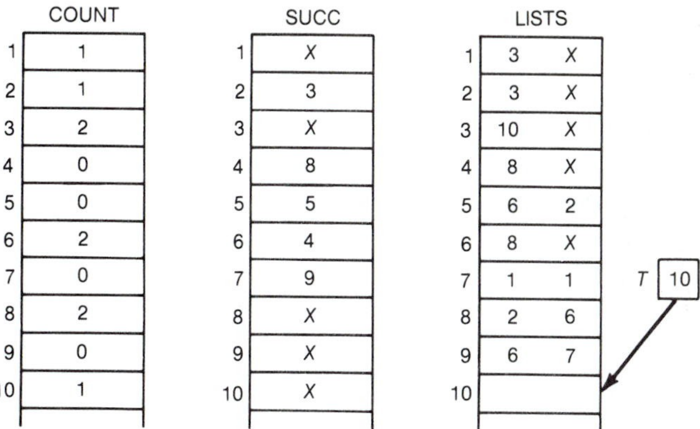

Figure 11.8 Data Structures of Figure 11.7 after Processing Last Input Pair of Phase I

new record is to be added, into the link field of the new record `lists[9].link`. Then place a pointer into `succ[7]` so that it points to the new record. In this case, 9 is placed into `succ[7]`. Since successors need not be kept in any special order, always adding records at the front of successor lists saves processing time. Adding the record anywhere else on the list would require traversal time from the head of the list to the insertion place. `T` must be incremented by 1 so that it points to the next available record in `lists`. The final situation after all nine input pairs have been read and processed is shown in Figures 11.8 and 11.9. An *X* indicates a null pointer.

We are now ready to consider the actual implementations for the functions of the data abstractions. Following is the code that might be used for those functions whose implementation may not be apparent.

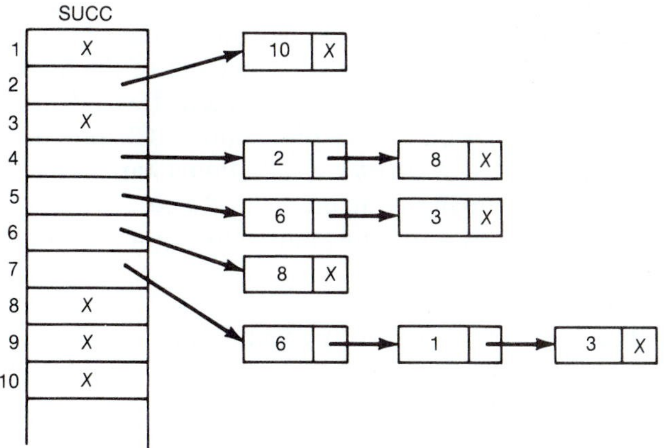

Figure 11.9 Graphic Depiction of Successor Lists of Figure 11.8

increase

```
count[j] = count[j] + 1;
```

decrease

```
count[i] = count[i] - 1;
```

iszero

```
return(count[i] == 0);
```

avail

```
static int t=0;
t++;
return(t);
```

`t` is an array index that points to the next available record in `lists`; it must be preserved between calls to `avail`

insert

```
pointer = avail();

setinfo(pointer,j);

setlink(pointer,succ[i]);
succ[i] = pointer;
```

get storage for the new record — `pointer = avail();`

copy `j` into its `succobj` field — `setinfo(pointer,j);`

copy the head of the successor list of `i` into its `link` field and set the head to point to the new record — `setlink(pointer,succ[i]); succ[i] = pointer;`

succinitialization

```
for (i=1;i<=n;i++)
   succ[i] = setnull();
```

set all heads of the successor lists to null

emptybag

```
emptybag =(bag == ranking.next);
```

the bag is empty when `bag` equals `next`

remove

```
*pobj = ranking.rank[ranking.next];
ranking.next = ranking.next + 1;
```

set `obj` to an object to be removed from the bag and remove it

Note that `avail` must correctly initialize and update `t`.

Task 5b of the better (or ''bag'') refinement of the algorithm could be done by writing the procedure `update` from scratch. Instead, it is done here using a tool that is available, the `traverse` procedure of Chapter 3. First, `traverse` is modified by adding `bag` and `count` as additional parameters of both `traverse` and `process`, and changing its name to `update`.

`Process`, called by `update`, must now be implemented so that `update` does its job. Its code is

```
currentsucc = info(recordpointer);
decrease(currentsucc,count);
if(iszero(currentsucc,count))
   {
      ranking.rank[*pbag] = currentsucc;
      *pbag = *pbag + 1;
   }
```

decrease the count of the successor pointed to by `recordpointer`, and if the count becomes zero, add the successor to the bag

A complete program using **topsort** follows. Notice that **topsort** has two parameters. It is the same as our version, except it copies the **rank** field of **ranking** into the output array as a last step.

Because of the implementation, some functions must have access to specific variables. C requires these variables to be either passed as pointers or declared as global. For example, **process** must have access to **rank**, and **emptybag** to **next**. Incidentally, as written, **topsort** does not depend on the medium assumed for the input pairs. Normally, we want programs to be independent of the form of the input. This has been accomplished here for the pairs by using the function **nextpair(i,j)**, which inputs the next pair and returns *true* if it is a nonsentinel pair. The program uses 0 0 as the sentinel pair.

```
#defineLIMIT 21

typedef  int outputarray[LIMIT];
```

sets the maximum value of n

global definition of type outputarray

```
main()
/* Reads the number of objects n and the input pairs
   specifying a partial order on the objects, and prints
   a topological sort of the n objects. Each pair should
   not occur more than once in the input and n should
   not exceed twenty. The sentinel pair is 0 0.
*/
{
   int n,i;
   outputarray topologicalsort;

   topsort(&n,topologicalsort);

   printf("\n A TOPOLOGICAL SORT IS");
   for (i=1;i>=n;i++)
      printf("\n %d",topologicalsort[i]);
}
```

storage allocated for the solution

topsort *inputs* n *and the partial order and places the solution in* topologicalsort

prints the solution

```
typedef int countcollection[LIMIT];

predinitialization(n,count)
/* Initializes all n counts to zero. */
int n;
countcollection count;
{
   int i;
   for (i=1;i<=n;i++)
      count[i] = 0;
}
```

implementation of the data abstraction countcollection *and its basic operations*

```
increase(j,count)
/* Increases the jth count by one. */
int j;
countcollection count;
{
   count[j] = count[j] + 1;
}

decrease(j,count)
/* Decreases the jth count by one. */
int j;
countcollection count;
{
   count[j] = count[j] - 1;
}

iszero(i,count)
/* Returns true only if the ith count is zero. */
int i;
countcollection count;
{
   return(count[i] == 0);
}
```

implementation of the list data abstraction and its basic operations

```
#define RECORDLIMIT 191
/* RECORDLIMIT should be at least
   (((LIMIT-1)*(LIMIT-2))/2)+1
*/
#define NULL - 1
typedef int listpointer;
typedef struct
{
   int succobj;
   listpointer link;
}listrecords,recordsarray[RECORDLIMIT];
recordsarray lists;
```

storage allocated for the array `lists` *to hold records of all lists*

```
listpointer setnull()
/* Returns a null pointer. */
{
   return(NULL);
}

anotherrecord(recordpointer)
/* Returns true only if recordpointer
   points to a record.
*/
listpointer recordpointer;
{
   return(recordpointer != NULL);
}
```

```
info(pointer)
/* Returns the contents of the succobj field
   of the record pointed to by pointer.
*/
listpointer pointer;
{
   return(lists[pointer].succobj);
}

listpointer next(pointer)
/* Returns the link field value of
   the record pointed to by pointer.
*/
listpointer recordpointer;
{
   return(lists[recordpointer].link);
}

setinfo(pointer,value)
/* Copies value into the succobj field
   of the record pointed to by pointer.
*/
listpointer pointer;
int value;
{
   lists[pointer].succobj = value;
}

setlink(pointer1,pointer2)
/* Copies pointer 2 into the link field
   of the record pointed to by pointer 1.
*/
listpointer pointer1,pointer2;
{
   lists[pointer 1].link = pointer2;
}

listpointer avail()
/* Returns a pointer to storage allocated
   for a list record.
*/
{
   static int t=0;
   t++;
   return(t);
}
```

implementation of the `succ_collection` *data abstraction and its basic operations*

```
typedef listpointer succ_collection[LIMIT];

insert(i,j,succ)
/* Add j into the ith collection in succ. */
int i,j;
succ_collection succ;
```

```
{
   listpointer pointer,avail();
   pointer = avail();
   setinfo(pointer,j);
   setlink(pointer,succ[i]);
   succ[i] = pointer;
}


succinitialization(n,succ)
/* Initializes all n collections of succ to empty. */
int n;
succ_collection succ;
{
   int i;
   listpointer setnull();
   for (i=1;i<=n;i++)
      succ[i] = setnull();
}


listpointer access_succ(i,succ)
/* Returns a pointer to the i collection in succ. */
int i;
succ_collection succ;
{
   return(succ[i]);
}
```

implementation of the `ranking-record` *data abstraction and its basic operations*

```
typedef struct
{
   outputarray rank;
   int next;
}rankingrecord;
rankingrecord ranking;
```

allocates storage for `ranking`

```
copy(n,topologicalsort,ranking)
/* Copies the rank field of ranking
   into topologicalsort.
*/
int n;
outputarray topologicalsort;
rankingrecord ranking;
{
   int i;
   for (i=1;i<=n;i++)
      topologicalsort[i] = ranking.rank[i];
}
```

```
typedef int bagcollection;

baginitialization(pbag,n,count)
/* Initializes the bag so it contains
   only objects whose counts are zero.
*/
bagcollection *pbag;
int n;
countcollection count;
{
   int i;
   ranking.next = 1;
   *pbag = 1;
   for(i=1;i<=n;i++)
      if(iszero(i,count))
         {
            ranking.rank[*pbag] = i;
            *pbag = *pbag + 1;
         }
}

emptybag(bag)
/* Returns true only if bag is empty. */
bagcollection bag;
{
   return(bag == ranking.next);
}

remove(pbag,pobj)
/* Sets obj to an object to be removed
   from bag, and removes it.
*/
bagcollection *pbag;
int *pobj;
{
   *pobj = ranking.rank[ranking.next];
   ranking.next = ranking.next + 1;
}

process(listname,recordpointer,pbag,count)
/* Decreases the count of the successor pointed
   to by recordpointer and adds it to the bag if
   its count has become zero.
*/
listpointer listname,recordpointer;
bagcollection *pbag;
countcollection count;
{
   int currentsucc;
   currentsucc = info(recordpointer);
```

implementation of the `bag` *data abstraction and its basic operations; notice that it shares storage with* `ranking-record`*, so* `bag` *and* `ranking-record` *are interdependent*

```
    decrease(currentsucc,count);
    if (iszero(currentsucc,count))
        {
            ranking.rank[*pbag] = currentsucc;
            *pbag = *pbag + 1;
        }
}
```

```
topsort(pn,topologicalsort)
/* Inputs the number of objects n and the
   partial order and generates a solution in
   topologicalsort.
*/
int *pn;
outputarray topologicalsort;
{
   countcollection count;
   succ_collection succ;
   bagcollection bag;
   int i,j,obj;
   printf("\n enter n between 1 and %d\n",LIMIT-1);
   scanf("%d",pn);
   predinitialization(*pn,count);

   succinitialization(*pn,succ);


   while (nextpair(&i,&j))
       {
           increase(j,count);

           insert(i,j,succ);
       {

   baginitialization(&bag,*pn,count);


   while(!emptybag(bag))
       {
           remove(&bag,&obj);


           update(succ,obj,&bag,count);
       }



   copy(*pn,topologicalsort,ranking);
}
```

from here on, the program is independent of the implementations of the data abstractions

- *storage allocated for* `count`, `succ_collection`, *and* `bag`
- *input* n, *the number of objects*
- *initialize the* n `counts` *to zero*
- *initialize the* n `succ_collections` *to empty*
- *input the partial order*
  - *increase the* `j`*th* `count` *by one*
  - *add* `j` *to the* `i`*th collection in* `succ`
- *set* `bag` *to contain only those objects whose* `count` *is zero*
- *generate a solution in* `ranking`
  - *set* `obj` *to an object to be removed from the* `bag`*, and remove it*
  - *decrease the* `count` *and place in the* `bag` *any successors of the removed object whose* `count` *has become zero*
- *copy the solution into* `topologicalsort`

```
nextpair(pi,pj)
int *pi,*pj;
/* Input the next pair and return true
   only if it was not the sentinel pair.
*/
{
   print("\n enter a pair \n");
   scanf("%d %d",pi,pj);
   return(!((*pi == 0) && (*pj == 0)));
}

update(succ,obj,pbag,count)
/* Update the counts of all successors of obj
   and place any whose counts become zero
   into bag.
*/
succ_collection succ;
int obj;
bagcollection *pbag;
countcollection count;
{
   listpointer listname,recordpointer,access_succ();
   listname = access_succ(obj,succ);
   recordpointer = listname;
   while(anotherrecord(recordpointer))
        {
            process(listname,recordpointer,pbag,count);
            recordpointer = next(recordpointer);
        }
}
```

this is a modification of the general list traversal function of Chapter 3

Note that the **ranking** and **bag** implementations are not independent. Thus, if it is desirable to change the implementation of one, the other is also affected. As written, the bag acts as a stack, but it may be important to pick the entry to be removed from the bag more selectively. One way to do this is to implement the bag as a priority queue. In any case, to make **ranking** and **bag** independent requires changing their declarations, definitions, and basic operations.

11.4 Analysis of Topsort

We will now analyze the time requirements of this implementation. Refer to the refinement shown in the implementation that used data abstractions on page 503. Reading n takes constant time. The **count** and **succ** array initializations take time proportional to n. The **while** loop read and test takes constant time. Reading the next input pair and tasks 3a and 3b, which involve executing five instructions, take constant time. Each repetition of the loop thus takes constant time. Since the loop is executed once for each of the m input pairs, the total loop time will be proportional to m. Phase I thus takes some constant time, plus time proportional to n, plus time proportional to m.

Initializing the bag at the start of phase II takes time proportional to n, since it involves traversing the `count` array and placing each object whose count is zero into the bag. The **while** loop body of phase II, unlike that of phase I, does not take the same amount of time on every repetition. Task 5a takes constant time, but task 5b depends on the number of successors of the object that was removed by task 5a. The loop itself is executed n times, once for each object output.

How can we determine the total loop time required? Notice that each of the n objects will eventually be output in *some* loop execution. We do not know in what order the objects will be output. However, the time taken in its particular loop execution for each object output is the same. This time is at most a constant plus time proportional to the number of successors of the object. Thus, the total time for the **while** loop in phase II is the sum of the time required to output each object. The total time is then a constant times n plus time proportional to the sum

[(number of successors of object 1) plus (number of successors of object 2) . . . plus the (number of successors of object n)]

This sum is just the total number of successors, m. Hence the total time for phase II is made up of the same kinds of components as the total time for phase I. We conclude that the total time for this implementation has the same form.

Note that the search-based algorithm could take time $O(n!)$. The straightforward implementation of the construction-based algorithm could take time $O(n \times m)$. `Topsort` takes time of the form $c_1 + c_2n + c_3m$ and represents a very substantial improvement. It was made possible because we were able to determine precisely, and to obtain efficiently, the information required to do the processing steps of the algorithm. The topological sort problem is more complex than earlier ones in this book, but it illustrates the same theme. The processing to be done determines the data structures that are most appropriate. Clearly, any implementation of an algorithm that does topological sorting must take time of the form $an + bm$, since it is necessary to read in all m input pairs and output all n objects.

How much storage does the implementation require? Suppose the program is to run correctly for values of n between 1 and 20. The only difficulty in determining the actual amount of storage required is in deciding what length to declare for `lists`. This depends on how large m may be. In general, if there are n objects, each object can have no more than $n - 1$ successors—that is, an arrow to every other object. There are then at most $n(n - 1)$ possible successors. Each successor requires one record of the `lists` array. Actually, because of the asymmetry property, at most one-half of the $n(n - 1)$ possibilities can appear. Hence we need a total of at most $1/2 \times n(n - 1)$ records for `lists`. If n is 20, then $(20 \times 19)/2$ records will do. The storage required is proportional to n^2.

Knuth [1973a] and Wirth [1976] give different implementations of the algorithm for the topological sorting problem. See Aho, Hopcroft, and Ullman [1983] for a somewhat different point of view on its solution.

11.5 Behavior for Replicated Pairs or Loops

In the solution to the topological sorting problem, it is assumed that each distinct input pair appears only once and also that the input contains no loops. Either assumption might be violated. Of course, more obvious errors could occur. For example, n or one of the input pair members could be negative or out of range. It is not difficult to add a validation routine to check for these kinds of input errors. Subtler errors, such as replication of pairs or the occurrence of loops, are not as obviously remedied.

What does happen if pairs are replicated or loops occur in the input? How would you recognize loops? Replication of an input pair i, j causes the `count` of j to be 1 larger than it should be. It also causes the successor j to appear on the list of successors of i one more time. When object i is eventually removed, its list of successors is traversed. This results in the `count` of j being reduced one additional time, so that the extra increase due to the i, j replication is cancelled. The implementation will thus work correctly as long as there is room for the extra successor records to appear in `lists`. If there is no room to accommodate these extra records, it is not possible to predict what will occur when the implementation is executed.

Loops, on the other hand, result in some objects never being output. Objects that are involved in a loop, or that are the successors of an object in a loop, will never have their counts go to zero, and will never appear in the bag of objects. In fact, had the test for completion been "S not empty" or "n objects output," loops in the input would cause an infinite loop in the program. It should now be clear that `next-1`, when the loop in phase II is exited, will be the actual number of objects that were output by the loop. If this is less than n, then loops occurred in the input. This can provide a simple test for loops.

11.6 Final Comments on Topsort

As already noted, the implementation of the output ranking and the bag are coupled because they share storage. As a result they are not independent. This means that a change in the choice of implementation for one will affect the other. In general, such a situation is to be avoided—and, as pointed out earlier, could have been avoided. Certainly the small saving in time and storage did not warrant the added complexity.

There are, however, some important storage considerations that were alluded to earlier. `Topsort` will run out of storage before it runs out of time, since storage requirements grow as n^2. The bulk of the storage needed is taken by the `lists` array. Suppose a maximum size, based on the available storage of the computer system, is declared for the `lists` array. Say its length is 50,000. Assuming each of its records takes two entries, this provides enough storage to guarantee the solution of any problem with no more than 25,000 successors ($m \leq$ 25,000). It makes no difference how the successors are distributed among the objects; only the total number is relevant.

Suppose, instead, that the decision had been to represent each collection of successors by dedicating an array to the collection. Since the programmer does not know in advance how the successors will be distributed, each of the required n arrays should have the same length. Lists are no longer necessary, since the successors can be placed sequentially in the proper array. Of course, a variable will be needed to keep track of the last successor in each array. An additional array may be used for these pointers. If n is to be no greater than (say) 500, then each of the arrays containing the successors can be declared of length 50,000/500, or 100. The upshot is that the solution may now be guaranteed for a different class of problems. These problems must have $n \leq 500$, and each object may have no more than 100 successors. Even though the total number of successors may now be 50,000 (twice as many as before), their distribution is critical. When storage is at a premium, such considerations are important.

Had dynamic memory been used instead of the `lists` array for storage of the successor records, the program would contain no explicit storage limitation (other than the declarations for the length of `count`, `succ`, and `rank`). Still, the maximum dynamic memory size would have imposed a limit on the value of m for which the program would execute.

11.6.1 An Input Validation

One final point involving time and storage trade-offs. Suppose an input validation must be added to `topsort` just prior to the processing of the current i, j pair read in phase I. The function is to check whether i, j is a duplicate of an earlier input pair. If so, it is to be ignored; if not, it is to be processed. One way to accomplish this, which requires no additional storage, is to traverse the current list of successors of object i. If j appears on the list as a successor, then i, j is a duplicate; otherwise it is not. This takes time proportional to the current number of successors of i and thus adds a *total* time to phase I that is proportional to m^2. Instead, the function can work in constant time if $n(n - 1)$ additional storage is available. Use the storage for an $n(n - 1)$ array that is initialized to all zeros. When i, j is read, simply test the (i, j)th array entry. If it is zero, the pair is not a duplicate. Then set the entry to 1 to indicate that this i, j pair has been processed. In this way, an entry of 1 will mean that the pair is a duplicate from now on. This adds *total* time to phase I of $O(m)$ but requires $n(n - 1)$ additional storage.

11.7 Reviewing Methodology

A topological sort produces a ranking of objects that satisfies constraints on their allowable positions within the ranking. The obvious algorithm for finding a topological sort, *searching* through all rankings until one satisfying the constraints is found, is not feasible. A feasible algorithm was developed by *constructing* a ranking that satisfied the constraints. The initial implementation merely produced an image of the input data in memory. It was improved significantly by using an array to contain predecessor counts, creating lists of successors, and introducing a bag to hold objects whose predecessor counts became zero. This solution was achieved by a process of stepwise refinement, stressing data abstraction, encapsulation, modularity, and the proper choice of data structures. The functional modularity of the final solution allowed immediate application of a routine developed earlier—the list traversal routine. Again, because of functional modularity, it was not difficult to determine where and how to build in appropriate checks of the input data.

More generally, the analysis of the storage and time requirements of a fairly complex program was demonstrated. Even though this cannot always be accomplished, or may be difficult for complex programs, it serves as an example of what we hope to be able to do.

■ Exercises

1. Within a textbook, chapters cover specific topics. The information required to understand each topic is expected to have appeared before the topic appears in the book. Suppose you are given a list of topics and the other topics on which each depends. How might you select an ordering of the topics for their appearance in the book?

2. Which of these binary relations is a partial order on S?

- **a.** "Square root of" on the set S of all real numbers greater than 1
- **b.** "Is older than" on the set S of all your relatives
- **c.** "Sits in front of" on the set S of all students in a class
- **d.** "Lives diagonally across from" on the set S of all people

3. Write down the graphic representation for the binary relation R on the first 10 integers. R = (3, 2), (4, 6), (7, 6), (8, 1), (9, 7), (9, 8).

4. Write a detailed modification of the algorithm of Section 11.2 that will check if a given ranking is consistent with the given partial order.

5. Write a program to implement the refinement of Exercise 4 and determine its worst-case time and storage requirements.

6. Apply the construction-based algorithm of Section 11.3 to the following data to obtain a consistent ranking. Always select the smallest integer for output.

S = 1, 2, 3, . . . , 12
R = (3, 2), (4, 6), (7, 9), (12, 10), (5, 6), (2, 4), (8, 9), (2, 6), (3, 6), (7, 12), (3, 4), (7, 10)

7. If the second implementation of the construction-based algorithm is applied to the input of Exercise 6, what integers are in the bag after 3 is removed?

8. State clearly and concisely what purpose the bag serves in the better "bag" refinement and why it was introduced.

9. Write an expanded version of the better refinement that will output integers from the bag by selecting the smallest possible integer first.

10. What will the `succ`, `lists`, and `count` arrays have in them after phase I, when the input pairs of the running example appear in the order 7 6, 5 3, 2 10, 6 8, 5 6, 7 3, 4 8, 7 1, 4 2?

11. What will the `count`, `succ`, and `lists` arrays look like after phase II as compared to after phase I?

12. Suppose the better implementation were modified so that no `count` array were stored in memory, and only the `succ` and `lists` arrays were available after phase I. Write a new phase II refinement under this constraint.

13. Suppose a solution to the topological sort problem had been constructed by determining what object should be at the bottom of the ranking. How would the better refinement be changed to reflect this new solution?

14. **a.** Suppose the bag is implemented in a separate record `bag` instead of using the `ranking` record. How must the data abstraction implementations change?

b. Suppose the output ranking is not kept in the `ranking` record but, instead, is simply printed. How must the program and data abstraction implementations change?

15. The function `process` is itself dependent on the ranking and bag implementations. Modify it so that `process` becomes independent of these implementations.

16. Suppose task 5b of the better refinement is further expanded to:

5b.i. For each successor of the output object, decrease its predecessor count by 1.
5b.ii. For each successor of the output object, if its predecessor count is zero, add the successor to the bag.

a. How should the implementation of the data abstraction algorithm (on p. 503) be modified to reflect this refinement?

b. Write implementations for tasks 5b.i and 5b.ii that use `traverse` as a tool. This should include writing the corresponding two `process` functions.
c. How will this expansion of task 5b affect the time required for the algorithm?

17. Suppose the input for Exercise 10 had the pairs below appended after 4 2. What would the graphic depictions of the successor lists be after phase I of `topsort`?

7 3, 5 6, 4 2, 7 3, 6 8

18. For the input of Exercise 17, what would be in the `count` array after phase I?
19. For the input of Exercise 17, show what will be in the `count` array, the successor lists, and the bag after 7 is output.
20. Take as input the Example 11.6 with pairs 10 4 and 10 1 appended after 4 2. What will the second implementation of `topsort` output in the `rank` array? What will be the value of `next` after phase II?

■ Suggested Assignments

1. Write and run a program whose input will be a series of topological sorting problems. For each problem the program should execute a slight modification of the `topsort` function called `newtopsort`. `Newtopsort` has parameters `n` and `topologicalsort`. `Newtopsort` is to read in and echo print `n` and all input pairs for the example it has been called to work on. It should print out the relevant portions of the `count`, `succ`, and `lists` arrays as they appear after phase I. When `newtopsort` returns, the program prints the topological sort contained in the `topologicalsort` array. Except for the modifications needed to do the printing, `newtopsort` corresponds exactly to the sample implementation of `topsort`, with one exception: Implement the bag as an array separate from `rank`. `Newtopsort` should work correctly for valid input and for any number of objects between 1 and 20. You should make up four input sample problems to use. Two should be valid. One should include replications, and one should contain loops.
2. Suppose, instead of using the sample implementation, you do the following to keep successor information: Declare `lists` to be an $n(n-1)$ two-dimensional array and keep the successors of object i in the ith row of `lists`. For the example, after phase I, `lists` would be

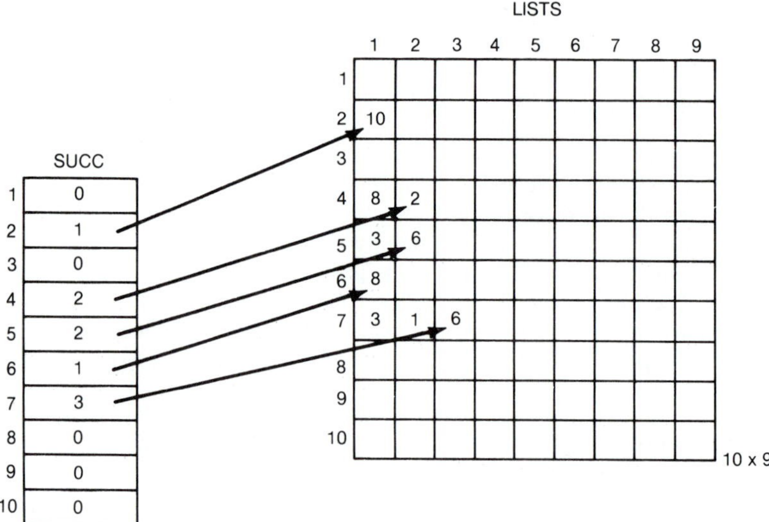

This two-dimensional `lists` array takes up the same total amount of storage as the one-dimensional `lists` array of the better implementation. For both implementations, the limiting factor on whether or not the program will run might then be the value of n beyond which available storage is exhausted. Suppose you are willing to give up the guarantee that `topsort` will always run correctly. This means you may attempt to run problems whose n is large enough that you are not sure whether the implementation of `lists` can hold all successors. Discuss the relative advantages of the implementations.

3. This is the same as Assignment 1 except, instead of the `lists` array, use dynamic memory to store the successor lists.

4. Assume your program for Assignment 1 treated the `bag` with the operations `emptybag`, `remove`, and `baginitialization` and `count` with the operations `predinitialization` and `increase` as data abstractions.

a. What does this mean?

b. Write a function, `number`, that also treats them as data abstractions and returns the number of objects in the `bag` when it is invoked. When it returns, the `bag` must contain exactly the same objects as before `number` was invoked. Assume `number` does not have access to information about the output ranking.

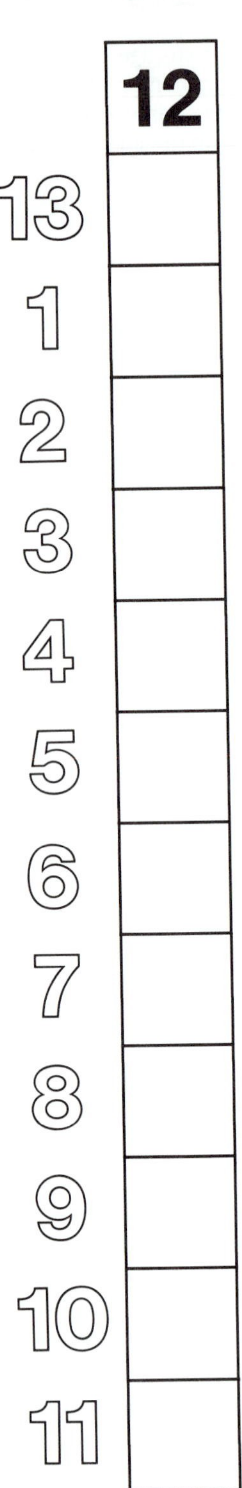

12 Huffman Coding and Optimal and Nearly Optimal Binary Search Trees

Three illustrations of the critical effect on program behavior of data structure selection are presented

Huffman coding, a text compression and coding technique, is used to show
- *good algorithm development*
- *the benefits of good data structure selection*

Optimal binary search trees, a related topic, are useful for storing static collections of information to be randomly accessed and traversed in sorted order; they demonstrate
- *the use of recursion*
- *how to develop efficient programs based on recursion*

Nearly optimal binary search trees are considered to emphasize program development

12.1 Techniques for Compressing Text or Storing Records

Many important techniques are available for the compression of text. Text compression is important when dealing with large collections of information, since internal memory is scarce and access to external memory is slow. Huffman coding is an elegant method that can be used profitably when characters do not appear with equal frequency in a text. This is the case with the letters of the alphabet in English text.

Binary trees can be used as the basis for encoding text and for the creation of Huffman codes. Binary search trees can also be used to generate more quickly codes of comparable efficiency.

The application of ''simple'' and balanced binary search trees for record storage and retrieval by key was demonstrated in Chapter 9. As shown there, ''simple'' binary search trees provide excellent average search times with random input when keys are accessed equally often. Also, AVL trees guarantee excellent worst-case search time. We shall see in this chapter that *optimal* binary search trees are useful when the keys have known, even unequal, frequencies, and when the trees, once grown, remain unchanged. Words in English text occur with known and unequal frequencies. An optimal binary search tree could be applied, for example, as a dictionary storing the 500 most frequently used English words, along with their definitions and their common misspellings. A search of the tree would then yield the definitions and misspellings. Once built, this tree would remain unchanged.

This chapter shows that the problems of finding Huffman codes and of finding optimal or nearly optimal binary search trees are related. The solutions illustrate the use of trees, heaps, and list-structures in the construction of good algorithms. The chapter also introduces the "greedy" heuristic. This method leads to an optimal solution for finding Huffman codes and to a nearly optimal solution for finding binary search trees. In both cases, the proper selection of data structures plays a significant role.

12.2 Weighted Path Length

An important measure associated with binary trees is the weighted path length. This measure underlies the entire development in this chapter. Suppose a numeric weight is assigned to each node of a binary tree T. The meaning of these weights is dependent on the intended application. When the application of the binary tree is to text compression or text encoding, only the weights assigned to terminal nodes have meaning. Each terminal node corresponds to a different character that can appear in the text. The weight assigned to the node represents the relative number of occurrences of the character in the text. When the binary tree is used for record storage, each node stores a record with a particular key. The weight assigned to a node represents the frequency of search requests for the key corresponding to the node. These weights must be estimated or determined empirically for each specific application.

The ***weighted path length of a node in*** T is the product of its depth and its assigned weight. The ***weighted path length of*** T, $W(T)$, is the sum of the weighted path lengths of all nodes of T. As an example, consider the binary tree in Figure 12.1(a), with assigned weights indicated for each node. Its weighted path length is

$$(1 \times 3) + (2 \times 17) + (2 \times 10) + (3 \times 15) + (3 \times 0) + (3 \times 20) + (4 \times 31) + (4 \times 4)$$

or 302. This was calculated directly from the definition of the weighted path length.

Another way to determine the weighted path length is to determine first the value of each node of the tree. The ***value*** of a node is the sum of the assigned weights of all nodes in the subtree with that node as root. Thus the root of a tree is assigned a value that is the sum of all the weights of the tree. The example would

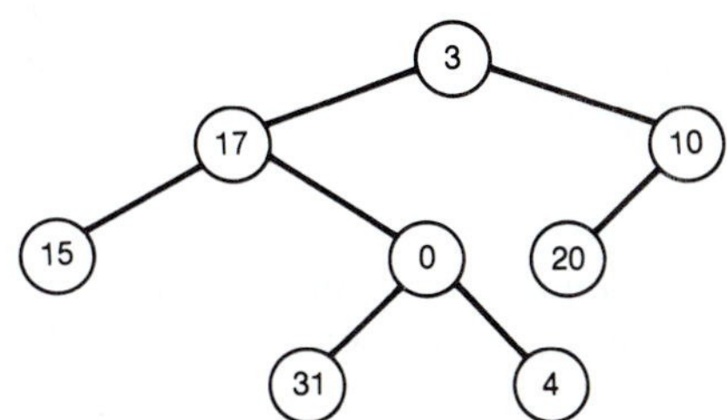

(a) Nodes Labeled with Assigned Weights

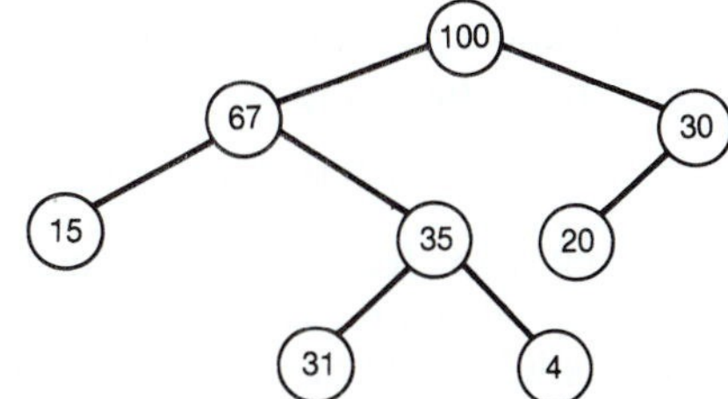

(b) Nodes Labeled with Values Derived by Adding Assigned Weights

Figure 12.1 Binary Tree T

have values assigned to each node as indicated in Figure 12.1(b). The weighted path length of the tree is then calculated by adding up the values of the nodes. Thus, from Figure 12.1(b), the weighted path length is

$$100 + 67 + 30 + 15 + 35 + 20 + 31 + 4 = 302$$

It is easy to see that adding the node values must always yield the weighted path length, since the weight of any node is counted once for every subtree in which it appears. For example, the weight 31 is counted in the value attached to each node from the node to which it is assigned to the root. This is a total of four nodes, exactly the number of times that the node's weight should count in the weighted path length.

The weighted path length can be viewed in still another way. It is given by the value of the root plus the weighted path length of the two subtrees of the root node. For the example shown in Figure 12.1(b), this is given by 100 + 152 + 50, where 100 is the root's value and 152 and 50 are the respective weighted path lengths of the left and right subtrees. Thus there are three ways in which the weighted path length of a binary tree can be calculated.

12.3 Huffman Coding

With this background, let us turn to Huffman coding itself. First we will look at how information may be coded based on a binary tree and how it is coded in computers. Consider a binary tree with n terminal nodes. Assign a zero to every left successor branch and a one to every right successor branch of the tree. *Encode* each terminal node with the sequence of 0's and 1's encountered when following the path from the root to the terminal node. Since this path is unique, the sequence or code assigned to each node must be unique. For example, in binary tree *T*1 (shown in Figure 12.2) the twenty-six letters of the alphabet and the space character designated by △ were assigned to the terminal nodes. Thus the code for the leftmost terminal node (*N*) in Figure 12.2 is the sequence 00000. Any character, word, or information associated with a terminal node is encoded with the unique code for that node.

The code assigned to the letter *S* in *T*1 is the sequence 00011 of length 5, one less than the depth of the encoded node to which *S* is assigned. In this way, a code is automatically generated for the twenty-seven characters associated with the terminal nodes of *T*1. Any string of these characters can then be encoded into a string of 0's and 1's. This string is simply the sequence of the combined sequences of 0's and 1's that constitute the codes for each of the characters in the string. For instance, the string of six characters "A△TREE" will be encoded

```
100101001100011111
```

of length 18. Again, because each path is unique, given any two code words, one can never be an extension of another. Consequently, no other sequence of code words will yield exactly this sequence of eighteen 0's and 1's, and any sequence starting with these eighteen 0's and 1's must start with A△TREE.

The tree *T*1 generates a ***variable-length code,*** since it does not assign the same length sequences of 0's and 1's to each character. A ***fixed-length code***

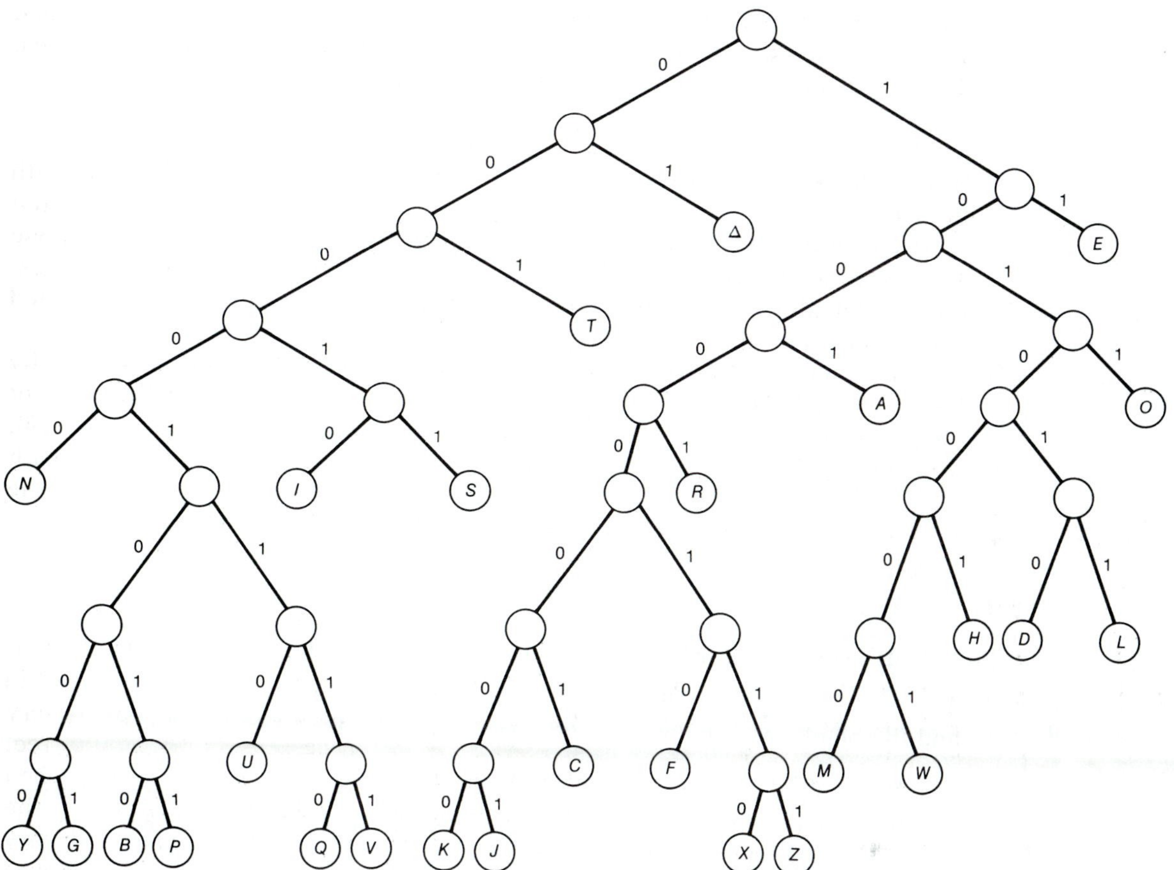

Figure 12.2 Binary Tree *T*1

assigns equal-length strings of 0's and 1's to each character. A fixed-length code would be generated by a tree if each terminal node of the tree had the same depth.

Since elements of computer memory actually store only sequences of 0's and 1's (by design), character information *must* be encoded. One way to encode the character set of a computer is by means of a standard fixed-length code, which uses six 0's and 1's per character.

The character set of a computer is the alphabet of characters that it can accept. For example, not all computers accept braces (that is, {}). Two important standard character sets are ASCII (American Standard Code for Information Interchange) and EBCDIC (Extended Binary Coded Decimal Interchange Codes). Both use fixed-length codes. ASCII uses a seven-bit code and EBCDIC uses eight bits. An n-bit fixed-length code can distinguish 2^n characters, and a sequence of l characters would then be represented by a sequence of $l \times n$ 0's and 1's. Variable-length codes are not constrained to using the same number of 0's and 1's for each character.

Using a variable-length code, a text in which the characters occur with different frequencies can be compressed. Shorter-length sequences would be assigned to characters used more frequently, and longer-length sequences to characters used less frequently. This is the idea behind the Morse code. Morse, in fact, estimated the relative frequencies of characters by looking at the frequency with which printer's boxes containing the different characters of the alphabet needed to be refilled.

The use of fixed-length codes makes it easy to decode a sequence of 0's and 1's to recover the original sequence of characters or text. It is not so easy for variable-length codes. A variable-length code must be chosen with care, if it is to allow proper decoding and avoid ambiguity. One way to achieve such a code is to use the scheme outlined for Figure 12.2, which associates a code to each binary tree. Decoding the code generated by a given binary tree would then proceed as follows:

1. Start at the root of a binary tree that is identical to the one used for encoding the original text.
2. Follow the branches according to the dictates of the sequence of 0's and 1's to be decoded—go left for a 0 and right for a 1.
3. When a terminal node is reached, the sequence of 0's and 1's that led to it is decoded as the character associated with that terminal node.
4. Start again at the root to decode the remainder of the sequence in the same way.

The relative frequency with which each of twenty-six characters of the alphabet and the blank space between words occur in English text is as follows:

△	A	B	C	D	E	F	G	H	I	J	K	L	
186	64	13	22	32	103	21	15	47	57	1	5	32	
M	N	O	P	Q	R	S	T	U	V	W	X	Y	Z
20	57	63	15	1	48	51	80	23	8	18	1	16	1

These relative frequencies are used to assign weights to the nodes of a tree such as $T1$. Each internal node is assigned weight 0, and each terminal node is assigned the relative frequency of the character associated with it. Thus, node S of $T1$ is assigned weight 51. The ***average amount of compression*** is measured by the weighted path length of the tree. In this way, the amount of compression achieved with different codes can be compared, since each tree has associated with it a unique code. The ***average length*** of the assigned codes is obtained by subtracting 1 from the weighted path length when the weights are *normalized* to sum to 1. Weights are ***normalized*** by dividing each weight by the sum of all the weights. The designer of a compression scheme can make this calculation directly or write a program for this purpose.

The weighted path length of $T1$ can be improved. Take the subtree with root at depth 5, and I and S as its successors, and interchange it with T to obtain binary tree $T2$ (shown in Figure 12.3). The weights of I and S, 57 and 51, will now each contribute one less time to the weighted path length of $T2$ than to $T1$, while T, with weight 80, will contribute one more time to the weighted path length of $T2$ than to

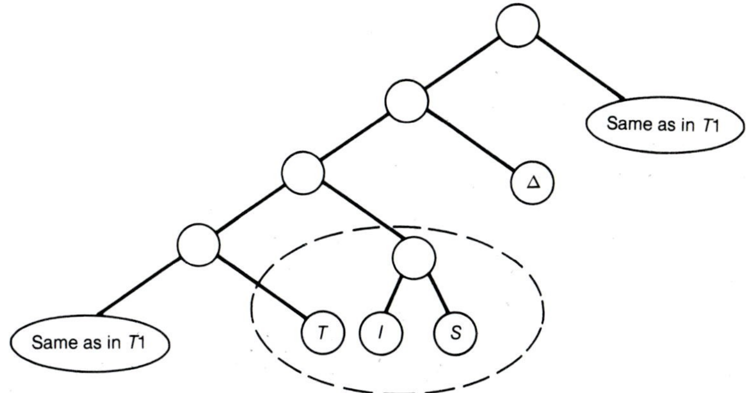

Figure 12.3 Binary Tree *T*2, Obtained by Interchanging Two Subtrees

*T*1. The result is that the weighted path length of *T*2 will be (57 + 51) − 80 less than that of *T*1.

The programmer's goal should be to find a binary tree, called the ***optimal binary tree,*** which has minimum weighted path length when the characters of the alphabet are stored at its *n* terminal nodes. Incidentally, the references here are to characters associated with the terminal nodes, but more generally they can be words or messages. A straightforward algorithm for finding this optimal binary tree is to generate each binary tree with *n* terminal nodes, associate the alphabetic characters with these *n* nodes, and calculate the weighted path length of the tree. A tree that yields the minimal weighted path length is optimal. Unfortunately, this algorithm is feasible only for small *n*. If $n = 13$, there are more than 10^{12} such trees, and the number of trees increases by a factor of almost 4 each time *n* increases by 1. We have to find a better way.

12.3.1 The Huffman Algorithm

An optimal binary tree generates what is called a ***Huffman code.*** Fortunately, the searching just described is not needed to find it; it can be constructed as follows.

1. Start with a collection of *n* trees, each with just a root. Assign an alphabetic character to each of these nodes. The weight of each node is the weight associated with its alphabetic character. The value of each of these root nodes is equivalent to its weight. (Value in this case equals the weight of the root itself, since these trees have no other nodes.)
2. Find the two trees with smallest values. Combine them as the successors of a tree whose root has a value that is the sum of their values. Remove the two combined trees and add the new tree obtained to the current collection of trees. Repeat the second step $n - 2$ times to obtain exactly one tree. This will be the optimal tree and will give the assignments of characters to terminal nodes.

When this algorithm is applied to the twenty-seven characters with their weights reflecting their frequency of occurrence in English, the first combination made is *J* with *Q*, since each has weight 1. The resultant tree has value 2. Next *X* and *Z*, also each of weight 1, are combined, yielding another tree with value 2. These two trees are combined, yielding a tree with value 4. The current collection now consists of twenty-four trees. The next combination involves weights 4 and 5 and yields value 9. Following this procedure, a final optimal tree that might result from the construction is shown in Figure 12.4. Other optimal trees could have been constructed, but all would have the same weighted path length of 5,124. This means that the *average length* (number) of 0's and 1's needed per character will be 4.124. The value 4.124 is obtained by normalizing the weighted path length (dividing it by the sum of the weights) and subtracting one. Thus $5124/1000 - 1 = 4.124$. This saves almost 20 percent over a fixed-length code of length 5 (the shortest fixed-length code that can distinguish twenty-seven characters).

This construction procedure is the ***Huffman algorithm.*** A proof is given later showing that it does, in fact, produce an optimal binary tree. Notice that a cumulative total weight can be kept as the algorithm is carried out. To do this, start with the variable **`weight`** set at the sum of all the weights of the alphabetic characters. Every time two trees are combined, add the value of the resultant tree to **`weight`**. When the algorithm terminates, after making $(n - 1)$ combinations, **`weight`** will contain the weighted path length of the optimal binary tree constructed.

The algorithm chooses the combination of current trees that yields a minimal value for the combined trees. It is in this sense that it is a "greedy" algorithm. It doesn't consider future ramifications of the current choice of subtrees to combine

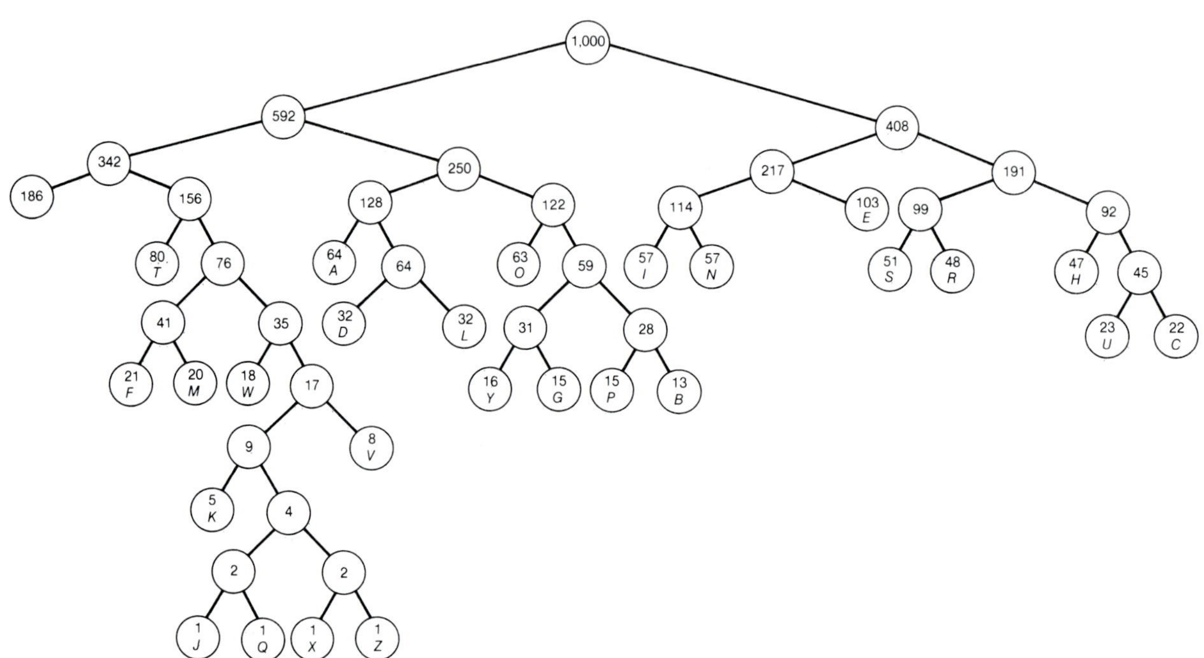

Figure 12.4 A Final Optimal Tree

but takes the current two "best" subtrees. In this instance, best means "of smallest value." The algorithm makes a "local" best or greedy decision. It is an example of the *greedy* method of algorithm design, which involves making choices on the basis of the immediate best alternative. This may lead to later choices being constrained to such poor alternatives as to lead to an overall suboptimal result. Being less greedy now may lead to better choices later, which in turn may yield better overall results. Hence it is not obvious that taking the best possible next combination, as done here, must lead to an optimal tree.

The greedy method does not yield optimal solutions in all situations. A traveler who applied the greedy method to selecting a route might always choose the next road because it is the shortest of all the current possibilities. This method will clearly not always yield the shortest *overall* route. When making change in U.S. currency using our system of 1-, 5-, 10-, 25-, and 50-cent pieces and dollar bills, we normally use a greedy algorithm. For instance, to give $3.70 change most people would give three $1 bills, one 50-cent piece, and two dimes (not seven 50-cent pieces, one dime, and two nickels). The algorithm is greedy because it always takes as many pieces of currency of the next largest value as possible. This always minimizes the total number of pieces of currency used to make change in our system. If a system had 1-, 5-, and 11-cent pieces and dollar bills, then making change "greedily" to give $3.70 would require three $1 bills, six 11-cent pieces, and four pennies. Fewer pieces of currency result from using three dollar bills, five 11-cent pieces, and three nickels, Fortunately, the greedy method does yield optimal binary trees.

12.3.2 Representation of Huffman Trees

Let us now consider how the binary tree constructed by the Huffman algorithm should be stored in memory. To this end we consider an example that shows that even though the weighted path length is as small as possible for a given set of weights, the depth of the tree can still be great.

Example 12.1 Suppose that the first n Fibonacci* numbers are assigned as weights to characters of an alphabet represented as terminal nodes in a tree. The task is to generate a Huffman code. ■

The Huffman algorithm would construct the tree shown in Figure 12.5. This tree has depth n. Hence the Huffman algorithm may generate trees whose depth is $O(n)$. If a sequential representation were used for such trees, considerable storage would be wasted. For large n, the storage would not even be available. A good alternative is a linked representation of the tree.

---

* The Fibonacci sequence is the sequence of integers $F_0, F_1, F_2, \ldots$ that starts with $F_0 = 0$ and $F_1 = 1$, with each succeeding integer found by adding its two predecessors. Thus the sequence is 0, 1, 1, 2, 3, 5, 8, 13, 21, 34, 55, . . . , F_{n-1}, . . . , where $F_0 = 0$, $F_1 = 1$, $F_{n+2} = F_{n+1} + F_n$, $n \geq 0$.

Figure 12.5 Tree Constructed by the Huffman Algorithm for Fibonacci Weights

12.3.3 Implementation

In this section the Huffman algorithm is implemented so that the Huffman tree and its weighted path length are generated. For a list of n records, a linked representation of the tree is illustrated in Figure 12.6(a) for $n = 5$ and weights 4, 3, 10, 2, 6.

The X's in the figure represent null pointers. The information field of each list record contains a pointer to a record representing the root of a binary tree. The records of the tree might be stored using pointer variables or in arrays. The records have `leftptr`, `info`, and `rightptr` fields. The `info` field contains the *value* assigned to the record's subtree by the Huffman algorithm. Thus each list record represents a tree. `Weight` is a variable initially set to the sum of the n weights and incremented by the value attached to each combined tree.

The implementation could proceed by traversing the list to find the trees with the two smallest values. These trees must be combined as dictated by step 2 of the algorithm into a new tree whose value is the sum of their values. The two trees that were combined must be deleted from the list, and the new tree added to the list. The result of these operations is shown in Figure 12.6(b) after one combination has taken place.

Every time step 2 is repeated, two trees are combined and the length of the list decreases by 1. The final list would contain one record; its information field would point to the root of the generated Huffman tree. `Weight` would contain its weighted path length. For this example, the resultant list would be as shown in Figure 12.6(c).

The list traversal required to find the two smallest value trees results in a worst-case time proportional to the length of the list for each traversal. Since the tree must be traversed $n - 1$ times, the worst-case time is $O(n^2)$. We can do better.

To improve the implementation, the two smallest values whose trees are to be combined must be found quickly without traversing the entire list. Recall that a

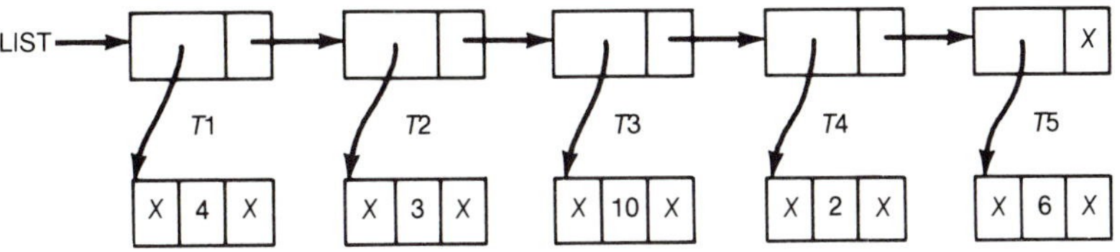

(a) List of Five Records Pointing to Five Initial Trees of the Huffman Algorithm

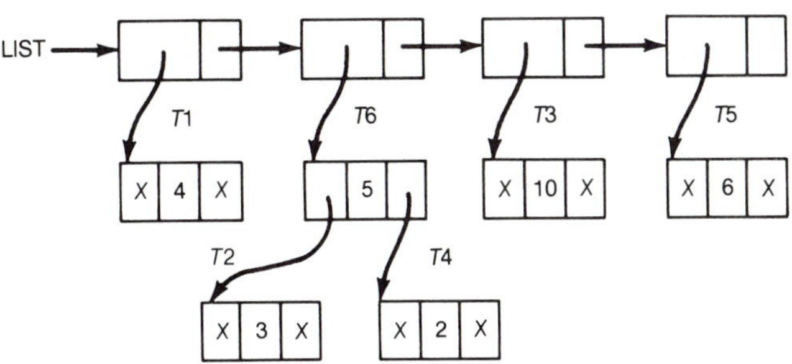

(b) List after Combining Two Trees with Smallest Values

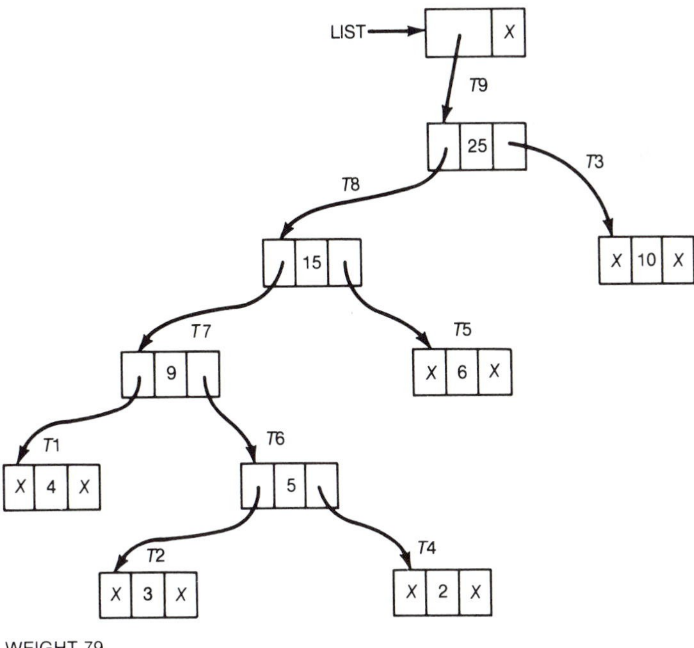

(c) Final List and Huffman Tree after Repeated Combinings of Values

Figure 12.6 A Linked List Representing the Trees Constructed by the Huffman Algorithm

heap, in this case a ***min heap,*** always has its smallest record at its root. Suppose the records of the binary tree are kept in a heap, or better, suppose the pointers are kept in the heap. Each pointer points to a corresponding record of the binary tree. The initial heap is shown in Figure 12.7.

To find the two smallest values, simply remove the top heap pointer *T4*, reheap, and again remove the top pointer, *T2*. The records corresponding to the two smallest values can be combined. The new pointer to the combined record can

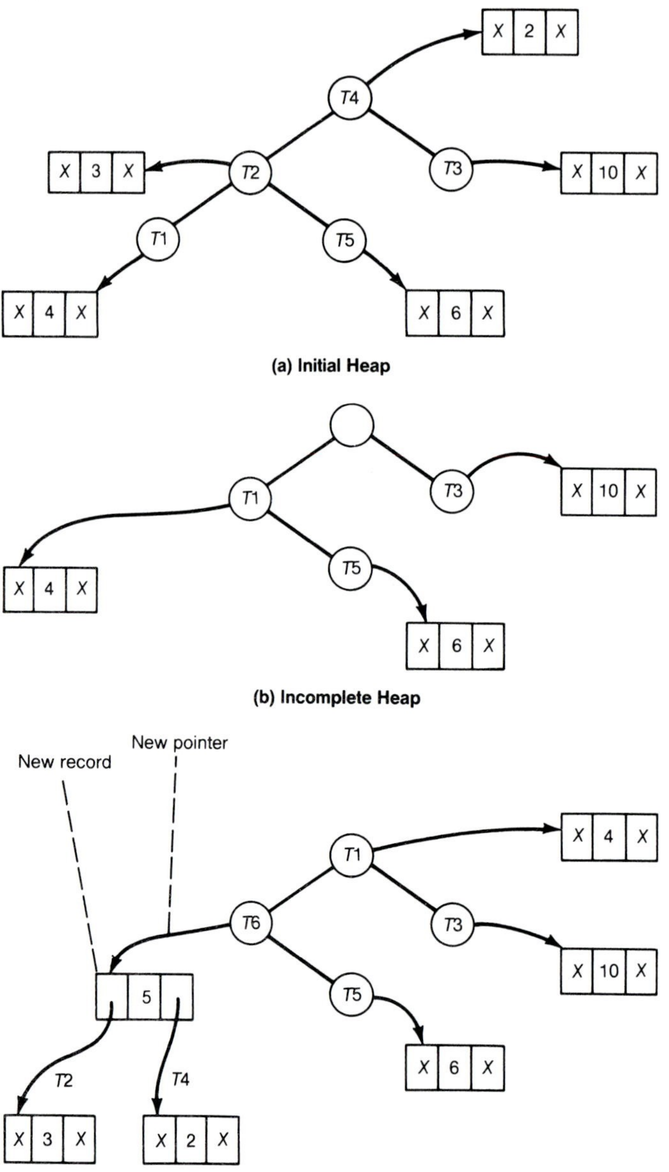

(a) Initial Heap

(b) Incomplete Heap

(c) Heap after Two Trees Are Combined and Reheaping Done

Figure 12.7 Heap of Pointers of the Huffman Tree

then be placed at the top of the heap (which was left vacant), and the heap reheaped. Figure 12.7(b) shows the heap obtained by removing *T*4, reheaping, and removing *T*2. The two trees removed are combined, and reheaping is done to obtain the heap shown in Figure 12.7(c).

With this implementation the computer time consumed in finding the two smallest values, combining their corresponding records, and reheaping is $O(\lg n)$. Since the entire process is repeated $(n - 1)$ times, the total time will be $O(n \lg n)$. It was the proper choice of data structure that made this improvement possible!

12.3.4 A Proof

For those readers who would like a proof of the Huffman construction, the following is an interesting example of the use of mathematical induction applied to trees. It can easily be adopted to prove that a recursive program for the Huffman algorithm is correct.

Assume the weights are $w_1, w_2, \ldots, w_n$ and are indexed so that $w_1 \leq w_2 \leq \ldots \leq w_n$. You should convince yourself that an optimal binary tree must be a full binary tree.* An optimal tree can always be found, since the number of full binary trees with n terminal nodes is finite. It is clear that the Huffman construction yields optimal trees for $n = 1$ and 2. This is the basis for the induction, which will be on the number of weights or terminal nodes, n. The induction hypothesis is that the Huffman construction yields optimal trees for any $n - 1$ weights. We must show that as a result, it must generate optimal trees for n weights.

Given any tree with n terminal nodes, T_n, in which Figure 12.8(a) appears as a subtree, let T'_{n-1} be the tree with $n - 1$ terminal nodes obtained from T_n by replacing this subtree by the terminal node shown in Figure 12.8(b). Then the weighted path length of T_n equals the weighted path length of $T'_{n-1} + (w_1 + w_2)$.

Given T'_{n-1}, inversely, T_n can be obtained from it. Therefore, T_n must be optimal with respect to weights $w_1, w_2, \ldots, w_n$, if and only if T'_{n-1} is optimal with respect to weights $(w_1 + w_2), w_3, \ldots, w_n$. This is because if only one tree were not optimal, it could be replaced by an optimal tree, thus improving the weighted path length of the corresponding version of the other.

By the induction hypothesis, the Huffman construction yields a tree, T'_{n-1}, with $n - 1$ terminal nodes, that is optimal with respect to weights $(w_1 + w_2), w_3, \ldots, w_n$. The corresponding tree, T_n, with n terminal nodes, is just the tree given by the Huffman construction for weights $w_1, w_2, \ldots, w_n$. Since T'_{n-1} is optimal, so is T_n. This completes the proof.

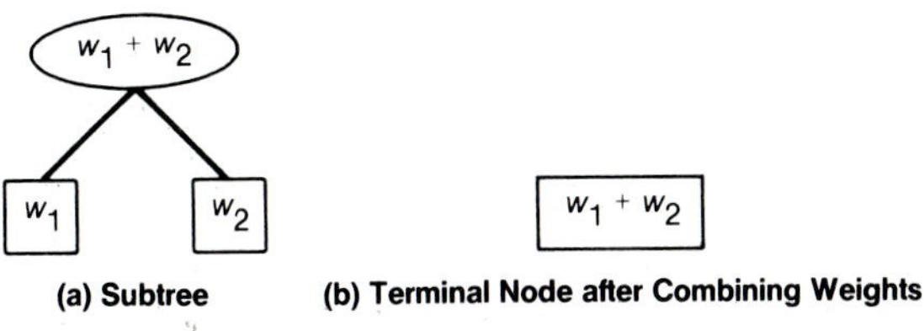

Figure 12.8 Subtree Replacement

---

* See Exercise 5 on page 548.

12.4 Optimal Binary Search Trees

So far we have been considering binary trees with nonzero weights assigned only to terminal nodes. Information (a character or message) has been associated only with their terminal nodes. We now consider ***extended binary search trees,*** which have keys stored at their internal nodes.

Suppose n keys, $k_1, k_2, \ldots, k_n$, are stored at the internal nodes of a binary search tree. It is assumed that the keys are given in *sorted* order, so that $k_1 < k_2 < \cdots < k_n$. An extended binary search tree is obtained from the binary search tree by adding successor nodes to each of its terminal nodes as indicated in Figure 12.9 by □'s.

Although the programming goal in this chapter is to find optimal binary search trees, extended binary search trees are used along the way. In the extended tree, the □'s represent terminal nodes, while the other nodes are internal nodes. These terminal nodes represent unsuccessful searches of the tree for key values. Such searches do not end successfully because the search key is not actually stored in the tree. They actually terminate when a null subtree pointer is encountered along the search path.

In general, the terminal node in the extended tree that is the left successor of k_1 can be interpreted as representing all key values that are not stored and *are less than* k_1. Similarly, the terminal node in the extended tree that is the right successor of k_n represents all key values not stored in the tree that *are greater than* k_n. The terminal node that is accessed between k_i and k_{i+1} in an inorder traversal represents all key values not stored that lie *between* k_i and k_{i+1}. For example, in the extended tree in Figure 12.9(b), if the possible key values are 0, 1, 2, 3, . . . , 100, then the terminal node labeled 0 represents the missing key values 0, 1, and 2 if k_1 is 3. The terminal node labeled 3 represents the key values between k_3 and k_4. If k_3 is 17 and k_4 is 21, then the terminal node labeled 3 represents the missing key values 18, 19, and 20. If k_6 is 90, then terminal node 6 represents the missing key values 91 through 100.

Assuming that the relative frequency with which each key value is accessed is known, weights can be assigned to each node of the extended tree. The weights

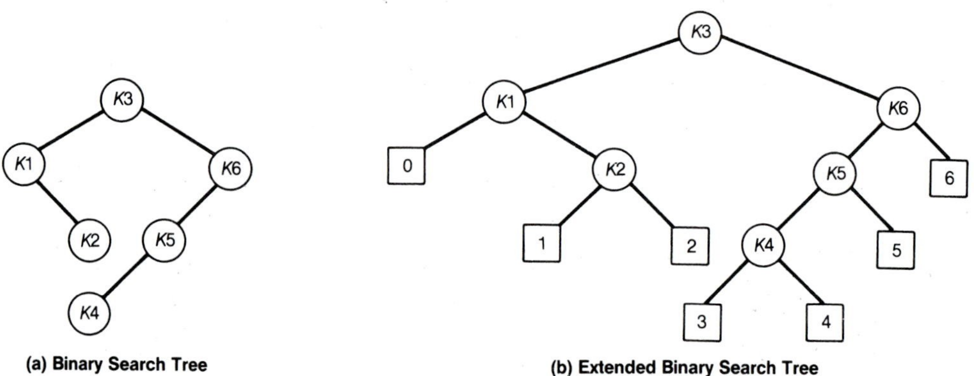

Figure 12.9 Extension of a Binary Search Tree

represent the relative frequencies of searches terminating at each node. The weighted path length of the extended tree is then a natural measure for the average time to search the binary search tree for a key.

Example 12.2 Find the extended binary search tree that has the minimal weighted path length. The optimal binary search tree is obtained from this tree simply by omitting the extended nodes. ■

Before dealing with this problem, we compare it to the Huffman coding problem that has already been solved. When the weights attached to the internal nodes of the extended binary search tree are zero, this problem is similar to the Huffman coding problem. The difference is that the task now is to find the binary *search* tree with minimal weighted path length, whereas the Huffman algorithm finds the binary tree with minimal weighted path length. Since the binary search trees are only a subset of all binary trees, the Huffman tree will yield a value of the minimal weighted path length that is never larger than that of the optimal binary search tree. The Huffman algorithm will not solve the current problem unless, by chance, the tree that it constructs is a binary search tree or can be converted to one with no increase in the weighted path length. An algorithm, the Hu-Tucker algorithm, has been developed for this special case, and requires, as does the Huffman algorithm, time $O(n \lg n)$ and $O(n)$ storage. Initially, its time was thought to be $O(n^2)$, but Knuth showed how to reduce this time by selecting the appropriate data structure. We now proceed to the general case in which the weights of the internal nodes need not be zero.

12.4.1 Finding Optimal Binary Search Trees

An obvious way to find an optimal binary search tree is to generate each possible binary search tree for the keys, calculate its weighted path length, and keep that tree with the smallest weighted path length. This search through all possible solutions is not feasible except for small n, since the number of such trees grows exponentially with n. A feasible alternative would be a recursive algorithm based on the structure inherent in optimal binary search trees. Such an algorithm can be developed in a way similar to that used for the construction of Fibonacci trees in Chapter 7.

How do we decompose the optimal search tree problem in Example 12.2 into components with the same structure? Consider the characteristics of any optimal tree. Of course, it has a root and two subtrees. A moment's reflection should convince you that both subtrees must themselves be optimal binary search trees with respect to their keys and weights. First, any subtree of any binary search tree must be a binary search tree. Second, the subtrees must also be optimal. Otherwise, they could be replaced by optimal subtrees with smaller weighted path lengths, which would imply that the original tree could not have been optimal.

Since there are n possible keys as candidates for the root of the optimal tree, the recursive solution must try them all. For each candidate key as root, all keys less than that key must appear in its left subtree, and all keys greater than it must appear in its right subtree. To state the recursive algorithm based on these observations requires some notation.

Denote the weights assigned to the n stored keys by β's and the weights assigned to the terminal nodes by α's. The weight assigned to k_i is β_i for $i = 1, 2, \ldots, n$, and that assigned to the external node labeled i is α_i for $i = 0, 1, 2, \ldots, n$. Let `obst(i,j)` denote the optimal binary search tree containing keys $k_i, \ldots, k_j$, and let $\boldsymbol{w(i,j)}$ denote its weighted path length. `Obst(i,j)` will involve weights $\alpha_{i-1}, \beta_i, \ldots, \beta_j, \alpha_j$.

The optimal tree with root constrained to be k_k and containing keys $k_i, \ldots, k_k, \ldots, k_j$ must then have `obst(i,k-1)` as its left subtree and `obst(k+1,...,j)` as its right subtree. Its weighted path length, $w(i, j)$, is given by $sw(i, j) + w(i, k - 1) + w(k + 1, j)$, where $\boldsymbol{sw(i, j)}$ is the sum of the weights $\alpha_{i-1}, \beta_i, \ldots, \beta_j, \alpha_j$. $Sw(i, j)$ is the value assigned to the root of `obst(i,j)`, the sum of its weights.

Finally the algorithm can be stated.

For each $k(k)$ as root, $k = 1, 2, \ldots, n$
    find `obst(1,k-1)` and `obst(k+1,n)`.
Find a k that minimizes $[w(1, k - 1) + w(k + 1, n)]$ over $k = 1, 2, \ldots, n$.

`Obst(1,n)` is given by the tree with root k_k, `obst(1,k-1)` as its left subtree, and `obst(k+1,n)` as its right subtree.
The weighted path length of `obst(1,n)` is $w(1, n)$.
$w(1, n) = sw(1, n) + w(1, k - 1) + w(k + 1, n)$.

The execution tree for `obst(1,4)` is given in Figure 12.10. Apparently this algorithm exhibits the same proliferation of recursive calls for identical component problems as did the algorithm for the Fibonacci tree construction in Chapter 7. These are summarized in Table 12.1. This inefficiency can be avoided by using a bottom-up construction, just as was done for Fibonacci trees. To do this requires a clear understanding of exactly which optimal subtrees must be retained for later reference.

All possible optimal subtrees are not required. Those that are needed consist of sequences of keys that are immediate successors of the smallest key in the

Table 12.1 Components Replicated by Recursive Calls

Replicated Component	Occurrences
$(\alpha_2, \beta_3, \alpha_3, \beta_4, \alpha_4)$	2
$(\alpha_0, \beta_1, \alpha_1, \beta_2, \alpha_2)$	2
$(\alpha_1, \beta_2, \alpha_2, \beta_3, \alpha_3)$	2
$(\alpha_0, \beta_1, \alpha_1)$	4
$(\alpha_1, \beta_2, \alpha_2)$	5
$(\alpha_2, \beta_3, \alpha_3)$	5
$(\alpha_3, \beta_4, \alpha_4)$	4
(α_0)	4
(α_1)	3
(α_2)	4
(α_3)	3
(α_4)	4

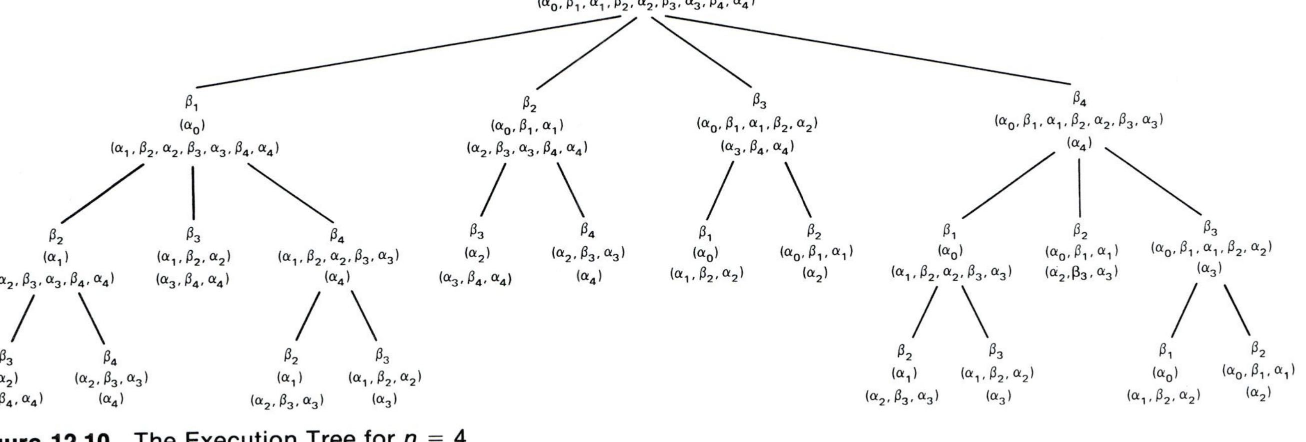

Figure 12.10 The Execution Tree for $n = 4$

subtree, successors in the sorted order for the keys. The final solution tree contains all n keys. There will be two with $n - 1$ keys, three with $n - 2$ keys, four with $n - 3$ keys, and in general $k + 1$ with $n - k$ keys, for $k = 0, 1, 2, \ldots, n$. Consequently there are a total of $(n + 1) \times (n + 2)/2$ optimal subtrees to be retained. Notice that to determine `obst(i,j)` requires knowing the optimal smaller subtrees involving weights:

(α_{i-1}) and $(\alpha_i, \beta_{i+1}, \ldots, \beta_j, \alpha_j)$
  i.e., `obst(i,i-1)` and `obst(i+1,j)`
$(\alpha_{i-1}, \beta_i, \alpha_i)$ and $(\alpha_{i+1}, \beta_{i+2}, \ldots, \beta_j, \alpha_j)$
  i.e., `obst(i,i)` and `obst(i+2,j)`

$(\alpha_{i-1}, \beta_i, \ldots, \beta_{j-1}, \alpha_{j-1})$ and (α_j)
  i.e., `obst(i,j-1)` and `obst(j+1,j)`

The bottom-up approach generates all smallest required optimal subtrees first, then all next smallest, and so on until the final solution involving all the weights is found. Since the algorithm requires access to each subtree's weighted path length, these weighted path lengths must also be retained to avoid their recalculation. Finally, the root of each subtree must also be stored for reference.

This algorithm requires $O(n^3)$ execution time and $O(n^2)$ storage. Knuth, who developed this solution, noticed an important fact that reduces the execution time to $O(n^2)$. He was able to show that the minimization need not be over all k from 1 to n. Instead, the minimization may be taken only over all k between $r(i, j - 1)$ and $r(i + 1, j)$, where $r(i, j)$ denotes the root of `obst(i,j)`. See Knuth [1973b].

Intuitively, this is plausible because `obst(i,j-1)` is the optimal binary *search tree containing keys* $k_i, \ldots, k_{r(i,j-1)}, \ldots, k_{j-1}$. Thus taking $k_{r(i,j-1)}$ as its root gives the tree just the "balance" it needs to be optimal, distributing keys to its left and right subtrees in the optimal way. `Obst(i,j)` includes k_j as well. If its root is also $k_{r(i,j-1)}$, then k_j will appear in the right subtree of this optimal tree adding more weight to its right subtree. Think of the optimal tree as "balanced." Its root should not be a predecessor of $k_{r(i,j-1)}$, since this would cause even more weight to appear in its right subtree. Reasoning this way, it is not unreasonable to expect the root of `obst(i,j)` to be $k_{r(i,j-1)}$ or *one of its successors*. Thus looking only at k where $r(i, j - 1) \leq k$ should suffice. A symmetrical argument should make it equally reasonable that looking only at k, $k \leq r(i + 1, j)$ should suffice. The actual proof is complex and adds little insight, so it is omitted here.

The bottom-up algorithm, incorporating the new minimization limits, may now be written.

1. For i from 0 to n
   a. Set $w(i + 1, i)$ to 0 and $sw(i + 1, i)$ to α_i
   b. For j from $i + 1$ to n
      Set $sw(i + 1, j)$ to $sw(i + 1, j - 1) + \beta_j + \alpha_j$
2. For j from 1 to n
   a. Set $w(j, j)$ to $sw(j, j)$ and $r(j, j)$ to j.
   (This initializes all `obst`'s containing 0 keys and 1 key.)
3. For l from 2 to n
   a. For j from l to n,

i. set i to $j - l + 1$;
ii. set $w(i, j)$ to $sw(i, j)$ + minimum$[w(i, k - 1) + w(k + 1, j)]$, the minimum to be over k satisfying $r(i, j - 1) \le k \le r(i + 1, j)$ and set $r(i, j)$ to a value of k corresponding to the minimum.

Actually, the $w(i,j)$'s will differ from the weighted path length of `obst(i,j)` by the sum of $\alpha_{i-1}, \alpha_i, \ldots, \alpha_j$. This does not affect the final tree but means that to obtain the true weighted path length, $\alpha_0 + \alpha_1 + \cdots + \alpha_n$ must be added to $w(1, n)$.

Arrays for w, ws, and r seem to be a natural choice for implementing this algorithm and provide rapid access to the information required for the processing involved.

Example 12.3 Find the optimal binary search tree for $n = 6$ and weights $\beta_1 = 10, \beta_2 = 3, \beta_3 = 9, \beta_4 = 2, \beta_5 = 0, \beta_6 = 10, \alpha_0 = 5, \alpha_1 = 6, \alpha_2 = 4, \alpha_3 = 4, \alpha_4 = 3, \alpha_5 = 8, \alpha_6 = 0$. ■

Figure 12.11(a) shows the arrays as they would appear after the initialization, and 12.11(b) gives their final disposition. The actual optimal tree is shown in Figure 12.12. It has a weighted path length of 188.

Since this algorithm requires $O(n^2)$ time and $O(n^2)$ storage, as n increases, it will run out of storage even before it runs out of time. The storage needed can be

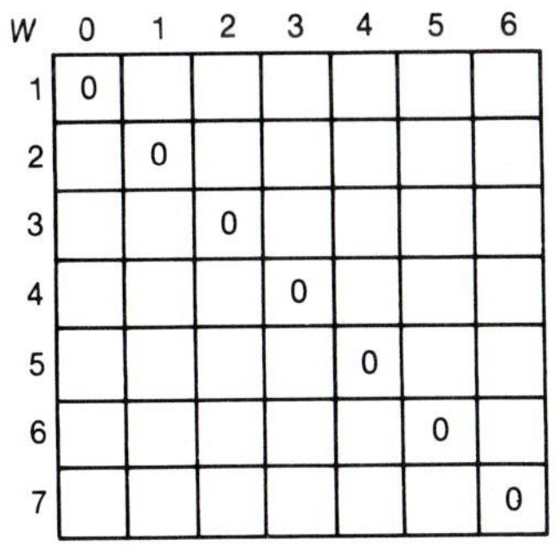

W	0	1	2	3	4	5	6
1	0						
2		0					
3			0				
4				0			
5					0		
6						0	
7							0

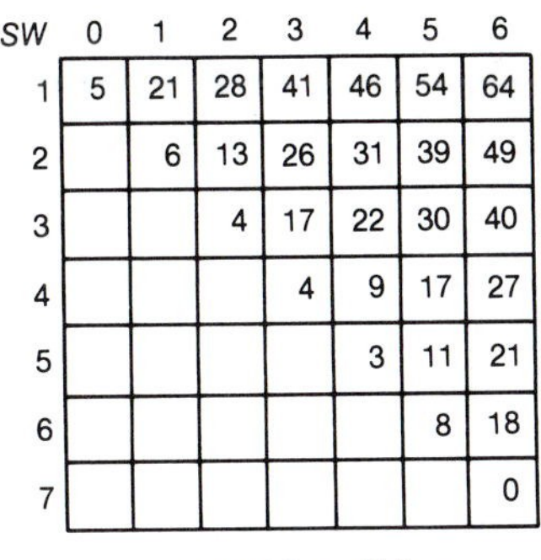

SW	0	1	2	3	4	5	6
1	5	21	28	41	46	54	64
2		6	13	26	31	39	49
3			4	17	22	30	40
4				4	9	17	27
5					3	11	21
6						8	18
7							0

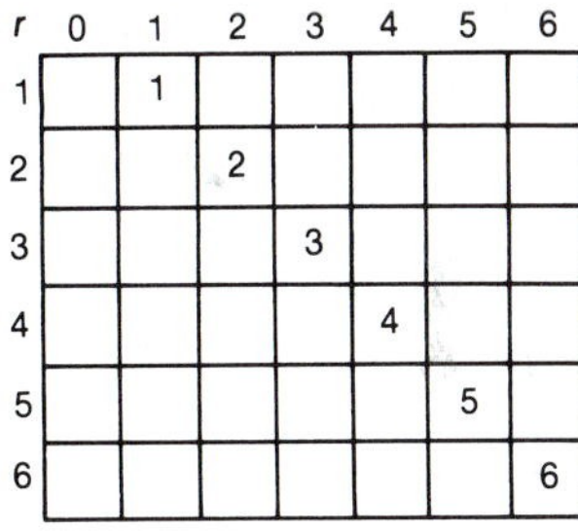

r	0	1	2	3	4	5	6
1		1					
2			2				
3				3			
4					4		
5						5	
6							6

(a) Initial Array Values

W	0	1	2	3	4	5	6
1	0	21	41	79	96	121	158
2		0	13	39	53	78	115
3			0	17	31	56	89
4				0	9	26	53
5					0	11	32
6						0	18
7							0

r	0	1	2	3	4	5	6
1		1	1	2	3	3	3
2			2	3	3	3	3
3				3	3	3	4
4					4	5	6
5						5	6
6							6

(b) Final Array Values

Figure 12.11 Arrays Used to Implement the Bottom-up Recursive Algorithm for Finding Optimal Binary Search Trees

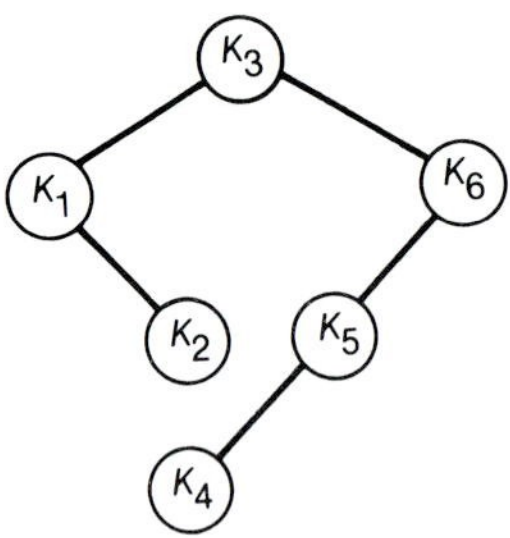

Figure 12.12 The Optimal Binary Search Tree Found by Means of the Bottom-up Recursive Algorithm

reduced by almost half, at the expense of a slight increase in time, by implementing the two-dimensional arrays as one-dimensional arrays using the technique of Chapter 2. Using one-dimensional arrays may enable problems to be solved that otherwise will abort because of insufficient storage. In any case, the algorithm is feasible only for moderate values of n.

In order to understand exactly how the algorithm creates the optimal tree, you should simulate the algorithm to reproduce the arrays of Figure 12.11.

12.5 Nearly Optimal Binary Search Trees

To date, no one knows how to construct the *optimal* binary search tree using less time or storage in the general case of nonzero α's and β's. For this reason it is important to develop algorithms that produce good, but not necessarily optimal, solutions with less time and storage being required. Algorithms have been found that construct ***nearly optimal binary search trees.*** The weighted path lengths of such trees cannot differ by more than a constant factor from the optimal value.

12.5.1 Greedy Binary Search Trees

One such algorithm produces ***greedy binary search trees.*** These trees are constructed by an algorithm using the greedy method. Unlike the Huffman algorithm, which is also based on the greedy method, they are not guaranteed to be optimal, but they are guaranteed to be nearly optimal. Other distinct, nearly optimal, tree constructions are found in Mehlhorn [1975, 1977] and in Horibe and Nemetz [1979]. A comparison of all these and other algorithms for the generation of nearly optimal binary search trees appears in Korsh [1982]. The proof that the following greedy method yields nearly optimal trees is in Korsh [1981].

In constructing a nearly optimal binary search tree by the greedy method, the programmer must ensure that the solution is a binary search tree. Looking at the optimal tree (Figure 12.12) found by the preceding section's algorithm will provide the idea behind the greedy tree construction. Think of the tree being generated by creating the subtrees shown in Figure 12.13, one after another, starting with the subtree with k_4 at its root and ending with the final optimal tree. Each subtree has its value (the sum of its weights) associated with it.

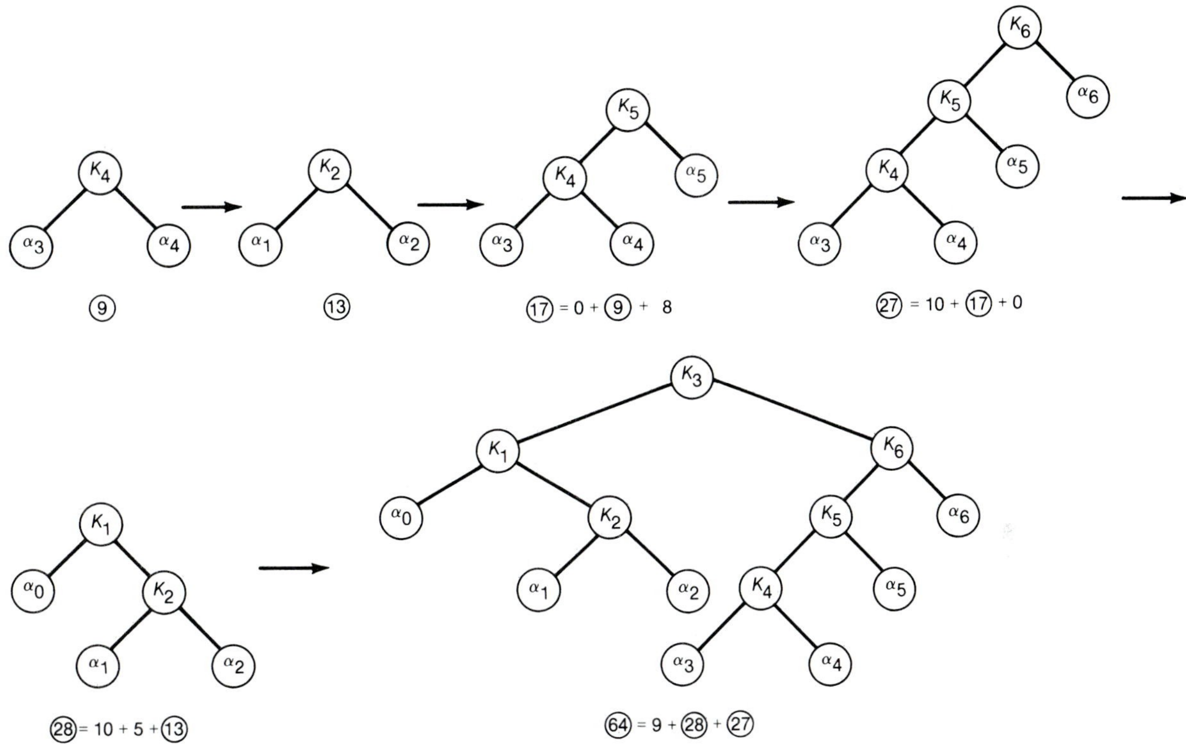

Figure 12.13 Trees Created from Subtrees (Circled Numbers Are the Trees' Values)

Each subtree is formed by taking for its root a key that has not yet appeared and adjoining a left and right subtree. These subtrees may correspond to an extended node (with weight some α_i) or to an already produced subtree. The value of the subtree formed is given by the β_i of its key plus the value of its left and right subtrees. These subtrees must be selected in a constrained fashion, or the resultant tree will not be a binary *search* tree. These constraints will be delineated shortly, but for now, the main point is that the weighted path of the optimal tree is the sum of the values of each of the subtrees. The greedy trees are built by always selecting the next subtree to generate as the one with smallest value from among all those satisfying the constraints. This is exactly how the Huffman construction works, except there are no constraints on the choice of subtrees since the resultant tree need not be a binary *search* tree.

12.5.2 Greedy Construction

To start the development, we use the α's and β's of Example 12.3 and array them as shown in Figure 12.14(a). In an inorder traversal of *any* binary search tree with the six keys, the weights assigned to the accessed nodes would occur in the order $\alpha_0\ \beta_1\ \alpha_1\ \beta_2\ \alpha_2\ \beta_3$, and so on. This sequence looks like *triples,* as shown in Figure 12.14(b). A value can be associated with each triple by summing up its weights. Thus the triples just shown have values 21, 13, 17, 9, 11, and 18 respectively. A greedy tree is constructed by always finding an allowed triple with minimal value and generating its corresponding subtree next. The weighted path length of the resultant tree is the sum of the weights of the $(n - 1)$ triples thus created. The greedy construction procedure is as follows. The allowable triples shown in the array have values 21, 13, 17, 9, 11, and 18. The triple with the lowest value (9) is

  2
4   3

Combining the corresponding key and terminal nodes yields the subtree shown in Figure 12.14(c). Its assigned value is the triple value 9. Delete that triple from the array, and replace it by a terminal node value of 9, as shown in Figure 12.14(d).

Now repeat this process. The next minimal value is 13, corresponding to the triple

  3
6   4

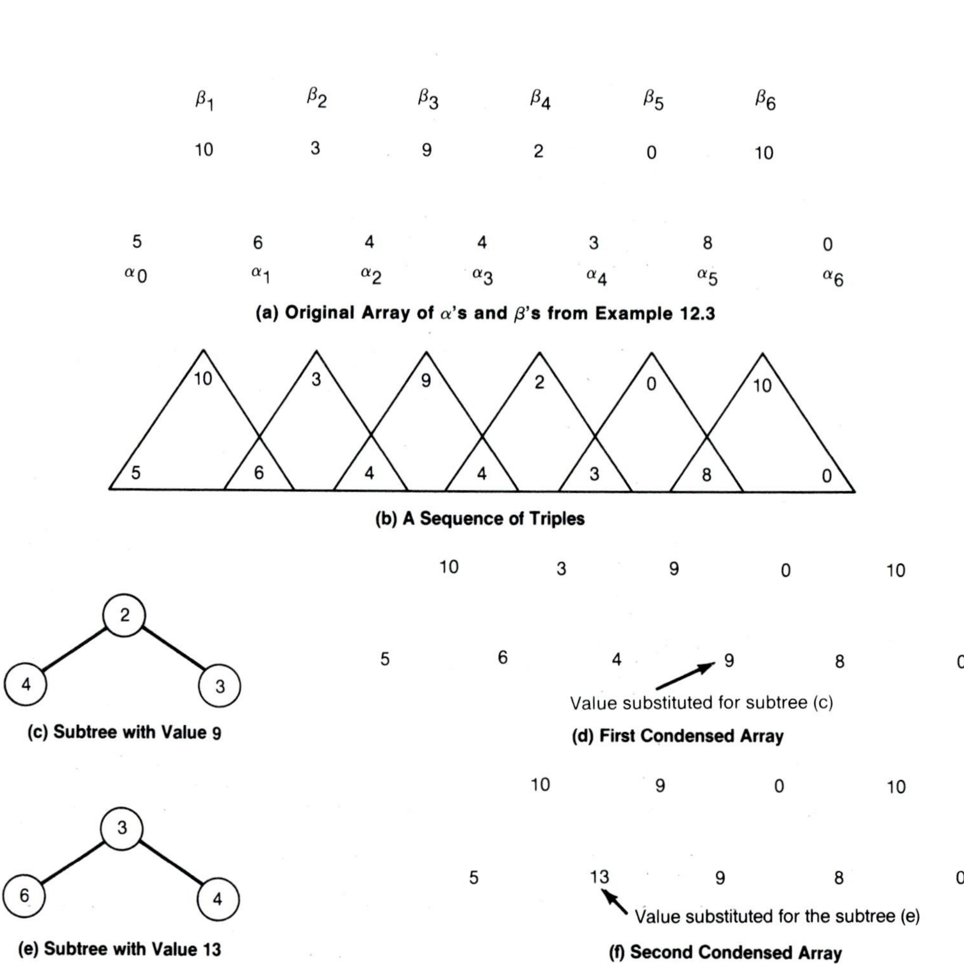

Figure 12.14 Construction of Greedy Binary Search Tree

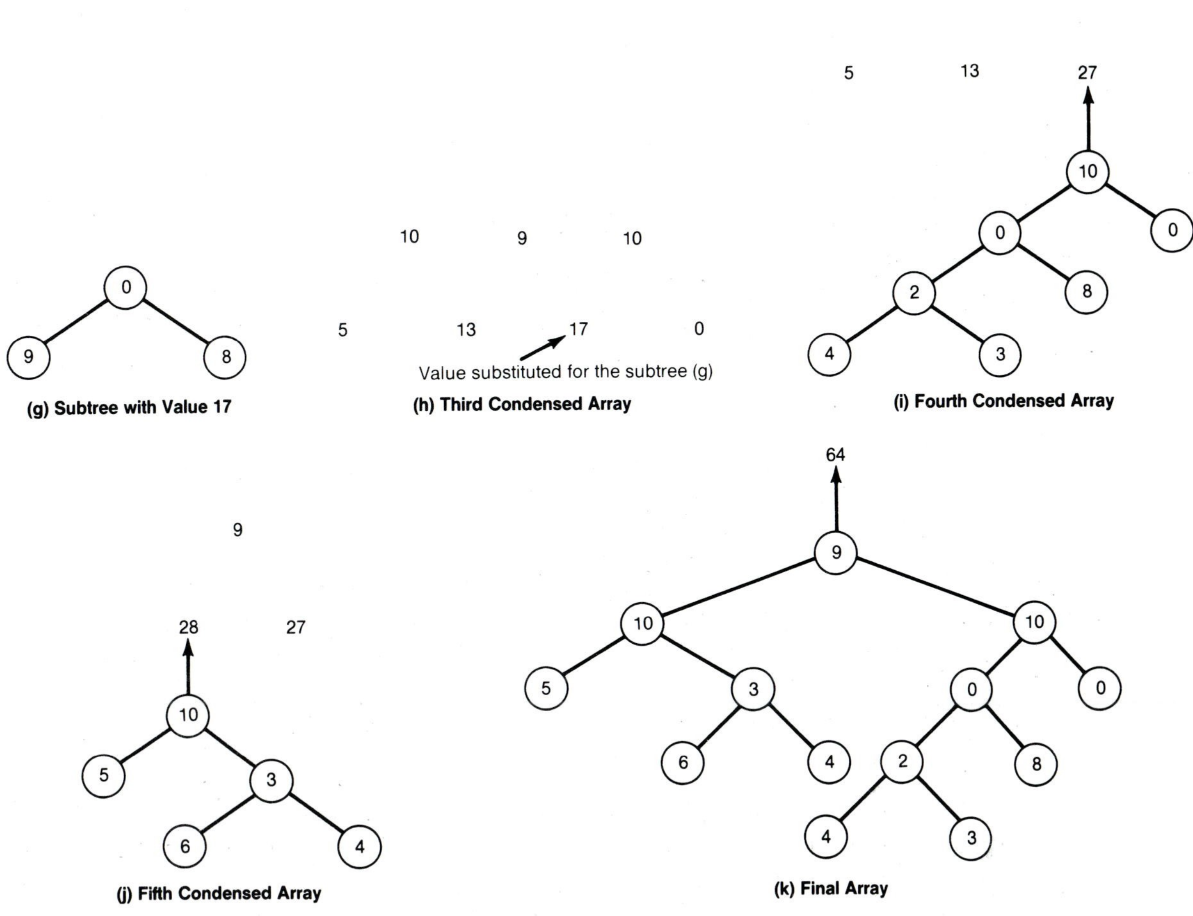

(g) Subtree with Value 17

(h) Third Condensed Array

(i) Fourth Condensed Array

(j) Fifth Condensed Array

(k) Final Array

Figure 12.14 *(continued)*

This gives the subtree shown in Figure 12.14(e). The condensed array is shown in Figure 12.14(f). Repeating the process finds the minimal triple whose value is 17. The corresponding subtree is Figure 12.14(g), and the new array is shown in Figure 12.14(h). Continuing in this fashion produces the arrays shown in Figure 12.14(i), (j), and (k).

The *greedy* tree thus constructed by always taking a minimal triple is shown in Figure 12.15. Its weighted path length can be found by keeping an accumulated sum, as in the Huffman algorithm. In this case the greedy algorithm actually yields the optimal tree.

12.5.3 Implementation

Just as in the Huffman tree construction, if we are not careful we will end up with an $O(n^2)$ time implementation. Instead, we can use a heap similar to that for the

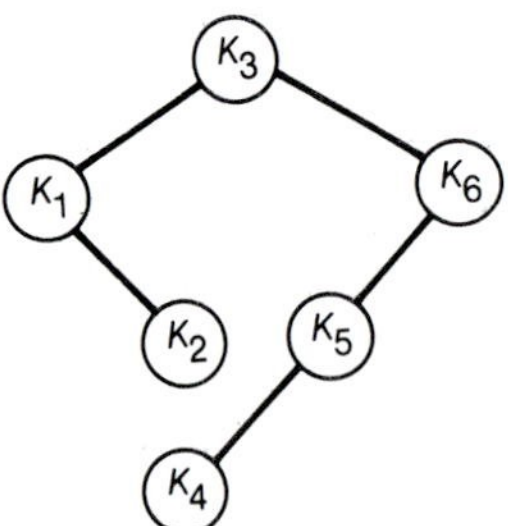

Figure 12.15 Greedy Binary Search Tree Constructed as Illustrated in Figure 12.14

Huffman construction to obtain an $O(n \lg n)$ time requirement and $O(n)$ storage. However, we can do even better.

The preceding method leads to a sequence of $n - 1$ combined triples with values $v_1, v_2, \ldots, v_{n-1}$. In this sequence $v_1 \leq v_2 \leq \cdots \leq v_{n-1}$. That is, the triples are generated in order, from the smallest to the highest value. The improved algorithm, introduced now, also generates a sequence of $n - 1$ combined triples, but their values will not necessarily be the same as $v_1, \ldots, v_2, v_{n-1}$, nor will they necessarily be generated in order by size. The improved algorithm, however, will produce the greedy tree that would have been obtained had they been combined in order by size when it is unique. A unique tree exists when there is exactly one smallest triple at each step. In general, the resultant tree will be greedy, but it will not necessarily be the same greedy tree generated by $v_1, \ldots, v_2, v_{n-1}$, nor will it necessarily have the same weighted path length.

We start with a list-structure illustrated in Figure 2.16. Each record represents a potential triple to be combined in the construction of a greedy tree. Traverse the list starting at the left and search for a *locally* minimal triple—that is, a triple whose value does not exceed the value of its successor triple. No triple to the left of this locally minimal triple can be combined before it in any greedy tree construction. In addition, any future combining of locally minimal triples to its right cannot cause the resultant tree to fail to be greedy. In other words, combining the minimal triple always allows a greedy tree to be constructed with the combined minimal triple as a subtree. Combine the locally minimal triple (say it is the ith), and obtain the new list-structure shown in Figure 12.16(b).

Here α'_{i-1} and α'_i were both set to the value of the combined triple $\alpha_{i-1} + \beta_i + \alpha_i$, the ith record was deleted, and the pointers changed as shown. The left-to-right traversal is continued, starting now at the $(i - 2)$th record, combining as before for each locally minimal triple encountered. Details involving the ends of the list-structure can be handled by special checking or by introducing artificial records with large weights at the ends. This results in the construction of a greedy tree. This procedure is reminiscent of the evaluation of an infix expression of Chapter 4. That algorithm is greedy in the sense that we look for the highest local priority operator to evaluate first in a left-to-right scan, evaluate it, and continue from that point.

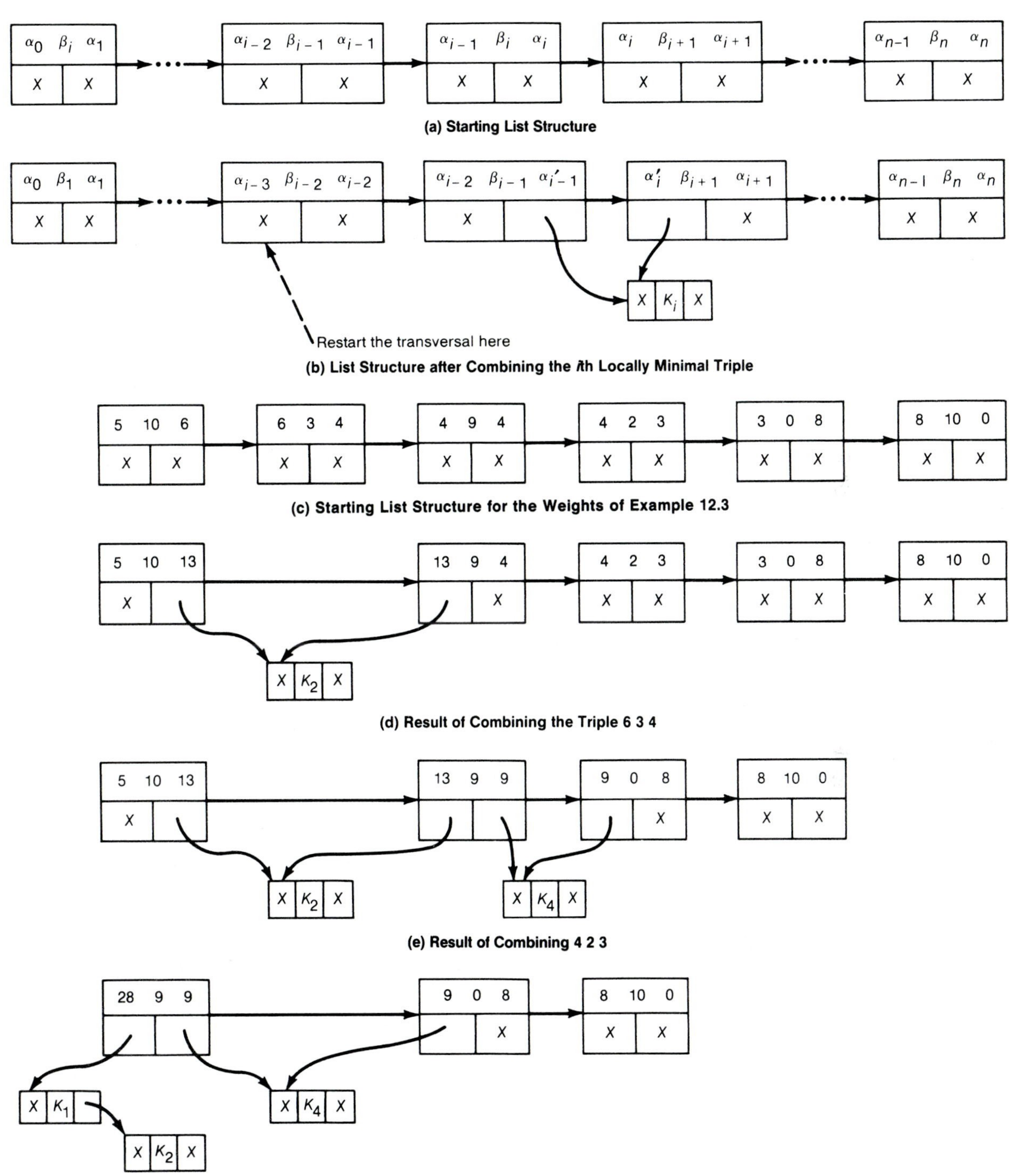

Figure 12.16 Implementation of the Greedy Algorithm

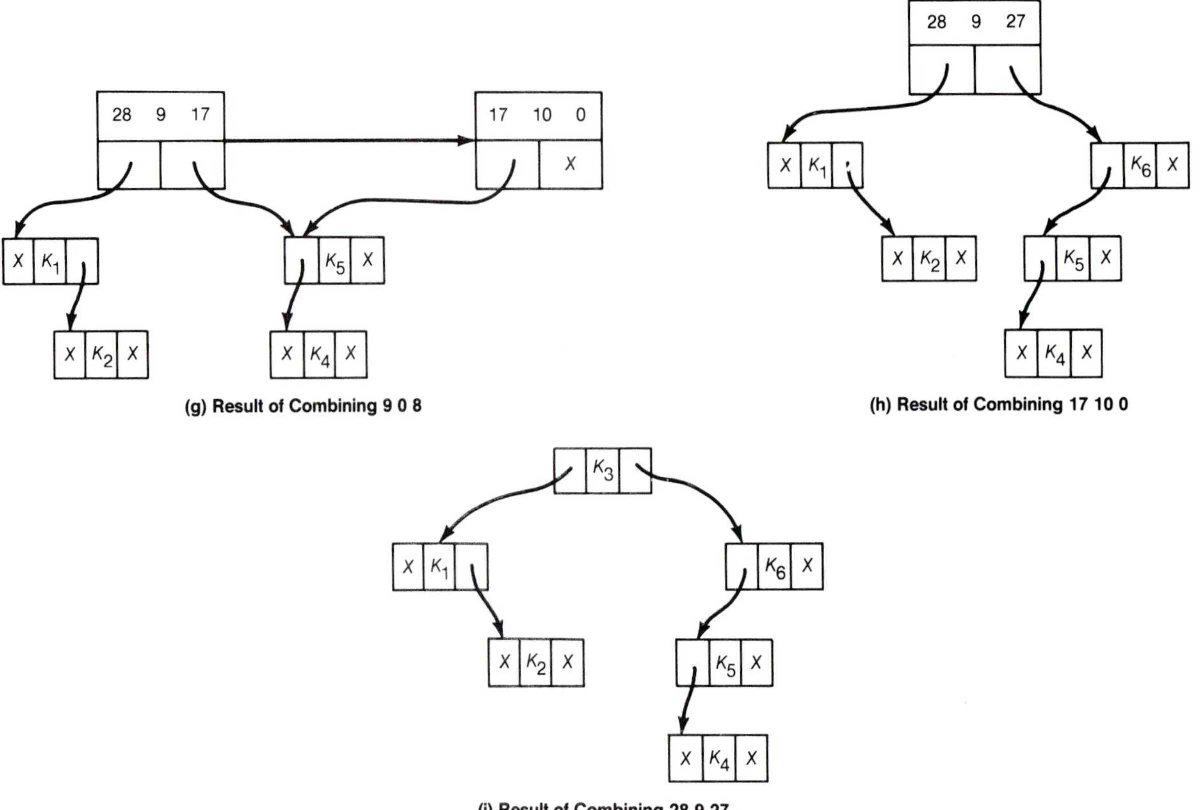

(g) Result of Combining 9 0 8

(h) Result of Combining 17 10 0

(i) Result of Combining 28 9 27

Figure 12.16 *(continued)*

Applying this improved algorithm to Example 12.3, the starting list-structure is as shown in Figure 12.16(c). The first locally minimal triple found is 6 3 4. The list-structure resulting from combining it is shown in Figure 12.16(d). Starting again at the first record, 4 2 3 is the next minimal triple, yielding the list shown in Figure 12.16(e). Starting again, the first record here is found to be the locally minimal triple to obtain the list shown in Figure 12.16(f).

Starting again at the next first record, 9 0 8, the next locally minimal triple, gives the list shown in Figure 12.16(g). Once again, we start at the first record. The next locally minimal triple is 17 10 0. Combining it results in Figure 12.16(h). Finally the triple 28 9 27 is combined to obtain the result shown in Figure 12.16(i).

We have constructed the same tree as before (in Figures 12.14 and 12.15). Again, this need not always occur. However, even when it does, as here, the order in which the subtrees were formed need not be the same. We generated subtrees with values 13, 9, 28, 17, 27, and finally 64, rather than in order from the smallest to largest as in the other method. Both trees in this example have the same weighted path length of 188.

This implementation takes time and storage only $O(n)$! This was made possible by the new method, coupled with the proper choice of data structure.

12.5.4 Alphabetic Codes

Consider the twenty-seven characters with relative frequencies given in Section 12.3 as weights. Order them as $\triangle < A < B < C < \cdots < Z$. Suppose we want to construct an extended binary *search* tree with these characters associated with the terminal nodes. We take the weights given there as the α's of this problem and take the β's to be zero. The extended binary tree will then generate what is called an ***alphabetic code.*** The optimal binary search tree will have weighted path length 5,200, and the greedy binary search tree will have weighted path length 5,307. Recall that the Huffman tree had weighted path length 5,124. Requiring use of a binary search tree rather than a binary tree results in an increase relative to 5,124 of only (5,200 − 5,124)/5,124 or 1.5 percent. The greedy construction yields an increase relative to 5,200 of (5,307 − 5,200)/5,200 or 2 percent.

12.6 Conclusion

Binary trees are useful data structures for encoding and decoding information. The Huffman algorithm generates optimal binary trees for this purpose and can do so efficiently. Binary search trees are useful data structures for storing information that is to be searched; they also produce good codes.

Greedy binary search trees, which are nearly optimal, can be generated very efficiently. The greedy method of algorithm design does not yield optimal solutions but may still yield very good solutions. Again it was demonstrated that careful selection of data structures can significantly change the time requirements of an algorithm.

■ Exercises

1. **a.** Using its definition, calculate the weighted path length of the following tree. The weight of a node appears at the node.

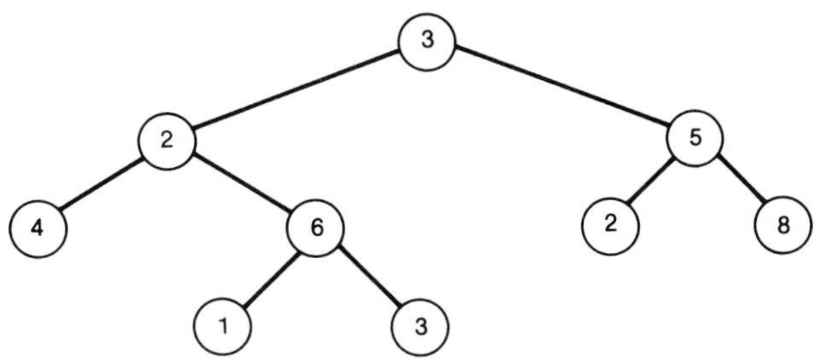

b. Calculate the weighted path length of the tree using the other method of assigning a "value" to each node and adding up all the "values."
c. Calculate the weighted path length of the same tree by adding the sum of all its weights to the weighted path length of its left subtree plus the weighted path of its right subtree.

2. Write a `process` function to turn a postorder traversal into a function for determining the weighted path length of a binary tree T based on the method of Exercise 1(b).
3. Determine the Huffman code (tree) for weights 1, 2, 3, 4, 5.

4. Determine the weighted path length for your solution to Exercise 3.

5. The Huffman tree for n weights will always have $(n - 1)$ internal nodes and n terminal nodes. This is because it is a *full* binary tree. That is, every internal node has exactly 0 or exactly two successors. Prove, by induction on the total number of nodes of a full binary tree, that this is true.

6. Write a nonrecursive function, `huffman`, with parameters `n`, `weights`, `tree`, and `code`. `Weights` is an array containing `n` weights, `code` is an array returned containing the `n` codes (sequences of 0's and 1's) assigned to each weight by the Huffman code, and `tree` points to the root of the corresponding Huffman tree upon return. Your function should take $O(n \lg n)$ time.

7. Write a recursive version of the function of Exercise 6.

8. Simulate the proof (by induction on n) that the Huffman tree yields a binary tree with minimal weighted path length for n weights for Exercise 3.

9. Write a function `decode` with parameters `n`, `alpha`, and `tree`. `Alpha` is a sequence of `n` 0's and 1's, and `tree` points to a Huffman tree for the twenty-seven characters of Section 12.3 (determined by their weights). `Decode` is to decode the sequence of `n` 0's and 1's into the corresponding characters. The sequence represents a coded version of a message composed of the characters.

10. Suppose you know the Huffman tree for the twenty-seven characters of Section 12.3 (determined by their weights). Write a function `encode` to encode a message composed of characters into the Huffman code. To do this you might consider using the following data structures:

- **a.** The Huffman tree.
- **b.** An array with twenty-seven records kept in sorted order by character, each record containing a character and its corresponding Huffman code.
- **c.** A hash table of records, each record consisting of a character and its Huffman code; the key is the character.

Discuss the relative advantages and disadvantages for each of these in the function `encode`.

11. Write a function `encode` to encode a message in a Huffman code.

12. Let $\alpha_0 = 10$, $\alpha_1 = 6$, $\alpha_2 = 8$, $\alpha_3 = 4$, $\alpha_4 = 2$, $\beta_1 = 2$, $\beta_2 = 5$, $\beta_3 = 7$, $\beta_4 = 6$. Determine the optimal binary search tree by generating all possible binary search trees storing the four keys with weights 2, 5, 7, and 6, and calculating their weighted path lengths.

13. The recursive approach of Section 12.4.1 is based on the idea that an optimal binary search tree must have an optimal left and an optimal right subtree. Can you use this idea to show that some of the trees you considered in Exercise 12 could have been ignored in searching for the optimal tree?

14. Simulate the bottom-up algorithm of Section 12.4.1 to reproduce the arrays of Figure 12.11.

15. Why do we want to find nearly optimal binary search trees rather than optimal binary search trees for large numbers of keys?

16. Find the greedy binary search tree for the weights of Exercise 12 using the definition of a greedy tree. Determine the relative difference between its weighted path length and the optimal value.

17. Find the greedy binary search tree for the weights of Exercise 12 using the implementation of the greedy tree construction. Is its weighted path length the same as the greedy tree of Exercise 16?

18. Write a nonrecursive function `greedy` to implement the greedy tree construction of Section 12.5.3.

19. Give a recursive definition of a greedy binary search tree.

20. Write a recursive function `greedy` to implement the greedy tree construction of Section 12.5.3.

21. Another method of constructing a nearly optimal binary search tree is to select the key to be placed at the root to be a key that minimizes the difference between the weights of its left and right subtrees. Having obtained the root, apply this procedure recursively to construct its left and right subtrees. This is a top-down construction, as opposed to the greedy tree construction, which is bottom-up. What tree does it generate for the weights of Exercise 12 and for the example of Section 12.5.2?

22. Write a recursive function for the construction method of Exercise 21. How much time does your function require?

23. Can you find a way to implement the procedure of Exercise 21 in $O(n)$ time, where n is the number of internal keys to be stored?

24. What will a greedy tree look like if the n β's are zero and the $n + 1$ α's are given by the first $n + 1$ Fibonacci numbers? Give two answers—one when the greedy tree definition is used, and one when the $O(n)$ implementation is used.

■ Suggested Assignments

1. a. Write programs to find and output optimal greedy trees and their weighted path lengths.

b. Explain why the greedy tree implementation with the list structure is linear in time. (*Hint:* When the next locally minimal triple is to be found, only list-structure records not previously accessed will be considered, as well as two records that were previously accessed.)

2. a. Write a function to read a file composed of the twenty-six letters of the alphabet, plus the blank character, the comma, and the period; produce an output file that is the encoded version of the input file. The Huffman code is to be used, with weights based on the number of times each character appears in the input text.

b. This is the same as (a) except that the "words" of the input text are taken as the objects to be encoded, and their number of occurrences is the basis for the code. Use any reasonable definition of a word. For example, take commas, periods, blanks, and any sequence of other characters to be words.

Note: For both parts, use a function `getnexttoken`. In part (a) it must return the next character in the input or `EOF`, while in part (b) it must return the next word or `EOF`. Also, there must be a table in which the tokens (characters or words) are stored. This table must be searched for a token, inserted into, and its entries updated. Your function must treat the table with these operations as a data abstraction, so the solutions to both parts should look the same except that the definitions of certain functions should change from one solution to the other.

c. Run your program for part (b) with the table implemented as

i. a binary search tree

ii. a hash table using double hashing

iii. a table composed of two parts—an optimal binary search tree storing the 25 most frequently used English words (take the α's to be zero) and a binary search storing any other words that occur in the input. The optimal binary search tree is to be built in advance of the input.

d. Write a function to read a text file consisting of the twenty-six letters of the alphabet, plus the blank and period characters, and produce an output file consisting of the text in Huffman code. Use the heap implementation in generating the Huffman tree.

13
1
2
3
4
5
6
7
8
9
10
11
12

13 Some Pointers on Storage Management

Applies the basic data structures to the management of dynamic memory
Presents alternative ways to structure the collection of unused memory locations
- *two-way circular lists*
- *the buddy system*
- *indexing methods*

Discusses problems that arise when structures share storage
Explains fundamental techniques for reclaiming unused storage
Illustrates data abstraction and functional modularization in the development of three stackless binary tree traversals
Calls attention to the problems of
- *garbage generation*
- *dangling references*

13.1 The Need for Storage Management

In languages such as C, arrays are ***static*** data structures. They do not change size or shape during the execution of a program. Chains, however, do change size, though they don't change shape. They are ***dynamic.*** List-structures, more complex lists, and binary and general trees can change both size and shape and thus are also dynamic data structures. The basic distinction between *static* and *dynamic* data structures relates to whether a fixed amount of memory is allocated in advance of program execution. Static structures can have a fixed amount of memory allocated for their sole use prior to program execution. For dynamic structures, the amount of memory required is not known in advance and thus cannot be allocated in this way.

In FORTRAN and COBOL, the total amount of storage needed by the variables of a program is known by the compiler and can be set aside before program execution. This means that a fixed amount of storage is allocated to variables for the entire execution of the program. This is not done in C, which is more versatile. It uses both static and dynamic storage allocation. Some storage is allocated for the entire execution of the program, while other storage is allocated when needed and is reused when no longer needed. This requires storage management *during* program execution. Dynamic structures such as lists and trees need even more complex storage management during program execution.

Consider a program that maintains a data base of stock portfolios for the clients of a brokerage house. Suppose each client's stocks are kept in a binary search tree ordered by stock name, with each node of the tree represented as a record containing information about the stock. It is not possible to predict in advance how much storage is needed, since how many stocks each client will buy is not known. Experience may show that all clients' stocks will never number more than 2,000, but the distribution of these stocks among the clients varies throughout the year. Thus it will be necessary to have storage available for 2,000 records. At a given moment this storage will be distributed among the clients' binary search trees. Whenever a stock is sold for one client, its storage must be deleted from that client's tree. It may be needed later to store the record of a stock just bought for another client. This allocation and reclaiming of record storage during program execution requires dynamic storage management. Some languages, such as C, provide needed storage management. Others do not, so the programmer must provide it.

This chapter discusses the fundamentals of storage management techniques. It offers insight into how programming languages manage storage and provides a better appreciation of the pitfalls that lie below the surface features of a language. Such insight is especially important when the programmer employs complex data structures that share storage.

You have already seen in Chapter 3 how the simple case of fixed-length records with no sharing might be handled. Problems arise when records have variable lengths and when data structures share memory. The remedies for these problems involve the creation and processing of data structures tailored to these needs. Sophisticated traversal algorithms have been developed to conserve storage. They are introduced here for three reasons. First, they are essential for the implementation of those data structures. Second, they are interesting in themselves. Finally, they serve as a good example of the use of data abstraction.

Although storage management is viewed here from the perspective of a single program's needs, these same techniques are employed by operating systems to deal with the allocation and reclamation of storage for a group of active programs.

In some problems, an upper bound on the problem size is not known in advance. One way to deal with this situation is to pick a reasonably large size and declare static data structures of this size. If the problem's memory requirement exceeds this size, an error message may be printed. When the number of available memory elements is fixed, there will generally be some problem size for which programs fail. However, it is possible that the program uses several data structures. During execution, when one data structure is large the others may be small, so that the *total* amount of storage required for all the structures may actually be available at all times. With static data structures, where memory is allocated and remains dedicated to a particular structure, storage must be allocated to accommodate the worst case. The worst case calls for the sum of the maximum storages needed for each data structure of the program. If, instead, the available memory can be used for the data structure that currently requires it and reclaimed for later use when that structure no longer needs it, then larger problems can be solved. This point is illustrated in the following examples.

Example 13.1 The `lists` array used to store successor records for the topological sort of Chapter 11 allows all successor lists to share storage. No storage is dedicated to any individual list. As long as the *total* number of successors on all lists does not exceed the length of `lists`, the program will execute correctly. This contrasts with the alternate collection of *n* arrays discussed in Section 11.6. With the latter approach, storage is dedicated to each list; although twice as many total successors may be accommodated, no list can contain more than its dedicated amount. ■

Example 13.2 Suppose five stacks are each implemented, as in Chapter 4, using static array structures, each with a maximum size of 5,000 elements. This requires 25,000 total memory locations. However, if the number of entries in all the stacks at any one time never exceeds 10,000, proper sharing of storage would allow a reduction of up to 15,000 in the amount of storage needed. ■

Example 13.3 A program can store, in linked representation, a number of binary trees that must be traversed using stacks. If the trees must be stored and traversed simultaneously, it is possible that available storage for the records of the tree nodes and for the entries of the stacks will not be sufficient for the worst case. However, if the available storage can be shared, so that it is used for tree records or for stack entries when needed, then the program might execute correctly. ■

In Example 13.1, the records sharing storage all have the same size. In Example 13.2, the five stacks can all store records of the same size, *or* they can store records of different lengths. Example 13.3 needs shared storage for records, which may or may not be of the same length for each binary tree, and for stack entries. Normally the record lengths would be significantly greater than that of the stack entries. One fundamental distinction between storage management techniques involves whether or not the storage allocated will all be the same size. When dealing with the fixed-size case, it is convenient to use the techniques for storage allocation and storage reclamation, discussed in Chapter 3, which involve a list of available space. When dealing with more general data structures or with variable-size records, additional complications arise.

13.2 The Heap or Dynamic Memory

As one or more programs execute, they may require storage for the creation of new records, which typically are to be inserted into dynamic data structures. How can a fixed amount of storage that is made available for the creation of these records be managed efficiently?

The records, or more generally, the components of dynamic data structures, are referred to as ***nodes.*** The region of memory consisting of contiguous elements that is dedicated to the storage of these nodes is called the ***heap*** or ***dynamic memory.*** We will use the term *heap* in the further discussion. In the heap all nodes need not be the same length, and nodes may appear as part of more than one data structure. Associated with each node is a length field, indicating the size of the node (that is, the number of memory elements it uses). If all nodes were the same size, there would be no need to store size information within each node. All dynamic data structures reside in the heap. At all times, the heap may contain three kinds of nodes:

- Nodes that are *in use* because they appear in dynamic data structures
- Nodes that are *not in use* and appear in no dynamic data structure but are on the current list of available space
- Nodes that are *not in use* because they are in no dynamic data structure but are *not* on the list of available space

Nodes on the list of available space are said to be ***known.*** Nodes that are available but not on the list of available space are called ***garbage.*** All *heads* (names) of dynamic data structures, which point to their first records, are outside the heap and are kept track of in some way. This means that at all times the program knows what dynamic data structures are in existence, since their names are known.

Example 13.4 Suppose `av`, `l`, and `t` are, respectively, the heads of the available space list, a list, and a binary tree. A heap containing these dynamic data structures may be visualized as in Figure 13.1. Each node has been labeled to indicate its current status:

1—in use since the node appears on `l` or `t`
2—not in use but on the available space list
3—not in use and not on the available space list, hence garbage ■

Storage allocation now involves three tasks:

1. Decide which node on the list of available space will be made available when a request for creation of a node is made.
2. Delete that node from the list of available space.
3. Set a pointer value to point to the node.

An `avail`-like function, discussed in Chapter 3, will perform these three tasks.

13.3 The List of Available Space for Variable-Length Records

When dealing with variable-size records, which is the usual situation, storage management is complex because of ***fragmentation.*** The fragmentation problem is as follows. When all records being allocated dynamically are the same size, then as long as unused storage finds its way to the list of available space, it can be reused. However, it is possible with variable-size records that storage for a large record is needed but is not immediately in existence. Suppose each available block of *consecutive* elements of storage is kept on the list of available space as an individual record, with a field of each record used to store its length. It is possible for records of length 10, 15, 3, 20, and 45 to appear on the list when a record of length 65 must be created, but no individual record is large enough to be allocated for it. However, a total of 93 elements is unused. This is the ***external fragmentation*** problem. Enough storage is unused to satisfy the need, but no record currently on the list of available space is, by itself, large enough to be used. The problem may be resolved by invoking a ***compaction*** procedure, which moves the field values in used nodes to contiguous elements of memory at one end of the heap. All unused elements then also become contiguous and can represent a node large enough that the needed storage can be taken.

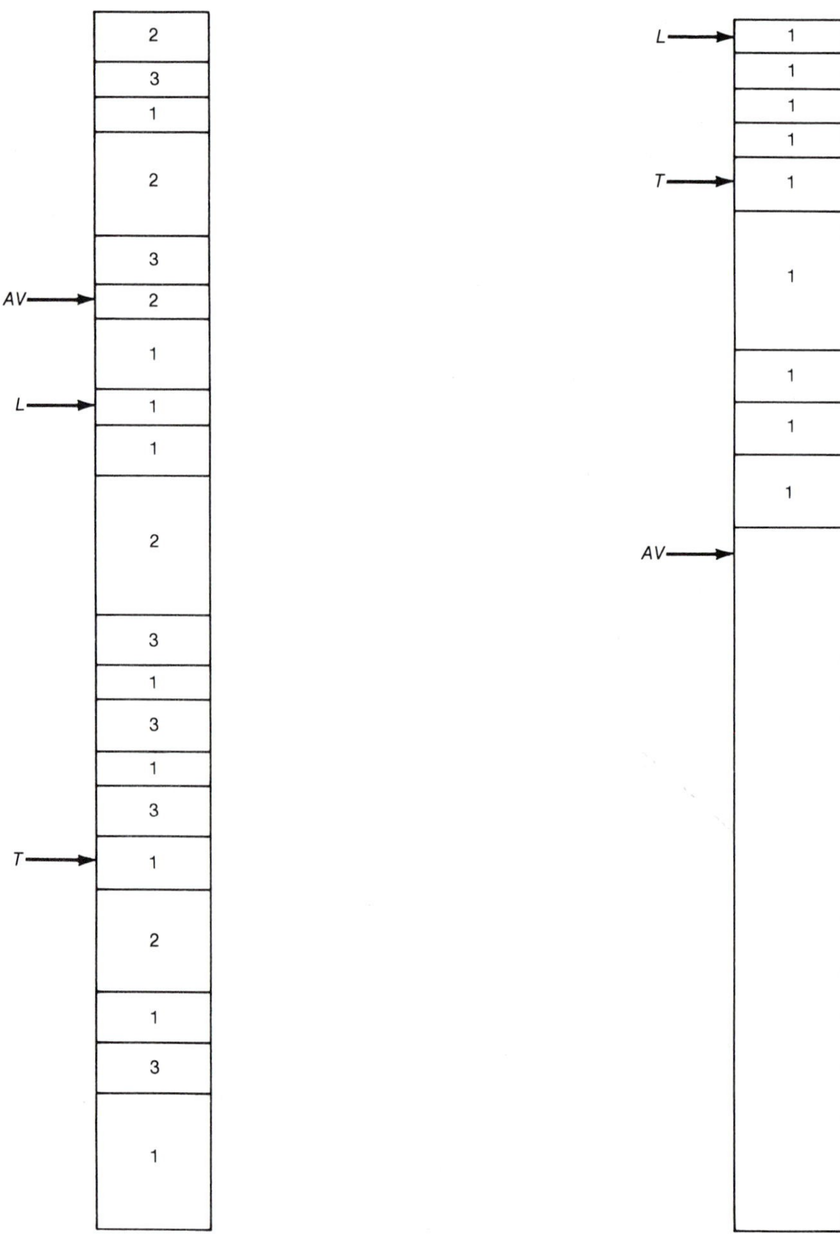

Figure 13.1 A Heap Containing the Available Space List (*AV*), a List (*L*), and a Binary Tree (*T*) and Nodes Labeled 1, 2, or 3 to Show Status

Figure 13.2 The Heap of Example 13.4 (Figure 13.1) after Compaction

Example 13.5 Suppose the compaction procedure is applied to the heap of Example 13.4, which was illustrated in Figure 13.1. The result may be visualized as in Figure 13.2. ■

Compaction, like garbage collection, is a time-consuming process that the programmer or computer system should only invoke infrequently. To overcome this, it is possible to organize the list of available space in an attempt to minimize fragmentation and thus the need for compaction. However, in limiting fragmentation the program should not spend too much computer time determining which node to allocate each time a request is made. Organizing the list of available space and using a reasonable policy to select the node to be allocated helps to reduce fragmentation. However, additional time is required to search the list to select the node to be allocated and to place a reclaimed node in proper position on the list to maintain its organization.

Fragmentation can also be reduced by creating larger nodes, by adding the freed storage to storage adjacent to it that is already free. This process is called ***coalescing.*** These policies and ways of organizing must be addressed by designers of compilers or operating systems and by programmers when they create storage management schemes for their own use.

Recall that the more structured or organized the data, the faster the access to required information. At the same time a price must be paid to maintain the organization. The primary considerations for a storage management scheme are the time to satisfy a request for a new node, the time to insert a node on the list of available space, the storage utilization, and the likelihood of satisfying a request. How well these characteristics turn out for a particular storage management scheme depends on the sequence of requests and returns. Mathematical analysis is generally not possible, and simulation must be used to evaluate different schemes. To provide some idea of the trade-offs and possibilities, three fundamental organizations for the available space list and appropriate allocation and reclamation policies are presented next.

13.3.1 Two-Way Circular Lists

The simplest organization for the list of available space is a two-way circular list, with nodes kept in arbitrary order, in order by size, or in order by actual memory address. Two-way lists are convenient for making insertions and deletions. They allow the list to be traversed starting from any list record, and in either direction. A request for a node of size l then requires a traversal of the list, starting from some initial node.

Two simple policies for selection of the list node to be deleted to satisfy a request are *first-fit* and *best-fit*. ***First-fit*** selects the first node encountered whose size is sufficient. ***Best-fit*** does a complete traversal and selects that node of smallest size that is sufficient to satisfy the request. Of course, if an exact fit is found, the traversal need not continue. For both policies, any leftover storage is retained as a node on the list.

When a node is returned to the list, its neighbors (in terms of storage addresses) are coalesced with it if free, and the resultant node properly inserted on the list. All nodes require tag and size fields, with the list nodes also needing backward and forward link fields. The tag field distinguishes nodes in use from those not in use, depending on which of two values it contains.

Allowing the starting node to circulate around the list, always being set to the successor of the deleted (or truncated) node, typically improves performance. This circulation provides time for the smaller nodes left behind it to coalesce so that, by the next time around, larger nodes have been formed.

Intuitively, spending more time fitting the size of the selected node to the size of the requested node should cut down on fragmentation effects. Surprisingly, this need not always happen, but it is the normal situation.

13.3.2 The Buddy System

Another organization, called the *buddy system,* provides faster request and return time responses than two-way circular lists. The buddy system requires the heap to be of length 2^m for some integer m, occupying addresses 0 to $2^m - 1$. Over time, the heap is split into nodes of varying lengths. These lengths are constrained to be powers of 2, and nodes are kept on separate lists, each list containing nodes of a specific length. An array `a` of length m contains the heads of these lists, so `a[k]` points to the first node on the list corresponding to length $2^{\mathtt{k}}$. Initially, `a[m]` points to the first address of the heap; all other array entries are null, since all other lists are empty.

To satisfy a request for a node of length n, `k` is set to $\lceil \lg n \rceil$. If `a[k]` is not null, a node is deleted from its list to satisfy the request. Otherwise, the next nonnull list is found. Its nodes will be of length 2^r, where $r >$ `k`. A node is deleted from that list and split into two nodes, each of length 2^{r-1}. That node created by the split with the greater address is placed on the appropriate list, while the other is used to satisfy the request if $r - 1 =$ `k`. Otherwise it is split and processed in the same way. Eventually a node of length `k` will be generated to satisfy the request.

During this iterated splitting process, each time a node is split, it is split into two special nodes called ***buddies.*** Buddies bear a unique relation to each other. Only buddies are allowed to coalesce. Although this can result in unused nodes being contiguous but not coalescing because they are not buddies, it is a rare occurrence. This restriction allows very fast coalescing of buddies, as will be shown.

When a node is to be returned to the list of available space (a misnomer now), its buddy is first checked to see if it is not in use and, if it is not, the buddies are coalesced. This node is, in turn, coalesced with its buddy when possible, and so on, until no further coalescing is possible. This coalescing process is the reverse of the splitting process that created the buddies in the first place.

At this point you must be wondering how a node's buddy is found. The scheme ensures that it may be done quickly because a node of size 2^k with starting address

$$b \; . \; . \; . \; b\underline{0}\underbrace{00 \; . \; . \; . \; 0}_{k}$$

has as its buddy a node of size 2^k with starting address

$$b \ldots b\underline{1}\underbrace{00 \ldots 0}_{k}$$

In general, given the address of a node of size 2^k to be returned, its $(k + 1)$th bit (addresses are expressed in binary notation) is changed from 1 to 0 or 0 to 1, and the result is the address of its buddy. A tag field is used to indicate whether or not a node is in use.

Example 13.6 How does the buddy system respond when m is 6 and a sequence of requests is made for nodes of size 8, 16, 4, and 6? ■

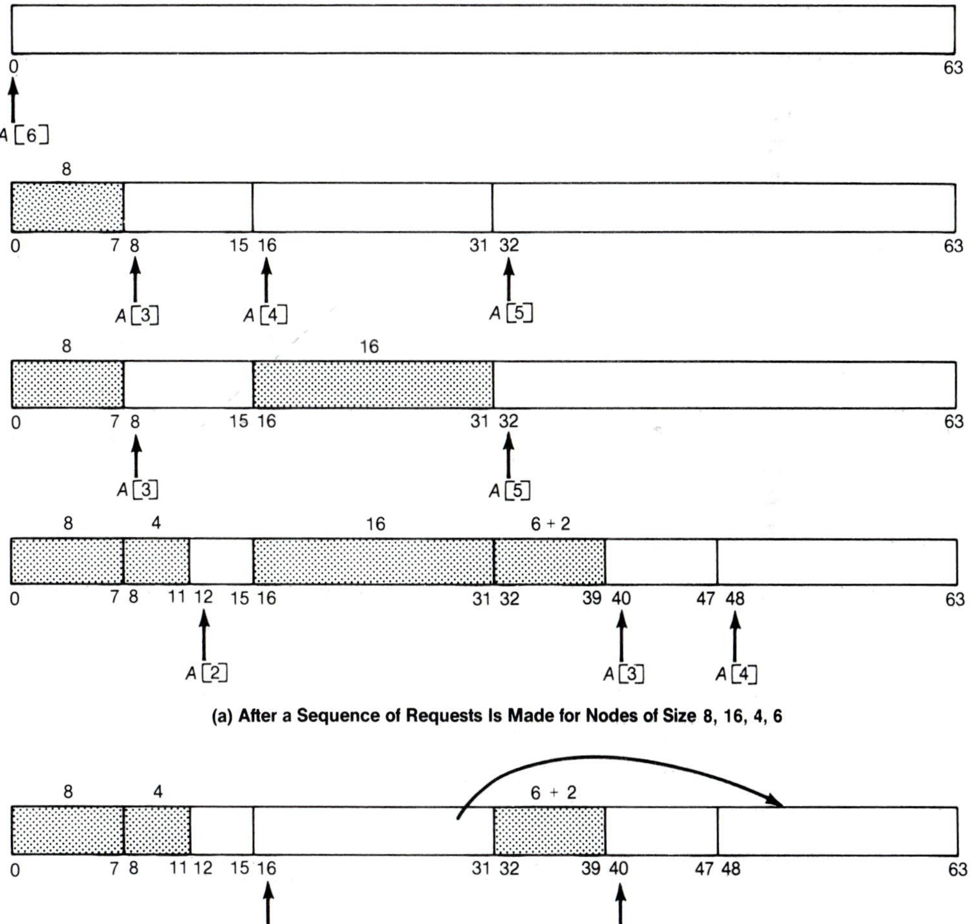

Figure 13.3 Sequence of Memory Configurations for Example 13.6

The sequence of memory configurations is as shown in Figure 13.3(a). If the node of length 16 is now returned, the configuration becomes as shown in Figure 13.3(b).

A[4] is now the head of a list with two nodes, each of length 16. The released node of length 16 starting at address 16 (10000 in binary) has the node of length 16 starting at address 0 (00000 in binary) as its buddy. Since it is not free, it cannot coalesce with it. Neither can it coalesce with the node of length 4 starting at address 12, since that node is not its buddy.

The distribution of nodes can be mirrored by a binary tree. This tree is a kind of derivation tree for nodes currently in existence and expands and contracts as nodes are split and coalesced. The tree shown in Figure 13.4 reflects the configuration for Example 13.6 before the node of length 16 is returned.

Buddies appear as successors of the same parent. Thus [12, 15] and [16, 31], although contiguous in memory, are not buddies and therefore may not be coalesced.

With the buddy system, lists are never actually traversed to find storage to allocate, although time is spent finding the proper list from which to take the storage. The result is quick response to requests and returns. However, in contrast to two-way lists, this scheme produces significant *internal* fragmentation. ***Internal fragmentation*** occurs when allocated nodes are larger than requested, resulting in wasted storage residing within a node. This is one of the drawbacks of the buddy system. Studies have been done on similar schemes that allow a greater variety of node sizes to appear. They also tend to be fast and to reduce storage loss due to internal fragmentation.

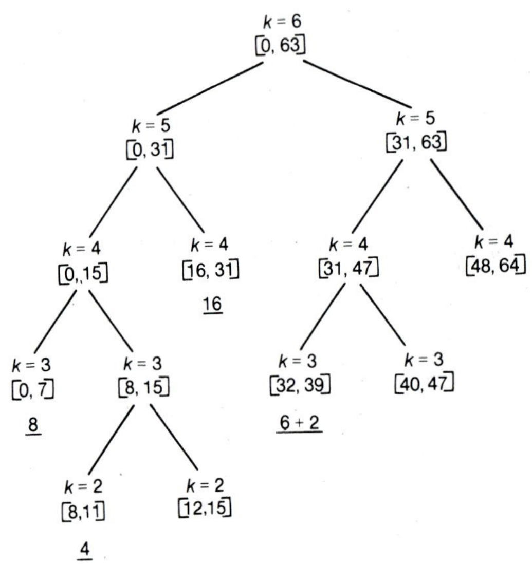

Figure 13.4 Binary Tree Reflecting the Memory Configuration for Example 13.6 Just before Return of Node of Length 16

13.3.3 Indexing Methods

At this point each of the two approaches, circular lists and buddy systems, seems to solve half the problem. Circular lists using the best-fit method utilize storage very efficiently, causing little internal fragmentation. Buddy systems produce significant internal fragmentation but offer fast allocation by narrowly focusing the search for a proper size node. The question is whether it is possible to achieve good storage utilization and allocation time by combining their features. As you would guess, it is. It can be done by using the appropriate structures. The means to do it is called the ***indexing*** approach. The indexing approach breaks up the list of available space into collections of two-way circular lists. Each of these circular lists contains nodes of just one size. Each node on the circular list represents a block of consecutive memory locations available for the storage of a record of the size of the node. Assuming that requests for nodes of sizes (say, 1 to 4) are very frequent, an array a contains pointers to each of the four lists corresponding to these sizes. The last array entry contains a pointer to an AVL tree. The nodes of this tree are circular lists, each list corresponding to nodes of specific size that are requested much less frequently. Thus a[2] contains a pointer to a circular list containing four blocks or nodes, each of size 2. In the AVL tree pointed to by a[5], the root node is a circular list containing three blocks of size 10. The tree is ordered on the basis of node sizes. A typical configuration might be as shown in Figure 13.5.

In this way, a specific request for a node of length less than 5 can be quickly satisfied if the exact matching list is not empty. If it is empty, the next nonempty greater-size list can be used, with one of its nodes truncated to satisfy the request. Any leftover is inserted on the appropriate list. For instance, with the situation of Figure 13.5, a request for a node of size 3 will be satisfied by deleting a node of size 4 from the list pointed to by a[4]. This node will be split into a node of size 3 to satisfy the request, and the leftover node of size 1 inserted on the list pointed to by a[1]. In the infrequent case when the requested node size is 5 or greater, the

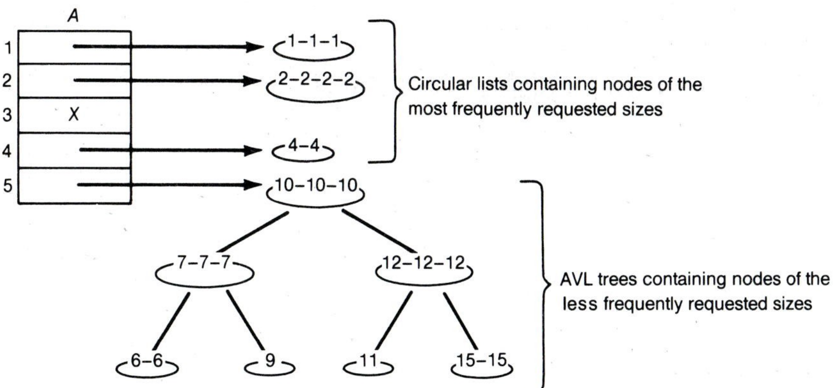

Figure 13.5 An Indexing Array Containing Pointers to Circular Lists and an AVL Tree Storing Circular Lists

AVL tree must be searched similarly. It is clear that this scheme can cause internal fragmentation, but the search times should be fast on the average. In fact the indexing approach is a compromise. It is not as fast as the buddy system but faster than simple circular lists. Likewise, the fragmentation is less than with the buddy system but more than with simple circular lists.

Thus choosing the appropriate scheme of storage management is a difficult task. It requires insight into the kind of request and return distribution involved in a given application. In the worst case all schemes may fail miserably. Intuitively, good performance should result when the distribution of node sizes on the list of available space reflects the distribution of requests and returns. In turn, this distribution should be reflected in the distribution of node sizes actually in use. This is analogous to the situation mentioned in Chapter 12 for the distribution of letters in printer's boxes. The distribution of letter requests is reflected in actual text, and the printer's ordering policy for letters should have caused the contents of the letter boxes to reflect this distribution.

The three techniques considered in this section, and other techniques, are compared extensively in Knuth [1973a] and Standish [1980]. See also Tremblay and Sorenson [1984].

13.4 Shared Storage

When components of data structures are identical and require significant amounts of storage, it is only natural to attempt to avoid component replication. This means that identical components will all share the same storage, so references to each will always be to the same place. As an example, consider Figure 13.6. The

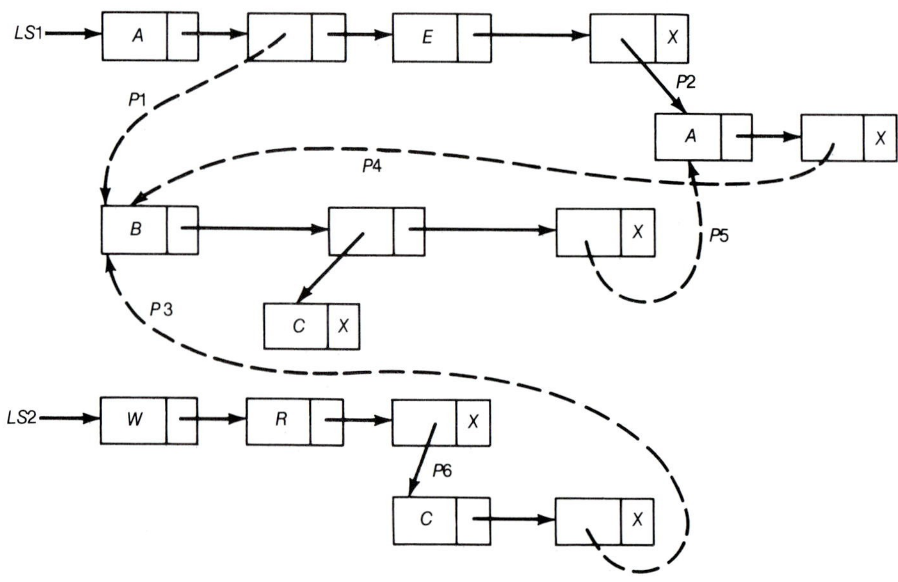

Figure 13.6 A Shared Sublist

two list-structures `ls1` and `ls2` share a common sublist. As a result, `p1`, `p3`, and `p4` point to the shared sublist.

As usual, what we gain in one area we pay for in another. Here, storage is saved, but the price is paid in more complex processing. In particular, suppose the sublist pointed to by `p3` is to be deleted from `ls2` by setting `p3` to null. Since `p1` and `p4` still point to it, it is not valid to return its records' storage to the list of available space, as would be the case without sharing. Deciding when and how to reclaim deleted records or sublists by insertion on the list of available space requires more sophisticated reclamation algorithms than those of Chapter 3.

13.5 Storage Reclamation Techniques

Saying that a node or component of a data structure is to be reclaimed for use means that the storage used for its records is to become known to the **avail** function. That is, the storage no longer needed by its records is to be inserted on the list of available space. There are two basic methods of reclaiming released nodes, ***garbage collection*** and ***reference counters.*** Other methods are essentially combinations of these. These methods are the two extremes with respect to the time at which storage is reclaimed. Garbage collection does not make storage available for reuse until it is needed, putting off reclamation as long as possible. Reference counters make storage available for reuse as soon as it actually becomes reclaimable.

13.5.1 Garbage Collection

The ***garbage collection*** method of reclamation is used when the available space list is empty or when the amount of storage that is known to **avail** becomes less than some given amount. Until that time, whenever a sublist is to be deleted from a data structure, the deletion is accomplished by updating appropriate pointers, but the storage vacated by the sublist's deletion is not made known. Initially, all records are assumed to be unmarked. The garbage collection routine works by traversing each data structure that is in use and "marking" each one of its records as being in use.

To accomplish this properly, the garbage collector program must know the names of all data structures in use. We have assumed that these are accessible through variables outside the heap. After marking, every record of the heap that is not marked will be made known (that is, placed on the available space list). Every record that is marked will be reset to unmarked so that the garbage collector will work properly on its next call. The marking phase of the garbage collector works by traversing all data structures in use. Thus marking routines generally take execution time proportional to the number of records in use and are therefore slow. Similarly, the collection routine, which inserts the unmarked records on the list of available space, takes time proportional to the heap size.

Example 13.7 Apply garbage collection to the heap of Example 13.4. ■

In the marking phase, the garbage collection would traverse `l` and `t`, marking all their nodes. The collection phase would then traverse the heap and collect all unmarked nodes on the available space list. Assuming the garbage collector recognizes when two unmarked nodes are adjacent and combines them into a larger node, the resultant heap would appear as shown in Figure 13.7. A better approach might be to garbage collect and compact together, thus producing an available list consisting of one large block, reducing fragmentation.

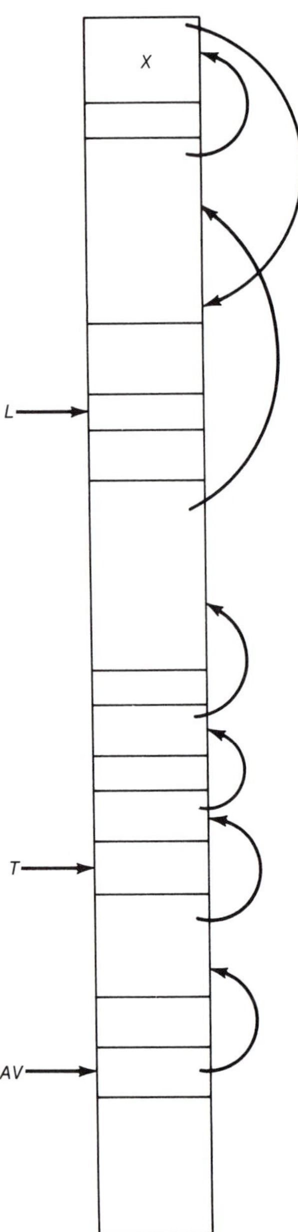

Figure 13.7 Heap from Example 13.4 after Garbage Collection

13.5.2 The Reference Counter Method

The ***reference counter method*** assumes that the first record of every sublist in use has information giving the number of pointers that point to it. This number is called the ***reference count*** of the sublist. The pointers can be stored in the name variables or in sublist fields of complex records. A "smart" header record may be used for this purpose. It is assumed here that only sublists may be shared. Each time a new pointer refers to a sublist, the reference count of the sublist must be increased by 1. Each time a pointer that refers to a sublist is changed so that it no longer points to that sublist, the reference count of the sublist must be decreased by 1. After a decrease that leaves the reference count at zero, the storage for records of the sublist may be made known. Again, a data structure traversal may be used to determine which storage elements are to be made known. No traversal algorithm has been given in this text for data structures that allow sublist sharing. Such algorithms differ from the list-structure traversal algorithm because of the possibility of looping or revisiting records. As an exercise you should modify the list-structure traversals of Chapter 6 to work for this more general case. The idea is to mark each accessed record and make sure that marked records are not revisited.

Deletion of a sublist whose reference count has become zero is similar to the traversal of successor lists for an object that has been removed from the bag in the topological sort algorithm. The sublist must be traversed and, in addition to the storage for all records being inserted on the list of available space, each sublist pointed to by a record must have its reference count decremented by 1.

Example 13.8 Associate reference counts with the first record of each of the sublists of Figure 13.6. The list-structures with associated reference counts would appear as shown in Figure 13.8. ■

Suppose `p1` is set to null. The reference count of its sublist would be reduced to 2. Since it has not gone to zero, no storage is available for reclamation. If `p6` is then set to null, the reference count of its sublist would be reduced to 0. Its storage could be reclaimed. This would require that `p3`'s sublist have its reference count reduced by 1. The result would be as shown in Figure 13.8(b).

A problem can occur with the reference counter method whenever loops appear, as demonstrated in the following example.

Example 13.9 Consider the loop in `ls1` of Figure 13.9. What happens when `p1`, `p2`, and `p3` of Figure 13.6 no longer reference the sublist? Then this sublist has no variables referencing it. It cannot be accessed, since we do not know where it is. It is serving no useful purpose, yet its storage was not reclaimed, since the reference count of records 1 and 2 never went to zero. This problem is analogous to the existence of loops in the input for a topological sort. Such unused storage, or garbage, can accumulate and clog the memory. ■

It is possible to share individual records as well as sublists. In this case, garbage collection will still work, as will the reference counter method. Now,

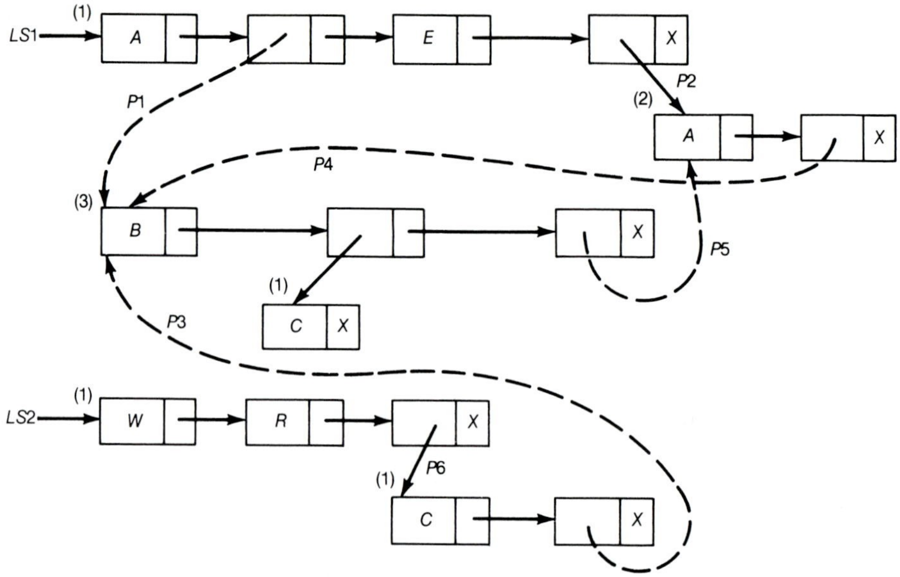

(a) Initial List Structures with Reference Counts

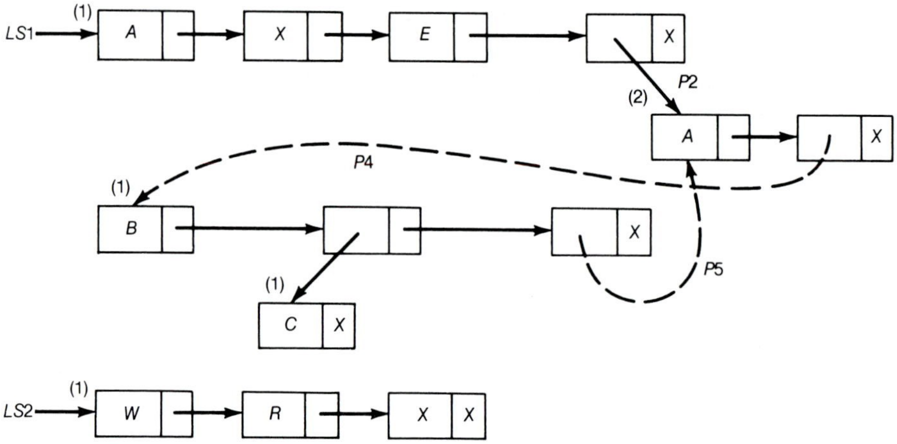

(b) Final List Structures with Reference Counts

Figure 13.8 List-structures of Figure 13.6 with Associated Reference Counts

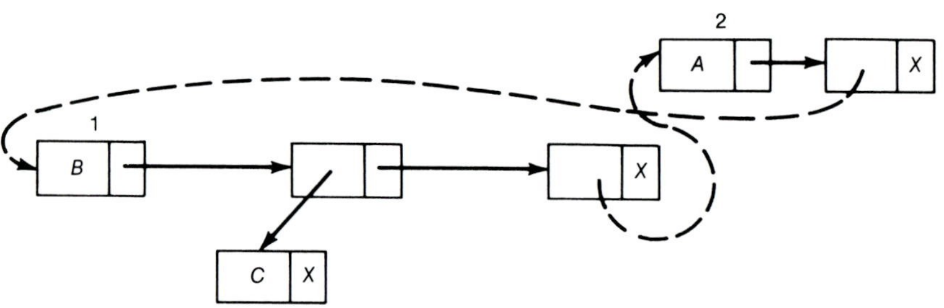

Figure 13.9 A Lost Loop

however, the individual records (not just the sublists) must have reference counters associated with them, requiring additional storage and updating overhead. Loops may cause the same problems for shared records as for shared sublists.

13.5.3 Overview of Storage Reclamation

There is a spectrum of reclamation techniques, but the two basic underlying approaches are garbage collection and reference counters. Garbage collection represents one extreme. Nodes that are no longer needed in a dynamic data structure are deleted from the structure, thus becoming garbage. They are not returned at that time to the list of available space, even though they are then reusable. Reference counters, at the other extreme, return such unused nodes to the list of available space as soon as possible, when their reference counters become zero. These methods of reclamation are done implicitly by the programming language in conjunction with the operating system.

In addition, programmer control allows the programmer to use commands signaling that nodes are no longer needed by a dynamic data structure. The nodes may then be returned to the list of available space directly, left for garbage collection, or, if reference counters are used, their reference counts will be decremented and tested for possible return to the list of available space. In C the standard library function `free` can be used for such signaling.

In the design of a specific reclamation system, a number of trade-offs are possible. For example, reference counters require additional storage and additional time to increment, decrement, or test when insertions and deletions occur. However, they do not always work. The reason is that garbage can accumulate when loops are present in the dynamic data structures (as in Example 13.9). If the amount of garbage generated in this way is significant, it can limit the size of the problem that can be solved. Still, reference counters allow the reclamation process to be spread over time. Garbage collection, in contrast, occasionally requires a relatively large block of time. Garbage collection is a more complex technique, involving more sophisticated algorithms. Recall that when garbage collection is invoked, even though many available nodes may exist, they are not known. It is not possible simply to look at a node of the heap to determine if it is in use.

To summarize, garbage collection works in two phases. The first phase, or marking phase, requires the traversal of all dynamic data structures in existence. Recall that the heads of such structures are assumed to be known. Initially, whether in use or not, every node has a field that is marked "unused." As each node of a dynamic data structure is accessed in the traversal, it is marked "used." When the marking phase is completed, the heap then consists of nodes that are marked "unused" and nodes that are marked "used." Consequently, it is now possible to look at a node and determine its status. The second phase, or collection phase, involves a traversal through the nodes of the heap. Each node marked "unused" is inserted on the list of available space. Each node marked "used" is merely marked "unused" so that the garbage collector will work correctly the next time it is invoked.

The marking algorithms known are quite elegant. The traversal of the dynamic data structures cannot simply use a stack, since no nodes are known in which to implement the stack. Instead, these algorithms allow the traversals to be accomplished by using tag fields, usually one bit, associated with each node. It is even possible to do the traversals with no tag fields, with a fixed amount of additional storage required. Of course, if we had an infinite amount of storage available, no reclamation would be necessary. Storage management would be trivial! The next section features three traversal algorithms for use in phase I of the garbage collector, or in other applications where storage is at a premium. See Pratt [1975] for more on storage management. The algorithms to be discussed next and generalizations are also given in Standish [1980].

13.6 Stackless Traversals

Garbage collection routines require the traversal of dynamic data structures that are more general than binary trees, such as list-structures and more complex lists. Algorithms for their traversal are generalizations of those we consider. For increased clarity, we will restrict our discussion to binary tree traversals and present three techniques that do not use extra storage for a stack.

These algorithms may be written assuming a particular binary tree implementation, such as arrays or pointer variables. Instead, to emphasize data abstraction and functional modularity, the following function, which is independent of the tree implementation, has been chosen. The function is a preorder traversal saving the path from the root on the stack.

```
preorder(pt)
/* Preorder traverses the binary tree. */
binarytreepointer *pt;
{
   binarytreepointer null,p,lptr,rptr;
   binarytreepointer setnull(),left(),right(),nextsubtree();
   stack s;
   null = setnull();
   p = *pt;                           ] initializes the current subtree to be
                                        traversed to t
   setstack(&s);
   while(p != null)                   ] test for completion of the traversal
      {
         process(pt,p);               ] process the current node p
         lptr = left(p);              ] set lptr to the left subtree of p
         if(lptr != null)             ] if the left subtree is not null
            {
               push(p,&s);            ] save p on the stack
               p = lptr;              ] set p to the left subtree
            }
         else                         ] otherwise
            {
               rptr = right(p);       ] set rptr to the right subtree of p
               if(rptr != null)       ] if it is not null
                  {
                     push(p,&s);      ] save p on the stack
```

```
                    p = rptr;                      ] set p to the right subtree
                }
            else                                   ] otherwise
                p = nextsubtree(&s,&p);            ] set p to the next nonnull right subtree to
        }                                            be traversed
    }
}
```

For each traversal, the basic concept is described. Then the appropriate implementation for the routines of the procedure is described.

Consider the binary tree of Figure 13.10, and suppose `node.p` has just been processed during the traversal using the `preorder` procedure. The stack will contain pointers `p1`, `p2`, `p3`, `p4`, `p5`, `p6`, and `p7`. At this point, the traversal of the left subtree of `node.p4` has been completed. The purpose of the `nextsubtree(&s,&p)` function in the preorder traversal algorithms is to find `node.p4`, to allow the traversal to pick up at its right subtree. In general, whenever the stack is not empty, a null `p` value signifies the completion of the traversal of the left subtree of some node. The traversal must then pick up at that node's right subtree. There may be more than one such node; it is the most recent that must be found. The stack allows this node, and its right subtree, to be found conveniently. `Nextsubtree(&s,&p)` is called after the terminal node pointed to by `p` has been processed. It finds the nonnull right subtree that must be traversed next, returns a pointer to it, and updates the stack to reflect the path from that subtree's root to the root of the tree. If no such nonnull right subtree exists, then it returns a null value. Each of the tree traversals we now consider actually uses stack information, but it is, in effect, stored in the tree, eliminating the requirement for additional stack storage. The `preorder` procedure treats the tree as a data abstraction, so it is independent of the tree implementation.

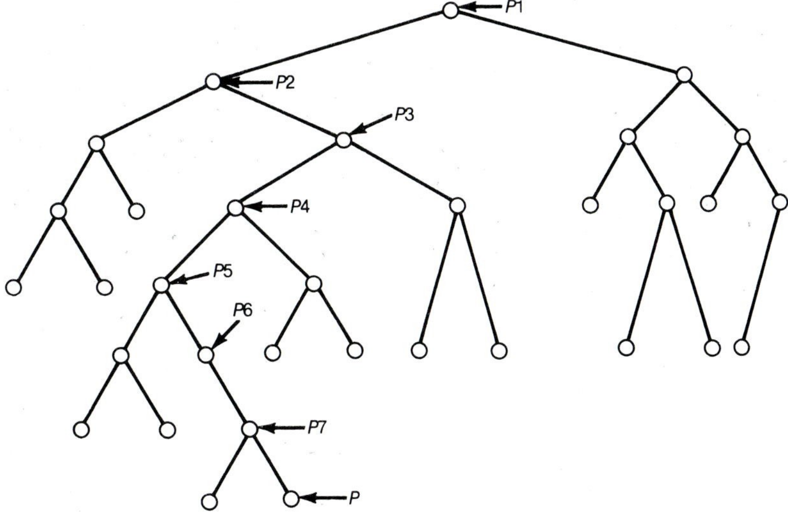

Figure 13.10 A Binary Tree *T*

13.6.1 Threaded Trees

A ***threaded tree*** implementation of the `preorder` traversal procedure is shown in Figure 13.11. It resulted from the replacement of the null left and right pointer field values of each node `t` by a pointer to the predecessor and to the successor, respectively, of that node in an inorder traversal of `t`. These pointers are called ***threads.*** The "leftmost" node of `t` does not have a predecessor, and the "rightmost" node of `t` does not have a successor. Their left and right null pointers, respectively, are left unchanged and are not considered threads. We assume that a field is associated with each node to indicate whether the node contains threads in its left link field, in its right link field, in both, or in neither.

To preorder traverse threaded trees, proceed as before, but whenever a node with threads is reached, follow its right pointer. This pointer leads directly to the node whose right subtree must then be preorder traversed. Notice, for example, that the right thread of `node.p` points to `node.p4`. The traversal is complete when a null right thread is encountered. Threaded trees may also be easily inorder and postorder traversed.

Procedure `preorder` may be used for the traversal of a threaded tree, with `stack` declared to be of type `binarytreepointer`, by implementing its routines as follows:

Routine	Task
`setnull()`	determined by the implementation (array or pointer variables)
`setstack(&s)`	sets `s` to null
`push(p,&s)`	sets `s` to `p`
`left(p)`	returns a copy of `leftptr.p` if it is not a thread, and a null value otherwise
`right(p)`	similar to `left(p)`

`nextsubtree(&s,&p)`	set `s` to `p`
	while (`rightptr.s` is a thread),
	`set s` to `rightptr.s`
	return a copy of `rightptr.s`

13.6.2 Link Inversion

Now consider the tree of Figure 13.12. It represents the binary tree `t` of Figure 13.10 during a ***link-inversion traversal*** after `node.p` has been processed. Notice that a path exists in the tree from `predp` back to the root. Each node has a tag field associated with it, and all tag values are initially zero. `Predp` always points to the predecessor of `p` in `t`, and every node on the path from `predp` to the root has its right pointer field pointing to its predecessor if its tag field is 1, and its left pointer field pointing to its predecessor if its tag field is 0. The root of the subtree whose left subtree traversal is complete after the processing of `p` may be found by following the backward links from `predp` until a tag value of 0 is encountered. As the path back is followed, a tag of 1 at a predecessor node means we are coming from the node's right subtree. A tag of 0 means we are coming from the left subtree. Again, for `node.p` this leads to `node.p4`.

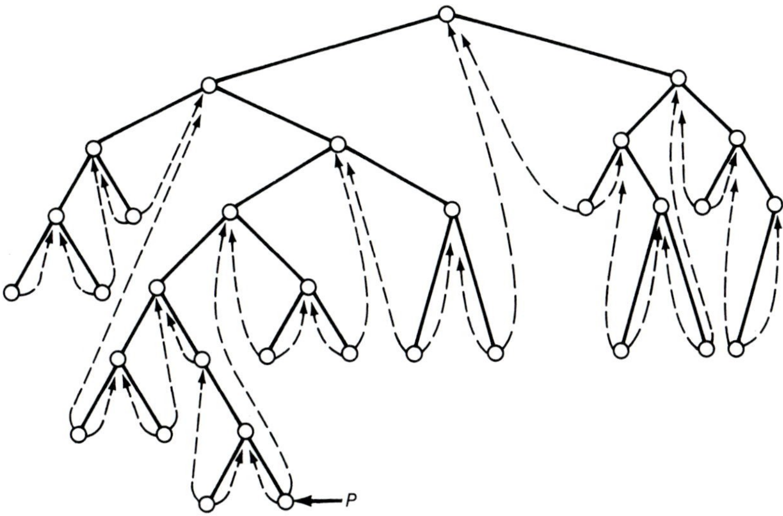

Figure 13.11 A Threaded Implementation of the Binary Tree *T*

Using the backward links with appropriate tag values to preserve the path to the root is the essential concept of a link-inversion traversal. During the traversal, the creation of appropriate links must be handled. For example, as the path to `node.p4` is traversed, after `p` has been processed, the nodes with `tag` values of 1 must have their correct right pointer values restored. Then when `node.p4` is found (`tag` = 0), its correct left pointer value must be restored, its tag field set to 1, its right pointer field set to its predecessor, and `predp` and `p` correctly updated

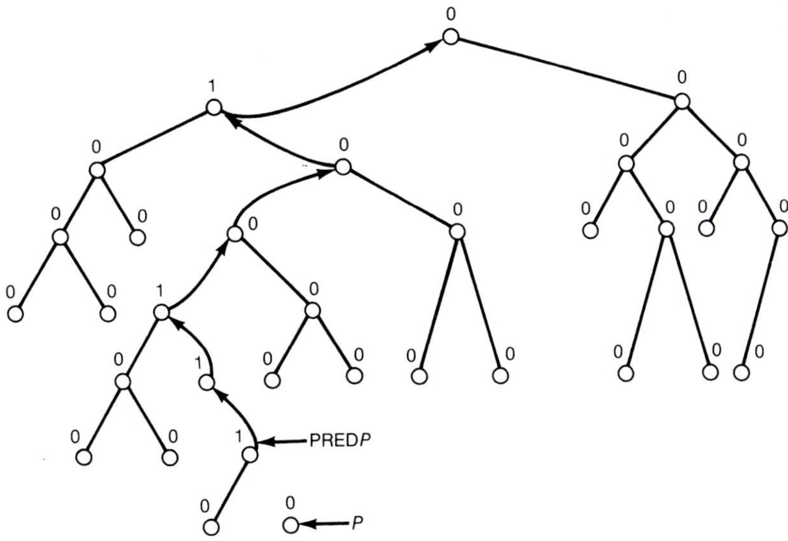

Figure 13.12 A Link-inverted Binary Tree *T*

before `node.p4`'s right subtree is traversed. The traversal is complete when the backtracking leads to a null `predp` value. Figure 13.13 shows the state of the tree just before `node.p4`'s right subtree is traversed. `Node.p` must now be processed, then its left pointer field must be set to its predecessor, `predp` updated to `p`, and `p` updated to the left pointer value of `node.p`. The traversal then continues with the left subtree of `p`. Initially, `p` must be set to `t` and `predp` to null.

Procedure `preorder` may be used for the link-inversion traversal if `stack` is declared to be of type `binarytreepointer`, and its routines are implemented as follows.

Routine	Task
`setnull()`	determined by the implementation
`setstack(&s)`	set `s` to null

`push(p,&s)`	if `leftptr.p` is not null, then
	    set `leftptr.p` to `s` and `s` to `p`
	else
	    set `tag(p)` to 1, set `rightptr.p` to `s` and `s` to `p`

`left(p)`	returns a copy of `leftptr.p`
`right(p)`	returns a copy of `rightptr.p`

`nextsubtree(&s,&p)`	set `found` to false
	while((not `found`) and (`s` not null))
	    if `tag(s)` = 1, then
	        set `pred` to `s`
	        set `tag(s)` to 0, `s` to `rightptr.s`,
	        `rightptr.pred` to `p`, and `p` to `pred`
	    else
	        set `pred` to `leftptr.s` and `leftptr.s` to `p`
	        if `rightptr.s` null, then
	            set `found` to true, `tag(s)` to 1, return
	            `rightptr.s`, and set `rightptr.s` to
	            `pred`
	        else
	            set `p` to `s`, set `s` to `pred`
	if `s` = null, then
	    return null.

In this implementation `s` plays the role of `predp`.

In a stack traversal, the storage required for the stack is proportional to the depth of the traversed tree. In the threaded-tree and link-inversion traversals, storage is not required for the stack but is required for the tag fields. This storage may actually be available, but unused, because of the implementation of the tree records. In this case, using it for the tag fields costs nothing. Otherwise, the additional storage is proportional to the number of nodes in the traversed tree. For the stack traversal, the constant of proportionality is given by the length of the pointer fields, while in the threaded-tree and link-inversion traversals it is given by the length of the tag fields.

The threaded-tree traversal is simpler than the link-inversion traversal and does not disturb the tree itself during the traversal. This allows more than one

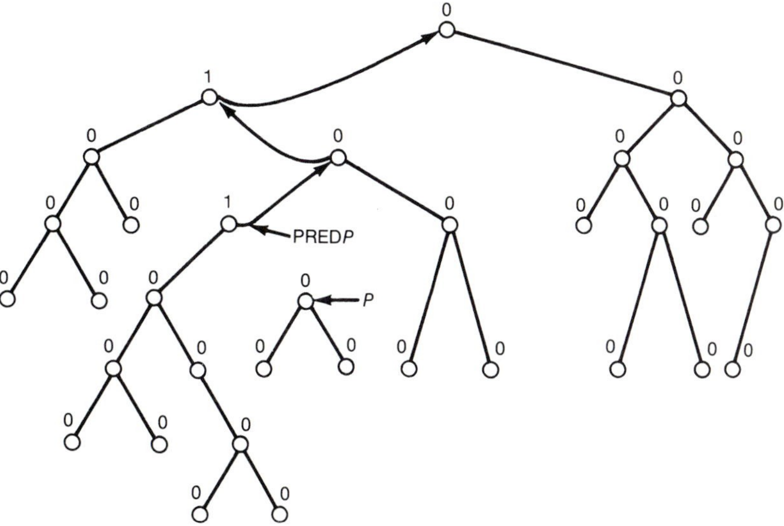

Figure 13.13 New State before Subtree Pointed to by *P* Is Traversed in Binary Tree *T*

program to access the tree concurrently. However, the insertion and deletion of nodes in a threaded tree is more complex and time-consuming. Inorder and postorder traversals may also be done using link inversion.

13.6.3 Robson Traversal

It is remarkable that an algorithm has been found which does not require a stack or even tag fields. This is the ***Robson traversal,*** the final stackless traversal we consider. Again, we give a preorder version, although it may be used for inorder and postorder traversals as well.

Consider the tree of Figure 13.14. In the link-inversion traversal, for every descent to the left from `node.p` (that is, every traversal of the left subtree of `node.p`), the left pointer field of `node.p` was set to point to `node.p`'s predecessor. For every descent to the right (to traverse the right subtree of `node.p`), the leftpointer of `node.p` was restored to its original value, the `tag` of `node.p` was set to 1, and the right pointer field of `node.p` was set to point to `node.p`'s predecessor. Consequently, having completed the traversal of the left subtree of some node `q`, it was possible to follow the backward pointing pointers to get to `q`. `Q` was the first node encountered with a tag value of 0, on the path back.

The Robson traversal does not have tag fields available for this purpose. Instead, a stack is kept in the tree itself, which will allow node `q` to be found. `Q` is the root of the *most recent* subtree, whose nonnull left subtree has already been traversed and whose nonnull right subtree is in the process of being traversed. A variable `top` is used, and kept updated, to point to the current node `q`. A variable `stack` is used, and kept updated, to point to the *next most recent* subtree whose nonnull left subtree has already been traversed and whose nonnull right subtree is in the process of being traversed. Variables `p` and `predp` are used, as in link

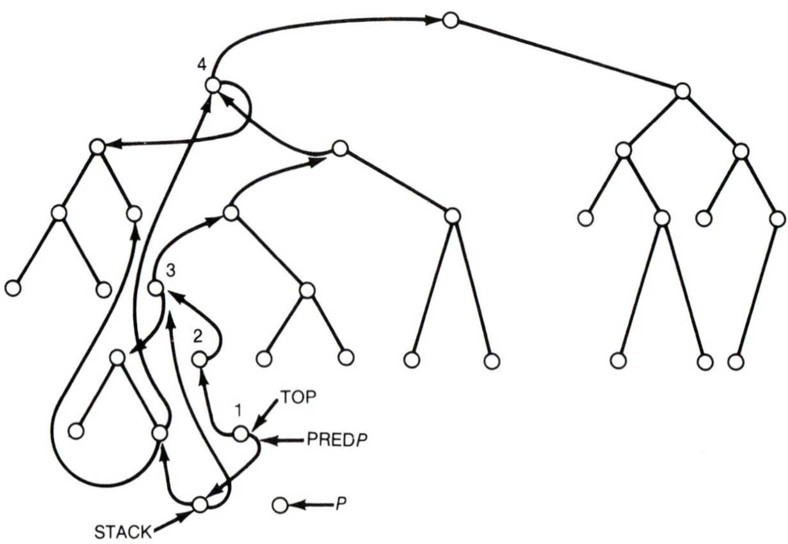

Figure 13.14 Robson Traversal Configuration of the Binary Tree *T*

inversion, to point to the node currently being processed and to its predecessor, respectively. Each stack entry, except the current top entry, is kept in the "rightmost" terminal node of one of the subtrees whose nonnull left subtree has been completely traversed, and whose nonnull right subtree is in the process of being traversed. In Figure 13.14, when `node.p` is being processed, there are four subtrees whose left subtrees have already been traversed and whose right subtrees are currently being traversed. Their roots are labeled 1 to 4 in Figure 13.14. Nodes 1, 3, and 4 have nonnull left subtrees. Each of these nodes has its left pointer field pointing to its predecessor and its right pointer pointing to the root of its left subtree. Node 2, which has a null left subtree, has its original null value, and its right pointer field is pointing to its predecessor. Nodes 1, 3, and 4 are thus the roots that must have stack entries. `Top` points to the most recent, node 1. `Stack` points to the stack entry corresponding to the next most recent root, node 3. This stack entry is kept in the rightmost terminal node of node 1's left subtree. This rightmost node has its left pointer field pointing to the node that contains the next stack entry, and its right pointer field pointing to its corresponding root (node 3 in this case). All stack entries (except the first, pointed to by `top`) have this same format. In Figure 13.14, the last stack entry points to node 4.

Notice that a path back to the root always exists from `node.predp`. In Figure 13.14, after `node.p` is processed, the traversal of node 1's right subtree has been completed. This also completes the traversal of the right subtrees of nodes 2 and 3 and the left subtree of node 3's predecessor. The Robson traversal now proceeds by following the backward path, restoring appropriate left or right subtrees along the way, until the predecessor of node 3 is encountered. At this point, its right subtree must be traversed. Figure 13.15 shows the situation just before that traversal. During the traversal of the backward path, if `node.predp`

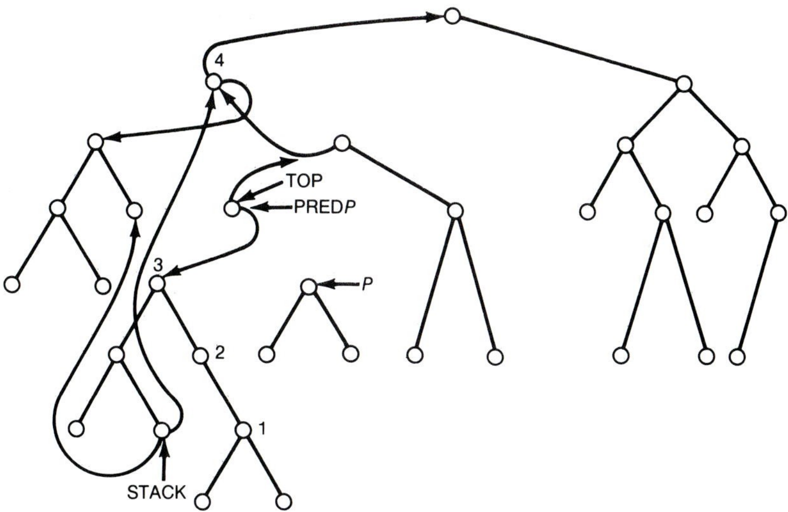

Figure 13.15 Robson Traversal before *P* Is Processed in the Binary Tree *T*

has a null right subtree, or `top=predp`, then we are coming from the left subtree of `node.predp`, otherwise from the right subtree. Thus the stack entries allow node `q` to be found even though no tag fields are used.

During the backtracking, the stack is popped, and `top` is updated as necessary. `Top` and `stack` are initialized to null, `predp` to null, and `p` to `t`. An additional variable `avail` is used and updated to point to a terminal node every time one is encountered, so that its pointer fields are available if a new stack entry must be created. In this case, the available node must retain a pointer to `node.top` in its right pointer field and a pointer to the current entry to which `stack` points in its left pointer field; `stack` must be updated to point to the new entry; and `top` must be updated to point to the new top root. At all times, the path from `predp` back to the root is stored in the tree, as well as the stack of entries pointing to roots of subtrees (with nonnull left subtrees), whose left subtree traversals have completed, and whose right subtrees are being traversed. Each node along the path from `predp` to the root is in one of the following states:

```
If the node's left subtree is being traversed, then
    its left pointer is pointing to its predecessor, and its right pointer is undisturbed.
If the node's right subtree is being traversed, then
    if the node has a null left subtree, then
        its right pointer is pointing to its predecessor
    else
        its left pointer is pointing to its predecessor, and its right pointer is pointing to
        the root of the node's left subtree.
```

The following routines are to be used with the preorder traversal so that it implements the Robson traversal. `Stack` is declared to be of the same type as `binarytreepointer`, and `s` plays the role of `predp`.

Routine	Task
`setnull()`	determined by the implementation
`setstack(&s)`	sets `top`, `stack`, and `s` to null

`push(p,&s)`	if `leftptr.p` is not null then
	    set `leftptr.p` to `s` and `s` to `p`
	else
	    set `rightptr.p` to `s` and `s` to `p`

`left(p)`	returns a copy of `leftptr.p`
`right(p)`	returns a copy of `rightptr.p`

`nextsubtree(&s,&p)`	set `avail` to `p`
	set `found` to false
	while((not `found`) and (`s` not null))
	    if `top` = `s`, then
	        save `stack` in `hold`, pop the stack by setting `top` to `rightptr.stack`, `stack` to `leftptr.stack`, and `leftptr.hold` and `rightptr.hold` to null. Save `leftptr.s` in `pred`, restore `leftptr.s` by setting it to `rightptr.s`, restore `rightptr.s` by setting it to `p`, set `p` to `s`, and `s` to `pred`
	    else
	        if `leftptr.s` = null, then
	            save `rightptr.s` in `pred`, restore `rightptr.s` by setting it to `p`, set `p` to `s`, and `s` to `pred`
	        else
	            if `rightptr.s` null, then
	                push an entry for `s` onto the stack by setting `leftptr.avail` to `stack`, `rightptr.avail` to `top`, `stack` to `avail`, and `top` to `s`. Return the value of `rightptr.s`, set `rightptr.s` to `p`, and set `found` to *true*
	            else
	                save `leftptr.s` in `pred`, restore `leftptr.s` by setting it to `p`, set `p` to `s`, and `s` to `pred`.
	if `s` = null, then
	    return null.

13.7 Pitfalls: Garbage Generation and Dangling References

This chapter has shown how a list of available space can be maintained to keep track of storage known to be currently unused. Storage may be allocated dynamically, during program execution, by deleting appropriate elements from this list when needed.

The need and means for storage reclamation have also been discussed. Garbage collection and reference counter techniques (or some combination) may be used for this purpose. When a node of a binary tree, a list, or other dynamic data structure is not needed, the programmer frequently knows at what point this occurs. Some high-level languages allow commands to be used by the programmer to signal this occurrence. For example, C provides the function **free**. Like **malloc** (and other allocation functions), its parameter will be a pointer type variable. When **p** points to a node that the programmer knows is no longer needed, **free(p)** may be invoked. This signals that the storage pointed to by **p** may be relinquished and reclaimed for use for another dynamically allocated data structure. Exactly how **free** uses this information is determined by the compiler.

High-level languages are usually designed with particular storage management schemes in mind. However, the language specifications, or standards, do not normally specify that these schemes must be used. It is possible for a compiler to use garbage collection or reference counters, to leave the reclamation entirely to the programmer, or to use some combination. If necessary programmers may even write their own programs to manage storage. We will not discuss these problems further except to illustrate two potential dangers.

Consider the following disaster segment as an illustration of these dangers.

```
(1)    p = q;
(2)    r = malloc(sizeof(binarytreerecord));
(3)    r -> leftptr = tree;
(4)    free(tree);
(5)    process(&s);
(6)    s -> leftptr = lefttree;
```

Suppose **p**, **q**, **r**, **s**, **lefttree**, and **tree** are all pointer variables pointing to nodes of the same type. Before the segment is executed, the situation might be as shown in Figure 13.16(a). Statement (1), when executed, results in the situation sketched in Figure 13.16(b).

The tree, pointed to by **p** originally, now has no pointer pointing to it. Hence there is no way the program can access any of its nodes. Also, the storage allocated to this tree, while no longer in use, has not been returned to the list of available space. Unless the storage management technique uses garbage collection or reference counters, that storage is lost. It cannot be accessed and will never be returned to the list of available space. It truly has become *garbage*. If **free(p)** had been invoked before statement (1), this might have been avoided, depending on whether **free** recognizes that the other nodes of the tree may also be returned. If **free** merely returns the storage for the node to which **p** points, this could have been avoided only by the programmer traversing the tree pointed to by **p** and "freeing" each of its nodes.

Suppose, instead, that **free** uses reference counters and, recognizing that the tree pointed to by **p** has no other references, returns its storage to the list of available space. Now statement (2) is executed. The result is shown in Figure 13.16(c).

After statement (4) is executed, assuming that **free** simply returns the storage allocated to the node pointed to by **tree** to the list of available space, we get Figure 13.16(e). However, the node pointed to by **r→leftptr** is now on the list of available space. **R→leftptr** is called a ***dangling reference*** because it points to a node that is on the list of available space. When **process** is invoked

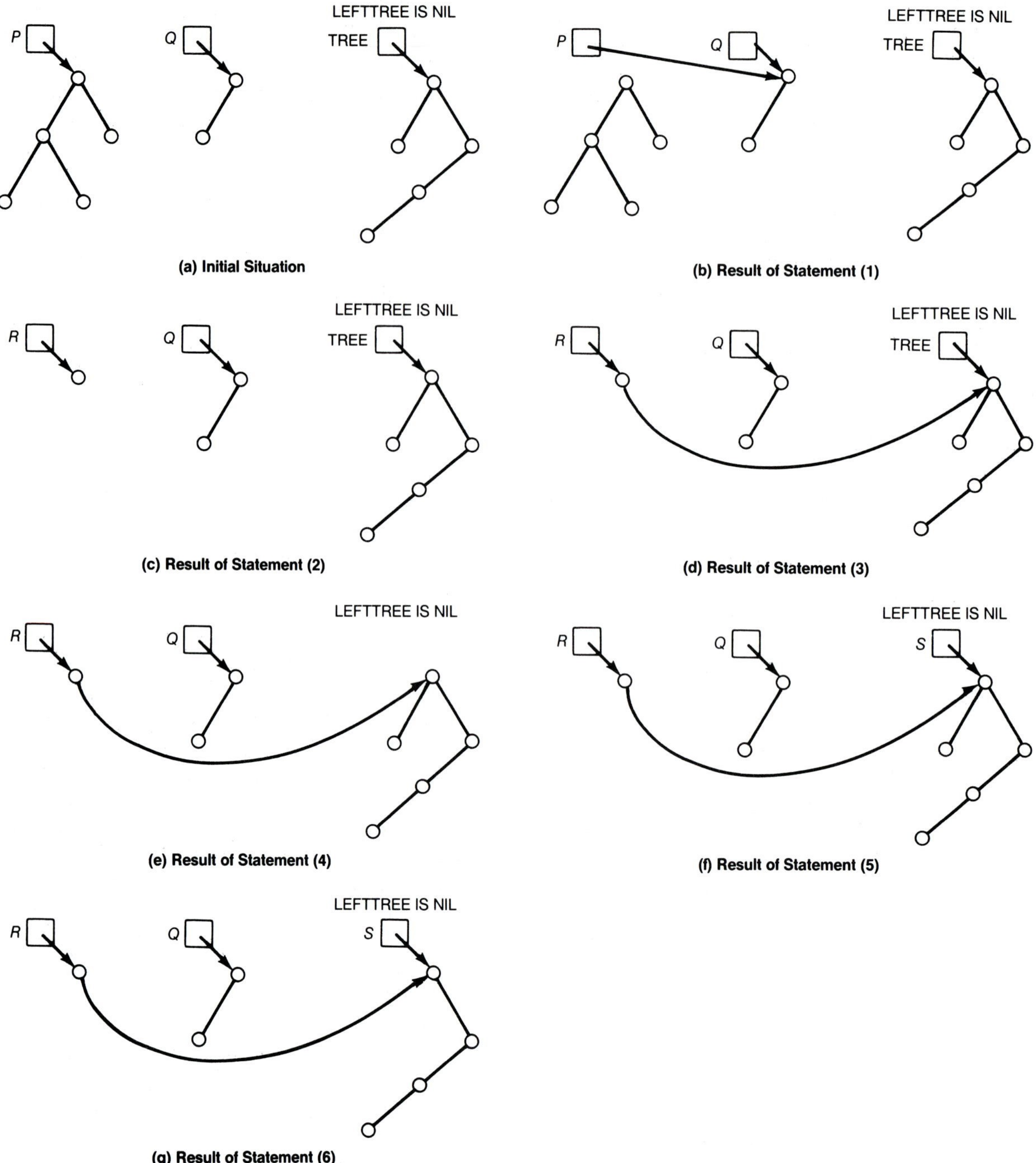

Figure 13.16 Simulation of the Disaster Segment

in statement (5), it is possible that it invokes `malloc`, so storage is allocated to `s`. Then we have the situation shown in Figure 13.16(f).

Statement (6) produces Figure 13.16(g). The binary tree that `r` now points to has been changed, because of the dangling reference. The programmer, unaware that this has occurred, may find the program's output incorrect and be unable to determine what went wrong. This is especially difficult to discover, since the next time the program executes, `process` may not need to invoke `malloc`. Even if it does, the storage allocated by `malloc` to `s` might not cause this problem. Still, the programmer may not realize that an error has occurred.

Of the two problems, garbage generation and dangling reference generation, the latter is more serious. Garbage generation may cause longer execution time, or, at worst, program failure. Dangling references, however, may cause serious errors undetected by the programmer.

13.8 Conclusion

Dynamic data structures require dynamic storage allocation and reclamation. This may be accomplished by the programmer or may be done implicitly by a high-level language. It is important to understand the fundamentals of storage management because these techniques have significant impact on the behavior of programs. The basic idea is to keep a pool of memory elements that may be used to store components of dynamic data structures when needed.

Allocated storage may be returned to the pool when no longer needed. In this way, it may be used and reused. This contrasts sharply with static allocation, in which storage is dedicated for the use of static data structures. It cannot then be reclaimed for other uses, even when not needed for the static data structure. As a result, dynamic allocation makes it possible to solve larger problems that might otherwise be storage-limited.

Garbage collection and reference counters are two basic techniques for implementing storage management. Combinations of these techniques may also be designed. Explicit programmer control is also possible. Potential pitfalls of these techniques are garbage generation, dangling references, and fragmentation.

High-level language may take most of the burden for storage management from the programmer. The concept of pointers or pointer variables underlies the use of these facilities, and complex algorithms are required for their implementation.

■ Exercises

1. a. Consider the Suggested Assignments of Chapter 11. Suppose only 200 memory elements are available for `lists` to store successors. Given an example of a problem with fewer than twenty objects for which the implementation of Assignment 1 will work but the implementation of Assignment 2 will fail. Assume `count` and `succ` have length 20, the `lists` array of (1) has length 200, and the `lists` array of (2) is 20×10.

b. Can you find such an example for which Assignment 2 works but Assignment 1 fails?

2. a. Consider two implementations. First, a total of 50 memory elements in an array are to be dynamically allocated and reclaimed so that a binary tree (in linked representation) as well as a stack may be stored in the array. Second, an array of length 35 is to hold the binary tree, and another array of length 15 is to implement the stack. Each array is dynamically managed. The binary tree is to be preorder traversed using the stack. Give an example of a binary tree, with fewer than 35 nodes, that may be successfully traversed with the first implementation but not the second.

b. Suppose that after a node is accessed and processed, its storage may be reclaimed. Give an example of a binary tree with fewer than 35 nodes that may be successfully traversed with the first implementation but not the second.

3. In Exercise 1, the `lists` array of (1) functioned as a heap. Why was its storage management so simple?

4. In Exercise 2, the arrays functioned as heaps. Why was the first implementation able to do traversals that the second could not do?

5. In the first implementation of Exercise 2(b), suppose that, after a node is accessed and processed, it is simply put onto the available space list.

a. Is the head of the tree a dangling reference?

b. Are fixed-size or variable-size nodes being dealt with?

c. After your answer to Exercise 2(b) is traversed, what will be garbage, and what will be on the list of available space?

6. This is the same as Exercise 5, except that, after a node is accessed and processed, it is not put onto the available space list. After the binary tree has been traversed, the head of the tree is set to null.

7. Why is compaction not necessary with fixed-size nodes?

8. Suppose Example 13.3 deals with three binary trees. Each node has an integer valued `info`, `leftptr`, and `rightptr` field. The stack needs elements that are also integer valued. An integer array of length `l` is used as a heap in which nodes of the binary trees and the stack are stored. Assume one additional field is used for each node to indicate its length. Design a storage allocation scheme and write an appropriate `avail` function.

9. a. Suppose in Exercise 8 that when a node of a binary tree is deleted, its predecessor node will be changed to point to the left successor of the deleted node. Write a function `delete` that carries out this deletion and also returns the storage used by the deleted node to a list of available space.

b. How would the `delete` function change if reference counters were used as a reclamation scheme?

10. Write `avail` for the two-way circular list implementation for

a. Randomly ordered list entries.

b. List entries in order by size

c. List entries in order by address

11. Write `avail` for the buddy system implementation.

12. Write a `reclaim` function for the buddy system.

13. Why will garbage collection take a longer time when many nodes are in use and a shorter time when few nodes are in use?

14. What are the disadvantages of reference counters compared to garbage collection?

15. Write a function to traverse a list-structure with shared sublists to reclaim storage of a sublist whose reference count has gone to zero.

16. Write a function to insert a node in a threaded binary tree `t`. The node is to be inserted as the node accessed next in an inorder traversal of `t` after `node.pred` is accessed.

17. Write a function to delete a node in a threaded binary tree `t`. The deleted node is to be `node.p`.

18. Write a function to return a pointer to the predecessor of `node.p` in a threaded binary tree `t`.

19. Write a function to read information into the `info` fields of a binary tree `t`, implemented using pointer variables. The `info` fields will contain character strings of up to twenty characters. The input is given in the order that the `info` fields would be accessed in a preorder traversal of `t`.

20. How will your solution to Exercise 19 change if the binary tree `t` is implemented as a threaded tree?

21. Implement the transformation of Section 7.6.1 using a list implementation for the stack. The binary tree is implemented using pointer variables as a threaded tree. Assume the general tree is given by a two-dimensional array of size 50 × 50. If the [`i, j`] entry of the array is 1, then `node j` is a successor of `node i`; if the [`i, j`] entry is 0, then `node j` is not a successor of `node i`.

22. This is the same as Exercise 21 except that the general tree will be given by a list of successors for each node. These lists should be pointed to by pointer variables, one for each node of the general tree. The binary tree should be a link-inversion tree.

23. Suppose input, representing a general tree, is given as a sequence of pairs. A pair `i, j` implies that `node j` is a successor of `node i`. A sentinel pair has its `i, j` values equal. For example, the general tree of Figure 7.13 might be input as B,F A,C D,J I,K I,L C,H B,E I,M A,D D,I A,B B,G X,X. Write a function that will create the successor lists of Exercise 22.

24. Simulate the preorder traversal implementation for the link-inversion traversal of the binary tree of Figure 13.10.

25. Simulate the preorder traversal implementation for the Robson traversal of the binary tree of Figure 13.10.

26. Why will there always be enough storage in the binary tree, during a Robson traversal, for the stack of root nodes whose left subtrees are nonnull, whose traversal has been completed, and whose right subtrees are being traversed?

27. What purpose does the stack of Exercise 26 serve in the Robson traversal?

28. Write a function to do an inorder traversal of a threaded binary tree `t`.

29. Write a function to do a link-inversion traversal of a binary tree `t` assuming the tree is implemented using pointer variables.

30. Write a function to do a Robson traversal of a binary tree `t` assuming the tree is implemented using pointer variables.

■ Suggested Assignments

1. Write and run a function to copy a list-structure with shared sublists. Use pointer variables.

2. Explain how storage may be reclaimed if all nodes of the copied list-structure that have nonnull sublists are deleted.

3. Why would we not write recursive versions of the three stackless traversals?

4. Simulate the different implementations for the list of available space of Section 13.3, choosing a number of request and return distributions.

Bibliography

Adelson-Velskii, G. M., and Landis, Y. M. [1962]. "An Algorithm for the Organization of Information." *Doklady Akademia Nauk. 146*(2), 263–266; *Soviet Mathematics*. 3, 1259–1263.

Aho, A. V., Hopcroft, J. E., and Ullman, J. D. [1983]. *Data Structures and Algorithms*. Reading, Mass.: Addison-Wesley.

Aho, A. V., and Ullman, J. D. [1972]. *The Theory of Parsing, Translation, and Compiling,* Vol. 1. Englewood Cliffs, N.J.: Prentice-Hall.

Aho, A. V., and Ullman, J. D. [1977]. *Principles of Compiler Design*. Reading, Mass.: Addison-Wesley.

Amble, O., and Knuth, D. E. [1974]. "Ordered Hash Tables." *Computer Journal 17*(2):135–142.

Austing, R. H., et al., eds. [1979]. "Curriculum '78: Recommendations for the Undergraduate Program in Computer Science—A Report of the ACM Curriculum Committee on Computer Science." *Communications of the Association for Computing Machinery 22*(3): 147–166.

Baase, S. [1978]. *Computer Algorithms: Introduction to Design and Analysis*. Reading, Mass.: Addison-Wesley.

Barnes, J. G. P. [1982]. *Programming in Ada*. Reading, Mass.: Addison-Wesley.

Barron, D. W. [1968]. *Recursive Techniques in Programming*. New York: American-Elsevier.

Bayer, R., and McCreight, E. M. [1972]. "Organization and Maintenance of Large Ordered Indices." *Acta Informatica 1*(3):173–189.

Bays, C. [1977]. "A Comparison of Next-Fit, First-Fit, and Best-Fit." *Communications of the Association for Computing Machinery 20*(3):191–192.

Bell, D. A., and Deen, S. M. [1984]. "Hash Trees Versus B-Trees." *Computer Journal 27*(3):218–224.

Bell, J. R. [1970]. "The Quadratic Quotient Method: A Hash Code Eliminating Secondary Clustering." *Communications of the Association for Computing Machinery 13*(2):107–109.

Ben-Ari, M. [1982]. *Principles of Concurrent Programming*. London: Prentice-Hall International.

Bentley, J. L. [1982]. *Writing Efficient Programs*. Englewood Cliffs, N.J.: Prentice-Hall.

Berry, J. T. [1986]. *Advanced C Programming*. New York: Prentice-Hall Press.

Bird, R. S. [1977a]. "Improving Programs by the Introduction of Recursion." *Communications of the Association for Computing Machinery 20*(11):856–863.

Bird, R. S. [1977b]. "Notes on Recursion Elimination." *Communications of the Association for Computing Machinery 20*(6):434–439.

Bitner, J. R., and Reingold, E. M. [1975]. "Backtrack Programming Techniques." *Communications of the Association for Computing Machinery 18*:651–656.

Brooks, F. P. [1974]. *The Mythical Man Month*. Reading, Mass.: Addison-Wesley.

Bunneman, P., and Levy, L. [1980]. "The Towers of Hanoi Problem." *Information Processing Letters 10*:243–244.

Comer, D. [1979]. "The Ubiquitous B-Tree." *Computing Surveys 11*:121–137.

Crane, C. A. [1972]. Linear Lists and Priority Queues as Balanced Binary Trees. Unpublished Ph.D. Dissertation. Stanford University, Stanford, Calif.

Dahl, O.-J., Dijkstra, E. W., and Hoare, C. A. R. [1972]. *Structured Programming*. New York: Academic Press.

Dijkstra, E. W. [1972]. *Notes on Structured Programming*. London: Academic Press.

Dobosiewicz, W. [1978]. "Sorting by Distributive Partitioning." *Information Processing Letters 7*(1):1–6.

Earley, J. [1970]. "An Efficient Context-Free Parsing Algorithm." *Communications of the Association for Computing Machinery 13*(2):94–102.

Elson, M. [1975]. *Data Structures*. Chicago, Ill.: Science Research Associates.

Fagin, R., Nievergelt, J., Pippenger, N., and Strong, R. H. [1978]. *Extendible Hashing—A Fast Access Method for Dynamic Files*. Research Rept. RJ2305. IBM Research Division, Yorktown Heights, N.Y.

Feller, W. [1975]. *An Introduction to Probability Theory and Its Applications*. 2nd ed. New York: Wiley.

Floyd, R. W. [1964]. "Algorithm 245: Treesort3." *Communications of the Association for Computing Machinery 7*(12):701.

Floyd, R. W. [1979]. "The Paradigms of Programming," *Communications of the Association for Computing Machinery 22*(8):455–460.

Fredkin, E. H. [1960]. "Trio Memory." *Communications of the Association for Computing Machinery 3*(9):490–500.

Garwick, J. V. [1964]. "Data Storage in Compilers." *BIT 4*:137–140.

Golomb, S. W., and Baumert, L. D. [1965]. "Backtrack Programming." *Journal of the Association for Computing Machinery 12*(4):516–524.

Greene, D. H., and Knuth, D. E. [1981]. *Mathematics for the Analysis of Algorithms*. Cambridge, Mass.: Birkhauser, Boston.

Harrison, S. P., and Steele, G. L., Jr. [1987]. *C: A Reference Manual*. Englewood Cliffs, N.J.: Prentice-Hall.

Hirschberg, D. S. [1973]. "A Class of Dynamic Memory Allocation Algorithms." Communications of the Association for Computing Machinery 16(10):615–618.

Hoare, C. A. R. [1962]. "Quicksort." *Computer Journal 5*(1):10–15.

Horbibe, Y., and Nemetz, T. [1979]. "On the Max-Entropy Rule for a Binary Search Tree." *Acta Informatica 12*:63–72.

Horowitz, E. [1983]. *Programming Languages: A Grand Tour*. Rockville, Md.: Computer Science Press.

Horowitz, E., and Sahni, S. [1976]. *Fundamentals of Data Structures*. Woodland Hills, Calif.: Computer Science Press.

Horowitz, E., and Sahni, S. [1978]. *Fundamentals of Computer Algorithms*. Potomac, Md.: Computer Science Press.

Hu, T. C., and Tucker, A. C. [1971]. "Optimal Computer Search Trees and Variable-Length Alphabetic Codes." *SIAM Journal of Applied Mathematics 21*(4):514–532.

Huffman, D. A. [1952]. "A Method for the Construction of Minimum-Redundancy Codes." *Proceedings of the Institute of Radio Engineers 40*:1098–1101.

Hull, M. E. C. [1984]. "A Parallel View of Stable Marriages." *Information Processing Letters 18*:63–66.

Johnson, D. B. [1975]. "Priority Queues with Update and Finding Minimum Spanning Trees." *Information Processing Letters 4*(3):53–57.

Jones, W. B. [1982]. *Programming Concepts: A Second Course*. Englewood Cliffs, N.J.: Prentice-Hall.

Kelley, A., and Pohl, I. [1987]. *C by Dissection*. Menlo Park, Calif.: Benjamin/Cummings.

Kernighan, B. W., and Plauger, P. J. [1978]. *The Elements of Programming Style*. 2nd ed. New York: McGraw-Hill.

Kernighan, B. W., and Plauger, P. J. [1981]. *Software Tools in Pascal*. Reading, Mass.: Addison-Wesley.

Kernighan, B. W., and Ritchie, D. M. [1978]. *The C Programming Language*. Englewood Cliffs, N.J.: Prentice-Hall.

Knuth, D. E. [1971]. "Optimum Binary Search Trees." *Acta Informatica 1*(1):14–25.

Knuth, D. E. [1973a]. *The Art of Computer Programming. Vol. 1: Fundamental Algorithms*. Reading, Mass.: Addison-Wesley.

Knuth, D. E. [1973b]. *The Art of Computer Programming. Vol. 3: Searching and Sorting*. Reading, Mass.: Addison-Wesley.

Koffman, E. B., Stemple, D., and Wardle, C. E. [1985]. "Recommended Curriculum for CSE, 1984." *Communications of the Association for Computing Machinery 28*(8):815–818.

Korsh, J. F. [1981]. "Greedy Binary Search Trees Are Nearly Optimal." *Information Processing Letters 13*(1):16–19.

Korsh, J. F. [1982]. "Growing Nearly Optimal Binary Search Trees." *Information Processing Letters 14*(3):139–143.

Korsh, J. F., and Laison, G. [1983]. "A Multiple-Stack Manipulation Procedure." *Communications of the Association for Computing Machinery 26*(11):921–923.

Kruse, R. L. [1984]. *Data Structures and Program Design.* Englewood Cliffs, N.J.: Prentice-Hall.

Lapin, J. E. [1987]. *Portable C and UNIX System Programming.* Englewood Cliffs, N.J.: Prentice-Hall.

Larson, P. [1978]. "Dynamic Hashing." BIT *18*(2):184–201.

Lin, S., and Kernighan, B. W. [1973]. "A Heuristic Algorithm for the Traveling Salesman Problem." *Operations Research 21*:498–516.

Linger, R. C., Mills, H. D., and Witt, B. I. [1979]. *Structured Programming Theory and Practice.* Reading, Mass.: Addison-Wesley.

Litwin, W. [1980]. "Linear Hashing: A New Tool for File and Table Addressing." *Proceedings of the Sixth International Conference on Very Large Data Bases.* Montreal, pp. 212–223.

Martin, W. A. [1971]. "Sorting." *Computing Surveys 3*:148–174.

Maurer, H. A., and Williams, M. R. [1972]. *A Collection of Programming Problems and Techniques.* Englewood Cliffs, N. J.: Prentice-Hall.

Maurer, W. D. [1968]. "An Improved Hash Code for Scatter Storage." *Communications of the Association for Computing Machinery 11*(1):35–37.

Maurer, W. D., and Lewis, T. G. [1975]. "Hash Table Methods." *Computing Surveys 7*(1):5–20.

Mehlhorn, K. [1975]. "Nearly Optimal Binary Search Trees." *Acta Informatica 5*:287–295.

Mehlhorn, K. [1977]. "A Best Possible Bound for the Weighted Path Length of Binary Search Trees." *Society of Industrial and Applied Mathematics, Journal of Computers 6*(2):235–239.

Miller, L. H., and Quilici, A. E. [1986]. *Programming in C.* New York: Wiley.

Morris, R. [1968]. "Scatter Storage Techniques." *Communications of the Association for Computing Machinery 11*(1):35–44.

Naur, P. (ed.). [1963]. "Revised Report on the Algorithmic Language ALGOL60," *Communications of the Association for Computing Machinery 6*:1–17.

Nievergelt, J. [1974]. "Binary Search Trees and File Organization." *Computing Surveys 6*(3):195–207.

Peterson, J. L. [1980]. *Design of a Spelling Program: An Experiment in Program Design.* Lecture Notes in Computer Science. New York: Springer-Verlag.

Peterson, J. L., and Norman, T. A. [1977]. "Buddy Systems." *Communications of the Association for Computing Machinery 20*(6):431–435.

Pratt, T. W. [1975]. *Programming Languages: Design and Implementation.* Englewood Cliffs, N.J.: Prentice-Hall.

Reingold, E. M., and Hansen, W. J. [1983]. Boston, Mass.: Little, Brown.

Robson, J. M. [1973]. "An Improved Algorithm for Traversing Binary Trees without Auxiliary Stack." *Information Processing Letters 2*:12–14.

Robson, J. M. [1977]. "A Bounded Storage Algorithm for Copying Cyclic Structures." *Communications of the Association for Computing Machinery 20*(6):431–433.

Robson, J. M. [1979]. "The Height of Binary Search Trees." *Austrian Computer Journal 11*(4):151–153.

Schorr, H., and Waite, W. M. [1967]. "An Efficient Machine-Independent Procedure for Garbage Collection in Various List Structures." *Communications of the Association for Computing Machinery 10*(8):501–506.

Sedgewick, R. [1977]. "Permutation Generation Methods." *Computing Surveys 9*:137–164.

Sedgewick, R. [1983]. *Algorithms.* Reading, Mass.: Addison-Wesley.

Shell, D. L. [1959]. "A High-Speed Sorting Procedure." *Communications of the Association for Computing Machinery 2*:30–32.

Standish, T. A. [1980]. *Data Structure Techniques.* Reading, Mass.: Addison-Wesley.

Stanfel, G. L. [1970]. "Tree Structures for Optimal Searching." *Journal of the Association for Computing Machinery 19*(3):508–517.

Stone, H. S. [1971]. "Parallel Processing with the Perfect Shuffle." *IEEE Transactions on Computers C-20*:153–161.

Stone, H. S. [1972]. *Introduction to Computer Organization and Data Structures.* New York: McGraw-Hill.

Stone, H. S. [1980]. *Introduction to Computer Architecture*. 2nd ed. Chicago, Ill.: Science Research Associates.

Sussenguth, E. H. Jr. [1963]. "Use of Tree Structures for Processing Files." *Communications of the Association for Computing Machinery* 6(5):272–279.

Tenenbaum, A. M., and Augenstein, M. J. [1981]. *Data Structures Using Pascal*. Englewood Cliffs, N.J.: Prentice-Hall.

Tremblay, J. P., and Sorenson, P. G. [1984]. *An Introduction to Data Structures with Applications*. 2nd ed. New York: McGraw-Hill.

Ullman, J. D. [1982]. *Principles of Database Systems*. Rockville, Md.: Computer Science Press.

Van Wijngaarden, A., et al. [1975]. "Revised Report on the Algorithmic Language ALGOL 68." *Acta Informatica* 5:1–236.

Walsh, T. R. [1982]. "The Towers of Hanoi Revisited: Moving the Rings by Counting the Moves." *Information Processing Letters* 15(2):64–67.

Weinberg, G. M. [1971]. *The Psychology of Computer Programming*. New York: Van Nostrand.

Wexelblat, R. L. [1981]. *History of Programming Languages*. New York: Academic Press.

Williams, J. W. J. [1964]. "Algorithm 232: Heapsort." *Communications of the Association for Computing Machinery* 7(6):347–348.

Wirth, N. [1973]. *Systematic Programming: An Introduction*. Englewood Cliffs, N.J.: Prentice-Hall.

Wirth, N. [1976]. *Algorithms + Data Structures = Programs*. Englewood Cliffs, N.J.: Prentice-Hall.

Subject Index

Function Index